Louisa Elliott

Louisa Elliott

A NOVEL BY
ANN VICTORIA ROBERTS

CB
CONTEMPORARY
BOOKS

CHICAGO · NEW YORK

Library of Congress Cataloging-in-Publication Data

Roberts, Ann Victoria.
    Louisa Elliott / Ann Victoria Roberts.
       p.   cm.
    ISBN 0-8092-4290-7
    I. Title.
    PR6068.O1414L68   1989
    823'.914—dc20   89-7362
                                     CIP

Published by Contemporary Books, Inc.
180 North Michigan Avenue, Chicago, Illinois 60601
Manufactured in the United States of America
Library of Congress Catalog Card Number: 89-7362
International Standard Book Number: 0-8092-4290-7

For my family
and
for Eileen and Bill,
whose love of York is unsurpassed

AUTHOR'S NOTE

Gillygate, the York street where I have located Mary Elliott's house in the novel, has a soft initial *g,* being named after the Church of St. Giles.

ACKNOWLEDGMENTS

Fiction though it is, *Louisa Elliott* is set against a background of events which actually took place and locations which largely still exist. To capture the atmosphere of the time necessitated lengthy research, and I am indebted to the staffs of York City Reference Library, York City Archives, and the National Army Museum, London. Dr. P. R. Newman, Keeper of Military History at the Castle Museum, York, was especially helpful in pointing a novice in the right direction, and I thank him for time and encouragement so generously given. Of all those who gave invaluable information, a special word of thanks must go to Colonel E. C. York (late, Royal Dragoons), Sister Elizabeth Bulmer, RMN, Ms. Christine Dean of Otley Museum, and Mrs. Revill of Metheringham.

From the many reference books consulted, three were invaluable, and my deepest appreciation goes to their respective authors: the Marquess of Anglesey for his *A History of the British Cavalry* (Leo Cooper); Frances Finnegan for her *Poverty and Prostitution—A Study of Victorian Prostitutes in York* (Cambridge University Press); and Peter Somerville Large for his *Dublin* (Hamish Hamilton).

Thanks, too, to T. R. M. Creighton for permission to quote from *Poems of Thomas Hardy—a New Selection* (Macmillan).

ANN VICTORIA ROBERTS

Book One
1892

Her laugh was not in the middle of her face quite.
   As a gay laugh springs,
It was plain she was anxious about some things,
   I could not trace quite.
Her curls were like fir-cones—piled up, brown—
   Or rather like tight-tied sheaves;
It seemed they could never be taken down . . .

And her lips were too full, some might say:
I did not think so. Anyway,
The shadow her lower one would cast
Was green in hue whenever she passed
   Bright sun on midsummer leaves.

From "A Countenance,"
by Thomas Hardy

ONE

The great bastion of Micklegate Bar loomed white and hazy in the gathering blizzard: dwarfed beneath its portals, two figures, very similar in height, trudged slowly homeward.

The man's hat and cape and curling beard were thick with snow, the young woman's enveloping cloak already dragging heavily. Holding his umbrella over her, he guided every step, following a sheltering path within the walls.

By the old railway station, eerily deserted at that time of night and strangely insubstantial, gas lamps flickered, dimmed by whirling, waltzing, moth-like flakes. Where that Italianate façade blended into mist, it was easy to imagine a religious house, ghostly friars still pacing empty cloisters, still tending, between those snowed-up tracks and the city wall, their long-vanished garden. Recalling a story heard in childhood, the woman stared hard and, shivering suddenly, moved closer to her companion.

"Ghosts," she murmured, aware that here the past was ever present.

He nodded; for him too, the place was charged. He thought of twenty years ago, when prosperity had made that mean little street one of the busiest in York, when it seemed the world trod those worn pavements and the shriek of trains in the night had come like a punctuation to every dream. Those days were gone forever, no more than shadowy memories, as ghostly as that vanished cloister.

"A new temple," he said ironically of those deserted buildings, "to less enduring gods."

Ahead of them, from a narrow alley an ill-clad figure emerged, sliding unsteadily toward a group of almshouses on the corner. Between those low roofs and the imposing gable of a more expensive hostelry stood a tall building, once fine, which had been their childhood home. "Elliott's Temperance Hotel," however, was now a somewhat seedy-looking eating house, its peeling paint and greasy windows but a poor reflection of the neighborhood. Not even the snow could disguise that its period of brief prosperity was over.

More than thirty years had passed since two young, unmarried women had defied convention, rented that four-story property in the name of an absent elder brother, and opened the house as a private hotel. One had a little money, the other a flair for business; both shared a sound if basic education, long experience as servants in grand houses, and one at least had a profound aversion to dependence on members of the opposite sex. Through sheer hard work and determination they made a success of the enterprise, and with the very name advertising moral cleanliness of the highest order, their clientele was similarly respectable. Ladies traveling alone with their maids, middle-class gentlemen not wishing to be importuned by drunken prostitutes, families taking advantage of the growing railway network, all were indebted to the Temperance Movement and the rash of hotels which sprang up in its wake.

Unimpeachable though the business was, the Elliott sisters, with their starched white cloths, shining silver, and excellent meals, had a less than respectable secret to hide. The elder one, so prim and spinsterish and grimly determined, was already a mother when the hotel opened, her son, Edward, fostered by elderly relatives in the north of the county. Not until the age of seven was he brought to Tanner Row, to be conveniently passed off as an orphaned nephew.

The younger sister, small, fair, and pretty, lacked the other's single-mindedness; it was her long-lasting affair with a married man which had wrecked that successful business partnership.

Swamped by a sudden plethora of memories, Edward Elliott sighed. "Do you remember, Louisa?"

"How could I forget?"

Together they paused and looked up. Louisa shivered again, wondering why her cousin had chosen this route instead of the well-lit thoroughfare of Micklegate running parallel only yards away.

"I haven't been this way in years," she confessed, knowing she never would by choice; for in Tanner Row lay the remains of childhood, its mysteries and uncertainties dredged up with too little pleasure. With her eyes on the recessed doorway, she recalled secret anxieties and the reassuring comfort of her cousin Edward's arms; then he had been the most important person in her young world: guardian, brother, confidant, and friend. Their mothers were always too busy, engaged in seemingly endless toil; the servants less concerned; and Louisa's two sisters too young at that time to understand the basic cruelties of life. Even her father, large and jovial, had been no more than another transitory visitor. Loaded with presents like an unseasonal Father Christmas, smelling of tobacco and raw wool from his business in the West Riding, he sat his little daughters on his knee and kissed them; but his time and attention went elsewhere. The significance of his absences, of the fact that he did not live with them but only visited, had escaped her for many years. Accused at school of being fatherless, Louisa had always hotly denied it, providing fuel for further accusations.

In those days, she thought, nothing was ever satisfactorily explained; even her father's death might have gone unremarked except for her mother's tears and the attendant minor scandal of his will. The outrage of his childless but legal wife had known no bounds, although the will was eventually proven, the bequests handed over.

The events of that year, which was Louisa's eighth and Edward's twentieth, prompted acrimony and ill feeling and a departure from Tanner Row. The anxiety of those last days, with Elizabeth Elliott preparing to go her own way, came back with sudden force. "I cried," Louisa confided softly, "because I thought you were leaving us, too."

Edward turned to look at her, the wistfulness of her expression catching him unaware. For a fleeting moment he was tempted to take her in his arms and kiss the pain away, as he had all those years ago; but she was no longer a child. With a small, embarrassed smile, he wiped a snowflake from her nose and said: "I know. I couldn't bear it either. And even though she finally saw that it was more practical for me to stay with you, my mother's never really forgiven me for it."

"But you went back to live with her in the end," Louisa said, a small edge of resentment in her voice.

He shrugged. "There wasn't much choice then."

It was a subject which had once been raw between them, the cause of much youthful heartbreak on her part; because of that, she merely commented: "You'd be better off on your own, Edward—you don't even get on with her."

"She's my mother."

And what has she ever done for you? Louisa thought but did not say. Instead, with forced lightness, she said: "So what would you do if you *were* on your own?"

"Oh, I don't know." He smiled. "Take a cottage in the country, write romantic verse for a living—lots of impractical things like that." Seized by the idea, he added: "And when you finally grow tired of looking after other people's children, you can come and minister to me instead."

Laughing then, Louisa shook her head. "As soon as I can afford to— I'll do that!"

"I'll hold you to it," he murmured; but the wind, as they rounded a corner, whipped his words away.

In the open reaches before the river, where strong gusts clutched at her skirts, she clung to him, glad of the shelter his body provided. She watched every footfall, steps uncertain in the treacherous leather boots she wore; but Edward's eyes were less concerned, taken more by the transforming beauty of the blizzard.

Like some misplaced remnant of a Rhineland castle, the round tower of North Street Postern sat dredged with snow, its crumbling tiles capped by a perfect cone of white. Once part of the city's defenses and latterly a shelter for ferrymen, it squatted by the river's edge, overshadowed by the cast-iron span of a new bridge across the Ouse. Below, the crusted masts of boats and barges loomed, each spar and halyard ghosted against the river's obsidian depths; while, bowed with snow, huge trees on the far bank bent their branches earthward. Edward's soul was stirred, too affected by the city's everyday grime not to feel the power of that silent magic.

Lifting his face to the tingling flakes, for a moment he forgot the reason for their journey and gave himself up to delight. Having seen so little of Louisa while she had been working away, the thought of sharing her company regularly made him feel quite ridiculously young again.

"It's so good to have you back," he said with heartfelt sincerity. "When the summer comes, we must spend more time together—like the old days." Fumbling in his pocket for coins for the toll, he asked: "And how's the new job going? It seems weeks since we had a chance to talk."

Sighing, reluctant to admit she was far from happy, Louisa simply nodded. "It is weeks." Edward's recommendation had secured the position, and it seemed churlish to complain that the hours were long and her duties onerous. Perhaps she had been spoiled in her last place, she thought; but with their profligate ways, her old employers had been forced to leave for Italy, where the living was cheap, if less convenient.

In describing her new employer, not quite jokingly, as a tightfisted old skinflint, she made her cousin laugh. He knew the family well, having been indentured to their firm as a boy. He was now senior bookbinder, a valued right hand when Albert Tempest was away on business. "I know the old man barks a lot," he admitted, "and I daresay he finds the girls a trial since their mother died, but I rub along with him all right. I'm sure you will too, once you get to know him better." After a slight pause, he asked: "Do you regret not going abroad with your other people?"

With a sad smile, she shook her head. "I miss them—and I imagine the weather's better in Italy!—but no, I don't regret it. If I'd been away, with Mamma suddenly ill like this—" She broke off. "Tell me honestly," she asked a moment later, "is she very bad?"

Guilty of having kept the truth from her, Edward said: "Well, she's taken to her bed—never a good sign with your mother. Apparently, she's been nursing one of the guests. He went down with something a few days ago—but he's recovering well."

She stopped and turned to look at him. "It's the flu, I suppose?"

Gravely, he nodded. Influenza was sweeping the country, rapidly reaching epidemic proportions: people were dying of it. "She's got a marvelous constitution," he said gently in an attempt to comfort her. "Don't worry—she'll be up and about in no time."

At the confluence with Lendal there was a muddle of carriages, horses, and coachmen having difficulty negotiating the tight corners in the snow; but Edward and Louisa tramped on, past the theater where jeweled coiffures vied with foyer lights, across Bootham to battle with wind and snow sweeping down the straight northern length of Gillygate.

Bessie met them at the front door, pulling off their wet things, fussing over the umbrella, ushering them through into the large kitchen at the back. A rich aroma of beef broth assailed their cold-sharpened senses, while coals glowed red beneath the simmering stewpot, a kettle emitted gentle puffs of steam, and the black-leaded range shone beneath a fringe of utensils hanging from a cluttered mantelpiece. Before the fire a tabby cat snoozed, regarding the newcomers with one half-open yellow eye before returning to its slumber. There was a scrubbing brush resting on the massive, part-scoured wooden table, its accompanying bucket of cold water beneath on the quarry-tiled floor.

"Mind that bucket," the old servant ordered as Louisa hugged her. "Sit yourselves down while I make a pot of tea. You must be starved through."

In spite of the circumstances, Louisa thought, it was good to be home. Breathing the aromatic steam of the broth, she was reminded of her mother's sumptuous dinners, and her mouth watered. Meals at the Tempests' were stodgy, tasteless, and unbearably repetitive. Like their arguments, she thought grimly, recalling the most recent confrontation, earlier that evening, between her employer and his elder daughter.

She was tired. With a sigh she acknowledged the fact and bent to examine her steaming skirts. The cat, disturbed, rolled over and stretched ecstatic paws toward the swaying hem of her dress. Its soft, mottled underfur was too tempting; she bent to tickle its stomach, and, affronted, the cat righted itself, reassessed its surroundings, and took a graceful leap onto Edward's knee.

"Daft creature," muttered Bessie. Pushing past Louisa, she reached for the teapot and poured a cup for each of them. Cutting two hefty slabs of Christmas cake, she silenced Edward's protests with a wave of one enormous, reddened hand. "You don't get enough down you, Mr. Edward—far too thin, always were. How's your dear mam, God bless her?"

"Not so bright at the moment, Bessie. This weather doesn't do a lot for her bronchitis, I'm afraid."

"Aye, she'll have to keep indoors, especially with all this flu about. You mind you take good care of her, Mr. Edward—it could carry her off, you know."

Catching Edward's glance, Louisa shook her head slightly. "Take no notice," she silently mouthed; but knowing Bessie's dire prognostications of old, Edward simply smiled and pulled his chair closer to the fire. "I'll do my best," he said and sipped the scalding tea.

A few minutes later Louisa drained her cup and made for the door. "I must go up and see Mamma and let Emily know we're here."

"I shall have to be going," Edward said, glancing at the clock. "But I'll call first thing in the morning, on my way to work. The old man will want to know the latest news."

"When I'm coming back, you mean," Louisa observed with some asperity. "Anyway, give my regards to Aunt Elizabeth. And thanks for coming for me," she added with a warm smile. "I'll probably see you in the morning."

TWO

*A*t the top of the stairs a gas mantle glowed, casting grotesque shadows as Louisa moved first toward and then away from it. Hearing her sister's footfall, Emily appeared in the doorway of the old dressing room, beckoning her away from the stairs to the second floor.

Louisa followed her into the tiny room where their mother lay. It was barely big enough for a single bed, a chair, and a small chest but sported a miniature cast-iron fireplace, the grate shaped like a shell. Louisa thought it charming and as a girl had longed for the little room to be hers; it was, however, usually reserved for guests.

"It's warmer here than upstairs," Emily explained. "And Mamma moved down to be handy for *him*." With a curt nod, she indicated the best bedroom next door. "He was raving day and night."

But Louisa was more concerned for their mother. Against crisp white pillows she looked like an aged china doll, her fifty-odd years revealed more in graying hair than in the smooth round face, flushed with fever, which a lifetime of insecurity had barely marked. Pale blue eyes fluttered open, and a weak smile touched her lips as she recognized her eldest daughter.

"I'm staying for a couple of days or so," Louisa explained, taking those burning fingers between her own cool ones. "Just so Bessie and Emily can get some rest."

"You're a good girl," Mary Elliott whispered. Her eyes flickered and turned toward Emily. "How's Mr. Devereaux?"

"Oh, don't be troubling yourself about him—the fever's gone, and he'll be up and about in no time. You concentrate on getting yourself better."

She nodded and was quiet for a moment, then, with evident anxiety, asked: "Did Blanche come yet?"

Louisa's heart sank. In times of emergency her other sister was always missing. She cleared her throat. "She'll be here tomorrow, Mamma. You get some sleep now."

On the landing, Emily stood in the shadows, her olive skin and gypsy eyes a startling contrast to her sister's autumn fairness. In obvious agitation, she said: "I wish she'd come. I sent word this afternoon."

"Oh, she'll come," Louisa promised grimly, "if I have to drag her here by her bootlaces. Don't worry."

"I can't help it," the younger girl confessed, chewing a corner of her handkerchief. "It's that dreadful man in there. He's young and strong, and *he* nearly died. What chance does Mamma stand?" Suddenly, dark little Emily burst into tears.

Louisa hugged her close. "Come on, Mamma's stronger than she looks. It's just a shock, seeing her ill and in bed. We're not used to it. She's not going to die—we'll make sure she doesn't."

But her sister was not to be comforted, turning her distress into anger and directing it at their unseen guest. "Some gentleman!" she sniffed, screwing her already damp handkerchief into a ball and rubbing furiously at her eyes. "Why did he have to come here to be ill?" she demanded, "with Harker's down the road and all the other big places to choose from? If he's as well-heeled as Mamma seems to think, what's he doing here?"

It was a valid question; one to which Louisa had no answer. She listened in silence as her sister questioned their mother's wisdom in letting the best room to a total stranger, almost smiling as she heard the list of all his sins. Not only had their guest lacked consideration by falling ill within hours of his arrival, but it seemed he bitterly resented their ministrations, cursing Emily particularly, in language which was hardly fit for a barrack room.

"Perhaps he's a soldier," Louisa observed, thinking of the garrison at Fulford.

"Well, he'd better be an officer is all I can say. Else he'll not have the money to pay Dr. Mackenzie's bills. He's been here every single day, dressing that arm of his."

"What's wrong with his arm?"

"Well, it's more his hand and wrist, really—looks like he's been stabbed or clawed, or something." Emily shuddered. "You should see it; it's horrible."

Wincing, Louisa shook her head. "No, I think I'd rather not." But at her sister's muttered forebodings, she smiled again, patting her shoulder. "I prescribe a cup of cocoa and some sleep," she said.

"Don't laugh, Louisa. I'm telling you he's *trouble*—I can feel it in my bones."

"Oh, you and your bones!" she teased. "You're worse than Bessie. You'll be reading the tea leaves next."

The man they discussed lay propped against pillows, a book open but unread beside him. He heard the whispered voices but paid little attention; there had been whispers, comings and goings on the stairs all day. Mary Elliott, of the gentle hands and insistent voice, was ill, perhaps near to dying, stricken by the same fever which had almost extinguished his own life.

With sudden, bitter longing, he wished she had left him to die. Death would have relieved him of his burdens, released him from every vow, wiped the ledger clean for all eternity. It had been so wonderfully attractive: soft, painless, inviting. But she had banished it; used his Christian name, invoked the memory of his mother, asked about Charlotte—God! What had he babbled about Charlotte?—and ultimately sworn at him, using his own curses to shock him into consciousness. And then she had called him a coward; a low, skulking, sniveling boy, afraid of life's realities, letting fear and misery persuade him that death was the easy way out. Even now he winced at the memory of that scathing tone.

He wished he could tell her, before it was too late, that he was sorry, not really a coward, merely tired and disillusioned, the bearer of too much guilt and pain.

Fatigue dragged at him, numbing his mind; those stinging thoughts sank like stones into black water, and he sank with them into sleep.

At half past ten Bessie looked into the dressing room on her way up to bed. She brought a jug of sweetened lemon juice for Mary Elliott and a pot of strong tea to keep Louisa awake, assuring her that their guest was settled for the night.

"I've been in to see him," she whispered, "and he's fast asleep. The fever's down, so he should rest quiet for a change—he's had us all up and running, day and night, since he arrived. Anyway, he's a lot better, quite the gentleman when he's in his right mind!"

Louisa grinned. "I'm glad to hear it. Emily was telling me about him. She sounded quite put out."

"Aye, we've had a rare education in curses," Bessie sighed. "Miss Mary's been a saint, though, she really has—but he wasn't so bad with her. And if he does start again," she said firmly, "don't try and tackle him on your own. Come up for me."

Promising to do that, Louisa closed the door and settled down with her book. By the time the clock downstairs struck twelve, she was well into Hardy's *Trumpet-Major,* a book she had read more than once, an old favorite guaranteed to see her through the long night vigil.

Her mother's breathing was harsh but regular, her temperature high but not rising. Every hour Louisa gave her a few sips of the lemon drink and watched the night tick slowly by. Sometime after two her eyes began to feel heavy; she dozed for a while, then something disturbed her, the book thudded to the floor, and, startled, she jerked upright.

Anxiously, she touched Mary Elliott's burning forehead, felt for the pulse at her wrist; but she was sleeping soundly enough, not even muttering with fever. As Louisa retrieved her book, there came from the other room a low, anguished cry, immediately repeated. With a sudden shiver of apprehension she contemplated calling Bessie and then decided not to; it seemed unnecessary and unfair to disturb her sleep. If their strange guest should prove impossible to quiet, then she would ask for help.

More from prudence than fear, she turned to ignite a taper before unlocking the communicating door. By that small glow she could see the bed's foot on her right and, with petticoats quietly rustling, tiptoed toward the bedside chest, where an oil lamp usually stood. As she reached out to light it, the deep, powerful voice cried out again; unintelligible, unnerving sounds which set her heart pounding, almost made her drop the burning taper. Sweating suddenly in the night chill, she turned slowly, hardly daring to breathe, dazzled by the small flame and unable to see clearly beyond it.

For several seconds she stood quite still, gradually realizing that the stranger was held fast by a dream.

Always he was going home, a seemingly endless journey across a storm-racked sea, plagued by the noise of wind and waves and the throat-catching fear of drowning. There was nausea too, so strong it would invariably almost wake him, but not quite. Enough for his conscious mind to reassure him; then, having got him in its grip, the scene would change, the nightmare would begin in earnest.

Lofty and sinister, the avenue of araucarias, bane of his childhood, blotted out the stars; he ran through it in the darkness, guided only by a tiny arch of moonlight ahead. The avenue at White Leigh was noted for its length and magnificence, but in the dream it seemed without end, every step weighted by fear and loathing, the dead spiked fingers of the trees reaching out, tearing at arms and face and clothes.

Eventually, sweating and shivering, he gained the open ellipse of lawn before the house, and in the moonlight all was as it should be: solid, familiar, and very beautiful. Once inside, however, relief turned to shock; for it was not White Leigh as he knew it. The rooms were lifeless, derelict, a single shutter hanging brokenly from an upper window. He wandered through those once-happy rooms, seeing ghosts amongst the dust-shrouds, pursued by memories, in search of something, or someone, he had loved and lost.

Then, at the head of the staircase, there was Charlotte, ethereal as ever, insubstantial as a shaft of moonlight in that dark and dismal house. Her hair rippled in silvery waves around her shoulders, and he stood transfixed until she called his name. Even as he mounted the stairs he was never sure that she was real, never caught her until she reached her room. And always it was there his terror began. For the room was not White Leigh, but the one they had shared in the beginning, at the Devereaux house, with its mirrors and those ice-blue, light-reflecting satins. He longed to take her away, out of that place, to somewhere with a blazing fire, where he could enfold her in his arms and warm her with his own lifeblood.

The longer he stayed, the less able he was to move. She stood by a long pier glass, a double diaphanous image, beckoning, tantalizing, laughing at his predicament, her eyes sparkling like white fire. Desiring, pleading, the more he begged, the more she laughed. Until, pitying him at last, she came and raised him up, drew him with her to the bed, kissing him with a passion and fervor she had never displayed in life, welcoming his lovemaking so wholeheartedly he was always fooled. That part of the dream was always the most real, the most shaming afterward, for he could feel himself entering her, experiencing the whole gamut of emotions she invariably inspired: love, hate, longing, loathing; a desire for mastery, for satisfaction; an overwhelming need to repay all the pain and anguish she had ever caused. But as he approached the point of climax, he always looked into her eyes, seeing not love, nor desire, only naked and terrifying hatred.

Nails raked his neck, attacked his face, became the talons of a predatory animal, clawing at his eyes. He tried to tear them away and could not; his hands sought her throat and found it, squeezing, squeezing, squeezing . . .

Sometimes his own cries woke him, and he would lie in the darkness gasping for breath, beset by the terrifying images which stayed so clearly in his mind. At other times the dream went on, Charlotte limp and lifeless, eyes blank and turned up, her lovely face bruised and contorted, like the face of a hanged man he had seen once as a child. And then it was sorrow that woke him, like an agonizing physical loss, as though his heart had been torn from his breast, leaving a bleeding, gaping hole. Wiping cold tears from his eyes, he was never sure for whom he wept, whether for Charlotte or himself.

The gentle but illuminating glow of the lamp revealed the room's old, familiar furniture, the large double bed and its briefly quiet occupant. He lay turned away from Louisa, his short, dark hair, ruffled by sleep, giving an impression of youth which was somehow less than frightening. Softly, she called his name, but there was no response. Leaning over, she saw that his black-lashed eyelids flickered constantly, following the dream. Reluctant to touch his naked shoulder, she called his name again. He began to moan afresh, hands clasping and unclasping the pillow, the muscles of his face twitching as though in pain.

Compassion lent her courage. Children were often subject to nightmares, and remembering their panic if suddenly disturbed, she began to soothe the man in a way that usually calmed her charges. Laying a cool hand across his brow, she lowered herself onto the edge of the bed, all the while whispering maternal, reassuring words. Within a moment or two, he was quieter.

For the first time, the pattern of the nightmare changed. While he pleaded and Charlotte laughed, another figure appeared, hazy and indistinct; as though reproved, Charlotte ceased her taunting, and as her power receded, relief flooded his mind, together with a feeling of being comforted. Words penetrated his consciousness, and an image of Mary Elliott's strangely youthful, twinkling smile; the voice became clear and firm but unfamiliar; he struggled to put a face to it and realized he was awake.

Elongated, forget-me-not eyes regarded him anxiously from beneath thick brown lashes. Bewildered, he stared back, wondering if she was as insubstantial as the terror which on previous nights had felt as real as her hand on his brow. Always the nightmare had stayed with him. He had been but dimly aware of Mary Elliott's presence and sometimes a dark-eyed girl he confused with his brother's wife. Yet now he recognized the dream for what it was, and like a man dragged into sunlight from a bottomless well of despair, he felt light-headed with relief.

Smiling, he caught hold of her wrist, half afraid she might disappear before he had a chance to gather his wits.

Looking into the man's face, Louisa realized he was older than she had thought at first. Thirty perhaps, or a little more, with strongly defined features and a curling black moustache. There were deep-etched lines at the corners of his eyes, eyes that in the lamplight were darkly blue and suddenly less bewildered.

He continued to stare, but she was conscious of neither offense nor embarrassment, rather of being invaded by a nameless, insidious warmth, as though she had known him intimately once, a long time ago. That strange sense of familiarity held her captive; but the relaxation of his fingers, sliding sensuously down over the back of her hand to her fingertips, broke the spell. On a sharply indrawn breath she looked away, conscious of the warmth in her face and an almost panic-stricken sense of shame. Hastily, withdrawing from both the bed and his grasp, she moved across the room toward the fire, tending it unnecessarily to cover her discomfort.

He spoke as she knelt before the hearth, murmuring apologies and the explanation of a nightmare. His voice still held the huskiness of sleep, but despite those educated vowels, she recognized immediately the lilting cadences of his native land.

Emily was right, she thought; he is Irish. And with that style of moustache, she decided, he might well be a soldier. Determined to find out, she was prevented only by manners from asking outright. She turned then and stood up, suddenly appalled by the sight of his naked chest and shoulders, black hair curling across the breadth of his chest. Instantly she dropped her gaze, reached for his dressing gown, and handed it to him with averted eyes.

The weight and richness of the heavy padded silk surprised her, and as he took it from her Louisa noticed for the first time the bandage which extended from just below the elbow to the knuckles of his right hand.

"You must have found it difficult to dress yourself," she coolly observed, guiding his injured arm into the robe's narrow sleeve.

"A valet would have made things easier," he admitted dryly, "although I've had little need for clothes these past few days."

He glanced up, seeing the brown pintucked fullness of her bosom as she bent over him, starched white collar and gold brooch; smooth cheeks and a generous mouth trying hard to be prim. A sudden surge of physical desire caught him by surprise; closing his eyes momentarily, he savored the tingling sensation where her fingers touched his skin and the clean scent of her, tinged with lavender. He wondered who she was. Not a servant, surely, with that intricate gold brooch at her throat; and why did her face seem so familiar?

"Thank you," he said simply, leaning back against freshly smoothed pillows; but the flash of panic in her eyes as he again caught hold of her hand made him release her immediately. "I'm sorry. I'm like the drowning man—longing to embrace his rescuer."

Color leapt to her cheeks, and he thought how lovely she looked, so young and fresh and alive, her eyes so bright in the lamplight; even her confusion delighted him.

"I shouldn't be here," she said at last. "My mother is very ill. I'm sitting up with her in the next room."

"Your mother?" he asked in some amazement. "Do you mean Mrs. Elliott? That is a surprise," he admitted, studying her with mock intensity. "I'd not realized she had another daughter."

"She has three," Louisa said, "altogether. Now, would you like me to leave the lamp like this, turned down, or do you want to read?"

For a moment he pretended to consider. "I might; you could turn it up a little—I doubt I shall sleep for a while. But before you go," he added as she turned away, "would you do something for me? Over there, on the mantelpiece, I think I left my cigar case and matches. Would you pass them to me?"

"I really don't think you should smoke in bed," she commented with heavy disapproval. "And if you've been as ill as everyone seems to think, I'm sure it can't be good for you."

Chastened, he assured her he was much recovered. "If you stayed awhile," he went on, "you could ensure my safety and that of the entire house."

Louisa shook her head. "*You* might be feeling better, Mr. Devereaux, but my mother is ill. I must see to her. Now, if you'll excuse me . . ."

Suddenly guilt-stricken by that reminder, he said: "I hope she's no worse . . ."

"I'm just going to find out, Mr. Devereaux; that is, if you'll allow me."

At the door he called her back. "Miss Elliott?"

"Yes?" Sighing, she turned to face him. "What is it?"

For a moment he hesitated, chewing at his lower lip. "There's something I feel I should say. My name's Duncannon, not Devereaux."

Louisa's left eyebrow arched quizzically; a sudden, dimpling smile appeared and was as quickly suppressed. "I see," she said crisply, as though he had explained everything; and with that, she closed the door.

Pulling the heavy robe around him, Captain Robert Devereaux Duncannon, of the 1st Royal Dragoons, stationed at the Cavalry Barracks, east of the city, eased himself out of bed and reached for the jug of lemonade. He would have preferred a good, stiff brandy.

With a sigh he found his morocco slippers and padded across to the fire, determined to have that cigar, no matter what the disapproving

Miss Elliott had to say. Gingerly he paced back and forth, trying to force some strength into limbs which seemed incredibly weak after a mere four days in bed, inwardly cursing the illness which had laid him low for so long. No matter, he would have to report for duty in the morning; no one knew where he was, and it simply would not do to be reported absent without leave.

So much, he thought, for the idea of a quiet few days in which to gather his thoughts and lick his mental wounds in private; the illness had put paid to that. For a moment, wondering what had possessed him to give his mother's family name instead of his own, Robert Duncannon shook his head. It was, he supposed, part of the morbid mood he had returned with; an irrational fear of meeting up with anyone he knew, of acquaintances hearing he was back in York, hazarding guesses as to the reason why.

That overwhelming need for anonymity now seemed foolish and pointless, like the impulse which had made him reveal the truth just now. What must she be thinking? he wondered. What had he said while delirious? How much did they know? The gruff little doctor had tried to question him earlier, when he came to bandage his wounds, and Robert knew his answers were too vague to be believed. He realized he would have to think of a more convincing tale for the regimental surgeon.

For the first time since Christmas Day, he was suddenly able to view the events leading to his injury with some kind of clarity. Of course it had been his own fault, as brother William had so brutally pointed out; and Anne, his brother's wife, had seemed to take delight in it even while she berated him. "You were warned," she said. "But as usual, Robert, you refused to listen. And now Christmas is ruined completely!" Finding a certain bitter humor in that, he laughed shortly. But the memory of his three-year-old daughter, hysterical and refusing to be comforted, was far from amusing.

Lost in unhappy contemplation, he barely heard the light tap at his door; its opening, a few seconds later, momentarily startled him.

They were both surprised; he by her sudden reappearance, she by the fact that he was simply standing there. And by his height. Even at that distance it was obvious to Louisa that their rather mysterious guest was several inches taller than she, and she was by no means a small woman.

Somewhat disconcerted, she apologized for disturbing him. "It's just that I heard you moving about and wondered whether I could get you something. A hot drink, perhaps?"

"No, no, the lemonade's fine."

"Well, then . . ." She turned, her hand on the door.

He relaxed suddenly, a warm smile dispelling the rather forbidding look she had faced on entering the room. "Please don't go. I—I'd appreciate some company." Running his fingers through his hair, he added with a small, slightly embarrassed laugh: "Bad dreams—they tend to linger."

Touched by that appeal, Louisa felt her earlier resolve begin to weaken; and sensing it, he pressed home that small advantage.

"You shouldn't, I know. It's most improper at this hour, and of course there's your mother to care for." Again that smile. "Why not leave the door open? Then you may keep an eye on two invalids at once." Marking her continued hesitation, he added: "I know I was raving for a while, but I assure you, I'm normally quite sane. And one loud scream would bring the entire household running, would it not?"

Unfolding a blanket which lay across the arm of a fireside chair, he wrapped it around his legs and sat down with a gratified sigh. "Oh, that's good. Forgive my poor manners, Miss Elliott, but these weakened limbs wouldn't hold me another minute. Come, do sit down where I can see you. And rest assured, had I a mind to chase you around the bedroom, I swear I'd make no more than a couple of yards!"

Hearing her anxieties so accurately expressed, Louisa felt a little foolish; to refuse would seem punctilious in the extreme. Nevertheless, there was a merry twinkle in those blue eyes which gave something of a lie to his words.

"Very well," she agreed, seating herself with grave dignity in the chair which faced his. "But I warn you, sir, having committed one impropriety, I intend to commit more with some very direct questions. In return for my company, you must tell me exactly who you are and what brings you to my mother's small establishment. *We* know its excellence, and so do our regular visitors, but I rather think you must be used to—shall we say something grander? Like Harker's or the Royal Station Hotel?"

Her frankness amused him. He chuckled quietly, on and off, for some time; but he introduced himself with correct if overdone formality, even to the extent of a mocking little bow from his chair. He talked about his regiment, giving some impressions of the city gleaned during a stay of almost six months, and even described a day in the summer, riding out toward Strensall, when he had chanced to pass the house.

In the heat and dust, he said, Gillygate had looked wilted and drab; but, with bright green paint, a man had been putting finishing touches to the sign which hung between the first- and second-floor windows. Recalling it well, Louisa smiled; she told him she had been at home that week of the house-painting, suffering from the smell of it.

Robert laughed at that but with unashamed sentiment said: "There were flowers at the windows and fresh white curtains. It looked clean and bright and very welcoming. I remember wondering who lived there."

"But you could have stayed in town," she insisted.

"That's true. But in the center of town," he pointed out, "I might have chanced across any number of acquaintances. I didn't want that. I wanted—oh, I don't know—time to myself, I suppose. Time to think, to make some sense of things." For a moment, seeing the concern in her eyes, Robert was sorely tempted to tell her everything. The low ebb of the night, the fall of coals in the grate, the intimacy of the bedroom, all conspired to bring the words to his tongue; but with a sad smile he shook his head.

Looking away from her, into the fire's glowing heart, he said heavily: "I was feeling ill, but it was such a bad crossing from Kingstown, I thought it merely the aftereffects. Had I known what it was, believe me, I'd not have come here. I'd probably have gone straight back to Fulford." After a moment's pause he added quietly: "And there, I imagine, I would have died."

"Oh, surely not—you have doctors . . ."

He shrugged. "Yes, if one had been called in time. What saved me, Miss Elliott, was not the little man who came to tend this—this wound of mine. He didn't save my life. Your mother did, with her excellent nursing." He could have said more, but refrained. Why burden her, he thought, with that depressed state which had longed so avidly for death? She would not understand, and with the strange lifting of that morbid mood, he could barely understand himself.

It was enough now to be alive; to be in the company of a young and very lovely woman, and to feel the blood coursing through his veins in response to her.

With a sudden smile he said: "I have a lot to thank your mother for. It's a debt I doubt I'll ever be able to repay."

"When I saw her this evening, you were the first person she asked about. I'm sure the only debt you owe her is to get well."

"You know," he smiled, "you're very like her."

"Indeed I'm not," Louisa protested, laughing. "We're very *unlike,* as a matter of fact. If you knew us better . . ."

"Oh, but you are," he insisted, charmed by the transformation of her smile and wondering if she laughed a lot. He could not remember Charlotte ever laughing like that; her amusement had been a rare thing, always with the hard edge of hysteria or cruelty. In the brightness of the fire's flame, this girl's eyes sparkled as she glanced at him, and the stray hairs of her close-cut curls were turned to gold, like an aureole.

He had always loved the luxuriant length of women's hair, but on Louisa Elliott the short, pert style seemed right and oddly attractive. Although it was a fashion many young and independent women had adopted, it seemed to accentuate her individuality. There was something very fresh and challenging about her, which he liked and respected; but there was warmth and wholesomeness too, which appealed in a far more basic way.

Disconcerted by that lingering appraisal and overly aware of the charm which had held her for far longer than was either necessary or proper, for a moment Louisa compressed her lips and looked away. "It's very late," she said, rising to her feet, "and I must leave you to get some rest."

Although he did not rise, as she passed his chair Robert caught her hand and held it. "I know it was selfish of me," he remarked, "to want to detain you. But thank you for staying, for giving me your company. I feel so much better for it."

"Not at all," she murmured politely while her heart beat hard against tightened stays and color mounted to burning in her cheeks. Beneath straight black brows, his eyes regarded her steadily; she waited for him to release her, but he did not.

"I have to report to the barracks tomorrow," he said at last, "so I shall be leaving quite early. Will I see you before I go?"

"In the morning?" Louisa asked stupidly, hardly crediting his words. "You're thinking of leaving!"

"I have to—no choice, I'm afraid." He smiled, and his thumb caressed the back of her wrist.

"But surely," she began, shaking her head in angry frustration, "you can't just walk out in the morning. It's snowing—bitterly cold. You'll catch pneumonia."

Robert shrugged. "So, I'll recover on the army's time. And as soon as I'm able, I'll call to see your mother. I want to thank her personally for dragging me back from the brink. Will you pass the message on for me?"

"Of course." Frowning, conscious of a quite ridiculous sense of disappointment, Louisa tried to withdraw her hand from his grasp; momentarily, however, his grip tightened, and he raised her fingers to his lips. Light though it was, she felt the quick thrill of that kiss run through her like a shock.

A little breathlessly, Louisa bade him goodnight. At the door, however, she paused, looking back. "Take care, then."

"I shall, don't worry."

He sat staring into the fire for some time, and when he did return to his bed, Robert Duncannon slept fitfully and later than he intended.

THREE

*T*here was a lot of fuss the following morning. Edward called at half past seven on his way to work, missing Louisa, who had just gone up to bed, and upsetting Bessie's usual quiet routine. At ten Dr. Mackenzie began his rounds with the Elliotts, and incensed by Robert's stubborn determination, the Scotsman ranted alarmingly. In his harsh Glasgow accent he prognosticated relapse unless the younger man returned to bed immediately; and as for walking out into the winter air, he could guarantee pneumonia at the very least. Finally, in the face of his erstwhile patient's implacable resolution, he shrugged his shoulders in disgust, scribbled his fee on a scrap of paper, and demanded to see Mary Elliott.

"And I sincerely hope *she's* not stirred from her bed," he muttered threateningly as he mounted the stairs.

Cowering under the blast of words, Emily followed him, leaving Robert Duncannon alone in the small front parlor. Beads of sweat stood out on his forehead, his face was pale, and his long legs trembled from the effort of appearing fit and nonchalant in front of the fierce little Scot. He sank heavily into a chair by the glass-fronted bookcase, a small pile of books beside him on the floor. After a while, he pulled himself together and returned the books to their rightful places, knowing now who was the owner of the name on most of the bookplates. Louisa Elliott: the signature was large, confident, the occasional appended date signifying that most of these books were the reading matter of her youth. Her taste had ranged from the romantic adventures of the Waverly novels, through Jane Austen and the Brontës, to that inexorable fatalist, Hardy. To Robert's mind, the beauty of Hardy's prose concealed too thinly the bitter pill of his philosophy; he was unable to read him without seeing, in part, his own life exposed under the novelist's pen.

With a small grimace he pushed the Hardy back, next to a slender volume of verse by Edward Elliott. It was inscribed with fondest love from the author to his dear aunt. Aunt who? Robert wondered. And who was Edward? The Elliotts as a family developed a new dimension, strongly defying all his preconceived notions of the English lower classes. Although he would have resented being called a snob, he had to admit that the men under his command did little to elevate his ideas. Yet here, in this comparatively humble little boardinghouse, he had been treated . . . with deference, yes, but there had been no false fawning, no apologies, rather a pride in what the family had to offer. He was beginning to understand that pride, but he wondered why their talents had not extended to a larger hotel in a more fashionable quarter of the city; custom would not have been lacking. And Louisa Elliott, with that luscious country bloom about her, so wholesomely desirable, like a delicious russet apple, waiting to be tasted. He wished quite fervently to see her, for her to come and say good-bye before he left.

Robert's eyes scanned the room, the heavy furniture rather too modern for a taste that had been educated by the faded eighteenth-century elegance of White Leigh; but, unlike his home, this house was possessed of a casual warmth and a comfort which he would long remember.

The door opened, and rising to his feet, he was disappointed to see that it was Emily who entered. As though uncertain how to address him, she hesitated, her dark eyes still full of suspicion.

"And how is Mrs. Elliott?" Robert asked, forestalling her need to decide upon a name.

"Dr. Mackenzie is quite pleased with her," Emily said slowly. "She's no worse, anyway, and that's supposed to be a good sign."

"Good. I'm very relieved to hear that. I told your sister I would call in the next few days to ask after your mother's health, but please pass on my best regards to her, and my thanks.

"Unfortunately, I have to leave very shortly. Do you think that you could make up my bill? And send someone to hire a cab for me? I doubt if I could or should walk very far today," he added with a small gesture of deprecation.

"I'll see to it," Emily offered. "Where will you be going, sir?"

Apparently preoccupied by the depth of snow beyond the window, he answered casually: "The Cavalry Barracks."

Over a pot of tea in the kitchen after their midday meal, Emily reiterated her surprise. "So when he said The Cavalry Barracks, I nearly dropped with surprise. You didn't tell me you knew already, Louisa. What is he, for goodness sake?"

Her sister shrugged. "I think he said he was a captain." But he never did explain about that arm of his, she thought.

"You don't sound very interested. He was certainly interested in you," Emily said. "Asked where you were, and when I told him you were sleeping, he said I must remember to pass on his thanks and his farewell to you. And," Emily added with great emphasis, "he not only paid his bill, he left an amount equal to his own doctor's bill for Mamma. Said he felt responsible for her illness."

Louisa remarked that it was the least he could do, under the circumstances. But she was intrigued nevertheless. "Still, I expect that's the last we shall see of him. In my experience, gentlemen can have the most charming manners, but their memories are short. Inside a couple of days he'll have forgotten all about us."

"No," stated Emily. "We'll see him again, of that I'm certain."

"You were certain he was trouble," Bessie reminded her from across the table. "Fair put the wind up me you did, Miss Emily. I wish you wouldn't get your *feelings* about people—I'd as soon not know about 'em."

Studying the leaves in the bottom of her teacup, Emily compressed her lips. "I can't help it," she muttered defensively.

"You can help telling me, miss," the older woman protested. "If I had a shilling for every time you've scared me, I'd be a rich woman by now. That poor young gentleman."

"Well," Emily insisted mulishly, "we haven't seen the last of him. You mark my words—he'll be back."

Abruptly Louisa stood up. "Isn't it time you went up to Mamma? I'm going to find Blanche."

The medieval church of St. Giles, after which Gillygate was named, was long since gone, all trace buried beneath more recent developments. Edward always said part of it lay under the Salvation Army Citadel further up the street, finding much irony in that small fact. But the blizzard of the night before had softened the citadel's harsh red brick, together with the neat new terraces of identical houses which flanked it.

In an old skirt and galoshes, Louisa paused to look up and down the street before setting off into town. Bessie had already cleared their step and frontage, but great swags of snow still clung to every windowledge and overhung the green-painted name-board which separated the top two stories. Recalling the captain's words, Louisa looked up, trying to imagine herself a stranger, trying to see it through his eyes. Beside the cobbler's old cottage next door, Elliott's and its adjoining neighbors looked very smart and new, although they had been built some forty years before, replacing half a dozen buildings no better than the cobbler's.

With a surge of possessive pride, Louisa noticed that their paintwork did look clean and shiny still, and despite the inevitable grime of winter, the letterbox and doorknocker shone and her mother's lace curtains were as white as the snow itself.

Gillygate was not as elegant as Bootham—its buildings were too hotch-potch—nor as good an address as Blossom Street, where the Tempests lived within sight of the city's main gate, the gate which formerly guarded the route from London and all points south. But it was busy and bustling, a main street of shops and hotels and inns, and on this side they had the privacy of long yards and gardens at the back and the city walls and ramparts to look out on. Which was more than the Tempests could lay claim to, Louisa thought happily as her eyes took in the picture-book aspect of the snow. Rusty pink brickwork was mortared in white, every pane of glass in smooth-fronted Georgian houses picked out by miniature drifts, the recessed doorways of shops piled high, leaving the tips of bootscrapers exposed here and there like black cherries on a frosted cake.

It was a bright morning, bitterly cold in the narrow, shadowed reaches of Gillygate, but where the sun flooded forth down Bootham and across the open expanse of Exhibition Square the air had a suggestion of spring about it, an invigorating sparkle which dispelled Louisa's weariness completely. Her eyes were suddenly attracted by a flash of scarlet by the De Grey Rooms, and looking across the road she saw two dragoon officers leaving the Yorkshire Hussars' Mess; as clear as though he stood before her, Robert Duncannon sprang to mind yet again. The strong features, easy elegance, and imposing height; how magnificent he must look in uniform, she thought with a surge of pleasure; and immediately reproached herself. Pursued, such imaginings would leave her as addle-pated as Rachel Tempest, besotted by vainglorious imagery and totally out of touch with reality. Whatever his social or military rank, Louisa harshly reminded herself, Robert Duncannon was just a man, with the same thoughts, desires, and indifferences as any other. If nothing else, five years with landed gentry had taught her that; and if she needed a further guard to romantic inclinations, she had only to conjure up pictures of her mother and Aunt Elizabeth, "fallen women" the pair of them, no matter how well buried the past.

Awareness of her own illegitimacy was something she lived with, as disabling in its way as a crooked spine or clubfoot; she was rarely relaxed or at ease with people outside the Elliott family, because it was impossible to be honest, impossible to share reminiscences about parents and child-hood, the common experience which drew people together. In a strange way, however, that sense of ambiguity, of being set apart, had been an asset in her chosen career. Notoriously suspended in the gap between servants and employers, governesses and companions were too socially awkward to be welcome in either camp; the loneliness could be killing, and for most, having to earn their own living was a humiliating step down in the world. For Louisa, however, it was a step up from what might have been; more than that, for she liked children, enjoyed teaching, and minded the solitude hardly at all. It was in fact her protection, and she fitted her chosen niche both cheerfully and well.

With plans for Emily's impending marriage upon them, Bessie often teased Louisa about her lack of suitors, but at twenty-five she had no hopes of marriage, nor any particular desire to relinquish the single state. She was pleased to see her sister engaged, because Emily was happy and the estate of marriage seemed to have been made for her; but Louisa was not envious. She found Emily's fiancé, John Chapman, worthy but dull, his family too patronizing for comfort.

John was a carpenter, apprentice-trained under his father and almost certain to follow on in the family business. He would no doubt do well, Louisa thought, and Emily would make him a good wife; she just wished Mrs. Chapman could be kinder, less keen to stress Emily's amazing good fortune; and having swallowed the unpalatable truth about the Elliotts, Louisa wished she would simply forget it. The only consolation was that the Chapmans were too concerned for their own snow-white respectability ever to admit the lack of it in Emily.

From snippets of conversation her sister occasionally divulged, Louisa knew the Chapmans thought her snobbish and superior, which was unpleasant; more hurtful still was their opinion that with her background Louisa Elliott had no right to seem so. There were times, when she felt most injured, that she thought her sister's dowry was an added attraction to her solid domestic virtues; for Emily's training had cost their mother nothing more than patience. What had been spent on Louisa and Blanche in their respective educations was given to Emily as her marriage portion.

But that brief twinge of pain was easily suppressed; Louisa considered herself too proud to submit to people like the Chapmans and, anyway, would rather have her freedom. Not for her the humiliation of having the past exposed and examined, the studied consideration of whether illegitimacy in the family could be borne; not for her the dashed hopes, the terrible disillusionment that had been Edward's a few short years ago.

Less than ten years, although it seemed a lifetime now; and the end of that affair had crushed him, with his honesty flung back in his face and permission to marry refused, and all because he lacked a father's name. Two years later the girl, Maud, was dead of consumption. Only too well did Louisa recall Edward's grief, his bitter vow to remain unmarried, and the gross injustice of it all.

Emily might marry her John, and Blanche would either make a fortune in her own right or manipulate some unsuspecting but well-heeled gentleman to the altar, but she and Edward would probably end their days as he often surmised: old maids the pair of them, reliving happier moments on either side of a shared hearth.

FOUR

Coney Street was the home of some of the finest shops in York. From the Mansion House at one end to the church of St. Michael at the other, it was filled with the kind of expensive establishments that attracted county families to the city for spending sprees when the capital was too inconvenient and the latest *arrivistes* who sought to camouflage their humble origins by aping their betters. Among the fashionable crowds strolling along the cleared pavements, Louisa felt like an outcast from an orphanage in her old skirt and second-best cloak. The galoshes were out of place, too, where crested carriages with liveried coachmen dropped ladies and gentlemen at the doors of milliners and outfitters, their shoes unsullied by the snow of the less exalted streets. Her chin lifted in unconscious defiance as she thought of Blanche and how she would wince when she saw her less than modish sister.

Blanche had risen, at the age of twenty-four, to the dizzy heights of senior seamstress to one of the most exclusive dressmakers in town. Her early affinity for good clothes and fine materials, inherited, it was quietly asserted, from her late father, had developed along with her flair for innovation and design until it was markedly obvious that an apprenticeship must be sought. Mary Elliott had used part of her controversial legacy to pay for the privilege, and Blanche had easily fulfilled every expectation. That her talents had gone to her head was indisputable; from time to time she increased her salary by threatening to take her considerable expertise elsewhere, which drove her employer into paroxysms of rage. The emaciated and dragon-like Miss Devine might rule her clients like a mandarin, but she made little impression on Blanche Elliott, who could match her demented outbursts shriek for shriek. But by and large they respected each other, and Blanche had no real intention of leaving; she would have been too insecure in her own business, and a desire for security was almost her only weakness. Once out of her apprenticeship, she had waved good-bye to the Gillygate house and taken rooms in a boardinghouse for young ladies on the other side of town. She did not get on with either of her sisters, and having to share a room with Emily in Gillygate was an imposition she had not intended to prolong beyond necessity.

Louisa passed the discreet frontage of Miss Devine's, a small Regency doorway and single half-bow window that belied the depths of the rooms behind, and entered a narrow passage which led eventually to a tiny yard shared by several adjoining properties. A path had been cleared, but dirty snow lay piled in heaps against damp, salt-encrusted walls. The stone steps she mounted were concave with age; like all these backs leading down to the nearby river, the building was much older than the face-lifted front it presented to the world. In the enclosed yard the air was dank; ancient bricks, unwarmed by the sun, gave off an eloquent miasma that reeked of blocked privies and successive river floodings. The muffled cries of men working in a warehouse close by competed with the rattle of sewing machines from Blanche's workroom as Louisa tapped upon its rickety door.

A young girl answered, face pale, eyes red-rimmed and squinting from sewing too many hours in too poor a light. Ten years ago Blanche had looked like that, Louisa recalled with a small shock; seeing her now, across the room, it was hard to believe. Taller than Emily, she nonetheless resembled her younger sister in features and coloring; but whereas Emily had a tendency to plumpness, Blanche's elegant figure was honed by nervous energy to a whipcord slenderness that her taut stays and black dress deliberately accentuated. Almost as black as the dress she wore, her hair was piled high on top of her head, the fringe frizzed, Alexandra-style; there was no rosy bloom to Blanche's cheeks; she preferred the city pallor which gave added luster to her intense dark eyes. Louisa often wondered whether her sister used laudanum drops to dilate the pupils; but perhaps it was simply the lack of light in this overcrowded workroom.

Those eyes registered surprise and annoyance as she realized who was at the door. Sharply she ordered the girl back to her work and bustled across the room toward Louisa.

"What have you come here for?" she hissed, at the same time taking in her sister's appearance with a single, horrified glance.

Again Louisa's chin came up; her generous mouth compressed itself into a thinner line, and she glared back at Blanche.

"Is it Mamma? I suppose it is," Blanche muttered, somewhat mollified. "I suppose you'd better come in and sit down a minute," she added, skirting several dressmaker's dummies, two large cutting-out tables, and four sewing machines from which part-made gowns cascaded in a riot of shimmering color.

Pushing aside the piece of crystal embroidery on which she had been working, Blanche pulled another chair toward her table and invited her sister to be seated. "Now," she said in a very businesslike way, "what's happened?"

"Nothing. Mamma's ill and wants to see you. That's all. I gather you were informed yesterday, and I do think you might've called to see her, even if you couldn't stay to help out."

"Of course I couldn't stay to help. I can't possibly be spared here— you can see for yourself the amount of work we have to get out."

"Why didn't you just look in? Surely Gillygate isn't that far out of your way?"

"I had to work late," Blanche replied defensively, earning herself a disbelieving look. There was a constant but uneven chatter from the machines, bursts of frantic treadling followed by short pauses as the women adjusted the satins and silks they joined together. Louisa cast a glance round the room; although the women were busy, only three dummies were being used, and one cutting table was quite clear. The fact that Blanche was whiling away her time with a piece of embroidery gave the lie to what she said.

"I trust you won't be working late tonight?"

Having the grace to look abashed, Blanche gave a reluctant reply. "No," she said slowly, "but I have an appointment later."

"Then cancel it," her sister said coldly.

She came to visit her mother that evening and the next, but it cut Louisa to the quick to see their mother's eyes light up with pleasure at the sight of her. Unable to bear Blanche's patent insincerity, Louisa trailed wearily down the stairs. In the kitchen they were pondering the same subject.

"She comes in here," Emily was saying, "dressed like a dog's dinner, full of poor Mamma this, and poor Mamma that. Fat lot she cares!"

"She wants her bottom smacking," pronounced Bessie, who might have said more had it not been for Louisa's sudden reappearance.

"It would warm the cockles of my heart to see you try," added Louisa, picking up a tea towel. They all laughed at that, glad to break the tension that Blanche's rare visits inspired. "Mamma seems a lot better this evening," she remarked as she stacked crockery in even piles.

"Aye," Bessie agreed, reaching up into the pine cupboard, "I made a nice hot mustard plaster and strapped it to her chest this afternoon. Does more good than all your doctor's medicines."

Emily nodded in agreement. "The fever's down a lot. I think she's going to be all right."

"I told you she would be, didn't I?" Louisa smiled. "But just you make sure she doesn't get out of bed too soon. You know what she's like—can't bear not to know what's going on. Have you any more guests booked in for next week?"

"Only two. We were expecting Mr. Rawnsley from Leeds, you know, but he hasn't turned up, nor has he sent word, so I'm wondering if he's gone down with the flu as well."

"More than likely, but the fewer the better while Mamma's ill. You've got enough to do, looking after her. Anyway," she sighed, "if you find yourselves stuck for money, just ask Blanche for some—she seems to have plenty."

As if on cue, the budding couturier swept into the kitchen, pulling a short, fur-lined cape around her shoulders. "What have I got plenty of?"

"Money," Louisa said bluntly, without turning round. "As guests are a bit thin on the ground, I thought you might help out."

Blanche was volubly offended, maintaining the fiction that she sent money regularly; had it not been for Edward's sudden and unexpected arrival, there might have developed an argument of serious proportions.

His normally serene face was flushed and agitated, but Blanche barely spared him a glance. With a curt nod, she took the opportunity to escape, flinging a few coins onto the table as a parting gesture.

"Conscience money," Bessie muttered, but Louisa left it lying there; angry though she was, her overstretched nerves registered immediately that something was terribly wrong.

Waving away Bessie's offer to take his coat, Edward reached for Louisa's hand, taking a deep breath to steady himself before he spoke.

"It's my mother," he said. "She's very ill. I think she may be dying."

There was a sudden, stunned silence in the room. Louisa gripped his hands, then, practical as ever, asked him why he had not sent a message instead of coming himself.

"They have people ill on either side of us, and there was no one in across the way. The street was deserted—nobody about at all. It was quicker to come myself," he added bleakly. "I must go on to Dr. Mackenzie's."

"No, I'll go," Louisa said, reaching for her coat. "You go straight home."

Bessie had not moved, but when she spoke, her voice was rough with emotion. "Can I come with you, Mr. Edward? I'd like to. I always loved your dear mam, and if she's going, it may cheer her to see my old face. And you'll not want to be alone.''

Edward would far rather have had Louisa as his companion through the long night watch, but with a brief nod and a final pressure on his cousin's hand he set off home immediately, leaving Bessie to follow as soon as she was able.

Beset by an epidemic which was gathering in virulence with each passing day, Dr. Mackenzie, like every other doctor in the city, found his attentions required by people who could not normally afford the price of a prescription. In desperation they called him, yet in so many cases it was too late. The virus killed with speed, and not only the traditionally weak; men and women in the prime of life were struck down as indiscriminately as ninepins.

The doctor was out when Louisa called, but she left a message, exchanged a few consolatory words with his exhausted wife, and returned home. Emily wondered what, if anything, they should tell their mother. It was decided ultimately to tell her nothing, to let the coming hours be peaceful for her at least.

With Emily sitting up till three, Louisa took a candlestick from the dresser and climbed the stairs to her top-floor room, the little flame casting leaping shadows on the steep and narrow wooden steps. It was bitterly cold at the top of the house, frost still crusted the windowpanes, obscuring the view of the Minster as effectively as any curtain. Nevertheless, she drew the pink gingham across and, shivering, rapidly unfastened the dozen buttons of her navy worsted bodice, pressed the stud from its starched white inner collar, and unhooked the heavy skirt she wore. Fumbling in haste, she eventually loosened the ties of her stays, relief fighting the chill as she struggled to pull on her nightdress. Sliding between icy sheets, only then did Louisa remove her undergarments, finally pushing her arms into the sleeves of her nightgown before curling up tight beneath the weighty covers.

As a tingling warmth gradually returned, she stretched out slowly, testing the cold areas of the bed as her feet made their way to the bottom. Her body began to relax, but her mind was resolutely wakeful, thinking of Edward, thinking with him, wondering if Elizabeth Elliott would divulge her secrets before she quit this world forever. Never once, to Louisa's knowledge, had her aunt spoken of Edward's father, nor of the circumstances which led to his conception; although it might have been a secret to which Mary Elliott was party, she had never hinted as much, and for Edward the mystery had always been something of an obsession. Sympathizing, sharing his dread of that knowledge going to the grave, she held her cousin's face, and her aunt's, in her mind, offering them both in mute prayer to a God she was unsure of. The Old Testament tenet of the sins of the fathers being visited upon generations of innocent children weighed heavily as always, fighting her desire to believe in a God whose love was too broad and deep to take account of such pettiness. Obeying childhood instruction, she prayed; her faith, however, was sadly lacking.

FIVE

Disturbed by a bleak sensation of doom, Louisa left her mother's side shortly after six and made a pot of tea before waking her.

"I have to go out," she said softly. "I want to see Edward before he goes to work." Still confused by the aftereffects of heavy sleep, Mary Elliott nodded unquestioningly. Louisa debated whether to say more. "Aunt Elizabeth is ill, and I want to see how she is." She looked long into her mother's eyes, and unspoken fear seemed to hang between them; patting the small hand on the coverlet, she abruptly turned away. "Will you be all right?" she asked from the doorway. "Emily's still asleep."

"Of course. You'd better hurry. Edward may need you."

Forbearing to say that Bessie had been with him all night, Louisa hurried down the stairs and was soon on her way through unlit streets toward Elizabeth Elliott's house.

It was a small house, two rooms upstairs, two down, without garden or proper hallway, so that its main door opened straight off the pavement into the parlor; for this reason, that door was always locked, and Louisa turned off before she reached it, into a lane that served the backs of these terraced houses. The yard door opened silently, and picking her way by the chink of light showing between heavy kitchen curtains, she reached the rear of the house without mishap. In the kitchen Edward was sprawled in an easy chair beside the range, the fire all but dead in the grate. In the soft light of an oil lamp, his thick brown hair was brushed with gold; long, waving strands falling forward across a high forehead. Purple lines of weariness showed beneath closed eyes and shadowed the hollows of his cheeks. Hidden by his curling beard, his chin lay wedged against his waistcoat, arms drooping across overstuffed chair arms, like those of a carved *pietà* Louisa had once seen in a book.

Alarm made her hasty. She shook him almost roughly, relief coinciding with his gasp of shocked awakening.

Stiffly he sat up, pushing back the hair from his forehead, light blue eyes cloudy with pain and confusion. He had never seemed his age, but suddenly, in this moment, Louisa realized that he looked all his thirty-seven years and more. Her hands went out to him. Without being told, she knew his mother was dead.

"When?"

He shook his head. "I'm not sure. A while ago—an hour, maybe." He made a sound that was surprisingly like a laugh. "I came downstairs and—just fell asleep. How stupid of me."

"Not stupid—you must be exhausted."

"Bessie's with her. Do you want to go up?"

"No. Not just yet." Still holding his hands, she knelt on the floor in front of him, her arms across his knees, eyes intently searching his. "Oh, love, I'm so sorry. So sorry," she repeated softly. Louisa looked away, knowing the answer to her question even as it was uttered. "Did she say anything—before she died?"

"For the last few hours, she wasn't even conscious," he wearily replied. "But I doubt if she had any intention of telling me." As the anguish in him suddenly surfaced, he gripped her hands fiercely, squeezing his eyes tight shut against hot, flooding, uncontrollable tears.

Unable to bear the sight of his contorted face, she looked down, watching his fingers tighten, feeling the pain of his grasp, willing herself not to cry out. But as suddenly as it had begun, the frustrated outburst was over; Edward pulled away from her, dashed the tears away with the back of his hand, found a crumpled handkerchief in a trouser pocket, and wiped his face quickly, ashamed of his weakness. "I'm sorry," he said huskily, not meeting her eyes.

"Why?" she asked gently. "If you can't weep with me, who can you weep with? I do understand."

From the depths of his bitterness, he turned on her. "How can you?" he demanded harshly. "You knew your father. He loved your mother, and she loved him, and you remember that. But me? I've never had the slightest idea about my father! He could quite literally be anything from a prince to a pauper. I don't even know if my mother loved him. I could be the result of a glorious passion or simply a passing fancy after the harvest supper!"

As Louisa winced, he laughed without humor. "But it's true, isn't it? Or do you think she was taken advantage of?" he asked sarcastically. "Always bearing in mind that my mother was over thirty at the time, of course!"

Distaste made Louisa turn away. She longed to block her ears, shut out the bitter mockery of his words, but his voice pressed relentlessly on.

"It's hard to credit her with any kind of loving impulse. I don't think she loved anyone in the whole of her life—not even me."

"Oh, Edward, you're wrong!"

"Am I?" His eyes held hers for a long moment, searching for the truth. All the antipathy she had ever felt for his mother seemed to be drawn to the surface, shaming her. She should have been mourning her aunt's passing, not remembering old resentments, Louisa thought as she looked away. Bewildered and unhappy, she simply pressed his hand.

"I was twelve before you were born," he said quietly. "You don't know how little love there was in my life before that date." The eyes which scanned her face were full of pain, and his hands, stroking her hair, so gentle, it was almost unbearable. Leaning her head against his shoulder, she thought of all the things that might have been and felt a surge of impotent anger.

"I was always passed off as her nephew when I was a child, never as her son. I was told so many conflicting tales in those early years, but never anything about my father. In fact the only consistency my mother ever displayed was in her refusal to tell me anything at all about him. Eventually, of course, I gave up asking. I've brought the subject up several times in the last few years, though to no avail. I thought, if she couldn't explain to a child, surely she could tell the truth to a grown man? But no. Do you know what she said the last time, Louisa? She said she couldn't see why it was of any interest to me!"

Feeling his pain, wanting to take it from him, Louisa hugged him closer, breathing in the familiar, reassuring smell of his working clothes. The scent of ink and leather took her back to childhood, except now the roles were curiously reversed. "She never understood you," she murmured.

"She didn't like me very much, either," he sighed. "Although I suppose the feeling was mutual. I think," Edward slowly confessed, "that I must have reminded her very much of him."

Louisa drew back and for the first time tried to see him objectively, as she might have studied a stranger. Except in coloring, he did not favor the Elliotts. The nose was too narrow, too aquiline; and his eyes, a light blue-gray, were deeper set. It was a sensitive, finely featured face, hardly disguised by the beard he had grown in his early twenties and kept ever since. Despite his strong, scarred hands and unremarkable clothes, Louisa had always thought the beard gave him a rather romantic, poetic air, which was not at all the impression he wished to convey. Remembering the teasing of long ago, she smiled and touched his cheek. If Edward truly resembled his father, she realized he must have been an extremely handsome man.

To put that thought into words, however, would have embarrassed him. Instead she asked whether he had approached her own mother on the subject.

"Once, a few years ago. She said they were working in different places at that time, and she knew nothing."

"Your mother's papers?"

"I doubt it," he replied shortly. "I shall go through them, of course, but it's hardly likely . . ." He broke off with a gesture of impatience and shook his head. "I'm sorry," he murmured. Raising her hand to his lips, he kissed the palm. "I shouldn't have burdened you with all this. Forgive me?"

"There's no forgiveness necessary," she said, kissing his cheek. "I told you before—I understand."

"I know you do," Edward whispered. "I didn't mean what I said."

Something in his eyes caught painfully at her heart, sparking memories and old emotions Louisa preferred to leave in peace. Deliberately brisk, she stood up and set about coaxing the dying fire back to life. Suggesting her mother's cure for all ills, she filled the kettle and set it to boil. "Because poor Bessie will need some refreshment, even if you don't!" she admonished Edward with a smile.

"Of course. Poor Bessie—I'd quite forgotten her."

Two candles burned steadily in the front bedroom where Elizabeth Elliott lay small and shrunken in a bed which seemed much too big for her. The gray hair was neatly plaited, her face composed, hands folded over her thin breast.

Bessie looked worn and very tired.

"She's not properly laid out, Miss Louisa, but I wanted to pretty her up a bit, so I did her hair and washed her face and hands. Mr. Edward'll have to get a woman in to do it right."

"Yes—yes, I suppose he will," Louisa vaguely agreed, having had no previous contact with the practicalities of death. "It was good of you, Bessie. Were you with her when . . . ?"

"No, miss, I wasn't. Mr. Edward was with her. I was downstairs, having a bit of a catnap. He came down looking terrible. I asked him had she gone, and he just nodded, sat down in the chair, and went to sleep. Just like that. Right odd, I thought. Anyway, I came up and sat with her—didn't want her to be on her own . . ." Bessie began to weep, huge, heaving sobs which made her flesh quiver. "She was a fine woman," she choked as Louisa comforted her, "so respectable, you'd never have thought . . ."

Louisa nodded and patted her shoulder, wanting Bessie to know she understood, there was no need to say any more.

"She worked that hard, and it was all for him—Mr. Edward, I mean. And she was so good to me. I don't mind telling you, Miss Louisa, if it hadn't been for Miss Elizabeth, I'd have been dead years ago." She sniffed noisily and found a handkerchief to wipe her eyes and nose. "She found me after I'd run away from the poorhouse, hanging round the station, begging. They took me out of the gutter, her and your dear mam, and made a decent woman of me." As her memories took over, Bessie burst into a fresh fit of weeping; it was all Louisa could do to persuade her to leave that cold and lonely room.

"You've repaid them both in good service, Bessie. No one could have had a better servant or a kinder friend. I know that—and so did Aunt Elizabeth. Now come down and get that cup of tea I've made."

Elizabeth Elliott had been a spinster, but for nigh on twenty years she had passed as a widow; it seemed too cruel to have to divulge her true estate now that she was dead. Although the problem seemed insurmountable, it was solved unwittingly by Dr. Mackenzie. In a state of exhaustion himself he completed the details of death automatically, murmuring odd, abrupt words of consolation.

"Well, Mr. Elliott, if you'll pardon my saying, it's a relief and a blessing. The poor woman suffered dreadfully with her bronchitis. A shock, yes, but you'll get over it. You're young, your mother was old. Save your pity for the widows and orphans."

Stunned into silence, Edward, Louisa, and Bessie left him to make his own exit. Looking at the piece of paper the doctor had left, they saw that Elizabeth Elliott was marked down as a widow.

The decision had been made for them.

Mary Elliott wept. She grieved for the suddenness of her sister's death when she had expected to die herself and for the fact that she was still too ill to do anything. As her nephew sat by her bed, she shed more tears, remembering that she and Elizabeth had visited each other rarely in the last fifteen years and more from duty than pleasure. The past welled up in her memory, and she looked at the man by her side, seeing in his place the withdrawn and solitary child he had been.

"You can't stay there on your own, Edward. You must come back to us."

He glanced up, and for a moment, as his eyes held hers, she saw a spark of old, half-buried resentment. With a wry smile he said: "You haven't the room."

Color mounted to her cheeks. "Nonsense," she assured him in a passable imitation of her normally brisk tone. "We made a place for your Uncle William when he needed us—you can have his old room at the top of the house and pay me what you gave your mother. You'll have a home and someone to look after you, and I shall have a room permanently filled, which will suit me very well."

"What about—?" He broke off, slightly embarrassed.

"Now there's no need to bring that up; it was a long time ago, Edward. The situation no longer applies. Besides, Louisa's living in with the Tempests, Blanche won't come back, and Emily will be married in the spring. What am I to do without all my chicks?" she asked with a coaxing smile.

"I feel we should both think it over," he said cautiously.

"Well, think about it. My mind's already made up, but take your time if you want to, and let me know. I'd love to have you back again— you'll do me good." She smiled suddenly, recalling long winter evenings when the girls had been young. "No one's read to me since you went away, and I've missed that, you know. All those lovely stories and your beautiful poems quite took my mind off all that boring mending!"

Although he felt he was being cajoled and flattered, Edward slowly nodded. To be closer to Louisa, he wanted to come back.

"Good," his aunt smiled. "I'm glad that's settled. Come whenever you're ready."

The funeral was held the following Wednesday. The group of mourners was small, the Lincolnshire brothers all dead now, their families prevented from sending representatives because of the severe weather. Cousin John wrote for them all, describing the frozen wastes around Blankney and Metheringham as something comparable only with Siberia; Mary Elliott had nodded as she read his letter, recalling only too well that flat landscape, having nothing to protect it as the east winds swept in from Russia, bringing snow in great, obliterating swaths. The Vale of York might be equally flat, but the wolds and moors of the East Riding stood between it and the bitter expanse of the North Sea; the city might not be as healthy, but with the onset of old age, a milder climate was preferable. And here, at least, the snow had turned to rain.

The hearse, drawn by two elderly black horses complete with nodding ebony plumes, moved off at walking pace, followed by the equally ancient carriage hired to transport the little band of mourners to the cemetery. Because of the epidemic, demand was high, and the old and dusty conveyance set Blanche alternately sneezing and complaining. Louisa calmly informed her sister that she had a choice: if the carriage was insufferable, she could walk the mile and a half to the cemetery. With a loud, unladylike sniff, Blanche shook her head and wedged herself more comfortably against Bessie's ample frame; she might have wished for a cleaner, more modish form of transport, but Blanche was unlikely to refuse this novelty. Indeed, there was an air of shared importance among the women in spite of their grief; accustomed to walking, or at best traveling by public horse-drawn tram, they savored this rare journey, and it showed in their faces as they glanced out at halted pedestrians, men doffing their caps as the hearse passed by. Past the soaring mass of the Minster's west front, down Petergate, with its steep-gabled medieval shops and inns, down narrow Colliergate, with a shared smile as Edward pointed to the sign of "Whip-Ma-Whop-Ma-Gate," and into Fossgate, where Albert Tempest had his printing premises. They all leaned across to look at Edward's place of work in the manner of tourists, although it was not entirely strange to any of them: a narrow, brick-built, eighteenth-century building which, like the one sober man in a group of inebriates, seemed to support the twisted and overhanging gables of its much older neighbors. The increasing air of genteel decay quickly degenerated into the obvious poverty of Walmgate, a long, shabby street which fronted a maze of tiny courts and yards to either side. Shopfronts were grimy and dark, windows broken and patched with filthy cardboard, the wares they displayed elderly and unappetizing. Gin shops and beerhouses abounded, doing regular business even on this wet Wednesday afternoon; unkempt women with painted faces touted for custom, shoving aside groups of ragged children who sheltered in the warm alehouse doorways.

Facing his aunt, Edward noticed her sudden pallor, the averted eyes, could almost hear the thoughts that flitted through her mind—"There, but for the Grace of God . . ." In her black alpaca dress, the cape with ruffled taffeta trim and gleaming jet embroidery, she looked the epitome of the respectable middle-class widow she purported to be. But her black-gloved hands shook as she clasped her beaded reticule and watered silk umbrella close upon her lap; her fingers fondled them like a rosary, seeking reassurance, as though these things defended her and set her apart from the women who openly plied their trade along this dirty street.

Blanche sniffed again. "Shameless. Quite shameless. I wonder someone doesn't attempt to clear them off. They're an affront to respectable people."

No one replied. In the embarrassed silence, it seemed that they were all, except Blanche, aware of the slur of illegitimacy, of the commonly held belief that any cohabitation outside marriage was tantamount to prostitution. Mary Elliott closed her eyes.

Edward was suddenly thankful of the opportunity to draw everyone's attention to the pillared Tudor house attached to the inner face of Walmgate Bar, to mention the hidden portcullis and the massive outer defenses of the barbican as they passed beneath it. The city's long and intricate history fascinated as well as saddened him; he hated to see crumbling, heaving tenements that had once been magnificent mansions and was glad of the new housing outside the walls. The open strays had all but disappeared, and cattle no longer grazed between the city and its surrounding villages, but the houses were neat and clean, and they relieved the crushing poverty of medieval slums where running water was unknown except on a day such as this.

But in spite of Edward's valiant efforts to distract them, the almost jaunty atmosphere in which they set out had deserted the little group. Not overly religious, they paid lip service to the Anglican Church, and yet as they stood beneath the daunting Ionic porticoes of the cemetery chapel, a feeling of judgment was upon them all. Cowed by the size and strangeness of this neo-Erechtheion, the six stood small in pews designed to hold three hundred mourners, alongside a sarcophagus which was surely too grand for Elizabeth Elliott's humble oaken coffin. It seemed they were all, in some way or another, a party to the sins of which she was guilty. The funeral service was a reminder of mortality, for them a haunting evocation that one day they too must meet their Maker and answer to the charges laid against them.

"... For we consume away in this displeasure: and are afraid at Thy wrathful indignation. Thou hast set our misdeed before Thee: and our secret sins in the light of Thy countenance. For when Thou art angry all our days are gone: we bring our years to an end, as it were a tale that is told ..."

There was little comfort in the words of the psalm, and even as the priest read the obsequies, praising Elizabeth's piety, each wondered at the depth of his knowledge.

Through lashing rain the bearers carried the coffin down the little hill toward the plot where William Elliott's grave lay opened and ready to receive his sister's body. The tall and simple headstone lay face up on the crushed and muddied winter grass, and as the words of the burial service were intoned, Louisa studied its inscription afresh.

In Loving Memory of
William Elliott
who died April 8th 1891
aged 71 years
Patient in great Tribulation

Again she thought how appropriate the inscription was. Her elderly, ailing uncle *had* been a patient man, good and kind, and he *had* suffered, particularly in his latter years. She had not wept for her aunt, but she wanted to cry for him.

The priest scattered a few lumps of wet clay onto the coffin. ". . . commit her body to the ground: earth to earth, ashes to ashes, dust to dust: in sure and certain hope of the resurrection to eternal life . . ." His voice droned on, the rain poured down, and for the first time Louisa noticed, and was horrified by, the number of fresh graves, heaps of mud and snow topped by beaten wreaths of laurel and yew. Shivering, she longed to drag her mother away, back to the carriage, out of this freezing rain.

". . . I heard a voice from heaven saying unto me, Write. From henceforth blessed are the dead who die in the Lord: even so saith the spirit: for they rest from their labors . . . Lord have mercy upon us."

Over the murmured responses of the women, Edward's voice rang out fervently: "Christ have mercy upon us."

"Lord have mercy upon us," echoed the priest.

At last the final words were uttered, the service was over. There was the sound of horses approaching slowly from the gate; looking round, Louisa saw that it was another cortege and that grave-diggers hovered, waiting to fill in the grave. There were so many more to be opened.

Reluctant to leave, Bessie wept openly and had to be helped by Louisa and Emily; Edward took his aunt's arm as they followed Blanche back to the hired carriage. Their driver carefully negotiated the turn, avoiding the second cortege and heading at a sharper pace for the cemetery gates, where he had to wait for a contingent of dragoons to pass on their way to the Cavalry Barracks a few hundred yards away. From her vantage point by the window, Louisa idly watched their approach, the oppression of the funeral still at the forefront of her mind. The officer at the head of the troop glanced briefly at the carriage, then at Louisa, his eyes holding hers for a second before he was crossing their path, obscured from sight by the carriage's interior. She turned her head to look out of the opposite window, but when he came into view she could see only his back. It had been hard to tell, because so many of them looked alike in those dark, enveloping cloaks, but she was almost sure that the officer was their visitor of the previous week.

By the time they reached Gillygate, however, she had put the incident from her mind, and in the domestic bustle of preparing the funeral tea and ensuring that her mother did nothing, Louisa forgot it completely.

Ham and tongue sandwiches in wafer-thin triangles of bread were served at the polished mahogany dining table in the front parlor. On the sideboard Louisa laid out trifles and cakes on lace-covered china plates; the Crown Derby tea set and monogrammed silver, relics of the Temperance Hotel days, were brought out for the occasion.

Her eyes full of tears, Mary Elliott fondled one of the spoons, remembering her sister, the good times they had had in those early years, flushed with their own success. "If only . . ."

"Try not to upset yourself," Edward murmured soothingly. "She suffered dreadfully these last few winters."

"I know. I suppose it was a blessed release for her, poor soul." Sighing heavily, she dabbed at her eyes. "Life's strange, though. You think you know what lies ahead, then something happens—something so unexpected, it changes everything." She sighed again, and the tears slid down her cheeks unchecked. "I ruined all her wonderful plans. I don't think she ever forgave me."

"I'm sure she did," Edward said, but he knew he lied. His mother had not forgiven easily.

"I wish I could believe that, Edward," she whispered. "And Will—poor Will. That they should both go within the year. There were six of us, you know—and now there's only me, and I was the afterthought! It doesn't seem possible, somehow—those days are gone forever, and now your mother's gone, nobody remembers."

"Remembers what, Mamma?"

"Oh, the old days, the days when we were people to be reckoned with round Blankney and Metheringham."

Blanche sighed and raised her eyebrows, but Edward silenced her with a sharp look. "Mother told me those stories," he said, wanting to comfort his aunt, to reassure her that the history of the family, or part of it at least, would always rest with him.

"I remember Uncle Will meeting us off the train at Lincoln," Louisa said fondly. "Do you remember, Blanche? When we traveled on the carrier's cart to Metheringham, before they got the railway. It seemed a hundred miles, that journey—I used to think we'd never get there."

"Oh, yes, that journey," Edward said nostalgically. "I stayed with Grandma and Grandpa every summer when I was small. They had the most beautiful garden, with an orchard. It used to seem like the Garden of Eden to me," he wistfully admitted, "and I always thought of it whenever that bit of the Bible was read. I felt so sorry for Adam and Eve, being cast out—because I never wanted to leave, either." He smiled to cover that painful recollection, being taken away by his mother like a prisoner under escort and the bleakness of her company on that long journey back to Darlington. It was not that the elderly great-aunt and her husband to whom he was taken were cruel, just that they had had no experience of young children, and the house by its isolated railway halt was as cheerless as the occupants. As a child he could never understand why he could not live with his grandparents the whole year through, and the explanation that Darlington was more accessible from York never seemed to hold water. His mother's visits were rare enough to make distance of secondary importance.

Edward shook his head, trying to recapture his image of summer, of tall trees and dense hedgerows, of corn poppies and wild roses and the rough dryness of his grandfather's callused hand surrounding his. He had grieved for the old man at his passing, as though for the father he had never known.

"I don't know how you could bear to leave Lincolnshire," Louisa said to her mother, and there was a sudden silence.

Edward saw her eyes darken as she looked first at her daughter and then at him. For a moment he felt uncomfortable under that searching gaze and wondered what she was thinking; but then with a tired smile she turned back to Louisa and said: "We didn't have much choice, dear. Lincoln was off the beaten track; York was thriving, with the railway and everything. It's central, you see, people passing through, north, south, east, and west. Good for business."

There was a lull in the conversation after that; Blanche stood up, smoothing her elegantly cut skirts. "I really must be going, Mamma, and you look tired. Why don't you let Louisa take you up to bed?"

Mary Elliott nodded. "I will, in a moment, dear."

Edward went to fetch Blanche's cloak from the hall, and as he did so the doorbell rang.

"It's all right," he called to Bessie. "I'll answer it."

The man who stood before Edward was a complete stranger, yet the distress in his eyes was obvious. His hesitation also betrayed a certain confusion.

"Sir, forgive my intrusion, but I believe there has been a bereavement in the family?"

Edward nodded, wondering who the gentleman could be. He took in the cut of his clothes at a glance, and the voice, despite its unusual cadences, suggested a privileged background.

"There has been a bereavement," he said slowly, "but—forgive me, I—"

"Of course, my card." The stranger produced an embossed visiting card from an inner pocket and handed it to Edward. "If Miss Elliott is too indisposed to receive me, would you please convey my sincerest condolences."

Beneath the formal phrases, Edward detected genuine grief and, for a second, was nonplussed. Aware of his own lack of manners, he stood

back, inviting the stranger inside, out of the rain. Under the hall light,
he looked at the name on the card: Captain R. D. Duncannon, 1st Royal
Dragoons. The name meant nothing to him.

"I doubt Miss Elliott is too indisposed to see you, Captain," he began
and then disarmingly admitted his confusion. "I'm sorry, which one do
you wish to see? I have three cousins by that name."

The captain removed his hat and gloves. "Miss Louisa Elliott."

Edward's surprise was quite transparent. He had expected Blanche's
name, not Louisa's. "If you would care to wait just one moment . . ."
And he went through into the parlor.

Robert Duncannon was scarcely less perplexed than Edward, and he
inwardly cursed the impulse which had led him here. Obviously he had
intruded upon a family gathering, which was unforgivable. He would
exchange the correct words and go, make an appointment to call at some
more convenient moment.

The door opened, and Edward invited him in. What seemed like a
sea of faces in that small room caught him unexpectedly, and he hesitated
in the doorway.

Louisa had not recovered from the shock of Edward's announcement;
cheeks pink with embarrassment, she advanced toward their visitor, her
hand extended in greeting. "Captain Duncannon, it really is most kind
of you to call."

His elegant bow over Louisa's hand took them all by surprise. Blanche
quite forgot that she was leaving and resumed her seat; looking the least
amazed and almost self-satisfied, Emily smiled across at her mother, and
as Mary Elliott turned her head to look up at him, she caught Robert's
sudden shock of recognition. His face drained of color. Glancing rapidly
from Mary Elliott's smiling face to her daughter's and back again, he
found himself clinging to Louisa's hand, totally bereft of words.

"Let me take your coat," Edward said quickly. "And do sit down.
Louisa, have Bessie make some more tea. I'm sure the captain will join
us in some refreshment." As he ushered Robert Duncannon to a seat
beside the table, it dawned on him that this was the mysterious visitor
of a week ago; however he had heard of their bereavement, he had
incorrectly assumed that Mary Elliott's death was the one being mourned.
"It's most kind of you to offer your condolences on the death of my
mother, Captain, but I must confess, I was not aware of your acquaintance. However, I believe you've already met my aunt, and Louisa and
Emily. And may I present their sister, Blanche."

Louisa returned from the kitchen, having regained most of her composure; but whereas she firmly ordered her eyes in every direction but
the captain's, his were not so well disciplined. He's in love with her,

Edward realized with a small but stabbing dart of pain; so intent on how and when this could have come about, he lost the thread of the conversation. Incomprehension was fortunately mistaken for natural grief, and the captain repeated himself.

"I was telling Mrs. Elliott how I saw your carriage this afternoon by the cemetery gates. Miss Louisa was by the window, and I chanced to recognize her. Of course, I leapt to the wrong conclusion—which I'm told is a great failing of mine—and, feeling quite distraught on my own account, came here to pay my respects as soon as possible. My brusqueness at the door must have been most distressing for you," he concluded sincerely, "and you have my humblest apologies for that."

As Edward nodded, the younger man's expressive gesture encompassed them all. "I pray you'll forgive my impulsive intrusion at such a time."

Offered more tea and cake, he tactfully declined, insisting that he must return to Fulford. As he rose to his feet, Louisa realized again how tall he was, his presence seeming to fill that little room. She fetched his coat and hat, which, like the suit he wore, were dark and plain, proclaiming by their very austerity the price he must have paid for them. A little smile played at the corners of her mouth as she helped him into his coat.

Mary Elliott attempted to leave her chair to see their guest out, but the captain would not allow it. Gratified by her sweet smile and warm invitations, he promised to call again.

In the hallway he bowed again, but this time his lips touched the back of Louisa's hand; the warmth of his voice softened his repeated, formal apologies and lent further sincerity to his avowed intentions to repeat this brief visit at a later date.

"If I may?" he asked.

"If my mother wishes it, Captain, I have no doubt that you'll be made welcome," she said, but the lowering of her voice robbed the words of any intended snub. "I don't live here."

His disappointment was obvious. "Then I can only hope that our paths will cross again. *Au revoir,* Miss Elliott."

As he closed the door behind him, Louisa found that her hands were shaking; it was several seconds before she could bring herself to rejoin the others in the parlor, where excited chatter and Emily's laughter were making an unseemly spectacle of what had been Aunt Elizabeth's funeral tea.

"For Heaven's sake, be quiet!" she demanded as she handed Blanche the cloak that Edward had originally gone to fetch. "Try to remember why you're here."

In the guilty silence, Edward spoke with unruffled understanding. "It's all right, Louisa. We can forgive a little excitement, surely? It isn't every day that the aristocracy drop in for tea." He smiled at her, but it was a tight, questioning smile.

Flustered, Louisa began to clear the tea things.

"Who's the dark horse, then?" Blanche asked archly as she arranged her cloak. "I notice it wasn't Emily he asked for!"

So had Edward, but he wanted to smack Blanche for her barbed remarks. "That's enough, Blanche," he said sharply and was immediately reminded of his mother as she eyed him coldly.

"Don't get high and mighty with me, Edward," she snapped back. "I was only teasing."

Louisa banged the best china onto a tray. "As he thought Mamma was no longer with us," she reminded them all, "I think it was quite proper that he asked for me. After all, I am the eldest daughter."

But Mary Elliott had the last word. "Such a gentleman," she sighed, "and so charming. . . . I do hope he calls to see us again."

SIX

*S*triding through rain that bounced up off stone-flagged pavements and drenched his trouser legs, Robert Duncannon hurried to the cab rank, questioning his own sanity. The last half hour, nay, the last two weeks, had been so full of conflicting experiences and emotions, carrying him along like a straw in the flood, that he felt he must rationalize his feelings or be in danger of making an even bigger fool of himself than he had done already.

As he leaned back against the hard leather of the hansom's upholstery, he thought of Louisa Elliott and the rather chilly rebuff she had just administered, so at variance with the glow of pleasure she had betrayed at his entrance. Or had that been mere embarrassment? It was difficult for him to decide. Recollecting their first meeting, he basked in the memory of her early warmth, reflecting, after a moment, that her sudden coldness should have put him firmly in his place, should have damped down any sentimental notions he was tempted to entertain. But his instincts told him otherwise. He suspected that hers was the iciness of formality and wariness, an exaggerated correctness which said quite plainly: "I am a female of inferior social rank, but I am also respectable, so take your upper-class philandering elsewhere." And she was quite right, he acknowledged. If he wanted a woman for purely physical enjoyment, then there were such women to be had; clean, high-class, relatively honest whores whose favors could be bought for the right price. He knew; he had purchased more than one such moment of pleasure during the last six months. But the brief sensation of physical release was merely a panacea to urgent bodily need that left him feeling hollow and dissatisfied and lonelier than ever.

Louisa Elliott attracted him deeply. She radiated good health and sanity in waves that were, for him, almost tangible; mentally calming, but physically exhilarating, like swimming in the river at home on a hot summer's day. He was aware of untapped reserves of strength in her and a corresponding need in himself, a longing to take hold of those cool, light fingers and submerge all his pain in the peace of her arms.

And she was as unaware of that as she was of her unconventional beauty. He had had enough of bored society women who were attracted by the uniform and the need for light-hearted diversions and their silly daughters who sought to trap him into marriage; he longed for honesty and stability, the kind of feminine company untainted by calculations or greed.

It seemed to him then that all he desired had been there in that small house on Gillygate. A fresh surge of relief flooded through him as he brought to mind Mary Elliott's lively, good-humored face. In the hour that he had thought her dead, he had suffered such agonies of guilt, believing himself responsible for her demise, that his joy at seeing her alive and well had bubbled forth unrestrained. Had he been guilty of such a social gaffe among the families with whom he was more generally acquainted, he knew he would have gone unforgiven; but the Elliotts had hardly seemed to mind his brightness; in fact he suspected that they had quite enjoyed his brief visit. He still squirmed inwardly, how-ever, remembering how close he had ridden to disaster, and made a mental note to think in future before acting on impulse, to plan his next visit with more care.

His thoughts were shattered by the driver's call; fumbling in his pocket for coins, Robert stepped down from the cab outside the double-fronted Queen Anne house he shared with three fellow officers and their servants. In choosing his lodgings six months previously, he had balanced the relative advantages of living as a guest with a local family against the less comfortable quarters inside the barracks. When the opportunity of living independently had arisen, he and Tommy Fitzsimmons had been the first to apply; they both appreciated their freedom, finding the company of brother officers less demanding than that of a family and living out less restrictive.

Harris, his servant, was returning a freshly pressed scarlet tunic to Robert's room as he walked in. Surprise at the captain's early return was evident on the man's face. "Everything all right, sir?"

"Yes, Harris, quite all right. Damnably wet out there, though. I shall have to change."

"Will you be dining in the mess, sir?"

Robert consulted his pocket watch and was surprised in his turn by the early hour. "Yes. Yes, I think I shall." He began to peel off his dark civilian clothes as Harris laid out the short red jacket, gold-frogged waistcoat, and high-waisted navy trousers that constituted his mess dress. Gold braid and insignia shone as the light caught them, but Robert pulled on the trousers and shrugged himself into the waistcoat as he would his oldest riding clothes at White Leigh. Pausing as Harris gave the jacket a final tug, he glanced into the long pier glass to make sure all his buttons were fastened correctly, ran a hand over his damply curling hair, adjusted the eagle-crested forage cap, and reached for the long, voluminous cloak which Harris held ready for him.

"Will you be going out again later, sir?"

"No, I shouldn't think so. An early night might be advisable—my arm aches abominably after riding out today. I doubt if I'll need you, so get yourself off if you want to. That is, if you can abide the torrential rain. And for Heaven's sake, don't catch the flu—I really cannot recommend it."

Harris gave one of his rare smiles. There was a nice little miss at the tobacconist's up the road; he might wander up there and buy some cigarettes. "Thank you, sir."

When the captain had gone, Harris sorted through his clothes, removing the wet things for cleaning and pressing.

Like all his class, Robert Duncannon was dependent upon the service of others, but he was not given to abusing the privilege. He treated Harris with a natural courtesy and was respected in return. Other servants might grouse about their officers and exchange intimate, often derogatory details and gossip, but Harris never did. Taciturn by nature, the young Kentishman was solitary and unpopular with his fellow troopers, but he gave his master little cause for complaint.

He was an orphan who had been brought up in institutions and regarded the army as a natural progression. While he did not much care for the life, he accepted the harshness much as anyone accepts cold winds in winter, with a shrug and a shiver. The captain's basic humanity within a regime which did its best to eradicate such finer feelings was to Harris like the first sun of spring, and he responded to those careless kindnesses with a devotion which would have surprised Robert Duncannon had he been aware of its depth.

Familiar with the silver-framed photographs of his master's sister and daughter and the view of White Leigh's south front with William and Anne in the open landau, Harris often wondered why there were no photographs of the late Mrs. Duncannon. At the time of his assignment, there had been some regimental gossip to the effect that the captain had married an heiress, who had died shortly after giving birth to their only child; that until his marriage, Duncannon had been the life and soul of the mess but, since his wife's death, had changed dramatically. It was common knowledge that the captain's home leaves were invariably followed by dense moods and heavy bouts of drinking, which information

Harris found to be true. Many were the times he had assisted him to bed, poured black coffee laced with brandy down his throat, and prayed for the brainstorm to pass. It worried him that these bouts had not lessened during his two years of service, and he had come to the conclusion that there was more to Robert Duncannon's heavy drinking than the memory of a motherless child left at home.

He had been prepared, therefore, for a very difficult week or so following his master's return and had been more than surprised to find him in the best of spirits, albeit weak from influenza. Those deep, raked gashes in his hand had been another surprise, and the explanation of a riding accident and a badly nailed fence seemed farfetched. Without a crack in that perpetually bland expression, however, the surgeon appeared to accept it, and it was more than Harris's job was worth to pursue the matter. Nevertheless, he would have laid a wager with anyone that the captain's wounds were not caused by a fall from a horse. All in all, his master's leave posed something of a mystery, and Harris would have given much to know what had really transpired over Christmas.

A group of younger officers were in the mess; sharp guffaws of laughter rang out from their corner, and as Robert glanced in their direction, one of them called a greeting. He raised his hand in acknowledgment but sauntered across to where Tommy Fitzsimmons was sitting alone. They were particular friends, since they had joined the regiment on the same day, and of the five others commissioned with them, only Robert and Tommy were left. Over the course of some twelve years the two had acquired a reputation which owed more to their peers' preconception of Irish temperament than had ever been proved by actual deeds, although Tommy occasionally felt himself beholden to reinforce the legend.

He came of an ancient family which could trace its line back to Norman times, a family which had collected far more genuine Irish blood along the way than ever the Duncannons could lay claim to, and he was possessed of that classic, paradoxical streak which could understand the most complex problems, yet fail to find an answer to the most obvious question.

He had introduced Robert to his future wife, for which he found it hard to forgive himself, and since then had taken on Robert's welfare as a kind of personal responsibility. He was one of the few people who knew the truth about Charlotte, and while she was rarely discussed, the secret hung between them like an attaching thread.

The two men walked through into the Mess Room, a magnificent oak-paneled hall whose vaulted ceiling supported the tattered standards and banners of past victories. To the newcomer it had the awesome atmosphere of a church, coupled with the equally awesome but luxurious splendor of an exclusive gentleman's club. Desultory conversation was easily swallowed by the plush hangings and tapestries, upon which artistically abridged versions of bloody battles were depicted.

Every year, on Waterloo Day, Robert ate the food and drank the toasts, half his mind enjoying the celebration of the most glorious victory the Royals had experienced; but his eyes dwelt on the elegantly posed dying in the paintings and tapestries. No horrible mutilations there, no pumping arteries to turn the stomach and spoil an excellent meal. He had seen men die in his own country, shot at close range, their chests shattered and bleeding over their scarlet tunics; men twitching impaled on hay forks, or dragged off their horses to be bludgeoned with any instrument that came to hand. He had heard horses screaming in agony, and if anything that was worse; but a single shot could put an end to that. Men died shrieking and cursing or lived with the remnants of their lives. The tapestries showed nothing of that, portraying death as a wonderful attainment; perhaps rewardable, Robert often thought, by a Valhalla of 365 days' hunting a year, society balls every week, and as much good claret as a man could drink.

A nudge from Tommy brought him back to the present. A group of young subalterns had entered and rather noisily took their places at the foot of the long refectory table; His Serene Highness, Prince Francis of Teck, was among them.

"Is today some kind of occasion?" Tommy muttered in an undertone. "We're not usually graced with his presence."

"He's not a bad young fellow," Robert remarked with equal circumspection. "But I do find the circle of sycophants rather tedious. No doubt he'll learn."

"He'll have to," was Tommy's cryptic reply.

Impeccably dressed regimental servants served the first course. Salmon salad was followed by a thick oxtail soup, hot roast beef with attendant vegetables, and a choice of cold cuts. Robert ate well, his appetite sharpened by the afternoon's ride and his emotional excitement at seeing Louisa again. As he beckoned another helping of pudding and custard sauce, Tommy's eyebrows rose.

"Lost your appetite and found a horse's?" he asked with a grin.

"Must build up my strength—doctor's orders."

Mellowed by the soporific effect of the meal, Robert planned a couple of drinks in the bar and an early bed, but that was not on Tommy's agenda. Going on past form, he knew that solitude was his friend's worst enemy; with a promise to stand the drinks, he inveigled him into the bar, regaled him with humorous accounts of social events over the

Christmas period, and finally persuaded two more officers to join them for a hand of whist. It was well after eleven when they left the mess and crossed the open parade ground together.

The heavy rain had ceased, leaving in its place a fine drizzle that formed a jeweled patina on their dark cloaks. Trapped beneath low cloud, the river's dank miasma spread outward, reminding the occupants of Fulford that, despite the City Fathers' efforts, the Ouse still carried the effluent of an overcrowded city toward the Humber and the open sea.

Having long connections with the military, the local inhabitants rather resented the influx of a new bourgeoisie between the city and the village. They struggled, ineffectually, to retain their quasi-military status by letting as much property as possible to officer's families and turning their backs, socially speaking, upon the incomers.

It was a situation that could only be advantageous to the visiting regiments. Invited into the homes of local people, they were quickly made to feel at home, introduced to every female relative of marriageable age, and generally treated like honored guests. It required a great deal of tact, wiliness, and diplomacy to avoid serious emotional involvements.

Over the years Tommy's natural defenses had become entrenched while his charm increased, so that he drifted in and out of amorous relationships with a lighthearted ease that was the envy of his contemporaries. Like the rest of the regiment, men as well as officers, his height bordered six feet; he was slightly shorter than Robert, heavier in build, and badly scarred down the left side of his face after what he described as a brush with some Fenian bastards in Dublin during the Royals' lads tour of duty in Ireland. In the presence of ladies, however, he referred to the Fenians as "rebels." Far from decreasing his popularity, the scars seemed to exercise a peculiar attraction, so that he was never seen socially without a rapt circle of female admirers.

This aspect of Tommy's character afforded Robert great amusement. Tommy needed the company of women as other men needed alcohol, and Robert was glad that the hideous day when his friend's face had been ripped open with a marlinespike had not curtailed his future pleasure. Physically attractive, unfailingly courteous, Robert had developed the habit of self-effacement in mixed company, so that he was often accused, though never to his face, of being morose and unsociable. But the somber expression was in truth a defensive mask, as Tommy well knew. Among friends, and in the company of women with whom he felt safe, Robert Duncannon displayed a natural charm and gaiety that was a much truer reflection of his nature.

"You're remarkably cheerful since your return," Tommy commented as they reached the Queen Anne house.

"Am I?"

"You know you are. It puzzles me," Tommy confessed. "I've grown so used to seeing you possessed of the black devils every time you return from White Leigh . . . but not this time." With a smile, he indicated Robert's arm. "And after this little episode?"

"Don't talk here. Come up and we'll have a nightcap."

Some time and several brandies later, Robert reached the end of his tale, having waxed lyrical on the subject of Louisa Elliott.

"You're smitten by her," Tommy pronounced, pouring himself yet another drink. "But if it makes you feel better, why worry? Enjoy yourself, have a good time. Who would blame you? Not me, that's certain. I've said long enough you should set yourself up with some accommodating lady. They do say mistresses are preferable to wives, and I'm bound to agree."

"You've never been married," Robert reminded him.

"Ah, no, that's true. But I've had several mistresses—lovely ladies, all of them."

Robert stared into the fire. A mistress was not what he wanted, yet while Charlotte lived there was little choice. He had tried to explain Louisa to Tommy, but Tommy seemed incapable of understanding the kind of person she was, and in the act of explaining Robert had finally seen the impossibilities for himself. She was the kind of girl who would naturally expect courtship to lead to marriage. His personal sense of honor forbade him to court her dishonestly, but he knew that once he disclosed the truth, he should expect nothing. The class to which she belonged would have no truck with mistresses.

Abruptly he drained his glass and sent Tommy on his way.

SEVEN

*B*eneath a leaden sky which threatened a repeat of the previous week's blizzard, Louisa returned to the Tempest residence on Blossom Street. There were squeals of joy from Victoria, a welcoming embrace from Rachel, and their father breathed several sighs of relief as he greeted her in the hallway.

In the schoolroom, even Moira interrupted her cleaning to say how much she had been missed. "Miss Victoria would not let me put her to bed. She cried for you every single night you were away."

"Now, Moira, you're exaggerating again," Louisa laughed.

"She did so! Miss Rachel could not pacify her, Mr. Tempest was fit to tear his hair out at the noise she was making, and even Mrs. P. was fair standing on her head, trying to distract her. Till Miss Rachel had a sudden idea—she said Miss Victoria could sleep in her bed. So that's where she's been since Thursday last."

"I'd no idea she'd become so attached to me," Louisa said, concerned and not a little alarmed by Moira's news.

"She has that. And it's no surprise—since you've been here, you've done wonders with that child, so you have."

"Well, it's nice of you to say so, Moira." Louisa smiled and set about preparing Victoria's lessons. "And how have things been with you?"

Moira struggled to pull out the heavy chest of drawers and smiled her thanks as Louisa lent a hand. "Oh, fine, you know. But my ma's worried about that young brother of mine, young Sean. He's no good that one, won't settle to a job, in with all the hard fellas—at least they think they're hard. Just bullies they are, I'm telling you. So now he thinks he'll go to America, but what on, I'd like to know." Having dusted the skirtings and polished the floorboards behind the chest, she sat back on her haunches and grinned. "He only thinks the rest of us should pay his way. Now would you believe that?"

"And would you?" Louisa asked as they pushed the chest back into place again.

Moira laughed again. "Sure, and it'd be worth it, just to get rid of the young . . . Ah, I'd better not say it, he is my brother, after all." On hands and knees, she continued along the edges of the carpet, rubbing and polishing as she went. "And how's your ma?"

"Much better, I'm happy to say. Upset about my aunt's death, of course, but better in herself."

"I was that sorry to hear about your aunt, Miss Elliott."

Louisa sighed. "It was something of a shock, I must admit. But she hadn't been well for a long time, Moira. My cousin is coming back to live with my mother and sister in Gillygate, which is a good thing for all of them, I think. Now, I must get on, and so must you. You won't forget to give my room a thorough clean today, will you?" It was a gentle reminder, but necessary. In the absence of a full-time housekeeper, the cook, Mrs. Petty, did most of the work with regard to provisions; Rachel Tempest was supposed to supervise the cleaning of the house but rarely examined the top floor with any interest. As long as her father's room and her own were spick-and-span, together with the two guest bedrooms, she tended to ignore the state of the schoolroom and the servants' quarters. Even Victoria's bedroom was left to Louisa's discretion.

Like most of her fellows, Moira was grossly overworked, rising early and going to bed late, her day an endless round of physical labor; sympathy prevented Louisa from seeming too harsh or too precise.

She spent the rest of the morning with the child, hearing her read, practicing the times tables, and taking her through a modicum of elementary geography. In the afternoon Louisa supervised Victoria's sewing lesson, which was not an easy task for either of them. The child had little coordination, and even less patience, and the presence of her sister Rachel, who had joined them out of boredom, only added to the difficulty.

Sensing that tempers were becoming frayed, Louisa went over to the window, her lips a thin line of exasperation. Beyond the glass the January afternoon was chill and overcast. Wind whipped ragged smoke from a score of chimneys, set thin scurries of snow flying across the rooftops, etching the slates and tiles with white. Lamps were lit in the shops, incandescent blobs of yellow on that otherwise colorless canvas, warmly inviting; but the icy blast kept custom away, driving a half-starved mongrel into the shelter of a grocer's doorway and an unkempt figure toward the liquid comfort of the Windmill Inn across the street.

Attracted by the approaching rattle of horses' hooves, she leaned further into the window, calling Victoria to come and look at the squadron of dark-cloaked dragoons emerging from Micklegate, their imposing figures dwarfed by the great creamy mass of the bar walls. The little girl clapped her hands at the jingling harness, the frustration of the sewing lesson forgotten; and as the squadron drew level with the house, Rachel joined them, marveling as she always did at their magnificence. Emanating an almost tangible aura of unity and strength, the squadron moved as though motivated by a single mind, each horse a part of its master, each man as one with his brother, heads up, backs straight, the simultaneous rise and fall both sensuous and hypnotic.

Rachel's heartfelt sigh found a secret echo in Louisa's heart, but she smiled a wry little smile, recognizing the changes a week had wrought. The military were a regular spectacle, a bright spot on a winter's day, entertainment in the summer as they displayed their prowess on the Kavesmire; and a week ago, that was all they had been. The advent of Captain Duncannon, however, had created a particular interest, which suddenly made Rachel Tempest's cravings seem almost comprehensible.

At nineteen years old, Rachel was less than a year out of the young ladies' academy where she had finished her education and already chafing at the reins her father sought to impose upon her. He had paid good money to make a lady out of his pretty elder daughter, and yet to Louisa Elliott it seemed as though he did not much care for the finished product. Rachel had developed a taste for her school friends' style of living, for the kind of society her father affected to despise and aped so assiduously; her plans had been thwarted by a year of mourning, but now the year was up, she seemed determined to pursue that life regardless of what her father wanted.

Watching her as she strained to see the last of the dragoons, Louisa suspected that Albert Tempest's ambitions for a prosaic and strictly mercantile alliance would receive short shrift from his daughter. She had her sights set on more flamboyant game.

Turning excitedly from the window, Rachel unwittingly confirmed her companion's train of thought. "I can't wait for Sophie Bainbridge's party—they have a captain of dragoons lodging with them, and Sophie says he's sure to bring some friends."

Annoyed by her heart's sudden, involuntary leap, Louisa bit back the impulse to ask the man's name; instead she said, with unaccustomed sharpness: "Have you asked your father if you may go?"

"Not yet," Rachel admitted.

"Then perhaps you'd better. When is it to be?"

"St. Valentine's Day—isn't that romantic?"

"Very," Louisa agreed dryly. "But it's less than four weeks away. Do you think you can persuade your father before you have to answer the invitation?" Privately she held out little hope, knowing that from the depths of his middle-class, Methodist soul Albert Tempest despised the military on principle and had scant regard for the Bainbridges with their army connections. Sophie's father was retired, but his eldest son, Arthur, was a lieutenant with the Yorkshire Hussars; they lived in some style at Fulford, not far from the Cavalry Barracks.

Before Rachel could reply, there was a tap at the schoolroom door. The girl, Moira, came in with a tray of tea and bread and butter, setting it down on Louisa's desk by the window.

"I can persuade him if you'll help me," Rachel said as soon as the maid had gone; and with a shrewdness of which Louisa had not thought her capable, added: "My father listens to what you say."

Her companion's fair skin flushed with embarrassment and anger. "You overestimate my position, Miss Rachel," she said sternly, turning away to pour the tea.

Two hours later, Albert Tempest passed beneath the arch of Micklegate Bar, busy now with the traffic of homebound railway and office workers. The refined whiteness of the pavements had been trampled back to soft brown sugar, the roadway ravaged by horse-drawn trams and carts. He hesitated at the corner of Nunnery Lane, while a dray squelched past through slush and dung, and finally crossed with great care for his boots and trouser bottoms. As usual, he bowed his head until he was past the convent; not as a mark of deep respect, but as a way of blotting its existence from his mind. Papists offended him. He detested having to allow his maid her hour off on Sundays to attend Mass; would not have employed her except that the Irish were generally willing to accept a lower wage than anyone else. With the raising of his chin, he looked spiritually ahead to the day when he could afford to move his home and family to the cleaner air of Bishopthorpe. No, not Bishopthorpe, he thought; more heathenish ways there with the Anglican archbishop and his palace by the river. Dringhouses, perhaps, or Acomb, where the land was higher, the air fresh from the country.

With his hand upon the bell, he wiped the worst of the filth from his boots onto the scraper by the door, his eyes ready, by the time it opened, not to look directly at the maid. Silently he handed over his gloves and bowler hat, staring at, but not seeing, the black cast-iron curlicues of the massive hallstand, waiting patiently while Moira removed first his ulster, then his coat, then bent to remove her master's boots. Equally silently, she handed him his slippers and bore the wet boots away to the kitchen to be cleaned. As the door at the far end of the hall closed, Albert Tempest stood beneath the double-shaded gas mantle and smoothed his hair, checking its graying wings in the oval mirror on the hallstand. Satisfied, he went through into the drawing room, where his daughters and Miss Elliott awaited him.

It was a richly furnished, although somewhat dismal, room, dominated by an elaborately framed likeness of the late Mrs. Tempest, her hollow, haunted eyes defying any foolhardy attempt at gaiety. Dark landseer prints almost receded into the maroon flocked wallpaper, and even the gas mantles gave off only a feeble glow.

Victoria thrust aside her dolls as her father entered the room, leaping up to greet him, her plump little arms winding about his neck, rosebud mouth puckering to be kissed. His response was genuine and spontaneous; the only spontaneous thing in his life, Louisa thought, as she unwittingly caught his glance above the shining gold of Victoria's hair. For a moment she wondered what truth there had been in Rachel's remark. For a man who rarely noticed the existence of his other servants, Albert Tempest's eyes had dwelt on her rather too often and for rather too long of late. Having disentangled himself from the child's passionate embrace, he received his other daughter's perfunctory kiss as usual and bestowed a smile in Louisa's direction, a smile she carefully avoided, although she returned a formal greeting.

With a vague air of disappointment he turned away, chafing his hands by the fitful flames of the carefully banked-down fire. He had a horror of blazing fires, maintaining that they were both dangerous and wasteful. Whenever Rachel complained, he simply told her to wear a warmer shawl.

It was but one aspect of his miserliness. Money spent on appearances was usually not begrudged, although even there he tried to cut corners. Like the daughters of the gentry he sneered at, Rachel must have her companion and Victoria her governess. Louisa Elliott performed both roles and after a mere four months was beginning to realize the iniquity of her position. After the carefree atmosphere of her last post, the Tempest household was oppressive; her duties, if not physically arduous, involved long hours and much patience, for the two girls, being so disparate in age, behaved like self-indulgent only children. Each seemed to resent time necessarily spent with the other, vying for her attention and that of their father when he was at home.

As Mr. Tempest seated himself, Louisa began to relax; she looked forward to these few minutes when he read his newspaper, relating suitable snippets of news while waiting for the evening meal to be served; it marked the beginning of the end of the day. She would still have to supervise Victoria until bedtime and prepare her lessons for the following day, but unless Mr. Tempest was going out or working alone in the library, she could sit in the schoolroom and read by herself.

With her eyes on her mending, she waited for her employer to settle himself. There would no doubt be a further bulletin on the progress of the Duke of Clarence; in her mother's paper Louisa had read of his illness, that he had fallen victim to the flu epidemic and was even now at Sandringham, attended by the royal physicians.

With a grunt that could have expressed either sorrow or satisfaction, Albert Tempest announced that the duke was dead. " 'Prince Albert Victor, eldest son of the Prince of Wales and Princess Alexandra, died in the early hours of this morning of influenza, at Sandringham House, a matter of days after his twenty-eighth birthday.' Well!" he exclaimed, "that's his future settled and no mistake. He won't make Viceroy of Ireland now!" Ignoring the stunned silence which greeted this remark, he read on: " 'H.S.H. Prince Francis of Teck, brother to Princess May, 2nd lieutenant in the Royal Dragoons, is naturally much affected and has left the city to join his family in London.' "

A wail from Rachel caused her father to lower his paper in amazement, but even Louisa had been surprised by his callousness.

"How could you?" Rachel demanded, tears apparent in her eyes and voice. "How could you be so heartless, Father? What does it matter if he was going to be viceroy? Just think how his family must feel! And poor Princess May—she was going to be married in the spring. What will she do now?"

Albert Tempest snorted. "Well, my dear, I'm sure they won't pack her off back to Germany or wherever it is she hails from. They'll find another husband for her, don't you fret. If she was about to marry a future king," he commented shrewdly, "she'll be too valuable a property to end her days a spinster. She'll be better off," he added cryptically, "without him. Better off, I daresay, with almost *anyone* else, from what I've heard."

As Rachel gulped and dabbed at her eyes, her father rattled his paper irritably. "Oh, for goodness' sake, stop that sniveling! I've heard enough of that lately to last me the year out." With a glance at the mantel clock, he slapped his paper shut and excused himself, closing the drawing-room door behind him with unnecessary force.

His elder daughter ceased her whimpering immediately. Round-eyed, she turned to Louisa and said: "Why should Princess May be better off with almost anyone else? What did Father mean, I wonder?"

Pursing her lips, Louisa shook her head. "Perhaps you should ask him."

"He wouldn't tell," Rachel declared with some disdain. "You know what he's like. Come on, Louisa, you know—what did he mean about the prince?"

"I don't *know*—and as your father says, Miss Rachel, I'm sure we shouldn't speak ill of the dead." Under pressure, however, she eventually said: "I have heard the prince led a somewhat dissipated life."

"What's dissipated?" Victoria wanted to know, and Louisa shook her head at Rachel in annoyance.

"It means a person who goes to bed *very* late and doesn't eat his greens," she explained severely. Most put out, the little girl returned to her dolls.

Rachel looked blank. "Is that *really* what it means?"

Irritably her companion began to pack away the sewing things. "The word covers a lot of sins, Miss Rachel, as I'm sure you are well aware. In the prince's case, however, I think it also means he drank a great deal. Far more than was good for him."

"Oh. How terrible." But Rachel sounded disappointed, as though she had hoped for more. As she added her embroidery to the sewing basket, the dinner gong sounded, cutting short further conversation.

They took their places in the dining room as Albert Tempest rejoined them. Before Louisa's arrival the little girl had virtually been confined to the schoolroom, and it had taken a great deal of tact on Louisa's part to persuade Albert Tempest that his younger daughter's difficult behavior was largely attributable to loneliness and grief after her mother's death. Although Mrs. Tempest had been a semi-invalid for many years, worn out by miscarriages and recurring illness, she had been their mother, and a governess was no substitute. Nor, Louisa privately considered, was a vain and silly elder sister. Rachel was too immature even to try to fill the gap, equating love with indulgence and denial with dislike. Sharing more of the family's life had certainly wrought improvements, however, and under Louisa's firm tutelage the child's manners were more acceptable, her appetite no longer giving cause for concern. It was a considerable step forward. As she bowed her head for the Grace, Louisa was aware that the privilege would not have been granted except for Albert Tempest's adoration of his younger daughter, and the fact that the experiment had worked made him view Louisa with greater respect. She hoped that was the only reason for his occasional little pleasantries.

Conversation between courses, however, was hardly the stuff of which soirees are made. Rachel tended to prattle endlessly about her friends and their social engagements, Victoria contributed the occasional unwelcome profundity of which only children are capable, and true to her position, Louisa never spoke unless invited to. But from the depths of his boredom, Albert Tempest invited her comments more and more often, for her candid and practical observations were refreshing enough to amuse him.

Not for the first time, he chewed reflectively and stole covert glances at the young woman sitting less than six feet away from him. Hardly a beauty, he thought, especially with that close-cropped hair, and taller by far than he liked a woman to be. But she was strong and healthy and looked more than capable of bearing a dozen strapping sons. Sons that his late wife had been quite incapable of producing. He had wanted sons; what was the use of building an empire without extensions of himself to carry it on? With a slight sigh, he acknowledged the near impossibility of such fantasies. He would have to marry again, and wives were such an encumbrance; even if he overcame that reluctance, he could never marry Louisa Elliott.

His quick, darting glances might have gone largely unnoticed by the object of his attention, who ate with downcast, inwardly reflective eyes, but they were not lost on Rachel. She had lived for too long under the gaze of eyes glazed by boredom not to notice the change in her father. He paid only little attention to what she said, and when he did listen, the only spark she provoked was that of irritability. After due consideration, she decided this was as good a time as any to begin her campaign for more freedom. Louisa must make of it what she could.

Engrossed in thoughts which concerned Prince Francis of Teck and Robert Duncannon, Louisa missed Rachel's first desultory remarks regarding the St. Valentine's Day party. It was Albert Tempest's heavy voice which jerked her to attention.

"I see. Miss Elliott thinks you should go to the ball, does she?"

"It's not a ball, Father," Rachel patiently explained, ignoring the sarcasm. "It's Sophie Bainbridge's twentieth birthday, and she's just having a small gathering of friends at home."

Louisa gathered her wits. "Please, Miss Rachel, do tell your father what I really said. That you should ask him. However, Mr. Tempest," she added quickly before Rachel could interrupt, "I cannot see any reason why Miss Rachel should not go. It's sure to be a pleasant occasion and a good opportunity for meeting people."

"But I don't care for the Bainbridges," he protested, belligerence creeping into his voice. "Empty-headed, the lot of them. And no doubt churchy. Rachel should be mixing with chapel people, do her more good in the long run. No, Rachel, I don't want you to go. Besides, who'd escort you? Different if you had a young man paying you court. Someone suitable, that is."

"And how is anyone ever going to court me, when I never get the chance to meet anyone?" she demanded, her voice registering several decibels higher.

Her father did not consider this to be a valid argument. "There are several young men I know who would be only too pleased to call on you or escort you to a social evening at the chapel."

As the color in Rachel's face mounted alarmingly, Louisa entertained a passing thought that Mr. Tempest was being deliberately provocative, but the argument had gone too far for her to intervene.

"These—these—so-called young men you speak of, Father," Rachel eventually spluttered, "must be at least thirty-five and unmarried simply because—because they are too repulsive for words! Arthur Grimshaw has warts as big as pigeons' eggs, Frederick Swales is scarcely taller than Victoria, and that awful Mr. Bickerdike looks like a scarecrow for all his money and has dewdrops hanging from the end of his nose!" She rose to her feet as Louisa struggled to hide her laughter at these terrifyingly accurate descriptions. There *were* others, as Louisa realized, but none of them had money. "If these—*men*—are the best you can offer me, then I shall remain a spinster and plague you for the rest of my life!"

As she stormed out of the dining room, her father waved his younger daughter away from the table. With the closing of the door his shoulders slumped and he was silent.

"I think she means it," he said at last. "In fact I'm sure she does. What am I going to do with her, Louisa?"

The use of her Christian name was instantly sobering. He had never called her that before, and yet in an unguarded moment it had tripped off his tongue with alarming ease.

"It really isn't for me to say, Mr. Tempest," she quietly replied.

His quick brown eyes rested on hers for a moment before dropping away with a sudden flash of annoyance. "No. No, of course not," he muttered, worrying at a small stain on the white damask with his thumbnail. He glanced up again. "All right, Miss Elliott, you may go."

The schoolroom, Louisa's room, and Victoria's opened into each other, the former being a good-sized room in spite of the low ceiling and warmer than the rest of the house because of it. But the latter rooms were small and narrow, having been carved from a larger one, with the fireplace in Victoria's bedroom. On particularly cold nights Louisa would leave the schoolroom door open while she worked, so that the warmth could permeate her spartan cell.

It had an iron bedstead, a large chest of drawers, a washstand, and a walk-in closet where she hung her few clothes. On the polished floor-boards beside the bed was a handmade clipped rug, warmly patterned in russet colors, the product of last winter's long evenings; it was the brightest thing in the room. The walls were papered in a faded blue Regency stripe which was probably original, and even the patchwork bedspread was old enough to have faded to an almost uniform beige, with mere hints of its former glory here and there. But it was a room of her own, and as she closed the door behind her at nine o'clock, Louisa breathed a sigh compounded of relief and exhaustion.

She dropped her shawl onto the bed and poured hot water from the jug Moira had brought into the flowered pottery basin. Holding the steaming flannel over her face and eyes, she felt some of her weariness seep away; it had been a tiring day, and she had not slept well the night before.

Albert Tempest's unexpected familiarity had unnerved her, and she found herself wondering what went on behind those quick, speculative glances. The thought that he might entertain any kind of desire for her was too repulsive to contemplate, and she thrust the idea away, seeking refuge in an image of Robert Duncannon.

His visit the day before had been less a surprise than a shock, severely denting her defensive conviction that Gillygate was unlikely to see him again. It left her doubting both his motives and her judgment, for while his concern for her mother had been obvious and, she thought, genuine, his pleasure at seeing Louisa had been equally apparent. That interest, unlike Albert Tempest's, was flattering, but in its way just as unwelcome.

Robert Duncannon's life was as far removed from her own as a Hottentot's. Perhaps not quite, she conceded, for by and large they spoke a similar language; but she knew she had far more in common with her employer, in spite of the dislike he inspired, than with the well-born Captain Duncannon. The news item concerning Prince Francis of Teck served only to heighten that awareness. He too served with the Royals, and she wondered how well the captain knew the man who was to have been brother-in-law to a king.

EIGHT

*A*fter her father's departure, Rachel dashed up the stairs to the schoolroom, full of excitement.

The morning's lessons were not quite under way, but Louisa glared, for her rules regarding interruptions before noon were quite specific.

"I'm sorry, Louisa, but I had to come and tell you—I would have said over breakfast, but Father took so long to move this morning, and I had to wait until he'd gone."

"What is it, Miss Rachel? Hurry up and tell me—I want to begin your sister's lesson."

"He's given me permission to go!"

"Go where?"

Rachel gave an exasperated sigh. "To Sophie's party, of course."

"Good. I'm very pleased for you. Can we talk about it later, please?"

Rachel stamped out of the room, but by afternoon tea she had quite recovered her spirits, the words tumbling out in her excitement at having cajoled her father into agreement. "But there's a condition attached—isn't my father just famous for his conditions? I must take a chaperon with me."

"I see. And who is that to be?" Louisa imagined it would be the wife of one of her father's friends.

Rachel's eyes sparkled with what she believed to be marvelous news. "Guess," she said, her whole body quivering with a desire to delay the amazing surprise.

"I really don't know," her companion replied, but the truth was beginning to dawn. "Oh, Miss Rachel! Not me? You can't possibly mean *me*. How can I be your chaperon? I'm in mourning—I can't go to a party."

The pleasure fell from Rachel's face like a slippery veil. A tantrum hovered threateningly. "But you must! We have no relatives in York, my father's friends are all too stuffily religious to even *ask,* and I cannot go without a chaperon. Father has put his foot down quite firmly over that. He doesn't want me to go at all, but I created the most terrible scene last night after you came upstairs—he had to relent.''

Louisa nodded. Rachel's scenes were infamous, and she could sense the next one closing in on her. ''Calm down,'' she pleaded. ''And for goodness' sake, don't cry. Tears solve nothing.'' She paused while Rachel collected herself. ''All right. If it means so much to you, I suppose I shall have to ignore the conventions for once. I'm flattered that your father thinks me suitable for such a responsibility, but there is another problem. I don't have anything to wear. This dress is too well worn, and my other black dress is even less suitable for a grand occasion like Miss Sophie's party.''

''Haven't you something in lilac or gray that would do?''

Louisa shook her head. ''I don't usually attend social functions, Miss Rachel.''

After a moment's thought Rachel brightened. ''Your sister, she's a dressmaker, I believe. Wouldn't she run something up for you?''

Louisa suppressed a laugh. What Rachel Tempest knew about dress-making would fill a short piece of notepaper, and she was entirely unacquainted with Blanche. ''My sister sews all day for Miss Devine. I doubt she'd be willing to sew all night for me.''

''But she's your sister.''

''Sisters are able to refuse with alacrity, Miss Rachel—only friends are restrained by manners.''

''Then we'll see her together,'' Rachel said, undeterred. ''She won't say no to me.''

Blanche did not refuse outright, but what help she offered, Louisa thought as they left that crowded little workroom, was most certainly from astonishment at Rachel Tempest's temerity in asking in the first place.

It was agreed that she would purchase some material on Louisa's behalf from Miss Devine, cut the gown and fit it, while Louisa did the sewing. It would mean bearding the housekeeper for a loan of the sewing machine, and some late nights, but it was more than Louisa had dared to hope.

Rachel was jubilant as they came out into Coney Street. ''There! I told you she'd be willing to help. Your sister may be brusque, Louisa, but I'm sure she has a heart of gold.''

''I'm sure your presence helped, Miss Rachel,'' Louisa dryly observed.

Her excited chatter ceased as they began the short, steep climb up Micklegate; when flanked by those imposing Georgian mansions, however, Louisa's thoughts strayed yet again to Robert Duncannon.

"By the way," she inquired, as casually as she was able, "this officer of dragoons the Bainbridges have staying with them—what is he called, do you know?"

"Oh, let me think," Rachel pondered, slowing as they breasted the rise. "It begins with a *D* I think . . ."

Louisa held her breath, her heart racing out of all proportion to the effort of their climb.

"Hugh—that's his name—Hugh Darnley. Sophie says he's *lovely*— I think she's got quite a pash on him!" Rachel confided with a giggle. "But why do you ask?"

"Oh, no reason," her companion sighed, aware of a crushing sense of disappointment. "It's just that I have difficulty remembering names. I like to fix them in my mind, if possible, beforehand."

NINE

*A*fter further consultations with her sister, Louisa decided upon a soft, fine wool crepe for the gown. The material was expensive, but infinitely wearable, which was more than could be said for Rachel's suggestion of exotic black lace. It was a high-necked, front-fastening gown with tiny jet buttons, sleeves puffed at the shoulder but tight in the forearm, smooth over the hips with gentle folds at the back falling into a small train. Rachel's passion for lace was catered for in a separate jabot, which retrieved the simple design from seeming too much the day dress and yet could be removed afterward. Carried away by her own imagination, Rachel thought it too plain and governessy, but Louisa was thrilled; in her eyes it was exactly right, saved from severity by the softness of the material and well worth the time, effort, and money it had cost. With care it would last for years. It was even worth Blanche's bad-tempered fussing over the set of the sleeves and her half-sarcastic, half-envious gibes at Louisa's social aspirations.

On the evening before the party Rachel insisted on a full dress rehearsal. With its scooped, shoulder-revealing neckline and short sleeves of ruffled lace, Rachel's pale yellow silk was beautiful; in yellow satin slippers and long satin gloves and with her rich brown hair piled into a shining heap of curls, she looked stunningly pretty. Beside her, reflected in the long wardrobe mirror, Louisa provided the perfect sober contrast. At last Rachel was forced to acknowledge the wisdom of her companion's choice.

Sighing pleasurably, she dragged her eyes away from the mirror and turned to the array of cloaks and mantles laid out on the bed. "What do you think to this?" she asked, holding up a short cape in moss-green velour.

Louisa shook her head. "It could be a cold night, Miss Rachel. A long cloak would be better."

Rachel studied and sorted, grumbling about her lack of suitable evening wear, until she eventually held up two cloaks, one in mulberry
wool, the other a dark brown velvet. Louisa indicated a preference for
the latter, and Rachel agreed. "But what about you, Louisa? What will
you wear? Not that old black cloak of yours, I hope—that won't do at
all. I know!" she exclaimed suddenly. "I have the very thing." She
rummaged among the clothes still in the wardrobe, producing a short
black cape heavily embroidered with jet beads. "I wore this for poor
Mother's funeral, and hardly ever since. It's a little old-fashioned, but
it will suit your new dress admirably, don't you think? Try it on, Louisa,
and we'll go down and show Father how fine we look."

Albert Tempest thought they looked very fine until his daughter
removed her mantle. His mouth fell open, and the color drained from
his face; as a livid flush returned to his cheeks, he seemed to have some
difficulty in finding his voice. "You—you—you can't wear that!" he
stammered. "It—it isn't decent!"

Rachel's shock was almost as great as her father's. The yellow silk
was her first evening gown, and accustomed as she was to choosing her
own clothes, it had never occurred to her that her father might object.
To the price, perhaps, but to the design, no.

"But it's the height of fashion," she whispered, her hands nevertheless
straying to her naked throat.

Her father leapt to his feet. "I don't care what it is—you'll not leave
my house dressed like that!"

"Father," Rachel pleaded, "it's an evening gown—all evening gowns
are cut low at the neck. Sophie and all the other girls will be wearing
very similar dresses."

Louisa looked at her employer and, for the first time, quailed inside.
She had witnessed his anger before, but had never seen him quite so
choleric.

"I don't care what they wear!" he exploded. "You are my daughter,
and I say you go nowhere dressed in that indecent fashion. When your
mother went out in the evenings, she wore proper clothes. I never saw
her half-naked in public." Or at any other time, he almost added, his
eyes glued in horrified fascination to his daughter's creamy shoulders.
"I thank Providence Miss Elliott hasn't succumbed to the same inde-
cency," he added with an almost regretful glance in her direction.

"But, but she's different," Rachel sobbed.

"Don't answer back, miss! Get up those stairs at once, and don't let
me see you half-dressed again!"

As Rachel rushed out of the room, Louisa turned to follow.

"Wait," he said before she reached the door. Making a visible effort to control himself, Albert Tempest inhaled deeply, clasped his hands behind his back, and rocked gently upon his heels. "I'm both surprised and displeased. I credited you with more discretion, Miss Elliott."

In the manner of an obedient servant, Louisa studied the carpet. "I'm sorry, Mr. Tempest. I didn't know you hadn't seen the dress before."

"How could you *think* I would approve?" he shouted.

Having been raised in an almost exclusively female household, Louisa was unused to being browbeaten by men. Albert Tempest's anger was frightening; even the pitch of his voice felt like an assault, but she refused to be cowed. Abandoning all pretense of humility, she stared back. "It's an evening gown," she said quietly, "and as such, in my opinion, quite modest."

"Huh! In *your* opinion. And what opinion's that, may I ask? Is my daughter's companion so well versed that she can venture to give me an opinion?"

Angered by his sarcasm, Louisa lifted her chin a little higher. "My sister makes evening gowns for some of the best families in the county," she said with spirit.

For a moment surprise curbed something of his fury, giving way to a more biting suggestiveness. "Oh, she does, does she? So tell me, Miss Elliott, would you wear a gown like that?" There was a distinctly unpleasant twist to his mouth as he spoke, and his foxy little eyes were bright with speculation.

Humiliated by the inference, Louisa cursed the blood which rushed to her face, but she refused to drop her eyes; her nostrils flared as she fought to keep her voice under control. "It's a beautiful gown, Mr. Tempest, and it suits your daughter very well, but both the color and the style would be unbecoming to me, especially in my position as Miss Rachel's companion."

His eyes glittering under the impact of her contempt, Albert Tempest coldly dismissed her, but she stood her ground, determined to say what needed to be said, even if it cost her her job.

"I told you to go."

"But I haven't finished, Mr. Tempest. You can dismiss me once and for all, afterward, but please listen for a moment. Miss Rachel may be willful and spoiled, but she isn't bad, nor would she willingly do anything of which you might disapprove. If you want her to marry well, and be happy, then you must allow her something of a social life. This—this party is the first occasion of her life. She's looked forward to it for weeks, had this gown specially made, and now you say it isn't suitable. She may have something else, I'm not sure, but that's not the point—she wants to wear this one.''

He paced up and down before the fire, apparently deep in thought. ''Miss Elliott,'' he said at length, in the tones of one explaining a difficult problem to a hysterical child, ''I'm not an unreasonable man. Contrary to your belief, my daughter's happiness is a matter very close to my heart, but so is her welfare. She does not leave this house in a state of near-nakedness, whether that is the fashion or not. Just imagine what people would think!''

And there lies the nub of the matter, Louisa thought wearily. ''So, she may go to the party, as long as her shoulders are covered?''

''Of course,'' he replied in the manner of one who sincerely wonders what all the fuss has been about.

Louisa resisted a triumphant smile. ''Then I think I may be able to solve the problem,'' she said cheerfully. ''The dressmaker left some odd lengths of silk and lace which I'm sure we can utilize to your satisfaction. May I tell Rachel?''

''You can tell her I want to see the results before she goes out tomorrow evening!''

''Naturally. Thank you, sir.''

Despite Rachel's pleadings, Louisa refused to give up her day off, which happened to be the day of the party. Having made a dainty, shoulder-covering shawl from the bits and pieces of material and transformed the gown into something acceptable to Rachel's father, Louisa needed a few hours of peace and relaxation. With a firm promise to return at five, she left for Gillygate, looking forward to her own preparations for the evening ahead.

Bathing facilities in the Tempest household were limited to the usual weekly plunge, hot water carried up in jugs by Moira to an enameled bath by a bedroom fire. Moira's tasks were so myriad, Louisa hated to impose any additional ones, the lack of warmth and complete privacy in her own room being an additional deterrent. Instead she bathed at home, before tea, every Saturday afternoon. Every other day of the week she wrapped herself in a towel and, using her one jug of hot water sparingly, performed the necessary ablutions. The habit kept her underclothes sweet and kept the heavy winter dresses from becoming too stale; nevertheless, each Saturday's bath and freshly laundered linen were sensual pleasures of which she never tired. Camisoles and petticoats felt smooth and cool against her fire-warmed skin, and the scent of lavender filled her nostrils; a new extravagance were the fine silk stockings, purchased in a moment of madness that morning.

She called Bessie to help with her stays. "Lace me good and tight, Bessie—I made the waist of my dress a bit on the small side."

"Breathe in then—there, how's that? I wish I still had a waist as neat as yours, Miss Louisa. It's a fine figure you've got. Let's see you in that dress."

"Not yet, Bessie, I haven't dried my hair yet. Off you go and keep Mamma company. I'll be down soon to show you how it looks."

A pair of iron curling tongs were heating by the fire. She tested them first on a piece of paper, took strands of hair at the crown, and expertly turned the golden brown waves into curls. Within a quarter of an hour she was finished and, teasing the curls above her forehead into a passable imitation of the Princess of Wales's, she surveyed her reflection with some satisfaction.

For weeks she had thought of the party with apprehension, had sat up late at night sewing, in dread that the dress would not be finished in time, wondering all the while what manner of people the Bainbridges were. Sophie and her elder sister had recently called to take afternoon tea with Rachel, amazing Louisa by their striking contrast of looks and temperament. Petite, feminine, and frivolous, Sophie could almost have been Rachel's twin, while the elder girl was thin and rather mannish. She had had little to contribute to their conversation, indeed seemed patronizing and superior; but when Louisa tried to draw her out, she realized Lily's attitude stemmed from a complete lack of interest in her sister's favorite topics. Miss Lily Bainbridge's passions were bloodstock and hunting, and social calls were decidedly low on her list of priorities.

With a wry quirk of a smile as she recalled that afternoon, Louisa thought that she might not be the only person feeling out of place at the party; anyway, she could console herself with the smart new dress, which was a pleasure in itself.

In the parlor Mary Elliott put down her crochet work and looked on approvingly as her eldest daughter pirouetted. "Turn slowly, Louisa. Let me see the back. Oh, yes, it's beautiful. The cut's superb."

"And what about the excellent sewing? It took me almost three weeks burning the midnight oil. Why should Blanche have all the credit?"

"I didn't mean it like that, dear. Of course the sewing's good; you've done a lovely job. But you know the secret of style lies in the cut of a thing."

Louisa sighed, but refused to let her mother's bias upset her. "What do you think, Bessie?"

Bessie's kind face was full of open admiration. "Lovely, you look a fair treat, Miss Louisa, even if you are in black. I bet there's none to touch you—you'll have all them gentlemen flocking round!"

Louisa laughed and kissed her cheek. "Oh, Bessie, I'm supposed to be Rachel Tempest's chaperon, making sure she doesn't overdo *her* quest for a husband, not looking for one myself!"

"Aye, well," Bessie sniffed. "It's about time you thought about it. Time you were married and having your own family, not looking after other people's."

"Now then, Bessie, poor Mamma would have a fit. She's got enough with Emily's wedding ahead of her. I shall have to give her a few years' grace."

When Louisa arrived at Blossom Street, Rachel's recriminations could be heard in the hallway. Quickly removing her cloak and hat, Louisa hurried up to Rachel's room, where Moira stood like a martyr while her mistress ranted over the disaster of her hair.

"Get back to answering the door, Moira. It's about all you're fit for!" Rachel exclaimed. "Just look at my hair, Louisa, just *look* at it. I asked her to pin these flowers at the back, and what did she do but pull all the curls awry. I'll never find a husband looking like this!"

"I thought you were going to a party, to enjoy yourself," Louisa calmly remarked, unpinning the shiny brown tresses and beginning again with the brush. "Hunting expeditions are rarely so successful, my dear."

"Oh, shut up, Louisa, and get on with my hair." A few minutes later, soothed by those steady strokes, she said: "You know I haven't got long to find someone. Father will have me married off to one of his awful friends before the year's out, mark my words. He can't wait to get rid of me."

"I don't think that's true, Miss Rachel."

"It is," she insisted. "You know it is." When Louisa did not rise to that, she said nastily: "It's all right for you—it doesn't matter if you work for your living and become an old maid."

Ignoring that barbed comment, Louisa continued her task in silence.

At last Rachel was ready, gloves smoothed, fan furled, mantle on, impatient and only half-listening to her father's repeated instructions. Stressing punctuality and abstinence, he escorted them outside, watching as the carriage turned into Nunnery Lane.

A few hundred yards beyond the Calvary Barracks the carriage turned left down a broad avenue, then left again into a short, semicircular gravel drive. The house was modern, quite grand with six steps leading up to a pillared portico, tall mullioned windows on either side, and a path leading off through extensive shrubberies. Experiencing more than a slight degree of trepidation, Louisa pulled at the bell; almost immediately the door was opened by an imposing manservant.

Rachel handed him their cards, following him through double glass doors into an oak-paneled inner hall where a maid waited to take their cloaks.

Giving Rachel a gushing welcome, Sophie announced that they were the very first to arrive, and Louisa instantly regretted Albert Tempest's fetish for punctuality. She hung back, relieved when Rachel at last recalled her manners, drawing her forward to be introduced to Major and Mrs. Bainbridge.

Short and stocky, his round red face foreshortened by a luxuriant moustache which joined abundant side-whiskers, the major was like a strutting pouter pigeon beside his nervous wren of a wife. In russet silk she fluttered to Louisa's side, inquiring sympathetically whether she was in mourning.

"I'm afraid so, Mrs. Bainbridge," Louisa confessed, "but Miss Rachel has no immediate relatives in the area, and Mr. Tempest did not wish her to make the journey unescorted."

"Quite right, I should feel the same about Sophie. But it was very good of you to agree, under the circumstances," she said, innocently assuming that Louisa had had a choice in the matter. "If you'd like to sit quietly, my dear, you'll find several peaceful corners in this rambling house. The young people tend to be rather noisy, I'm afraid," she admitted with the air of one who has her retreats well mapped out.

Louisa thanked her kindly, following Sophie and Rachel upstairs, where Sophie's bedroom was set aside for the ladies' use. She showed them into the bathroom, a recent installation and the source of much family pride. Rachel insisted on a demonstration for Louisa's benefit, turning on taps and laughing delightedly at her companion's amazement. Full of enthusiasm, Sophie explained that the huge contraption at one end of the bath was for heating water, that the family could take hot baths as and when they wished; it was a great saving on work for the servants. Louisa was both impressed and entranced; under the gaslit chandelier, white enamel gleamed, bottle-green, lotus-flowered tiles shone, and around the fireguard thick towels were draped invitingly. A small stab of envy pierced her normally serene soul.

Sophie moved to the door. "We really should go down. I want to introduce you to my brothers, and there will be more guests arriving. But do feel free to use the bathroom."

"As long as we don't spend the entire evening in here?" Louisa asked dryly, and the two girls giggled all the way down the stairs.

Larger overall than the Tempest residence, this house consisted of several smaller rooms, lacking the elegant proportions of Blossom Street, but brightly lit and furnished in glowing colors. William Morris designs adorned the walls, portraits and prints hung from picture rails, and displays of hothouse flowers were reflected in the long French windows leading to an elevated terrace. Adjacent to the window, more glass doors led through into a charming conservatory, and Louisa eyed this avenue of retreat as Rachel was introduced to Sophie's elder brother, Arthur, and Captain Hugh Darnley, the Bainbridges' current lodger.

Arthur Bainbridge was an unmistakably male version of his sister Lily, earnest and horsey, and apparently just as unimpressed by Sophie and her suddenly awestruck friend. The young dragoon, however, seemed more than pleased to be in their company. Immaculate evening dress lent elegance to a tall, angular frame, and as he bent his head toward Rachel's upturned face, soft brown hair fell forward across eyes as soft and appealing as a spaniel's.

Tactfully edging toward the conservatory, Louisa exchanged a few pleasantries with Lily, who looked awkward and uncomfortable in a harsh blue taffeta, smiled at two younger brothers sitting in rigid silence on a massive horsehair sofa, and as a fresh group of guests were ushered into the room, made her escape.

There was an old brocade chaise longue in the conservatory, almost hidden by potted palms and aspidistras, wreathed about with ivies and exotic ferns. It faced the night-hidden garden, but by bending her head every now and then Louisa could see through the ferns into the room she had recently left. In dresses of every hue, Sophie's friends mingled like pretty butterflies among the ever-increasing groups of young men, anonymous in black and white. Laughter filtered through, and the tinkling notes of a piano being played for fun.

Part of her would have liked to be with them, to have been accepted as an equal with Rachel. But Louisa thought of herself as practical and realistic; she refused to let herself be sad, so enjoyed it vicariously, pushing the small twinge of loneliness and envy resolutely aside. Engrossed in her efforts to see and not be seen, to pursue and protect her solitude, she would have been most put out if anyone had come into the conservatory to talk to her.

She had been there for perhaps half an hour, her eyes following Rachel around the room, pleased to note that the yellow gown with its quaint little neckerchief of lace and silk was quite as fashionable as and prettier than most, when she became aware of a newcomer to the group. He was dark-haired, half-hidden behind another man, older and heavier than the slight young hussars who were Arthur's friends. The two girls laughed in unison at something the thickset man said; as he turned in Louisa's direction she saw that he was badly scarred down the left side of his face; then his companion moved, and it was as though the rest of the room faded and blurred in that split second of recognition.

Breathless, shocked, her heart pounding painfully, Louisa sank back against the ferns. After a few moments she edged forward and looked again, almost convinced that she was the victim of hallucination. But he was still there, with the same group. It was impossible to mistake his height and that crisply curling hair. From behind a palm frond she watched his every movement, studied the polite smile, his occasional laugh, always at some comment of his friend's, noticed the guarded expression in his eyes, and even counted the sips he took from his glass; with some surprise, she realized he was bored.

One of the girls spoke to him; he bent his head to listen more carefully, and Louisa craned her neck to see which one of them it was. With a pang very akin to jealousy, she saw that it was Rachel. But his interest was barely more than polite; he smiled and nodded and replied, then turned and spoke to Lily, hovering on the edge of the group, ill at ease in her stiff blue gown.

Within a few moments gaunt, unattractive Lily was talking animatedly, and Louisa would have given almost anything to know the subject of that conversation. White teeth flashed suddenly as Robert threw back his head and laughed; abject misery coursed through Louisa's veins. Who would have thought Sophie's sister could be so witty? But he was moving on. With a backward glance and a genuinely amused smile he left Lily's side, not seeing, as Louisa did, the look of regret which followed him across the room.

As he approached the conservatory, Louisa ducked back among the plants; when she dared to look again, he was talking to Mrs. Bainbridge, who, like Louisa's mother, was blooming beneath a charm few of the younger ladies had been able to elicit. He was also very close to the conservatory door, almost facing her. Panic-stricken, Louisa retreated once more.

Moments later the glass door opened. Startled, she looked up into the kindly, smiling face of Mrs. Bainbridge.

"I see you've found my favorite retreat, Miss Elliott. May I send in a glass of something for you? Lemonade, or perhaps a little wine? There is some punch, but I understand," she added with a little laugh, "that it may be rather heady."

Rising to her feet, Louisa politely declined. "Not just at the moment, thank you, Mrs. Bainbridge."

The older woman said something more, but Louisa hardly heard; Robert Duncannon was standing just a few feet away, staring with such frank and delighted amazement she could do nothing but smile and blush and shake her head like some bemused foreigner dropped in a strange but pleasant land.

Caught between the two, Mrs. Bainbridge read their expressions, eloquent as the pages of the romantic novels to which she was addicted; feeling, as her husband would have phrased it, extra to requirements, she tactfully slipped away.

"What a delight this is," Robert remarked, closing the conservatory door behind him. Smiling, he raised Louisa's hand to his lips. "Can I really believe it?" he asked. "Truly, Miss Elliott, you are the very last person I expected to see this evening—and to think I very nearly refused the invitation!"

Unable to trust her voice, Louisa simply smiled, her eyes unwittingly revealing as much as they absorbed. The stark black and white of evening dress suited his dark good looks; as though aware of her innocent appraisal, his eyes sparkled with sudden amusement, and as she quickly glanced down, Louisa found herself blushing furiously.

"I had no idea you were acquainted with the Bainbridges. Why haven't I see you here before?"

"I'm not," she said with unintentional abruptness; cross with herself, she found it hard to be civil. "At least not personally." She paused, glanced up into expectant eyes, and wondered why it was so hard to admit to being a paid companion. She forced a light laugh. "You know, Captain, you really shouldn't be blocking my view of the proceedings— after all, I am supposed to be a chaperon."

Laughing heartily, Robert moved away from the window and took a seat on the chaise longue. "I don't believe it!" he said at last. "Surely the first requirement of a chaperon is to be that certain age, old enough to have forgotten one's youth totally, yet not so old that youth is all one *does* remember?"

His light, teasing tone brought a smile to Louisa's lips. "I'm sure you're right. Unfortunately, there was no one of that description to oblige. And in my position as Miss Tempest's companion I was—shall we say, pressured?—into it."

"And which of the little hothouse flowers is Miss Tempest?" Robert asked, peering between the overhanging ferns. "Ah, yes, the little girl in yellow," he murmured as Louisa pointed across the room. "I'd say she'd keep you on your toes."

"What makes you say that?"

The black moustache twitched again. "Hmm. Instinct," he admitted and turned back to Louisa. "Am I right? Yes!" he laughed, "I see that I am, and I do not envy you your charge!"

"It's not as bad as you think," she said defensively, feeling suddenly bound to explain her position in the Tempest household, her sympathy with the two girls after the tragic loss of their mother.

"You have a kind heart," he observed. "But then, I knew that already. I hope the Tempest family appreciates you."

At a loss for words, Louisa studied her hands, strangely calm despite an inner trembling; she was overwhelmingly aware of his close proximity, an arm resting nonchalantly along the back of the chaise longue, and one black-clad knee only inches from her own.

"You know, I've wondered what you did and where you lived ever since our first meeting. You very cleverly let me talk about myself on that occasion and revealed practically nothing about yourself. But in spite of that, I formed certain ideas about you." He paused, and she glanced up, again catching that amused twinkle in his eyes. "I decided that here was a young lady of great independence, a young lady, I told myself, accustomed to giving orders and to being obeyed. No, don't frown," he admonished, tapping the back of her hand. "Independent ladies never frown—they are quite above criticism!"

As she laughed, his left hand closed lightly but firmly over her own; with a quickening heart she looked down, noticing two long, livid scars which reached from beneath his starched cuff almost to the knuckle. She stared in horrified fascination, wondering what could have caused those wounds, for in places it was obvious they had been deep.

Apparently unaware, Robert leaned closer, whispering like a conspirator in her ear. "I had you down for a nursing sister," he confessed. "Or perhaps a teacher—in a very proper girls' school. What do you say to that?"

"I—I don't know what to say," she admitted, forcing a smile. "Except— I doubt I could have made a nurse . . ."

Her eyes gave her away. He withdrew his hand, and for a moment the laughter went out of him. "I'm sorry," he murmured. "I shouldn't have taken off my gloves. I'd forgotten about those scars—not very pretty, I'm afraid."

As he pulled on one white kid glove, she said, "What happened? You never did say."

"I didn't, did I?" He sighed and briefly touched her cheek. "And now I'm thinking I should have." For a long moment his eyes held hers, but in spite of the little smile which touched his mouth, there was no amusement. "But this is neither the time nor the place for that kind of confidence. One day, perhaps . . . ?"

The question, left hanging on the air, was shattered by the sudden opening of the door; as Tommy Fitzsimmons joined them, voices and laughter invaded that precious moment of intimacy.

"So this is where you've gone to earth, you old fox!" Turning to Louisa, he bowed, begging forgiveness for the intrusion. "My old friend has such a habit of disappearing, I have to be sure he's not eluding his social obligations. However," he added gallantly, "I see that on this occasion he is not."

Covering his displeasure tolerably well, Robert performed the introductions.

"I'm delighted to make your acquaintance, dear lady," Tommy murmured as he bent over her hand, but Louisa was strangely embarrassed; afraid that she had taken up far too much of Captain Duncannon's time already, she excused herself at the first opportunity.

It appeared that she had neglected her duties shamefully, for Rachel was nowhere to be seen.

The two men watched her as she crossed the room. Taking a glass of wine from a passing servant, Robert drank deeply. "Your arrival, my old friend, was most inopportune."

Surprised, Tommy stared at him. "Was it? Sure and I thought I was rescuing you from unwelcome clutches!"

"Far from it."

"My sincere apologies! Had I known . . . why did you not say? Who is she? I've not seen that face before."

"She's the one I was telling you about."

For a moment or two Tommy thought hard. "Not the one you met all those weeks ago, in the hotel?"

Robert nodded. "And would you believe it? She's here with a friend of the Bainbridge girl." He laughed suddenly and shook his head. "It's incredible—seeing her here, of all places! God, but she's beautiful. Don't you think so?" Lost in private reverie, he failed to notice Tommy's hesitation.

"Well—yes," his friend finally agreed, but it was a gallant rather than sincere assent. Tommy's taste ran along more obvious lines, and recalling Charlotte's exquisite and ethereal beauty, he found Robert's rose-colored vision hard to appreciate.

Louisa returned, her movements sharpened by anxiety.

"Could you not find her?" Robert asked, putting down his glass.

"Oh, I found her. In the hall with Sophie and the young man who's staying here, giggling quite helplessly, I'm afraid. I couldn't get any sense out of her. I'm sure she's been drinking."

Tommy laughed. "I'll say she has! Downing the punch like it was lemonade. I said she'd regret it, but she'd not listen."

Louisa closed her eyes tight against a sudden vision of Albert Tempest. "Oh, goodness! Her father will be furious—he doesn't hold with strong drink. What am I to do?"

"Food," Robert said, taking her arm and ushering her out of the room. "Get something inside her to soak up the alcohol and give her lots of black coffee. It's only ten o'clock; she's got time to sober up before you have to leave."

The scene in the hall was exactly as Louisa had described it. All three were sitting on the stairs, with Rachel propped up against the newel post. Darnley was very recently promoted and, at the look on Robert's face, immediately sprang to his feet.

"Be so good as to escort Miss Bainbridge in to supper, Captain Darnley, and I will escort Miss Tempest."

The young man did not question his instructions; only Rachel had the temerity to protest. Between them, however, Robert and Louisa urged her to her feet.

"What will your father say?" Louisa demanded. "If he should see you like this, he'll never let you out of his sight again, you silly girl."

"But it was only punch!"

"Laced with wine and brandy," Robert assured her.

"Oh, dear—Father will be cross!" She giggled.

"He will indeed—unless we sober you up," Robert muttered grimly. "Lots of food—that's what you need, my girl, so start eating." He found her a chair, leaving Louisa in charge while he went to the buffet table. Less than five minutes later he was back with three plates, each substantially filled.

Under the eyes of two such determined guardians, Rachel did as she was bidden; halfway through her second cup of coffee, she complained of feeling sick.

"Fresh air," Robert pronounced, hauling her to her feet once more. "Come on, don't be ill in here, you'll never be asked again."

In the hall, they met Tommy.

"Grab our cloaks, Tommy. We're in need of some air."

He joined them outside, wrapped his evening cloak around Rachel, and handed Robert's to Louisa. The garments, which were long on the men, trailed behind the two women as they walked the length of the gravel drive and back toward the house. A narrow path led through the shrubbery, spidery fingers of winter-naked trees and vines forcing them from four abreast into two. Staying by Louisa's side, Robert dropped back, while Tommy, eager to make amends, tactfully went ahead with Rachel.

"I should have been watching her," Louisa said guiltily, "not hiding in the conservatory."

"Were you hiding?" he asked in some surprise. "Why?"

"Oh, you know how it is," she began, then stopped. She gave a little laugh, then said: "Well, no, I don't suppose you do. To be perfectly honest, I was afraid of feeling out of place."

For a moment he said nothing; then, as a sudden gust of wind shook the trees, he slipped a comforting arm around her shoulders. "I do know what you mean," he said seriously. "I often feel out of place, in spite of knowing most of the people by sight or even name . . . in spite of knowing what is expected of me, the level of conversation, even how much I may eat and drink!" He laughed suddenly and squeezed her shoulder. "I often stand there, listening, wondering what on earth I'm doing. In fact, the only reason I attend is because it is expected. Part and parcel of the job, I'm afraid."

"Really?"

"Really. The part I've not enjoyed for a long, long time. Tonight, now," he confessed with a smile, "has been quite remarkable. And do you know why? Because you were here, because we talked—because it was . . ."

"Different?" She laughed.

"Now don't be cynical, Miss Elliott. I'm trying to pay you compliments."

"Why should the truth be cynical?" she demanded. "I *am* different, at least from the young ladies who are present this evening. I'm twenty-five years old, I work for my living, and by and large I'm responsible for my own behavior. Nobody worries whether *I'm* escorted or chaperoned each time I set foot outside the house. But if I happened to be the daughter of a wealthy and privileged family, I doubt I'd be here alone with you!"

Robert smothered a laugh. "*Touché,* Miss Elliott! Most decidedly *touché!* Did I hear, 'Unhand me, knave!' in that little speech?"

"If you think you did," she said tartly, "then do!"

He laughed again. "If I thought you were in the least bit frightened of me, I would. But you're not, are you?"

"No," she lied. "Of course I'm not."

"You're shivering simply because you are cold?"

"Naturally."

"I thought so," he murmured, seeming vastly amused by the idea. "You're quite delightful, do you know that? I just wish you could spare a little pity for the wealthy and privileged, however. Money and social position aren't everything, I do assure you."

His tone was bantering, but she caught his underlying seriousness. "I'm sure they're not, Captain. But how many people truly understand that?"

"I do," he said.

They walked on in silence, along gravel paths which skirted lawns and flower beds, following Tommy and Rachel, who were already some distance ahead. Occasional giggles, carried back by the wind, signified a rapid return to her earlier buoyant spirits.

"Ah, the resilience of youth," Robert observed. "Which reminds me— how is Mrs. Elliott?"

"Much better; quite her old self, in fact."

"I'm glad. I must call on her again, to thank her properly this time."

"I'm sure she'd appreciate that."

"I hope I may call often—to see you."

She stiffened and knew from the sudden relaxing of his arm that he was aware of it. She wanted to see him again, longed to share more of that lighthearted banter and his sudden, disconcerting moments of seriousness. He was attractive, and so very charming, and she knew she was more than flattered by his attentions; but he belonged to a different class. With a great effort, Louisa told herself that it would be futile to pursue the relationship. However much he wished it, she could never be part of his world, and he would never be truly accepted in hers.

"Is that a good idea?" she gently asked.

"I don't know," he admitted. "Perhaps not. But I do want to see you again."

Their tour of the garden completed, Tommy and Rachel stopped on the drive in front of the house. As they looked back, Robert discreetly dropped his arm.

"I feel much better now," Rachel announced, "but I think I'd like to sit quietly for a while."

"Try the conservatory, Tommy," Robert advised. "Miss Elliott and I will join you directly." As they went inside he cut across Louisa's protests. "She doesn't need you for a moment—she's enjoying Tommy's company, and he'll see no harm comes to her, I promise you."

He turned to face her, pulling her cloak closer around her shoulders; she could feel his fingers in her hair and against her jaw. In the flickering portico light, his eyes were dark and very serious.

"I want to see you again, Louisa. And I very much want to kiss you."

Beneath tight-laced stays, her heart skipped several beats. With an attempt at lightness, she said: "Do you think you ought to?"

With a quirky little smile, Robert shook his head. "I'm sure I shouldn't—it's most improper. But I do so want to."

As he bent his head, she reached up on tiptoe, lightly brushing her lips against his cheek. It was intended as a gesture of thanks for an evening she would never forget and as a small diversionary measure which might avoid the temptation his mouth presented. Before she could draw away, his arms encircled her.

Sensing her apprehension, he responded to the butterfly lightness of her kiss with gentleness, and his kiss lingered on her lips like honey. The temptation she had sought to avoid was suddenly there in all its sweetness, calling to emotions she had tried so hard to suppress. In sudden confusion, she did not pull away, but stood transfixed, eyes wide and questioning, lips parted in silent supplication.

Then he began to kiss her again, and she was aware of relief, and a blossoming warmth, an overwhelming response which cried out for the submission of self to greater and more urgent demands. As tenderness gave way to passion, her very soul seemed to swell and soar, exploding in a dazzling and deafening cascade. Stunned and dizzy, she clung to him, aware of nothing beyond that transitory and unforgettable sense of union.

For Robert, the experience was equally shattering. Having longed for her all evening, he had intended nothing more than a brief taste of those tantalizing lips; yet while he held her in his arms, the world had been forgotten, and he had known in those moments a depth of emotion, a physical desire so intense, almost every curb had snapped. Aware only of a desperate need to take her there and then, he had forced himself to stop, kissed her face and hair, and held her away from him, very firmly. Angry with himself, he was afraid his apology had been too abrupt; her eyes had looked hurt, even accusing, as she handed him his cloak and turned to go.

Pulling his cloak closer, Robert leaned against one of the pillars and with trembling fingers lit a much-needed cigar. Dragging the blessed smoke into his lungs, he exhaled on a shuddering breath, wondering whether anyone had seen them at the foot of the steps, locked in that all-consuming embrace.

With the calming of mind and body, he began to think more rationally, glad that he had held her, briefly and gently, whispering some desperate words of reassurance before finally letting her go. He could not remember what he had said; he simply hoped that it had been the right thing, that she had not returned to Rachel bearing obvious signs of distress.

Whatever her demeanor, Tommy would know what had happened, or make a very good guess. With a sigh of resignation, Robert crushed his cigar butt and hoped his friend's tact was still in force.

Incredibly, it seemed no one had remarked upon his absence. As he walked through the crowded drawing room, all were laughing and talking; Darnley was playing the piano while Sophie sang to a small circle of admirers; not one accusing eye turned in Robert's direction. The ormolu clock on the mantelpiece registered a quarter before eleven.

In the conservatory Tommy was regaling the two ladies with his endless fund of anecdotes. Apart from one raised, eloquent eyebrow, he made no comment. Rachel was pale but cheerful, too flattered by Tommy's practiced charm to notice that anything might have been amiss; and Louisa, by the look of things, was eager not to distract either of them.

She stood a little apart, among the ferns, pale green tendrils softening the stark black elegance of her dress; her cheeks seemed paler, her lips rosier than before, and her eyes when she looked up at him were so infinitely vulnerable, he was stabbed to the heart. Forgive me, he silently begged, holding her gaze; for I love you and want you more than anyone or anything I've ever known.

And then he thought of Charlotte.

He looked away, afraid that Louisa would see too much.

TEN

*T*he following day Rachel complained of a headache and stayed in bed. As usual, Louisa accompanied Albert Tempest and his younger daughter to morning service at the chapel on Priory Street.

The vast, galleried building was almost full, the visiting preacher inspired, but Louisa's mind closed itself to the endless, ranting prayers, presenting instead picture after picture of Robert Duncannon: sitting beside her; standing with Rachel; leaning against the conservatory door, his impeccably tailored form reflected in the glass. She saw his face, animated, appealing, eyes intent upon hers; laughter wrinkled that long, straight nose, exposing strong white teeth beneath the curling black moustache. Her body echoed the feel of him; her lips burned as she remembered his kisses. She heard again that tender, despairing plea, soft as a caress: "Why can't you stay with me forever?" And afterward, that terrible sadness, tearing her apart because she did not understand the reason for it.

There had been no further chance to talk, and afraid her eyes might give everything away, Louisa had avoided the merest glance. Disturbed, she had ushered Rachel toward the carriage at eleven-thirty, reassured only at the last moment by the lingering pressure of Robert's hand as they said their good-byes. Thankfully, Rachel had been too full of her own success to ask embarrassing questions of Louisa. Content to relate every compliment paid by the handsome dragoon officers and the looks she had intercepted from young Arthur Bainbridge, she gave her companion only one cause for disturbance. Robert Duncannon had apparently intrigued her, and listening to Rachel's ill-formed impressions of the man, Louisa was simply grateful for the secret darkness of their carriage.

Mrs. Petty's Yorkshire puddings were good, and Sunday dinner was normally enjoyable; faced with so much food, however, Rachel and Louisa were overfaced. Over his mountain of roast beef, sprouts, potatoes, and mashed turnips, Albert Tempest surveyed their plates and feeble appetites with stern disapproval.

"Now I see what social gallivanting does for you. The pair of you make an excellent match for the tablecloth."

"It was a lovely evening, Father. But I had a vast amount to eat last night, and I'm not very hungry today."

"God's good food is not to be wasted. It's a wicked sin, Rachel. Make sure you clear those plates, both of you—I'll not have waste in this house. More meat, Victoria? Sprouts, my dear?" He heaped more food onto the child's plate and emptied the turnip tureen onto his own.

Rachel looked distinctly ill, but she obeyed her father and ate her dinner, asking permission to visit the Bainbridges that afternoon. She explained that they would think it impolite otherwise. Struggling with his belief that Sunday was the Lord's day, to be spent in worship and Bible-reading, her father finally agreed. He could not afford to have it said that his daughter was ill mannered, that she had delayed her thanks for hospitality received; the need to do it on a Sunday, however, was another black mark against the Bainbridges.

"Be sure you get back before dark," he muttered. "I don't want you passing the barracks when the riffraff are heading into town."

Wearing her new black dress, but with her own cloak this time, Louisa accompanied Rachel to the tram stop across Blossom Street. The horse-drawn vehicle proceeded down Micklegate, across Ouse Bridge, along Clifford Street, and past the Castle, picking up passengers along the way. Being Sunday, they were few, most of them alighting at the cemetery. A young woman, no more than Louisa's age, struggled past them with a baby in her arms and a grimy toddler hanging on to her skirts. Rachel drew her knees aside as they brushed past, her face expressing severe distaste. The young woman saw it and hung her head, her cheeks aflame as she stepped off the tram.

"Miss Rachel, that was most unkind of you."

"I don't care—they were dirty. Couldn't you smell them?"

"That's not the point," Louisa said coldly. "If you were young and widowed, and poor through no fault of your own, would you like to be despised?"

Rachel flushed angrily and tossed her head. "I really do wish, Louisa, that you would remember your position. You are my companion, *not* my governess. I do not want to be reprimanded like a child again—do you understand?"

"Perfectly," Louisa said quietly and with some relief noticed the terminus ahead. They walked the rest of the way to the Bainbridge house in silence.

It seemed more imposing by daylight, with rhododendrons lining the drive and ivy softening the harsh red brick of the east wall. As she climbed the portico steps to ring the bell, Louisa found herself wondering, as had Robert the night before, whether anyone had witnessed that brief display of impropriety. Acutely embarrassed, she lowered her eyes as the same manservant admitted them.

She was aware of Robert as soon as they were shown into the drawing room, but in the first flush of greetings and rearranged seats she was able to avoid the intensity of his gaze.

The gathered company acted like a tonic; her spirits thoroughly recovered, Rachel proffered pretty thanks for the party, was fussed over by Mrs. Bainbridge, and laughingly shook her head at Sophie's whispered questions. Young Captain Darnley offered her his apologies, which she accepted, and even Sophie's brother asked solicitously after her health.

Having nodded politely to Louisa, Robert continued his conversation with the major while Louisa found interest in a series of hunting prints and tried to preserve an attitude of calm.

Mrs. Bainbridge sent for more tea and with its arrival turned to Louisa, exchanging small talk about the previous evening. In an undertone, she referred obliquely to Rachel's misdemeanor with the punch.

"Such a responsibility for one as young as yourself, to act *in loco parentis,* as it were."

"Really, Mrs. Bainbridge, Miss Rachel was quite well again by the time we left," Louisa insisted. "A slight headache this morning, but that was probably due to the excitement."

"I'm sure you're right. But these young girls are so silly—and Sophie's no better. As for Lily . . ." She rolled her eyes and sighed eloquently. "She's a different problem, of course. I can't prize her away from the stables, which is where she is at the moment. I couldn't persuade her to stay and receive our guests, I'm sorry to say."

Louisa perceived that Mrs. Bainbridge was not in complete control of her household, but she did not condemn her for it; she was basically kind, and Louisa could feel her generosity in the relaxed atmosphere of the house. It was so much pleasanter than Blossom Street. "Please don't worry on Miss Rachel's account."

"Oh, but I do. Ah well, I must not bore you with our little difficulties. Tell me—are you a York girl?"

Louisa said that she was.

"And your father?"

With practiced ease, Louisa explained that her mother was a widow and that she had two sisters.

"And do they also earn their own livings?"

"My younger sister is still at home, but Blanche is employed by Miss Devine."

"Ah," Mrs. Bainbridge interjected with a knowing smile. "I thought I detected style in the cut of your dress. It really is most elegant—did your sister make it for you?"

"Well—almost," she said dryly.

"And, tell me, have you been long acquainted with Captain Duncannon?"

Color washed into Louisa's cheeks and out again, provoking a conspiratorial smile from the older woman. "Don't worry," she said, patting Louisa's hand gently, "your secret is safe with me. Such a charming man, but something of a lone wolf, I fear."

"I don't know him well," Louisa protested. "We met quite by chance some weeks ago."

Mrs. Bainbridge smiled again. "If you want my opinion, my dear, he's quite taken with you. And he couldn't make a better choice, you being so good with children."

Mystified, Louisa shook her head. "I'm sorry?"

"Why, he's a widower, didn't you know? With a small daughter. And I have it on excellent authority that he's quite wealthy—estates in Ireland, you know."

Louisa did not know, but she perceived that Mrs. Bainbridge was even less in control of her tongue than of her household. Anxious lest their conversation be repeated with embellishments, she sought an effective reply. "I know nothing of Captain Duncannon's personal circumstances, Mrs. Bainbridge. Our conversations have been brief and quite superficial, and I doubt his interest in me is anything more than kindly. My social position," she added heavily, "is far too humble for any deeper interest on either side. Now, if you'll excuse me, Miss Rachel and I really must be leaving. Mr. Tempest said we were to be sure to return before dark."

The older woman looked genuinely hurt, and Louisa was sorry. "Forgive me, I know you thought to be kind, but—we really do have to go." Embarrassed, she stood up, signaling to Rachel, repeating their thanks for the previous evening's hospitality. She was aware that she had been hasty and ungracious, and that Rachel was far from pleased by this abrupt leave-taking.

As the manservant brought their cloaks, Robert followed them into the hall, suggesting very casually that he escort them back to the main road.

Doubly mortified, Louisa wished him a thousand miles hence; but Rachel was flattered and thanked him with a winning smile, reserving her stony expression for Louisa's eyes only.

It had begun to rain, and the pavements were wet. Complaining, Rachel raised her umbrella and hoisted her skirts with a complete disregard for the amount of ankle and petticoat she displayed.

"In Ireland, we'd say it was a soft day," Robert commented with an amused smile.

Catching up the train of her dress, Louisa did not reply. His twinkling, downward glance was not lost on her, however, and she was tempted to drop her skirts into the muddy path.

"Don't do it," he said. "You'll spoil that lovely dress."

Infuriated, she averted her eyes, inwardly raging at his lack of discretion. His actions gave the lie to what she had said to Sophie's mother, and considering those comments, she squirmed afresh, unconsciously speeding her footsteps as though she longed to be on the tram and back in Blossom Street.

"Goodness me, Louisa, do slow down. We're not in a race, you know," Rachel crossly reminded her. "You were inordinately eager to leave the Bainbridges, but there's no need to run!"

"Is anything wrong, Miss Elliott?" Robert asked evenly.

"Mr. Tempest wanted us to be back before dark."

Mystified by her obvious ill temper, he sought her eyes, but she resolutely refused to look at him. Anxious, a little hurt, he began to think that she was angry because of what had passed between them the previous evening.

He addressed himself to Rachel. "Do you have a long journey, Miss Tempest?"

"Long enough," she admitted. "Blossom Street, just a few doors down from the nunnery, which doesn't please my father."

Making desultory conversation with Rachel, Robert waited with them until the tram arrived. In spite of Louisa's frosty attitude, he assisted them both onto the platform, then with a part wave, part salute, he strode smartly away toward the barracks.

In a fierce undertone, Rachel ranted furiously all the way home, commenting with great irony on Louisa's lack of manners both to the Bainbridges and to Captain Duncannon, whose interest it was important to encourage. Louisa stared blankly out at the pouring rain and said nothing. When they arrived back home, she asked to be excused, pleaded a headache, and retired to the safe solitude of the schoolroom.

Two days later, a letter arrived for Louisa. In a plain, good-quality envelope, it was addressed in a bold and unfamiliar hand, but the York postmark provided a clue to its sender. Ignoring Moira's questioning eyebrows, she slipped it into her pocket.

It was evening before she had chance to read it. Making the excuse of lessons to prepare, she took a tray of tea up to the schoolroom; pulling her desk and chair closer to the fire, for it was a bitterly cold and windy evening, she lit the oil lamp and spread out her books.

Only then did she open Robert's letter.

"My dear Miss Elliott," he began, "I hesitate to address you less formally, recalling your silence, and I fear anger, at our last meeting. I can only assume that you were outraged by my lack of restraint the evening before.

"The presence of Tommy Fitzsimmons and Miss Tempest, and the press of people later, prevented the quiet words I longed to share with you, the things I wanted to say. I attended the Bainbridges on Sunday afternoon not only to thank them but in the express hope of seeing you, of hopefully arranging another meeting where we could talk privately.

"For there are things I must say. I long to see you again, if only to beg your forgiveness in person. Since the night we first met, I have thought of you almost constantly. So, Miss Elliott—Louisa—I beg you from the depths of my erring being—please forgive my hasty embrace. And believe that it will not be repeated, should you agree to see

> Your obedient servant,
> Robert Duncannon."

She read the letter through twice and then a third time, savoring every word of it. Aside from family missives, and replies to job applications, she had never had a letter from a man before. She looked at the signature and smiled. "Your obedient servant" sounded both dignified and humble and also touchingly funny. Remembering his kisses, she touched her lips, knowing that if she lived for a hundred years, she would never forget. Mentally she consigned Mrs. Bainbridge to penal servitude for the words which had provoked that angry reaction which had made him think that he had offended her.

Glancing at the letter again, she wondered what it was he longed to say. If Sophie's mother was to be believed, he was a widower and a father, roles which cast him in a different, softer light. It occurred to her that his wife's death might have been quite recent, perhaps after a long and protracted illness, which would explain the depth of sadness she had seen in his eyes. His reference to the night of their first meeting made her think again about those scars, the "accident" he had so carefully glossed over, and having spent a great deal of time deliberately *not* thinking about Robert Duncannon, she suddenly realized that she knew very little about him. She was seized by a desire to know *all* about him, every little detail that made up his life, from school days through to adulthood. He had a daughter; what was her name?

Impulsively she began to write a reply to his letter, but halfway through she stopped, tore the page into small pieces, and burnt them.

In trying to explain the cause of her anger that Sunday afternoon, she realized just how dangerous a liaison with him could be. York was a city, but it was small with gossip. People knew people who knew people. Louisa's background would be checked by interested parties, and even supposing that she told him the truth, that by some wild, incredible stretch of the imagination he loved her in spite of it, the gossip would be too much to endure. The slur upon both of them would be bad enough, but to have her mother subjected to all that again was intolerable.

Had he been an ordinary serving soldier, it would have been so simple; but Robert was too well born and too eligible for a relationship with Louisa Elliott to go unremarked.

Sadly she went into her room, placing Robert's letter with those sent by her mother and Edward when she had lived in the North Riding. She knew that she would have to reply, but the letter would need thought and careful phrasing, and at the moment she was too tired for either.

ELEVEN

Moira was allowed Tuesday afternoons off, usually returning to Blossom Street at half past eight in the evening. At half past nine, however, it was Mrs. Petty who brought a tray of tea into the drawing room.

Rachel did not look up from her book, but Louisa thanked the cook with some surprise.

Mrs. Petty sniffed loudly. She was little and thin and perpetually irritated by every circumstance of life; her mouth had a dissatisfied, downward turn; wispy gray eyebrows met in a constant frown, and her shrewish nostrils quivered uncontrollably. "Moira's not back yet," she said crossly. "And that girl Ellen has a streaming cold. I've sent her to bed—for all the use she's been to me today, she might as well have been there all along."

"That was kind of you, Mrs. Petty," said Louisa equably. "Have you told Mr. Tempest that Moira's not back?"

With another disapproving sniff Mrs. Petty shook her head. "Taken herself off, I shouldn't wonder. All the same, these Irish—no sense of duty."

"I'm sure you're wrong, Mrs. Petty. She's usually back by this time. She may have had an accident, or something may be wrong at home— we don't know. I think you should inform Mr. Tempest. He should be in his study."

When Mr. Tempest was informed, the facts annoyed him. By the following morning, when Moira had still failed to return, he was extremely irritated. Mrs. Petty said she could not possibly cook *and* serve breakfast, which left the kitchen waif, Ellen, sneezing abominably, to lay the table and fumble with sausages, eggs, and bacon. Louisa winced at her nervousness and longed to help her; Rachel clucked her tongue at every mistake, and her father's color rose each time he checked his watch. Furious, he declared that the porridge was the only edible item on the table; the eggs were broken, the bacon cold, his toast like leather. Rachel and Victoria wilted under his thunderous complaints. Louisa was driven to offer her services for the next meal, but at this Albert Tempest turned puce. Flinging back his chair, he vehemently rejected the offer.

"But if you want to help, Miss Elliott, go and look for her. Ask Mrs. Petty where she spends her time off and see if you can find the stupid girl. If she's left for good, I want to know—then we can make other arrangements." With a final glance at his pocket watch, he stormed out of the house.

In the kitchen the skivvy sneezed and wept into a sinkful of washing-up while Mrs. Petty glowered at her over a reviving cup of tea.

In answer to Louisa's inquiry, Mrs. Petty wrote down the address from a greasy notebook she kept in her apron pocket. "You'll have your work cut out to find it, I reckon. No good asking me—I've never been down Walmgate in my life. Nor would I want to," she added, smugly pulling down the corners of her mouth. "I should take care if I were you, miss."

"Oh, I shall take care, Mrs. Petty, don't you worry."

After a hurried consultation with Rachel, who reluctantly agreed to supervise Victoria's lessons for the morning, Louisa went to her room for her hat and cloak. The black velour she had so recently refurbished was rejected in favor of an old brown felt hat with an unfashionably wide brim and dusty petersham ribbon. She sucked in her lips, regretting the fact that her old coat had been left in Gillygate; her black cloak was hardly new, but she had the feeling it would be noticeably smart in Walmgate. As an afterthought, she took some silver and copper coins from a small box in her top drawer and slipped them into her pocket.

It was a cold, dank day, the leaden sky already darkened by a pall of smoke hanging over the city; mist swirled over the river, obscuring barges and cargoes, muffling the cries of men, eerily revealing masts and spars, booms and winches, the upper half of warehouses by Ouse Bridge. There would be a fog by evening, thick and sulfurous; Louisa knew the signs well and shivered, praying she would find Moira and return with her before dark.

She hurried through the town center, passing Albert Tempest's printing shop on Fossgate and crossing the narrow bridge over the stagnating waters of the river Foss. A thick mist fortunately obscured the shallow, canalized river, into which the sewers of the area drained. It was little more than an open cesspool, meandering through the poorest quarter of the city, a source of disease which flooded the low-lying streets to either side each winter and released choking odors in the heat of summer. Behind the semirespectable facade of Fossgate, to the rear of Tempest's, lurked some of the most squalid houses of ill fame in York; there were reports every week in the papers of respectable men being accosted and robbed by prostitutes and their bullyboys. Louisa kept her eyes about her, amazed that anyone could be tempted by vice in such evil, malodorous surroundings and pitying the female remnants of humanity whose degradation led them to such a way of life. The very thought of them made her blood run cold, and she was glad that her journey was in daylight.

For a moment she wondered about Edward and Mr. Tempest, going home on dark winter nights. Had they ever been accosted by the women of the streets? How did they view the half-world that bordered Fossgate? Gentle, restrained, and fastidious, Edward was so lacking in obvious sexuality that she could not imagine him feeling anything more than pity for those unfortunate women; but Albert Tempest would have little sympathy to spare. Yet he was the kind of man she believed would be tempted by vice as long as the price was right and the sheets tolerably clean. He strove so hard to give the impression of well-bred gentility, but his passionate temper gave him away, together with those strange looks she had sometimes surprised, the looks that made her grow hot with embarrassment, that made her feel like something which could be bought. With a shiver of distaste, she renewed her determination to keep the distance of formality between herself and her employer. Too many girls fell by the wayside within the confines of the house in which they worked; and all too often that fall led them to streets such as these.

Walmgate had more pubs and alehouses than any other thoroughfare in the city; even at this hour of the morning men were hanging about in groups by warm doorways, their eyes following her, watching every hesitation in her step. Glancing down each dark and noxious alley, searching for name-boards, Louisa despaired of ever finding Butcher's Yard, not knowing which side of the street it favored or how far it was into the maze of courts and passages beyond. She dared not approach the men, and even the women she thought to ask returned her inquiring glances with hostility, their eyes taking in her good warm clothes with obvious resentment. Almost resigned to walking the length of Walmgate twice, she suddenly spotted a solitary child, a boy of about seven or eight years, gazing longingly into the window of a bread shop.

She approached him slowly, apparently a casual customer also interested in the loaves and baps displayed behind the grimy glass. Very carefully, she withdrew a penny from her pocket and asked him if he knew the address she sought. The child was startled, wary, but with the street knowledge of a half-starved urchin, he saw the penny was within his grasp. A pair of ancient eyes looked up at her.

"I might," he said, studying the coin.

"If you can take me exactly where I want to be—exactly, mind; I want to see the people first—you shall have this penny."

"Butcher's Yard, you say. What's the name of the people?"

"Hanrahan."

"It's off the yard. You'll never find it on your own. I'll take you."

He walked ahead of Louisa. Her heart twisted as she looked at his filthy rags and blue-mottled legs. Diligence, thrift, and luck had kept her own family away from the maelstrom of poverty; she had seen enough as a child, however, to know that for some the grip on decency was at best a tenuous one, too easily swept away by the downward spiral of illness and unemployment.

Butcher's Yard was less than fifty paces away, on the same side of the street. The child paused at the entrance, his old eyes raking her face.

"Are you from the board?"

"The School Board? No, there's no need to worry about me."

"Board of Guardians, workhouse, I meant. Have you come to take her in?"

"Who?" Louisa asked with a frown.

"Old Ma Hanrahan—they reckon she's dying."

"Is she? How dreadful—that must be why . . ."

The child stared at her. "Who are you?"

"I'm not from any institution," she replied quietly. "Moira Hanrahan is a friend of mine. I've come to see what's the matter, to see if I can help," she added, extemporizing.

Evidently satisfied that she was not an enemy, he nodded. "All right, lady. I'll take you, but you'd better keep close by me." With that, the skinny child disappeared into the alley, emerging in a muddy court with a pump at the center, around which several ragged and disheveled women gossiped. One stared at Louisa, and the rest turned, silent as statues, suspicion and hostility radiating from them in almost solid waves. In the close, dank air, the vile stench of privies assaulted her nostrils, causing her to swallow hard; she hurried in the boy's wake, fishing in her pocket for a scented handkerchief with which to cover her nose and mouth. He disappeared again, into another passage, between a row of tiny brick-built cottages and a stinking slaughterhouse. The fetid reek of blood and excrement coming from the passage halted her; fighting nausea and the overwhelming urge to run away, to put miles between herself and this disgusting place, she called out to the boy to wait.

He returned for her, his eyes taking in the horror of her expression, hardening at her disgust. Impatiently he tugged at her cloak, pulling her into the black bowels of the alley. Something wet touched her face and she screamed, but the boy muttered that it was only somebody's washing and dragged her on, till a subdued light showed the existence of another yard behind the first, and Louisa almost ran toward it.

Clutching her handkerchief to her mouth, she clung for a moment to the wet wall by her side, her eyes on the squelching mud at her feet, refusing to take in the filthy piggery, the agitated and screaming animals, the dungheap piled against one side of the tiny court, its liquid contents leaking over the mud and presumably into the cottages which formed its sole support. She closed her eyes and breathed shallowly through her mouth, trying hard not to smell the stench trapped in that small, sunless area.

As she opened her eyes, the child extended a skinny arm in the direction of the far corner. "That's Hanrahan's," he stated flatly.

"Are you sure?" she asked feebly, unable to believe that dear, funny, cheerful Moira could originate from such appalling surroundings.

Her small, hardened companion nodded dumbly, his contempt reserved for Louisa. Stung by the realization that he probably lived in equally squalid conditions, she gritted her teeth, lifted her chin, and, abandoning her skirts to the mud, crossed the unpaved yard. A tiny child who had been playing outside an open cottage door was whisked inside as she passed, the door slammed behind it. She had a fleeting impression of faces at grimy windows, hurriedly withdrawn; of eyes watching every sliding footfall, taking in the minutest details of her progress, her appearance, and her scarcely hidden disgust.

The door of the Hanrahans' hovel hung lopsidedly in its frame, no more than a fragile demarcation of privacy. Louisa's light tap brought no response, but, as she knocked harder, the door opened of its own accord, revealing a miserable earth-floored room with rickety wooden steps leading to an upper chamber. A black and empty fireplace faced her, with the remains of a broken chair beside it; a straw palliasse lay in one corner, and as she and the boy stepped tentatively inside, a rat scuttled into deeper darkness beneath the stairs.

"But there's nobody here," she whispered to the boy.

He shrugged. "Might be up there," he said, indicating the upper room.

Louisa cleared her throat, but as she called Moira's name, her voice sounded small and squeaky with nerves, even to her own ears. She called again, more strongly this time, and was rewarded by the sound of someone moving above. The door at the head of the stairs scraped open a few inches, and a female voice, harsh and unrecognizable, shouted down for them to state their business.

The boy was nervous and demanded his penny of Louisa. Fiercely she shook her head and grasped his thin shoulder. She shouted her own name and asked to speak to Moira Hanrahan. At that the door opened fully, a pair of booted feet appeared, followed by skirts and petticoats; but the light entering the dingy hovel was so feeble that the figure was almost at the foot of the stairs before Louisa was able to distinguish Moira's face. Her black, curly hair was disarrayed, her normally rosy cheeks white and pinched with cold; she almost fell into Louisa's arms.

"Miss Elliott—oh, Miss Elliott—thank God!" she cried as Louisa hugged her.

"Can I have my penny now?" the boy demanded.

"Of course," Louisa said, releasing herself reluctantly from Moira's arms. In her relief she took two pennies from her pocket, and giving a lopsided grin, the boy curled his fingers around the coins and dashed away.

Moira was weeping openly, the kind of helpless, silent tears which slide unbidden and unchecked. "I swear by all the saints, I'm glad to see you, miss. But I'm that ashamed for you to see this place. Don't tell on me, will you? Promise you'll not tell Mrs. Petty or Miss Tempest what a hole this is?"

"Now why should I do that? Hush yourself and tell me what's wrong."

"My ma's dying," the girl said and began to sob. It took Louisa some time to calm her, to decipher the story between her outbursts of grief, but she finally understood that Moira had arrived home the previous afternoon to find her mother terribly ill with the flu and the house full of gossiping women. It was, however, empty of what little furniture the family had possessed. Jumping to the wrong conclusion, Moira had berated the lot of them and cleared the house, only to discover later that her young brother Sean was the culprit.

She had gone to the pub where he worked behind the bar, to hear a tale that reduced her to more tears in the telling. Having talked for months about his ticket to America, having saved at his mother's expense, young Sean had finally taken their few salable possessions and pawned them. Choking and sobbing over his ingratitude, Moira cursed his name for leaving their mother without food or fire, for leaving a sick woman to die of a broken heart.

"And he had the nerve to tell Ma she'd be all right—I was coming in the afternoon and I'd look after her!"

With some trepidation, Louisa followed Moira up the rickety steps. The old Irishwoman lay on a narrow truckle bed, apparently sleeping; several thin blankets and Moira's coat were laid across her, but there was no warmth in the room, no fireplace, and aside from a pile of straw and an old wooden sea chest, no furniture.

"She *will* die if you leave her here," Louisa said, feeling the woman's burning forehead and cold hands, the barely flickering pulse at her wrist. "She needs warmth and care. Why don't you get a doctor?"

Moira looked down. "There isn't enough money for doctors."

"But she should be in hospital," Louisa protested.

"You mean the workhouse," Moira said bitterly. "Ma would rather die here than wake up in that place."

Louisa turned on her angrily. "That's a wicked thing to say! How can you let her die? *You* can't look after her. There isn't even a fire in here!"

Stubbornly Moira shook her head. "She's not going to the workhouse. I'll manage somehow."

With a sigh of frustration, Louisa looked around. "Then we must get her downstairs and make the fire. Can you get one of the neighbors to help?"

"They don't care much for me since I moved away," Moira admitted. "And I cursed them all yesterday when I thought they'd made off with the chairs and things."

Eventually the girl was persuaded to go to the bar where Sean had worked; Louisa reasoned that the landlord might offer some constructive assistance out of sympathy. To ease things, she gave Moira most of what money she had.

It seemed an age till her return, but return she did, with a burly friend of Sean's who was willing to help. He eyed Louisa like a nervous horse, but with the coals and kindling he had brought he managed to coax a small fire into life and reluctantly handed over the miniature of brandy that the landlord had sent. He moved the truckle bed and carried the sick woman downstairs.

The activity drew forth observers from the other hovels. A female child of indeterminate age, with red-rimmed eyes and a sore, runny nose, was pushed forward by one of the women. Hesitant, fearful, she asked if there was anything to be done. Before Moira could send her away, Louisa thanked her kindly and went with her to where her mother stood, shawl pulled down across her forehead.

"If any of you have the time and kindness to sit with Mrs. Hanrahan, I'm sure her daughter would appreciate it," Louisa said slowly and clearly. "There's a warm fire, and I intend to send out for some food."

The woman's eyes met hers for a fleeting second; the broken toe of her boot pushed at the mud in front of her. Finally, she nodded. "I could," she said at last.

"There aren't any chairs, I'm afraid."

"I'll bring a stool," the woman said and turned toward her own door.

Returning to Moira, Louisa told her to take the rest of the money to buy food. "I have to get back to Blossom Street, or Mr. Tempest will think I've absconded, too. This fog's getting thicker, and it will be dark soon. I'll try and come again tomorrow, but I can't promise. If you should need me, go to the printing shop on Fossgate. It isn't too far, and Mr. Tempest will let me know."

But this drove the girl into an even greater state of panic.

"He'll have her taken inside," she wept. "She's going to die, I know she is, but I don't want her to die in there. Mr. Tempest will send the guardians, I know he will."

"Moira," Louisa said firmly, "I have to tell him what's going on. If I don't, he'll think you've run away and get another maid. You can't afford to lose your job, now can you? I promise I'll make it all right— I promise."

Only half convinced, Moira let the woman and her daughter in, taking Louisa back through the maze of stinking alleys to the main road; they parted by the bread shop where Louisa had met her young guide that morning, and the smell of fresh bread reminded her that she, too, had not eaten all day; but it hardly seemed to matter.

In the broader reaches of Walmgate, the fog was thicker. Solitary figures passed, ghost-like, their footsteps muffled; it was impossible to see across the street and getting darker by the minute. Louisa began to be afraid. All that she had read and heard about the area, coupled with what she had seen today, conspired to activate her imagination, so that she shrank from shadows and halted to listen to muted noises. She saw the glow of a lamplighter's pole ahead of her and hoped that she could follow him to Fossgate and the more familiar parts of the town; but he was coming toward her, leaving only the gas lamps, like feeble glowworms, to guide her through the dense, swirling fog. It stung her eyes until she was sure she could see its particles dancing before them; it filled her nose and mouth so that she could taste its acrid edge and distorted her sense of hearing until she was sure she was being followed. All thoughts of Blossom Street were abandoned; the printing shop on Fossgate was the safety she was aiming for. Would she never reach the bridge? Panic ate into logic; she began to hurry, broke into a run, realized suddenly that the lights had disappeared, cobbles were beneath her feet, and she was lost.

The sound of horses' hooves and heavy wheels increased her panic. In desperation, she ran forward, tripped over a pavement edge, and fell sideways against a brick-built wall.

TWELVE

*B*oth Edward and Albert Tempest were horrified at the state in which Louisa arrived, to the extent that Mr. Tempest gave her a cup of tea in his own china cup and offered to call a cab to take her back to Blossom Street. He insisted that he had known nothing of Moira's circumstances.

That, as much as Louisa's badly bruised and grazed cheek, infuriated Edward. "He should make it his business to know," he muttered as he helped Louisa into the cab. Edward's eyes were anxious, showing more of his true fears than he realized. "It's a bad area, Louisa. You were very lucky—it could have been so much worse."

"I'm all right," she assured him, but she understood what he was trying to say: she might have been mistaken for a prostitute.

"You mustn't go there again. Promise me?"

Louisa sighed. "I've already promised Mr. Tempest," she said quietly. "But I doubt he'll do anything about Moira."

"If she comes here for help," Edward promised, "I'll see to it myself."

Stark images of Walmgate haunted Louisa that night. Hovels with thin walls and broken roofs, the damp earth floor of that downstairs room, and Moira's mother, breathing feebly in the scant warmth from that smoky fire.

She had washed her hair and dried it in front of the schoolroom fire, had washed herself and donned fresh clothes, but hours later she could still smell the dank air of those filthy courts.

Tired and restless, the next day she was edgy to the point of anger, her patience with Victoria, and particularly Rachel, stretched to the breaking point. The promise not to reveal the sordid facts of Moira's existence had to be honored, and she said little beyond the fact that the girl's mother was ill, that Moira needed help, and that this had delayed her return to Blossom Street. She was glad that the cause of her accident had been so mundane. After a while, both girls stopped asking questions.

Moira returned that evening. Albert Tempest saw her in his study, with only Louisa present. He did not want his daughters' ears sullied by unnecessary details.

Shaking with cold and shock, Moira gave him the bald facts: that her mother had died in the early hours of that morning, that the doctor had come to verify her death, and that her mother's body had been taken to the mortuary. She would be buried in a public grave, as there was no money for a proper funeral.

Albert Tempest grunted a few conventional words of condolence, but Louisa privately suspected him of being unconcerned. The fact that Moira's mother was a Roman Catholic seemed to relegate her, in his eyes, to a position beyond sympathy; to him she would be one of the undeserving, feckless poor, to whom it was immaterial where they were buried. He did, however, give Moira permission to attend the funeral.

Ever observant, Louisa took Moira into the kitchen for a warming drink and something to eat, and ignoring Mrs. Petty's clucks and sniffs, made the girl comfortable beside the blazing kitchen fire.

Later she went up to Moira's little room on the second floor, needing to talk to her for her own conscience's sake as much as to give comfort.

She asked whether Moira's family had always lived in Butcher's Yard; the girl's eyes filled with tears as she shook her head. "When we first came to York, we lived in a proper house by Fishergate Postern. Pa had a good job on the railway, and never did he touch a drop, God rest his soul. He was killed, though, when I'd be ten—after that things got a mite desperate. Ma tried hard, but she was never what you'd call a good manager—the older ones left, you know, sent a few shillings when they could, nothing regular. Ma ended up in Butcher's Yard a couple of years after I was sent into service. Just a skivvying job, you know, like Ellen. It was a good place, though—I don't know why I moved. Still," she said with a shrug, "it's a job, to be sure, and now Ma's gone I can be thinking of moving on. I've a sister in London—maybe she'd look out for me something."

Her voice, strangely quiet, was still so rich with the accents of Ireland that Louisa said she had imagined Moira a more recent immigrant.

"Ah well," the girl said with a smile. "When it was secrets they were keeping, Ma and Pa still talked the Gaelic. And you know it's all Irish they are down Walmgate—a real home from home for Irishmen, whether from Donegal or County Cork. And don't they all hate each other," she said, laughing, "fighting in lumps on a Saturday night!"

Louisa laughed too, but she wondered why; fighting did not seem to her a very amusing pastime. "So which county were you born in?"

"Me? I was born in Waterford—the city, that is. Not that you'd be knowing it for a city, Miss Elliott—excepting the slums, it's nothing like York, nothing at all . . ." She went on to describe the poverty, the lack of work, and her own parents' reasons for leaving, while Louisa listened in horror.

The mention of Waterford brought Robert Duncannon vividly to mind; as though he whispered in her ear, she heard him saying that wealth and privilege were not everything, and his sincerity sickened her. It might not be everything to him, but even a tiny portion of that wealth could work miracles for people like Moira and her family. The knowledge that his family's position was founded on the suffering of others was intolerable; she thought she would never be able to look into his eyes without seeing Moira's mother in that appalling hovel and the image of that little boy, old before his time.

THIRTEEN

When Louisa arrived home on Saturday morning, Bessie was black-leading the cold kitchen range. A little packet of soft graphite stood with a stone mixing jar and several brushes and cloths on a paper by the hearth. Polishing energetically, she looked up at Louisa's greeting, revealing black hands and a comically smudged nose. Louisa grinned as she dropped a kiss on the older woman's forehead.

"You look nearly as pretty as I do, Bessie, with that black blob on the end of your nose."

Almost as a reflex action, Bessie wiped it with the back of her hand, and Louisa laughed outright. "Now you've made it worse!"

Bessie grumbled and stood up, seeing Louisa's grazed cheek for the first time. "Oh, my lamb, is that what you did the other day? Mr. Edward told us—"

"It's not so bad, Bessie. The bruise is coming out now, which makes it look worse than it is. I must admit, though, I was glad I didn't meet anyone I knew coming through town."

Gathering up her brushes and cloths, Bessie grunted. "Aye, well, you've a visitor coming today."

"A visitor? Who?"

"That gentleman who stayed here, the one who called the day of Miss Elizabeth's funeral."

Louisa rescued the tabby cat from Bessie's feet, burying her face in its soft fur to cover her sudden agitation. "You mean Captain Duncannon?"

"Aye, that'll be him," Bessie replied with a sniff and proceeded to light the already laid fire. While it burned up, she whitened the hearth with hearthstone, her eyes constantly checking the condition of the fire, fortunately ignoring Louisa, who stood with the cat in her arms, absently fondling its silky fur. The tabby purred and nuzzled her, its paws ecstatically kneading her shoulder and breast.

"He called the other evening—Thursday I think it was. I know it was still foggy, but I think he came by cab . . . Talked to Miss Mary in the parlor, I took them some tea in. Anyway, she must have told him about your fall, because she said he was calling today to see how you were."

Inwardly Louisa groaned. He *would* decide to call today, when she was looking and feeling dreadful. "You don't sound very approving, Bessie," she commented, wondering whether she should refuse to see him.

Bessie sniffed again as she sat back on her haunches and surveyed the fire. "Well, Miss Louisa, I'll be honest—Miss Emily put the wind up me when he was staying here. She said he was trouble, and I can't help but think she was right. I know you're a bonny lass, but it's what his intentions are that worries me."

The cat gave a little cry of protest as Louisa involuntarily squeezed it to her breast. Suddenly she was very angry. No matter what she herself thought of Robert Duncannon, Bessie had no right to cast aspersions upon his character. "You needn't worry on that score, Bessie," she said coldly, adding for good measure, "He's nothing to me, whatever his intentions. Just because Mamma seems dazzled by his station in life doesn't mean to say that I am. I thought I might be out when he called, but I've changed my mind. Perhaps if he sees me like this, it might just put him off for good." She dropped the cat unceremoniously onto a chair and opened the gladstone bag she had brought from Blossom Street.

"Can you get these things clean for me? They're badly stained around the hems, I'm afraid."

Bessie took the bundle of linen and examined the damage to Louisa's dress. "Oh, I'll have these clean in no time. Look, why don't you sit down and let me make you a nice cup of tea?" she added, half regretting her outspoken remarks.

While Bessie continued with her jobs, Louisa sat and sipped her tea, feeling strangely exhausted. The cat sidled onto her knee, turning itself round and round until it was comfortable, and she stroked it absently, gazing with unseeing eyes out of the kitchen window at the long, narrow yard, shadowed by the looming city wall. The sky above was brightly blue, with little scudding clouds driven by a sharp wind, heralding the gales to come. It was almost the end of February, and tomorrow would be Leap Year's Day. A mocking half-smile appeared on her lips as she thought of the old custom. What a pity today was not the twenty-ninth, she thought bitterly, else she could have asked the captain to marry her, and what would he have said to that?

Interrupting her thoughts like a warning knell, the booming bells of the Minster beyond the wall struck twelve, and a glass on the window-ledge vibrated in unison against the pane.

Emily and her mother returned from market laden with groceries in wicker baskets and vegetables in string bags. They both commented and commiserated over Louisa's accident and Moira's personal tragedy, the continuing story of which had to be repeated for Edward's benefit.

Immediately after their meal, as if on cue, Edward said he intended to work in his room that afternoon, something he rarely did on Saturdays. Emily announced that she would be going out, having made plans to see her John and to take tea with his family afterward. Seeing her mother's hand in these convenient absences, Louisa felt uneasy, then irritated by the conspiracy, and as she carried water upstairs to bathe in her room, she wondered what her mother was thinking of. By the time she was ready to join her in the parlor, Louisa's nerves were tuned to concert pitch, liable to screech at the slightest clumsy touch.

With a pile of crochet work upon her knee, Mary Elliott was seated by the fire in her favorite wing chair. She wore her Sunday black with jet jewelry, and beneath a starched lace cap her graying hair was piled into a neat chignon. The furniture bore witness to some ardent polishing, and in the firelight the brass fender and firedogs winked cheerfully; dancing points of light were reflected from the glazed family photographs, hanging straight and symmetrical as soldiers on the opposite wall. Taking it in at a glance, Louisa sighed and took a seat near the window with her back to the light, hoping her disfigured cheek would be less noticeable.

"Have you any embroidery I could do? I don't like to appear to be just waiting for someone to call."

From her sewing basket, Mary Elliott produced a half-completed table-runner, which Louisa took up with a singular lack of enthusiasm. After a moment's thought, she spoke again. "Did Captain Duncannon say why he wanted to see me? Other than to check on the state of my health, of course?"

"No. Should there be another reason?"

"Possibly," Louisa admitted. "He wrote to me the other week—just after the Bainbridges' party—and said that there was something he wished to discuss with me, but I put him off. Quite honestly, Mamma, I don't think there's anything to be gained by encouraging him, and I do wish you hadn't said he could come here this afternoon."

With a sigh, Mary Elliott privately acknowledged the error. She had a genuine affection for the man she had nursed and virtually bullied back to life. He had been ill, very ill, but he had not wanted to live; that had been the difficulty. He had wept and cursed in his delirium and shouted more than one woman's name. His secrets, however, remained undisclosed. She still wondered why he had been so anxious and afraid, what it was that had so deprived him of his will to live. And yet, seeing him on the day of her sister's funeral, she had been amazed at the change in him. It still puzzled her.

"It would have been difficult for me to refuse without seeming rude," she said slowly. "Don't you want to see him?"

Studiously selecting a strand of yellow silk, Louisa considered her reply. "I'd have preferred not to," she admitted. "Oh, I know you think he's charming, Mamma, but if you'd been in Walmgate with me the other day, and heard what Moira had to say—well, you'd think differently."

"I'm sorry, dear, I don't follow . . ."

"Mrs. Bainbridge told me he owns estates in Ireland, which I imagine includes hundreds of starving tenants, people like Moira and her family, who had to leave Waterford because it was either that or die. If you could see the conditions those people live in *now,* it would horrify you, Mamma, absolutely *horrify* you."

"Surely the captain—"

"Probably has no idea what's going on. Probably doesn't care. Anyway, if he's coming here to see how I am, he's going to get more than he bargained for!"

"Don't be so quick to judge, Louisa. You may be wrong." After a moment's thought, she asked, "I wonder what it is he wants to discuss with you?"

"I've no idea. Unless he wants to offer me a job," she added grimly.

"According to Mrs. Bainbridge, he's a widower with a young daughter."

"A widower, is he? I hadn't realized that." Suddenly much of the mystery seemed clear. A young man, recently bereaved: that would explain his reluctance to fight for life. But if he was anxious about the welfare of his child . . . ? "Would you accept?" she asked seriously.

"What?" For a moment, Louisa wondered what her mother meant. "Oh, Mamma—no, of course I wouldn't. Look" she began and then broke off; the truth of the matter was far too personal. "It isn't quite proper, I know, but I think it might be as well if I saw him alone."

"Well, dear—"

"Please, it is important."

Studying the tension in her daughter's face, Mary Elliott slowly nodded. "Very well. I won't ask you why."

"Thank you, Mamma."

Nothing more was said after that, but Louisa glanced repeatedly out of the window, wanting to see Robert Duncannon's approach, to be prepared for his arrival; but while she watched so assiduously in one direction, the captain approached from the other.

Wearing a crisply starched cap and apron, with her sleeves rolled down and neatly buttoned, Bessie answered the front door, showing him into the parlor with just the right degree of deference. Waiting until the formal greetings were over, she asked her mistress whether she should bring tea now or later.

"We'll have tea in a quarter of an hour, Bessie," Mary Elliott graciously replied, her eyes alight with pleasure at this opportunity of playing the genteel hostess. Her eyes brightened even more as the captain presented her with a prettily wrapped box of chocolates and gave a posy of early primroses to Louisa. Her daughter's tight-lipped acceptance of the flowers caused her to suppress a sigh, however, and she chattered inconsequentially to cover the awkwardness. While Louisa fetched water from the kitchen, she noted the healthy color a brisk walk had brought to the captain's face and the slight increase in weight which made him look fit and well. His obvious recovery pleased her, and she felt a quite irrational twinge of regret on his behalf. No matter what his intentions toward Louisa, she felt sorry for him and wished circumstances could have been other than what they were.

As Louisa came back into the room, the captain's eyes followed her, his expression betraying more than compassion as he looked at her bruised cheek. He asked about her visit to Walmgate, more concerned with her unfortunate experience than the suffering of those she had gone to visit. "You were lucky," he said, unconsciously echoing Edward's words. "From what little I've seen of the area, I'd say things could have been much worse."

"I'm luckier than Moira, that's true," Louisa commented coldly, and her mother's heart sank. She hoped Louisa was not about to lecture the captain on what she considered to be his responsibilities. "At least I don't have to live in those dreadful conditions." After a short pause, she stared hard at him and went on. "Her parents are from your part of Ireland—Waterford, I believe."

"Indeed?" he said evenly. "What name do they go by?"

"Hanrahan."

Mary Elliott saw the startled surprise in his eyes and, in her daughter's, a small gleam of satisfaction.

"You know the name?"

He hesitated, dropping his glance. For a moment a strange little smile played about his mouth. "Oddly enough, I do. But I doubt your girl's related—it's a common enough name."

"Some people on your estate, perhaps?" Louisa pressed.

"Not my estate," he corrected. "My brother's." He smiled at her expression, at the sudden color which flooded her cheeks. "Did someone tell you I was an absentee landlord, living off the unremitting toil of my tenants?"

Uncomfortably Louisa studied her embroidery. "Not quite in those terms," she said primly, and her mother suppressed a smile.

"But someone intimated I was a wealthy landowner?" He searched his pockets for his cigar case, begging Mary Elliott's permission to smoke. She nodded, afraid that the conversation was getting a little out of hand. "I wonder who it could have been?" he mused aloud. "It wasn't by any chance Mrs. Bainbridge?"

"You mean the mother of Rachel Tempest's friend?" Mary Elliott asked, although she knew quite well whom he meant.

"The same. A very pleasant lady, but talkative, and sometimes a little misinformed, I'm afraid."

"Ah, yes, Louisa mentioned that you were at the party, Captain. Wasn't it a fortunate coincidence? Louisa was so afraid she wouldn't know anyone."

"The pleasure was entirely mine," Robert insisted.

"Of course she shouldn't have gone at all, being in mourning for her aunt—but Mr. Tempest would have her go, and she couldn't really refuse."

"A difficult situation," Robert agreed with a glance at Louisa.

It was something of a relief to all of them that Bessie arrived with the tea tray. The lighter aspects of the party were discussed, the tea and cakes handed round, and then Mary Elliott left them, insisting that there were matters of pressing importance for her to attend to. For the captain's sake, she was pleased that Louisa had been proved wrong, but his real reasons for calling nagged at her, and she wished Louisa could have confided more; it might have been possible to advise her.

FOURTEEN

*P*ouring more tea for them both, Louisa asked, "Why did you want to see me, Captain?"

The tone of voice and her formal address were not encouraging, but he strove to ignore both. "Will you tell me first what Mrs. Bainbridge had to say?"

Somewhat taken aback, she handed him his cup. "Is it important?"

He nodded, conscious of a sudden dryness in his throat. "It's a beginning," he said at last. "You were obviously upset that afternoon, and as I said in my letter, I thought I was to blame. But when I received your reply, I realized that Mrs. Bainbridge must have said something silly, something that offended you. What was it?" When Louisa did not immediately reply, he gave a wry smile and added, "She's a notorious matchmaker. Did she tell you I'd be a good catch?"

Her sudden blush provided his answer. "I thought so," he nodded. "Well, she couldn't be more wrong, I'm sorry to say. I'm far from wealthy—in fact my personal assets are rather limited. A house in Dublin which once belonged to my mother's family and a small legacy which augments my army pay. The estate belongs to my brother, William, but I'm afraid White Leigh eats more money than it produces, in spite of the fact that he's no absentee! However, enough of my family for the moment. Tell me about Sophie's mother."

"She said you were a widower with a small child," Louisa abruptly replied, determined to reveal nothing more than that.

He chewed his lower lip, aware of a desperate need for courage. With a heavy sigh, he said, "I rather thought she might have said something like that. It isn't true."

"You mean she lied? Why?"

"Oh, no," he said quickly "She didn't lie. She thought she was telling you the truth. Everyone is under the impression I'm a widower, excepting Tommy. But I'm *not*. My wife isn't dead."

There was a long silence. Outside, a cart rumbled by. The footsteps of passing strangers echoed past the window, and from the kitchen, Mary Elliott's light laugh mingled with Bessie's heavier voice. Steadfastly, Robert held Louisa's shocked and staring gaze, willing her to let him explain.

"You're married?" The question was barely a whisper. As he nodded, she shut her eyes against belief. "And I was angry because I thought you owned estates in Ireland," she said faintly, a sharp sense of irony cutting through her emotional pain.

The touch of his hand brought her back to reality. He knelt at her feet, his eyes shadowed by intense self-reproach. Blinking rapidly, Louisa looked away, across the room, seeing her father's portrait on the far wall, sharply focused by a trick of the light. Not again, she thought desperately; this cannot happen twice. Why? Why me?

She passed a hand over her eyes, shutting out both faces. "I'm such a fool, Robert," she whispered. "I never dreamt you were married."

"I'm sorry," he murmured huskily. His fingers tightened, and the heavy gold signet on his little finger bit painfully into her hand. "I wanted to tell you, that night we first met. You asked about my arm— and I nearly told you. I wish to God I had!" he bitterly exclaimed. Abruptly he stood up and, in short, staccato sentences, began to relate the happenings of Christmas Day. Shocked and confused, Louisa struggled to follow his rather disjointed story.

"You mean—your wife tried to kill you?" she asked incredulously.

Distractedly, Robert shook his head. "I don't know. I imagine so." With a short laugh, he clenched his right fist and showed her the scars, still pink, along the back of his hand. "Scissors did that. A pair of scissors. And if she hadn't thrown the contents of a bottle of perfume in my face to begin with, it might have been my eyes."

With a sudden quiver, Louisa pictured it and recoiled; tried to speak and had to clear her throat of a sudden constriction. "Robert," she managed eventually, "I feel very stupid. Won't you begin again—at the beginning?"

"The beginning?" he sighed. "It feels like a hundred years ago—and must be all of five."

"It doesn't matter. I've got time to listen." And the rest of my life to understand, she thought but did not say. As she met his gaze, a sense of loss overwhelmed her; she had expected nothing, had grasped at reasons to dislike him, yet hope had lingered, and with its dying she felt bereaved.

"Tommy introduced us," he said shortly and looked away. He went and stood before the fire, extending his hands toward the warmth, for he was suddenly cold. As he lit another cigar, he thought about that time, the first ball of the season in Dublin, the crush of guests, violent colors of silks and satins and uniforms, himself on a crest of pride and achievement, recently promoted. And amidst the laughter and the braying voices, the great hilarity which followed what had been a difficult few months in Ireland, there was the small, still presence of Charlotte. Slender, fine-boned, with a mass of silvery hair; that pale, pale skin and eyes like the shadow of a cloud on water. He had called her his Diana, his Goddess of the Moon, and only afterward, much, much later, had he realized the true irony of it, for Diana was also a virgin goddess.

A cynical smile lifted the corners of his mouth as he began to talk about that evening, to describe the events that followed, and his voice took on a mocking tone, which in spite of being directed at himself, Louisa found unpleasant. She stared into the fire, envisaging the scene, the entire situation, now that Robert was relating it calmly. But the machinations of those people were harder to understand.

"Tommy, of course, had a head start—his late father was a close friend of Charlotte's uncle, the earl, and in fact they were related by marriage. But I could see Charlotte didn't much care for him. I think his scars frightened her—she had a horror of anything ugly, disfiguring—and they were recent then, very livid. I remember he was rather jealous of my success, although he's more than thankful now," he added with a bitter smile.

From then on, Robert had found that he was seeing Charlotte often, at balls, concerts, and receptions; no discouragement was offered, and he was even invited to the earl's Dublin home, which had been tantamount to a seal of approval on the courtship.

"I was quite besotted by her beauty," he admitted. "Even by her quietness. She had a curiously remote air, which I thought romantic and mysterious at the time. I kept congratulating myself on my good fortune," he said contemptuously, and although Louisa made no comment, he begged her to understand. "Imagine—she was well born, beautiful, and of a wealthy family. In fact, she was due to come into a small fortune at the age of twenty-one, although I was not aware of it at the time. It never struck me as odd that her family should welcome me so hospitably. If I thought anything at all, I assumed they were genuinely pleased that a little happiness had come into her life.

"One of the aged aunts told me about her parents. A little over ten years ago they were killed—murdered, in fact—during riots in Ulster. Charlotte must have been about fourteen then—an only child, at a very impressionable age. Apparently she was inconsolable for months."

"No wonder, poor child."

"Yes, it was tragic. But, sadly, not unique." He sighed heavily. "I should have paid more attention to that old lady—it's possible she was trying to tell me something, trying to warn me. I don't know. Oh, Louisa, when I think of that time, I wince at my naïveté and sheer conceit! I was twenty-five, and thought myself a man of the world. I'd achieved my captaincy and was so puffed up with my own self-importance, so blinded by infatuation, I never asked the obvious questions. Such as why this titled family with vast estates and business interests should welcome *me,* the almost penniless younger son of an undistinguished family. Now, of course, I see it all too clearly—I had no money of my own with which to fight them, and no influence. And by the time Charlotte inherited her fortune, it was too late to use it. We were well and truly married by then, with a child to prove it," he added bitterly.

"What age was she then?"

"Eighteen when I first met her." Robert paced up and down before the hearth, unable to meet Louisa's eyes. "Nineteen when I married her. I asked her uncle for her hand, and he agreed—with just the right amount of reservation, the attitude of a concerned guardian, bestowing youthful innocence upon an impetuous young man!" Robert laughed, but the sound was harsh. "He did it very well, Louisa, very well indeed.

"Still, there were problems. I had to have permission from my commanding officer. Marriage is forbidden to subalterns and hardly acceptable under field rank. Well, that's how it was, officially at least. Now there are quite a few of us married. So, my first application was turned down. I was treated to a lecture on the duties and loyalties of a young officer to the regiment, told that the regiment must always come first, must be as wife and family to me while I served within it. If a wife was more important to me, then I must seriously consider whether the Royals truly needed my services! In other words, that I must choose between them. To my credit, I did think twice, more than twice. The regiment was, and is, my life. I never wanted anything else—and I could not have given it up simply to idle my life away on Charlotte's money!

"But instead of letting the whole thing drop, I discussed it with Charlotte's uncle. He advised me to apply again. Within the month, I did so—and my application was accepted without a word. Even in the light of what happened afterward," Robert continued, "I hold no ill feelings toward the colonel. He was just a pawn in the game, part of the earl's efforts to dispose of his niece in the most civilized and respectable manner. She would then become *my* responsibility, and he could wash his hands of her while pretending complete and utter innocence. But he must have known," Robert said bitterly. "Even allowing for the fact that her illness was slow and insidious in those early years, he could not have had her under his roof for almost five years without realizing that something was very wrong.''

Louisa shook her head, as though the whole story was too bizarre to be credible. "But your family—didn't they meet her? Didn't your parents advise you?''

Wearily Robert sat down, leaning back against the sofa cushions in an attitude of utter exhaustion. "My mother died when I was fifteen. At the time I met Charlotte, my father was already too ill to know or care what I was about. Anyway, her family made a whole mint of excuses as to why she couldn't travel down to Waterford. Eventually William and Letty—my brother and sister—traveled up to Dublin to meet her. Letty came several times. And for some peculiar, God-forsaken reason, actually liked her! There was none of this 'Oh, my goodness, you're stealing away my favorite brother' nonsense. Not with Letty. She spent half the time before my marriage entreating me to be good to Charlotte, that poor, innocent orphan. Even now she sees good in her, in spite of what she's done. In fact, Christmas Day was partly Letty's fault. She praised Charlotte so much, told me how much recovered she was—I actually fell into the trap of believing her.

"No,'' he said after a moment. "That isn't strictly true. I *wanted* to believe her.'' He closed his eyes, and the argument with Anne came back to him: her insistence that he should accompany them to morning service and his refusal; a burning determination to see Charlotte alone, while the house was quiet. The thought of seeing Charlotte again, for the first time in six months, with every ear strained to catch the first obscenity, had appalled him. So he had stood at the window and watched them go before climbing the stairs alone. "I exchanged a few words with Charlotte's nurse—not the brightest of women, I must admit, but a kindly soul who loves and cares for her like a child. Even she reinforced Letty's optimism—told me that Georgina had been visiting her mother regularly, with no apparent problems. She said Charlotte was taking an interest in herself again, which I knew she had not done for a long time—not since before Georgina's birth. So, feeling quite optimistic, I asked Mrs. Hanrahan to wait in the anteroom. Oh, yes, the nurse's name is Mrs. Hanrahan—you see now why your friend's name surprised me?''

Louisa nodded, and he went on. "Charlotte was at her dressing table, brushing her hair. She paid no attention to me whatsoever, but I knew she'd seen me in the looking glass. She really is very beautiful, you know—if you ever saw her, Louisa, you'd understand. And she looked—'' Sighing, he passed a hand over his eyes. "She was wearing a white robe. I was mesmerized, thinking of our wedding, how much I had loved and wanted her, thinking of everything in between." Robert paused again, remembering that sudden leap of desire, knowing how easily his senses had betrayed him. His eyes had seen her, innocent, virginal, and his mind had accepted the image as reality. "I had brought presents for her—a pretty dress ring and a bottle of perfume. She liked the ring," he said and saw again the moment of pleasure as she ceased brushing her long, rippling hair. Delighted, he had watched her turn her hand this way and that, admiring the pretty design of seed pearls and amethysts; had been tempted, reaching out with trembling fingers, to touch that beautiful hair. He had longed, just once, to convey that he cared about her.

His touch had been light, momentary, but Charlotte had whipped her head back, the glacial fire in her eyes shockingly intense. Recoiling, he had nerved himself for a more violent reaction, but with an effort she had controlled herself. Nervously Robert had sought to distract her with the second present, but as he opened it, talking all the time, she had wrenched it from his grasp.

"She had the glass stopper off that bottle of perfume in a second— no more. Before I had a chance to move away, out of reach, she'd flung the contents in my face." Involuntarily his hands went to his eyes; the vaporous liquid had stung, blinded, suffocated him; and while his hands protected, Charlotte had found those scissors, carefully hidden but so readily to hand. "I remember thinking I must stay on my feet, keep upright, as far out of reach as possible. The thick tweed of my jacket took most of her attack, fortunately. But of course, where my hands and wrists were exposed . . . Anyway, at least it was only one hand.

"Her screams brought Mrs. Hanrahan running within seconds. She rang the bell, and help came pretty quickly. I was dragged out of there with very little ceremony and, of course, when William and Anne came back, no sympathy either."

"Why, Robert?"

"Well, everyone kept telling me it was all my fault. They were quite right, of course, but it didn't help. Only served to increase my self-pity, I'm afraid," he admitted with an apologetic smile.

"Why does she hate you so much?"

"Oh, my dear, what a question! Several reasons—most of them founded in fantasy, or so eminent medical brains would have me believe. She hears voices, has intimate conversations with all kinds of people, alive and dead. If it weren't so frightening, it might even be quite amusing! If I recall correctly," he added lightly, "Her Majesty was always most gracious, quite a good influence on Charlotte, had it not been for her aversion to men!" He laughed and for the first time seemed genuinely amused.

"Oliver Cromwell was a little hard to accept, however, in spite of being a fellow soldier. God!" Robert suddenly exclaimed. "When I think of the times I've sat with her, listening to that stream of nonsense, wondering what to do! Cromwell came on the scene at Aldershot—his arrival persuaded me that it was time to take Charlotte back to Ireland. Her behavior had become so bizarre, I dared not leave her alone, and the servants were beginning to gossip—and to leave. I persuaded William and Anne to have her at White Leigh, and before you credit them with great philanthropy, Louisa, let me assure you the arrangement is a legal one. Charlotte's fortune pays their bills. And believe me, Anne knows how to spend money!

"Joan of Arc made herself known about the time of Georgina's birth," he said quietly, but did not elaborate. "And then Charlotte gained the ear—and the voice—of the Almighty Himself. Since then, my dear, I've been what you might call a marked man. Charlotte's God, in His wisdom, has informed her that I am the devil incarnate, the Prince of Darkness himself. Rather a backhanded compliment, don't you think?"

Louisa shivered. "Don't, Robert, don't joke about it."

"My dear, I couldn't be more serious. It's Charlotte's bounden duty, as she sees it, to rid the world of my evil influence."

Coals fell into the grate and, thankfully, Louisa stirred to mend the fire. Kneeling by the hearth, she turned to look up at him, almost angered by the intensity of her feelings. Love, compassion, and a sizable amount of jealousy provoked her to ask, "Do you still love her?"

He shook his head. He wanted to say that he had never loved her, but it was not the truth. Hard as it was to recall, he had loved her once, in the beginning; but the memory which lingered was that of physical desire unfulfilled. And moments of searing hatred, when he could so easily have killed her. The memory shamed him, and to cover it he laughed. "Love died a long time ago." He wondered when, and how, and found it impossible to pinpoint the manner of its dying. "I suppose I must still feel something for her. I can't bear to think of her suffering, when I seem to have been the cause of so much of it."

Something in the tone of his voice, the way he avoided her eyes, made Louisa study him intently. "She makes you feel guilty, doesn't she, Robert? Why?" When he shook his head, she pressed him further. "You may as well tell me—you've told me so much already."

He sighed, searching for an adequate reply. "Shall we say I added fuel to the flames?"

"In what way?"

Obviously agitated, he studied his hands, worrying the signet ring. "I don't know how to answer that," he said eventually. "At least, not in a way that won't shock you."

"I wasn't born yesterday, Robert," she said heavily. "Anyway, one more shock on top of all the rest I've had today won't make a lot of difference. Go on."

"Well, shall we say that when I first married Charlotte, she confused me. Completely. I thought—oh, I thought all kinds of things, Louisa. Innocence in an ivory tower, that kind of nonsense. That theory held up quite well for a while," he said sadly, remembering the long nights of tenderness, endless words of patience in the face of torment. And the end of patience, which he could rationalize but never really forgive. On a shuddering breath, he said: "I loved her—I wanted her. But once she understood that, once she understood what marriage entailed, she used it to torment me. Eventually, one night, she went too far—my temper got the better of me, I'm afraid . . ." His voice trailed away. "Do I have to say more?" he asked quietly.

Angry and embarrassed, Louisa poked at the fire, sending showers of sparks flying up the chimney. "If truth be known, you're not the first, and I'm sure you'll not be the last. If that were a prime cause of insanity, Robert, the inmates at Bootham Park would double overnight!"

"No doubt," he said, but his agreement was halfhearted. "Still, I can't forget. If I had accepted the situation, and simply left her alone, she might not have collapsed so totally. I don't know," he added distractedly. "The doctors say not. In their opinion, she would have reached that point sooner or later, no matter what. But you see, Louisa, if I had accepted her rejection of me as her husband, then she would never have borne a child. It was the birth of Georgina which finally tipped her over the edge into madness. Before, she'd been unpredictable—afterward, her behavior became . . . terrifying, there's no other word to describe it." He stopped again, and Louisa looked up; she saw that his hands were trembling, that tiny beads of sweat glinted across his forehead.

"She did dreadful things to herself—indescribable things," he said, suddenly closing his eyes against an image of Charlotte, spread-eagled across the bed, her thighs and abdomen a mass of blood. "She thought she was bearing another child, tried to kill it, and in the process almost killed herself.

"They'd taken Georgina away—fortunately. And Letty's looked after her ever since, been a mother to her in all but name for the last three years. If ever Letty should marry," Robert began and then stopped again, spreading his hands toward Louisa in a gesture of mute appeal. "You see how many people's lives are affected? Can you begin to understand *why* I feel so responsible?" As she nodded, he stood up and pulled her to her feet. "But all that, all that's *nothing* compared to the regret I feel now."

His eyes held hers, and she was suddenly afraid that his regret was centered on herself. Sighing, he let go of her hand and moved toward the window, staring out at the darkening sky. "If I had accepted her rejection of me, Louisa, there would have been no marriage. It could have been annulled. I would have been free."

In the silence, the ticking of the clock sounded unnaturally loud.

"As it is," he continued, "only death—either hers or mine—can release me."

Stunned, Louisa stared at him. Of all the things he had said, for her that was the most chilling. "Robert," she said quietly, "please don't say that."

He turned, a bitter, mocking smile on his lips. "But it's true."

"I don't care how true it is—you mustn't even think it!" Angrily she pulled the heavy chenille curtains together and drew him back toward the warm fire. While he talked, she had kept apart from him, feeling compassion above a dozen different emotions; knowing her mother or Bessie might enter the room at any moment, she had not expressed it. Now, afraid, she embraced him, trying with the force of love to stem that insidious stream of guilt. She sensed a curious imbalance in his nature, something oddly self-destructive. He would not harm his wife, of that she was sure; but he might prove too careless of himself.

"You mustn't see her again!" she muttered fiercely. "Forget her—let her forget you. Think about yourself and your daughter. She needs you—she always will."

Moved by the urgency in her voice, by the underlying concern which took no account of herself, Robert held her tightly. He brushed his lips against her hair and longed to taste the sweetness of her mouth. "I want you so much," he breathed. "With you, I could be happy. I know it."

"You mustn't say that," she whispered, and he heard the anguish in her voice.

"Why not? It's true." His fingers caressed the nape of her neck, then raised that bowed head until she looked at him. "Don't you want me too?"

A moan escaped her as he touched her parted lips; twisting free, she covered eyes which might have betrayed, and shook her head. "Don't say such things, Robert—please." Trembling, she sank down into the nearest chair, her face turned away. "I could have loved you," she whispered, "had things been different. But even if there can be nothing more between us—*and there cannot be!*—I need to know that you are safe and well. Not constantly tempting danger. Promise me that."

Feeling a coldness around his heart, Robert slowly nodded. "I promise."

There was a firm tap at the door, and Bessie came in to collect the tea things. Under cover of her skirts, the curious tabby cat sidled in and, with a plaintive cry, looked up at Louisa. Glad of its protection, she gathered the sly creature into her arms, burying her face against its silky fur.

"Mrs. Elliott thought you might like something before you go, sir?" Bessie said pointedly to Robert. "Another cup of tea, perhaps?" As he shook his head, she turned to Louisa. "And she asked me to remind you that it's past five, Miss Louisa."

With tense, unsmiling acknowledgment, Robert said he was just about to leave; unable to trust her voice, Louisa said nothing at all.

Bessie's sharp look encompassed them both. "Well then, don't make yourself late. And don't," she added from force of habit as she retired with the tray, "let that cat claw the furniture."

As she disappeared, Robert gently removed the cat from Louisa's arms and set it down, unprotesting, on one of the velvet sofa cushions. As it began to purr ecstatically, he knelt beside Louisa's chair, begging her not to turn away. He raised her hands to his lips, and for a long moment neither of them spoke.

"It was just that I didn't want to deceive you," he said at last.

"I know that," she whispered, embracing him with a passion which belied fine words and better intentions. For the first time she knew and understood her mother's predicament all those years ago. It was so tempting to say: *I'm yours, take me—what do consequences matter?* Mary Elliott had done that, but in this case Louisa knew in advance the price to be paid, and it was far too high.

Very slowly, she eased herself away. "I'm sorry," she said huskily, "but it isn't possible. I wish it could be, but it can't, and that's that. Forgive me."

"Forgive you? What for?" He gave a quirky little smile and softly traced the outline of her mouth. "For your tender heart, or that lovely smile? Or maybe," he added, framing her face with both his hands, "you think I should forgive your funny hair. Well, I can't, I'm afraid. I love it too much." He kissed her face where the healing graze disfigured it. "I'm going to miss you, Louisa Elliott," he whispered. "How I'm going to miss you! Don't ever change."

Quietly Robert took up his hat and coat and, without looking back, let himself out.

FIFTEEN

*I*n the Minster's great nave, the vaunting tread of soldiers' feet disturbed a thousand echoes. A capricious cacophony of sound, like holy souls in protest, assaulted every ear, catching the unwary, halting the fainthearted, till each booted and spurred man of war filed into place on tiptoe. For several minutes, voices and footfalls echoed, a ghostly, murmuring resonance in the upper reaches.

Someone coughed, and the cough was repeated to muttering infinity, swallowed at last by the first tentative notes of the organ; as it swelled to fill the Minster with tangible, thrilling sound, Robert's tensions eased, and in those calming minutes before the service began, his thoughts began to drift. Late April sun filtered through medieval glass, suffusing the air with a golden radiance, throwing jeweled harlequins of light across stone floors and soaring, pillared piers. Ruby and sapphire, emerald and topaz, glowingly magnified, rivaling the secular brilliance of scarlet and gold in the nave.

The dean's sonorous voice broke into his reverie, welcoming them all into this house of God, reminding them that they were gathered here to pay their respects to the memory of a dead comrade, Prince Albert Victor, Duke of Clarence and Avondale, stricken in the prime of his youth, a royal victim of the scourge which throughout the winter had made mourners of almost every family in the land.

Fifteen other royal victims, bearing crowns and swords, gave witness to the transitory nature of life on earth; carved into the stone of the choir screen, they gazed blankly down on the gathered congregation. Robert stared back at them, only half-listening to the dean, following other, more personal considerations. Prince Francis stood a couple of rows in front; already it was rumored that his sister would marry the duke of York. So she still had the prospect of a throne to enthrall her, Robert thought, while he wondered at the nature of royal romances. Were they so different, in the long run, from commonplace ones? Talk had it that Albert Victor had been unbalanced; if so, he thanked God that she had been spared. But perhaps she had preferred the brother all along?

On his knees, Robert prayed not so much for the repose of their dead comrade's soul but, with a fervency which would have horrified the dean, for Charlotte's rapid demise, as much for her sake as his own.

Not knowing which was most painful, her absence or her presence, he thought of Louisa, finding honor small consolation for the deprivation of her company. In the past eight weeks he had cursed his sense of fair play and tried to console himself with the knowledge that she would never have agreed to be his mistress; that had he been free, it would still have been difficult for them to marry.

But not impossible, he thought bitterly, tormenting himself yet again with memories.

Listening to Rossini's *Stabat Mater,* Robert was thinking of Louisa three weeks ago, on the Knavesmire; with Tommy and Darnley and some others, he had been making arrangements for the Royals' annual steeplechase, riding the course and giving the horses some exercise. Racing the last few furlongs with Tommy, he had suddenly noticed two women and a little girl alongside the winning post, talking to Darnley. The shock of recognizing Louisa had destroyed his concentration, and Tommy streaked ahead, laughing like a banshee, swearing, as he cantered back, that he would take the Regimental Plate this year, and Robert must eat humble pie for a change. But Robert, patting his horse, breathing hard, had eyes only for Louisa.

Automatically he had nodded to Rachel Tempest, returning her laughing commiserations with a formal smile, glad when Tommy dismounted to envelop the girl with his usual easy charm. While Tommy and Darnley fought a friendly duel of wits for Rachel's attention, Robert sat on his horse, looking down into Louisa's serious, upturned face. She was thinner, he noticed, and her eyes, echoing the color of the sky that day, were more gray than blue.

The child at her side was older, but blonde and blue-eyed like his daughter; he smiled at her and she responded eagerly, demanding that Louisa pick her up to stroke the big bay. Taken by Victoria's appeal, Robert dismounted and, holding Gay Gordon's head, invited the little girl into his arms. But it transpired that, after all, she was too shy. Louisa picked her up, standing close beside him while Victoria patted and stroked the bay's nose and neck, her eager questions covering the silence between himself and Louisa. He wished most fervently that it could have been his own daughter in her warm and capable arms, in almost any place but this, the three of them alone, without constraints, able to laugh and talk and touch . . . He was almost afraid to look at her, in case his eyes should reveal too much. Finally he found his voice, asking in clipped, formal tones whether she would be at the races the following Saturday; with downcast eyes, she shook her head, explaining that it was her day off, while silly Rachel Tempest volunteered that she would be there, accompanied by the Bainbridges. As though he cared for them.

And so, cheered on by an enthusiastic crowd which lacked the only witness who mattered to him, he had gone on to win the Regimental Plate for the second year in succession. It had been an excellent birthday present, with protracted celebrations in the mess afterward; but at the end of it, drunk and maudlin, he had told Tommy he would rather have lost and had Louisa by his side. Tommy had not been sympathetic, and Robert had later regretted his tactless and ungracious remark.

The party cost him a large proportion of the thirty guineas in prize money and an appalling hangover. In the mood of depression and remorse which followed, he felt ashamed of himself, knowing his reactions were rapidly becoming those of a callow, inexperienced boy rather than a thirty-one-year-old man. Louisa would not have approved; aside from all other considerations, the prize money would have covered her salary for a year.

With a mental shake, he forced himself back to the present. Properly modulated voices, filled with gloom and regret, droned on, followed by a specifically composed requiem in memory of the departed duke. As the pipes of the Royal Scots took up a haunting lament, Robert bowed his head, hating the stirring sentiment of the pipes and what seemed to him the sheer exploitation of his personal feelings. The strange, eerie music echoed hollowly throughout the Minster, so exactly mirroring his despair, he had to force himself not to march away in outraged protest. He hated the Minster and what seemed to him this farce of a memorial service; he loathed the men and women who were gathered in the guise of mourning for a man whose private life, if rumor were to be believed, would have made many of them blanch. So long as the conventions were observed, the great god of Society was placated; step out of line, answer your true inclinations openly, and you were finished—as unacceptable as a trooper suddenly gone berserk in the noonday heat. Society would say that what he felt for Louisa Elliott was sinful, and therefore wrong, yet on his knees for the final prayer, Robert Duncannon placed those feelings before a God he only partially believed in, and his supplication was for release.

SIXTEEN

*I*n a dove-gray dress, carrying a bouquet of white orange blossoms and wearing the same fragrant flowers in her glossy brown hair, Emily gave shy responses to her wedding vows.

In the vestry afterward, looking pretty and demure, she pushed back her veil and hugged her husband and sister, her dark eyes aglow with happiness. The two respective families filed out after the bride and groom, Louisa with the best man, Edward with John's mother, Mary Elliott with old Mr. Chapman, and Blanche bringing up the rear, proudly declining the arm of the groom's younger brother.

Outside the church, Blanche tolerated a warm embrace from Emily, giving proprietary care to the silk dress and little adjustments to Emily's veil as she did so; Edward, having given his cousin away, kissed her warmly on both cheeks. Overcome by this, the first wedding of a daughter in the Elliott family for almost eighty years, Mary Elliott had to be revived with Blanche's smelling salts. Mrs. Chapman, however, was somewhat less impressed by the originality of the occasion.

With the parlor of the Gillygate house packed tight, the guests overflowed into the kitchen, where Louisa and Bessie worked with the speed and regularity of automatons, handing out food and drink, rescuing precariously balanced cups and plates and preparing more. With a wisdom born of past experience, they left the handling of the Chapmans, which needed a delicate sense of social balance, to Edward and his aunt; Louisa, for one, had no desire to provoke barbed remarks.

She was engrossed in the task of slicing wedding cake into reasonably even pieces when a hand slid familiarly around her waist. Startled, she gasped and tried to pull away, but the owner of the hand caught her to him, dropping a kiss on her cheek as she turned to see who would dare such an act.

"John Elliott! I might have known it was you. How dare you make free with me, and you a married man these past eight years!"

Eyes that were so like her own crinkled as he laughed. "And why aren't you married? All that governessing isn't good for a pretty girl like you. You'll soon be saying you're on the shelf and turning sour—and that, my lovely cousin, is not what you were made for."

"Oh yes? Then what was I made for?" she asked with a laugh, turning back to her task.

With his hands still on her waist, he leaned over her shoulder. "Loving," he whispered softly, his lips against her ear.

Her eyes filled with sudden tears. She laid the knife down carefully, afraid of slicing something other than the cake. "John—please don't tease. It isn't funny."

His fair, still handsome face expressed surprise and more than a little concern. "Why so sad? What have I said? This isn't like you, sweetheart. Here—" He drew a yellow handkerchief from the top pocket of his new tweed suit and wiped her eyes with great tenderness.

"Leave the cake," he said. "Isn't there somewhere to sit down?" He glanced around the kitchen in some desperation. Guests laughed and talked, oblivious to the little drama in the corner; eventually he caught Mary Elliott's attention and, at her direction, took Louisa upstairs.

Sitting beside her on the large double bed where Robert Duncannon had slept, Louisa's cousin took her into his arms and held her till the sobs abated. "Now then, sweetheart, what's it all about? I wouldn't have thought you'd cry like this at a wedding feast. A funeral, maybe, but not your sister's wedding—unless she married the man you wanted? But no—he's not your sort, is he? You'd go more for a fellow like me, now wouldn't you?" he teased. "A good-looking chap with something to say for himself—a bit cheeky, maybe—just like me!"

A watery smile fought its way through the tears, and with his soft Lincolnshire burr, John Elliott gradually drew out the story of Robert Duncannon. When Louisa had told him everything, he pulled her close again. "I said you were made for loving—I knew it years ago. Remember when I was living around the corner? Used to pop in here for my dinner, see your mam, tease you a bit. You had a passing fancy for me in those days, didn't you?" he asked, chuckling at the memory. "But you were too young, sweetheart, and, alas!" he exclaimed, dramatically striking the region of his heart. "I was promised to another!"

With her face hidden against the rough tweed of his jacket, Louisa blushed and smiled, finding the revelations embarrassing after so many years. She had almost forgotten, but he was right: she *had* thought him attractive, and in the bitter resentment of Edward's leaving, she had flirted shamelessly with her Lincolnshire cousin. And unlike Edward, John had responded. But she had been no more than a girl then, and he a man; in the intervening years she had grown to adulthood, while he remained much the same, impudent, roguish, and oddly likable. Aunt Elizabeth had never cared for him, nor Edward; but her mother had always kept a soft spot for her young cousin, welcoming him with open arms and the choicest cakes.

For Louisa his earthy masculinity was something of a relief. The faint tang of tobacco reminded her of Robert, and the simple physical comfort of being held in someone's arms was reassurance in itself.

"Are you happy, John?"

"Bless you, of course I am," he said with a laugh. "I love my Jenny and she loves me. We've five fine babies to prove it."

"She should have come with you. I'd like to have met her."

"With five to look after and another on the way? Impossible!"

Louisa sat back and looked at him. "Another one? How on earth do you manage?"

He chuckled slyly. "Oh, I manage fine—it just comes naturally."

Color rose to her cheeks and she looked down, but she could not hide a smile. "Really, John! It's a good job my mother can't hear you."

"Don't you believe it! She'd have a good laugh, and that's better than crying, sweetheart, now isn't it?"

"You're dreadful! But I do feel better," she admitted with another sidelong smile. "Thanks for listening to my woes—and not judging." After a moment she added: "You won't say anything, will you? To my mother, I mean—or Edward."

"What? I'd be afraid to say *anything* to Edward. Don't worry, I'll keep all your secrets. I kept the last one well enough, didn't I? Seriously, sweetheart, what are you going to do about this grand fellow of yours?"

"What can I do?" She shrugged.

He thought for a moment. "As I see it, you've got two choices. Three really, but I wouldn't recommend the third. You can follow your inclinations—be his mistress and live in the lap of luxury—or you can marry the next man to ask you. Don't be an old maid; Blanche would make a good one, but with you it'd be a waste."

"You make it sound so simple," she said with a broad, genuinely amused smile.

"You know, I love it when you smile like that—your mouth turns up at the corners, your eyes sparkle, and you're lovely." Taking hold of her shoulders, he pulled her toward him, watching her through narrowed, smiling eyes. "For old times' sake?" he asked and, before she could pull away, kissed her fully and lingeringly on the mouth, easing her gently backward until they were both lying on the bed. "I just wanted to know what it would feel like," he whispered, "kissing you."

Halfway to anger, Louisa pushed at him, then relaxed, burying her face against his neck. "You're a rogue, John Elliott. Isn't one woman enough for you?"

"Usually," he admitted, brushing his lips against her ear. Relaxing their grip, his hands traversed her narrow waist, taking sensuous pleasure in the swell of her hips beneath the soft black crepe.

Before he could kiss her again, Louisa pushed his hands away and stood up, leaving him lying nonchalantly across the bed. "You'd better go," she said coldly, "while we're still friends."

"Don't be angry, Louisa," he pleaded with pained surprise. "It was only meant in fun. I wanted to cheer you up, that's all." He had all the appeal of a mischievous and misunderstood little boy, and he knew it. Louisa wanted to smack him.

"Oh, get yourself back to Blankney, John, and stop trying to misbehave with me. What would your Jenny say if she knew what you were up to?"

The long blue eyes twinkled yet again. "And what would your captain of dragoons say if he'd seen you a minute ago?"

Sharply Louisa raised her hand, but he backed out of reach, laughing. "I'm going, I'm going!" he protested, diving for the door. "But I can't go back to Blankney. I'm staying here tonight."

After he had gone, Louisa first sat on the bed, then lay full-length in the place Robert Duncannon had occupied when she first set eyes on him. "What have you done to me?" she whispered, knowing that what had so recently transpired would never have happened before she knew Robert. She would have pushed John Elliott away, told him not to be stupid. Instead she had allowed John to kiss her and imagined it was Robert; enjoying the sensation, she had wanted it to go on, and the knowledge shamed her. "What have you done, Robert?" she murmured again. "What have you made of me?"

There was a gentle tap at the door, but she was deaf to it; when Edward laid a gentle hand upon her shoulder, she jerked round, afraid that it might be John.

Disconcerted, Edward stared at her. "What's wrong?"

"I'm—I'm all right," she stammered. "Honestly, I was just coming down."

Knowing that his cousin had been upstairs, Edward made a fair assessment of the situation. "What's John been up to?"

"Nothing." Shaking her head, Louisa pulled herself up and straightened her dress.

Impatiently Edward waited for an explanation. "He always had an eye for you, didn't he? He ought to be horsewhipped!" There was a deep antipathy between the two men, and Edward greatly resented his cousin's presence in the house. "What did he do?"

"Nothing, Edward! I felt unwell, and he brought me upstairs to lie down. Ask Mamma if you don't believe me."

"Then why have you been crying?"

"I told you—I don't feel well."

"Something's bothering you, isn't it? What is it?" he asked sharply. "There's been something wrong for weeks, hasn't there?" he said, more gently now. When she did not reply, he sighed irritably; several hours of social nicety had sorely worn his patience. "Oh, Louisa, I do wish you'd tell me what it is!"

"I don't *know* what it is," she lied, wishing she could have confided in him rather than John, yet knowing that Edward was too close. "Perhaps the wedding upset me—or maybe I'm going down with something . . . I don't know."

He frowned, conscious of a gnawing anxiety. She had looked pale and drawn for too long, and he had remarked on her loss of weight to his aunt. "Have you a cough?" he asked, suddenly alarmed by the thought of consumption. Leaning over her, he touched the back of his hand to her hot forehead. "I think you should go to bed."

Peace and silence, the thought of being fussed over like an invalid, of being absolved from the effort of living, at least for a little while, were suddenly very seductive. There would be no need to go back downstairs, no need to wave Emily off with her new husband, and the Chapmans would hardly remark on her absence. It was too tempting. She nodded and lay back with relief.

"I'll write a note to Mr. Tempest and have it sent across to Blossom Street. Go upstairs now and get into your own bed. I'll make your excuses to Emily and John—although she'll probably want to come up and say good-bye to you. And I'll put a flea in the ear of John Elliott while I'm about it," he added shortly. Louisa was too exhausted to reply.

Some hours later, when the guests had all departed, John Elliott crept up to Louisa's room to apologize. For once, he appeared genuinely contrite. "Say you forgive me, sweetheart. I'd hate to leave tomorrow thinking we'd never be friends again."

She studied him for a moment. "It's all right—my fault, too. I didn't realize, until today, just how badly I felt about—everything. Maybe the tears have done me good," she added with a small smile.

"Sure?" asked John, and she nodded, her mouth firm. With a sheepish grin, he went on. "Your mother asked me what was wrong with you.

I said you weren't well, and stuck to that, but I think she knows there's more to it. She said she wouldn't force me to break a confidence."

"Oh dear, I thought she'd forgotten about Robert."

"Maybe she hoped *you* had." Awkwardly he sat on the edge of the bed and laid his large, square hand over hers. "Why don't you come and see us this summer? We've asked Cousin Mary many times, but she doesn't come, and you haven't been to Blankney since you were so high. Won't you come and stay with Jenny and me?"

Louisa gave him a long, searching look, and he grinned. "Oh, Jenny will keep me in line, don't you worry."

Touched by his attempt to make amends, she smiled. The idea of summer in Lincolnshire was very appealing. "I promise I'll think about it," she said.

SEVENTEEN

Called in by Mary Elliott, Dr. Mackenzie had diagnosed general debility brought on by overwork, recommended a strengthening diet of oysters and porter, beef broth, liver, plenty of eggs and milk, and as much rice pudding as Louisa could eat. She played up this diagnosis to her mother, skillfully sidestepping her apparently casual references to Robert Duncannon and taking refuge in sleep. She was curiously reluctant to talk about him. To say why she was so unhappy would have meant telling the whole sorry story, and she could not admit to her mother that he was married.

Whenever Louisa looked back on those few days, she realized that the giving in had been necessary. Even John Elliott was forgiven. As a man, he had behaved badly, but then, his reputation was less than spotless, and she should have known better; as a catalyst, he had provided a much-needed reaction.

She had had a girlish fancy for John, but Robert had come into a woman's life and had shaken her image of herself as a cool, detached spinster, interested in neither marriage nor men. The revelation that he was married had illumined a part of herself she had not known to exist, had stripped away protective layers which remained even after those briefly shared moments of passion. Her shock had not been that of a prude, but of knowing bitter disappointment, of having unacknowledged hopes and desires blighted forever. Of realizing, for the first time, how much she loved and wanted him.

She had shared his pain, had felt it doubled by his declaration, by his sense of honor; and then the shutting down of feeling, that sense of moving in a world of cotton wool, where every action required super-human effort and nothing was real, least of all herself.

John Elliott had unwittingly released her, had put her back amongst living, breathing people. She had to thank him for that, if for nothing else.

She prayed daily never to see Robert again, fought regular battles with Rachel over their afternoon walks, insisting on the Museum Gardens, the riverside, anywhere but the Knavesmire where the Royals exercised their horses. Each time she lost the argument, Louisa walked in dread; the memory of that other time, when they had conversed like strangers, ate into her even now. The only blessing seemed to be his aversion to the same old places; he was rarely at the Bainbridges', and while Rachel had been used to bemoaning his absence, of late she had become rather taken with Sophie's brother, Arthur, an attraction which seemed to be reciprocated.

Rachel had been invited to accompany Sophie's family to the Field Day that afternoon, for which Louisa was grateful; otherwise Louisa would have been pressed into service for the event, and the Knavesmire, with its press of people, was the last place she wanted to be on a hot June afternoon. While the citizenry of York watched a display of formation riding by the Royals and the 14th Hussars, she intended to take a chair into the back garden and read a book.

On an impulse, Louisa mounted the steps at Micklegate Bar and walked the section of wall which led to Lendal Bridge. Way below, on the road which followed the line of the old moat, trams and cabs formed a constant and noisy stream; a series of staccato protests announced the departure of a gleaming express from the station's great arcade, and Louisa stopped to watch it, wondering whither it was bound. She liked the station, its noise and bustle having an aura of excitement and importance which she felt her life sadly lacked. Behind her, in dark and silent shadow, stood a group of freight wagons and sooty, ancient engines, mute caricatures of another generation, the dirty old station beyond lost against the backdrop of Tanner Row. For a minute she looked and remembered. For all their lives' upheavals, Elizabeth and Mary Elliott had traveled frequently and quite extensively in those early days, and Louisa felt a stab of envy for their supreme independence. Then, with a sharp admonition to herself, she walked on.

The sight of the Minster lifted her flagging spirits. She loved this view on such a day, the white wall stretching like a ribbon ahead, broken by the town's rusty pink brick, white towers, and pinnacles soaring above those humbler roofs, in perfect poetry of form against a bright blue sky. There was a sense of eternity about it, a comforting continuity which proclaimed all else as transitory. In a hundred, two hundred years, it would still be there, while she, with all life's little anxieties, would be nothing more than a handful of dust. Nothing was so important after all.

There was salad, cold meats, and potatoes for dinner, with early strawberries and cream, Louisa's favorite and a rare luxury at this time of year. They ate early, which surprised her, and afterward Mary Elliott disappeared upstairs, to return in her best summer dress and attendant finery, announcing that they were going out.

It was too late for Louisa to plead illness or a headache. She tried to protest on account of the crowds there were sure to be on the Knavesmire, but her mother would not be swayed. She had made up her mind that they were all, including Bessie, going to see the Field Day and would brook no refusals.

Edward rolled his eyes in mock despair while Louisa controlled her panic under a thin veneer of laughter. Under the pretext of finding a prettier hat and a parasol to protect her face against the afternoon glare, she dashed upstairs to calm herself in private. Dabbing her face with cold water, her wrists with cologne, she breathed deeply, finally reassured by the thought that the dragoons would be at some distance and therefore indistinguishable.

A horse-drawn tram took them past the Tempest house on Blossom Street to the terminus. Crowds were already walking down the Mount toward the racecourse, well-heeled citizens mingling with a lesser breed, albeit with some disdain. In high good humor, Mary Elliott stepped out more smartly than she had done for some time, chivying her daughter and exchanging amusing comments with her nephew, whose arm she had appropriated. Even Bessie, her face hot and rather flushed, seemed happier than Louisa, whose cheeks grew paler with every step.

They found a place with a good view, quite close to the rails. The huge green arena created by the course was empty, but at last, to enthusiastic cheers, the dragoons and hussars rode in, their full dress uniforms a brilliant sight, their chargers magnificent, gleaming in the afternoon sun. Riding by squadrons, in single file, by sections, they performed their intricate, perfect maneuvers to cheers and applause and yells of delight. The cavalry were the flower of the armed forces, a perfectly disciplined symbol of invincibility. The thought was in every mind that day: what ragged bung of rebels could hold out against such might? With such men at its head, the empire would live forever!

Mary Elliott praised and exclaimed as loudly as the rest, her eyes never leaving the red-tunicked Royals; squeezing her daughter's arm, she constantly tried to pick out the captain. While the squadrons were moving, it was impossible to tell one face from another, but as they advanced by gallop in line to the rails, wheeling off to right and left, Louisa suddenly spotted him and could not tear her eyes away.

The two regiments displayed their dexterity with swords, silver blades flashing in the sun; and suddenly they were at a gallop again, pursuing some imaginary enemy for the benefit of the crowd. At a gallop and away.

His ears ringing with cheers, Edward stood in silence, watching not the retreating body of men, but Louisa, studying every fleeting change in his cousin's face. There had been tense, unsmiling vigilance, a momentary flush of pleasure, and now this wistfulness. He knew now what brand of unhappiness burned within her, the reason for that lack of appetite, the pale and slender visage which had formerly been so rosy. He admired her stoic silence, but he wished she could have confided in him, as once, long ago, he had confided in her.

Drawing her hand through his arm, he looked into her eyes. "I understand now," he said softly under cover of his aunt's bright observations. "Won't you tell me about it sometime?"

Louisa tilted her frilly parasol until it shaded her eyes. With a half-smile, she nodded. "I'd like to," she confessed. "Although there's not a great deal to tell."

"Isn't there?"

Sighing, she patted his arm. "Well, perhaps there is."

"I'm always here," he reminded her, adding lightly, "and both shoulders are waterproof."

She laughed at that. "I don't deserve you, Edward, but I'll remember—I promise."

EIGHTEEN

The summer wore on, the usual mix of sunshine and showers, gray days succeeding clear skies of palest eggshell blue, which were followed in their turn by brilliant sun. There was a spate of election fever during the dry days of late June and early July. The Tories and Liberals fought a bitter duel, every harsh criticism and dire insult reported at length in the papers and jubilantly repeated by Albert Tempest. On July 16th, with the promise of Home Rule for Ireland, Gladstone was returned to power. Wondering how Robert felt on that particular issue, Louisa read that his squadron had completed a successful two weeks of maneuvers at Strensall Camp and that they were due to be replaced by the group Tommy commanded.

By the middle of August there was talk of a drought. Trapped by a sulfurous veil of coal fumes, the city sweltered in the afternoon heat. The sky took on a brassy, unnatural tinge, giving a jaundiced look to the streets. Doors and windows stood open to catch any stray breeze; old women sat on doorsteps, high collars open at the neck, sleeves rolled up, toddlers playing listlessly at their feet, while wealthier citizens went about their business dreaming of open countryside and Sunday picnics. Dogs panted in the shade and horses plodded by, heads drooping, too exhausted to flick or toss at the flies which swarmed about their heads. Each city water trough had a seemingly permanent group of animals surrounding it.

In the schoolroom, Louisa stood by the open window, brushing Victoria's hair. With deft fingers, she plaited the long golden tresses, looping the braids and pinning them up off her neck for coolness. Straightening the child's collar, she reached for the starched white pinafore, tying its ribbons in two neat bows at the back. They were invited with Rachel to tea at the Bainbridges', and it was with now customary reluctance that Louisa prepared herself for the journey to Fulford.

She felt that these increasingly frequent visits annoyed Albert Tempest; he was barely civil to Sophie and Arthur when they returned the compliment, but more often he was out, leaving Louisa to do his chaperoning for him. He still insisted that she accompany Rachel everywhere, which, in the case of the Bainbridges, was something of an embarrassment; Louisa had never been quite forgiven for her rudeness that Sunday afternoon, and she was still afraid of meeting Robert, although in two months she had not seen him at all.

Albert Tempest's blind neglect of his responsibilities worried her, however; she was afraid that he left too much to her discretion, afraid that, in the period of insensibility following Robert's departure from her life, Rachel and Arthur Bainbridge had taken advantage of the situation. Not wishing to tell tales, and reluctant to bring her father's wrath down upon Rachel's head, Louisa had tried reasoning with the girl, to little avail. A lifetime spent with Albert Tempest had taught Rachel to be both secretive and stubborn. Louisa had sought opportunities to mention her fears to her employer casually and, hopefully, discreetly; the opportunities, however, were too few, and Louisa too discreet. When she did see him alone, he was strangely dismissive, as though the subject of his daughter bored him, as though he wanted only to sit in silence, feasting his eyes on the woman before him. His speech, breaking into these long moments of highly charged unease, seemed deliberately abrupt, almost offensive. Louisa began to dread his company, torn between her anxiety over Rachel and her fear of an unreasoned and perhaps uncontrolled outburst from the girl's father.

The forthcoming holiday would be something of a relief, releasing her, for a week at least, from some of her anxieties. The Tempests would soon be off on their annual pilgrimage to Bridlington, and she had decided at last to take up Cousin Jack's invitation; her mother had been very persuasive, and even Edward had agreed that she should get away from York, have a complete break for her health's sake.

At the rear of the house, Sophie and Lily were playing croquet with two other young women, whose nasal and somewhat strident voices competed with the excited cries of children playing a noisy game of skittles at one end of the terrace. At the other end, stretched out in a reclining wicker chair, languidly fanning herself, Mrs. Bainbridge greeted Rachel with a complaint about the heat.

"My dear, we hardly expected you this afternoon. It really is too hot to go anywhere. You must be exhausted. Do sit down and have some of this fresh lemonade."

As Rachel took a seat, Mrs. Bainbridge bestowed a civil nod in Louisa's direction, noticing Victoria for the first time. The child clung to Louisa's hand, shy and uncertain at first; eventually, lured by the older woman's smiles and lavish compliments, she consented to sit beside her, accepting a sugared almond and a glass of lemonade.

"Now, dear, why don't you go and make friends with the other children? I'm sure they'd love you to join them."

Victoria was less sure of their welcome; with Louisa in tow, she approached them hesitantly. The two boys were boisterous, greeting each other's scores with boos and yells, to the nervous reprimands of their nanny, a young woman in her early twenties. The girl, who at nine was the eldest of the children, fortunately decided to play the little mother; taking hold of Victoria's hand, she led her over to the far end of the terrace steps, where she had her small collection of dolls. The gesture pleased Louisa, who was ever unsure of Victoria's reactions; she seemed content, however, and, with a sigh of relief, Louisa sat down next to the pink-faced nanny.

The little scene reminded her so very much of her last employment: children's parties in the grounds of that magnificent though decaying mansion; excited, piping voices; the tinkle of teacups as nannies and nurses took tea and gossiped. The heady scent of jasmine and honeysuckle, tumbling over the low balustrade in front of her, heightened the memories, bringing a wave of nostalgia so painful she closed her eyes against it; but she could not shut out the voices, nor the perfume.

Against the fraught, unnatural atmosphere of the house on Blossom Street, this moment, this echo of another day, was so unbearably normal, so perfect that she longed to wind time back twelve months and petrify it, as it had been then, without the Tempests, without Robert. She had been happy then, secure and sure of herself; a little dull, perhaps, but unencumbered by the daily stresses which seemed to have taken such toll recently.

With an effort, she pushed the memories away, turning to the young woman at her side, asking questions about the children and their families. She learned that all three belonged to Sophie and Lily's second cousin, the lady in the pale blue dress, and that the other lady was her sister. The children's father was with the 14th Hussars, the regiment which had recently joined the Royals at the Cavalry Barracks; they had not been settled long, and their rented house was small, too small for guests as well as children and servants, so the younger cousin was staying with the Bainbridges for the duration of her visit. It was suddenly borne in upon Louisa that the Bainbridges were wealthy, presumably in their own right, for a major's pay in a volunteer regiment could not maintain their lifestyle without assistance. With the arrival of Arthur, she wondered how they would view an alliance by marriage with the Tempests. Albert Tempest had money, but it was new money, accrued by business acumen, not inherited; they obviously liked Rachel, but would they approve of her as a daughter-in-law? If the Bainbridges did not need money, Rachel could be in for a difficult time; that is, if her sights were really set in that direction. Louisa suspected that she loved the idea of Arthur Bainbridge, and what he represented more than the young man himself.

Louisa chatted on, but her eyes never left Rachel for a moment. Coquettish, provocative, the girl played up to the uniformed young lieutenant, allowing him to put his arms around her, an ostensible lesson in croquet, but an alarmingly sexual display to Louisa's eyes. Sophie giggled, lending encouragement, but as Arthur caught his mother's disapproving stare, he dropped his arms, contenting himself with verbal instruction.

Engrossed in her own thoughts, Louisa failed to notice Hugh Darnley's quiet presence on the terrace behind her; Tommy Fitzsimmons's firm step and hearty greeting startled her, and afraid to turn her head, she listened avidly for Robert's softer, deeper voice. She heard only Darnley's reply and turned to find Tommy's eyes upon her, his mouth twisted into a peculiar half-smile. He acknowledged her presence with a slow, deliberate inclination of his head.

Whether from disappointment or relief, Louisa felt light-headed. Her sudden pallor provoked a solicitous question from the young woman at her side.

"I'm all right—really. It's just the heat." Accepting a glass of lemonade from her companion, Louisa studiously avoided the temptation to look around again and tried to ignore the lilting richness of Tommy's brogue, for she was reminded too much of the night of Sophie's party. Robert's name was mentioned, however, and almost against her will, she began to listen. It seemed that his squadron had performed with exemplary efficiency at the summer camp at Strensall and that Tommy found this fact highly amusing, especially since he had suffered the usual fiasco at musketry training and fared little better on maneuvers.

Louisa thought that Tommy laid a little too much emphasis on Robert's name, as though he spoke for her benefit as much as Darnley's, and by the tone of Darnley's monosyllabic replies, she understood he did not share Tommy's sense of humor.

As Rachel and the rest of the group left the croquet lawn, Darnley moved off to join them; a footstep on the terrace behind her warned of Tommy's approach, but she was not prepared for his invitation to play.

With an apologetic smile, she shook her head emphatically. "I'm sorry, Captain Fitzsimmons, I'm afraid that croquet is *not* on my list of accomplishments."

"Then why not let me teach you, Miss Elliott?"

Recalling Arthur's attempts to improve Rachel's game, Louisa suppressed a smile. "I don't think so, but thank you, Captain."

Tommy was not to be put off, however. Louisa's presence that afternoon was too much a heaven-sent opportunity for him to let it go easily. He was too genuinely concerned at the change in his old friend and not a little disturbed that all his attempts to alleviate the gloom had met with rebuff. Bob Duncannon had never been one to run with the pack, and yet he had been glad of Tommy's company in the past. They shared a similar, somewhat irreverent sense of humor, which even Charlotte's worst outbreaks had not been able to suppress for long. It seemed to Tommy that, while the catastrophe of Charlotte had drawn them together, the advent of Louisa Elliott had closed a door on all that.

If only she would agree to become Bob's mistress, Tommy was convinced that all would be well. Bob would satisfy his passion and regain his sense of proportion; sooner or later he would tire of her and the old friends would be back once more on their usual footing.

"Well, now," he murmured with his usual indolent smile, "I must confess your refusals are most frustrating. You see, I had hoped to sound you out—as an informed source—on the rumors I hear of an engagement. Miss Tempest is such a fascinating young lady, and I'd not wish to press my suit where it'd not be welcome."

The young woman at Louisa's side looked first at the tall dragoon, lounging so casually against the balustrade, and then at the prim governess, and seemed unable to believe that this conversation was taking place.

Louisa's smile disappeared. "I don't think you should worry about that, Captain. Common knowledge is rarely accurate and should not be taken too seriously. Is that not so?" she pointedly asked.

He laughed. "*Touché,* Miss Elliott." For a long moment his eyes studied her, their expression unfathomable. "So, you won't play. Well, how are you? What shall my report be? That you look a little slenderer than I recall at our last meeting? That life is treating you fair, or ill?"

Rising abruptly to her feet, Louisa unsteadied the little wooden table at her knee. She bent to rescue it, righting the empty glasses and flushing uncomfortably as she did so. "Really, Captain, you are almost insulting!"

But before she could move away, Tommy was beside her, apologizing, his arm beneath her elbow. "Leave the table—the croquet lawn awaits your first lesson. Please excuse us," he added in an aside to the other young woman and proceeded to steer Louisa down the steps.

"I would appreciate it if you'd remove your hand from my arm," Louisa hissed at him. "What will Mrs. Bainbridge think? Not to mention the children's nanny!"

Having achieved his object in removing Louisa from the terrace, Tommy dropped his hand. "I'm so sorry, Miss Elliott, I thought you might appreciate news of Bob—or do you call him Robert?"

"I don't call him anything," said Louisa stiffly. "I haven't seen Captain Duncannon for some considerable time, as I'm sure you are well aware."

Handing her a mallet, Tommy demonstrated how to tap the wooden ball. "Ah, yes, I am indeed. It's a matter, in my humble opinion, for grave regret. He misses you most dreadfully."

For a second Louisa's heart lurched, and she was unable to speak. Undisturbed, Tommy tapped the ball through a hoop and bent to retrieve it. "You know about Charlotte? Yes, of course you do. So, you will understand that his life does not lie easy. And I feel some responsibility for that—because, you see, it was I who introduced them, and by the Grace of God, he married her, with me standing by as best man. I loved her too—and you see how things turned out? His life could have been mine . . . so easily." He might have been discussing the finer points of the game, so pleasantly did he speak of these personal matters.

"For twelve years now we've known each other. Taken a drink or two when the going got rough—lived with Charlotte between us, you might say. The worst times being after home leave. But speaking as what you might call a connoisseur of Bob's somewhat volatile temperament, I'd say that now things are worse than they've ever been."

Louisa sent the ball wildly off course. "Charlotte?" she asked faintly, wondering what more damage Robert's wife could have wrought. Her heart was pounding painfully beneath her tight stays, and the heat of the afternoon seemed suddenly unbearable.

"No, it's himself I'm worried about. He spends far too much time on his own these days, brooding. Refuses most invitations and hardly ever drinks in the mess. Did I not know him better," Tommy added with a laugh, "I'd swear he was hell-bent on promotion, and his men almost fainting from the effort! He goes on leave tomorrow week—the poor devils can hardly wait for that. I swear even Harris will heave a sigh of relief!"

"Harris?"

"His servant. A most devoted fellow. So you see, Miss Elliott, why I'm so concerned."

Louisa did not see. She did not understand that Tommy Fitzsimmons was deliberately trying to sow the seeds of doubt and confusion. "I'm sorry, Captain Fitzsimmons, but I really don't understand. What are you trying to say?"

Tommy sighed, and for the first time looked quite exasperated. "He's going to Ireland, to White Leigh."

"Well, yes, I imagined that was where you meant," she said. "He's going home, to see his child."

With a defeated shrug, Tommy let his mallet fall to the grass. "After all that's happened in the past, Miss Elliott, and in his present frame of mind, White Leigh is the last place for him. I've tried to tell him, but he'll not listen to me. I thought—but no." He turned, as if to leave her, but Louisa caught his arm.

"What did you think?"

"I thought perhaps you might try and persuade him *not* to go."

"Me? But how? Captain Fitzsimmons, you don't understand—I cannot see him, no more than I can tell him what to do!"

"Forgive me—I thought you cared for him. It seems I was wrong," he said flatly and began to walk away, his patience apparently exhausted.

Louisa hurried after him. "Wait, please!"

"No, it hardly matters. Forget what I said—indeed, I should not have mentioned it."

Suddenly within excellent earshot of the terrace, Louisa bit back her reply. Cross and frustrated, she hung back, trying to force a smile at the teasing comments directed at them both.

Laughing, sipping lemonade, the ladies looked so coolly at ease in their pretty pastel dresses and wide-brimmed summer hats; even the men, in high-necked uniforms, seemed undistressed as they lounged in the shade. Louisa hated them all. Tommy Fitzsimmons had made her look a fool out there in front of them, but that was as nothing compared to the feeling of mental stupidity which burned inside. He had tried to impart a warning, a warning so wreathed about in obscurity that it left only anguish and frustration. His hasty assumptions were so bitterly unfair, she longed to hit out at him, to wipe the smiles from all their faces.

She was saved by the insistent pulling of a small hand at her sleeve. Victoria had grown tired of the other child's dolls and wanted to go home.

NINETEEN

Walking up Micklegate hill that Friday evening, Albert Tempest cursed inwardly. The hot pavements made his feet ache abominably, and after a day spent cooped in his airless office, he longed for a cool breeze to restore his temper. For the umpteenth time he considered his lonely estate, and self-pity welled like a spring within him.

He had his regular appointment to keep this evening, but she was damned expensive. He could do what he liked, as long as he paid extra for it, and the house charged enough for her usual services. There were times when he was tempted to pick up a cheap streetwalker, but he was too afraid of the consequences.

Recently his desires seemed constantly at boiling point, furnaced, he was sure, by the presence of Louisa Elliott. Perspiration oozed wetly beneath his hat brim as he thought of her, always so damnably cool and self-contained these days and impossible to provoke. He despised docile women, and had he not seen something of her spirit, he would not have been so obsessed with the need to possess her. Remembering the occasions when she had outfaced him, he felt a twinge of pleasure which quickly turned to anger as he recalled the times he had tried in vain to annoy her. Nothing seemed to touch her. In his daughters' company, she said little; on the rare occasions when he was alone with her, she refused to rise either to his baiting or to his veiled suggestiveness. Her detachment had become unbearable, provoking absurd and almost uncontrollable desires. He wanted Louisa Elliott. He wanted her so much he almost hated her.

It was well past the hour of their evening meal when she arrived back with Rachel and Victoria.

Albert Tempest had fumed and fretted and finally demanded his tea, an entirely unsuitable meal of cold mutton and greasy fried potatoes, followed by hot rhubarb crumble and custard sauce. The windows in the dining room stood open, although the heavy curtains were pulled close against the fading effects of the sun. It was unbearably hot, and his temper was dangerously high.

Before Moira could open the door, he was behind her. "Send them into the drawing room," he abruptly ordered. "And take Victoria upstairs."

Although there was no fire, he took up his usual stance before the hearth, legs straddled, hands clasped behind his back, and chin thrust forward, ready and eager for the attack.

Having marched first into the room, Rachel took a step back on seeing her father's face and almost cowered behind Louisa's shoulder. As Moira closed the door behind them, Louisa glanced back in alarm, feeling suddenly trapped.

"I really do apologize, Mr. Tempest," Louisa began, but he cut her off with a sharp gesture and turned to his daughter, demanding the explanations from her.

Rachel's stammering reply that they had taken tea with the Bainbridges and forgotten the time set fire to the smoldering fuse of her father's fury. Cursing the Bainbridges and all they stood for, spitting his contempt of their patronage, he allowed his rage to feed upon itself and grow. Until he mentioned Arthur's name, Rachel cowered and wept; her beloved's name sparked a reckless defiance, however, and she straightened to face her father.

"He's not a useless fop!" she cried angrily. "And neither is he stupid. He knows more about horses than you'll ever know or care about, *and* he has good manners. What's more, he loves me and wants to marry me. And when he does, I shall leave this house with the greatest of pleasure and never—ever—come back!"

There was a stunned silence as each of them digested what Rachel had said so impetuously. Louisa shut her eyes and prayed. Horrified, Rachel bit her knuckles and stared like a frightened rabbit at her father's face, which changed with alarming rapidity from livid puce to pasty white. His graying side-whiskers stood out darkly from his cheeks, heavy brows arched in exaggerated surprise.

"If you think that I would allow a daughter of mine to marry into a heathen family of idle, posturing, thick-witted military clods, then you are very much mistaken," he declared, his voice quieter but tense with barely suppressed fury. "I blame myself to some extent—allowing you to mix with such unsuitable people—but that can fast be rectified. You'll stay within the four walls of this house until we go on holiday, miss, and afterward, a protracted visit to your aunt and uncle in Bradford might enable you to cool your heels. You'll find dashing hussars a little thin on the ground over there!''

"I won't! I won't go to Bradford!" Rachel screamed at him. "And if you make me, he'll come after me and take me away!"

The beacons of rage were lit afresh in Albert Tempest's eyes. He started across the room, and as he did so, Rachel fled. Her father wrenched open the door she had slammed behind her, almost knocking Louisa down in his haste. His feet made but four steps on the stairs, and Louisa heard a sharp crack as his hand made contact with Rachel's face, then a scream, and the sound of her bedroom door slamming, the key being turned in the lock.

Shivering, shocked, Louisa tried to leave the room. She had some thought of taking refuge in the kitchen until her employer calmed down, but he was before her in the hallway, advancing with a terrifying expression in his eyes. He closed the door behind him and leaned heavily against it.

Rage burned: strong, just, and overpowering. His body throbbed with it, from the palm which had cracked across Rachel's face, through ears and eyes and chest and limbs. How dare they defy him? He was a man, and master not only in *this* house; he could make or break lives as and when he wished.

Rachel could starve for a week; that would bring *her* to her knees. But this one would spit before she would beg, and the knowledge excited him. It was time she saw her true position, the true position of all women, and he was the one to teach her!

She knew; he could see it in her eyes.

As she began to back away, power surged through every muscle, centering at his loins. Exultant in that thrusting hardness, past impotence was forgotten; he almost laughed at her shaky demand to open the door.

In the gloom, her foot caught against a low stool, and she grasped at the arm of a nearby chair for support; too late did she see her wrong direction. As she twisted toward the shrouded window, he was on her, wrenching her around and against the table. She cried out; he silenced her with hands and mouth, brutally gripping her jaw; she fought, and he pinioned her against him, tearing at the front of her gown. The strong, fully-lined material held, but threads which caught buttons and seams gave way, exposing fair and vulnerable flesh beneath. He sank his teeth into the soft curve of her shoulder and squeezed her breast hard, immune to the cries of pain, the violent kicks and blows aimed at shoulders and shins. Far from hurting him, her struggles acted like a goad, till thought was lost and mastery was all, centered on the need

to dominate and degrade, to have her sobbing and quivering as he thrust
deep and ever deeper . . .

Yanking at her skirt, he pushed her backward across the table, fumbling in haste at his flybuttons; for a second she resisted, kicking frantically at his thighs; then, panting and gasping for breath, she suddenly
lay back, wide-eyed.

Smiling, glad of that acquiescence and the close-curtained, twilit gloom,
Albert Tempest released the last button, thrusting her skirts high and
clear. With his hand at her waist, even as he pulled at the fine batiste
of her underthings, she twisted round, kicking out at his stomach. As
he doubled over, she fell to the floor, heavily, but before he could recover
she was on her feet, behind the table, dragging at the heavy curtain.

Light flooded the room, fine net drapery fluttering in the slight breeze
from the open window. In horror he noticed the little group of onlookers
beyond the glass, already retreating like eavesdroppers disturbed, and
with panic-stricken haste rapidly covered the already wilting thing which
hung from his trousers.

Shielded from their gaze, gathering the tattered remains of her bodice
together, she turned her wild eyes upon him. She was shuddering convulsively, but between gritted teeth she swore at him, spitting her hatred
and contempt.

"Let me go—now! Else I swear to God I'll stand before this window
and show the world what you've done to me!"

Trembling with shock and revulsion, her first thought was to get
home to Gillygate, to weep and sob and tear her hair, to call a thousand
curses upon the name of Albert Tempest; to be cosseted and comforted,
soak in a hot bath for hours—anything to cleanse away the feel of those
ugly, defiling hands. When she thought of that patent intent, felt the
horror sweep through her at what he had so nearly done, Louisa shuddered and moaned, hardly crediting her own presence of mind.

Had it been conscious, that instinct to relax? Or sheer animal terror?
What reserve of courage had fueled that gesture of defiance by the
window?

There was no answer, and it frightened her. Staying here, in this
house, terrified her; she could think of one thing only: to get home,
home to the comfort of her mother's arms and Bessie's fuss and sympathy, to the safe, calm security of Edward's protection. *He* wouldn't
let her be hurt; he had always defended her; he would show Albert
Tempest he couldn't get away with that; he'd tackle him face to face
and—

—and be dismissed.

That realization hit like ice-cold water, and with dreadful clarity Albert Tempest's words came back to her. "Tell one living soul," he had rapidly threatened before that door was unlocked, "just one—and I'll drag your name through every bit of mud I can find. I'll tell anybody who listens, you begged for it, you've shared my bed for months, I kicked you out because you threatened to blackmail me. And whose word will they take, eh?"

She closed her mind against the rest.

Edward, Edward, she cried in silent anguish, knowing her cousin could never keep silent on this. Quiet and unassuming he might be; but he was also an honorable man. What Albert Tempest had done ran against every precept of Edward's life; it would be dragged into the open, and the resulting scandal would be ugly, dirty, and resounding. It was too terrible to contemplate. And would he ever find another job? She doubted it. Could the hotel support them both, when it was barely supporting itself? A scandal would drive even the regulars away.

For several minutes the sheer inequity of her position made Louisa despair. But even while she muffled her sobs against the pillow, from the other room a small girl's voice called out to her, like some pathetic echo of her own childhood.

Her name, called over and over with desperate persistence, eventually roused Louisa to action. Bathing her face and pulling off what remained of her pretty cotton dress, she clothed herself again with trembling fingers and flung a few essentials into an overnight bag.

About to go to Victoria, she met Moira on the landing.

"Dear Mother of God!" the girl whispered, wringing her hands. "What did he do to you? I heard the noise and went to Mrs. Petty for the key, but she wouldn't give it up, the old witch. Said it was none of our business and locked me in the kitchen till just now. What happened to you?"

Louisa shook her head, afraid that if she started to speak the tears would come again. Dumbly, she led Moira into her room.

"Are you leaving?" she asked, noticing the bag, the scattered things on the bed. "Did he sack you?"

Louisa's mouth twisted into the semblance of a smile. "Oh, yes, he sacked me. I'm leaving. I won't be back. I shall have to send for my trunk, although it's not packed," she added distractedly. "Would you do it for me?"

"Sure I will. Jesus, Mary, and Joseph!" she exclaimed, sinking onto the bed. "If this isn't a cue for me to leave, I don't know what is! Sure and he's mad, locking Miss Rachel up like that, doing what he did to you. Dear God, he shouldn't have touched *you!*"

"No, he shouldn't have," Louisa shakily agreed. Unable to bear Moira's well-meant sympathy, she turned to the door. "I'm sorry, but I have to go. I must get out of here before he comes upstairs. And I want to see Victoria—she's crying her heart out, she doesn't understand—"

"I'll see to her," Moira said firmly. "You get yourself gone, now."

"Keep your eye on them, won't you? Especially Victoria—"

"I will, and I'll keep in touch whenever I can—I promise."

She turned to Victoria's door and, with a sad little wave, watched Louisa creep quietly down the stairs. Not quietly enough, however; Rachel banged several times upon her door, calling shrilly to be let out. For a moment, as a final act of defiance, Louisa contemplated doing just that, then decided against it. In her present mood, Rachel was liable to do something stupid, like flying to the Bainbridges for help. What she needed was time to calm down.

At the half-landing she hesitated; with her eyes firmly fixed on the closed drawing room door she descended the last few steps almost at a run. A shudder of relief, and she was across the hall and out, slamming the heavy door behind her.

She turned to the left simply for fear of passing the drawing room window.

TWENTY

*T*he early evening air was like velvet, but it felt fresh against her face after the close and stifling atmosphere of the house. Without a backward glance, Louisa walked quickly away, her legs shaky and weak, chest aching as though she had run for miles. Uncertain what to do or where to go, she was aware only of a need for distance, a place to sit and think, before she returned home to a barrage of questions.

There were seats on the Mount, facing the main road, and plenty of people about, enjoying a walk after the almost intolerable heat of the day. Her bag felt heavy and, exhausted, she sat down, thinking not of Albert Tempest, but of earlier events; it seemed an age since Tommy Fitzsimmons had spoken to her that afternoon. Remembering her anger and frustration, she sighed and shook her head. What had he meant? Why had he spoken? It had puzzled her all the way back to Blossom Street, and now that sense of anxiety returned. But she was too tired to think clearly, and the questions simply buzzed around her mind like trapped flies.

A man's voice jerked her back to the present, and she stood up, feeling sick and faint. Aware that she had dozed, she glanced up at the sky, trying hard to assess the time. Eight? Half past? The sun had set, the sky was in flames.

An empty hansom pulled out of the turning ahead, and without thinking, she hailed it, regardless of the few coins in her purse. The driver asked where she wanted to be dropped, and she paused, her mind a blank. Where was she going? Gillygate? No, not there, not yet; her mind balked at the thought of the lies she would have to tell.

After a moment of silence she said: "The Cavalry Barracks," and the driver looked surprised, his eyes taking in her neat, dark dress, her lack of flamboyance. With a shrug and a click of encouragement to his tired horse, he turned the vehicle and headed in the direction he was bidden.

Hazily Louisa sought to justify her decision. A vague idea that it was imperative to see Robert before he went to Ireland presented itself. No more than that. She was beyond coherent thought, beyond realizing that Robert Duncannon was the only person she trusted not to stand in judgment, not to make trouble for her family.

He had been in the mess for less than ten minutes. The fine evening had let him out onto the stray, behind the barracks, where he had been walking for over an hour. As usual, when alone, he had been thinking of Louisa, wondering when, if ever, he would forget her. The pain of wanting desperately to see her and resisting the temptation was lessening; or had been, until this evening, when Tommy returned from the Bainbridges' with news of seeing her there. Tommy's indolent and much abridged report of the croquet lesson had infuriated Robert, to the extent that he had left the mess abruptly after his meal, returning only for a small nightcap before going home.

He had almost finished his drink when the servant handed him an old envelope, folded over, on a silver salver. He was startled to see Louisa's name and address, in his own hand, crossed out in pencil on the back. Opening it, he read the message: "Please come to the gate if you are able to do so. L.E."

Shattered by the unexpectedness of it, amazed that his desire to see her should so speedily be realized, he banged down his glass on the bar and without a word of explanation walked out of the mess.

The hansom waited to one side of the main gate, its occupant seated well back, out of sight of casual passersby.

"Louisa?"

The deep, familiar voice penetrated the mists of oblivion which tugged so attractively at her mind. She heard him give directions to the cabbie, and then he was beside her.

"What on earth are you doing here?" Robert asked, but as he saw her face he gave vent to a sharp exclamation. "For God's sake, what's the matter? Are you ill?"

Louisa opened her eyes, took in the fact of his presence, and smiled wanly. "I—I was worried about you," she said faintly.

The incongruity of her words frightened him. Frowning, he asked no more questions, contenting himself with the possession of her hand, so chilled between his own warm palms. A moment later the cab pulled up beside the Queen Anne house. Pressing Louisa's arm, he told her to sit still, he had to find Harris.

The front door was open and the house quiet, its usual occupants apparently still in the mess. He walked through to the servants' quarters, where Harris was sitting outside the kitchen door, polishing four pairs of riding boots. Surprised, he came raggedly to attention, reaching hastily for his jacket.

"Money, Harris. Quickly. Enough to pay a cab from the far side of town—a couple of shillings should do it. There's not time for me to go upstairs."

"Anything wrong, sir?" Harris asked as he fished in his pocket for the remains of last week's pay.

"I rather think there is. I'm about to bring a young lady in, so get yourself into the hall and make sure the coast's clear, will you? I don't want her presence broadcast throughout the town."

The house was empty, but Harris scanned the street anxiously as his master escorted Louisa into the house. She moved slowly, like a sleep-walker, giving him excellent opportunity to be surprised. The captain was not given to entertaining ladies of any class in his rooms, but if he had wondered what to expect, the silent Kentishman had certainly not thought to see a plain, somberly dressed young woman who looked more suited to the classroom than either ballroom or bordello. As he relieved Robert of the one small piece of luggage, Harris noticed that there were fresh bruises along her jaw, and judging by the captain's grim expression, he had noted them too. Harris decided he would not care to be the person who had caused them.

"Upstairs, Harris—and open that door," Robert muttered before pick-ing Louisa up bodily. She was no small burden, but he carried her up the stairs, laying her gently on the bed in his room. Brushing aside her faint, stammered apologies, he persuaded her to drink a few drops of the brandy Harris thoughtfully provided.

"Excuse me, sir," Harris said in an undertone, his normally impassive face troubled. "Oughtn't you to, er . . . persuade the young lady to . . . er, loosen her clothing? I mean—young ladies—fainting—clothing too tight, sir," he added hastily as Robert shot him a murderous look.

Realizing the wisdom of the suggestion, Louisa struggled to release the top button of her dress and the hook and eye which fastened her high collar. "Do you think I might have a cup of tea?" she asked. "I'm sure that would make me feel much better."

As Harris disappeared to see to it, she tried to sit up, anxious to show that she was, in fact, feeling better already. The movement revealed an ugly red mark at the base of her throat. Horrified, Robert stared at it, his expression changing to angry, flushing dismay; as he turned sharply, Louisa saw his black brows draw threateningly together.

"I'll wait outside," he said tersely. "Perhaps you should do as Harris advised. I'll see if he has any witch hazel to dab on those bruises."

Louisa had been aware, before she left Blossom Street, that her face was swollen and pink with weeping and also rather tender in places; she had not realized that it was bruised. With an effort, she stood up, moving unsteadily across to the long pier glass by the window. There were marks on either side of her jaw, where Albert Tempest's fingers had gripped her face, and her lips seemed fuller, unnaturally red. With a shudder of distaste, she drew the back of her hand across her mouth, noticing, for the first time, the crimson mark on her throat. A hot wave of shame burned through her as she realized that this was what Robert had seen before he turned away.

Shuddering convulsively, her fingers fumbling with the tiny buttons, she opened her bodice, seeing two more such marks: one on the curve of her shoulder, the other where her camisole skimmed the fullness of her left breast.

Without warning, she was sick. She retched twice more, but had had little to eat that day, and the results were hardly more than a dark stain down the skirt of her dress. Shame and revulsion, a desire to run from the world and hide—but where?—battled with a total inability to rise to her feet.

Robert knocked twice, and having allowed what he considered sufficient time for her to call out or cover herself, he walked in, to find her still kneeling on the floor.

Clutching the two halves of her bodice together, she weakly resisted his attempts to raise her, and almost angrily he pulled at the restraining neck of his high-collared mess jacket. Together with the choking waist-coat, he flung it off, bending down to her in his shirtsleeves. His breath came in angry gasps, as roughly he clutched her to his breast, fierce, protective instincts battling with a rage so towering he wanted to yell at her: who? and how? and why? But he bit the questions back, afraid that his rage would come like a second assault, that he would terrify her into silence.

Aching, his limbs stiff and cramped, Robert held her until his anger was controllable, until her shuddering ceased. Aware of his own trembling, he gently persuaded her to lie down on the bed and, with a supreme effort of will, forced some semblance of calm into his voice. Handing her one of his shirts, he told her to remove her dress so that Harris could deal with the stain; he ordered fresh tea and thin slices of bread and butter, waited patiently in the darkening room, refusing to let her speak until she had finished. He sat in his chair, with the brandy bottle by his feet, sipping at the overly generous measure in his glass, resisting the urge to down it in two swift gulps.

The long summer twilight was almost gone; from the bed, Louisa could barely discern his face across the room. In his chair by the screened fireplace he sat quietly, his eyes on some distant point beyond the window. She wished that she could see him more clearly, although she was glad enough of the shadows which hid her face from him; it was easier to pretend that she was merely present in spirit, as she had often longed to be. The room she had tried so hard to imagine was surprising in its lack of ornament, its spare austerity. She had thought he would live luxuriously, but the bed was hard and narrow and the furniture functional; the only clue to his interests lay in the shelves of books beside the fireplace, the photographs of family and, presumably, favorite horses, which stood on his desk by the window. Robert's one concession to rank seemed to be his excellent servant.

Breaking the silence, she commented on the good cup of tea Harris had made for her. "He's quite a magician, your man."

"What? Oh, Harris. Yes," Robert agreed, "he is good. A very silent character. He won't breathe a word of your presence, and I've told him I'm not to be disturbed—not even by Tommy."

"I saw him today, at the Bainbridges'."

"Yes, I know," he replied shortly, his mind concerned with other things.

"Something he said," Louisa hesitantly began, "made me anxious about you. I don't really know what he was trying to say, but he worried me. It might sound very foolish, but that was in the forefront of my mind when . . . after . . . I really came here to make sure you were all right," she whispered.

"To make sure that *I* was all right?" Robert repeated incredulously. Sighing deeply, he came across the room toward her. "Oh, my dearest love, of course I am. Or should I say," he added with a wry smile, "as well as can be expected. I thought I was beginning to recover, until Tommy came into the mess and told me he'd seen you. I wanted to punch him on the nose because he'd been to the Bainbridges' and talked to you, and I could have gone and wouldn't."

"Because of me?"

"Because of you," he said softly. He took her hand and stared intently through the shadows, the glimmer of his eyes betraying something of the trial he had endured on her behalf. And then he uttered her name, a whispered, begging plea which seemed to be dragged unwillingly from the very depths of his being.

She turned away, for a moment too moved and too afraid to answer him. "You want me to tell you what happened? After I left the Bainbridges'?"

In agonizing uncertainty, he slowly nodded, wondering who would have dared to molest her, who would even think of it, afraid that it might be someone he knew. "Yes," he said at last. "No. Oh, my God," he swore and gripped her hands convulsively. "Of course I want you to tell me, but I don't want to know. Can you understand that? I can't bear to think that—that anyone could hurt you—in such a way."

And suddenly Louisa understood the depth of his fear. "He didn't," she said faintly. "He didn't get the chance. I got away."

"You mean he didn't rape you?" Robert asked, hating the word, yet needing absolute confirmation that that was what she meant. As she shook her head he released his breath slowly, unable to speak.

"Who?" he asked eventually, his voice strained and angry.

"My employer," she whispered "Rachel's father." The mere thought of that hot, wet mouth on her skin, his bruising hands and the stale, acrid smell of the man, was enough to bring back shuddering revulsion. She clung to Robert, burying her face in the crook of his shoulder, the fresh scent of his body blotting out that other memory. Haltingly she explained the angry scene with Rachel, up to the moment when Albert Tempest locked the door.

"I knew," she said, "right from the first, what he was going to do. Don't ask me how—I just *knew*. I fought him, Robert—but that only made him worse! It seemed to go on for *hours* . . . I screamed for help, but he'd locked the door . . ."

Holding her, he felt her shudder, then gently asked: "How did you get free?"

Louisa's mind veered away from the horror of that momentary pause. She simply said: "I kicked him."

"Good for you!" he muttered grimly. "Right where it hurts, I hope?"

Unfamiliar with the phrase, she nodded innocently. "Yes, in the stomach."

Something like a laugh escaped him. "Oh, God!" he exclaimed, "I thought you were so worldly-wise! Didn't your mother ever tell you? Any man ever tries that again with you, my love—you kick him right in the—" He broke off. "Between the legs," he added viciously. "That's where it *really* hurts."

She shook her head. "If I'd had a chance to think—yes, I should have known that. But I was too terrified to think at all." Her voice sank to a whisper again as she tried to explain her actions after that.

Listening, Robert was aware of mingled pride and anger; understanding the aftereffects of shock, he attempted to rationalize those actions for her; what he failed to understand at first was why she had come to *him* instead of going straight home. The blackmail he was inclined to dismiss as the natural reaction of a man hoisted by his own petard; he did not take it seriously until Louisa explained about Edward.

"All right, I understand that it must be hidden from your family—especially your cousin. He can't do anything about it, but *I* can. And I will. I swear it!"

"No, you mustn't! Please, Robert!" Suddenly frightened, Louisa gripped him by the shoulders, begging him to do nothing, say nothing, for fear Albert Tempest should fulfill those appalling threats. But she could not bring herself to reveal what seemed to her then an even worse truth, nor repeat the filthy names Albert Tempest had hissed at her, the disgusting references he had made to her parentage. And Edward's.

Anxious to calm that rising agitation, Robert gave her to understand he would do nothing; but he very carefully made no promise. Soothing her, he rocked her gently in his arms. "So, you came to me," he whispered at last, lips against her hair. Amidst all the anger and pain, he felt strangely happy, as though, having taken the side of honor against inclination, he was being rewarded. The temptation to take advantage of that trust, however, was very strong. It would be so natural to lie down beside her, to ease mind and body with tender kisses; the step from tenderness to passion was such a small one . . .

Taking a deep breath, he held her away from him. "Try to put it out of your mind for the moment. What you need is sleep—a good eight hours of undisturbed rest. I'll take you home if you want me to, but somehow I don't think that's a very good idea right now. You'd be better facing them in the morning." Before she could protest, he added: "There's a camp bed in my dressing room somewhere. I'll sleep in there. We can talk in the morning." He rose to his feet, but Louisa caught his hand.

"Do you still care for me?" she asked in a very small voice. Her uncertainty tore at his heart.

"How can you doubt it?" he whispered. When she did not reply, he returned to her side. "Do you think what's happened could alter my feelings so radically?"

The sense of having been permanently tainted was too strong for mere verbal assurances, however; modesty battled with a desire for more tangible proof and lost. Louisa longed, with a fervor so intense it astounded her, to feel again the joy of his lips on hers, to erase once and for all the taste and feel of Albert Tempest. "Then kiss me before you go."

For a second he crushed her fingers between his own, then abruptly stood up and moved away. "No," he said flatly. "I'm sorry, but no. You came to me in trust. Don't make me betray it."

The quick, upward movement of her head caught some small residue of light; without reading her expression he sensed the unspoken hurt.

"I love you," he said softly, knowing the aching truth of it, "and I need you—far more than you can even imagine. If I kissed you now, believe me, I'd not be able to stop at that." He paused to let his meaning sink in, then, in a barely audible whisper, added: "Tomorrow—next week—*any* other time. But not now, my darling. Please, not now!"

He leaned against his dressing room door, aware that he was shaking uncontrollably. "Do you understand?"

Her assent was faint but audible. For a long moment Robert stared at the bottle of brandy, then wearily closed the door on it. Alcohol might help him sleep, but it was far more likely to make him change his mind.

As he had expected, he slept little, but the long, silent hours were not wasted. Before dawn he had devised a plan which could take time to bring to fruition but was worth pursuing. He was determined to hear Albert Tempest squeal, if it took the rest of his time in York to achieve that satisfaction.

It also came to him that he was supposed to be duty officer that day, which had been the reasoning behind his planned early night. He rose at five, splashing the exhaustion from his eyes with water cold from the night before and, pulling on a pair of trousers, rang the bell for Harris.

In the bedroom the curtains were slightly open, revealing the shirt Louisa had worn, together with her flounced white petticoats, at the foot of the bed. Her arms and shoulders were roundly exposed, pale as alabaster in the early morning light; he moved closer, realizing with a sharp pang that a sleepless night had curbed not one whit of his desire. Smooth and flushed with sleep, her face had the innocence of a child's, he thought, until he saw again those dark bruises. Desire gave way to a fresh surge of anger, and he turned away, hardening his resolve of the predawn hours.

In the still and silent house, he heard Harris's soft step on the landing and had the door open before he could knock. After a whispered exchange, he took the tray of tea and hot shaving water, closing and relocking the door as gently as he had opened it.

Small, unfamiliar sounds disturbed Louisa; in the midst of a dream she turned, her eyes opening on a strange room with strange furniture, a cup of tea steaming on a bedside table, and beyond it an open door, framing a man's naked back. She blinked several times, but he was still there, arms raised, muscles rippling as he moved. The small splash of water, his attitude of concentration, the faint scraping sound, were as unfamiliar as her surroundings; as she raised herself against the pillows, memory came flooding back, and with it consternation at her own semi-naked state.

As she reached for the shirt Robert had lent her, he heard the movement and turned; hastily she covered herself, afraid that her brief camisole was immodestly revealing.

"I'll close the door while you dress," he said unsmilingly. "Let me know when you're ready."

Clean and pressed, her cotton dress was laid carefully over a chair back. Buttoning up the neck, she stared miserably at her reflection in the glass; the bruises along her jaw were darker, more noticeable this morning. Touching them gently, she wondered at Robert's attitude and, remembering her forwardness of last night, blushed furiously. In that moment she would have given anything to recall her words or, having said them and listened to his mortifying reply, to be relieved of the necessity of facing him now. But he had to be faced. With downcast eyes, she tapped on the dressing room door.

A moment later he emerged, smelling freshly of soap, with his hair brushed, a starched white shirt tucked neatly into tight, high-waisted overalls, his manner as crisp as his appearance. Beside him, Louisa felt somewhat disheveled.

"Do you always start the day this early?" she asked, having noticed the time with some amazement.

He shook his head. "I must apologize for the hour. I'm duty officer today, and last night I'd quite forgotten. I have to be present for morning stables at six, but I can be back here about nine. There should be time to whisk you discreetly away from here, if that fits in with your usual scheme of things. Or would you rather wait until this afternoon?"

"I can leave now," she said quietly. "At this hour there'll be less chance of me being seen—I hope."

"That's true, but how will you get home? And what about your family?"

"I'll walk. By the time I get to Gillygate, it won't be much earlier than usual."

He opened the curtains and made her turn to the light. "What will you do about those bruises?" He studied her face intently, his eyes concerned but distant, as though he preferred to ignore the intimacy of the situation. "Have you any rouge or face powder?" he asked, displaying a surprising knowledge of female artifice.

Louisa shook her head. "But I suppose I could always buy some," she conceded, feeling suddenly very gauche. His brusque manner upset her, making her painfully aware that they were strangers, that she was irrevocably compromised, no matter that he had behaved with such a bitter sense of honor. There was tension in his face, in every muscle of his body, a harshness which in the early morning sunlight made him seem unbearably remote.

Harris knocked and entered, handing Robert a highly polished pair of boots on his way through to the dressing room. Leaving Louisa by the window, he sat down to pull them on. "What are your plans?"

"I don't know," she said, which was untrue, but Harris's presence was inhibiting. She wondered what he was thinking as he folded sheets and put away the camp bed. He reappeared with the high-necked frock coat which was Robert's regimental working dress, helped his master into it, and brushed nonexistent specks of dust from the shoulders with a small, stiff brush. Awkward and embarrassed, Louisa looked out of the window at a pretty but neglected garden and the open fields beyond. Both Robert and his servant seemed so undisturbed by her presence, she began to wonder if a steady procession of women visited these rooms and watched him dress in the mornings. A sharp pang of jealousy swept through her, together with a mixture of regret and relief that he had left her to sleep alone. Furious with herself, she pushed out her chin and forced herself to be thankful that he was going to Ireland.

"So," he said, breaking into her thoughts as Harris silently departed, "you don't know what you are going to do with yourself."

She turned abruptly. "I had arranged to go to Blankney next Saturday while—the Tempests—were on holiday. But I think I shall go sooner than that and stay longer. It will be good to get away from here for a while. After that," she added, "I have no plans. Probably, I'll help out at home until something suitable presents itself."

"Where's Blankney?"

"A few miles south of Lincoln," she said dismissively, "but I hardly think it's on the map."

"And a week from today I shall be in Ireland, for three weeks, I think, unless I decide to return early. But I shall follow your advice," he said kindly, allowing his eyes to meet hers for the first time that morning. "I shall spend more time with my daughter and try to ignore other distractions. Should it prove too difficult, I may take Letty and Georgia up to Dublin for a while. Letty will enjoy the change of scene."

Immediately she forgave him everything, allowed herself to show the concern she felt. "Tommy was worried about you going to White Leigh."

"Tommy fusses like a mother hen," he said tersely. "He doesn't know what's passed between us." He went into the dressing room and returned with his forage cap. "By the way, how does Tempest spend his evenings? Is he out often?"

Startled, Louisa looked up at him, her eyes wide with apprehension. "He goes to a couple of religious meetings, I believe. Wednesdays and Fridays. Why?"

"Oh, I merely wondered what manner of man he was," he casually replied. "And now I know I was right to be suspicious of religious maniacs. Does he dine at home?"

"Always. Look, Robert, you're not thinking—you wouldn't—?"

"Wouldn't what? Call him out? Swords at dawn?" He smiled as he said it, but his eyes glittered, and Louisa knew he would have loved to do just that. "No, my dear, I couldn't kill a man in cold blood."

"What is it that Browning says? 'Tis God shall repay'?" Or furnish the means, he thought grimly. "I have to go. Are you sure you'll be all right, walking all that way home?"

"It's a fine morning. It will do me good."

"What about your bag?"

"It's not so heavy," she assured him. "I shall manage."

"Well, it's better we're not seen together. Harris will spy out the land for you. I'll send him up with some more hot water, and you can tell him when you're ready to leave. The rest of the house won't stir for another hour yet." Now that the moment had come, he did not want to let her go. He wished she could be there, waiting for him, when he came back later in the day. "Write to me tomorrow—tell me how things go at home or *I* shall be the one to worry. And give me your Lincoln address so I can write to you from Ireland. Promise me?"

She nodded miserably, and in a final moment of weakness he pulled her close. "My dearest love," he murmured, "I'm so very sorry for all that's happened. Forgive me for last night. I didn't mean to hurt your feelings."

"I understand," she whispered. "Forgive me, too." With a brave attempt at a smile, she stood back. "You must go, else you'll be late. Good-bye, Robert, and thank you. For everything."

His eyes were bright and very blue as he took his leave of her. "Not good-bye, Louisa—never say good-bye."

TWENTY-ONE

She wasted time by walking slowly along the riverside, sat for a while in the gardens by Skeldergate Bridge, then, as the first shops began to open, went into town to purchase face powder and vanishing cream. Making a detour to the railway station, in the privacy of the ladies' waiting room Louisa carefully camouflaged the worst of her bruises.

Her mother's nearsightedness was a blessing; nevertheless, Louisa kept her back to the light and tried to avoid Bessie's sharp eyes. On the pretext of wanting to talk to her mother in private, she retreated to her room, keeping the curtains closed while they talked. Having dropped the bombshell of her dismissal from Blossom Street, Louisa found it impossible not to tell the truth about Albert Tempest. Swearing her mother to absolute secrecy, she related the events of the previous evening with remarkable calm; only when questioned did she falter; then the whole truth came tumbling out.

Aghast, her mind reeling from one shock to another, Mary Elliott was temporarily speechless. "Good God in Heaven!" she exclaimed at last. "You mean after all that, you went to the barracks? You spent the night there?"

"No, not at the barracks. Robert shares a house. Apart from his servant, no one else knew I was there."

Bemused and shaken, the older woman stared at her daughter, shattered not just by the facts, which were appalling enough, but by such totally unexpected behavior. "Have you taken leave of your senses?" she demanded.

"Yes, Mamma," Louisa murmured contritely. "Under the circumstances, it certainly seems that way. But I swear to you," she added, "that nothing happened between us. Nothing untoward, that is. The captain gave me his bed and spent the night in his dressing room."

"Oh, my God!" Mary Elliott prayed, covering her face with her hands. "You told him, of course? About—about Albert Tempest, I mean?"

"I hardly needed to, "Louisa murmured. "It was patently obvious at the time."

"And how did he take it?"

"He seemed very upset."

"Have you seen much of him in the last few months?"

"No. I've hardly seen him at all since that Saturday he came here, and certainly not to speak to."

"I see. Would you mind telling me why not?"

Louisa's cheeks flamed with sudden guilt. "I . . . didn't think it was a sensible thing to do."

"So what on earth possessed you to go to him last night?" Mary Elliott angrily demanded. "You could have gone to Emily—even Blanche would have found room for you under the circumstances! How foolish of you—you, of all people! I'd never have believed it possible!"

Louisa sighed and turned away.

"Well? What happens now? I suppose you'll go on seeing him?"

"No, I'm going to Blankney," she declared. "I just want to get away from here."

"Well, I hope he doesn't come calling on me while you're away—else I'll give him more than he bargains for!"

"Oh, Mamma—it wasn't his fault! Anyway, he won't come here. He's going home on leave to Ireland—and I've no idea when he'll be back."

Mary Elliott gave a grunt of satisfaction. "Best place for him, if you ask me. I sincerely hope he has a busy round of engagements to take his mind off you. There's no future there—you realize that? He couldn't marry you, Louisa, even if he wanted to—his family would never allow it," she declared emphatically, then paused as another, more disturbing thought struck her. "I just hope Albert Tempest never gets wind of this, that's all." With a shudder, she stood up, nervously smoothing her apron. "Now—what am I to tell Bessie? And Edward when he comes in?"

Out of the depths of her anxiety, Mary Elliott managed to gather sufficient wit to tell Bessie the barest of truths and, having done so, sent her off to do the Saturday shopping. It was fortunate that Bessie regarded the disgrace of dismissal cause enough for her mistress's gray face and Louisa's desire to keep to her room. Remembering that Emily was to have called for tea, her mother sent a note putting her off; there was enough to contend with without inviting further inquisitions.

The real problem was Edward. Vague though he often was, where Louisa was concerned he was perhaps just a little too shrewd not to suspect that something was very much amiss. When he came in at half past twelve, however, Mary Elliott made sure that she was too busy to talk, answering his query with the brief information that Louisa had a headache and was lying down.

It was extremely hot in the kitchen. Hanging up his jacket, Edward went out into the backyard, inhaling the scent of herbs ranged in pots along the wall. Purple sage and green marjoram, a spiky bush of rosemary, and three varieties of mint were overshadowed by the fiery red of poppies growing wherever there was a small residue of soil. The first seeds, he was told, had come from Lincolnshire, many years before, together with the lavender growing in a built-up bed beneath the scullery window. He pulled a few of the fading flowers, absently crushing them between his fingers. He thought of Louisa, lying on her bed in what was often the hottest part of the house when she should have been outside, sitting in the shade; perhaps he would put out a chair for her later and read to her; she always enjoyed that.

As he washed his hands at the kitchen sink, Edward noticed his aunt making up a tray; curious, he asked who it was for, but his question went unanswered.

"What's wrong?" he repeated, following Bessie through into the cool parlor, where the table was set for two.

"It's too hot to eat in the kitchen," Bessie said by way of explanation, hurrying back to serve their three guests in the dining room.

He sat down, feeling quite bemused. His aunt refused to discuss anything until they had eaten, and not until Bessie had brought in two cups of tea did she embark upon an explanation. With her opening words, she came straight to the point.

"Albert Tempest's given Louisa the sack."

"What? *Why?*"

"Oh, it's quite unreasonable, Edward. Something to do with that spoiled brat of a daughter misbehaving herself. Not even that, really," she added with a weary sigh. "He doesn't like the company she keeps and has accused Louisa of encouraging her. There was an almighty row last night—Rachel said Arthur Bainbridge had asked her to marry him, and that set the sparks flying, I gather. Louisa tried to defend both herself and the girl—" She stopped suddenly, closing her eyes against the unfortunate dual meaning of that phrase, then continued as firmly as she could. "Anyway, he didn't like it and dismissed Louisa on the spot—no references, nothing."

"Arthur Bainbridge? Didn't Louisa say she'd tried to talk to the old man about that? I'm sure she's mentioned that more than once to me."

"Yes, she did try to tell him what was going on, but he wouldn't listen. And now she's got the blame for it."

"That's ridiculous."

"Of course it is, but what can she do? She's extremely upset about it."

"Well," Edward said sharply, "I don't know what *she* can do, but I shall certainly speak to him. He can be hot-tempered and hasty—no doubt come Monday he'll have had a chance to think things over and will probably be sorry."

Inwardly Mary Elliott quailed. Pressing her hands together to still their trembling, she shook her head firmly. "I don't think so, Edward, and Louisa is far too upset to accept the job, even if he came on bended knees, apologizing all the way."

"She should have references, Aunt Mary, if nothing else!"

With a shrug of her shoulders, his aunt sighed. "Look, dear, if I were you, I wouldn't bother. Leave things as they are—Louisa doesn't want any fuss."

"But what about your education? How can you waste that? And all those years of experience?"

The room was still shrouded against the penetrating sunlight, but Louisa watched her cousin anxiously as he paced the room. She felt exhausted, but his words provoked a small spark of anger, enough to prompt a sharper answer than she really intended. "And what use has it been to me? I'm nearly twenty-six years old, Edward, and what am I fit for, apart from looking after other people's children?" Bitterness at her invidious position made her add: "I'd have been better off as a nursemaid—at least I wouldn't have been educated out of my class!"

Edward spun around and faced her. "How can you say that? It was what you always wanted. Nobody stood over you and made you do it. *You* were the one who wanted to get away from York—to bury the past."

"So I came back and had it resurrected for me."

"What do you mean?"

Afraid that Edward would notice the marks on her face, Louisa turned away from that searching gaze. Fresh recollections of Albert Tempest knotted her stomach with anxiety and set her whole body trembling. "I mean that the so-called gentleman for whom you've worked all these years reminded me of my past in a most unpleasant fashion. He dragged it *all* up, Edward—Tanner Row, the scandal, everything. He even brought your name into it. So, after that, I'm afraid I wouldn't work for him if he came crawling to me on bended knees. References or no—I've finished. As long as I can keep body and soul together, I really don't care what I do for a living."

It came as no real surprise to Edward that Albert Tempest knew of their respective backgrounds; nevertheless, he felt the cold chill of personal betrayal, as though his employer had returned the years of faithful service with a sneering laugh. He was shocked and stunned, because he had always thought of Albert Tempest as an honorable man. "Exactly what did he say to you?"

Aware that she had perhaps revealed too much, Louisa struggled for an adequate reply, a reply that required the fewest lies. To tell the truth, to quote him directly, would mean explaining so much more. "He implied that a person of my unfortunate background was quite unfit to look after his children."

"Surely he must have known your background all along?"

"Of course he knew. But I've come to the conclusion that in Albert Tempest's book, it's a question of what suits him best at the time. He's an opportunist, after all. You must have realized that."

"But what did he actually *say,* Louisa?"

Stubbornly she shook her head. "I refuse to repeat it. It would serve no purpose—except to make you as angry and hurt as I am."

Poised on the verge of argument, he turned away and, with a shrug, conceded defeat. He knew that look, that tone of voice. Further questions would be a waste of breath. "I shall at least demand that he give you a reference," he said quietly.

"You'll demand nothing, Edward!" she exclaimed, her voice breaking with agitation. "Do you hear me? *Nothing*! If you want to keep your job, forget this. Forget what I've told you—forget there's any connection between us." The hurt surprise on his face made her add more gently: "Pretend it never happened—please. That's the way I want it—no fuss, no recriminations, nothing."

Uneasily, with a deep feeling that much was being withheld, Edward slowly nodded. Her obvious lack of trust hurt him deeply, preventing further probes, and his sense of personal aggrievement toward Albert Tempest was so great, he knew it was impossible to raise the subject and still go on working for the man. Gratifying though it might be, an outburst of self-righteous anger would surely mean dismissal, and jobs were not so plentiful that he could afford the risk of being out of work for long. For the time being at least, Edward reasoned, he must swallow his ire, hard though it was to do. With a frustrated sigh, he looked long and searchingly at his cousin before turning away.

As she heard him close the door of his own room, Louisa squeezed her eyes tight shut, hating herself for lying to him. Even if it was simply by omission, he knew and was hurt by it; and after his support and kindness in recent weeks it was unforgivable. Bit by bit she had told him something of her feelings for Robert Duncannon, although, as with her mother, she had balked at the ultimate reason for rejecting him. Edward had listened sympathetically, his comments restricted to simple confirmation that she had done the right thing. Although he had never said as much, Louisa suspected he had little liking for the Irishman; whether it was personal or a simple matter of distrusting his motives, she could not have said; but it seemed strange that Edward should dislike Robert, who loved her, even while he defended Albert Tempest. Shuddering at the images which leapt to mind, she curled up, weeping hot, silent tears of humiliation and regret. With all the sudden and concentrated force of a tornado, the night before had changed every single thing in her life, scattering the carefully built bricks of her defenses against Robert and damaging, probably beyond repair, her relationship with Edward. What it had done to her mother she could scarcely begin to guess.

Almost squirming with shame, Louisa thrust those painful considerations aside. She had to get away from them, physically as much as mentally. The prospect of Blankney, with its peace and tranquility, its rolling fields and open skies, beckoned like a seductive dream.

TWENTY-TWO

*E*nlisting the help of Harris, Robert had Albert Tempest watched. Twelve years of army life had given him a deeper insight into the baser forms of human nature than Louisa would have cared to contemplate, and a deviousness in dealing with it which was not entirely gentlemanly. He had joked with Louisa about swords at dawn, because the thought of it had been with him for half the night; a fantasy in which he unsheathed that honed steel blade and terrified the life out of Albert Tempest with swirling, slashing, cutting strokes, strokes which merely touched the skin, laying breast and back open in a thousand tiny cuts. But from the depths of his contempt, he realized that a man like Albert Tempest, with such unbridled appetites, must seek an outlet for them somehow, somewhere. There were enough bawdy houses in the city, and double standards were so prevalent that Robert found nothing incongruous in the idea of a staunch chapelgoer taking his pleasure with a prostitute.

It merely remained to find out where he went and when. Each evening that week, Harris took the tram to Blossom Street and watched the doorway of the Tempest house from the saloon bar of the Windmill. There were few comings and goings, but on Wednesday night Albert Tempest emerged, his impeccably dressed figure unmistakable. He did not go far. Harris followed him at a discreet distance into Priory Street, to the Wesleyan Chapel hall, and with a shrug of disappointment settled down to wait, thankful for the fine summer evening.

He could not help but wonder at the captain's motives, sending him out on this wild-goose chase; unless the camp bed had been a blind, and the young woman really was his mistress. Harris was sure the captain would have liked her to be, no matter how hard he tried not to show it. The whole situation intrigued him, yet no matter how often he went over his sparse accumulation of facts, no satisfactory explanation presented itself.

A shy man, his personal experience was limited to occasional halting conversations with shop girls or even less frequent forays in search of sex. But that was always a straightforward business matter, for which he was prepared to pay. Anything in between was sadly foreign to him. From the usual loose talk among his peers, however, Harris believed that women who were raped or assaulted almost invariably asked for it, and it was hard for him to reconcile those assumptions with what he had seen of Louisa Elliott.

Decent and respectable, he would have said, and with a living to earn, probably hardworking too; he could not imagine a young woman like her giving any man come-hither looks, not unless she meant it. And whether marriage was part of the bargain or not, with Robert Duncannon on offer, why would she give the other miserable-looking old sod more than the time of day?

This Tempest character must be a randy old goat, Harris decided, unable to have a woman under his roof without wanting her in his bed as well. Disgusted, he stubbed out another cigarette and continued his watch.

At dusk the old goat left his religious meeting and went straight home. There was nothing at all to report on Thursday, but on Friday evening, shortly after seven, Albert Tempest again set off toward town. With a quickening of the pulse, Harris watched his quarry pass Priory Street and continue across the city.

The house was in a quiet, respectable quarter off Bootham, and had it not been for a visibly furtive glance up and down the street, Harris might have been deceived. That one look, however, was enough to make him suspicious, and in the two hours of his watch, five other equally well-dressed men approached the house and were let in by a tiny maid-servant who could not have been more than twelve or thirteen. Harris slipped into the shelter of an alley as Albert Tempest was shown out again, and discreetly followed him back to Blossom Street.

After his return on Wednesday evening, the house had been locked up for the night. But this evening was different. The maid was waiting for him at the door; lamps were lit upstairs, and from his position across the street, Harris could see the man moving from room to room. Intrigued, he continued his surveillance. When Albert Tempest reemerged, almost running in his haste, Harris hurriedly stamped out his cigarette and followed. In Nunnery Lane, his quarry stopped a passing hansom; lack of a second cab stopped Harris from dogging him further, but he had been close enough to hear the destination given.

"So you lost him?"

"I'm sorry, sir, but I did hear him tell the cabbie to take him to Fulford."

"Fulford! What urgent business could he have here, at this time of night?" Robert queried.

"No idea, sir. He came out pretty sharpish, though. And before that, it looked as though he was searching the house for somebody."

Deep in thought, Robert stared at the clock. "Rachel," he said suddenly. "His daughter. What was it Louisa said? She said he was furious because of his daughter's friendship with the Bainbridges, particularly young Arthur. So," he mused, "I wager you anything, Harris, that she's run to them, or rather to him. With any luck," he commented cheerfully, "she's eloped with the young fool. Keep your ear to the ground—it's an interesting little development, and I'd like to know how the land lies. The Tempests were supposed to be going to Bridlington tomorrow, but if Rachel's taken herself off, then our teetotal printer may not be going on holiday after all. Which means that I may pin him down before I go to Ireland, and the sooner the better." Robert rubbed his hands in great satisfaction. "You've done well, Harris, and I'm more than grateful for your help. Now—expenses for the week—will a guinea cover it?"

"That's more than generous, sir—"

"Never—you deserve it. I shall not forget. All that remains is to establish beyond doubt the nature of that house he visited. It's not one I've heard of, but I'll take a chance and go there myself tomorrow evening."

"What about your other plans, sir?"

"Ireland will have to wait. I'll send a telegram in the morning. At the moment, Harris, this other matter is more important. I want to see that swine squirm."

In the mess the following evening, Robert sought out Hugh Darnley. His soft brown puppy's eyes were troubled, and he was genuinely reluctant to talk about the Bainbridges, for he was fond of them; to gossip about the family he lodged with seemed to him a form of betrayal, especially as the mess was buzzing with speculation.

"I don't deal in gossip, Hugh, and neither do you, I know that. I'm not asking out of idle curiosity, believe me. Do you remember Miss Elliott, Rachel Tempest's companion?"

Darnley looked surprised. "Yes, of course I do. I've seen her often."

"Don't ask me how I came by the information, but I happen to know that she was dismissed only last week because of Rachel Tempest's friendship with young Arthur—dismissed without a reference. I happen to think it was extremely unjust, and—well, I'm simply interested to know what happened last night.''

Darnley was several years younger than Robert, softhearted and sentimental where women were concerned, but no fool. He gave Robert an intensely speculative glance before replying. ''Well, the first anyone knew of it was when the girl's father came pounding on the door, demanding the return of his daughter. The major was out, and Mrs. Bainbridge apparently collapsed after five minutes' onslaught. Poor Sophie was in hysterics, and even the butler couldn't get rid of old Tempest, so he came for me. I'd just got back from the mess and hadn't had time to change. When I went down into the drawing room, Lily was giving the old bastard hell—there is one thing about that girl, she's got guts. Painfully awkward in society, but she's spent so much time with the grooms in the stables, she swears better than any of them! Tempest was shocked rigid, I can tell you—it didn't need me to put a flea in his ear.''

''Good for Lily,'' Robert said admiringly.

''Anyway, once she'd shut up, I tried to find out what it was all about. He said Rachel had run off, that he knew she was here, and if not here, then with Arthur, and he wanted her returned to her rightful home, et cetera, et cetera. Whereupon I assured him that she was not in the house, that Arthur was at his mess, as far as I knew, and no one knew anything about his daughter. At that point he began to berate the Bainbridges as a family, and I'm afraid I lost my temper. When he refused to leave the house, I took his arm, twisted it up his back, and marched him to the front door.''

''Did you?'' Robert breathed, his eyes gleaming. ''By God, I wish I'd been there. You didn't by any chance kick him down the steps while you were about it?''

''No,'' Darnley modestly replied. ''But I should have done—he was most insulting to me personally and Her Majesty's Cavalry in general.''

Robert snorted derisively. ''Was he, by God? He'll eat his words before I've done with him, I promise you that.''

''Really? And what's provoked you? Or shouldn't I ask?''

''Don't ask,'' Robert replied grimly. ''Anyway, go on—you didn't finish your story.''

''Yes, well, after I'd thrown him out, and the ladies had recovered from their hysterics, we all decided that the man was mad, that Rachel had been quite sensible to leave home, that she had probably gone to a relative, and that Arthur would be back at any minute to prove us correct. About eleven o'clock, the major returned—he'd been to the Yorkshire hussars' mess and seen nothing of Arthur. When the lad still hadn't returned at midnight, Mrs. Bainbridge was almost out of her mind with worry. Sophie was quite prostrate with grief—how could her best friend betray them like this?—you know the sort of thing."

"Yes, I can imagine," Robert said as he signaled the servant to bring two more drinks. "Very romantic when it happens to someone else, a little less amusing when your brother's career is in jeopardy."

"If only the young fool had talked about it, asked permission. The Bainbridges aren't unreasonable people; in fact they're quite indulgent to their children—nothing like my parents," Darnley said with a bitter laugh. "And the volunteer regiments are hardly the Royals, with all our so-called inflexible regulations. He could have asked, and waited a while. He'll have to marry her now, of course," Darnley added with a sigh, "having compromised her utterly."

Robert nodded, a tight smile marring his otherwise expressionless features. "Of course."

"It's the heat, you know," Darnley said with an air of great profundity. "They say people go off their heads in India, and I can quite believe it. It's been so hot for so long—and we're just not used to it." He pulled at the tight neck of his uniform and glanced out of the window at the clear evening sky. "God, I wish it would rain."

"But not tonight," Robert protested with a grin. "I have an appointment in town, and I really must go and change. But I thank you for the information—and don't worry, it'll go no further."

An hour later he was alighting from a cab by Bootham Bar, the northwestern gateway into the city, and with the bar behind him he glanced up Gillygate, experiencing a small stab of longing for Louisa as he did so. She had not written as he had asked her to do, but she had left her Lincolnshire address, and he intended to write as soon as his business with Albert Tempest was complete.

Anxious, he nevertheless forced himself not to hurry along Bootham; he wanted to appear to be merely taking the air, in company with so many other innocently strolling citizens. The panoramic expanse of the asylum's grounds caught his attention, and he shivered, thinking momentarily of Charlotte; with an effort, he dragged his eyes away, concentrating on the street names, looking for the one Harris had named. It was on his left, leading down to the river, a smart street of well-kept houses, presenting as innocuous a face as all its neighbors. As he mounted the steps and rang the bell, he wondered briefly how much a place like this charged for services rendered. If Tempest was as tightfisted as Louisa had intimated, then he must place his personal comfort high on the list of priorities. No wonder he wanted it for nothing, Robert thought bitterly; with a compliant mistress installed at home, he would save a lot of cash.

The little maid was reluctant to let him in until he said that he had been recommended by a friend. A tall, thin, quietly dressed woman of indeterminate age came into the hallway; for one appalling moment, Robert thought he had made a mistake, that this was the meeting place of some learned society, that his judgment of Albert Tempest had been sadly wrong. Mind racing, seeking a legitimate excuse for his presence, he bowed low; but as he raised his head, he caught the unmistakable calculating glance, the look which weighed him up in pounds, shillings, and pence and found him worth cultivating.

Playing for time and confirmation, he gave a slow smile, allowing his eyes to show generous appraisal; as the woman responded, he begged her forgiveness for the intrusion. "A friend of mine spoke most warmly of you, madam, and as I happened to be in the neighborhood, I chanced to call."

"And which friend would that be?" she asked boldly, her eyes never leaving his.

"Mr. Tempest," he answered, wondering suddenly whether Albert Tempest might have used another name. He let out a slow sigh of relief as she smiled.

"Ah, yes, one of our most valued clients," she said with practiced smoothness. In fact, he was troublesome, and she wanted nothing to do with his friends. "Unfortunately, Mr. . . . ."

"Captain—Captain Devereaux," he said with a quick smile, praying that his mother, wherever she was, would forgive him for the use of her name in such circumstances.

Hard brown eyes brightened at the rank; hers was a relatively recent establishment, and the right military connections could be useful. "I cannot imagine how you know Mr. Tempest," she said with a swift, ironic smile. "But no matter. As I was saying, Captain, we usually keep to an appointments system here, and most of my girls are engaged at present."

Robert tried to sound disappointed; he virtually had the evidence he needed; it was hardly necessary to go upstairs. "Of course, my friend did mention that. I had hoped . . . but never mind, some other evening perhaps?"

The woman consulted a list. "You see, we like to match personalities wherever possible, Captain. I'm a great believer in people enjoying some kind of rapport, if you see what I mean," she added with another of those knowing smiles.

"Oh, yes—indeed," he agreed with alacrity, suspecting that the clients must pay dearly for that kind of service.

"I don't suppose," she asked with a small frown of consideration, "that your tastes are anything like your friend's?"

"Well . . ."

"I see they are," she commented coyly, and the coyness sat ill upon that hardened face. Like an aunt who has been tantalizing a favorite nephew with a special gift, she announced that Miss Leonie happened to be free and that Albert Tempest always favored her with his attentions. "If you are prepared to wait a few moments, Captain, I will see if Miss Leonie is able to receive you."

"But of course," Robert replied suavely, wondering if this were wise.

"Do come through into the salon." She led the way from the sparsely furnished hall into a sumptuous waiting room, but before he could take a seat on a red plush sofa, she named the price he would have to pay.

She must be good, he reflected, as he handed the money over; what Albert Tempest paid out for pleasure would keep an average family very comfortably for a week.

Copies of Italian Renaissance paintings littered the walls. Botticelli's *Birth of Venus* competed with a reclining Venus by Titian, while yet another faced him, an obscure but erotic picture which aroused nothing more than a smile from Robert as he studied its crudity of posture and expression.

The little maid disturbed his amusement. In her black and white uniform she led the way upstairs, her slender back provoking such feelings of disgust that he was afraid he would be unable to go through with the coming interview. Prostitution was one thing, but he hated to think of corruption, and the corruption of children was abhorrent to him. Not for the first time, he wondered what kind of tastes were catered to in this beautiful house.

The child halted before a door at the far end of the corridor. With a curtsy to the woman within, she announced him and left.

In common with most of his colleagues, Robert had had experience of high-class prostitutes, so he was not unprepared for the opulent, highly perfumed boudoir; nevertheless, his heart was beating as fast as it had on the very first occasion, when he had been little more than a raw and callow boy. Then he had been afraid of making a fool of himself in the act of love; now he was nervously wondering how he could maintain her interest in him without having to take the goods for which he had paid.

Leaning against the closed door, he gave as genuine a smile as he could muster, allowing his eyes to take in the voluptuous presence of Miss Leonie. In a diaphanous silk peignoir, she reclined on a pink chaise longue, her long, dark hair falling in fetching waves around her plump shoulders. She was perhaps twenty years old, but those dark and deep-set eyes were far older; she would not be easy to fool, he thought, as he approached her.

"So—you're a captain?" she asked provocatively, her voice light, the accent well schooled. "Infantry or cavalry?"

"Cavalry," he replied automatically.

"Really?" she said slyly, eyeing him up and down. "You should prove a novel experience, and no mistake. Come and sit down," she insisted, patting the cushion beside her. She caressed his shoulder, her hand sliding down the muscles of his arm, one fingernail raising a pleasurable and involuntary shiver.

He recognized the expertise with a wry smile and inwardly acknowledged the temptation she presented. Beneath the austere and rather monkish image he preferred to cultivate, he was a sensual man, physically fit and in the prime of life; he was also very much aware of his sexual needs. The fact that he had on occasions paid for that particular hunger to be assuaged bothered his conscience not at all. To Robert, it was like eating or sleeping, only less frequently required; and far less immoral, in his eyes, than using pretended affection as the currency of exchange. There were women of easy virtue among his own class, but he had had his fingers burned and learned to steer clear of them. After Charlotte, emotional involvement seemed something he would never know again; and since meeting Louisa, he had remained celibate, not from any conscious decision, but largely from lack of desire for any other woman. The fires which had been so carefully banked down had recently been rekindled with a vengeance, however, and for the past week he had lived on a knife edge of physical desire, remembering her, longing for her, castigating himself for not making love with her on what could prove to be the only opportunity he would ever have. She haunted his dreams, ever elusive at the point of satisfaction, so that he woke feeling drained and angry with himself and, scorning the simplest solution, mortified his recalcitrant body with cold baths and brisk early-morning walks. He felt that he was being faintly ridiculous, but his renunciation of Louisa a week ago had resolved itself into a kind of vow. Sooner or later, he and she would be together, with or without the church's blessing; and for that day he was prepared to wait.

But he was only human, and he knew that his self-control was a fragile thing. He must confess his intent to Miss Leonie before she tempted him too far.

"I won't remove my jacket, if you don't mind," he said with a gentle smile. "Really, all I want to do is talk to you."

"Talk, love?" Miss Leonie asked, her astonishment sending the genteel accents fleeing.

"You're a lovely girl," he said sincerely and steeled himself to lie. "The fact is that I'm a happily married man—otherwise, I would be only too pleased to avail myself of your generosity."

"But—"

"But I'm here on business, to ask you to betray a confidence, for which I am quite prepared to pay. I want to know about one of your clients, how often he visits this excellent establishment."

"Look here," she said sharply, "you're not a policeman, are you? 'Cause if you are, I want you to know we have an arrangement with one of your superiors—"

"Do I look like a policeman?" he interrupted.

"Well, no. But you can never be sure these days. Getting quite posh, some of 'em."

"I'm not a policeman. I want information for a private reason. One of your clients is blackmailing a friend of mine, and I intend to put a stop to it with a bit of blackmail of my own. Will you help me?"

She eyed him shrewdly. "Well, now, that rather depends on who it is. If I tell, that bloke's sure to stop coming here, and Mrs. Dodsworth won't like it. She's trying to build the place up, not run it down."

Robert said that he would make it worth her while, but Miss Leonie was still unsure. "Tell me who it is first."

He took a deep breath. "Albert Tempest."

The girl laughed, a free unrestrained guffaw of pure mirth. "Oh, *him!* My God! Tell me what you want to know and I'll spill the beans. I shan't miss that nasty old sod, that's for sure, and neither will Mrs. Dodsworth. Tight as a tick's arse, he is. Give us a couple o' quid and I'll tell you all you want to know."

Robert sighed at the price, but handed over two gold sovereigns.

"Well, love, he comes here once a week, every Friday—has done for the last few months," she said as she locked the money away in a small wooden box on the dressing table. "Let me see, must have been not long after we came here—end of February, beginning of March—somebody introduced him, I forget who. Anyway, as I say, he comes here every week, and every week we go through the same performance. He has to insult me, I have to get mad—really mad, shouting at him, calling him all sorts, which, the way I feel about him, isn't too bloody difficult, I can tell you. But it's bloody exhausting, love, far harder than the usual things I get paid for. And he'll like as hell pay extra for it, the mean old bugger."

"Did he visit you last Friday night?"

"Yesterday?"

"No, the week before."

"Yes—yes, he did. Now that was queer, 'cause he was late for his appointment, and he isn't usually—like bloody clockwork as a rule. And funny you should mention last week—he didn't want the insults neither. Easiest half hour I've had in a long time," she added with a grin.

"Hmm, I'm not surprised," Robert murmured, feeling his anger rise afresh.

Miss Leonie watched his face, noted the hardening of his mouth and jaw; his eyes were veiled, but she knew intuitively that Albert Tempest was about to suffer, and the knowledge excited her. She resumed her seat, began to stroke the fine hair at the back of his neck; this one was handsome, not an ounce of fat on his tall frame, he had to have a lovely body beneath that expensive suit. "Sure you won't stay, love?" she whispered persuasively. "Your wife won't miss this once, will she? I bet you're not a high days and holidays merchant."

Robert grinned at her. "You'd be surprised."

"I'm sure I would, if only you'd give me the chance, love."

He stood up, smoothing a hand over his ruffled hair. "You're very tempting, Miss Leonie, but I've got what I came for, and I can't thank you enough for your help." Before he opened the door, he turned and smiled at her. "As a small recompense, would you like me to recommend you?"

Her eyes held his for a long moment, her regret obvious. "I never say no, love."

TWENTY-THREE

*T*he days were long and hot, sun beating down on the cornfields from a sky so deeply blue it seemed to touch the horizon in a solid mass. Billowing columns of white cloud, sometimes edged with gray, threatened from time to time, while village sages shook their heads and clicked their tongues, prophets of doom enjoying every pessimistic warning, urging the work force on. In their efforts to reap the early harvest, to gather all in before the glorious weather broke, as break it must, whole families worked the fields from dawn to dusk, traditional rivalries forgotten.

Enjoying the spirit of rare fraternity, John Elliott worked along with the rest, organizing teams of horses for the hay wains, loading the stacks to ever-increasing heights. Man could work all hours God sent, but the great shires were protected and cared for like nursing mothers, pulling the enormous loads for only a few hours a day, their heads guarded against sun and flies by soft straw hats, each plunging footfall accompanied by a nod, each nod by a flopping whisk of the brim. They were strong, beautiful creatures, and John's love for them was deep and abiding, his tenderness and pride in the shires far exceeding his regard for the squire's overbred hunters, which he considered vain, silly animals, too temperamental by half.

Each time he passed the cottage, his younger children dashed to the gate, demanding a ride beside him on the trip to and from the fields. Sometimes he would take them, but only if Louisa would come; he was too afraid of the little ones being hurt without someone to watch them. William, who was six, and Johnnie, the eldest at seven, were already busy with the other village children, gathering gleanings from the shorn fields. He was sorry that Louisa had lost her job, but glad that her misfortune meant a longer stay, for her help and assistance eased the burden on his wife.

Making another trip to the fields with Tom and little Beth, Louisa glanced sideways at her cousin; the role of husband and father suited him. He was gentler and more considerate than she had imagined he would be. He adored his Jenny, her patently pregnant state such a source of great joy to him that Louisa wondered how he behaved when she was not pregnant. After much initial embarrassment, she had come to accept this unself-conscious behavior, even envying their easy, affectionate relationship.

Jenny seemed to find almost as much delight in her happy brood of children as did her husband, although Louisa thought she looked very tired by the heat.

"Don't you worry about her?" she asked John as he negotiated a bad bend in the land.

"Who? Jenny?" Louisa nodded, and he was silent for a moment. "Yes, I suppose I do, sometimes. At times like this, I worry. We could do with you living here permanently," he joked.

"I can't do that, John, however much it appeals to me. The money I've saved won't last forever, nor even very long, I'm afraid." Remembering the children at her side, she chose her next words carefully. "She can't go on indefinitely, you know. Like this every year, I mean—it will destroy her health. Don't you realize that?"

His sun-bleached brows drew together in a frown, and he did not answer her.

Louisa cleared her throat. "There are *ways*, John, means of preventing—these situations."

"Nonsense!" he exclaimed. "Old wives' tales, indecent, too. I'm surprised at you, Louisa."

"They are *not* old wives' tales, John. Don't you ever read a book? No, I don't suppose you have access to books like that in Blankney. But believe me, there are means—proven, if not necessarily approved of. Perhaps they're not totally foolproof, but they lessen the risk. Oh, dear, I'm not explaining this very well," she said distractedly, blushing furiously at her own temerity in introducing such a forbidden topic. "I wish I knew Jenny better; I'd be able to explain what I've read to her."

Her cousin turned and looked at her, his light blue eyes screwed up against the sun. "Are you serious? You're not fooling me?"

"No, of course not. I would hardly have spoken, had I not been so anxious about Jenny."

"I'll tell her," he said decisively. "I'll get her to speak to you about it. She hasn't been so well the last few months, and I have been worried about her. I suppose anything's worth a try," he conceded. With that, he turned the horses into the field, and further discussion was impossible.

The following evening, being Saturday and John's night out at the pub in Metheringham, Jenny tentatively brought up the subject with Louisa. After many blushes and false starts, Louisa explained to her cousin's wife the principles of contraception which she had read in an expensive and not widely circulated magazine two or three years earlier. A doctor in Leeds was still giving advice and selling contraceptive devices, despite being struck off the Medical Register for his beliefs. With the lack of an effective and appealing male sheath, he had made certain modifications to a female method of protection, which was considered to be the safest and least harmful way of ensuring freedom from pregnancy. Louisa described illustrations of a cone-shaped device, which could be sent for, together with a full set of instructions for use.

"I don't pretend to know how it works, Jenny," she said, "but I do recall being very impressed by what I read. You see," she explained hesitantly, "it seems very wrong to me that women should have no say. I'm not married, I know, and perhaps I should not talk of these things— but if I was married, I should hate to face the prospect of bearing a child every year until either my health or my sanity gave out. I do love children, and it saddens me to think that I may never marry and have babies of my own. But still," she added with a smile, "I wouldn't want one every year."

With a rueful grin, Jenny patted her bulging pinafore. "I'd like to think that this one would be my last—and not because I may die before I conceive another. Oh, don't look so anxious!" she said reassuringly. "There's a lot of life in me yet! But with every child, we all of us face that thought . . . I think I shall persuade John to take me to see that doctor in Leeds. I love the children dearly, as you know, but they do wear me out, especially just now. And I love John too much . . ." She stopped, afraid that she was being indiscreet. "Perhaps Emily would advise me?"

Louisa colored again. "I don't know—I doubt it. We don't discuss these matters, I'm afraid. I think she would be shocked."

"Well, I'm grateful," Jenny said firmly. "We are cut off here, and the old wives' methods are a bit hit and miss to say the least, although every wife I know seems to have a method she swears by." She laughed suddenly. "I've tried them all, believe me."

When Jenny had gone to bed, Louisa sat on for a while, reluctant to go upstairs. All the heat of the day would be contained in the tiny bedroom under the eaves, and she was afraid of disturbing Beth and baby Mary Ann if she could not sleep. The kitchen door was open, and she looked out into the moonlit garden, wondering how life would have been if her mother and Aunt Elizabeth had stayed here. Either or both might have married and brought a dozen children into the world, all tied to the land as her cousins were. It was a slower, simpler way of life, as full of unremitting toil and beset by as much poverty in its way as city life, but at least the air was clean, the children, though poor, were healthy and well fed. The false, materialistic values of the city were less in evidence here. Blankney was cut off, behind the times, but at least people knew who they were, knew who and what *she* was; there was no need to lie, for here everything was known and accepted. Truth was honored, and modesty was not false; respect was something to be earned, not donned like a cloak to cover actions which would not bear the light of day. Here you were either a landowner or a land-tender; the squire owned the land, and the squire was next to God; everyone else was more or less equal. It was a simplistic view, and Louisa was aware that even here things were changing, but for the time being she did not correct herself, for the simplistic view was comforting and healing.

She went out into the garden, pleased by the feel of the cooler night air; it was good to be here, even if her journey had been in the nature of flight from people and things with which she was unable to cope. It was impossible to think of her employer by name, nor could she contemplate the reasons behind his assault, but as the marks beneath her dress faded, so the horror of it lessened with each passing day.

In the five days that she had been here, she had also tried to come to terms with her other emotions and found it oddly more difficult. Hatred and revulsion for a man she need never see again, a man she could push down into the recesses of her mind, were relatively simple to dispose of; he was less than nothing, he did not matter, and even his disgusting behavior, the fear she had experienced, that too would fade into memory, given time. But Robert Duncannon was different. He was dangerous, and infinitely more disturbing, because she loved him. Coming so close on the heels of Albert Tempest's attack, the rawness of Robert's emotions had had a stunning effect; she was still amazed by that frank revelation, to the extent that she quite regularly scrutinized her face in the mirror and found nothing there with which to answer herself. The face which regarded her so searchingly seemed just as ordinary as it had always been, a little more refined perhaps with the loss of weight and less like a dairymaid's, but plain nonetheless.

She sighed, remembering Robert, how small and feminine she felt beside him; how, when he looked at her, she could almost pretend that she was beautiful. He was such a joy to behold, he was everything she was not; even his voice, lilting and musical, was like a caress. With that latent charm, and the warmth which seemed always to envelop her, it was easy to explain his attraction, why she had fallen in love with him; less easy to understand what such a man saw in her. He found her easy to talk to, that was obvious, and had he regarded her solely as friend and confidante, she would have been honored enough; the rest was a mystery. And yet, she thought, those feelings had been real enough that night. Unwittingly she had presented herself to him, almost on a plate, as her mother would have said, and she blanched at the recollection. He had proved himself a gentleman, but was she a lady?

In the seclusion of the orchard, with the harvest moon coming to fullness in the warm night sky, she was very much afraid that she was not.

The click of the gate rescued her from these disturbing thoughts; expecting it to be John, she turned to face him as he came around the corner of the cottage.

"It's only me," she assured him, afraid that her pale dress among the trees would startle him.

"Couldn't you sleep?" he asked, and she could smell the aroma of beer and tobacco which clung to his clothes. Against the ruddiness of his tanned face, sun-bleached hair and eyebrows shone white in the moonlight; his eyes were bright, too. She was suddenly wary of him; he was not drunk, but sufficiently intoxicated to make her recall Emily's wedding.

"It was too warm earlier, but I think I'll be able to sleep now."

"Don't go just yet," he said persuasively. "I haven't had a chance to talk to you since you arrived, and I've been wondering how things went for you. Did you see your dashing dragoon again?"

A sadly ironic smile flitted across her pale features. "Yes, I did. Last week, oddly enough."

"And did you take my advice?" he asked with a twinkling grin.

"No, I did not," she said on an indrawn breath and made to go inside.

John swung her around to face him, sighing as he saw the anger in her eyes. "All right, all right," he murmured gently, but he cupped her face in his large brown hands. "Remember what I said—you're too lovely to go to waste, sweetheart."

"Do you know something, John? If we hadn't had that conversation yesterday, I would swear you think every woman's sole purpose in life is the bearing of children. Now, just let me go. You've had too much to drink, and it's gone to your head."

Laughing, he dropped his hands. "That dashing dragoon of yours ought to be horsewhipped, Louisa—he doesn't know what he's about. If I ever meet him, I shall tell him so."

"Thank God that's hardly likely," she muttered and turned to go.

He said something else, but she only caught the word *geldings* as she ran up the stairs. His coarseness was nothing new, but suddenly it disgusted her. She undressed quickly, shaking as though with cold, eager to get into bed and to close her mind to conflict.

TWENTY-FOUR

"*I*rish, are you?"

From his vastly superior height, Robert looked down on Albert Tempest and smiled. "I would say so, but your maid might disagree with me."

Momentarily disconcerted, the older man glanced again at the engraved visiting card. "Well, you'd better state your business quickly. Some of us do observe the Lord's day," he said with heavy sarcasm, "and I must be at chapel in half an hour. If it's about my daughter Rachel, I'll tell you now, you're wasting both my time and yours. That little madam ought to be thrashed—she'll not darken my door again."

"I haven't come about your daughter," Robert said evenly. "You may not have noticed, but *my* regiment is the Royal Dragoons. I believe your daughter ran off with a lieutenant of the Yorkshire Hussars." Noting his adversary's aghast expression, Robert added: "Yes, it's a small world—these things get around."

Swallowing hard, Albert Tempest stared first into the hard eyes of the man in front of him and then at the portrait of his late wife, as though for inspiration. He took refuge in a display of temper. "Then what do you want? Tell me your business and get on your way. I haven't too much time."

Robert stared back, his eyes glacial. "I want you to write a reference—an exceedingly good reference—for Miss Elliott."

"*What?*"

"I think you heard me."

"Oh, I heard you, all right. But I don't believe it! What's she got to do with you?"

"I don't think that's any of your business," Robert said coldly. "But I happen to be a friend of the family."

"You?" Albert Tempest laughed. "A friend of the Elliotts?" He snorted derisively. "Now I've heard it all. Her fancy man, more like!"

Robert clenched the slender ebony walking stick he still carried. Moira had taken his hat and gloves, but he had insisted on keeping the stick with him. It was an antique, a curiosity which his late grandfather, George Duncannon, had carried in days when Dublin was even less safe for Englishmen than now. "Just write the reference."

"Or else what? You don't frighten *me,* Captain—whatever your army rank, you've no jurisdiction here. I've no intention whatsoever of writing a reference for a woman I dismissed."

"Tell me why you dismissed her," Robert demanded.

"Because she was inadequate. Because she failed to chaperon my daughter, allowing her to dally with the type of person she knew I disapproved of."

"You knew where they were going," Robert pointed out. "Why didn't you put a stop to it yourself?"

He blustered at that, eventually denying the accusation but without much conviction. Robert stared at him, taking in the well-fed paunch beneath that cleverly tailored suit, noting the belligerent jowls and crafty eyes. He remembered Louisa and knew his anger burned on a short fuse. It was time to stop playing, to come to the point.

"You dismissed Louisa Elliott because she would not submit to your advances. Which, as I understand it, are somewhat perverted." He paused for breath, his nostrils flaring at the sudden memory of her bruised flesh. "You *will* write that reference," he insisted coldly, "because if you do not, I shall send to the elders of your church a list of dates and times when you visited Mrs. Dodsworth's brothel and availed yourself of the services of one particularly talkative Miss Leonie."

Like a deflated balloon, Albert Tempest sank into the nearest chair, his jaw hanging slack in disbelief. For a moment he wondered how he had been found out, but did not bother to ask; the details were too incontrovertible. The bastard had him cornered, and he knew it. "Blackmail," he whispered. "That's blackmail."

Robert nodded, his lips a grimly compressed line. "But more effective than yours, I think." Before Albert Tempest could recover himself, Robert raised his hand to the bellpull, and a moment later Moira appeared, her eyes flickering nervously at Robert before she addressed herself to her almost supine employer.

"Mr. Tempest would like a pen and ink and some paper," Robert said quietly, but the unexpected order startled her almost as much as the lilt in his voice. For a brief moment she stood and stared, then hurried to the study. The two men said nothing until her return. Robert thanked her; Albert Tempest dismissed her with a vague nod, and when the door had closed once more, he moved slowly across to the table.

Unbuttoning his jacket, Robert reached into an inner pocket and withdrew a piece of paper. "To save time and effort, I have already made out a suitable letter of recommendation. A fair copy on your own headed notepaper, in your usual hand, will suffice."

The reference was short and to the point; avoiding excessive praise, it simply said that Louisa Elliott was honest and diligent, that she had performed her duties as companion and governess to the signatory's children for a period of eleven months, and that he had regretfully released her from her employment at her own request.

There was something approaching a sneer on Albert Tempest's face as he added his careful, copperplate signature. "I wish you well of her," he said, holding the paper up to dry. "Of course she's no better than she should be, you realize that?" When Robert did not reply, he added: "Like mother, like daughter, don't they say? And the old woman was a bit of a whore in her day. Kept a Temperance Hotel, you know— pretty good cover, eh?"

Robert was stunned; for a moment he could neither move nor speak. He had expected unpleasantness, but he had not expected . . . Had he heard correctly? Albert Tempest's gloating chuckle assured him that he had.

"Shocked you, have I? The old woman never married, and nor did her sister. There's a whole family of 'em," he said with obscene relish. "No wonder young Elliott keeps his head down."

The short fuse reached the tightly corked keg of his rage and exploded. Robert's fist smashed into that foul mouth with such force that Albert Tempest spun around before he fell against the table, bringing the mahogany top off its central pillar in a splintering crash.

When his head cleared, some minutes later, he found that his adversary was standing over him, the expression in his eyes giving deadly earnest to the long, slender blade which hovered over his heart.

"I could have killed you with my bare hands," Robert said with deceptive softness. "I could kill you now, but, fortunately for you, you're not worth it. However, you'll give me the pleasure of taking back what you just said." The sword point moved, splitting the heavy broadcloth waistcoat with the ease of a scalpel.

Albert tried to raise his head; with bulging eyes, he watched that deadly edge withdraw slightly, saw it hover again, this time over his private parts. He swallowed, tasting blood in his mouth, and almost vomited with nerves. He was ready to agree to anything. Almost.

"Yes, yes—all right," he mumbled through his gashed lips. A tooth was broken, and it tore at his tongue. "Maybe I did—overstate—the case. I'm sorry."

"You lied," Robert insisted, bringing the point nearer.

"No," Albert stated emphatically. "I didn't lie. Louisa Elliott and her sister are—" he was going to say "bastards," but he thought better of it "—baseborn. And their cousin. It's the truth!" he cried desperately, seeing the hand that held the sword shake, the eyes above it flash with anger.

It seemed an eternity before that silvery blade lifted, before the man relaxed.

With a sudden movement, Robert swept up the two pieces of paper, secreting them inside his jacket. He sheathed the sword inside its slender ebony scabbard, and it made an ominous, hissing sound in the silence, then became again what it had seemed before: an innocuous, if old-fashioned, walking stick.

He turned sharply away toward the door, and with a heaving, shuddering sigh, Albert Tempest heard him leave the house.

TWENTY-FIVE

A curious sense of detachment dogged him. Unable to concentrate on preparations for the journey to Ireland, he instructed Harris to pack and left the house in his riding clothes.

The barrack square was deserted. Not a breath of air stirred the white dust beneath his feet. Shuttered and still, the mellow brick buildings slept on in the bliss of Sunday afternoon. Acknowledging the sentry's salute, Robert entered the stable block, inhaling the sharply ammoniac smell of the straw, walking past the empty lines to the tack room, where he selected his own mount's saddle and bridle. On the way back, the guard sergeant approached him, eyebrows arched in surprise.

"Riding out, sir?"

"That is my intention, Sergeant."

"Very good, sir. I'll send one of the men to help you saddle up."

"That won't be necessary. I'm quite capable of doing it myself."

The sergeant hesitated, disconcerted by the rarity of the situation. It was not the done thing, and he was not at all sure that it was not against regulations. "Well," he said slowly, "if you're quite sure, sir?"

"*Quite* sure, Sergeant."

The man hovered for a moment until, ignored, he turned on his heel, annoyed that the sentry had disturbed him for nothing.

Irritated by this reminder that mundane tasks were supposed to be beneath the attention of officers and gentlemen, Robert hoisted the saddle and marched out toward the near paddock where the hunters were munching quietly. Resting the saddle on the fence, he took the bridle and whistled for the big bay gelding. Pricking his ears, the horse looked up and, recognizing his master, ambled slowly toward him. He nuzzled Robert, taking the bit with no more than a token protest, and stood patiently while the saddle went on and the girths were tightened.

In the yard, the guard sergeant was waiting; after a rather stiff salute, he gave the captain a leg up into the saddle and watched him ride out onto the Fulford Road.

Once clear of the village, he left the high road, heading through fields toward the river. Reluctant at first, the big bay cantered along the towpath, then, at Robert's urging, broke into a gallop. The sensation of speed was release in itself; the wind roused Robert's blood so that he began to feel the pain which had eluded him earlier, and the pain made him dig his heels in, driving the horse on to greater effort. He was almost at Naburn before he eased back, the preceding miles a blur of golden fields and trees in dark summer leaf. By a small coppice he slowed his mount to a walk, turned in among the trees, and halted by the riverbank; his lungs ached, and he slid to the ground with a gasp, looping the reins around a low branch before he dropped down onto the grass.

The full force of Albert Tempest's words hit him then. Wincing at the man's obscene insinuations, he wondered how Louisa had ever become involved with a man like that, how she could have worked for him, when he obviously knew so much about her past. For Albert Tempest's words had carried the ring of truth; under those circumstances, Robert knew he had not lied, although in retrospect he hated even to think of it. He particularly hated himself, his foolhardy sureness, the conviction that he could avenge a dreadful wrong. The words he had uttered to Louisa came back to him: " 'Tis God shall repay." Good old Browning! Did he also know that pride preceded a fall? No wonder Louisa had been so afraid of Tempest, so terrified her cousin would tackle him, and so adamant that he, Robert, should not. There was so much at stake: not only her own reputation, but her mother's as well.

Mary Elliott came into his mind, and no matter how hard he tried, he could not fit her into the image of a Miss Leonie or Mrs. Dodsworth. She was no retired madam, he would stake his life on it; and surely Albert Tempest would never have employed Louisa if she had been. Much of what the man inferred was the product of an overheated and lascivious imagination.

With a sudden, piercing sense of the irony of life, he realized that the father of Mary Elliott's children could have been in his own position, tied to a loveless marriage without the possibility of release. He supposed he must have found love and happiness with Mary Elliott, a happiness that he, Robert, sought with her daughter. But in seeking the physical satisfaction of that love, he ran the risk of placing Louisa in the same position as her mother, of giving her children without the benefit of his name, who would themselves be illegitimate.

The enormity of that appalled him. His thoughtlessness, his monumental selfishness, rose suddenly to mock him. Never before, in all his casual encounters and brief affairs, had he considered the consequences;

at least not in any serious way. He was considerate enough, usually, to practice a certain technique which seemed to have worked over the years; as far as he knew, there were no fatherless children to his account. But perhaps that was luck as much as good management, and luck had a knack of running out.

He tried to imagine what Louisa's life had been like as a child and failed. With a rare flash of insight, however, he saw that strength and resilience he so admired as having less secure foundations than he had imagined, and her innate reserve seemed founded less on middle-class morality than a deep-seated reluctance to become involved with anyone.

She had not written. He had searched the mail each day, but there had been nothing from her. It seemed, in the light of what he now knew, very significant. She did not want him. How could she want him? In his distraction, Robert thanked Providence that she had left him the address he had asked for. He could at least write and tell her he loved her.

And if you really love her, a small voice said clearly in his mind, you will let her go.

Standing with the luggage, Harris watched the tall figure standing before the train departures board. He wanted the Leeds train, to change for Liverpool; what was taking him so long? He sighed, wishing the captain would hurry, wondering what was the matter. He had been so full of himself yesterday morning, but since then Harris had been able to get nothing out of him, not even proper instructions for packing. He hoped he had included everything and sighed again, glancing up at the station clock. If he stood there much longer, the train would be gone.

"At last!" Harris muttered beneath his breath.

"I've changed my mind," Robert said carefully. "I'm taking the Lincoln train instead. There's something I must attend to before I go to Ireland."

Having changed trains at Doncaster, Robert arrived in Lincoln shortly before noon. He purchased a map at the station bookstall, registered at the gloomily imposing Great Northern Hotel, picked at an indifferent lunch, and studied a railway timetable. The nearest station to Blankney was Metheringham, about a mile from the village, on the line to Spalding. He had just missed one train, but there was another in a couple of hours; the last one to return was shortly before eleven. Time enough, more than time enough to find her and talk to her.

As he handed in his ticket at Metheringham station, he asked the road to Blankney, finding the man's thick burr hard to comprehend and gathering more from gestures than words that there were two ways, the long route by the road or the shortcut by footpath across the fields. Once out of sight he consulted his map, finding no footpath marked, but willing to trust to luck and further directions, he set off in that general direction.

Crumbly chalk walls gave way to verdant hedges, and sure enough, at a bend in the road was a gate and a stile, the field beyond already laid waste by the reapers. Hunched figures picked over the ears of wheat left behind, some women, but mostly children, too far distant for him to hail. They stood and stared as he passed, but he walked on, treading the well-worn path between the stubble. It was good hunting country, he decided, visualizing the fallow fields of winter; a broad, undulating land with woody pockets, surprisingly familiar, like the Vale of York. Even the cottages with their mellow terra-cotta tiles lent conviction to the feeling that he had strayed but a short distance from his point of departure.

Banks of white cumulus swathed the southern horizon, but the sky above was blue and clear, the sun drawing beads of perspiration beneath his eyes and across his forehead. At the next stile he rested for a while, fanning his face with the brim of his hat. Although the suit he wore was a light tweed, it was still too warm for the day; with a shrug for the proprieties, he took off his jacket and slung it across his shoulder, continuing on his way.

To the right and beyond a belt of young trees, he suddenly saw a towering group of Gothic chimney stacks and, as he breasted a slight rise, gray roofs and mullioned windows, shimmering like a mirage above a golden, blood-spotted field. Pennons should be flying, he thought with a quickening of the pulse, and lances glinting in the sun.

And then in the stillness came shouts and laughter, jocular voices from behind the trees, and he saw the mirage for what it was, not a castle, not even an ancient fortified manor, but a group of cottages, the bold embodiment of another man's romantic dream.

Beyond the coppice, a knot of farm laborers with a reaping machine were gathered by the gate, calling to another who led a pair of heavy shires up the lane. As Robert approached, the men quietened and stood back, a couple faintly hostile, most frankly curious. The older ones touched their cap brims in polite deference to the stranger, and he bade them good afternoon, intending to seek further directions. But, with the other man's arrival, he hesitated, resting on the stile, his eyes taken, as always, by the sight of well-cared-for horses. With some lighthearted banter from the group, the man hitched the shires to the reaping machine, standing back as it was maneuvered through the gate and into the field.

He was well built, tanned, his thinning hair bleached almost white by the sun; as he turned, Robert experienced a slight shock of familiarity. The face was nut-brown, but the eyes which met his inquiring gaze were so like Louisa's, long and blue with thick-fringed lashes, and the shape of his mouth so very similar to hers: the man had to be an Elliott.

A broad grin spread slowly across the man's face as Robert made his inquiry. He took in the size and build of the stranger, the cut of his clothes, and the curling, military moustache and knew that this was Louisa's dashing dragoon. Who else would come looking for the home of John Elliott and not know he spoke to the man he sought?

"Well, sir, you've found the man, if not his home. In what way can I be of service?"

Stepping down off the stile, Robert extended his hand. "Robert Duncannon," he said with a smile and nodded toward the pair of shires. "Fine horses you have there, Mr. Elliott."

"If only they were mine," John replied with a grin. "Now, what can I do for you, Captain?"

Surprised, Robert met his gaze and held it, the struggle for explanations suddenly unnecessary. "I gather my reputation has gone before me," he murmured wryly. "Obviously, Miss Elliott has—mentioned me." The other man's eyes were more expressive than his nod, and Robert looked away, feeling curiously betrayed.

"Don't worry, Captain, I surprised her one bad day, months ago. It was the day her sister was married. I doubt she'd have told anyone, otherwise. But what brings you here? I gather she's not expecting you."

"No." Robert put on his jacket, wondering what to say, how little he could get away with. "Things have taken rather a surprising turn in York since she went away. I was going to write, but I had some leave due and thought to come in person. I hope you don't object?"

"That's Louisa's prerogative," John said with a laugh. He looked Robert over, rather as he would a new addition to the stable, noting the strong bone structure, steady eyes, and absence of affected mannerisms. With a smile, he nodded and began to lead the way toward the village.

On the left, a high gray wall screened the grounds of Blankney Hall; at the end, by the deserted little schoolhouse, they turned onto the dusty white high road, where the butler's house faced the hall gates, and in descending order of grandeur, miniature Gothic mansions sat back on either side. In every tiny garden, bees hummed amongst the flowers, hollyhocks and snapdragons, pinks, and scented stocks; Robert's hand brushed against a fading lavender hedge, and the sudden, familiar perfume lent presence to his thoughts.

John Elliott's cottage was the last and smallest, but, like its neighbors, the front garden was a riot of color, the side strip rich with soft fruits; at the back was a small orchard, dividing vegetables from the golden wheat beyond. A ripely pregnant woman pulled sheets and baby clothes from a washing line, and two plump toddlers played by the kitchen door.

"We have a visitor, Jenny. Where's Louisa?"

"In the kitchen," she replied with a shy smile of welcome for the stranger.

John strode into the house while Robert hesitated in the doorway, his tall frame blocking the light, so that Louisa looked up from her ironing, recognizing the shape of him, yet doubting it. She stood there by the kitchen table, flatiron paused in mid-stroke, sleeves rolled above the elbow, collar open, face flushed, her blue eyes wide with surprise.

Caught thus, off guard, she looked so very beautiful that for a moment words deserted him. John rescued the iron from Louisa's hand, covering the moment with laughter as he ushered them both through into the parlor.

"A mug of ale, Captain?" he asked and, without waiting for a reply, left them alone.

Transfixed, they stared at each other, one too surprised to speak, the other too reluctant. Robert's heart was racing, and he was afraid his apprehension showed like words on an open page.

"Robert, what's wrong? What brings you here?"

Sighing, he shook his head. "Must something be wrong?" he whispered, raising her hand to his lips. "I simply wanted to see you—had to see you—before I went to Ireland."

But Louisa was searching his face. "Are you sure?"

"Quite sure," he lied, standing away from her as Jenny came in with cool drinks for them both. At John's insistence that he should join them for their evening meal, Robert glanced quickly at Louisa, and at her smiling assent, he agreed.

"And in the meantime," John said, "why don't you get yourselves out for a walk? You must have plenty to talk about." Aware that he was needed elsewhere, John set down his empty tankard and made for the door. "I should take the path across the park—over toward the old lodge. It should be quiet that way, with everybody working at the harvest."

Catching the puckish twinkle in his eye, Louisa hoped Robert had missed it, but when she dared to glance up, she saw that he was smiling too.

"I should go and change," she said, blushing. "I can't go out looking like this."

But Robert insisted she looked delightful as she was and, taking her hand, followed Jenny through into the kitchen. As they came out of the house, John was already turning the corner; with a smile for his retreating back, Robert explained how they had met in the lane. "Quite a character," he commented, but Louisa simply laughed and shook her head.

Passing the gates to Blankney Hall, he turned to look at the imposing residence at the head of a curving drive. Palladian in style, but much rebuilt and added to over the years, it was a huge place, lacking White Leigh's uncluttered lines.

"It's up for sale," Louisa informed him, glad of a chance to change the subject. "If Edward's mother was still with us, she'd be delighted."

"Oh? Why's that?"

"Oh, she always loathed the squire's family, blamed them for the loss of the family fortunes. How true that is, of course, I wouldn't like to say."

"What happened?"

"To tell the truth, I'm not sure. Something to do with the Elliotts being great landowners here at one time, when Aunt Elizabeth was a little girl. According to her, the squire of the time—who would be this man's uncle or great-uncle, I think—tricked her grandfather out of what was truly his and made paupers of them all. But my mother says the old man was greedy and quite a gambler, so maybe he contributed to his own downfall. Apparently he invested heavily in some grand scheme or other and it failed. The land was lost, and the family were forced to sell up to pay the old man's debts. The shock of it killed him, but my mother's parents had to live with that humiliation for the rest of their lives. Aunt Elizabeth never got over it—she lived on grand memories for the rest of her days."

"And your mother?"

"Oh, Mamma's not like that. She was born after the fall, so to speak— her inheritance was no more than a good upbringing and a sound education. She escaped the bitterness, thank Heavens. But it's ironic, you know," Louisa added, looking back at the hall. "John was just telling me that the reason for the sale is because of the squire's heavy gambling debts." She laughed and shook her head. "Full circle."

But Robert was not impressed by that particular irony. Louisa had just revealed some interesting facts about her family, facts which he had already pieced together without her knowledge. "So," he said carefully, determined to have it from her own lips, "your mother and Edward's mother were sisters?"

All the amusement left her face. She glanced quickly up and away and, with a flat little sigh, said: "Yes, Robert, they were sisters. And no, they weren't married—either of them. I don't know who Edward's father was, because Aunt Elizabeth took that secret to the grave. But my father was a wool merchant from the West Riding. My mother idolized him: he was the one love of her life. Sadly, she wasn't his only love—he was married, you see."

"Just as I am," Robert said quietly.

"Just as you are," she repeated. "Life seems to go round in circles, doesn't it?"

For a while they walked on in silence. Then, crossing the high road, negotiating the dry ditch beyond, he took her hand. "Tell me something. Did you mean I should know? Or did you not realize what you were saying?"

Louisa did not immediately reply. As they climbed a slight rise, she turned and looked back at the village, the outlines of the cottages blurred by a shimmer of heat. "Does it matter? It wasn't something I intended to keep from you, if that's what you mean. You never asked about my father. If you had, I would have told you. Anyway," she sighed, "it's out in the open, and I'm glad of it. You had a right to know."

He moved in front of her and looked directly into her face. "I have no right to anything," he reminded her. "But I love you, even so."

Smiling then, her face lit up with sudden happiness. "Do you, Robert? It doesn't matter?"

He shook his head. "How could it?" he asked and reached for her hand, entwining her fingers with his. Hand in hand, they breasted the low hill, each intensely aware of that small physical contact; Robert's reasons for being there were quite forgotten.

Her face was largely hidden from him by the cotton sunbonnet she had swept onto her head as they left the cottage, but the neck of her plain cotton dress was still undone, revealing several inches of white throat and, as he looked down at her, the softly shadowed hollow beneath. She kept pace with him, the rise and fall of her skirt revealing a lace-edged petticoat and feet which were bare inside their thin leather slippers. There was an unusual softness and fluidity of movement about her which mystified as much as tantalized him, until he realized that she had abandoned those severely structured undergarments which were as harsh in this heat as they were restrictive. His grip on her hand tightened, but he looked away, suddenly realizing that the village with its white ribbon of road was out of sight, that fields and woods were all that lay ahead. He paused to peel off his jacket. "We may as well look as though we match," he said with a grin. Unfastening cuff links and collar studs, he rolled back his sleeves and removed his tie. "Wonderful," he breathed, relishing the cooler air on his skin. "Takes me back to my misspent youth. I loathed formal clothes—was the despair of my mother—so what did I do? I joined the army and have hardly been out of stiff collars since!"

Louisa laughed and pulled at his collar, which he stuffed into his jacket pocket along with the other items. There was a crackle of paper, a crackle which brought his reasons for this visit abruptly to mind.

"Is anything wrong?" she asked, alarmed by the sudden change in his expression.

After a moment's pause, he withdrew an envelope and gave it to her. "I could have posted this—but I didn't know what to write, didn't know how to explain it. There was too much chance of misunderstanding. Before you open it," he added tautly, "say you forgive me."

"For what, Robert?"

"For my crass stupidity."

Disturbed, she opened the envelope clumsily; when she saw Albert Tempest's handwriting, her fingers shook so that she could barely discern the words. She was silent for some time, her face such a blank mask that Robert could not tolerate it. He looked away, torn by self-recrimination.

"How did you get this?"

"Louisa, I'm sorry—"

She backed away from him, out of reach of his imploring arms. "How did you get it, Robert?"

He shrugged, at a loss for explanation. "On a calculated guess, I had him followed. He had a guilty secret with which I blackmailed him. Not very pleasant, is it? I'm sorry."

"He can't have given in easily," she observed, her mind racing over all the things Albert Tempest might have said.

"No, he didn't." The murmured admission was revealing.

"He told you, didn't he?" she cried. "You knew what I was before I said anything; that's why you weren't even surprised!" Angrily she thrust the letter back at him. "Keep it, I don't want it. It isn't important anymore." She turned on her heel and ran, down the side of the hill, toward the stream and the lane which ran beyond it.

He caught her as she hesitated on the bank, but she shook herself free. "How could you?" she demanded. "How could you go there after what he did to me and listen to the dreadful things he must have said?"

"If it's any consolation to you, I nearly knocked his head off for that. He has at least one broken tooth to remind him to watch his tongue!" As she gathered her skirts to cross the stream, he pulled her back and into his arms. "Don't be so damn stupid—it doesn't matter now. Believe me, Louisa, it doesn't matter!"

She continued to struggle against him, and through the fine linen of his shirt he could feel the angry heaving of her breasts. The thin veneer of his self-control broke apart. His mouth closed on hers almost roughly, silencing her protests; his tongue traced the outline of her lips beneath his own, parting, probing, setting fire to his blood. Pressing down on the hollow of her back, he drew her hard against him until her striving ceased, until he felt again that passionate response which had surprised him all those months ago. Anguish, guilt, longing, the reasons for that brief display of fury burned up like kindling in the hot desire which surged through both of them. Overwhelmed by its raw intensity, Louisa barely heard his whispered "Not here, my love, not here," and was aware only that his kisses were more tender, the pressure of his fingers lighter.

"There's a gate further up," she said breathlessly as his eyes scanned the impenetrable thorn hedge beyond the stream and led him toward it, to where the trees of an ancient wood overhung the lane.

At its heart stood a massive oak, its branches wreathed about with mistletoe; a place of magic and slanting sunlight and easy, pagan charm; an old trysting place for lovers which John Elliott had once known well.

Robert dropped down beside Louisa on the soft, springy grass. He lay on his side, not quite touching her. From the unfathomable depths of his eyes surfaced a flicker of amusement, and he released the bow of her sunbonnet, casting the offending article aside.

"I very much want to kiss you," he said at last.

Remembering the words, she gave him a sidelong glance. "Do you think you ought?"

Slowly he shook his head. "I'm sure I should not, for I want to make love to you."

Momentarily she closed her eyes, unable to prevent the rush of color to her cheeks. He was giving her every chance to back away, to say no; yet refusal was beyond her. Nothing mattered, as he said; the past was irrelevant, the future a haze of uncertainty. All that was important was here, in this moment, and she ached with longing for him. Her fingers trembled as she raised them to his lips, marking the lines of mouth and jaw, sliding up and around his neck, and, with gentle pressure, bringing his head down to hers.

Not knowing that he thought of Charlotte, she nevertheless sensed his reticence, attributing the curb he put on his passion to a fear of hurting or frightening her, a fear she was powerless to alleviate. Knowing what the ultimate act of love entailed was not the same as experiencing it; she gasped with surprise so many times as his hands gently explored her awakening body that she was aware of adding to his nervousness and wished for his sake to be more knowing in the ways of love. On another indrawn breath, his fingers touched her bare thighs, and for the first time he smiled, whispering teasing words of love at her lack of proper underthings, cutting short her murmured excuses with another kiss. She shivered as he found the soft warmth of her, his touch rousing emotions so intense, all thought ceased to be.

For a moment, the pleasure was withdrawn; she opened her eyes and he was above her, his face intense, almost afraid.

There was pain. Sharp and severe, so that she stifled a cry as he entered her, holding him tight and still. In the fleeting seconds which followed, she remembered all the whispered horrors she had ever heard, the pursed lips, the knowing eyes, the savagery to which men subjected their wives, and almost gave way to panic. But then that lilting, loving voice soothed her, and as she relaxed the shock abated. He began to move slowly, until deep inside her rose a strange, languorous pleasure, erasing pain and drowning memory, rising like a flood tide within. She wanted it to go on forever, was afraid she might die of it; but in those seconds before death he pulled sharply away, shuddering, crushing her against him with almost unbearable force.

"Oh, my love—I'm sorry, so sorry," he whispered at last, and she clung to him desperately, burying her face against his shoulder. "I couldn't, just couldn't wait for you." Cradling her in his arms, he kissed her gently. "Next time will be better. I promise."

With returning calm came awareness and understanding. She was suddenly conscious of the sun on her face, birds singing in the silence, dry twigs sticking into her back, and Robert's weight, which threatened to crush the breath from her body. But she was happy, ridiculously so. She kissed his eyes and mouth and tasted salt on her lips; smoothed rough waves back from his brow and saw the beads of sweat which clustered there; felt his shirt, damp and crumpled, clinging to her breast, and regretted nothing.

But the eyes which met hers were distressed and concerned; with a tender smile she touched his cheek, eager to dispel the anxiety which clung to him like a shroud. "I love you, Robert," she whispered, and the words were like magic; the shadows fled.

"I love you, too," he said softly, seeking her mouth afresh, "and I know I always will."

An air of normality, delicately precarious and constantly threatened by John Elliott's twinkling, knowing smile, was somehow maintained throughout the meal. Louisa had hurried upstairs to wash and change the moment they returned and, in an effort to preserve the secrets of the afternoon, kept her eyes modestly downcast. But her expression was overly demure, and her cousin was not deceived. The captain's unmistakable air of relaxed well-being added confirmation to John's suspicions, and his pagan spirit was exultant.

Louisa felt not guilty, but embarrassed, although Jenny affected ignorance and treated her with the usual kindly deference. It was something of a relief when the meal was over and Robert insisted that he must leave for his return train for Lincoln. She walked with him as far as the fields.

The men who had begun their task that afternoon were toiling still, far enough away and too engrossed to notice a pair of lovers standing in the shadows of the hedge. Above the western horizon the sky was streaked with red, Blankney's Gothic chimneys stark silhouettes between the trees.

Caught again by the magic of the place, Robert sighed, a sigh of such depth and contentment it brought a smile to Louisa's lips. He pulled her closer, delighted by the feel of her in his arms. "No regrets?"

"No, Robert, none."

"Nor me."

Neither of them spoke again for some time. The violet evening deepened to indigo, and in the fields the men called their farewells.

"Till tomorrow then," Robert whispered against her lips. As she murmured her assent, he took her hand and, feeling for the third finger, slipped onto it the warm gold of his own signet ring. "I wish it could be different," he said earnestly, "that I could be meeting you in that little church we passed this afternoon, making my vows to you publicly and legally . . . Without benefit of church or state, my love—nevertheless, with this ring I thee wed, and with my body I thee worship . . ."

Gently he touched his lips to hers, and for a moment she was too moved to speak. As she stared at the heavy gold ring, at the scratched but clearly distinguishable initials on the face, he said: "It will have to do for the time being—we can choose a proper one later."

It was too big, and hung heavy on her slender finger, but Louisa shook her head. "If you don't mind, Robert, I'd rather keep this one. It's all the wedding ring I want or need. I shall treasure it always."

Although Robert had assured her there was no need to worry about the hotel, Louisa paid minute attention to her appearance before setting off for Lincoln. She was terrified of letting him down in some way, very much afraid that even the best of her summer clothes lacked the style and expense befitting a cavalry captain's wife.

She arrived on the first train of the afternoon, wearing her newest dress, a cool blue and white print which enhanced the color of her eyes. In her lace-gloved hands she carried a frilly parasol, and perched atop her freshly washed and curled hair sat a tiny straw hat trimmed with blue silk roses and lilies of the valley.

Waiting for her on the platform, Robert bent to kiss her cheek as she stepped down. "How dare you tell me you don't look the part?" he breathed. "You're beautiful."

The porter he had appropriated took care of Louisa's trunk, escorting the couple the short distance to the hotel. She took Robert's arm, answering his desultory questions regarding her journey in monosyllables, praying that to onlookers her nervousness might seem to be boredom. In the foyer of the hotel, she unconsciously raised her chin, looking, as Robert laughingly said later, as though the place was less elegant than what she was used to.

With the servant tipped, the door of their room closed and locked, Robert swept her gaily into his arms, spinning her around in an excess of happiness. "I hardly dared believe you'd come," he said, laughing. "I was convinced you'd change your mind at the last moment or that your cousins would forcibly detain you!"

Remembering John's face, Louisa laughed with him. "My cousin is a wicked and devious man. You realize he sent us off toward that wood on purpose?"

With a wry smile, Robert removed his jacket and tie and tossed them onto a chair. "I rather thought he did. Does it bother you? That he tried to engineer things between us?" He grinned as she shook her head. "And what about the good Jenny? What did she have to say?"

Louisa shrugged her shoulders, but her cheeks were suddenly a deeper pink as she remembered the conversation they had had, the advice she had given Jenny so artlessly. "Nothing. I doubt she approved, but I said I was going home to York, and she didn't question it."

"How long dare you stay? Three, four days, perhaps?"

"What about Ireland?" she asked.

"Ireland can wait," he said and pulled her down beside him onto the bed. Ireland held no more terrors for him. His wife's rejection and denigration, her madness, the wrongs to which she had once driven him were now laid to rest beside the oak in that unnamed wood.

With a confidence which had not been his the day before, he slowly began to unfasten the tiny buttons of Louisa's dress, teasing her all the while, this time for the amount of underthings she wore. Naked, she was lovelier than he had imagined, full-breasted and long-legged, her skin smooth and creamy-fair, warm and receptive to his touch. In spite of her diffidence, and the modesty which drove her to seek the cover of the sheets, she did not flinch at the sight of him, and he loved her the more for that.

Relaxed in the knowledge that she both wanted and trusted him, Robert was content to take his time. He learned ways of pleasing her and taught her with gentleness the secrets of his own body. His patience was rewarded, for he discovered in Louisa a sensual nature which more than matched his own.

In the days that followed, they woke early, made love, and breakfasted, going out to enjoy the pleasure of walking in a place where they were strangers. Arm in arm, they climbed the hill toward the cathedral, browsed in shops, bought mementos, and talked. About Ireland, about White Leigh and the past; about York and more recent upheavals. Robert told her of Rachel Tempest's elopement, an event which he had almost forgotten in the heat of all that had happened since. The news distressed Louisa, but she was more concerned for Victoria, knowing the fretting and nightmares to which the child was subject, than for Rachel. Rachel would survive, and Louisa felt sure her father would swallow his antipathy to the Bainbridges, given time, although Robert was not so confident that they would forgive him for that intemperate display the night the young couple disappeared.

But their concern regarding these matters was distant, muffled by the increasingly sultry weather and their obsession with each other.

Late in the evening of the third day, the heavens opened; amidst a thunderous, flashing storm, they lay side by side, watching lightning rip jagged rents in the night sky. They talked about John Elliott with affection and wondered about the harvest at Blankney, although, from the warmth and safety of their little haven, even the importance of the harvest seemed remote.

After some minutes of companionable silence, Robert reached for his cigars and padded over to the window, watching the rain and hail beat a steady tattoo on the glass. "And your other cousin?" he asked quietly, for the reality of life in York was beginning to impinge upon his present happiness.

The cigar glowed, and as the lightning leapt again, his chest and thighs gleamed palely in the gray darkness. Louisa watched him, her thoughts uncomfortably echoing his. "Edward?"

"And your mother and sisters. What about them?"

"I don't know. I haven't thought about it."

"But we must. Tomorrow you have to face them, and I won't be with you." She did not reply, and after a moment he added: "I have to be able to go on seeing you, Louisa, which means they're going to find out sooner or later. Wouldn't it be better to be truthful from the beginning?" Still there was no answer, and he went on, searching for words he would much rather not have had to say. "How will your mother react to me as—well, as your lover? She virtually saved my life. She might think this a poor way to repay that kindness."

"I don't know. I didn't tell her you were married." She sighed and, with a shiver, pulled the sheets up to her chin. "My mother's attitude does concern me, but not half so much as Edward's. I dread to think . . ." But Louisa could not complete the sentence; it was impossible for her to frame Edward's disapproval into coherent thought. All her life she had been his favorite, and together they had shared so much. How would he react if she told him, baldly, that she was Robert Duncannon's mistress? He was so unworldly; how could he understand the kind of love that refused to be denied, the deep and overmastering passion she shared with this man? She saw Edward's face, eyes hurt beyond enduring, with perhaps a twist of contempt to that sensitive mouth, and thrust the vision away, unwilling to acknowledge just how much her cousin's opinion meant, how barren life would be without the security of his affection. For a fleeting second she sensed the void surrounding her, knew the awful truth of Robert's words, that he could not be with her, that he would never be with her when she needed him most. Because she was frightened, and even more afraid that Robert would sense her fear and mistake it for regret, she took refuge in bravado. "As for Emily and Blanche . . . well, dearest, to use one of your more eloquent phrases— I really don't give a damn what they think."

He laughed and came back to her. "Nor do I. So you'll tell them?"

"No, I couldn't Robert. They'll just have to find out in their own good time."

Staring down at her through the gloom, he gently laid a hand against her cheek. "Do you think that's wise?"

Seeking the comfort of his arms, she pulled him down beside her. "Perhaps not, but I'll have plenty of time to think things over while you're in Ireland."

"You really shouldn't put things off, Louisa. It would be better to tell them—get the anguish over quickly. Theirs as well as yours."

She looked up at him, and for the first time he noticed the rather stubborn set of her mouth and chin. "They're my family, Robert. Let me do things in the way I think best."

He would have challenged that, but he knew it might be weeks before they were together again; it seemed pointless to waste the time in argument. With a small sigh, he kissed that stubborn, pointed chin and gave himself up to the warmth and softness of her arms.

They traveled together as far as Leeds, parting with dry eyes and unsmiling lips beside the hissing Liverpool express. Robert's final kiss, almost filial in its brevity, went unnoticed among the covey of other embraces, noisy good-byes, entreaties, and promises to write.

A porter held the door of a first-class carriage, and as the couplings gave a sudden, warning creak, Robert stepped inside. There was a final banging of doors along the platform, a shrill whistle, a shriek of steam, and then, with a final groan of protest, the Liverpool train pulled slowly away.

As Louisa waved, she experienced a feeling of such desolation that, had it been possible to turn back the last few days, she would have done so. The void yawned, and she wondered what she had done. The past, in all its safe familiarity, was over, and the future lay before her like another country, peopled by strangers whose language she did not speak, whose customs she would never understand. Abruptly she turned and walked away.

Book Two
1892–1893

Let us off and search, and find a place
Where yours and mine can be natural lives,
Where no one comes who dissects and dives
And proclaims that ours is a curious case,
Which its touch of romance can scarcely grace.

From "The Recalcitrants,"
by Thomas Hardy

ONE

The week following Louisa's departure became more intolerable with each passing day. Edward's unease grew like a monstrous thing until he was illogically convinced more harm lay in wait for her in the depths of Lincolnshire than had ever walked the courts and alleys of Walmgate. Yet he could put no name to it, could find no rational reason for the anxiety which kept him awake into the early hours.

He dwelt on their brief interview that Saturday until he thought he would go mad for want of some explanation. It seemed against all reason that she should shun him so, especially after their recent weeks of closeness. He had basked in that renewed warmth, shared confidences with her, and gradually learned something about Robert Duncannon. Louisa's view, naturally, but allied to what he recalled of the man, he began to understand in part the feelings which had wrought such devastation. Whatever his intentions, she had turned him down, for which Edward was profoundly thankful. He supposed the man was handsome; he was certainly possessed of great charm; but the Irish, Edward considered, were renowned less for their fine morals than their sense of expediency. Anyway, the captain was of a different class; it would never have worked, even had marriage been on his mind, which Edward severely doubted.

Suppressing his own opinions, Edward had listened patiently and with compassion, delighted by the intimacy of her hand on his arm as they walked together, a tentative smile and the first spark of genuine amusement. Confident she was over the worst of it, he had begun to relax, secure in the knowledge that they were friends again.

Then, in one fell swoop, Albert Tempest's irrational behavior had destroyed that illusion. Louisa's trust in him was shattered; he knew not why. He wished desperately that she could have told him exactly what had been said; nevertheless, his imagination burned with possibilities.

In Fossgate, the temperature was arctic, and while Louisa's name was never mentioned, she stood between Edward and his employer like an invisible block of ice, freezing what had once been a passable relationship of more than twenty years' standing. Edward could not, in all honesty, say that he liked Albert Tempest, but he respected him, saw him as a straight, if occasionally ruthless, man of business who, in common with the rest of his class and contemporaries, attended chapel regularly and paid his dues toward the relief of the deserving poor. Admittedly, he was irascible and intolerant, but he rarely interfered with the bookbinding side of the business, which was all that mattered to Edward. Beyond the common knowledge of the workshop, and casual comments from Louisa, he knew little of Albert Tempest's private life and had no reason whatsoever to suspect the depths of his sexual proclivities.

Nevertheless, the fact that his employer had revealed his knowledge of the Elliotts' past, and with such apparent contempt, made Edward wonder for the first time what other festering sores lay behind that bluff and blustering exterior.

For some other, less explicable reason, the atmosphere at home in Gillygate was also strained. Mary Elliott was uncharacteristically sharp with Bessie and abrupt with the guests; whenever Edward mentioned Louisa, she either ignored him or changed the subject. She made it so abundantly clear that her daughter was not to be discussed that Edward's anxiety doubled, and he began to suspect there was far more behind Louisa's dismissal than he had been told.

Plagued by insomnia, he tried to take consolation in his writing, but the banal verses he composed to order were impossible to execute. Pain brought forth words which shamed him, an agony of longing and frustration so intense he could scarcely bear to scan the lines. In the close hours of the night, he examined his conscience until its tender fabric was almost threadbare, morbidly afraid that his feelings for Louisa surpassed the bounds of fraternal affection. Love, to Edward, meant the abnegation of self, a desire for the happiness and well-being of another, in which purely personal gratification had no place. By that rigorous yardstick, his affection for Louisa measured well, but the fact that they were first cousins, brought up within a much closer relationship, made him uneasy about the nature of that affection.

Toward the end of that unbearable week, he longed as never before for the seven days' holiday which was to follow and, in an unprecedented gesture of desperation, answered a long-standing invitation from a fellow poet in Whitby.

They had corresponded for more than two years; each summer it had been suggested that Edward stay for a few days as the elderly schoolmaster's guest. Edward had never refused outright, but the visit had been deferred each time as he found pressing reasons to keep him in York. For the first time, however, the city failed him; the heat was claustrophobic, and his unhappiness seemed locked within the walls of the Gillygate house. Longing to get away, he stood over Bessie as she laundered his best linen and pressed his only lightweight suit.

With a sense of relief that was almost euphoric, he set forth on the Monday afternoon.

The broad plain with its rolling wheatfields and open skies gave way, beyond Pickering, to the steep-sided valleys of the North York Moors. Climbing with dogged, chugging determination, the train twisted and turned its way through dark, sun-dappled woods, past narrow strips of cultivated land and rocky, dried-up streambeds. By the open window, Edward listened and watched, delighted by each turn of the track, surprise after surprise revealed like a nest of Chinese boxes and as quickly whipped away. At Levisham the valley broadened, climbed again; thinning coppices gave way to steep, sparse moorland, ocher against a fresh blue sky. Sheep grazed between purple cushions of heather, scattering in alarm before the engine's noisy, gasping approach; here and there, blackened, smoldering patches bore witness to the summer's dryness. Firewatchers studded this length of line, armed with besoms and spades, but while Edward wished them rain, he hoped for a few days' grace.

The fine, dry weather held, breaking in a series of storms the night before his return. In borrowed oilskins Edward was escorted to the station by the schoolmaster and his wife; they were a jolly pair, after forty years' experience on that exposed coastline quite undaunted by the weather. As rain dripped off roofs and gurgled in gutters, he thanked them for their kindness and hospitality, while the elderly lady presented him with a small, well-wrapped parcel, a suspicious twinkle in her eye. First, Edward pressed it, then he sniffed at it, and then he began to laugh. Four days' close proximity to the smoking sheds along the east cliff had quite dispelled his partiality for kippers.

"A little reminder of your holiday!" she said wickedly, and in spite of the rain, their parting was full of warmth and laughter.

Amidst pressing invitations to return, Edward left them, two cheerful, sou'westered figures waving on the deserted platform. He opened a book, but did not read it; his thoughts were too full of the friends he had made and long sunny days spent walking the cliffs, discussing poetry and prose, favorite authors, and cherished ambitions. At dawn they had watched the fishing cobles leave and in the evening counted their return, decks awash with gleaming herring; walked the length and breadth of Whitby, climbed the steep way to the church and visited the abbey ruins, where once, more than a thousand years before, the poet Caedmon had been befriended by the Abbess Hilda.

Halfway across the Vale of York, with the Minster in sight, he suddenly realized he had given Louisa barely a thought since leaving. Momentary guilt gave way to reason: he had needed to get away, as she had. Recalling the fears which had plagued him previously, he almost smiled; they seemed faintly ridiculous now, as much the products of insomnia as of grief and disappointment. During his time away, he had slept like a child, relaxed by the sun and the soft sea air. Happier, more confident, he looked forward to her return, hoping her holiday had been as beneficial as his own.

It seemed auspicious that he should see her tall figure ahead of him in the crowd beyond the barrier. Impatiently he handed in his ticket and hurried after her.

"Louisa! This is a delightful surprise!" He kissed her warm pink cheek. "What train did you come on?"

"What train?" she repeated faintly, suddenly bending to retrieve the parasol which had slipped from her grasp. "Oh, I—I came from Leeds. Wouldn't you know, I fell asleep and missed the stop at Doncaster."

"How fortunate," he said, smiling. "If you'd been earlier, you'd have had to struggle alone. Look, it's still raining—shall we have a cup of tea before we set out? It'll give the weather a chance to clear."

"If—if you want to," she replied, making a fuss of her basket and gloves and the trunk which seemed to be in everyone's way.

Having settled her with the luggage in a corner of the tearoom, Edward sat opposite, a smile lighting his eyes as he studied her. "You're looking very pretty," he remarked and was both amused and gratified to see a small blush come to her cheeks. "Is that a new dress?"

Louisa glanced down in surprise. "No. I've had it some time."

"Perhaps it's your bonnet," he said with a grin, pretending to study it from every angle; her blush deepened. "Anyway, whatever it is, you look remarkably well. How was Blankney?"

"Beautiful—it doesn't change."

"I keep saying I'll go back there one day. Perhaps I will, next year. Do you know," he suddenly observed, "you don't seem the least bit surprised to see me." Over the rim of his teacup, Edward looked at her, saw the momentary flash of guilt in those wide blue eyes and the confusion which forced her glance away.

"Oh, Edward, I'm sorry. I was miles away. Still in Blankney, I think," she added with a faint, uneasy smile.

"You were certainly miles away," he agreed, serious now. "I hope you're not still worrying?"

"About what?"

"About Albert Tempest."

The color which had rushed so easily to her cheeks now drained away; she swallowed, hard. "Oh, him! No—no, I'm not worrying about that. I've put it quite out of my mind, I assure you."

"Good," he said softly.

"Now you're looking worried!" she said with a laugh. "I really had forgotten it. You startled me, mentioning it, that's all. Coming home's made me realize that I've got a job to look for, and it won't be easy."

"You could stay at home, help your mother."

"For a while, yes. Anyway," she added brightly, "don't let's worry about that. Tell me where you've been. Out in the sun somewhere, I can tell—you're as brown as a berry!"

He laughed. "Whitby," he confessed, and as he began to tell her of his visit she relaxed visibly, laughing about the kippers. Encouraged, he went into greater detail, describing his friends and the little seaport with infectious enthusiasm; he told her everything that had happened, but not the reason for his going.

In the days that followed, he noticed an indefinable difference in her. To all intents and purposes she was pleasant and cheerful; nevertheless, he understood that Albert Tempest was not to be mentioned. It also seemed as though the wall Louisa had erected around herself in the days of her distress had been immeasurably fortified, as though she held a secret to which she was determined Edward should not be party. It nagged at him, and he watched her covertly, but the bland facade never slipped. She was always there when he came home from work, and fitting into the habit which had been reestablished, she sat with her mending and listened as he read aloud in the evenings.

Gradually his anxiety seeped away. Although he knew she was searching for some suitable employment, had been through more than one unsuccessful interview, it was something of a shock when she announced that she intended to take rooms of her own once everything was settled.

Only when her mother took refuge in tears did Louisa's guard show signs of breaking down. In a voice which shook with equal reproach, she begged her mother to understand that she could not go on indefinitely without properly paid employment; Emily had really worked for what she earned, but since her departure the two older women had organized themselves very well. Louisa's help was superfluous and largely inefficient; furthermore, she had grown used to her independence and wished to continue it.

The truth of what she said could not be denied, but it did not prevent their attempts to dissuade her.

Some three weeks after her return from Blankney, Louisa applied for a position at the Royal Station Hotel as a clerk. She wrote an excellent copperplate hand and had always been familiar with elementary book-keeping; providing her references went unchecked, she reckoned she might succeed.

As Edward took her through some intensive revision, he brought up the problem. "They're bound to want to know what you've been doing for the last twelve months. What will you say?"

She shook her head, unwilling to reveal Robert's hand in her affairs. "I don't know. Perhaps my old references will be enough."

"She can say I've been very ill," Mary Elliott said, looking up from her sewing. "She's been running *this* hotel—for me." Her face, set, determined, challenged either of them to find the flaw. "They won't check, and if they do, I'll tell them exactly what they want to know."

Despite Edward's unease, Louisa pretended to leap at the suggestion: she knew enough about the day-to-day running of a small boardinghouse to satisfy the most informed enquiry, and her experience could be an added bonus. Albert Tempest's letter, safe for the time being in Robert's hands, dispensed with any need to lie.

After her interview, she returned home flushed with the joy of success: the job was hers, subject to a month's approval, and both pay and hours were reasonable. She would work in a private office with two other young women, checking and filing accounts and preparing clients' bills. They did not handle cash: that side of things was dealt with by their immediate superior, a man.

"Dear me," Mary Elliott sniffed at this piece of news. "Don't they trust you? Or mustn't young girls sully their hands with filthy lucre?" She sniffed again as she totted up the week's takings. "You should tell them your mother's been running her own business for nigh on forty years—and never been within sight of the workhouse, thank God!"

Louisa sighed. "It's just a job, Mamma—"

"No, it isn't. It's the attitude. Men never credit us with more than half a grain of sense—frightened to death in case we get a bit of authority and make them look stupid!"

"When did a man ever try to make you look stupid?" Louisa demanded.

"Not for many a long year, my girl, not for many a long year."

"They're not *all* like that."

"No, but the worst type are the ones you'll be working for—the petty clerks and under-butlers of this world. The jumped-up nothings, bent on improving their lot over the backs of women like you. You do the work, they reap the reward. So just be careful, and don't try to be clever."

Thrilled as she was at the prospect of independence, Louisa refused to be influenced by her mother's opinions; after the iniquities of Blossom Street, she had high hopes of enjoying the job and doing well. Within the week, however, she was beginning to appreciate a spark of truth in her mother's statements: there was pettiness, there was snobbery, there was the kind of jealous hierarchy she had heard about in servants' halls, but never personally experienced. For the first time she began to realize that the position of governess, particularly in a grand house, had much to recommend it. A governess was alone, neither family nor servant, but she was her own mistress; a female clerk in a large establishment such as the Station Hotel was very low in an extensive pecking order.

With downcast eyes and occasionally gritted teeth, she did her work self-effacingly and well, so that there should be cause for neither reprimand nor envy. The money she earned represented the independence she coveted, the freedom to spend part of her life, at least, with Robert Duncannon.

On one of her rare visits, Blanche announced patronizingly that there was a room available in the ladies' apartment house where she lived, but Louisa dismissed that idea. Barely two weeks later, she was planning to move her books and belongings into furnished rooms off Marygate.

Until then, none of the family had seriously believed she would go, but it proved useless to remonstrate. Against all their arguments of cost and inconvenience, she simply repeated what had been said a dozen times before, until Mary Elliott begged Edward not to argue with her, and for his aunt's sake he kept silence after that.

On the Saturday afternoon, he halfheartedly helped to pack her things onto the hired cart. As it drew away down Gillygate, he offered to walk down with Louisa to her new home; she refused, but he insisted, strangely gratified to see her look genuinely upset as she bade her mother good-bye.

"Mamma! I'm not going far—don't cry."

"That's not what I'm crying for, and you know it!" Mary Elliott muttered fiercely and abruptly stepped back into the house.

Edward saw Louisa's chin come up, noted the now familiar shuttered expression close in. He turned away, walking slowly until she should choose to catch up. A moment later, as though nothing had happened, she remarked brightly on the fine afternoon, thanking Providence that yesterday's rain had not continued. He stared blankly ahead, neither caring nor seeing the fitful sun which illumined the far side of the street.

She was leaving, and a downpour of rain would have better suited his mood.

After a lengthy pause, he said: "Why do you have to do this?"

Exasperated, she dropped her hand from his arm. "Anyone would think I was going to darkest Africa! I'll be living less than half a mile away—you'll see me often. Why are you all being so possessive?"

The sudden anger surprised him. Until this moment, she had managed to preserve a patient and equable front. "Is that how it seems?" he asked with genuine contrition. "It isn't meant that way. I—we—are simply concerned for you, that's all."

"I'm sorry," she said with a sigh. Her hand stole back to its former place. "It's just that I need to take responsibility for my own life, make my own mistakes for a change, instead of having them thrust upon me. That way, I've only myself to blame. Can you understand that?"

Edward shook his head; he did not understand, knew only that he would worry about her, living alone.

"In a few days," she added gently, "I shall be twenty-six. I'd like to spread my wings a little before I'm too old and too afraid to leave Mamma's cozy nest. It may come to nothing," she murmured, half to herself. "I shall likely be back in a month or so, with wings well and truly clipped. But I have to know, first."

"Is it so important to you?"

"Yes, Edward, it really is."

TWO

*P*erched on the window seat in Louisa's tiny sitting room, Robert Duncannon stared out toward the river. It was a mild, hazy day, with leaves falling idly, one by one, like large yellow butterflies. A whole carpet of them had collected in the lane, and two small boys gleefully kicked their way through, leaving a brown wake behind. It was quiet along the river, barges and keelboats tied up and idle by Marygate Landing, but as the boys' laughter receded, from somewhere in the city came the sound of two distinct church bells, pealing the call to morning prayer.

Conscious of a feeling of deep contentment, he yawned and stretched, poured himself another cup of coffee, and reached for his cigars. "So, my darling, what shall we do today?"

In the bedroom, Louisa adjusted her collar, pinning her gold brooch just below the throat. In the doorway she paused, her eyes full of affectionate regret. "Didn't I tell you? I'm expected in Gillygate at one, for dinner."

Frowning, Robert shook his head. "No, you didn't."

"I thought you were going to be away," she reminded him with slight reproof.

"I know, I'm sorry. They had a death in the family, so the house party was called off. Tommy's quite put out—he was making some headway with the honorable Cecilia, but all that will have to go by the board for a while." He looked up at her, his eyes full of unconcealed desire. "How I wish it weren't necessary."

"What?" she softly asked, stirred again by his frankness, by that habit he had when they were alone of caressing her with his eyes.

"All this keeping up of appearances. You know I refuse far more invitations than I accept, but every now and then I *have* to say yes. However," he added, and there was suddenly a twinkle in that bright blue gaze, "I do have next Saturday to Monday free—no invitations and a late duty to follow. So don't make any other plans!"

"No, sir!"

Laughing, he caught her to him, pulled her onto his knee. "Do I detect a note of insubordination, Miss Elliott? Let me tell you, it simply will not do!" She kissed him lightly and made to free herself, but he refused to let go, returning her embrace with playful, half-teasing passion. "Come back to bed with me," he whispered, delighted by the conflict in her eyes.

Not far from the house, over Scarborough Bridge, a train gathered speed as it left the new station, and with its passing the house shook. As always, Robert winced, cursing the untimely intervention as Louisa smilingly escaped him.

"You chose this place," she laughed as he swore again, and evading his gasp, she began to clear the breakfast dishes.

"I saw that magnificent view across the park and down the river," he admitted with a rueful grin, "and never so much as thought of the railway. I think the landlord checked the timetable before he agreed to see me."

A firm, decisive rap at the door halted Louisa's reply. She paused, her hands full of dishes, shaking her head at his inquiring glance. Pushing the pots behind the screened area which comprised her tiny kitchen, she gestured toward the bedroom, and Robert stood up, gathering his cigars and jacket as he went.

Cautiously she opened the door. The visitor was Blanche, standing with pursed lips a matter of inches away.

"Well? Aren't you going to invite me in?" she demanded as she pushed past Louisa, her eyes raking the room, nose immediately detecting the pungent aroma of cigars. "Who on earth were you talking to?"

"No one. I—"

"You were, I heard you. Or should I say," Blanche corrected severely, "I heard a man's voice, presumably talking to you."

"Your ears did not deceive you, Miss Elliott," Robert said, and Blanche spun around, her eyes twin beads of shocked astonishment.

While taking in the fact that Robert had donned both tie and jacket in those few seconds, Louisa inwardly quailed. However much her mother might have suspected, now that Blanche had seen Robert here the secret would be well and truly out; there was little point in making excuses. Defeated, she shook her head wearily and sat down.

"Well!" Blanche finally exclaimed with eloquence. "Captain Duncannon! And what might you be doing here at this hour on a Sunday morning? But perhaps," she added with a scathing glance at her sister,

"I should know better than to ask?" With a sniff of disgust, she turned on her heel and made for the door, but Robert was there before her.

"Your assumptions could be wrong," he said softly.

She glared at him. "I don't think so."

"And no explanations are required?"

"I prefer not to sully my ears, thank you!"

"Yet I'll warrant you caught a whiff of scandal from somewhere and came to find out if it were true. I'll even wager you stood outside for quite some time before you knocked."

"How dare you!" Blanche hissed. "Stand aside, I wish to leave!"

"For goodness' sake, Robert, if she wants to leave, let her!"

He hesitated, then with a shrug he moved away from the door. "I'd appreciate it if you'd inform Mrs. Elliott that Louisa will not be there for lunch."

Angrily Blanche swept past him and, without a backward glance at her sister, was gone.

"I disliked Blanche on first meeting," Robert said into the silence. "Now I know why. She reminds me of my sister-in-law."

Blanche went straight to Gillygate with her news, inwardly raging with self-righteous indignation. Robert Duncannon's accusations had been humiliating. The man was insufferable. So typical of his class to launch an attack as soon as he was seen to be in the wrong. Her visit had been a chance one, a sisterly call before accompanying Louisa to dinner at their mother's house; she had suspected nothing, or almost nothing; although when she came to think of it, Louisa's ability to afford that cozy little apartment had been something of a mystery. With a flush of spiteful pleasure, Blanche realized that all was now explained. He paid for the place, of course he did, and she would tell their mother that for good measure. Suddenly she remembered two good new dresses Louisa had worn recently, a similar mystery until today. Tossing her head, Blanche marched briskly into the house; her sister was nothing but a kept woman, and she would take great pleasure in telling her mother so.

Distraught and agitated, Mary Elliott wrung her hands. "Blanche! How could you say such wicked things in front of Bessie?"

"What does it matter? They're true. And the whole of York will know about it soon enough!"

"Not if you keep your vindictive little mouth shut!" Edward shouted, and Blanche recoiled at his livid anger. "You've had your say and now forget it! I'd like to hear Louisa's side of things before I listen to any more from you!"

"Oh, that's right, stick up for her! You always did, didn't you? She could never do any wrong in your eyes, could she? Well, as far as I'm concerned, she's shown herself in her true colors at long last—she's a shame and a disgrace!"

"Be quiet, Blanche! You've got Bessie weeping in the kitchen and your mother sobbing in here. Haven't you said enough?"

"Haven't *I* said enough? Hasn't she *done* enough, more like! You're incredible!" she cried furiously. "Anyone would think it was all *my* fault that Louisa is living in the lap of luxury and behaving like a prostitute!"

She reeled as Edward's open hand cracked across her face. "Don't ever use that word again—not in this house and *never* about your sister!"

"Where—where are you going?" she sobbed as he grabbed his coat and began to struggle into it.

"Where do you think I'm going? To see Louisa, of course. And don't you dare leave this house till I get back."

Edward strode along Bootham as far as the village of Clifton, past the Green, down the lane called Water End, and back along the muddy towpath. Ten days previously the river had flooded, leaving a silted tidemark on either bank, but he plowed through it angrily, heedless of shoes or spattered trousers. An elderly gentleman in galoshes stared at him curiously, but despite the hazy sun there were few other people about. By the time he reached Scarborough Bridge he was calmer, already regretting the stinging slap he had administered to Blanche. For a few minutes he stood in the shadow of the arch, watching little convoys of leaves floating past; some were caught by the dead flotsam of a tree branch, others clustered thickly by the bank, obscuring the water's edge. It was a strangely depressing sight; hypnotic, too. With an effort, he dragged his eyes away, wondering what he was going to say, how to broach such a subject in front of a man who was a virtual stranger. Although Robert Duncannon was no stranger to Louisa, he reminded himself bitterly.

Suddenly, the full force of Blanche's words swept over him. Looking back, adding up all the little inconsistencies, he felt he should have known what was going on, that in some way he had failed Louisa; yet now that his anger was gone, every muscle of his body felt leaden, weighted by apprehension and a terrible, aching foreboding. But finally he forced himself to move, to walk the last hundred yards which led to the house.

The small garden was neglected. Graying banks of hydrangeas flanked the path, and beside the front door a skeletal rose hung, its single surviving bloom a pathetic memorial to better days. Edward opened the front door and slowly climbed the stairs, his mind blankly refusing to frame even an opening sentence. Numbly he rapped twice at the door. There was no reply. He knocked louder, but the silence of empty rooms remained within; he knew they were out, yet a peculiar sense of disappointment kept him standing there. He did not know what to do.

A moment later a door banged somewhere below; a man came running up the stairs, two or three at a time. Edward turned to see the tall figure of Robert Duncannon come up the last few steps at a slower pace, almost hesitant as their eyes met.

"We saw you from the other side of the river," he said quickly and paused to catch his breath. "I ran across the footbridge—didn't want to miss you. Louisa will be along in a moment." He took a key from his pocket, opened the door, and stood aside for Edward to enter. "We didn't expect you, but in a way, I'm relieved you've come."

Removing his hat and coat, he offered to take Edward's and was halfway across the room with them when he suddenly turned, laid the coats across a chair and the hats side by side on the table. Edward stood by the open door, reluctant to take the offered seat. With each unconscious act, Robert Duncannon confirmed Blanche's every word. Although Edward was conscious of the other man's tension and embarrassment, his own emotions were numb. He was powerless to understand it, shook his head as though to prompt some return of feeling, and bit the inside of his lip, hard, to test physical sensation.

"I don't know what to say," the other man confessed, and Edward felt an absurd echo in himself. "Except that I love her."

"Do you?" Edward heard himself ask and saw those black-lashed eyes close momentarily, hands gripping the chair on which he leaned.

"I wish it were possible to tell you how much," he said. "You'd not condemn me then."

Wouldn't I? Edward thought, suddenly seized by an angry desire to voice a thousand condemnations. He passed a hand over his eyes, afraid that once he found his voice, the act of speech would rob him of all self-control. He felt, rather than heard, Louisa behind him, turned, and she was standing in the doorway, her eyes wide with apprehension. There was nothing brazen about her; she looked unhappy and very frightened, her glance flickering nervously toward her lover and back again. Edward held her gaze, trying desperately, in that one unguarded moment, to convey all his innermost feelings: sorrow, reproach, regret, the anguish of the scene with Blanche; above all, his love, unconditional and unchanged.

He saw the tears in her eyes, felt the unspoken plea for forgiveness, then she was in his arms and he was overcome by a riot of conflicting impressions and emotions. Conscious of Robert Duncannon's presence in the room, he tried to resist that embrace, but as his arms closed around her, all sense of propriety broke down. He held her fast, knowing that he must do his utmost to persuade her to return with him to Gillygate.

"Why didn't you tell me?" he whispered as her arms slid from around his neck. He felt her fingers against his cheek, and he held them there. "If *only* you had told me!"

"I couldn't, Edward, I'm sorry. And the longer I left it, the more impossible it became."

"But Blanche, that it should be Blanche!"

"I know, I'm sorry, I didn't expect her, truly I didn't."

"You must have known you couldn't keep a secret like this?"

"Robert begged me to tell you—he said this would happen. But—"

"You've upset your mother terribly—you realize that?"

Louisa began to weep; he pulled her close, holding her gently this time. "Enough now—stop your crying. You must pack your things," he said firmly, "and come home with me."

Breaking free, she stood away, her eyes meeting his. "No. I'm not going back."

"But you must. This can't go on—" He looked around, but Robert Duncannon was gone; the faint aroma of cigar smoke, the partly open bedroom door, revealed his whereabouts, and Edward dropped his voice. "It isn't right, Louisa. No matter how much he pretends to love you—"

"It's not pretense!"

"All right, I'm sorry." In a gesture of mute appeal, he spread his hands. "But tell me this," he said at last. "If he loves you as much as he says he does, why doesn't he marry you?"

"He can't, Edward; it's not possible."

"I suppose he thinks you're not good enough?" he demanded angrily.

Before she could find an answer, the captain returned, his eyes hard with resentment and hostility. Crossing the room to Louisa's side, he slipped a protective arm around her shoulders. It was obvious he had overheard every word.

Cold blue eyes bored into his, but Edward refused to look away. "Well?" he challenged. "Why don't you marry her?"

Briefly the captain lowered his gaze. A cynical smile touched his lips. "And add bigamy to my other sins?"

For a second the whole room seemed to darken and recede; Edward gripped the back of a fireside chair for support until his head cleared.

It seemed incredible that this should be happening, really taking place. How, in the name of God, could Louisa be involved in a situation like this? His mind resolutely refused to accept it.

Feeling as though his limbs were turned to liquid, he sank into the chair. Beside him, Louisa lifted his unprotesting hand to her cheek, murmuring meaningless apologies.

From somewhere, the captain produced a bottle of brandy, poured a generous tot, and handed it to him. "I'm sorry," he said, with unexpected sincerity. "That was below the belt."

With some reluctance, Edward accepted the proffered glass and the apology. He watched the other man pour himself a drink and down it before Edward had had a chance to sip his own. Unused to spirits, Edward drank the brandy like medicine, quickly and with distaste, but his wits cleared at once.

"I had no idea, Captain Duncannon, that you were married."

"No," the other man acknowledged in the same conversational tone. "It's been a well-kept secret. One day, if you give her the chance, Louisa might tell you about it."

"I'd prefer to hear it now," Edward said. "From you."

"Would you, now?" There was a momentary spark of anger, followed by a suddenly weary smile. "Well, as I'm not disposed to bare my soul at this precise moment, Mr. Elliott, I'll give you the facts.

"I was married a little over five years ago. I have a daughter aged four. My wife is . . ." He paused, stared at his empty glass, and rose to pour another drink; Louisa gripped Edward's hand convulsively.

"She's quite mad, I'm afraid. Were it not for my long-suffering family, she'd no doubt be locked up in a place like Bootham Park. No," he amended, "more like the Retreat, I think. The Quakers are a little more enlightened, thank God."

Edward was stunned. There was nothing he could say, not even to question the man's veracity. In the face of such anguished brevity, to seek for proof would be an insult.

"It may perhaps sound a little trite," he went on, "but knowing Louisa has made a vast difference to my life. Until I went back to Ireland this last time, I hadn't realized to what extent. I really enjoyed being there," he admitted with a smile. "Spent time with my daughter and had not the slightest desire to see my wife. And before you condemn me for that, let me assure you that *not* seeing Charlotte is probably the kindest thing I've done in years." With a sudden chuckle at his own irony, he raised his glass to Louisa.

"You know, Mr. Elliott, for a moment there—earlier on—you had me worried. I thought—I really thought I might lose her!"

Jerked out of his momentary pity, Edward tightened his grip on Louisa's hand. "And when you leave York, what then?"

"Oh, the odds favor Dublin, I think. The promise of Home Rule is both tantalizing and troublesome, wouldn't you agree?"

Edward's jaw tightened with irritation. "I meant what about Louisa? What will she do when you've gone?"

"She'll come with me, of course."

Shocked beyond speech, Edward gazed from one to the other, amazed that such feckless immorality should wear a seemingly cohesive face. "How can you even consider it? And Ireland, of all places! If Gladstone gets his way, there'll be trouble from the Unionists, and if he doesn't—

"—there'll be trouble from the rest, landowners and peasantry alike. But Louisa will be safe," he said patiently. "Do you think I'd endanger her life?"

"I don't know. You seem to have scant regard for her future happiness and even less for her reputation!"

Again there was that sudden flash of anger, sustained this time. "I'll let that pass," he said icily. "Under the circumstances, you're entitled to think that. Nevertheless, it's not true."

"Isn't it?" Edward demanded. Suddenly he was furious. How dare this stranger, with his fine clothes and cool self-confidence, walk into Louisa's life and so blithely ruin it? However miserable and unfair life had been to him, he had no right to assuage his sores at Louisa's expense. For she would be the one to pay in the end, of that Edward had no doubt whatsoever. Furiously he wished her elsewhere; her presence forced too tight a rein, and he would rather be damned than exhibit such belittling emotion in front of her.

Abruptly he stood up, his gaze traveling between the two of them. "It's wrong," he said shortly. "However you phrase it to yourselves, it's quite wrong."

"I think that rather depends on your point of view."

"No, Captain. Morally, practically, ethically—it's wrong. Louisa will suffer, not you. I should have thought you were intelligent enough to see that."

Before he could reply, Louisa stepped in. "Edward, you don't understand; the decision is mine to make."

"Then you're a fool," he said bitterly, before the words could be stopped. "I expected better of you than this! People will talk, you know— and you, above all, should know how malicious they can be. And what of your mother? Don't you think she's suffered enough?" He knew she was hurt, but he could not hold back the final thrust. "What if *she* should disown you?"

"That's a matter for her to decide," Louisa said bravely, but her lip trembled nevertheless. On a shuddering breath, she asked: "And you, Edward? Now that you know, will *you* disown me?"

He saw that her decision was made. Saddened beyond measure, he gathered up his coat and hat and walked toward the door. "Would it matter if I did?" he asked quietly, and as he uttered the words, he felt sick and defeated.

She grasped his arm, made him turn to face her, and he saw his own anguish reflected in her eyes. "Of course it matters!"

"It would be easier to deny my own existence," he whispered. Removing her hand from his sleeve, he closed the door quietly behind him.

Later that night, as he lay in bed with Louisa curled up beside him, Robert stared into the darkness and thought about Edward Elliott. Having met the man only once before, Robert's impressions had come largely through Louisa, and it seemed she had omitted far more than she had revealed.

Forgetting that little volume of verse, Robert had imagined a father figure without benefit of wife or child; an inflexible man, old before his time. Now he knew the error of that assumption, for Edward Elliott was far from old, and while he possessed a fine sense of duty and the morality of his class, he was obviously willing to sacrifice that, and more, on the altar of his love for Louisa.

Briefly he relived that palpitating moment of her return, seeing again, like an intruder, the naked intimacy between those two; felt the same astonishment as she flew to her cousin, and his arms, at first raised in protest, slowly tightened across her back. In the darkness that contorted face came back to him; angrily Robert turned, trying to block the image which stayed so clearly in his mind. Louisa had never so much as intimated the depth of that relationship, and the revelation shocked him still.

Disturbed by that sudden movement, Louisa stirred; her voice, blurred by sleep, murmured his name.

"I ought to go," he said. "I'm on early duty."

"It can't be morning *yet*," she protested sleepily.

"It's just after two, and I haven't slept at all. If I fall asleep now, I'll never wake in time, nor will you."

"But if you go now," she recited, "the remarkable Harris will make sure you don't oversleep."

Disengaging her arm, he sat up. "That's right. That's what he's there for."

Louisa yawned. "Why haven't you slept? Were you thinking about yesterday?"

"What else?"

"Oh, Robert, I'm sorry. I thought we'd said it all, and I was so tired, I'm sure I fell asleep before my head touched the pillow." Lightly her fingers touched his arm. "Won't you tell me what's on your mind?"

Privately he acknowledged the justice of her words. They had talked for hours, covering every imaginable aspect, every contingency which could possibly follow the events of the day; discussed all bar the one thing which lay at the forefront of Robert's mind. In the silent, sleepless hours, he had tried to view the relationship between Edward and Louisa from every conceivable angle; each time, however, he returned to his original conclusion. Now he must face her with it.

"That's better," he murmured as he lit the bedside lamp. "I can see you now."

Her eyes, large and lustrous in the gentle glow, blinked as they scanned his face. "Are you angry with me?"

"A little," he admitted.

"Whatever for?"

As always, he was touched by that quality of innocence she had when newly woken, as though for her each night's sleep erased the cares and irritations of a heartless world. He tried to suppress the tension in his voice, to speak gently and reasonably. "Why didn't you tell me about Edward?" he asked. "I'd have tried to understand."

Perplexed, Louisa shook her head. "What is there to understand? I don't know what you mean."

With a sharp sigh of frustration, he lowered his eyes, trying to control the jealous anger which threatened, suddenly, to erupt. "To my mind, Louisa, there's a lot you haven't explained. You might have told me how important you are to him."

"Of course I'm important to him—he practically brought me up. He's been like a brother to me. No," she corrected," more than a brother; he's been a friend, too."

"If that's all he was," Robert said tensely, "why were you so reluctant to tell him about us?"

Crossly Louisa turned away. "After what happened this afternoon," she said, "I should have thought it was obvious."

"Oh, it is," he whispered. "Believe me, it is."

"What do you mean?"

"Do you really not know?" Robert demanded. "The man's in love with you!"

THREE

After Robert left, Louisa slept little. She rose at six and made a pot of tea, but breakfast seemed out of the question. Her stomach threatened revolt at the thought of food, cramps knotted her abdomen, and her head ached.

Shivering in the damp chill of early morning, she recognized the symptoms for what they were, but instead of relief, she felt merely betrayed, as though her body had joined a painful conspiracy to make her suffering complete. It seemed grossly unfair that the curse of womankind should inflict itself upon her on a day when she was least able to cope with it. She found her supply of neatly hemmed and folded sheeting, washed carefully, and began to dress.

Wearing a large apron, she set about her everyday tasks, carrying the covered chamber pot down two flights of stairs to the privy in the backyard; the ashes from yesterday's fire were riddled and tipped into a bucket, and, with an effort, coal was brought up the same two flights, the fire laid ready to light. After scrubbing the hearth and polishing the brass fender, she washed her hands and made the bed, desiring nothing more than to creep back into it, to sleep away her anguish and physical distress.

A second cup of tea, hot and sweet, revived her a little; donning her cloak, she set off in the half-light toward the river. There was a shortcut to the station via a footpath attached to the railway bridge; too short a journey to improve the circulation, yet long enough to chill the bones.

With pinched cheeks she warmed herself for a moment by the office stove, chafing her hands in an attempt to restore the flow of blood. She was earlier than usual; and by the time her chattering companions arrived, Louisa had managed to regain something of her normally efficient demeanor. The high stool did nothing to ease her physical discomfort, however; throughout the day she worked slowly, her mind preoccupied more with Robert than with columns of figures. He was wrong about

Edward, she knew it with every fiber of her being; yet last night it had been impossible to convince him.

Robert had absolutely no conception of the kind of life she and Edward had led, marked by the secret stigma of illegitimacy, terrified to form close relationships for fear of being found out. It had thrown the family in on itself, made each dependent upon the others, protected by a conspiracy of love which had existed for so many years they were hardly aware of it. Back in Tanner Row, Louisa thought, they had all been party: her mother, Aunt Elizabeth, Bessie; and afterward in Gillygate it was carried on, the pact stronger than ever, because at last the secret appeared to be safe. Blanche had years ago blotted out the past and, in her own way, escaped; Emily had stepped right out into marriage and respectability. The enclave had grown smaller, and had it not been for Robert, Louisa knew she would never have wanted to break away. The pain she was suffering now was largely because the security of that life was all she had known, was all she was ever likely to know; she had been desperately afraid that, with Robert, her bridges were burned and was even now unsure of the way back, should she need to return.

Only through Robert's stubborn insistence did she begin to see the peculiar insularity of the Elliott household. He thought her work as a governess should have broadened her outlook, helped her to understand its abnormality, but that had not been so. The world of great houses was too far removed for it to have had any bearing on her own life. Children lived apart from their parents, belonging to the realm of nannies and servants. Sent away to school, often at an early age, family became for them a part of duty and heritage, abstract and strangely impersonal. Louisa thought it unnatural and said so. Affronted, Robert accused her of exaggeration; his life, for one, had followed a different pattern. If anything was unnatural, he had cruelly added, it was Edward's relationship with her. In his opinion, Edward should have been married years before, and so should she. Robert loved his sister, but had he ever been guilty of such a display of unrestrained passion, people would have thought him very odd indeed.

On that bitter, accusatory note, he had left. Anguished and smarting, Louisa relived the words and emotions of their first quarrel, wondering when, and if, he would be back. He had muttered something about Tuesday, but she doubted him. His anger had been intense, his convictions so opposed to hers, she wondered how either of them could forget it, if their former intimacy could ever be recaptured.

Walking wearily home through town, she bought fresh bread, bacon, and eggs at a grocer's on Bootham. It was not a meal she particularly relished, but it was easy enough. For her, cooking was more of a trial than a pleasure. The newfangled gas cooker unnerved her, so that she served vegetables either half-raw or burned; nothing tasted as it should, and she longed, suddenly, to go home, to have her mother set a beautifully prepared meal in front of her. She could have found her appetite then.

Robert always laughed at her apologies, stoically eating all she presented. Secretly it was a relief to her that he ate most of his meals in the mess, that his demands for food were usually limited to breakfast or an occasional light supper. Occasionally he took her to a discreet hotel where they were able to eat in comparative privacy. The first time, she had worn her best black dress, but after that he had insisted on something a little less somber, had even accompanied her to a dressmaker's to view a selection of evening gowns. Knowing her sense of frugality, her fixed impression of herself as a plain woman, he had not trusted her to choose the kind of gown he had in mind. Envisaging arguments, she had been surprised and forced to admit he had excellent taste. He had chosen a rich russet velvet, simply and, as a concession to her sense of propriety, modestly cut. As Louisa held the soft material against her shoulder, she saw that it brought out gold lights in her hair and, by sheer contrast, heightened the color of her eyes.

"You're as lovely as the autumn," he had whispered the first evening she wore it. "And autumn was always my favorite season."

And was their affair to be as briefly beautiful? she wondered. With a heavy heart she mounted the two flights of steps, found her key, and let herself into the cold and strangely lonely apartment. It had lost its charm; as she bent to retrieve a letter from the mat, she swore she would not stay.

Staring at the envelope, she wondered who could have sent it. The writing was open and unformed, like a child's. She thought of Victoria Tempest, then dismissed the idea; her handwriting was surely neater than this. Quickly she tore the envelope open, glanced at the bottom of the flimsy sheet, and saw that the sender was Moira Hanrahan.

"Dear Miss Elliott," the letter began, "I hope ye are well as I am. I no ye be workin now from ye last Letter but Dearly would I like to see ye Miss. I will call Tuesday near seven. If ye be out dont upset yeself. Ye obdnt servant Moira Hanrahan. P.S. I niver went to shcool much. I hope ye can read dis."

Sitting down suddenly, Louisa pressed the letter to her breast. Dear, dear Moira! She had seen her once, while still in Gillygate, but not since. Well, she would make an effort to be back for seven and would try to make a decent meal for them both, something easy which would surely be an improvement on Mrs. Petty's leftovers.

Strangely heartened by the letter, Louisa set to lighting the fire, then made herself a cup of tea. Hastily she penned a reply to Moira, telling her to wait if she should happen to be delayed, then a few lines to Robert, informing him of Moira's visit, asking him to delay until later in the week.

Glancing at the clock, she hurried out, determined to catch the post from the main office on Lendal.

It was bitterly cold, full moon and stars struggling to shine through the usual pall of smoke; her face tingled, and her hands, in woolen gloves, were bloodless by the time she returned.

While she fumbled for her key the door was opened, and by some undeserved miracle, Robert was standing there, eyes troubled and apologetic.

They faced each other for a moment, then he reached for her and held her close. "I'm sorry," he whispered. "I was angry and jealous—forgive me."

Louisa nodded. "I've had an awful day," she admitted.

"Me too," he said and kissed her forehead. "By the time I'd walked all the way to Fulford, I was thinking rationally again. There's nothing like a cold night and a long walk to restore a modicum of sanity," he said with a short laugh. "But I've had the very devil of a day—couldn't wait to get back to see you. Then, when you weren't in, I thought you'd gone home."

"Did you?"

"I did indeed. Then I saw the fire and guessed you'd be back sooner or later."

Louisa explained where she had been and why. Studying her face intently, he asked whether she had eaten; when she shook her head, he tut-tutted impatiently.

"If you gave up that ridiculous job, my love, you'd have time to cook yourself proper meals. But we won't argue the point," he added hastily as her chin came up. "What is there?"

With a heavy sigh, Louisa indicated the packet of bacon and the small bag of eggs.

"Very well. Sit yourself down in front of that fire while I attempt to cook them. You look absolutely dreadful—not at all fit to look after yourself." Removing his jacket, he tied one of Louisa's capacious white aprons around his waist and proceeded to light the gas.

Smiling at the picture he made, she said: "And when did you last cook yourself a meal, Robert Duncannon?"

"Ah, every now and then, the remarkable Harris gives me what he calls survival lessons. He's afraid that in the rather unlikely event of war, he may be killed, and I shall subsequently starve!"

"You're a terrible liar, Robert!"

Cutting thick slices of bread, he emphatically shook his head. "Not at all. I can make a fire, brew tea, make a disgusting cup of cocoa, fry bacon, and draw a chicken. Harris informs me my next lesson will be rabbit stew." Sticking the slices of bread onto a toasting fork, he handed it to Louisa. "Here, toast that while you toast your toes!"

"But first catch your rabbit!" she taunted, her nose twitching pleasurably at the aroma of sizzling bacon.

"No problem," he assured her. "I was poaching my father's game and outwitting the keepers when I was twelve years old. Of course," he admitted with a shrug, "it was simply a jape to me, but for my companions, a little more serious. A slight matter of life and death to some of them. I suppose they involved me because they knew I'd get them off if we were caught."

"And were you?" she asked, amazed by that casual revelation.

As he set a tray with plates and cutlery, salt and pepper, Robert shook his head. "A man is easier to stalk than a deer. Than most game, come to that. I had some rare companions," he said reflectively. "I sometimes wonder whether they're still at it. I hope not—William's not nearly so tolerant as my father was."

"Do you ever see them—when you go home, I mean?"

"We exchange words in passing. And Letty," he added cryptically, "keeps her eyes open for me." With a sudden, soft curse, he said: "I'm afraid I never passed the egg test, my love. Your eggs are more scrambled than fried!"

"Never mind, they'll taste the same." She watched him buttering the toast, hands capable, eyes calm and good-humored, so very different from the man who had slammed out of the house the night before. This morning she had thought never to see him again, yet here he was, displaying a most unexpected side of himself.

"You're a remarkable man, Robert Duncannon."

"Of course."

"You're also insufferable," she muttered, taking another forkful of the crisply delicious bacon. "You even cook better than I do."

"But I don't look as pretty in an apron," he retorted and promptly removed it. "Feeling better?"

"Mmm."

"Good." Reaching into the cupboard where she kept the brandy, Robert poured himself a tot and sat down, stretching his long legs out toward the fire. For a moment, with a contented sigh, he closed his eyes. "I think I might just allow you to make your own cup of tea, darling—you're decidedly better at that than I am."

Louisa laughed. "It might not be much, but we've all got to be good at something!"

Slyly, watching her from beneath lowered lids, he said: "Oh, I don't know, I can think of other things . . ."

Blushing, she dropped her gaze. "No," she whispered, "not tonight."

With a theatrical groan, Robert clapped a hand to his forehead. "My God, when I think of the invitations I've turned down!" Laughing, he reached for her hand. "Never mind, sweetheart, I could do with a night in my own bed. Didn't get an awful lot of sleep last night, what with one thing and another. Tell you what," he added, dropping a kiss on the end of her nose, "I'll stay till you go to sleep, then get a cab back to Fulford."

FOUR

Wearing her best hat, a lavishly decorated bright blue straw which, in view of the weather, was hardly suitable, Moira was waiting on the upper landing when Louisa arrived home from work. Panting from the climb, Louisa set down her heavy baskets and greeted the Tempest's housemaid like an old friend.

"You look cold, Moira, come inside. I'll soon have that fire blazing, don't you worry." She preceded the girl into the room, amused by her wide-eyed and innocent appraisal of its contents. "Apart from the books and pictures, it's all rented," she informed her with a smile.

"It must set you back a bit," Moira replied and then clapped a hand over her mouth in dismay. "Oh, I am sorry. Sure, I never meant to be rude."

With a slight smile, Louisa shook her head. "I know, it's all right. As a matter of fact," she said with what she hoped was disarming frankness, "there are certain drawbacks to living here. The trains, for instance." Remembering Robert's curses, she laughed nervously, adding: "It isn't as expensive as you'd think." She crossed her fingers at the outright lie, for she knew now that the rooms were far from cheap; it had been difficult for Robert to find an accommodating landlord away from the immediate area of the barracks.

Moira's eyes took in the comfortable fireside chairs of deep-buttoned oxhide, the warm Turkey carpet, chenille curtains, and matching table cover. There was nothing stiffly new about the furnishings, rather an inviting coziness born of age and use, and as Louisa bent to light the fire, she hurried to her side. "Let me do that, Miss Elliott. You sort out your shopping."

Thanking her, Louisa set about preparing their meal. She had bought pork chops with the kidney attached as a special treat, baby brussels sprouts and potatoes, and a curd tart to finish with. Bessie would have had a fit at the thought of buying curd tart, but there had been no time to bake, even had Louisa been confident enough. "This may take a little while, Moira. Will it matter if you're late back to Blossom Street?"

"Oh, I'll be in no more trouble than usual."

"How are things these days?"

Intent upon supplying coals to the burgeoning fire, Moira sighed dramatically, launching into a long diatribe against the iniquities of the Tempest household and the new governess in particular. "And she's a nasty old biddy and that's a fact. She's why I came—I thought to myself, if I don't go and tell somebody about it all, I shall go mad and no mistake. The old bag—oh, sorry, Miss Elliott, but she is indeed—in her way, she's worse than Mrs. Petty, and that's saying something, now don't you agree?"

With her back turned, Louisa allowed herself a smile. "Does this formidable creature have a name?"

"Miss Maitland, if you please. Forty-two she's supposed to be, but she's fifty if she's a day, always going on about the grand houses she's been used to. I told her, you don't want to bandy names like that about, not in this house. But she's pretty quiet when Mr. Tempest's about, which is not often these days, I can tell you. And she likes her drop."

Louisa spun around, almost spilling the pan of potatoes. "You mean she drinks?"

"She does that. Straight after breakfast she's to her room—you can smell the gin and peppermints a mile away."

"What about—?"

"Mr. Tempest? Like I was saying, he hardly ever sees her. And with only me to see to Miss Victoria, it's hardly a minute I have to breathe. And that poor mite hardly gets a couple of hours of lessons a day; she's on her own and miserable as sin since you and Miss Rachel left. You'd not know her, Miss Elliott—thin as a rail she is, and her always plump as a chicken."

Bereft of words, Louisa tried to digest this torrent of information while supervising the chops and vegetables. Louisa knew Moira's slap-happy ways well enough to realize that a situation had to be bad to upset her to this degree.

As they sat down to eat, she said, "I gather Rachel still isn't reconciled with her father?"

"He's banned her from the house," Moira said, watching with round eyes as Louisa served the food onto two very hot plates. "She was after calling a couple of weeks back, but Mrs. Petty answered the door, and there was no chance to tell her a thing. So—not knowing what the devil to do, miss, I thought I'd better be seeing you. Did Miss Rachel never get in touch?"

Apparently concentrating on her dinner, Louisa thought carefully before replying. Rachel had not contacted her, but through Robert she knew very well where Rachel was living and in what style. Having recovered from the *fait accompli* of Arthur's quite legal Scottish marriage, the Bainbridges had swallowed their recriminations and with some aplomb set up their son and his wife in a pleasant little villa off the Fulford Road. How long the financial honeymoon would last, with Rachel's propensity for spending money, Louisa had no idea, but she seemed to be making the most of things. Robert had been invited, along with Darnley and several other Bainbridge acquaintances, to afternoon tea some weeks ago; largely under pressure from Tommy, he had accepted, returning to Marygate with a fund of cynical anecdotes. He despised Rachel Tempest, as he persisted in calling her, and refused two subsequent invitations, finding the company too young, the gaiety rather overdone for his taste. Louisa made a mental note to ask him to accept the next one when it came; his acquaintance with Rachel and Arthur Bainbridge could prove the only means by which Victoria might be helped.

"If I remember correctly, she's living near the barracks. I'll see if I can find her address and get a message to her somehow. But I don't see that I can do much more than that. If her father thought I was even remotely involved, he might make things worse for Victoria. So don't ever say to anyone that you've been here—not even Rachel, if you should happen to see her."

With her fork halfway to her mouth, Moira looked at her curiously, but she agreed to the request. As though realizing it was as well not to press the matter further, she commented appreciatively on the excellence of the meal, and with a small smile of satisfaction, Louisa had to concede that she was right. Almost for the first time, she had produced something which was not only edible, but well cooked and most enjoyable. She wondered reflectively whether, with Robert, she tried too hard. When Moira had cleared her plate, asking for a piece of bread to mop up the last of the gravy, Louisa set the curd tart on the table and, as an afterthought, fruit and cheese also. Robert always finished a meal with an apple and a piece of Wensleydale, and while Moira might not be used to that, it would fill another corner should she still be hungry.

With one of Louisa's china cups poised, the girl sighed her satisfaction. "Miss Elliott, that's surely the best meal I've tasted in years. Thanks."

There was such a wealth of sincerity in that simple word, Louisa felt ridiculously touched; and as Moira gossiped over the washing-up, she was relieved to find the mention of Albert Tempest's name affected her so slightly. She did not want to hear about him, how often he came and went, what incidents had caused his wrath, yet, as Moira's tongue ran on, she might have been talking of a complete stranger. Only when she broached that last evening at Blossom Street did Louisa feel herself shrink inwardly. Almost brusquely, she sidestepped the subject, going on to describe her holiday in Blankney, her cousin's children, the fact that John's wife must now be near her time.

For some reason, Moira then recalled Robert's visit to the house and, apparently unaware of his connection with Louisa, proceeded to relate the curious incident which had occurred little more than a week after Louisa's departure.

She listened impassively until Moira began to paint that anonymous visitor in glowing colors; then she laughed to cover her embarrassment. "It seems this military gentleman created quite an impression!"

"He did indeed," Moira said and began to giggle. "And not only on me! Why, he knocked the very devil out of Mr. Tempest. I heard the crash as the table went. Mr. T. stayed in his room all the day, and I had to take bowls of soup up to him—it was all he could manage, the poor soul!" She dissolved into gales of laughter at that. "Wasn't his face a mess! His mouth all swelled up and a tooth broken—I couldn't hardly tell a word he said. Ah—it did my heart good to see him! A good thing he wasn't at work that week—else all York would've been talking."

"It's no more than he deserved," Louisa said bitterly, but she found that her hands were shaking, and her knees; with relief, she sat down beside the fire.

"You'll be right, at that," Moira said, but again she gave Louisa a curious look. "A bit of justice from the Almighty, would you say?" she asked slyly, then added: "I wish he was *my* guardian angel, I don't mind telling you!"

Feeling her color rise, Louisa bent to the fire, stirring it with unnecessary vigor. "Yes, indeed," she murmured and rather pointedly looked at the clock. It was almost half past nine.

She went through into the bedroom and fetched Moira's threadbare little jacket together with the too-cheerful hat; somehow, they symbolized her, and for that reason alone Louisa felt sad and was possessed of a sudden desire to see her dressed in something warm and sensible.

"Take care of yourself, Moira—and do all you can for Victoria. Give her my love, but swear her to secrecy when you do, for goodness' sake."

"I will that, miss, and she'll keep it. She was too fond of you not to."

"It won't be easy," Louisa said, "but I'll try to do something. It may take time. Anyway, keep in touch."

They went down the stairs together, and with Moira's profuse thanks echoing in her ears, Louisa waved her good-bye, watching that jaunty little figure as she disappeared into the darkness of the lane.

FIVE

bove the blackened roofs and smoking chimney stacks of Walmgate, a pale November sun rose slowly into a fragile sky. In the
dry air, clouds appeared and disappeared with every breath, and
like unquiet wraiths conjured at a séance, cart horses clattered by, enveloped in their own steamy haze. Underfoot, a crystalline rime edged
pavements and cobbles, while in the gutters, frozen on its overnight
passage to the Foss, effluent lurked blackly.

Dodging drays and workmen, Edward hurried into Fossgate, heedless
of the treachery beneath his feet; his mind was occupied by other be-
trayals.

At Tempest's front entrance, the boy who served in the shop was
waiting, his eyes reproachful as Edward unlocked the door. Hurrying
through the drafty workshops, past bookstore and composing room,
Edward wrestled with bolts and padlocks and finally admitted the rest
of Albert Tempest's work force, fully ten minutes after the usual time.
Amidst much stamping of feet and ostentatious blowing of hands, the
men filed in, one or two commenting, in half-jesting fashion, on the
tardiness of his arrival; but he was in no mood for witticisms and ignored
them. Entering his own tiny cubbyhole of an office, he removed his
overcoat and hat, donned a brown coat of cotton drill, and sat down to
study the order book. He rubbed his eyes, trying to erase all personal
preoccupations, to focus his mind on the day ahead; but like dancing
black spots the problems floated back. He had slept badly since Sunday,
the shock of that day's events superseded by the twists and turns of his
aunt's efforts to surround and contain the situation.

Like a Machiavelli come suddenly out of retirement, Mary Elliott had
thrown off the vestments of grief and shock and set about protecting
her eldest daughter and, along with her, the man who was her lover.
Edward was stunned by the speed with which she had apparently recovered. Still reeling, he had listened in amazement as she repeated,

verbatim, her orders to Bessie and Blanche and, yesterday, to Emily. The only ones yet to be interviewed were the chief protagonists; it was to be their turn on Sunday next. She had already written to Louisa summoning them to dinner. Bessie's protests had been waved aside; Edward's insistence that he would not condone such behavior by sitting at the same table as Louisa's lover was met by an icy stare. "You'll swallow your indignation along with your meat," she had said. "And don't forget your origins while you do it."

Effectively silenced, he had quietly accepted her formal apology along with her regrets that he, of all people, should need such a reminder. Afterward, of course, he had thought of all the things he should have said: that Louisa ought to be reminded of her own origins, of the unhappiness illegitimacy had caused. She had no friends; none of them had. The stigma did not end with childhood torment; it was a shameful deformity the victim constantly strove to hide, so that reticence and suspicion became second nature, lies and half-truths the only means to survive.

The more Edward considered Louisa's position, the less he understood. Love? Yes, he could recall the joy of it, the almost miraculous wonder of realizing one was loved in return; also the torment, both physical and mental, when, like a pretty bubble, the miracle burst. Louisa had gone through that, he was sure. Why, then, had she succumbed? Was her moral sense so ill developed? And if it was, which he did not believe, surely her experiences were such that she would suffer anything rather than bequeath the same to her own children? She could not be so naive as to think she could evade that fateful responsibility. How had she fallen prey to Robert Duncannon? And when?

The how and why of it escaped him completely, except that he began to see her attachment to the captain as a kind of derangement, fed and supported by the very presence of the man. Before, Louisa had been possessed of reason; now, however, she seemed blind to everything. The change in her, Edward thought, could be pinpointed to her dismissal from Blossom Street. There was more to that event than had ever been admitted, and it seemed logical to assume that Robert Duncannon was involved, that she had been seeing him at the same time as Rachel Tempest was conducting her romance with young Bainbridge. No wonder the old man had been so angry. If that was indeed the case, then Albert Tempest's references to their respective backgrounds became suddenly understandable, as was Louisa's reluctance to quote him directly.

Having placed Louisa squarely in the wrong, Edward's attitude toward his employer began to soften. A modicum of sympathy for his difficulties crept in, and it no longer seemed so important to look for another place.

Resolving to ease the atmosphere between them as best he might, Edward turned once more to the order book; the working day, at least, was clearer now.

That evening, he again attempted to clarify things with his aunt. While Bessie attended to the guests in the dining room, he finished his meal at the kitchen table and raised the subject of Louisa yet again.

"Won't you even tell me what stance you're going to take? Surely you can't condone this situation? She must be persuaded to come home before things get really out of hand."

"Out of hand, Edward? I should think things were already out of our hands. Or do you think Louisa's merely playacting?"

Embarrassment and annoyance colored the skin along his cheekbones; he fought to keep his voice under control. "You know what I mean," he said gruffly.

"Of course I do, but it may be too late for tears, and if it isn't, a few days aren't going to make that much difference. These things must be done properly. It's no good weeping and wailing. We must be calm and strong. Above all, we stand together—no matter what happens—as we've always done."

"That's all very well," Edward protested. "But you haven't even spoken to her yet. You don't know what you're up against."

"Don't I? Anyway, I'm going to see her this evening."

Edward's frown lifted slightly; he tugged at his beard, a habit he had in times of stress. "I see." After a short pause, he added: "You will try to make her see the folly of it?"

Exasperated, Mary Elliott swept plates and cutlery off the table and banged them into the sink. "I shall do my best."

"About Sunday," he continued hesitantly. "Do you think you should be the one to talk to him? Won't it be difficult for you? Perhaps it might be easier if I spoke to him—man to man, I mean."

She stared long and hard at him and sighed. "You've had your opportunity, Edward. How far did you get?"

"Well, not very far," he admitted. "But Louisa was there, and at the time I was too stunned to think clearly."

"Precisely. Which is why I've done nothing until now. I wasn't born yesterday, you know—I'm more than capable of talking to the captain myself. Don't forget," she added in gentler tones, "that I nursed him when he was too ill to know where he was or even *who* he was. I've fed him and bathed him and seen him naked as the day he was born. He's no different from any other man—he hasn't got horns, and he's no more Old Nick than you are."

"I don't—" Edward began.

"Yes, you do. You think he's magicked her away and is holding her against her will. You're wrong. It's nothing more or less than the feelings the Good Lord blessed and cursed us all with."

"Base nature, you mean!"

With an abrupt gesture, Mary Elliott waved her nephew's angry protest aside. "Call it what you like, I won't argue the matter. It's part and parcel of us *all,* whether you admit to it or not."

Stung, Edward kicked his chair back and turned to leave; but before he could reach the door, his aunt called him back. "Are you so perfect," she asked, "that you can cast the first stone?"

That hit home, as she had known it would. Slowly he returned to his chair, leaned heavily on it as he apologized. "I've cast no stones," he said quietly. "I don't mean to judge her; it's just that I don't understand. I really *don't* understand," he repeated. "I know she loves him, but that doesn't make it right." Anguish tore at him, and abruptly he turned away. He paced the few steps before the fire, stopped, and stared into the glowing coals. "Believe me, it's not just her soul I'm concerned for."

With a deflated sigh, Mary Elliott sank into her chair. "I know. I'm sorry, Edward." Bessie came and went with crockery from the guests' table; as she returned again, her mistress stood up. "I'd better go and tidy my hair."

"Shall I walk down with you?" Edward asked. "I'll not stay, but I can call back for you later." She shook her head, but he insisted. "I need the walk."

Warmly bundled against the bitter wind which swept down Gillygate, Mary Elliott leaned on her nephew's arm, clutching a basket of newbaked bread and scones under her cloak. Dead leaves scurried past them, brown and brittle, catching and chattering in doorways. The wind brought with it the sharp scent of winter, of plowed fields and open skies less than a mile hence, and with sudden, downward gusts, another smell, sooty and sulfurous. Forever afterward, Edward was destined to remember that evening, to have it conjured up perfectly by wind and leaves and unswept chimneys.

Perhaps that redolence of open country prompted other memories, for Mary Elliott said suddenly: "There never was much talk of sin when your mother and I were girls, you know. People were always too busy. We went to church on Sundays, of course, but the parson's sermon was always a good opportunity for father to have forty winks undisturbed. I don't remember anybody pointing the finger at girls who had babes out of wedlock in those days. If anything, it was the man who was hounded, to do the right thing by the girl. And if he wouldn't, he was made to pay, which was only just and right. A nine days' wonder then, that's all it was. None of all this fussing and fretting and secrecy. No need for it—everybody knew what was what, anyway. Still," she reflected sadly, "I'm getting old, and times were changing even then, even in the country. New parsons, new ways—hellfire and damnation if father took a drop too much on a Saturday, and God help you if you were poor, for nobody else could."

Edward listened intently, aware that these thoughts were but a summary of all that had been in his aunt's mind for several days. In all the years that he had lived beneath her roof, he had never before known her to speak so freely of the past. Part of him was faintly shocked, for he was a product of a different age, of a far more straitlaced environment; yet he realized that this was one of the secrets of her philosophy and was probably why she was so much easier to live with than his mother had been. There was no bitterness in his aunt; she had lived her life according to her own lights, accepting the consequences with little more than a shrug. Her ideas had been formed years before he was born, in a place where he had spent some of the happiest times of his childhood. With another, greater shock, it dawned on him that friends and relatives in Lincolnshire had always known him as Elizabeth Elliott's child; no one had ever remarked on his lack of a father. If there were no secrets in Metheringham, as his aunt maintained, then perhaps there his father's identity was known.

Carefully, for he was afraid his anxiety to know the truth would set a guard on her tongue, Edward formulated a reply. As casually as he was able, he said: "You make life in the country sound eminently desirable, Aunt. Perhaps we should persuade Louisa to retire to Lincolnshire? In fact," he continued, "under the circumstances, it sounds like such a good idea, I can't help wondering why my mother found it so necessary to leave. Won't you tell me? I'm sure you know, and I'd appreciate the truth. My mother's dead now—it can't possibly matter anymore."

Under a flickering street lamp, his aunt glanced up and realized her mistake; but lies seemed suddenly pointless, and she was heartily sick of deceit. Sighing, she said: "Your mother left because she was pregnant, because your father's family forced her to leave. And she made me promise never to tell you because she was afraid you'd go back—afraid you'd try to contact them. It was vital to her that you shouldn't."

"Why?"

Mary Elliott sighed again. The reasons seemed old and trite and trivial compared to current anxiety; the more so because history seemed so depressingly set on repeating itself. "Oh, some document was involved. I suppose they were terrified of a scandal, so they made her swear on oath that she'd never reveal your father's name. In return for that—and quitting the country—she was given a lump sum and a small annuity for your upbringing. She was lucky," Mary added dryly; "they were quite generous."

Caught by a sudden wave of revulsion, Edward stopped dead. "You mean she was paid off?" he demanded and in the next second wondered why he was so surprised.

"Oh, be your age, Edward! She didn't have a choice, for goodness' sake! If she'd refused, and stayed in Metheringham, what would it have meant? Think about it—think hard!—try to imagine what life was like for us in those days. Our parents had nothing, and they were getting old. For twenty years they'd worked like slaves—and for what? Trying to pay off old Tom Elliott's debts—a shilling here, a guinea there— struggling to give us younger ones a decent start in life. Then Elizabeth, thirty-one—and still not married, in spite of all the offers she's had— comes home and says she's expecting!"

With a snort of disgust, Mary Elliott continued walking, not caring whether Edward followed or not. Elizabeth! she thought bitterly, remembering her sister as she had been then: pretty, clever, and vain. Haughty, too, always harking back to the old days, when her father and grandfather had been men of property and substance, and she the only daughter, apple of her father's eye. Mary, born after the fall, remembered only the genteel poverty of the cottage in the High Street, where a few remaining pieces of fine furniture moldered against damp walls. Their father's books consisted of favorites salvaged from the sale, dog-eared with use and hard for young minds to comprehend, but they were read over and over again. Year after year their mother's gowns were altered and turned, until the once-good cloth was threadbare, hardly fit for rag rugs. Everyday matters to Mary, who had known nothing else; but to her sister they were daily recriminations she did everything to avoid.

Elizabeth, with her mincing manners and passion for fine clothes; she did well as a lady's maid, Mary thought, wishing her sister had possessed enough sense to see the folly of wanting more. But pregnant, and with the specter of poverty hanging over her, reality had been hammered home then; it was no good ranting at fate, swearing marriage had been promised, and cursing the family whose name she had coveted; the old baronet had the upper hand and knew it. So did the Elliotts.

Distraught and helpless on Elizabeth's behalf, at least her parents were realists. Experience had taught them that little could be achieved without money, and their elder daughter had been granted enough to make a future of sorts. Mary was summoned from Lincoln, and with her help Elizabeth was finally brought to her senses. Between them the practicalities were ironed out. They had relatives near Darlington in Yorkshire, who would take her in until the child was born; and after that, with that generous lump sum, Elizabeth might set herself up in some kind of business. Eventually she agreed, but that surrender had not been won without sacrifice on Mary's part. She would go only, she said, if Mary would accompany her.

Then she had had no real regrets, but later Elizabeth's unconcealed distaste for Mary's problems had hurt deeply. The trouble was, Elizabeth had never wanted the encumbrance of a child; had been quite happy whenever her son could be fostered by those elderly relatives in Darlington. She had never understood Mary's attachment to her own daughters, the need to have them with her from birth. It was that need which had started the gossip; that maternal love which had led, ultimately, to the end of their partnership. And the end of that had meant the end of friendship, the end of sisterly affection. An angry little sob broke in her throat as Mary hurried along, and she was suddenly aware of Edward beside her, catching anxiously at her arm.

He forced those angry steps to slow, and gradually, as she regained control of herself, the threatening tears subsided, and she was able to speak with relative calm. In a low voice she related the bare circumstances of his coming into the world, glossing over the less pleasant aspects of his mother's character.

"I suppose she must have loved him—she'd had plenty of other offers and turned them all down—but like an awful lot of others, dear, he disappeared when he was most needed. Tragic, because she never got over it, but at least she didn't end up on the streets, like thousands of others in her position. I don't know." She sighed. "Men have the pleasure, we pay the price. It's an unfair world. And whatever your father's intentions, they obviously didn't stand up too well in the face of his family. That's what I tried to tell Louisa—but then, I didn't know the captain was married."

"You seem to have told me everything," Edward said, "except who my father was."

"That's because I don't know. Oh, I can tell you the family name— your grandfather used to hunt with the Blankney pack when I was a girl—I've seen him many a time, and you have the same look. But you see, dear, there were three sons and a daughter, all much of an age, and none of them married. And whatever your mother's faults, Edward, I'll say this for her—she stuck to her oath and never uttered his name again."

Angrily he turned to face her. "This isn't another lie, is it? Another excuse not to tell me the truth?"

Mary Elliott stood her ground. "I didn't lie to you before. You asked if I knew who your father was. I didn't then, and I still don't. It was the bare truth."

After leaving her at Louisa's door, Edward turned back toward town, conscious of a desperate need to walk. There was a kind of solace in the bleak, blustery evening, in the empty city streets. Lights still burned in a few small shops, but there were few people about, and those he passed paid him scant attention.

Blind to his surroundings, he crossed the river twice and, without realizing, found himself on Fossgate, outside Tempest's. Like a sleep-walker suddenly come to, he stood and stared at the shopfront, wondering how and why he was there. Then he blinked and, with a surge of irrational anger, turned sharply away. He had gone no more than a few yards when, from a recessed doorway, a painted face leered at him suggestively. Stonily Edward walked on, ignoring her, but the prostitute caught at his arm and, with an obscene gesture, named her price. In what seemed no more than a reflex action, he twisted free and grabbed the woman, pinning her against a shop window. As her terrified eyes stared into his, he felt, rather than heard, the window begin to crack. He pulled her to him and, locked like lovers, the two stood fast.

Cheap perfume, mingled with the odor of her unwashed body, assaulted his nostrils; as she opened her mouth to scream, he released his grip and flung her aside. "Get back home," he hissed, "to your children, if you have any!"

Pursued by a round mouthful of curses, he strode on, away from the shadowy half-world and into broader, brighter thoroughfares. At the head of Pavement, the lantern tower of All Saints stood pale against the night sky; on impulse, he sought refuge within.

Shuddering, trembling, he sank to his knees in the shadows of the Lady Chapel, his mind racing, reliving the scene in Fossgate over and over, until he was convinced he had half-killed the woman in his rage. His reactions, usually so controlled, horrified him. Prostitutes had approached him before; they were a fact of life, regrettable, like poverty, and as ever present. Usually he ignored them or, if pressed by the old and destitute, found a piece of silver, however small, to give them.

In the sanctuary, candles burned, tiny lights shining in the darkness, symbols of a greater light, of hope and peace and love in a bitter and unfeeling world. In spite of his mother's peculiar brand of piety, Edward had never lost sight of that, even though there had been times when his faith was strained to the breaking point. Shame burned as he realized the power of frustration, the seductive pull of darkness and despair, the ease with which even a sane, intelligent man could descend to violence.

Most of all he was aware of deep betrayal: by his mother, who had never trusted him, and by Louisa, who rejected all that he, Edward, stood for. All his life he had believed in decency and kindness, gentleness and moral precepts founded on his Christian faith. He was no whited sepulcher; he hated extremism and loathed the double standards which seemed so distressingly prevalent. In trying to understand without condemning, he had also sought to pass on those beliefs to his cousins. In Blanche's case it was wasted effort; Emily was more easily swayed, going the way of the prevailing wind; but Louisa was strong and sure, and with her he had imagined he shared a deep and lasting rapport. He had trusted her, believed in her, relied upon her, and most of all *loved* her for what he thought she was. Now it seemed he did not know her at all.

Remembering her face that day, the way she had wept as she embraced him, Edward knew, in spite of that later bravado, that what she did was not done lightly; she loved him still, it was simply that she loved Robert Duncannon more.

But that it should be *him!* Edward inwardly raged. A married man with nothing to offer her; a married man who would discard her as soon as he grew bored. She was good, intelligent, and kind; she was also very lovely; she could have had *anyone*. Why had she chosen him? How could she be so blind to the folly she was committing?

He wanted to pray, but found it impossible. It seemed that even the Almighty, who could have prevented this catastrophe, had laughed and flung Edward's belief back in his face.

Drained and numb, he rose from his knees with only one thought to comfort him: he had a name. Out of all this chaos had come the answer to a lifelong question, and he would use every wit he possessed to pursue the truth of his paternity. Hornet's nest or no, to Edward it did not matter: his mother was dead, and her fears and bitterness were buried with her. He would have the truth, whatever the cost.

SIX

*D*espite the honesty of that lengthy conversation with her mother, in which they had talked as equals for the first time, Louisa was nervous as she walked the length of Gillygate. She had not seen Edward since the previous Sunday, and not even her mother's assurances could erase the memory of his face as he left the apartment. Bessie she had not seen at all. Knowing her fierce protectiveness, Louisa feared the worst kind of reaction; dreading it, she took a deep breath and slowed her quick, anxious steps, trying to look as though she was making a regular visit home without a care in the world.

The long, straight road seemed longer, the gusting breeze colder as it tugged at her cloak. Under a fitful noonday sun children ran home, kicking up dusty leaves as they went, and stiff young men escorted self-conscious girls from chapel and church. Although it was quieter than a weekday, with shops shuttered and no heavy carts moving, Louisa was suddenly glad to be alone; a neighbor, unfamiliar in his Sunday best, raised his hat to her, and further on a little girl smiled a shy greeting as she passed. On this day of all days, Robert's presence beside her would have been a great comfort, but at the last minute each had agreed to bow to discretion: while she took the direct route, he had decided to walk through town via Monk Bar and Lord Mayor's Walk, to approach her mother's house from the opposite direction as he had on his last visit, all those months before. He had started out ahead of her, but with the hotel in sight she slowed her steps still more, reluctant to arrive alone.

Feeling like a stranger uncertain of a welcome, she rang the bell, in her nervousness studying the doorway with its deep, paneled architraves as though she had never seen it before. The fanlight above was mirror-clean, and she could almost see her face in the spotless green paintwork. Bessie must have worked very late last night, she thought, noting the freshly whitened doorstep, else she was up exceedingly early, before anyone should chance to see her working on the Sabbath.

Anxiously Louisa looked up the road once more, but there was no sign whatever of Robert. The farmhouse and buildings on the corner of Lord Mayor's Walk were bathed in sleepy Sunday quiet, and the elms and chestnuts beyond lent that usually busy corner an illusory air of rural peace. As a child, it had been her job to go there each morning for the milk; she had loved seeing the cows chewing contentedly in their stalls, the dairymaids milking with their foreheads resting against the animals' sides; but most of all she had loved the clean dairy, with its buttery, cheesy tang, the scrubbed stone floor and shiny brown tiles. Remembering the farmer's wife with her enormously fat forearms and starched white bonnet, Louisa smiled, wondering whether she was still ladling gills of milk and dispensing bits of cheese to local children . . .

The door opened suddenly, and Bessie was standing there stiff as a guardsman, her eyes gimlets beneath furrowed brows.

Louisa sighed. "I'm sorry, Bessie . . ." she began tentatively.

"Aye," the older woman muttered brusquely. "And no doubt you'll be sorrier still before you've finished. You've not got all your bread baked *yet,* you know," she added tartly.

As Louisa's chin came up in angry defiance, Bessie brushed past her. "He's here already, by the way," and she nodded toward the parlor, leaving Louisa to go through alone.

"Do you catch everyone unawares?" she asked as Robert rose to greet her, but he saw beneath her brightness, and knew Bessie had met her frostily.

"The element of surprise," he replied, including Mary Elliott in his disarming grin. "Actually, I cheated. I picked up a cab in Exhibition Square and asked him to drop me by Monk Bar. Ridiculous really, because he turned around and brought me up Gillygate and along Lord Mayor's Walk—so I had to retrace my steps! But it didn't matter at all. It was pleasant walking along the moat."

With a smile, Louisa shook her head. "I'm afraid he's quite unpredictable, Mamma, and utterly incorrigible."

Her mother nodded. "I can see he is," she admitted quietly and then, into the suddenly embarrassed silence, said: "I'm sorry about Bessie. She's getting old, I'm afraid, and all this has been a terrible shock to her."

Surprised, Robert raised his eyes, startling her by the compassionate intensity of his gaze. "I'd have thought," he said slowly, "that it had been a greater shock to *you,* Mrs. Elliott."

"Well, Captain," she murmured with a small deprecating gesture, "as I'm sure you are aware, I am not entirely ignorant of the world. And Louisa is my daughter. Do you think I'd abandon her?"

"Not at all. I simply meant—"

"Bessie is a servant, but she's been with us for almost thirty years, through good days and bad. While I don't approve of her attitude at the moment, I do understand it. In time, I'm sure she'll grow used to the idea. Until then, I hope you'll bear with her."

Robert had the feeling that the same little speech, or something very like it, had been used several times already. Utterly crushed, he gazed appealingly at the older woman. "I feel I should apologize," he said in some embarrassment, "but that would denigrate Louisa. However, I am sincerely sorry for the pain we've caused you . . ."

Mary Elliott laid a small hand over his. "May we talk about it later? Edward will be joining us in a moment, and I think Bessie is wanting my help in the kitchen."

Like Louisa, Robert dreaded the meeting with her cousin. In spite of her protests, the lengthy explanations he had listened to, Robert could not forget that first, shattering impression, nor the austerely phrased opinions which had set him so squarely in the wrong. That slight man, with his passionate eyes, had severely unsettled Robert; in his anger he had longed to strike back and in doing so had only succeeded in hurting Louisa. For her sake and her mother's, he knew he must make a supreme effort to conquer both his antagonism and his pride.

When Edward did appear, the eyes which met Robert's were still wary, still hostile, and although he did not look at Louisa even when he spoke to her, he seemed to be making an effort for her sake. His self-control was admirable under the circumstances, Robert thought; with Mary Elliott's light, inconsequential chatter, it was almost possible to forget the previous week's appalling sequence of events. He followed Louisa to the table, taking the place indicated by her mother; Edward said a short Grace and, with the arrival of the first course, commented dryly on his cousin's culinary expertise, his manner suggesting that Louisa's lack of skill in the kitchen was something of a family joke. She flushed uncomfortably, and Robert was tempted to say a word in her defense, but her mother cut across him with "you'd improve in a month, Louisa, if only you'd apply yourself properly."

Again he had the feeling that this was a set speech, the subject a bone of contention between them.

"You know I've never had the time, Mamma."

"Well, dear, until you *make* time to learn, you'll never improve." Mary Elliott glanced across at Robert as though making a mental note to add that to their later discussion. A little bemused, he took another forkful of the crisp and delicious batter pudding, smiling his enjoyment as he did so.

Bessie brought in the beef, sizzling in its ring of golden roast potatoes, and placed it before Edward at the head of the table; while he carved, she served the vegetables, leaving a sauceboat of piping-hot gravy in the center of the table.

As Robert ladled a spoonful onto his beef, Edward addressed him directly for the first time. "Tell me," he asked, "we read so much these days about reform, but I often wonder what army life is really like. The food, for instance—is it as poor as some of the newspapers would have us believe?"

"Not in the Officer's Mess," Robert emphatically replied. "But then, it should be good; we pay enough for the privilege. As for the men, well, their rations are vastly improved on what they used to be, and we're constantly exhorted to check their quality. The raw victuals are usually quite good, but," he added with a wry smile, "I think the food would be more palatable if Mrs. Elliott were doing the cooking! And, come to think of it, ours would be a deal better, too!"

With a deprecating comment, Mary Elliott offered him more meat; as he accepted another slice, Edward said to him: "You must forgive my lamentable ignorance, Captain Duncannon—but beyond watching the occasional display on the Knavesmire when persuaded to attend by my aunt, I have no experience whatsoever of military life." He paused, and Robert looked up into eyes which belied the softness of his tone. Such cold and open resentment was nothing new to Robert: he had seen it in the eyes of recruits when their sergeant's back was turned; seen it in the eyes of sergeants when brought to book by a junior officer. It was both familiar and understandable, and twelve years of army life had taught Robert how to deal with it. What he could not bear, and could not deal with, was raw emotional pain, and he thanked Providence that Edward was man enough to have put that behind him.

"So, Captain, what do you actually *do?*"

Relief brought a smile to Robert's face. "Well, in the winter," he said evenly, "very little. The usual parade-ground drill, of course, and training of recruits. And the horses have to be exercised, whatever the weather. Usually, though, we ride to hounds two or three days a week, which is one of the great advantages of being stationed in York—lots of good hunting within easy distance.

"But in the summer," he added, "we really do work, wherever we are, as long as there is daylight. Maneuvers, musketry practice, training for the displays you mentioned earlier. If you'd ever seen a bunch of raw recruits in the riding school, you'd understand the amount of work that has to be done to achieve that seemingly effortless coordination." He laughed suddenly. "There are times when I despair, but in the end it all comes right, and there lies some of the satisfaction of it."

Edward nodded, adding, with deceptive innocence: "I believe there's a school of thought which dares to question the viability of cavalry in modern warfare. Is that not so?"

Faintly nettled, for a second Robert stared at him, seeing the half-hidden provocation which lurked beneath that bland facade. With what he hoped was a disarming grin, he said, "Well, as the young subaltern said to the general: 'I suppose we're there, sir, to give tone to what would otherwise be a vulgar brawl!' "

Amidst the laughter, Edward acknowledged the joke with a cold smile. "But how do *you* see your role?"

"How do *I* see it? Well, Mr. Elliott, that is—if you'll forgive me—a leading question. My pet hobbyhorse. I could bore you and these good ladies for the entire afternoon with my ideas about the role cavalry *should* be playing in these modern times. I won't, however," he added in an aside to his hostess. "Shall we say I don't agree that bravery and a willingness to die gloriously in a medieval set piece are enough? Modern arms are far too accurate and deadly for the charge to have much effect. All right against a bunch of ill-equipped natives, of course—the sound of even a single squadron at the charge will break them every time— but not much use against well-aimed carbines and shell-firing guns. That much was illustrated at Balaclava—and if we've learned nothing from that, the 'Tally-ho boys!' generals should be pensioned off here and now. Unfortunately, we still have a lot of the old diehards in command."

"So what's the answer?"

"Change is the answer, but like all other things in the army, it will take time. Horses will always be needed, of course—and in an increasing variety of roles—but men will have to change. Instead of relying on the old principles, we'll have to become like a kind of—may God forgive me!—a kind of mounted infantry, experts with gun and carbine, as well as sword and lance. And tactics will have to change, too. It may take time, but it will come eventually. Of course—" Robert laughed at his own seriousness—"my opinions don't make me very popular with *everyone* in the mess!"

"I can imagine," Edward murmured, but Robert saw that he had earned a certain grudging respect. He released a barely perceptible sigh of relief and was glad when the meal was over.

There was some desultory conversation over the fruit and cheese, then a chance remark evidently reminded Mary Elliott of other things. She disappeared into the kitchen and came back holding a letter for Louisa.

"This came for you yesterday. I almost forgot. From Blankney—the writing looks like Cousin John's. It'll be news of the baby, I expect," she remarked as Louisa slit the envelope with a knife. "Do hurry and read it," she urged, "and tell us what he says."

Louisa scanned the page quickly, initial tension giving way to smiles as she informed them that John Elliott was the proud father of yet another son, strong and healthy, God be praised, although the birth had taxed poor Jenny's health severely and she was compelled to rest.

"She must be ill to have had the doctor," Mary Elliott said, clucking sympathetically. "Poor thing, how ever will she manage with a new baby and all that brood to look after?"

"That's just it," Louisa said with a sigh. "She can't manage. Cousin John asks if I can go down and help out for a week or so."

Glancing quickly around the table, Robert caught the gaze of both Edward and his aunt; both revealed surprise that was just a little too eager for his liking.

"Then you must go," they said, almost in unison, to Louisa.

"But he doesn't know," she began, coloring with embarrassment. "I mean, he thinks I'm still here, helping out. He doesn't know I'm working at the Station Hotel."

Robert stifled an exclamation. He did not want her to go away, even for a few days, but it would be a small price to pay if she could be persuaded to give up working. He longed to provide for her, to lavish on her every luxury, if only she would accept. In effect, she was the least extravagant woman he had ever known excepting his sister Letty, and the most impervious to any form of bribery.

Unconsciously taking up the argument which was to end her daughter's attempts to remain at least partially independent, Mary Elliott sniffed and said, "But you don't even like the job." Robert could have hugged her.

"That's not the point—"

"The point is—John needs help, and he's asked for you. You had a good holiday down there in the summer, Louisa, and one good turn deserves another . . ."

Robert chewed the inside of his lip and stared hard at the tablecloth, praying that the details of that particular holiday would never come to light.

". . . so you must ask for a leave of absence from the hotel, and—well, if they won't give it, then you must leave. You can always look for something else when you come back."

"Easier said than done," Louisa sighed. Beset by such decisiveness, she knew better than to look to Robert for support; he wanted her to give up working completely. Instead she sought Edward's eyes, and Robert remarked her disappointment. It was easy to imagine the thoughts leaping through his agile mind: that she could be away for weeks, weeks in which the "bored dilettante" would hopefully turn to other consolation.

With a little tug at his beard, her cousin murmured, "If they really need you in Blankney—and it seems they do—then you must go, Louisa."

With the arrival of coffee, Edward tactfully excused himself, taking his into the kitchen. A few minutes later, Louisa joined him, her cheeks burning with suppressed indignation.

"Has Bessie gone out?"

"She has, but there's a pot of coffee here," he said evenly, pointing to the hearth.

"I don't care about the coffee!" Louisa expostulated, striding angrily toward the sink. Alert and troubled, Edward's eyes followed her, watching as she drank half a glass of water and stood gazing rigidly out of the window. Beyond the leaf-strewn yard, the trees on the ramparts were almost bare; behind her he could see the city walls white against a darkening sky. He thought irrelevantly how much he liked winter, simply because he could see the Minster's towers from his tiny room at the top of the house; in summer the view was obscured by flourishing sycamores, and from ground level the whole year-round by the walls; but it was always possible to hear the bells pealing out the hours of daily service. The call to Evensong began, and, without glancing at the clock, he knew it was almost four.

"You wouldn't believe it, would you?" she said at last. "You'd think Mamma would berate him, weep, make a scene—demand the restoration of her poor demented daughter to the family home? But no, she's got a mind like a cash register: mention money and she's all ears!"

"What on earth are you talking about?"

"He's talking of changing his will," she said with slow emphasis, as though it was important to pace her words to the ringing of the bells. "And would like to make me an allowance. But I don't want that, either."

Distracted by their melodious accompaniment, Edward found it hard to digest her words, harder still to understand the reasons for her anger. "Why ever not?"

Louisa turned. "Because I love him," she said, amazed that he should need an explanation. "I don't want to be his *kept woman!*"

At a loss, Edward stared back. He wanted to say: but you are! Then he realized why she had been so insistent on keeping her job: it gave her a certain amount of independence. Without it, she would have to rely on Robert Duncannon; either that or come back home.

Beset by his own distrust, he said: "Don't you trust him?"

"Of *course* I trust him!"

"Then why are you so distressed?"

"Can't you see? It would be like—like receiving payment for services rendered. I don't want that."

"Nonsense!" he said sharply, but even as the word was uttered, he recalled his own reaction when Mary Elliott had told him his mother had accepted money. He could see Louisa's point, although he still believed the summons from Blankney was Heaven-sent. Get her away from York, he thought, and in a few weeks this madness will cool. She might be hurt, but better such pain in the short run than long-term anguish and an illegitimate child. Oh, God! he prayed fervently, please don't let that happen!

The inequity of her situation infuriated him, the more so because it seemed the folly of women that they should continue to walk such pitted but well-trodden paths. With an exasperated sigh, he said: "Yes, I do see what you mean. But I think you're being oversensitive. If you were married, you'd expect him to provide for you and—and any children of the union."

"But we're not married. It makes a world of difference."

"It certainly does," he agreed heavily. "But I don't think you're being very practical, which is most unlike you."

"I'm being far more practical than you give me credit for," she said enigmatically, but she turned away and refused to be pressed as to her meaning.

Eventually he simply let it go, returning to the matter of her job. "If I were you," he said as calmly as he could, "I'd follow your mother's advice. Tell John Elliott you'll go to Blankney and see what the hotel has to say about it. And if—if the captain wants to provide for you, then let him. It seems quite natural to me that he should want to protect you financially, since it seems he's unable to do so in any other way."

"I love him," she said suddenly and with such intensity that Edward recoiled, as though from a blow. "I love him so much it frightens me. But if he went away tomorrow and never came back, I'd not regret one minute of the happiness we've shared. Can you understand that?"

No, he thought painfully; I can't, nor do I want to. Chilled, he moved closer to the fire, chafing his work-scarred fingers as he stared into the glowing coals. "It almost sounds as though you expect him to leave you," he accused, while pain and longing fused once more into bitter exasperation. Turning to face her, he exclaimed: "I don't know how you can be so stupid! Does the past mean nothing to you? Your childhood—mine? You were taunted and ridiculed—so was I. I even remember you coming home from school one day with your arms black and blue, your scalp bleeding where one little fiend had pulled out a great chunk of hair."

As she winced from the memory, Edward added viciously: "And our mothers paid the price, too. I remember people spitting at them on Tanner Row, just before we left; I remember the names they were called," he whispered bitterly, "even if you don't."

Slowly Louisa shook her head. "I haven't forgotten."

"But it doesn't matter? You think it can't happen to you?"

With a sigh of despair she shook her head again; still he pressed on. "Just thank God they had money behind them, Louisa—because without it they'd have ended up either on the streets or in the House of Correction, pride beaten, spirits broken. And what would have happened to us then?"

"Oh, stop it!" she cried, blocking her ears. "You were twenty, Edward; you had a job. They had money. We weren't paupers!"

"No," he said softly, "we weren't paupers. Money protected us from the ultimate disgrace. We were reviled, but not, thank God, degraded."

For a moment he searched her face in the twilight, seeing the flush of mortification deepen. Despite the anger, she looked so very young and vulnerable that Edward instinctively reached out, wanting to hold her, build a wall around her, protect her from herself; but she jerked away as though burned.

"You don't know what love is!" she spat out. "If you did, you'd understand."

Pain shot through him, turning his bones to water. In need of support, he turned and leaned against the mantelpiece. As he steadied himself, he strove to regain some of the detachment which had always proved a defense against his mother; to suffer and to show it was to invite greater pain, and he was loath to experience more.

When he had found his voice again, he said tautly: "Perhaps you're right. But still, I think you should accept that allowance. Even if you don't need it now, there may come a day when you'll be glad of it."

She did not reply, but he was aware of her standing a little distance away. On the mantelpiece stood a little porcelain replica of Lincoln Castle; he stared at it for several minutes before it impinged upon his consciousness.

"When will you go to John Elliott's?" he asked.

The question seemed to exasperate her. "Oh, Lord, I don't know. Next week sometime, I suppose. How can you ask that at a time like this?"

He sighed. "I don't know. I was just thinking, I have some business to conduct in Lincoln."

SEVEN

The halt, on a little branch line running southwest from Lincoln, was almost a mile from the village it served. Watching the train puff noisily away, Edward felt strangely deserted, as though an old friend had accompanied him as far as the lion's lair, then suddenly discovered a more pressing engagement.

Until this moment, it had been merely an idea, a fantasy which had grown and taken on shape. In his imagination, Edward had seen himself arriving here like some invisible observer, but with the rich scent of wet earth in his nostrils and the feel of the wooden platform springy beneath his feet, he recognized reality. He was a stranger, and with the curiosity of villagers the world over, the people here would mark his presence, take note of his clothes and the slightly shabby valise, try to classify him, and wonder what he was doing in their community. They would examine his face for familiar features, speculate upon possible relationships; he was bound to be questioned. For a second resolve wavered; had it not been for the searching wind, Edward might have waited for the down-train to return to Lincoln, his curiosity unassuaged.

But there was rain in that sharp wind, and he was already chilled; with a shiver, he picked up his small case, fingered his beard reflectively, and set off along the muddy road.

A local directory in Lincoln Library had provided all the details he required of the village and its environs. There was an inn, a church, a post office, and three shops. Burke's Peerage had furnished a potted biography of his paternal grandparents, now deceased, and their descendants. Sir Alfred Gregory, born under the rule of George III in 1795, had lived through four reigns, finally quitting this life in the year of Victoria's Golden Jubilee. His wife, who predeceased him by some thirty years, had been a peer's daughter, remarkable in that age for her devotion to the poor. Of their three sons, the eldest and present baronet, Sir Oswald, had married his lady in the year 1859, subsequently siring two daughters. His listed interests were the predictably traditional ones of the landed gentry, no doubt funded, Edward thought, by the family's extensive holdings in Nottinghamshire coal.

Alfred, the second son, was a Tory MP for a constituency in the Midlands. He too was married, with two sons and three daughters. There seemed little chance of catching a glimpse of him, with his residences in London and Warwickshire, but Edward planned to make a journey to London for the next important political debate. The way things were going in Parliament, that would probably be quite soon; since the election of the Liberals in July, the question of Home Rule for Ireland was a constant leader in every newspaper. The Tories, with their commitment to the Union, were up in arms; Alfred Gregory dare not miss the vote on that bill, except he was on his deathbed.

Edward's chances of seeing the lord of the manor were remote; it being the hunting season, he could well be away, but there was a possibility he would be in church the following morning. Certainly there was a more than even chance that the youngest of the three brothers would be present.

The youngest son, George, who would have been a mere twenty-three years old in the year of Edward's birth, had never married; taking Holy Orders in 1860, he had been this parish's incumbent for over twenty-five years. He seemed the least likely candidate, but in his desire to know who and what this family were, Edward was determined to view them all with an open mind; and if the vicar took his duties at all seriously, then the likelihood of his preaching the sermon at morning service was a strong one.

As the threatened rain began in earnest, Edward raised his umbrella. He had been walking at an even pace for some ten minutes, along a road that wound between plowed open fields on one hand and dense woodland on the other. A low wall, crusted with gray lichen spirals and topped by velvet cushions of moss, divided the woods from the road; the house itself stood a half mile distant according to the map, beyond some forbidding trees. Although his eyes could not penetrate that deliberately set veil of privacy, he was drawn to look that way, searching for a gap where he might suddenly glimpse it. Then, as the road snaked to the right, he saw a gray lodge, and beyond, set in a semicircle of crenellated wall, a pair of elaborate cast-iron gates. But the gravel drive curved between banks of mature rhododendrons, so that even here the house remained invisible to the casual passerby.

He stood and stared, aware that he might be watched from the lodge, wishing that he had the courage to go back, climb the wall, and creep upon the place unobserved, but the real possibility of traps in those woods, the indignity of being caught by a patrolling keeper, urged his steps toward the village. With a sigh, he pressed on.

The muddy country lane became the village street, meandering like a soft brown ribbon between steep-gabled cottages, mostly thatched and whitewashed, an occasional red-brick house standing like a guardsman in between. A broad lane led off to the right toward the church, whose tower could be seen above the rooftops, and on the left stood the inn, square, two-story, its yard and stables behind.

After a moment's hesitation Edward entered the bar, waited while the landlord served a bent old character his pint of ale, then made himself known. He had telegraphed two days previously, requesting bed and board for one night. While the landlord went off to find his wife, Edward glanced around, catching the expected curious stares from a group of elderly farmworkers by the fire. The room was a typical barroom, stone-flagged, with wooden settles and benches, but the sawdust was clean and the brassware well polished, and logs blazed cheerfully in the grate.

The landlord returned with a boy, whom he installed behind the bar, and led Edward through to an inner hall which obviously served as a snug, for there was a tiny bar with bottles of spirits, easy chairs, and a desk in the corner. As he signed the register, Edward was subjected to a string of oblique questions; reluctant to lie, he smiled and shook his head and, remembering details from the directory, murmured something about interesting monuments in the church. At that, the short, round man visibly relaxed. Apparently other visitors came to the village, although usually in the summer months, to view the tombs of a family dead these 400 years. There was even a brass plate, very old indeed, which always aroused great excitement, although the innkeeper himself could never understand why. Nevertheless, proud of this claim to fame, he willingly revealed every scrap of fact and fiction he could remember, until Edward thought he would never see his room.

At last, her feet heavy on the creaking wooden stairs, his wife appeared, and the landlord excused himself. Without a word, she led Edward upstairs and opened the door to his room. As she turned to leave, he thanked her and said, "Could you tell me—" for a second he hesitated— "what time is morning service?"

"Half past ten, sir," she replied curtly.

He was about to inquire whether Sir Oswald and his family were in residence at the hall, but her abrupt, faintly hostile manner threw what remained of his confidence. He glanced at his pocket watch: it was just turned three. Time enough to unpack and take a leisurely walk over to the church; there he could examine the more recent memorials, mark the position of the family pew, and prepare himself for the morrow.

For such a small village, the church was a delight, a combination of early and late Gothic styles which had been sympathetically restored some twenty years before. Edward's opinion of the family had risen several degrees as he noted the fine Early English porch, unspoiled lancet windows in the aisles, and beautiful hammerbeam roof. Only the east window jarred; it seemed an arrogant gesture to have a great armorial window above the altar, although it was compatible with the tombs of long-dead knights and their ladies in the nave.

Fascinated though he was by the early monuments, it was the more recent ones which really interested him. Judging by the inscriptions on those marble tablets, the forebears of the present family would seem to have been patriotic paragons of great virtue, exceptional sportsmen, soldiers, and public benefactors. Over the years there had been several clergymen, younger sons of course, but only one had achieved the purple; judging by the present incumbent's length of service in this humble sphere, it seemed unlikely that he held any such ambition, and, almost unwillingly, Edward's heart warmed to him.

As he waited for the service to begin, he took surreptitious glances at the newcomers. Several prosperous-looking farmers, surrounded by wives and offspring, took named pews; laborers with scrubbed, weather-beaten faces; dairymaids in their Sunday finery; servants and shopkeepers. Gradually the church filled, but still the family pew at the rear remained empty. Aware of a quite unreasoned disappointment, Edward stood to let two young women file past him into the pew. Each of them blushed; the prettier one, nearest him, sucked in her cheeks to suppress a wayward smile, and he felt his own mouth twitch a little as he stole covert glances at them on their knees. They were farm girls by the look of them, with heavy boots beneath their best serge skirts, and their hands, clasped in spurious prayer, were coarse and red. But the curve of the pretty one's cheek, her full mouth and firm chin, reminded him of Louisa; he found it hard to drag his eyes away.

When he looked back, the pew he had been watching so carefully was filled. For a second his heart seemed to halt in his breast and with a sudden rush began to beat fiercely; quickly he glanced down, fiddled with his prayer book, found the relevant page, and then, when he had gained control of that sudden sense of panic, looked around again.

A rather bloated, elderly man sat farthest away from him. He had prominent eyes and thick white hair; the yellow stains on his heavy moustache proclaimed an addiction to tobacco and, judging by his red face, to good port also. Edward viewed him with a mixture of distaste and disappointment. On the flimsiest of grounds, Edward had judged him as favorite for the role of his mother's one-time lover, for he was closest in age and the eldest son. As such, a well-placed marriage would have been most important to him. Looking at the desiccated and haughty woman at his side, Edward wondered if he had been happy and suspected not. There was a young couple with them, the girl a younger, haughtier version of her mother, the man remarkable only for his fine clothes.

With his eyes upon his prayer book once more, Edward reflected that his mother had also been haughty in her way; perhaps Sir Oswald was always attracted to the same type of woman. The realization that this man could be his father filled him with instant disillusion; he wished he had not come, that he had merely gathered the information and returned to York with fantasies intact. Even to the blindest, it must be obvious he had nothing in common with this man, nothing at all; even without vanity, Edward knew he bore no physical resemblance to him and had none of his tastes. But, with disturbing insight, it came to him that few sons favored their fathers closely; contiguity seemed to force them to be different. Yet he had not resembled his mother, either.

Was he really Elizabeth Elliott's son? Suddenly the terms of her will came back to him: "And to my reputed son, Edward Thomas Elliott . . ." That had hurt, wickedly. In a riot of confusion, his thoughts tumbled over one another, and he covered his eyes, afraid that someone would see the panic he felt.

The congregation rose. George Crispin Gregory, vicar of this parish, followed by his curate, entered the body of the church and took his place on the right of the chancel. Edward barely glanced at his book. The opening hymn was a well-known one, and he knew most of the words by heart. His eyes were transfixed upon the priest, Sir Oswald's youngest brother; yet so unlike were they, Edward began to doubt the identity of the man behind him. The vicar was a small, spare man, on paper a mere five years younger than his eldest brother, yet to look at them there could have been almost twenty. He was balding, but what remained of his hair showed traces of its original fairness among the gray; his nose was high-bridged and narrow, he wore no beard or moustache, and his eyes and skin were parchment-pale. So many years had passed since Edward had last seen himself clean-shaven, he could hardly recall the shape of his own mouth and jaw, but there was a distinct familiarity about the vicar's face; Edward felt that he was looking at an older version of himself.

Suddenly, without warning, knowledge hit him; chills ran up his spine and his knees seemed about to give way beneath him. It was pure, unreasoned instinct, but Edward knew, with every fiber of his being, that the man who stood at the head of this congregation was his father. As he grasped at the wooden ledge in front of him for support, he questioned it, examined it, and thrust the knowledge away as ridiculous. The man who wore those priestly robes would have been a mere twenty-two years old at the time of Edward's conception, a full nine years Elizabeth Elliott's junior. It seemed incredible that a young man, who must even then have had strongly religious inclinations, should consort with a servant, a woman so much older than himself. It was easy to imagine Sir Oswald deflowering housemaids almost as a matter of course, but that image refused to fit the cleric. Aside from his calling, the fact that he had never married precluded an obsession with fleshly pursuits.

On his knees, Edward forced himself to concentrate on the words of the General Confession, but his own sins were far from his thoughts; as that light, dry voice pronounced the Absolution, he remembered Mary Elliott's words, her repetition of his mother's insistence that her lover had promised to marry her. In his anger and frustration that night, he had thought it simply a trite excuse for wrongdoing. Faced with the man himself, for the first time Edward believed it might be true. Perhaps the young George Gregory *had* loved Elizabeth Elliott, but parental pressure had ensured he did not commit the folly of marrying her.

Edward thought of Maud and parallels in his own life. He had accepted her parents' decision with a broken heart but little protest; Maud herself had wept and pined, but for her to defy them was unthinkable. In this man's case, Edward reasoned, he must have had so much more to lose than mere parental regard.

Framing the words of hymns, uttering responses which were automatic, Edward paid attention only to his father's face and voice. The sermon was based upon the lesson for the twenty-first Sunday after Trinity, the story of King Nebuchadnezzar and the three defiant Jews, Shadrach, Meshach, and Abednego, who were delivered unscathed from the fiery furnace. The theme was faith and the rejection of false gods; the content was not particularly inspired, nor was it delivered in tones of ringing conviction; instead the vicar gently exhorted his flock to set less store by earthly possessions, to reject temptation in the form of an easy life, and to have faith in God alone.

Privately Edward thought such choices could hardly apply to half the congregation, for judging by their poor clothes and honest faces, faith in God was about all they had; and as for the rest, the area's comfortable middle class, to them social position was all, and faith a very abstract concept. In a quick backward glance he noted Sir Oswald's bowed head and closed eyes and his wife's glazed expression. They've heard it all before, he thought, and was suddenly sorry for the man in the pulpit.

Too soon, it seemed, the service was over, and the baronet's wife, daughter, and son-in-law were sweeping out after the barest few words with their relative. Instead of following them, however, Sir Oswald stood beside his younger brother, affably shaking hands with the most worthy, nodding pleasantly to the rest, generally presenting a united front of beneficent church and state.

Keeping his seat as much from curiosity as politeness, Edward waited for the crowd to thin; standing to let the farm girls leave, he followed them to the door. The vicar acknowledged their brief curtsies with a smile, but his eyes lingered on the stranger. Edward inclined his head at that kindly curiosity, but before he could make his escape, the now familiar voice addressed him.

"How pleasant to see a new face in our congregation! Will you be with us long, Mr.—?"

It was a moment Edward had not envisaged. Yet as he grasped the extended hand and gave his name, he knew he could not have lied had his life depended on it. "Elliott," he said. "Edward Elliott."

He wondered if he imagined the flicker in those calm gray eyes, but in the following momentary silence, the hand that held his tightened perceptibly. "It—it's a short visit only—I came to see the church," he stammered, aware of a warmth in cheeks and brow. He withdrew his hand from the other man's grasp, but those eyes still held his, searching now, and more than merely curious.

"Yes—people do. It's quite famous. Have you seen all the monuments?" he asked, gesturing toward the north wall. "Quite fascinating— the older ones in Latin, of course, and not very good Latin at that!" He laughed shortly, then glanced at his fidgeting brother, who was obviously keen to be gone. The church was empty but for the three of them. "Perhaps you'd care to call at the vicarage tomorrow afternoon, Mr. Elliott?" he suggested. "Then I could show you around. It's no trouble, I assure you—the church and its monuments are one of my enthusiasms."

Momentarily overcome, Edward bit his lip. "I wish I could take you up on that kind offer, sir, but unfortunately I must be back in York this evening. Nevertheless, I thank you most sincerely."

The older man seemed genuinely disappointed. "That is unfortunate. But perhaps you'll visit us again?"

"I most certainly will," Edward promised warmly and, with a polite bow, bade the two men good morning.

As his footsteps echoed in the stone-flagged porch, he heard Sir Oswald say: "Deuce take it, George! D'you have to befriend every waif and stray that admires this heap of old stones? I'm off before Hermione has me hung. Will we see you for dinner?"

The reply was inaudible, but Edward could verify the baronet's words as he passed the carriage beyond the gate. Lady Hermione watched with gimlet eyes; and in part-apology for having kept her waiting, Edward smiled and tipped his hat. So exultant was his mood, it seemed his heart performed somersaults; he had no proof beyond that wild surge of instinct, but he was convinced that the invitation had more to do with his name and who he was than any ancient monument, however interesting. But his reasons for refusing had a double foundation.

It was true Albert Tempest had been severely put out by Edward's sudden request for two and a half days of absence, and in the end he had had to explain that he was called away on family business which was impossible to deal with on a Sunday. The series of half-truths had caused Edward no compunction, and even now he was tempted to ignore his promise to be back on Monday morning. It was less the promise that put a brake on his inclinations than a fear of things going too fast. He felt he needed time to digest what he had learned, time to arrange his thoughts and emotions in suitable order; time, if necessary, to prepare himself for disappointment.

EIGHT

*O*n a wooden tray covered by a starched white cloth, Harris brought the usual pot of tea, together with the morning's mail. There were two slim, buff envelopes with York postmarks, which looked like bills, and a heavy white one, postmarked Lincolnshire, addressed to the captain in a neat copperplate hand. That should cheer him up, Harris thought as he laid the tray down; in a week's absence, this was her first letter, and the captain had been crusty as an old colonel for the past four days.

Pushing back the curtains, Harris announced that it was a fine morning. "A bit of mist lingering, sir, but that should soon clear. Chilly, though—should I light the fire, sir?"

With his eyes still closed, Robert murmured his assent. He listened to the rattling and scraping sounds for a minute or so before pulling himself into a sitting position. The cold air on his skin woke him fully; with a shiver he hitched the quilt around his shoulders, reached for the tea, and suddenly noticed the letters.

"Good God, Harris, there's mail. Why did you not say? Pass me the paper knife, will you?" He cast the two bills aside and weighed Louisa's letter in his hand. "Well, she might not write as often as one would wish, but . . ."

Eagerly he slit the envelope open and extracted half a dozen pages of close-written script. The first page, dated Sunday evening, described the chaos of her cousins' house, with children running wild, Jenny fretting herself into a fever, and enough laundry to keep a washerwoman busy for a week. Robert smiled at the image conjured up by her description of John Elliott's misery, his evident relief at Louisa's capable management of household and willing but disorganized neighbors.

There was a break, occasioned by a sudden crisis, the narrative not resumed until Tuesday. Having sung the praises of her cousin's eldest daughter, an adorable five-year-old, Louisa was prompted to ask after Victoria Tempest.

With a heavy sigh, Robert turned the page and read on. "Did you see anything of the Bainbridges or Rachel in the last week? I do hope so. The thought of Victoria nags at me dreadfully, but Rachel is the only one who can do anything, and I am afraid she may be too taken up with her recent success in society to bother.

"Thinking of home reminds me of how much I am missing you. This week has been so busy, I have hardly had time to think and have fallen into bed each night utterly exhausted! Together, the older children are like a barrel of monkeys; they try my patience dreadfully, but the baby is a little cherub. He sleeps all night and hardly ever cries, which is quite remarkable, I must confess you now have a rival, Robert, as I have fallen in love with my little cousin! Jenny says she is afraid I may take him home with me when I go!

"I am pleased to say that she seems much improved even in the last few days, although the doctor said yesterday that he hoped I would stay at least until the end of the month.

"Hopefully I shall be back with you by the first week in December, and by then we shall be thinking of Christmas, which I can hardly believe, the year has gone so quickly. How strange it seems that this time last year I did not know you, nor had any inkling that you were about to enter my life and my heart. Now I cannot imagine a time when I did not know you, did not love you. How strange, yet how wonderful it is.

"I hope you have not missed me too much, my love, and that there has been some good hunting weather in Yorkshire. It has been ideal here. I saw the Blankney pack one frosty morning last week, and they are indeed a most stirring sight. Sometimes I wish I had learned to ride, but other than plod around a field on somebody's old mare when I was a child, I never had the opportunity. One day, perhaps when we go to Ireland, you might teach me?

"I really must close now and take this letter to the post in the morning. My eyes will barely stay open, but I go to bed in hopes to dream of you until we are together again—from your ever-loving Louisa."

At the bottom of the page was a hastily scribbled postscript: "Thanks for your note which arrived just now. I'm sorry you were worried, but there was no need. Glad you've seen Mamma. If you go again, give her my love and any news as I may not have time to write again for a while. P.P.S.—Do not tell her this, however—I have had a letter this morning from Edward. His few days in Lincolnshire proved most worthwhile— more about that when I see you. Love, Louisa."

Robert frowned, wondering at that last cryptic comment. Shaking his head, he turned to the beginning and read the letter through again. It was so typical of her, revealing in ways she did not dream of, ways he loved, even while part of him disapproved. It was hard work she was doing, servants' work, and he regretted the somewhat reproachful note he had sent the other day, instructing her to write as soon as possible; but he knew from past experience she was not much given to writing letters, and he had been anxious that she would not bother at all.

In seven days he had missed her with an intensity out of all proportion to the length of her absence, and because she was so out of reach, he longed for her both mentally and physically, was victim of a restlessness which had little to do with the enforced idleness of winter.

Sighing again, he returned the closely written pages to their envelope and, leaning back, allowed himself the luxury of a prolonged, tendon-cracking stretch.

"Well, Harris," he said at last, "it's about time I moved. I think an appearance on the parade ground is required this morning."

Naked, he stepped out of bed and thrust his arms into the robe his servant held ready. "Wish I'd known it was going to be fine today—could've made arrangements to go out with the York and Ainsty. Will it last, do you think?" he inquired, peering at the high arc of blue above the low-lying mist.

"Might be foggy tonight, sir, but it should be clear in the country."

"Hmm. Well, we can try it tomorrow. I could do with a spot of exercise. I'll see what the duty roster has in store and fix something up with Tommy."

"Right you are, sir."

Having brought up the hot water for his master's bath, Harris automatically checked each item of uniform for the morning's mounted parade: frock coat, pantaloons, knee boots and jack spurs; sword with sabretache, white sword sling and belt, white gloves, and last but not least, the round pillbox hat. From separate drawers he took out a freshly laundered shirt and clean underclothes, found fresh white towels, and set them to warm by the fire.

While the captain took his bath in the dressing room, Harris proceeded to strip the narrow bed, smiling to himself as he recalled that warm summer's evening, the night she had slept here, and the curious train of events which followed.

He continued to smile as he remade it, squaring the ends of each sheet and blanket, laying the eiderdown and counterpane with exact precision. He and the captain had a tacit understanding about Miss Elliott; in case of emergency, he had the apartment's address, knew how often the captain visited her and for how long; and despite that solitary meeting, Harris felt he knew Louisa Elliott intimately, simply because his master reflected her every mood. In her own very original way, she had the man dangling from her finger as neatly as any courtesan. The situation afforded Harris much innocent amusement.

He pushed the bed back into place, then took two warmed towels through into the dressing room. Picking up the tray from the bedside table, he winked and nodded at Louisa's photograph in its silver frame; as always, he could have sworn those long eyelashes dipped slyly and that enigmatic mouth broadened into a conspiratorial smile. Still grinning, Harris turned, tray in hand, and saw his master was already out of the bath, watching him. His name was spoken with deceptive softness.

"Sir?"

Robert tucked one towel around his waist and slowly rubbed his arms and chest with the other. "Do you make a habit of leering at that particular portrait?"

"No, sir!"

"Good. I'm relieved to hear it. I should so hate to lose you to the drill sergeant."

With tray in hand, Harris endeavored to come to attention. "Sir!"

As his servant stiffly left the room, Robert picked up the guilty picture. He stared at it for a long time, a half-smile on his lips, remembering the afternoon they had gone to the studio on Lendal. Quite deliberately he had stood behind the camera and stared at her, and the result had been three quite delightful portraits. She often looked like that: amused, secretive, slightly challenging, wearing that ladylike reserve as she would a high-necked gown. It was part of her charm, he decided, and felt again the familiar response within himself. Firmly he set the frame down in its usual place and strode back into the dressing room, slamming the door shut behind him.

"Blast Harris!" he muttered and reached for his clothes.

He returned at six, having turned out for the mounted parade at ten that morning, performed a stables inspection at twelve, and done a spot check of the men's victuals an hour later. Following his own meal, there had been an interview with the adjutant regarding Christmas leave, after which he had been relatively free, choosing to spend the rest of the afternoon in the riding school, watching half a dozen recruits and two new subalterns being put through a form of purgatory by the riding master.

As a diversion on free afternoons, it was generally entertaining and often very revealing. The riders cantered around and around the ring, with saddles, without saddles, without harness, over jumps, hands clasped behind their backs, while Robert watched and smiled grimly, knowing at once who could be relied upon, who must be curbed, and who encouraged. The riding school was no place for vanity or pride; with each sickening thud to the sawdust, reality was hammered home, and in the end most of those men would sit a horse as though born to it, controlling the animal instinctively. In the fray of battle, this would be vital.

Tommy had joined him for a while, to make hopeful arrangements for the following day; but as they left after evening stables, the feasibility of riding to hounds was very much in question. By noon the brief sun had disappeared, swallowed by a thick pall of fog rolling upriver from the coast. It was certainly not exclusive to the city, although as the two men laughingly struggled to find their way home from the barracks, they could taste sulfur in the saturated air; the effort of finding the Queen Anne house seemed to preclude any idea of returning later to eat in the mess. On a decision to review their hunting prospects the following morning, they parted outside Robert's door.

Inside, the fire was blazing a warm welcome, the lamps were lit, and Louisa's photograph seemed to send him a happy smile. Throwing off his damp cloak, Robert sank into the chair beside the hearth and yawned. His eyes were stinging from the fog, and he was unaccountably tired, glad of the excuse not to have to turn out again within the hour. Momentarily he closed his eyes, then Harris came in and, following the set routine, removed Robert's boots before beginning to lay out his clothes for the evening.

"There's no need, Harris; I'll not be going out again. I'll write some letters and have an early night. Anything will do for supper—bread and cheese, a slice of ham, anything. And some coffee, a pot of good hot coffee with a tot of rum in it to thaw me out."

Less than an hour later he was ensconced at his desk, with a reply to Louisa's letter already under way. He lit a cigar and began a fresh page.

"Bearing in mind what was discussed before you left, I accepted an invitation to tea at the Bainbridge (*fils*) villa on Tuesday afternoon. After two refusals, I was afraid I might be coolly received (not that it would have mattered in the least), but in fact Rachel welcomed me most warmly. She seems to regard my presence at her little gatherings as something of a feather in her cap. (I cannot help but wonder what her attitude would be if she knew of our relationship!)

"Before I went, the thought of what I should say caused me some considerable anxiety, yet once she gave me her attention, it was quite surprisingly easy. I began by commenting on the length of time she had been married, and playing the role I had set myself, referred to the elopement as a truly romantic gesture. (Yes, you may laugh, my darling!) I asked how had her father taken the news, and had he forgiven her yet?

"To expect concern from Rachel was perhaps naive, but I did. There was none that I could see. She laughed and said her father was quite implacable. Then I asked after her little sister. Did she not miss the child or think the little one might pine for her? At that, I admit, the laughter ceased. I saw I had struck an exceedingly painful blow and was almost sorry for it.

"Improvising as I went along, I said I had met up with the child on the Knavesmire, in the company of a servant (describing Moira as well as memory served), that I had not immediately recognized Victoria, she being so much thinner than I recalled, but she had hailed me as I rode by.

"Rachel was much affected by this imaginative tale, whereupon I went on to suggest that she might communicate with either her sister or the maid, perhaps arrange a meeting one afternoon. She said her father would recognize her handwriting! (Does she have no intelligence at all? Truly, I had thought her more practiced in the art of subterfuge!) So then it was necessary to explain that if she printed the address badly and posted the letter in town, her father would be none the wiser.

"So, my love, distasteful though it was, I have done as much as you asked of me, and I hope that is an end of it. I can understand in part your concern for the child, although why you or I should continue to inconvenience ourselves on the Tempests' behalf is quite beyond me. The child is no longer your responsibility, and now that Rachel is aware of the problem, you must try to forget it. It concerns me that the father may see your hand in this kind of interference, and he is too vindictive not to find means of making you suffer for that."

With a sigh, Robert laid down his pen and stood up. Throwing the butt of his cigar into the fireplace, he bent to the warming coffeepot; the liquid was bitter and black, just palatable with an added tot of rum. As he drank, his eyes scanned the pages he had written. At the last line, he sighed again, hoping it really was the end of Louisa's involvement with the Tempests; even their name gave him a feeling of severe disquiet. In many ways, much as he had grown to love York, he knew he would be glad to leave. In some other place, where Louisa was a stranger, gossip would present less of a problem. Although it was only an educated guess, if his next posting was to Dublin, practically his own home ground, there she could be protected. The Duncannons might not be in the same league as Charlotte's titled relatives, but they were not without friends amongst the older Irish gentry. Having led the social life of a hermit since his marriage, Robert felt that perhaps the time had come for him to refresh some of those old connections, and if sympathy had to be bought at the cost of a few words in the right ears, then he was quite prepared to do it. Once, he would have died rather than admit to Charlotte's insanity, but not any more. The price had been paid a hundredfold. In future, Louisa would be by his side, and he was determined she should be accepted.

Taking up his pen again, Robert wrote: "Since you are to be away rather longer than we first thought, I have asked for leave at the end of next week. Not to come to Blankney, although that would have been delightful, but to go to Ireland. There are some matters of business to which I must attend, and while you are otherwise occupied seems a good time.

"Also, the adjutant informs me today that I am rostered for duty at Christmas, so my heart searching on that score is now settled. I intend to persuade Letty to come over here for Christmas, bringing Georgina, of course.

"It will be good to see the child again, for I confess she grows more and more delightful, and I long for you to meet her. I am sure you will love her, for like her father she is both intelligent and charming. She is, however, prettier and more modest!

"In the meantime, I shall take the opportunity to view the worst of the Dublin house. If we are to live there, then certain rooms must be refurbished. It shames me to admit this, but the place has been sadly neglected, and I cannot bear for you to see it in its present state.

"No doubt I shall be in York again before you, counting the hours and minutes to your return. I have missed you most dreadfully and am determined you shall not leave me again, not even on a mission of mercy! Having said that, however, I should like you to give your cousins my warmest regards, also good wishes for Jenny's speedy recovery.

"Until we meet again, my darling, I send you all my love—Robert."

NINE

*T*hree days before Christmas, Robert walked briskly into the station, consulted the arrivals board, purchased a penny ticket, and descended the steps of the subterranean walkway which led to the far platforms. The walls were covered with advertisements for household goods: Reckitt's Paris Blue, Wright's Coal Tar Soap, Van Houten's Cocoa, Rowntree's, and further on, Fry's. He hurried along the tunnel, wondering whether the nation would fall apart without its favorite chocolate drinks: one brand even claimed no breakfast table was complete without it. Shuddering at the thought, he climbed toward daylight, feeling the cold, sooty air catch at his throat.

An east wind funneled round the station's long curve and, chilled, he hugged his overcoat closer. The clock showed twenty-seven minutes past eleven; five minutes to wait if the train was on time, five minutes of mixed anticipation, eagerness to see his daughter and Letty, and unease at thoughts of what lay ahead.

Porters hovered, blowing on mittened fingers, ready to offer assistance to the next batch of alighting passengers; slipping a silver sixpence into one ready palm, Robert issued instructions, promising another when the luggage was safely delivered to the Station Hotel. He glanced at the clock again, marking the fact that the train was a minute late; as he did so, he heard its rumbling approach, seconds later seeing it, gleaming black livery wreathed about with steam, easing gently around the western curve, hissing and groaning past him, until, like some monstrous animal, it came to rest with a heaving sigh.

He saw Georgina's face first, hands waving excitedly from the window, then Letty's tall figure, hair awry as usual, broad-brimmed hat perched like a boat atop a wave. As soon as the door opened, Georgina flew into his arms, her warm and eager little body clinging hard, as though she would never let him go. He swept her up with delight, hugging his sister with a free arm, greeting the maid by name as she bobbed a curtsy, her rosy Irish face full of smiles.

While Bridget directed the porter toward their luggage, Robert took his daughter to see the engine, still hissing quietly, still emitting an occasional puff of steam as though anxious to be gone. Awed and impressed, Georgina watched with round eyes as a cleaner bravely polished brass rails and plates, running a soft cloth over red, gray, and cream lines on engine and tender. Catching her eye, the fireman winked and smiled, a pink and white beam in that grimy face; the driver touched his cap to them, and Robert smilingly returned a half-salute of thanks as he led Georgina away. She went reluctantly, constantly turning, until the walls of the subway finally cut the engine from view.

In the tunnel she found her voice, relating the high points of the journey and asking questions so fast there was no space for anyone to reply.

"I thought children were supposed to be seen and not heard?" Robert ruefully asked, noting the several heads which turned and smiled at that high, piping, demanding little voice.

"Not this one," Letty replied equably. "She has everyone organized, from Bridget to the butler. Isn't that so, Bridget?"

"Then I don't stand a chance," Robert commented, returning the brightly beaming smile his daughter offered.

"Do you know, Daddy, the boat was going up and down and round and round—such fun it was! And I was liking it, but Auntie and Bridget made me lie down. They weren't liking it at *all!*"

Letty pursed her lips at this reminder of their seasickness. "That's quite enough, dearest!"

As a tactful diversion, Robert said, "Was the crossing very bad?"

"Bad?" His sister raised her eyes in supplication. "Had I known, I'd never have left Dublin!"

"But you've crossed before."

"In the summer!"

"It can be unpleasant, even then," he remarked with feeling. "Never mind—it's dry land you're on now, and the suite I've booked for you should be comfortable. At least you can dine and relax in privacy—public rooms are no place for children."

Gratefully Letty glanced at her brother. "It sounds ideal."

"I hope so," he murmured fervently, which made her think it must also be expensive. Pushing her hat squarely down on its luxuriant bed of springy curls, she followed him up the steps and into the Royal Station Hotel's grand foyer, ready to be appreciative because of the trouble he had taken. But, with a sinking feeling, she realized it was not the sort of place she greatly cared for: it was too modern, too overbearing with its crimson walls and heavy furniture. A large, gilt-framed portrait of the queen glared balefully at the turn of the magnificent staircase, while Landseer stags threatened from Scottish mountain crags. The royal passion for all things Scottish had also been echoed in the tartan carpet. It was all very different to White Leigh, with its Chippendale and Sheraton furniture and mild-eyed Stubbs horses gazing from even milder landscapes.

There were people everywhere, milling about, seated on plush sofas, all showing off their latest and most elegant clothes; catching sight of herself in a floor-length mirror, Letty made a face: overtall, thin as a whip, as their father always said, and dressed no better than a poor parson's daughter. Guiltily she looked away, wishing she had taken her sister-in-law's advice and bought a whole new wardrobe of clothes; but resentment at Anne's spending habits, and foolish pride in her own thriftiness, had made refusal instantaneous and adamant. With a regretful sigh, she grasped her niece's hand and climbed the stairs.

Their suite was much more to Letty's liking, decorated in light floral colors and not overburdened with heavy tables and chairs. With pleasure she went to the window, pulling back green velvet curtains to let in more light. The view caught her by surprise: an expanse of charmingly laid-out gardens, which must be a delight in spring and summer, and the city beyond, white cathedral towers disembodied above the city's smoky haze.

With a satisfied smile, Robert slipped an arm around her shoulders. "See the Minster? Magnificent, isn't it? And wait till you see it close to—I swear there's not a sight to equal it in all England."

A quizzical smile lit his sister's slate-gray eyes. "That's not what you thought when you first came here," she reminded him.

"It must have been a foggy day," he said, grinning.

"I'm thinking you were the foggy one!"

"Perhaps." His eyes traveled upriver, finding the railway bridge and, beyond that, guessing the location of Louisa's apartment; back again, and there were the ruins of St. Mary's Abbey showing white between winter-naked trees, the half-timbered Hospitium close by the riverbank. "Do you see the ruins?" he asked. "The gardens there are quite beautiful, even at this time of year. I must show them to you. Quite a collection of rare plants and trees—nothing like the size of White Leigh, of course, but the setting is delightful."

"I should enjoy that," she said with obvious pleasure. Gardening for her was both a hobby and an obsession. "Perhaps this afternoon?"

"If you say so," he agreed. "We'll have a walk around while the weather holds."

While Bridget unpacked their luggage, Letty agreed that they should take their midday meal downstairs, although as they entered the high-ceilinged dining room, she swore to herself that she would not make a habit of it.

With its white napery and banks of hothouse chrysanthemums, the room had the atmosphere of a church, gathered diners eating in hushed intensity, their conversation, unlike their plates, small and insignificant. Having given vent to a brief burst of energy upstairs, Georgina once again subsided into silent awe, for which her aunt was thankful. She loved the child like a mother, but like a mother she had the same clear-sighted view of both faults and virtues.

Georgina could be as bossy as she was mischievous and in some ways seemed old beyond her years. "Walked this earth before, that one has," Bridget often said, and on occasion Letty was inclined to agree. Usually, and more logically, she attributed the child's shrewd remarks to the peculiar circumstances at home; the difficult atmosphere was bound to have its effects. The child knew Charlotte was her mother, knew also that the poor woman was as sick in mind as others were in body. Letty made a point of stressing that, taking Georgina with her when she visited the old and ill who were part of White Leigh's responsibility. But even at the best of times, it was never easy, with William and Anne maintaining a stiff-lipped endurance, ignoring Charlotte's presence in their house as well as they were able. They suffered her, as Letty well knew, simply because the interest from Charlotte's fortune paid their bills.

At the worst of times, it was almost unendurable. She still blamed herself for what had happened a year ago, knew she would carry the terrible memory of it to her dying day.

But Charlotte had been so good, for so long! Lucid, eager to please, happily content to watch her little daughter playing with her toys. Never alone, of course, but Letty's blood still ran cold whenever she thought of what might easily have happened, picturing the child lying bleeding and broken . . . That sudden obsession with cleanliness and appearance might have been a clue, but Charlotte's quietness had lulled all suspicion, while she waited like a spider for her intended victim. And like a fool, Letty thought, I encouraged him to walk into the trap.

Until that day, she had pitied her, feeling that in many ways she was an injured party; but the way she had been duped, the evil slyness of it, had ended that. Letty would never forget the scene which met her eyes that Christmas morning: returning from church, seeing the abject confusion on the servants' faces; racing up the stairs to find Robert lying across the bed where he had collapsed, his shirt covered in blood. She had thought him dead. So had Georgina. Her sudden, panic-stricken screams had filled Letty's ears, never to be forgotten.

Even now the child's nightmares were not entirely gone. For weeks after his departure she had wept for him at night, asking for him, demanding to know where he was and why he would not come back. For some inexplicable reason, she adored her father; yet until recently he had shown little more than perfunctory interest in her. Letty had thought he could not love the child, that she represented too clearly the thorns which stabbed his conscience. Something had broken his obsession with Charlotte, however; thawed that frozen expression and dammed the seemingly endless flow of alcohol, restoring him to thinking, feeling life.

She had known it was a woman, of course. The only difficulty had been in restraining her own bubbling curiosity. Who was she? What was she like? How had it come about?

Once or twice in the summer, he had seemed almost on the point of speaking, then shied away, as though his happiness was too new, too fragile to risk in the hands of another. Then, a month ago, he had telegraphed from Dublin, and she had arrived to find him in the midst of alterations, surrounded by samples of curtaining and wallcoverings and eager, at last, to share his plans for the future.

Her pleasure at this badly needed refurbishment of their mother's house was tempered by Robert's proposals. She did not begrudge him his mistress, but the idea of her living there while the Royals were stationed in Ireland was nothing short of madness.

One reason for accepting this invitation of Robert's had been the hope of meeting Miss Louisa Elliott. From his description she sounded decent and sensible, not at all the sort who wished to flaunt herself at Robert's expense; although one could never tell, Letty thought. Where women were concerned, men could be inordinately blind. At some suitable moment, she decided, she would ask him to bring the young woman to dinner; probably tomorrow evening, for he would be otherwise engaged on Christmas Day. Then, with Georgina safely in bed and asleep, she would have a chance to assess Miss Elliott's character.

Certainly she was deserving of gratitude, whatever her personality; Robert was in marvelous spirits, relaxed and lighthearted, his sense of humor bubbling forth in laughter which evoked memories of other, happier times. Watching him now with Georgina, eyes bright as he listened to her confidences, she knew this journey was already worthwhile, whatever the outcome of the other matter. Bringing the child here, to celebrate Christmas with her father away from White Leigh, had been the only true incentive. God willing, the terrors of a year ago would soon be forgotten.

TEN

Since returning from Blankney, Louisa's days had no routine about them at all. Unexpectedly and almost guiltily delighted by this newly acquired freedom, she came and went at will, sometimes rising early, like the ideal housewife buying meat and vegetables at their freshest and best, on other occasions lying in bed till lunchtime, surrounded by books and journals. In the past her reading had been restricted to a stolen hour before bed; now she read voraciously, indulging that particular passion to the full. It was a novelty, and for the present she relished it, aware that eventually her days would develop a pattern of their own.

But as she tidied away her books and clothes, Louisa was very conscious of a stomach-tightening anxiety. Robert had arranged two days' leave of absence in lieu of his duties over Christmas, and while dressing that morning he confessed to feeling, for the first time, like an adulterous husband.

"Which is what I am," he had declared somberly, "but it never occurred to me before. Must be the thought of Letty—wondering how she's going to take all this."

At that Louisa had begun to panic. Mistakenly, it seemed, she had assumed all was arranged beforehand; now it was obvious he had told Letty very little indeed. For fear she would refuse to make the journey at all, he had not asked her to meet Louisa; but blithely overriding all her fears, he maintained it was of no account. "All I want is for you to meet Georgina, and somehow I shall arrange it."

And somehow he would, Louisa thought, feeling a small tremor of excitement lighten her anxiety. Seeing father and daughter together would reveal another dimension of the man she loved, a side she very much wanted to know and share. His sister, Letty, was quite another matter, however; despite the glowing portrait Robert painted, Louisa had had enough experience of well-born ladies to know that even the best of them could crush lesser beings like walnuts in a vise.

Having killed an hour or more about the apartment, she could stand the tension no longer; changing her clothes, Louisa donned new coat and bonnet and set off toward town, up the hill to Bootham, through the bar and into Petergate.

There was the nerve-tingling expectancy of Advent in the streets, a special excitement which seemed to alert every sense to sights and sounds and smells which only a week before had gone unnoticed. The smoke-grimed medieval buildings looked like Hansel and Gretel houses, huddling secretly together, their windows brightly dressed feasts to tempt the buyer inside. Passing a better-class inn, the warm smell of cigars and wine reminded her with unexpected poignancy of Robert; outside a greengrocer's, the mixed scent of evergreens and fruit made her want to go in and buy a dozen of everything. People were different, too: gentlemen tipped their hats, ladies smiled as they crossed her path, and Louisa smiled back, loving the few days before Christmas when the world was a kinder place and all things seemed possible.

She lingered in front of the toy shop where, a few days before, Robert had bought an exquisite china doll with blue eyes and real hair, its garments complete in every tiny detail. Like a child herself, she had exclaimed over it, laughingly envying the small girl for whom it was intended. Her own dolls had been robust rather than elegant, but loved and cared for all the same. With a secret smile she thought back to those days, remembering the eager anticipation, wondering what treats Mamma would have in store for them. Always there had been stockings filled with apples and little, bitter oranges, freshly minted pennies which gleamed like golden treasure in the dark of a winter's morning, and an extra, special surprise for each of them, different every year.

Christmas in the North Riding had been a grand affair, almost eighteenth-century in its lavishness, she thought, with cook busy for a week or more beforehand and the children rehearsing plays, making presents, and gathering holly and mistletoe by the cartload. It had all been such tremendous fun, she had hardly minded being unable to get home before New Year.

Last year, however, had been curiously lacking in joy of any kind. The Tempest celebration, if celebration it could be called, was almost puritan in its austerity. Officially the household had been in mourning still, Mrs. Tempest having passed away with the Old Year; but in the absence of any suppressed delight, Louisa suspected there had never been much fun, even at Christmas.

On a sudden impulse she went into the shop and, after much sighing and searching, eventually purchased a gift which could pass unnoticed in the Blossom Street schoolroom. It was a stiff booklet which, with diligent use of paste and scissors, should turn into a miniature theater, complete with characters and scenery. A little advanced for Victoria, perhaps, but she would enjoy it. To ensure delivery to the child, she thought she would address it to Moira, with a covering note. Rachel, of course, was in need of neither presents nor sympathy; her Christmas would be assured of parties and jollity if nothing else; even so, Louisa wondered whether she would spare a thought for her little sister.

Retracing her steps, Louisa passed beneath the huge trade sign of Seale's brush and mat warehouse, feeling very brave as she did so; memories of childhood, when she had imagined the enormous broomhead poised and ready to sweep them all away, brought a smile to her lips. It had terrified her for years, and she had always gone to incredible lengths to persuade her mother to pass on the other side of the street; but across the road lay Merriman's, the pawnbroker's, a place her mother was equally keen to avoid, for reasons which in childhood had never been clear. Glancing at the dusty finery hanging on poles outside, Louisa wondered whether her mother had once had cause to use Mr. Merriman's facility and was anxious never again to catch a whiff of that fusty air.

Turning into Stonegate, she made her way to a small jeweler's where she had noticed a pair of cuff links, tiny enameled shamrocks within a ring of gold. There was no price marked, but feeling the supreme importance of buying Robert a good gift with her own money, she had withdrawn some of her savings; as she walked into the shop, she hoped it was enough. On inquiry, she found the price was less than she had feared; with a small sigh of satisfaction she nodded, and the present was boxed and wrapped; feeling very grand indeed, she stepped out of the shop and made her way toward home.

It was quicker, and also pleasanter, to walk through the Museum Gardens. With Victoria's book tucked beneath her arm, and Robert's present safe in her small drawstring bag, Louisa willingly paid her penny for the privilege. As always, she looked out for the child; they had often come here, sometimes with Rachel, and while she had given up hope of seeing Victoria, she still glanced automatically at groups of children and nannies out taking the air. But it was cold today, the brief spell of midday brightness fading fast; apart from a few disconsolate peacocks, the gardens were practically deserted.

There were three main paths, one breasting the rise where the museum's neoclassical facade looked out over the river, a low path skirting the riverbank, and another which ran diagonally from one to the other, past a small octagonal observatory partially screened by shrubs and trees. Louisa took this central path and had begun to descend the hill when between the trees she saw Robert in the distance by the half-timbered Hospitium, his back turned, apparently looking for someone. Her first instinct was to run toward him, but remembering his sister she stopped, edging backward into the cover of the shrubbery. For a second she stood with her back to the wall of the little octagonal building, aware that her heart was thumping crazily beneath tight-laced stays.

Her intention was to catch her breath, then go. To run into them now would seem prearranged, and Louisa had no desire to antagonize his sister in such a way; but she could not resist another look. She wanted to see Letty Duncannon; even more did she want to catch a glimpse of Georgina.

The spreading branches of a cedar obscured her vision; bending slightly, she peered beneath, seeing the lower halves of two people standing on the lower path. In the same moment, a whispered greeting startled her.

Round blue eyes in a delicately featured face surveyed Louisa with disarming frankness. "Would you be hiding too?"

If there had been a moment's doubt, the lilting words dispelled it. Here was Robert's daughter, after all the plotting and planning, virtually introducing herself. Weakly Louisa chuckled at the irony.

"I would indeed," she softly confessed, noting silvery plaits beneath a deep blue bonnet, fair brows and lashes, and a pink and white complexion. Other than the shape and color of her eyes, the child bore little resemblance to her father. She was, in fact, as dainty as a piece of Dresden, and with a sudden chill, Louisa wondered whether she was looking at a younger version of Charlotte.

Mustering all her years of self-control, she smiled and whispered: "But you mustn't tell."

"Who mustn't I tell?" Georgina asked, bright eyes scanning trees and empty lawns in search of other children.

Disconcerted, Louisa tried to think. "Well," she said at last, "that's a secret for the moment."

"It's Auntie *I'm* hiding from," the little one confided, then, with a frown, added: "And Daddy, too. They're being such a terrible time, looking at all the plants and things. And I'm wanting to see the—the ex—exhibition. And Daddy's being naughty—he won't tell me what it is."

Her little figure expressed such a vast amount of pique, Louisa had to suppress a laugh. She agreed that it was most unfair of him. "But I think you should give yourself up now, before he begins to worry. You could be anywhere—he won't know where to look."

"Yes he will." With elaborate care, Georgina peeped around a corner of the observatory wall, darting back immediately with a giggle of excitement. She pressed herself against Louisa's skirts. "He's here!"

Rooted by panic and indecision, Louisa waited to be discovered, quailing at the prospect of meeting Robert's sister in such undignified circumstances. She closed her eyes, opened them, waited, but no one appeared. The child peered cautiously out. Louisa did the same.

"Well, I'll be damned!" a male voice exclaimed behind them. "Haven't I caught more than I bargained for!"

With a delighted squeal, the child launched herself into Robert's arms. "Didn't I say you'd find me? May we go now? May we? Please?"

"Not so fast! Auntie is walking the other path, looking for you—and where are your manners? What about this lady you've waylaid? Introductions are called for, don't you think?" He looked at Louisa then, his eyes sparkling with mischief.

"I don't know her name," Georgina confided to his coat lapels.

"But I do," he said softly, his eyes never leaving Louisa's. "Her name is Miss Elliott. I'd appreciate you being kind to her, for she's a very dear friend of mine."

Between parted fingers, Georgina peeped at this very dear friend of her father's; for his benefit, she was determined to be shy. "Hello, Miss Elliott," she whispered.

Louisa's lips quivered as she smiled, but she took the little gloved hand in hers. "Hello, Georgina. I'm delighted to make your acquaintance at last. I've heard a great deal about you." Conflicting emotions swamped her heart and mind; she blinked rapidly, wanting to stay and knowing she should go. Loving Robert, she loved his child, too; but there was sudden envy, painful and shocking. The longing for motherhood hit her like a hammer blow.

Avoiding Robert's eyes, she said with difficulty: "I really must get home, I'm afraid—"

He laid a compassionate hand on her arm. "No, don't dash away. Please, not yet."

"What will your sister think of me?"

"I think we're both about to find out," he murmured.

Following his eyes, she looked up to see a tall figure coming toward them from the top path, striding across the grass without apparent care for either skirt or boots.

"So there you are!" she cried. "I was thinking I'd lost the pair of you."

Georgina ran to her, breathless with importance, babbling incoherently about the game of hide-and-seek. Robert followed slowly, his hand still beneath Louisa's elbow, gently urging her forward.

Louisa wondered whether it was possible to die from sheer embarrassment. She hated herself for preempting this meeting, for placing a woman she had so wanted to impress in a difficult position. Expecting the worst, she was unprepared for the amused, if slightly wry, smile which lit that thin, attractive face.

Letty Duncannon shook her head and wagged an admonishing finger at her brother. " 'Tis a desperate man you are!" But she laughed as she came abreast of them.

Raising his hands in mock defense, Robert pleaded innocence in a brogue so thick Louisa stared in astonishment. The child's delighted giggles brought a smile to her lips, however, a smile which broadened as she recognized the playacting for what it was. She grasped Letty's outstretched hand as much in gratitude as greeting.

"Miss Elliott, you must forgive us! We're all slightly mad, you know, across the Irish Sea."

"I don't believe that for a minute," Louisa smiled. "Indeed, I hope you'll forgive me, intruding like this. I was on my way home when I bumped into Georgina." She gave an embarrassed laugh. "We ended up playing hide-and-seek together!"

Letty glanced fondly at her niece. "Bread and water for a week, you little minx!"

Fresh giggles and a tugging at her father's hand gave the lie to that statement, however; their high spirits signified such an easy affection, Louisa was once more afraid she had intruded on time which was precious to them all.

"Well," she said with a brightness she was far from feeling, "I really must be on my way. It's so nice to have met you, Miss Duncannon—"

Briefly Letty's eyes met her brother's. "Robert has promised to take us to the exhibition—won't you join us? That is, unless you're expected somewhere?"

Beset by her sense of what was right and fitting, Louisa hesitated. "Thank you, but—"

"Oh, don't be so stuffy, Louisa. Say you'll come!" Grinning like a schoolboy, Robert squeezed her arm. "You haven't been, and it finishes tomorrow."

"What *is* it, Daddy?"

Playfully he tweaked her nose. "Shall we find out?"

In the Winter Garden of the Exhibition Hall was an extensive display of Australian curios, staged largely, Robert suspected, as a means of stimulating the flow of emigrants to that distant land. Its entertainment value was certainly immense; even in the midst of Friday afternoon, the place was packed with a wide cross section of lively and interested onlookers.

There were minerals and models, pictorial views of mountains and mines and giant anthills, solitary sheep stations and empty deserts; there were living plants and lifelike animals, gaudy birds in glass cages, and two noisy laughing jackasses; and as a further attraction, in case any were necessary, sweet stalls and a shooting gallery.

Reluctantly Robert allowed himself to be coerced. Taking up a rifle, he shot two ducks, not well enough to knock them down, then three more, fair and square.

"Should've known you for a military gentleman, sir," the stallholder muttered ruefully, offering a selection of cheap prizes.

"There are a few of us about," Robert replied. "But don't worry, with guns like these, you won't go out of business!"

Georgina was delighted with her monkey on a stick, inordinately proud of the expertise which had won it; like a little lapdog she kept close to his heels as he led them round the rest of the show, interested and obedient.

Robert kept up a wittily amusing commentary which, intended or otherwise, effectively covered Louisa's quietness. Bringing up the rear of the little party, she obligingly looked and smiled at all he pointed out, but her mind was occupied elsewhere. To her, Robert and his sister were infinitely more fascinating than any duck-billed platypus or aboriginal artifact.

No stranger, meeting them for the first time, could be mistaken as to their relationship, although the resemblance was not totally physical. They shared similar coloring and bone structure, but it was their facial expressions which were most alike; and the longer he was in his sister's company, the more noticeably Irish his accent became. Louisa's amazement went deeper, however: Robert had always possessed the ability to surprise and confound her; that Letty should do the same was uncomfortably disconcerting. It left her doubting the validity of her own beliefs, the upbringing which, in spite of illegitimacy, had always been strictly observant of moral and social codes. It was one thing for Robert to break those rules: he loved her; but for his sister to condone it so lightly was quite beyond Louisa's understanding. Perhaps, as she had said, they were all slightly mad; or was Ireland a different world, where English codes of conduct did not apply?

Her acquaintance with Tommy Fitzsimmons was slight, and with his obvious idiosyncrasies, she thought him simply eccentric. Robert she had thought to be unique. His anecdotes of society and regimental life were often wickedly amusing; they would laugh together like naughty children poking fun at humorless adults; and she was often as bad, relating ridiculous incidents never shared before. Yet the laughter, on her part at least, was tinged with guilt, because they mocked the very structure she had been taught to revere. For the first time she began to suspect that, as an outsider, Robert had never revered it. His thinking had been shaped not by the rigidity of the English upper classes, but by a looser and far more complex society, whose roots were meshed with a culture no Englishman would ever understand.

She remembered that he had not been sent to school until the age of thirteen; his father, Robert once explained, had not quite trusted the public school system, employing tutors until he felt his sons' characters were sufficiently formed to withstand those particular rigors. Letty had never been to school at all; as a result, Robert said, she was far more intelligent and well informed than most men of her age and class. Louisa wondered if that was why she had never married.

Watching them together, Louisa saw how wrong she had been before in making facile assumptions about his background. In spite of that soft lilt in his voice, she had always thought of him as basically English, yet he was not, and if Letty was a yardstick to measure him by, there had been nothing truly English in his upbringing.

This sudden realization distanced him; smiling, he turned and spoke to her, but for one unnerving moment his face was that of a stranger. Was this the man she loved?

His hand was on her arm. "Are you all right?" She shook her head, but his tender concern dispelled the panic. "It's warm in here. Let me take you outside."

"No—no, honestly, I'm all right." She gave a small, tremulous smile. "A goose on my grave—that's all. I'm all right now, really."

His eyes searched her face, not totally convinced. "Sure? We can leave now, if you like. We've seen most of what there is to see."

"No, Robert," she said firmly. "I'm all right."

"Refreshments are being served somewhere. I saw the sign as we came in." He turned to Letty. "A cup of tea, don't you think? We could all do with one."

Georgina slipped her hand into Louisa's. "Was there *really* a goose on your grave?"

Laughter banished the remaining shadows. "I don't think so, dear. It's just an expression."

The child frowned at that, uncomprehending. Louisa bent down to her. "An expression is a way of saying something. 'A goose on my grave' means that I shivered suddenly, for no good reason. Geese on graves are supposed to be unlucky, I think, and bad luck makes you shiver, doesn't it? Because you are frightened.''

"Were you frightened?''

With a smile and crossed fingers, Louisa shook her head. "No, of course not.'' Straightening, she saw Letty grasp an outstretched hand in greeting, then Robert moved to introduce his daughter, revealing Hugh Darnley and Sophie Bainbridge and, hovering uncomfortably, one of the younger Bainbridge boys.

"Oh, isn't she a dainty little thing!'' Louisa heard Sophie say, her little trill of laughter producing an uncertain smile from the child. "And what has she got there? A monkey on a stick! How amusing!''

Georgina retreated to the safety of Letty's skirts, and Sophie laughed again; in startled surprise, Darnley caught Louisa's glance and held it, while with just the right amount of hesitation, as though he had almost forgotten, Robert included her in the introduction. "I believe you already know Miss Elliott.''

Manners under control, Darnley smiled and bowed, but Sophie stood and stared, openly taken aback.

"But of course,'' she said at last. "I'd quite forgotten you were acquainted with Rachel's companion, Captain. How are you, Miss Elliott?''

"I'm very well, Miss Bainbridge.''

"How strange—Rachel only mentioned you the other evening. We wondered what you were doing now?''

Louisa felt herself bridle at this tardy concern; but before she could reply, Robert turned to her with a rather dangerous smile.

"How touching to be so well remembered, Miss Elliott! I'm sure you'll be quite an asset to us in Ireland. Don't you agree, Letty?''

"Oh, indeed! I'm most impressed by all I've heard.'' Faultless as a star performer, she softly patted Louisa's arm. "And Mrs. Delaney-Jones spoke so warmly of you before she went abroad, my dear.''

Out of her depth, Louisa bit her lip, for once thankful for the warm color which flooded her cheeks.

"Well, I've promised these ladies some tea,'' Robert announced heartily, "so I'm afraid we must leave you. It's an excellent show, Darnley. Make sure you see all of it.''

With little nods and bows, they separated, the other party so obviously bemused that Louisa found it impossible to control a smile. In the foyer, Robert steered them past the refreshments and toward the open door. "Let's have tea in the hotel—this place is far too crowded. That's if you don't mind, Letty?''

"Not at all—I should think our new governess deserves it!'' she laughed, pressing Louisa's hand. "How very *rude* that young woman was!''

"Who on *earth*," Robert asked, "is Mrs. Delaney-Jones?"

"I've no idea. She simply sprang to mind. Quite inspired, though, don't you think? And their faces were perfect pictures! All their questions answered, and so ambiguously—the conjecture will go on for days!"

Louisa giggled, then laughed. She laughed, on and off, all the way to the Station Hotel.

When Edward arrived home late on the afternoon of Christmas Eve, his heart leapt as it always did at the sound of Louisa's voice; then memory mocked, and he was left with the usual aching aftermath. Since her return from John Elliott's, his hopes that the affair might fizzle out had been decisively dashed; not only had she come to terms with the loss of her financial independence, Louisa seemed to be reveling in the situation, taking cookery lessons from her mother two or three times a week, even discussing recipes and fashions in the latest women's journals, which was something she had never done. It had become so familiar, he simply sighed as he placed his parcels on the hall table and picked up the evening paper.

The plainly wrapped parcels were his Christmas presents for the family: a desk diary for his aunt, with the name of the hotel engraved on the cover; a large box of her favorite chocolates for Bessie; and good leather gloves for Emily and Blanche. Louisa had admired Emily's wedding present, a leather-bound album for photographs; racking his brains to think of a suitable Christmas gift for her, he had finally decided that nothing else would do. It was impossible to match anything Robert Duncannon might buy her, but he thought she might appreciate the hours of loving workmanship which had gone into the album. Its soft morocco was the finest, each mount engraved with a delicate motif, the heavy pages edged with gold; to him it was a symbol, a most important one, that he still loved her in spite of everything. He hoped she would understand.

Sniffing appreciatively at the soup simmering on the hob, he announced to Bessie that it was cold enough for snow, smiled at her ungracious reply, and went through into the parlor. All the guests were gone, returned to their families for a couple of days at least, and his aunt was relaxing in her favorite chair, feet propped on a small stool in front of the fire. Someone, perhaps Louisa, had decorated a tiny Christmas tree, and colored candles on the mantelpiece lit the gathering gloom of a bitter winter's evening. He poured himself some tea, grimacing at its orange strength as he added milk and sugar.

"Something smells good in the kitchen. Are you eating with us, Louisa?"

"Not this evening—I'm on my way out. But I'll be here tomorrow for Christmas dinner."

"Blanche is coming," his aunt said, stifling a small yawn. "But Emily's going to the Chapmans'. It'll seem strange without her." With an effort, she pulled herself upright. "Goodness me, I'm tired, and there's still plenty to do. Edward, you can't possibly see to read in this light. Fetch some more hot water for the tea, there's a dear, and light the lamps before you strain your eyes."

Putting down his newspaper, Edward did as he was bidden. As he poured a weaker cup of tea for his aunt, he asked whether Louisa wanted more.

"No, I shall have to move myself. Robert will be here soon."

As her cousin reached up to light the lamps, she left the room, returning a few moments later with her hat and cloak. "Goodness, it's cold out there! I think you're right, Edward, we will have snow before morning. Won't that be lovely? A white Christmas!"

Smiling, she turned to the mirror, hat and pins in hand, her eyes taken with the problem of the silly little bonnet, no more than a froth of ribbons and veiling, which on her short curls had little to cling to. As she stood there, arms raised, Edward saw with a sudden catch of his breath how very beautiful she had become. Her face, reflected in the glass, had lost those anxious shadows; her eyes and skin, warmed by the fireglow, were soft and lustrous in a way he had never before noticed. His glance, traveling downward, took in the rich dark blue velvet of her gown, high-necked and long-sleeved, yet perfectly cut to reveal every contour of a perfect hourglass figure. There was a new voluptuousness about her, as though in its very softness her body reached out and begged to be touched.

Knowing nothing of the subtleties of Blanche's trade, he was suddenly disconcerted by a fleeting and perfectly natural response; also antagonized, as though she had flaunted herself deliberately.

Having settled the hat to her satisfaction, Louisa turned to him with a coquettish smile. "How's that?" she asked, much as she had often done in the past. "Will I do?"

For a brief moment his eyes held hers. "Of course," he said, resuming his seat.

As he picked up the newspaper, Louisa leaned over him; he caught her perfume, heavier than the lavender he normally associated with her. "What's wrong?" she asked. "Are you all right, Edward?"

"Perfectly," he murmured, not looking up; but as she turned away, he saw the eloquent shrug, and his aunt's silent response; furious with them both, he turned his eyes to the day's news, but it was ridiculously hard to concentrate.

"Is that clock right, Mamma?"

"It's as close to the Minster bells as I can make it," Edward tersely replied.

"He's late then. It's not like him—he's usually so punctual." She went over to the window, peering out between shrouds of lace.

"What on earth are you so anxious about?" he said with a sigh.

"We're invited out with Robert's sister. I don't suppose she'll mind if we're a couple of minutes late, but he's got tickets for the theater. The show starts at half past seven."

"The theater? Are you mad?" he demanded. Exasperated, Edward rattled the paper. "I don't know why you don't advertise your—your *liaison*—in the press!"

Stung, Louisa glared at him. "Robert's sister will be with us."

For a long moment he glared back. "You think that will make a difference?"

The sound of a carriage drawing up outside broke the tension. Louisa flew to the window, almost upsetting the little Christmas tree. "Where's my mantle? Oh, here it is—thank you, Mamma," she whispered breathlessly as her mother arranged it around her shoulders. She was halfway to the door as Bessie showed Robert in.

A gust of cold air came with him, and a sense of excitement. Through narrowed eyes Edward noted the elegant evening clothes, the proprietary hand on her arm, his aunt's almost involuntary brightening. Then there was a kiss for her, a prettily wrapped gift and a small posy of Christmas roses for Bessie. With apologies for not being able to see them all on Christmas Day, he shook Edward's hand heartily and, on a flood of seasonal best wishes, ushered Louisa to the door.

"Your umbrella!" Bessie called after them. "Don't forget your umbrella. It'll be snowing tonight, most like . . ." And Louisa dashed back, kissing Bessie and her mother before the door closed finally behind them, leaving a strange and empty silence in their wake.

ELEVEN

*I*n the darkness of the carriage, Robert kissed her lingeringly. "Sorry I was late," he whispered. "I was held up in the mess— they're celebrating already. Forgive me?"

"I might," Louisa teased, "if you kiss me again."

"Mmm," he breathed against her lips, "that's a terrible penance." Beneath her mantle, his hand slipped down from shoulder to breast. "You look lovely in that gown—so lovely, I can't wait to see you take it off . . ."

Giggling, Louisa pushed his hand away. "Stop that this minute!"

"Yes," he said with a laugh, "I think I'd better." Leaning back, he began to search his pockets, finally producing a small, square box. "I have your Christmas present—a little early, but I thought perhaps you'd like to wear it. That blue velvet should set it off perfectly. Here." He opened the box, and in the darkness something glittered.

Hardly daring to breathe, Louisa took out a small brooch, a star of sapphires and diamonds. "Oh!" she exclaimed. "Robert, you shouldn't—"

"Don't say it!" he warned. "Don't say I shouldn't have or that you can't possibly accept it, or I'll be angry. It's more than just a Christmas present," he went on hurriedly, before she could interrupt. "I want you to think of it as a little insurance policy."

"Insurance?" she repeated, puzzled by both words and tone, which were incongruously businesslike.

"Yes, an insurance policy. After all, my love, none of us knows what the future holds." He stopped suddenly, pulled her close into the crook of his arm, and kissed her forehead. In a much gentler tone, he added: "It's a little 'just in case,' don't you see? There may come a time when you need money quickly, and if so, then this should raise a fair amount. Enough to cover immediate necessities, at least."

Rescuing the brooch from her suddenly nerveless fingers, he pinned it to the velvet of her gown. "There, it looks beautiful, and I want you to enjoy wearing it. Don't look so sad," he whispered as he kissed her again. "It's Christmas, and I love you."

Chilled, she clung to him. "Oh, Robert, I love you too," she murmured, wishing all the while that it had not been necessary for him to say what had just been said.

Letty's eyes as she admired it were almost as bright as the brooch itself. Louisa summoned a smile and tried to forget that cold chill of presentiment. Awareness, with her, was never far from the surface, although Robert rarely spoke of the future, and never of a time when they might not be together. That he should have done so, especially at this their first Christmas together, cast a shadow over Louisa's happiness.

The play, a light farce with a seasonal flavor, was sufficiently amusing to lift her out of the blue mood which had threatened earlier, and the first flakes of snow, falling onto frosty pavements as they left the theater, banished it completely. Like two enchanted children, Letty and Louisa exclaimed over it, congratulating themselves and Robert on the delight of snow for Christmas, as though it had been specially ordered.

Over dinner in Letty's suite, Robert gazed at his two ladies with fond, indulgent eyes, charmed by their laughter and the ease with which they had made friends. Knowing well the unpredictability of women, he had hardly dared hope they would like each other; that they did, and with such genuine lack of constraint, amazed and delighted him. He knew he could not have wished for a more pleasing Christmas gift, although, as he fingered the cuff links Louisa had given him, he was again quite extraordinarily touched.

With the coffee he begged to be excused, making the attraction of an excellent billiard room his reason for leaving them to talk.

Letty smiled as he closed the door. "Old habits die hard," she commented and, from a silver case, casually offered Louisa a cigarette. Her round-eyed amazement made Letty laugh.

"Robert doesn't approve either," she confessed. "But as I keep trying to tell him—it's preferable to drinking oneself to death!" Suddenly serious, she poured two cups of coffee, handing one across the table. "I thought that's what he was doing, you know. A year ago, he was never without a glass in his hand—at home, at least. I can hardly believe the difference in him now. I can't thank you enough."

Stirring cream into her cup, Louisa glanced up in surprise. "Me?"

With a little laugh, Letty nodded. "Of course. There hasn't been anyone else."

Louisa blushingly denied that she had had anything to do with Robert's drinking habits; privately, she thought he still drank far more than was good for him, but in the mess she supposed they all did. Nevertheless, Letty's assumption that the improvement was due to her influence was pleasing.

"May I ask you something rather personal?" As Louisa nodded, the other woman went on: "How do you feel about living in Ireland? Robert's almost certain the regiment will be in Dublin by the summer—so certain, in fact, he's having the Devereaux house completely refurbished. Not before time, I hasten to add! We've been trying to persuade him to do something about it for years. However," she hesitated a moment, "I wonder how you feel about it."

"I don't know. It's hard to imagine—a little nervous, I suppose." She was, in fact, extremely daunted by the prospect. After a moment she added: "I do know he lived there with Charlotte."

"Ah, I was wondering about that, too."

Hesitantly Louisa asked: "Don't you approve of my living in your mother's house?"

"Oh, goodness me, no—it's not that—not that at all!" Coming to sit beside her on the sofa, Letty pressed Louisa's hand. "I'm worried for you," she confessed and, with a heavy sigh, added: "Dublin isn't London, you know. Robert has the idea he can install you in the Devereaux house, then walk out with you on his arm, and people won't turn a hair. The prince of Wales might get away with it—and many of his friends—but Robert's not of that circle and never will be.

"Oddly enough," she continued, "if you were a married woman, or a widow, it could perhaps be brazened out, but a young woman, unmarried . . ." As her voice trailed away, she shook her head. "It won't work, not the way he envisages it. Believe me, I do know."

Watching those soft gray eyes, Louisa felt she did know, and from experience which must have been personal. Unwilling to face the problem of Dublin, she would have preferred to hear what sadnesses had shaped this woman's life, what comforts sustained her now; but early training silenced the question before it reached her lips.

Not before it reached her eyes, however. Catching that unguarded, quizzical glance, Letty gave a rueful smile. "Oh, yes, there was someone— a long time ago. Years older than me, and married, of course. His wife caught scent of it and whipped him back to Dublin. He's a member of Parliament now, fighting on Gladstone's side for Home Rule." Soft laughter, edged with self-mockery, made a joke of it. "You see, I follow his career with interest!"

"Do you ever see him?"

"Not in fifteen years, nor do I want to. I suffered for him once; I'd not do it again," she said with feeling. "So, in life there are no happy endings." She laughed again, dispelling the sadness. "His wife's still going strong, I'm afraid, and will no doubt outlive us all."

The bright, irreverent humor was infectious. Louisa laughed, glad of the warmth between them, the friendship which seemed to spring as naturally as her love for Robert. Suddenly, however, a dampening thought curtailed her amusement.

"And Charlotte?" she murmured. "What can you tell me about her, Letty? Will *she* outlive us all, do you think?"

The rueful laughter faded. "Had I Bridget's faith," Letty admitted, "I'd probably make the sign of the cross and mutter several fervent prayers. But as I don't have much faith in anything anymore, what can I say? I wish I could give you hope—but on that score, sadly, there is none to give. Short of murder or suicide," she said heavily, "and believe me, there have been moments when either could have been possible, she could live for years. A normal life span.

"If there was any justice in this world," Letty commented bitterly, "she'd die tomorrow and release us all from this ghastly merry-go-round."

For a moment there was silence between them. "It must be terrible," Louisa murmured at last, "having to live in the same house."

"It is. Robert doesn't realize the strain. He thinks he's being kind to her, but—" She broke off suddenly. "It's hard for us, living there. And I worry about Georgina. When I think of what happened a year ago—" Breaking off again, she sighed. "But I mustn't heap those worries on your shoulders, my dear. Robert will never forgive me."

Her sudden smile was warm and very bright, like sunshine after rain; pouring more coffee for them both, she said: "At least, now it's possible to talk to Robert, we may get some sense on the subject before long!"

Before Louisa could ask what she meant, one of the interior doors opened, and Georgina wandered in, blinking sleepily in the room's bright light. Although she asked for her father, when she saw Louisa she smiled bewitchingly, taking refuge against her knees.

Laughing, she hitched the little girl onto her lap and squeezed her, waving Letty's disapproval aside. "Your daddy's downstairs, but he'll be back in a minute. If you get into bed, we'll ask him to come in and say goodnight."

"Will you come, too?"

"I'll come now and tuck you in."

In the bedroom, they discussed the matter of Father Christmas and where he would leave her presents; Louisa assured her that Robert had written a note to the bearded gentleman, telling him Georgina was in York and to leave her presents at the foot of the bed. Happy again, the little girl lifted her face to be kissed.

"But you won't forget to tell him, will you?"

"What's that?"

"Tell him to come in and give me a kiss."

Louisa smiled. "I won't forget—promise."

In the sitting room, Letty was pouring two glasses of sherry and looking very smug. "Good health, Louisa, and Merry Christmas! I think I have the problem solved."

"What problem's that?"

"Yourself and Robert—the Devereaux house! If the regiment can come to Dublin, then so can we. Georgina and I, that is. It would be the best thing for her, getting away from White Leigh. And the most natural: she *should* see more of her father."

"I'm sure she should," Louisa agreed, "but I don't quite follow."

Gaily Letty laughed. "But it's so obvious, don't you see? You *are* a governess, are you not? So why don't we offer you a job, my dear, one you are quite well qualified to perform? After all," she added mischievously, "I understand you have most excellent references. Didn't I myself tell Miss Bainbridge so?"

TWELVE

As a concession to Christmas, Mary Elliott brought out a bottle of her best elderflower wine. While Bessie supervised in the kitchen, she cast a critical eye over the dining table before sitting down to take a glass of the pale, golden liquid, pronouncing it excellent, which it was. Had anyone described the wine as alcoholic, she would have been mortally offended; nevertheless, it was extremely heady, and after only one glass Blanche began to thaw visibly. After two, with flushed cheeks and bright eyes, she became positively friendly toward her sister, gossiping in her usual malicious but amusing way about Miss Devine and some of her more noted clients.

She was an excellent mimic, but even while she laughed, Louisa found herself recalling other occasions in childhood, when burning indignation had produced devastating impressions of their mother or Bessie. As her laughter died, she wondered how well and how often she herself had been impersonated, especially to Emily. Since their sister's marriage, Blanche had taken to visiting the Chapmans from time to time, which was odd, Louisa thought, since she professed no particular liking for Emily and thought John very common. Louisa had recently begun to suspect her sisters of indulging themselves at her expense, their respective primness no doubt titillated by salacious speculation. Emily had never revealed an opinion of that most intimate aspect of marriage, and Louisa wondered whether her younger sister regarded it in the light of duty rather than pleasure. As for Blanche, she would think it right to be shocked, no matter what her private feelings were.

When she thought of Letty Duncannon, with her blithe acceptance of the situation, her spirits lifted; but like her brother, Letty seemed to have grasped the fashionable nettle of unbelief, whereas her sisters still paid their respects in church every Sunday, as they had been taught to do since childhood.

Blanche had arrived with the scent of St. Maurice's on her, and as Edward returned from morning service in the Minster, Louisa wondered who was right; whether her relationship with Robert Duncannon, sinful as it was in the eyes of religion, had condemned her forever in the eyes of God.

In her present quandary, she would have liked to embrace Robert's rather fatalistic philosophy, which took little account of personal sin, regarding all as part of some grand practical joke perpetrated by an omnipotent and rather cruel Superior Being. Lacking his appreciation of such irony, however, she found it difficult. She was not even sure that he believed it, although from time to time he would quote odd, relevant verses from *The Rubáiyát* with great amusement. In Edward Fitzgerald's translation, Louisa had found disturbing echoes of the questions which often tormented her; in his bittersweet lines, the insistence that life is transitory, that death is close and all too final, underlined her need to grasp what happiness there was, here and now.

In her desire to be understood by Edward, she had bought a beautifully illustrated copy for him as a Christmas present; it lay beneath the tree, unopened as yet; with a flutter of nerves, she wondered what he would think of it.

When he joined them, he bestowed a chaste kiss on Blanche's cheek; all Louisa felt was the soft brush of his beard against her skin. Accepting a glass of wine from his aunt, he sat down on the sofa, avoiding Louisa's gaze.

The presents were opened and exclaimed over; opening Edward's gift, Louisa had an idea what it was, and, afraid of making too much of it in front of Blanche, she pushed the beautiful album beneath her chair, trying to catch Edward's eyes in order to thank him discreetly. It seemed he was resolutely determined not to be thanked, however, for he refused to look at her.

As ever, when it came to opening his own presents, he was as much embarrassed as pleased, politely thanking each of them but not making overmuch of anything. Louisa watched him closely, although, beyond a careful examination of the spine, he exhibited little reaction to the book of verse. The brief smile he gave her as he murmured his thanks, however, was oddly at variance with the bleak look in his eyes.

All through dinner he seemed preoccupied, although he remembered to compliment his aunt on the plump roast goose and the excellence of her Christmas pudding. Afterward, when the table was cleared and Bessie had served them with candied fruits and peppermint creams and tiny cups of coffee, Edward was prevailed upon to read from Dickens.

Clear and mellow, his voice enunciated the familiar words of that master storyteller, taking them through Dingly Dell with Mr. Pickwick, who was a favorite of his aunt's, on to passages from *The Chimes* and *The Cricket on the Hearth*, until by dusk both Bessie and her mistress, exhausted by their morning's efforts, were fast asleep, and under the influence of the elderflower wine, Blanche was nodding gently. Staring into the fire's glowing embers, only Louisa heard the last of Mr. Scrooge and Tiny Tim.

With a sigh, Edward placed *A Christmas Carol* beside its companions; he looked up and held her gaze for a moment, his expression unfathomable. In a sudden movement he bent to the hearth and, taking a lighted taper, touched the candles on their small tree to life.

As he passed her chair, Louisa caught his hand. "A cup of tea?" she softly asked, and he nodded, blowing out the taper. She rose to her feet, wanting to thank him for the album, to ask what he thought of her small gift, perhaps offer an explanation, if one were needed. Touched by the sadness which for some reason he had worn like a shroud all day, on a sudden impulse she kissed his cheek; but as her lips touched him he froze, turning such a look of accusation upon her that she half-expected to hear the name "Judas!" upon his tongue.

Involuntarily she flinched and stepped back. Edward brushed past her, bent to his books, and began to return them to their correct shelf.

"Yes, I would like a cup of tea," he said stiffly, and she fled from the room, determined he should not see the depth of that unexpected wound.

Mechanically she filled the kettle, set it on the hob, and stirred the fire. As she laid a tray with cups and saucers, milk and sugar, the front doorbell jangled; with a hasty glance in the mirror she smoothed her hair, just as Bessie ambled through into the kitchen.

"Miss Emily's here."

"Yes, I know, I'll be through in a minute. You go and talk to her."

With a penetrating glance, Bessie said, "What's up?"

"Nothing." Attempting a smile, she added, "Except Mr. Dickens—Tiny Tim always did make me want to cry!"

"Aye," Bessie laughed. "I'm glad I dropped off to sleep—else I'd have been sniveling!"

She disappeared, and Louisa stood by the window, waiting for the kettle to boil. It was dark outside, but deep swathes of snow illumined both yard and ramparts, reminding her of the last great fall, almost a year ago. Tired and anxious, she had come home that night accompanied by Edward and met Robert Duncannon. How much, she thought, had happened in just one year. How impossible to think then that Edward, dear and devoted, would ever turn on her in such a way. Even after that initial shock, he had been good to her, a little more reserved perhaps, but not unkind. Wondering what she had done to deserve that dreadful snub, she could think of nothing, nothing at all.

As she leaned over to close the curtains, she saw a dark shape leap delicately onto the cleared path, running with an anxious, stiff-legged gait toward her. She opened the door, and the cat mewed its gratitude, rubbing piteously against her skirts until she smiled and went to the pantry. With a guilty glance toward the door Bessie had left ajar, Louisa pulled a few scraps of meat from the carcass of the goose, leaving them, together with the cat, on the scullery floor.

Strangely heartened by that small act, Louisa made the tea and sallied forth into the parlor.

John Chapman stood up as she entered and with a brief nod wished her the compliments of the season; Emily's greeting was similarly lacking in enthusiasm, her eyes taking in every detail of Louisa's blue velvet gown. With the addition of a new paisley shawl, Emily was wearing the same dove-gray silk in which she had been married.

Once the weather had been discussed, conversation flagged; seeking another neutral topic, Louisa mentioned the Australian Exhibition. Emily glanced at her husband, pursing her lips.

"Yes. We saw the exhibition," she said. "We saw you, too."

For a moment the statement hung in the air. Feeling both accused and guilty, Louisa inwardly cursed the color which flooded her cheeks. "That's strange," she said evenly. "I didn't see you. Why didn't you say hello?"

"Oh, goodness me, you were far too busy with your fine friends—whoever they were—for John and me to interrupt."

Stung, Louisa retorted sharply, "You're well enough acquainted with the captain—and I would have introduced you to his sister."

"You were with another couple and some children."

For a moment Louisa was puzzled. "Oh, yes, we were for a minute or two. Sophie Bainbridge and—and her brothers. I'd quite forgotten about them."

Having discomfited her sister, Emily sipped her tea with an expression of smug self-satisfaction, while Blanche lowered her lashes and gave a superior little smile. Emily had gained weight, giving her a matronly look, yet for a moment she and Blanche seemed so alike Louisa wanted to smack them both. With shaking hands she poured more tea for her mother and Edward. As she passed his cup, he looked up at her, his eyes eloquent with pain and apology; she was too angry to acknowledge it, sitting stiff and silent while her mother tried to smooth the ruffled atmosphere.

Over Christmas cake and mince pies they gradually began to play their parts with some degree of conviction. With Louisa at the piano, they all joined in the carols, Edward's light baritone and John's deeper voice providing the foil for Emily's pure soprano. But to Louisa the gaiety had a disturbingly hollow ring; she was relieved when the clock struck nine. In the kitchen, she made excuses to her mother.

As she bent to kiss the soft, upturned cheek, Mary Elliott hugged her eldest daughter close. "You've been brave—I appreciate it, dear. It isn't easy for you, I know that. And," she added with a bright, quizzical look, "I suspect you could have been elsewhere this evening?"

"Yes, Mamma, I did have an invitation to join them."

"Well, it was good of you to refuse it." She paused, then said: "Blanche and Emily don't understand. They can't. But I do. Don't forget that."

Eyes suddenly brimming with tears, Louisa hugged her mother close. "No, Mamma, I won't forget. Thank you."

"Whatever for?"

"Nothing. Everything. For just being you."

"Away with you!" Mary Elliott exclaimed, turning abruptly to the tray of dirty crockery. "Will you be all right, walking down Gillygate?"

"I'm sure I will. Robert's meeting me on the corner."

Before she could return to the parlor to take her leave of the others, Edward appeared in the doorway, coat on and hat in hand.

"I'll walk you home," he said quietly.

"There's no need. But I expect Blanche could do with an escort—she's to go through town."

"Emily and John have already offered."

"Well, I don't want you to put yourself out on my account—"

"It's no trouble," he assured her.

"Look, Robert is meeting me on Bootham, and I'm sure I can walk that far on my own, thank you."

Her coldness cut him, the more so because he knew it was justified. "I'd rather make sure," he insisted. "It's bad underfoot, and there may be revelers about."

Mary Elliott suddenly clicked her tongue, and they both turned in surprise. "Don't tell me you two are falling out now! I've never known such a family, and at Christmas, too. Edward's quite right—you'd better let him walk down with you."

"I'm sorry, Mamma," Louisa murmured. Without looking at him, she said, "All right, Edward, if you're ready, we'll go." Kissing her mother again, she went through the ritual of departure with the others and bade Bessie good-bye at the door; after the suffocating atmosphere of the house, the cold, sharp air of Gillygate was a pleasure.

Longing to beg her forgiveness, Edward could not find the words. Apologies meant explanations, and how could he explain the feelings which had torn him apart at her touch? He could not even think of a half-convincing lie. The change in her, strangely underlined by that most unlikely Christmas gift, repelled him, even while his whole being longed to leap to her protection. He burned, just thinking of Emily and Blanche.

Had Robert Duncannon not been waiting for her at the end of the street, he thought he might have tried to speak to her, but the fact that Robert was waiting to take her home, waiting to take her into his arms and into his bed, strangled any attempt.

They walked side by side, not touching, the silence between them as frozen as the snow beneath their feet. As once before, he watched her every footfall, anxious lest she should slip; remembered that other night, an age ago, when she had leaned on him and he had lifted his face in pure delight to the soft, cold kiss of the snow.

The folly of that momentary happiness hit him hard. On that night, as now, he had been taking her to another man, the only difference being that then he had not known it.

THIRTEEN

*J*f the long climb up to Christmas had been fraught with hazards and pain, it had also, Louisa thought, had its beautiful moments. She was sorry to say good-bye to Letty and Georgina and, on being exhorted to write often, had promised she would. Her moments alone with Robert's daughter had been rare and, in retrospect, precious, although whenever she thought of the child she became aware of maternal longings which were not easily quelled.

In spite of Letty's warnings, she began to look forward to Dublin, to the prospect of teaching Georgina and living with Robert and his sister as family. He had agreed to the plan quite readily, said nothing would please him better than to have his daughter permanently in Dublin; Letty could set herself up as chaperon if she liked, but he had no intentions of allowing Louisa to hide herself away. The two women had been forced to accept that, and although Letty had voiced some misgivings, Louisa felt sure that between them they would eventually make Robert see sense.

The wintry slide down the New Year to Easter was quieter, with life settling into the kind of mundane routine which bred contentment even while it dulled the senses. Once or twice a week she visited her mother, usually in the afternoon, for she was reluctant to invite further rebuffs from Edward. When their paths did cross, which was rarely, his manner seemed set to reflect the weather, which continued cold and bitter. It was depressing, yet she could not discuss it with Robert, who was still touchy on the subject of Edward; and while she felt sure her mother noticed, Mary Elliott was obviously reluctant to air the matter.

News of Emily's first pregnancy did not help to heal the breach between the sisters; as though she sensed Louisa's envy, Emily preened like a well-fed cat, while Blanche cooed and fussed over her, declaring her delight at the prospect of becoming a doting aunt. Louisa tried to distance herself, although she was drawn in by her mother's subsequent distress at news of the young couple's decision to move away from York. It had been discussed for some time; with the country in the grip of depression, John reckoned he could do better for himself in Leeds, where the cheap clothing industry was booming and people had money to spend on furniture and funerals. It was eminently plausible, but Louisa saw other reasons behind it, reasons which were understandable though not endearing.

Although she took pains not to show it, Robert sensed her despondency and tried hard to cheer her. He bought a small second-hand piano which fitted awkwardly behind the sofa; they spent many a pleasant hour during the long February evenings playing duets and songs old and new. When the mood was on him, he would make her laugh, striking dramatic chords and singing sad Irish songs in a mock-mournful voice; but when she played for him, he was tempted into seriousness and sang the songs as they were meant to be sung.

He would rarely be drawn on the subject of Gladstone and the proposed Home Rule Bill, but Louisa knew that his loyalties were very much divided. He felt that his first allegiance should be to the regiment and his brother officers, yet because of his background Robert believed implicitly in an independent Parliament for Ireland. Almost a century before, the Duncannons, together with many other old, established families, had opposed the Act of Union which abolished the old Irish Parliament and with it the ideal of a separate identity for Ireland. As landlords, they had suffered at the hands of successive inept and arbitrary English governments, not least during the years of the famine, when attempts to alleviate that terrible tragedy had been frustrated by legislation from London. Robert's grandfather had almost bankrupted the estate in his efforts to stem the tide of hunger and disease which ravaged the local population, opening his own kitchens and later financing escape for those who wished to emigrate.

Louisa had felt chastened at that, recalling the accusations which had gone through her mind at the time of Moira's personal tragedy; even more so when Robert said: "So don't talk to me about absentee landlords—the Duncannons were never that, no matter what other sins may be to their charge. We never recovered from the famine, nor have many of our closest neighbors. At least I married Charlotte," he added bitterly. "If I'd not married her—or some other willing heiress—White Leigh would be crumbling now, like so many other estates in the south. William, God bless him, married a wife with even fancier ideas and less money than he had. They're all so damned feckless!" he swore angrily as he poured another drink. "God save us from the Irish gentry."

Nevertheless, he firmly believed that Ireland should be governed by people who understood the country and the problems peculiar to it; the English would never get things right, if they tried till doomsday, yet they seemed bent on dying in the attempt. He was well aware that his colleagues were mostly Conservative and Unionist; they were for the expansion of the empire, with themselves lending a hand in the expanding, not its reduction, and as such would have cursed Gladstone to perdition given half a chance. So Robert learned to keep silent, except with Tommy, while they both read and reread the reported debates, arguing vociferously as to the outcome.

There were rumors that Ulster was secretly arming, that should the bill become law, the possibility of civil war in the province would become fact. One editorial even went so far as to suggest that ninety-nine percent of the army's officers would hand in their papers rather than accompany their regiments to Ireland on an expedition which would require them to fire upon the Loyalists.

"They have the gall to call it cold-blooded and murderous tyranny," Robert snarled as he read the piece aloud to Louisa. "The double-dyed hypocrites! So democracy is only fair when it works in their favor, I suppose, and the army may only be employed against rioting Catholic peasants: Carson and his bunch of Loyalist bullyboys don't count! Of course we mustn't forget that he's an industrialist," Robert added sarcastically, "and one of their own kind. No, we mustn't lose sight of that small fact. But in my book, Louisa, a mob is a mob, and incitement to riot is a crime, no matter the name or title. Carson should be arrested now, before he does any more damage."

Louisa had asked then whether he knew the man, but he said not. "Although, oddly enough, I believe he's distantly connected to Charlotte's family by marriage. For that reason, too, I'd like to see him silenced." It was a strangely chilling revelation.

The hitherto unconsidered power of Charlotte's family preyed on Louisa's mind for some time, and she began to have severe qualms about the wisdom of moving to Dublin. Robert, apparently, had none.

While never-ending debates wore on in the House of Commons, he refused to let natural anxiety color his life and, apart from the occasional furious outburst, refrained from lengthy comment. He hunted regularly, attended the occasional house party, and went to the usual semiofficial functions alone; but as plans for the regiment's leave-taking gathered momentum, he began to entertain what seemed to Louisa a quite ludicrous idea.

There was to be a Regimental Ball at the end of April, a gesture of thanks toward neighboring gentry and civic dignitaries alike, a small return for hospitality rendered. When Robert first suggested she should be his partner, Louisa refused outright, firstly because such an indiscretion would be folly and secondly because she had not danced for years and had quite forgotten how. Robert suggested lessons, and when she modestly balked at that, brought Tommy over to play the piano while they practiced a few basic steps.

Even with half the furniture removed to the bedroom and the rest pushed back against the walls, the space left for dancing was pitifully cramped. After much initial embarrassment at Tommy's first visit, toes stubbed and shins bruised on protruding chair and table legs, the lesson dissolved into hilarity. By the third afternoon, Louisa began to relax, to appreciate Tommy's laconic sense of humor, understanding for the first time that in spite of a basic difference of temperament, the two men were much alike. Both were equally irreverent, having little regard for English social mores; and once it had dawned on her that Tommy cared not a whit for the facts of her relationship with his friend, Louisa was able to ignore his presence.

At last the two men agreed that she was quite able to dance the night away without disgracing herself. But that, as far as she was concerned, was only part of the problem. Later that evening, when Tommy had gone, Louisa voiced her real anxiety, which was of coming face to face with Rachel Tempest.

"You know, I dread her seeing us together." She paused, pushing an erring chair back into place, and turned to look at him. "At one time, she'd have given anything to add you to her list of admirers."

"Oh, what nonsense," he muttered.

"No, I'm serious. If you'd given her even one ounce of encouragement, Robert, she'd have played up to you like she did to Arthur Bainbridge. You were far more eligible."

"I wasn't eligible at all," he corrected her, picking up the book he had been reading earlier. "But Darnley was, and Tommy, and a whole host of others. It was just that poor Arthur was the first to take the bait."

"Precisely. That's exactly what I'm saying. But you were her first fancy, Robert. Believe me, you were. She hardly stopped talking about you in those few weeks after Sophie's party—it nearly drove me mad, especially after . . . well, after you told me about Charlotte. It was only because you were keeping out of my way—because she never saw you for long enough—that she started chasing after Arthur. And she only went after him because—"

"Because she wanted to be the first of her set to have a ring on her finger."

"Yes! That's just it!"

"Sweetheart," Robert said wearily, "I've seen it all before . . ."

"But you think she's just silly and empty-headed," Louisa declared passionately. "You don't know her as I do. She has a greedy, envious little heart. All right when things are going her way, when she can have the best of everything, but not so pretty when she's thwarted. I was her *paid companion,* Robert—she didn't like me that much, but she enjoyed playing Lady Bountiful occasionally, when it suited her. How do you think she'll feel when she sees I've walked off with the prize? She'll *hate it,* and if she can't get back at me in any other way, she'll gossip as maliciously and vindictively as she knows how!"

"I refuse to let the Rachel Tempests of this world dictate my actions. Or yours, for that matter," he added dourly, slapping his book shut as though the matter were closed and done with. But his frown deepened as he paced the room, and a moment later he exclaimed: "That damned family! Must they always overshadow our lives? Does it matter what any of them think? They're *nothing,* Louisa, nothing at all."

"I don't much care what they *think,*" she said in agitation. "It's what they'll say to other people." Edward's words were in her mind, and those last days in Tanner Row as a child: abuse and scorn, salacious comments, laughter, a woman spitting at her mother. Swallowing hard, she busied herself with small, tidying movements, plumping seat cushions, placing the newspaper in its rack by Robert's chair; anything to dispel the vivid pictures in her mind, the stomach-knotting fear which suddenly possessed her.

"It's her father you're frightened of, isn't it?" Robert asked, his voice gentler now, more willing to understand. "But you needn't be, you know. He's cut her off without a penny, won't even let her across the doorstep. And we'll soon be in Dublin; he can't touch you there."

"It's not her father!" Louisa cried distractedly. "She'll talk to anyone who'll listen. The past will all be raked up—Mamma's name will come into it—Edward's—"

"Good God Almighty!" Robert exploded, his anger refueled by her cousin's name. "Do we have to worry about him, too? He can take care of himself!"

She did not answer, but simply stood there, hands clasped tensely, eyes downcast, lips compressed in a tight little line; looking at her, for a brief moment he hated all she represented. "Do you have to be so bloody English?" he demanded, making the word an insult. "So bloody prim and proper? There are women who'd give their eyeteeth to go to this ball, and you stand there, making excuses, frightened by a bit of gossip! For God's sake, where's your courage?"

His contempt cut her like nothing else could. For a moment she quailed beneath it, terrified of the gulf which yawned between them. Not for the first time, their relationship seemed little more than a fragile bridge between two vastly different worlds, and in the depths a raging torrent of ignorance and misunderstanding. In other circumstances she might have kept silence or tried to placate him, but the inference of cowardice stung her into furious retaliation.

Brushing past him, she exclaimed, "It's not a question of courage. I'm talking about discretion, which is said to be the better part of valor. But that's something you don't seem to understand!"

"Oh, I do understand it," he avowed, catching her arm. "I've practiced it for eight long months. Coming here under cover of darkness, never taking you out except on the rarest occasions, pretending—even to Tommy, for long enough—that you meant nothing to me. I've done it because I love you—not because I enjoy it."

She recoiled then, fighting against his grip, appalled by that unexpected revelation. For Louisa, the months since Christmas had encompassed the happiest moments of her adult life. Free from care, cocooned and protected by a veil of secrecy, for the first time she had learned to relax, and in the sun of Robert's love had blossomed as a woman. If she had alienated her family in the process, it had, until now, seemed worth the sacrifice; yet in one fell stroke, and for what seemed to her the most trivial of reasons, he was threatening to destroy that precious security, threatening the very fabric of their life together.

"Dublin is only a matter of weeks away," he reminded her. "You must learn to conquer your fear. Can't you see how much easier it will be if you let me introduce you now? Your presence later will seem far less remarkable. And in such a crowd," he added reasonably, "who will notice you and me? Especially with half the county's nobility present!"

The argument was now on well-worn territory. Exhausted by its familiarity, Louisa sank slowly into a chair, resting her forehead against his arm. Was she really a coward, she wondered, afraid their love would wither in the light of day? It was a question she had never asked herself before, and it was frightening to think what the answer might be. The months of happiness: were they simply illusion? That was the most daunting question of all. They had seemed to share so much; how bitter to realize that for him the pleasure had been blighted by the very secrecy she clung to. In weary confusion, she silently shook her head.

Unaware of those despairing questions, Robert saw only that negative gesture and, misinterpreting it, gave way to an exasperated sigh. On past form, he had hardly expected capitulation; nevertheless, disappointment bit deep. Although he loathed being at odds with her, there were times when Louisa's very intractability seemed to demand a show of anger, when he saw through that soft defenselessness and was forced to recognize a will as strong as his own. And while he might on good days respect it, at times like this he was left feeling resentful and very much alone. Somewhere deep inside, hidden and unacknowledged, lay a kernel of fear that, one day, love would not be enough, and she would leave him. It nagged at a corner of his mind, intensified by the unaccustomed humility of that bowed head. In a gesture of contrition, he touched her hair and kissed it, and the traitorous fear was drowned in the sudden awakening of physical desire.

Always after disagreement he wanted her. Not perversely, but as a form of reassurance, a reaffirmation that, in bed at least, there were no barriers between them. He lifted her chin, making her look directly at him, and was faintly disturbed by the expression in her eyes.

"Come to bed now," he whispered with a kiss. "It's getting late, and we're both tired."

She undressed silently, holding his gaze with that strange element of disappointment and pleading; even as Robert drew her into his arms, he was conscious of a difference in her, not unwillingness exactly, more a disconcerting passivity. A spark of residual anger flared in him, so that his kisses were suddenly more brutal than he intended, his hands hard and bruising. When it came, her response was fierce, almost unexpected, so that their lovemaking took on the nature of a desperate struggle, the moment of conquest brief and bitterly intense.

On a wave of reaction he clung to her, emotions still raw, tactile need unassuaged, knowing that small victory for what it was: a mirage, an illusion. Fear possessed him, bleak and recognizable. Convulsively he gripped her shoulder, burying his face against those warm, full breasts. "I'm sorry," he whispered. "I didn't mean it."

Oh, but you did, she thought as his desperation reached her, and a confusion of half-formed thoughts and conflicting emotions tumbled through her mind. Shame and sorrow, guilt and desire, a wanting of something frighteningly absent in their first coupling made her draw him closer. She wanted to talk, to explain, but the words were locked behind a wall of uncertainty and despair; needing his compassion, she was suddenly afraid it was limited, that her own fears were in danger of driving him away. Their argument's basis seemed so trivial, yet it revealed the gulf she had been so afraid of in the beginning. Robert had crossed it to possess her, and now he was demanding she do the same for him. As a gesture of faith it was necessary, but still the words refused to come.

She looked down at him. A thin shaft of moonlight illumined rumpled sheets and blankets and the outline of his body, wrapped around hers; a deeply shadowed indentation marked the length of his spine, smooth, hard muscle curving up in cleanly defined lines across back and shoulders. Against the round whiteness of her breast, his face seemed tanned, the black smudges of brows and lashes like charcoal on dark paper. Not for the first time she was stirred by his masculine strength and beauty, by the fact that such a man found delight in her; she knew she could not bear to lose him, to have him look at her with the shadow of regret and disappointment in his eyes.

Her fingers stroked the short, crisp hair, found the soft waves at the nape of his neck, and traveled downward, over those powerful shoulders. Like a child he stirred, seeking comfort at her breast; and as the nipple rose to touch his lips he slowly began to caress her, rousing and controlling with such delicate, exquisite tenderness it was almost unbearable.

"Slowly," he murmured as she moved against him. "No more fighting."

"Did I fight?"

"Like a tigress." The words, whispered against her mouth, became a kiss. Gently this time, he entered her; and with the fusion of their bodies all else was forgotten. But with the climax of their passion came a different kind of release. As he kissed and cradled her in his arms, Robert felt the chill of wintry tears in her hair. Patiently he hushed her sobs of distress, tried to make sense of the gulped, disjointed phrases until at last, when she was still and sleeping in the curve of his arm, he began to understand. She would not fight him anymore. The battle, such as it had been, was over. He had won. He wondered why he felt so ashamed.

FOURTEEN

*S*implicity: recalling the battle for it, Louisa almost smiled. Madame Marcelle had paled at the suggestion that she could create a ballgown in less than two weeks and threatened tears over Louisa's insistence on a simple design. Ridiculously simple, she had said, and quite impossible for such a grand occasion. Studying the result in the long pier glass, Louisa wondered why dressmakers were so in love with frills and flounces; she felt uncomfortable in fussy clothes, and anyway, Robert preferred her in simple gowns. He said simplicity showed off her figure to advantage, and with another half-smile, she acknowledged that he was right.

It was a beautiful gown, silk, in a soft midnight blue, cut low to reveal the perfect whiteness of her throat and shoulders. She felt that it was very daring and nervously ran white-gloved hands over the drapery at her breast, the tautly boned bodice beneath accentuating a neat waist and rounded hips. Half a dozen tiny rosettes caught up the hem, and as she turned to view the train her petticoat frothed and swirled, revealing extravagant yards of lace beneath.

"Wonderful," she murmured. "Exactly what I wanted. Thank you, Madame."

Unaccustomed to thanks, Madame Marcelle fluttered deprecatingly. "It is nothing. So simple, I confess I did not think it would work. Ma'm'selle will look like a poor governess, I said—I know, I remember! But I was wrong. Ma'm'selle has the regal look—ah yes, I insist! I have titled ladies who would give their all for the figure, the form, like Ma'm'selle."

Louisa blushed, provoking a mischievous grin and a stream of rapid French, of which she caught only Robert's name. On the two or three occasions he had accompanied her, the old woman had flirted outrageously, Louisa thought, and now she sighed dramatically, giving the impression that even thirty years ago she would have given Louisa a run for her money. Obviously she understood the situation. On that first visit, months before, without any embarrassment, Robert had made it quite clear that all bills were to be sent to him, yet he had made no attempt to pass Louisa off as his wife. With a Gallic shrug of supreme indifference, Madame had taken her new client under her wing and set about transforming the dowdy cygnet into a swan. That the cygnet's own ideas had caused many a tug-of-war seemed not to have affected Madame's pleasure in the task; and if she was aware of her client's unease, she made no reference to it.

While Louisa donned her outdoor clothes, Madame Marcelle made arrangements for the blue gown to be delivered the following day. With a tight smile and a sigh of relief, Louisa stepped out into Lendal, crossed busy Museum Street with care, and paid her penny to walk home through the Museum Gardens.

It was worth that small fee for such peace and tranquility, for the pleasure of close-clipped lawns and neat gravel paths and the ruined Gothic purity of St. Mary's Abbey. She found a bench sheltered by the walls and sat down; after the stuffy, highly perfumed atmosphere of the salon, the open air with its myriad scents was a tonic to be savored. In the warmth thrown back by those ancient walls a solitary bee droned, attracted by the wallflowers growing in ragged profusion above Louisa's head. Watching it idly, she envied its single-minded simplicity of purpose, for a moment regretting the diversity of human choice.

Two weeks ago, in the aftermath of that dreadful quarrel, agreement had seemed the only salve to a burning sense of shame, yet fear and apprehension had returned tenfold, increasing as fast as the ball approached. It had taken on a kind of graphic importance, illustrating in black and white all the differences between Robert and herself. No longer were there any comforting shades of gray, and the starkness of all she surveyed was little less than terrifying. As camouflage, the dress itself was small comfort; she was less afraid of not looking the part than of making some dreadful social gaffe. If people snubbed her, she knew she would never have the courage to repeat the experiment, and that worried her even more, for she had given Robert her promise . . .

Lit by the glow of the westering sun, an ornamental cherry stood out in clear relief against darkly rolling clouds; rain threatened, but still Louisa sat, captured by its fragile perfection, a brief, exquisite flowering, unbearably poignant. With the first spots of rain, a sudden gust scattered a thousand petals like snow upon the grass, the wallflowers shed their heavy scent, and on the breeze came a sharp, earthy smell, cold as the grave. Shivering, she gathered up her parcels and went home.

Three evenings later, pulling on white kid gloves over ice-cold hands, she awaited Robert's arrival, wondering how and why she had ever agreed to this. Her mother had come to help her dress, and without her Louisa knew she would still have been in her robe, rigid with fear. It had been impossible to eat; at the last minute Mary Elliott had forced a glass of milk and some biscuits into her hand and stood over her until they were gone. Now she looked at Louisa and clicked her tongue disapprovingly.

"You looked better at your Aunt Elizabeth's funeral."

"Thank you, Mamma."

"Your face, I mean; you look like death itself. Where's that brandy the captain's never short of?"

"Brandy? I don't want that."

"Yes you do—this is a medicinal purpose if ever I saw one. Where does he keep it?"

Sighing, Louisa perched herself on the edge of a dining chair. "In the far cupboard—with the glasses." Her eyes widened at the generous measure, but Mary Elliott pushed it across the table, insisting she drink it.

"There, get it down. It'll put some warmth into you—and maybe some roses in your cheeks."

Sipping at it, Louisa pulled a face, then with great distaste drank the rest in one gulp. Her eyes watered as the spirit burned its way down her throat, and she coughed twice, wondering how Robert could drink it for pleasure. Within a minute or two, however, she was feeling better, and by the time his step was heard on the stairs, warmth and feeling were beginning to return.

It was the first time either of them had seen Robert in dress uniform, except at a distance. Mary Elliott sighed and walked around him several times; Louisa simply smiled, drinking in every detail of his magnificent appearance. From the high, gold-braided collar of his scarlet tunic to the toes of his highly polished boots, Robert was immaculate and impressive. Epaulets, insignia, buttons; all gleamed beneath the shaded light above his head. He was quite dazzling.

Amused by their appraisal, he smiled down at them, the curled ends of his luxuriant moustache curving upward in happy echo. "Will I pass?" he inquired, eyes twinkling as he glanced from mother to daughter.

"You certainly will," Mary Elliott conceded. "And you've put a bit of weight on—it suits you."

"Louisa suits me," he said boldly, taking her hand. His eyes traveled over her approvingly. "You look beautiful."

Her mother sniffed. "She looks better now she's smiling. Go on, get on with you," she said, pushing them toward the door, but there was a suspicious brightness in her eyes as she watched Robert arranging Louisa's mantle. "I'll lock up when I've gone, so don't be worrying. And for goodness' sake have a good time!" she ordered sternly.

"We will," Robert promised, but a few moments later, as the carriage pulled away, he touched Louisa's face with tender concern. "Are you very nervous?"

"Worse than having a tooth pulled," she admitted and tightly gripped his hand. Closing her eyes, she sank back into the seat, trying to concentrate on the steady, rhythmic clopping of the horses' hooves, willing the tight knot of tension away.

Watching her in the half-light, long curling lashes soft against the faint flush of her cheek, Robert felt a glow of possessive pride; the diamond and sapphire brooch held a small corsage of white roses, a coronet of tiny buds nestled amongst golden-brown curls, and around her neck, so white and slender, hung an oval locket on a thin gold chain. Recalling her agonies of indecision over the brooch, he smiled; in the strident glitter of necklets and tiaras, bracelets, rings, and pendants, Louisa's discreet display of jewelery would seem small indeed. Giving her hand a reassuring squeeze, he glanced at his watch.

"We've timed it right, I think. Tommy said he'd be there and waiting on the half hour, and it's almost five-and-twenty to ten now. There'll be enough arriving to cover our entrance."

Looking out of the carriage window, Louisa shivered. They were passing the end of Gillygate, and she suddenly wished herself at home, tucked up before the fire with a good book and a pot of cocoa. In spite of the brandy, she was cold again, and inside her new gloves, her hands were clammy with fear.

"I know you're frightened," he said softly. "Don't be. There's nothing to be afraid of—Tommy and I will take good care of you."

At the junction with Duncombe Place they paused; the Minster's twin towers rose palely into the night, and Louisa offered up a silent prayer for any kind of deliverance, but as they passed the brightly lit Assembly Rooms, none was forthcoming. Narrow little Blake Street was already thronged with carriages, many of them liveried; their own turned at the junction with Stonegate and proceeded to join the queue. Each minute seemed an eon; eventually, when she thought she could bear the suspense no longer, the carriage halted before the enclosed awning which had been erected in case of rain. With pounding heart, Louisa waited for Robert to alight and hand her down, waited hours until his hand beneath her elbow gently guided her up pillared steps into the Assembly Rooms' oval foyer. True to his word and magnificently uniformed, Tommy Fitzsimmons awaited them, a pair of ladies by his side, sisters by their similarity of feature and attire.

Afterward, Louisa felt sure they were introduced, but at the time, with ears deaf and eyes blind, scarcely able to breathe, she moved and spoke as if through a veil, registering nothing beyond the security of Robert's presence. Uniformed servants took their cards and dealt with the ladies' cloaks. In the first reception room the frond of a potted palm touched Louisa's arm, and she jerked away as though stung; Robert's fingers tightened, and as they moved forward, he murmured reassuringly.

"You're doing beautifully, my darling," he whispered. "Just keep it up for another minute or two." He turned to face her, holding out one white-gloved hand. Almost imperceptibly, it was trembling. "You see? Me too." But his eyes, blue with that peculiar intensity only excitement engendered, crinkled into a smile, and she thought miserably that he was enjoying the fear.

In the second reception room, the little party ran the gauntlet of all but the very senior officers; dazzled by that array of scarlet and gold, Louisa felt her face stiff in a half-smile as Robert introduced her to friends and colleagues. While he smiled and joked, she stood rigid beside him, hands clasped tight around her fan. A dozen paces, no more, as many moments which dragged like hours before that bright, circular room, with its ring of interested onlookers, was behind them.

The small ballroom was another world entirely. She paused, terror momentarily suspended, caught by the sheer unexpectedness of it: softly lit, scented, draped with silks and damasks of almost Oriental splendor, the long, narrow salon was like a picture from the Arabian Nights. Giant palms shadowed intimate groups of tables; smaller varieties, with azaleas and ferns, formed secluded arbors, while here and there amongst the greenery, like members of some Sultan's seraglio, brilliantly clad ladies fanned themselves, covertly watching each new arrival. Through a screen of drapery and leaves the vast Egyptian Hall awaited the first waltz, its soaring Corinthian columns illumined by thirteen crystal chandeliers.

Nodding pleasantly to more than a dozen acquaintances, Tommy led the way. Having previewed the arrangements, he had already decided which was the most secluded corner with the best view of the main ballroom; after some discreet haggling, his contact on the Ball Committee had placed Tommy's name upon the requested table.

As they sat down, Robert whispered: "What do you think of it?"

Louisa's lips curved into their first smile. "I feel like Scheherezade," she admitted, her eyes sparkling as she caught his swift glance.

"But I'm not interested in fairy tales," he reminded her. "You'll have to think of something else to keep me amused! Anyway," he added dryly, picking up her dance card as a distraction, "you're supposed to be impressed. They've spared no expense, you know."

"It's beautiful," she insisted. "And the ladies will love it."

"You're probably right," he acidly agreed, casting a practiced eye over the gathered company, most of whom were known to him. "They're dressed to match." With an indulgent smile, he patted her hand, proud of her simple elegance amongst all that finery. "However, I shall have to play my part and dance with some of them. But don't worry, you won't be short of partners."

With a smile, he begged the pleasure of a dance with each of Tommy's ladies, and like puppets operating on the same strings, they handed over their cards, embellished with the Royal Garter surmounted by the French Imperial Eagle, symbol of the one captured by the Royals at the Battle of Waterloo.

Stylish and pretty, Amelia and Flora, the Misses Conyingham, were alike enough to have been twins, so mentally attuned that often one began a sentence only for the other to finish it. With Blanche and Emily in mind, Louisa watched and listened in absolute fascination, amazed by the complete lack of rivalry between them, for it was obvious both were quite besotted with Tommy Fitzsimmons. With the benign ease of an Eastern potentate, Tommy basked in their dual adoration, apparently regarding it as no more than his due; and aside from an occasional twitchy grin, Robert gave nothing away of his opinions. Louisa began to wonder if their surroundings were to blame, if the opulent atmosphere temporarily suspended rational behavior; then it occurred to her that for them, perhaps, this was normal, and she was faintly shocked, although she could not have said why.

Tommy addressed the sisters as one, and after a while, Louisa found herself doing the same. Amelia and Flora were pleasant in return, although apparently incurious and far too interested in Tommy and the rapidly thickening stream of new arrivals to pay more than polite attention to the couple who shared their table. Quietly, for Louisa's benefit, Robert named some of the more distinguished guests being escorted to central tables, titles tripping easily off his tongue. Lords and ladies seemed commonplace, and there were enough colonels to staff a dozen regiments; county names like Fawkes and Fairfax, Deramore and Howard were scattered throughout the room, all familiar to her through society gossip columns; some had been regular visitors to that decaying mansion in the North Riding where once she had been governess. She found herself more titillated by the novelty of being among them as a guest than seriously afraid of recognition, but she kept her eyes open for the Bain-bridges.

As his commanding officer's party entered, with the lord mayor and other civic dignitaries, Robert drew Louisa's attention to a young man who seemed little more than a boy against that group of older men and their full-bodied wives.

"There you are," he whispered. "His Serene Highness, Prince Francis of Teck. Great-grandson to George the Third."

Louisa was unexpectedly overawed by that succinct utterance, and also faintly surprised. "I thought his family were German?" she murmured, with sudden, disturbing clarity recalling a remark of Albert Tempest's more than a year before.

"The Georges *were* German, weren't they?" he reminded her with a grin, deliberately misconstruing her question. "No, you're right. His father's German, mother first cousin to Her Majesty. But Francis was born and educated over here. Far more English than I am," Robert added with a mischievous smile. "But he's decent enough. He has a sense of humor, at least."

"I should think he needs one, the company he keeps," Louisa murmured, gazing at those well-fed, overdignified faces. "Is it true, Robert, that his sister will marry the duke of York?"

With a great show of secrecy, he leaned close. "I have it on good authority that an announcement is expected any day."

Half to herself, she said softly: "So Mr. Tempest was right," and felt rather than saw Robert's sudden stiffening at mention of that name. "He said the Princess May was too valuable a property to end her days a spinster," she explained with a humorless smile. "Poor Rachel was horrified. Which reminds me—have you seen her? Or any of the Bain-bridges?"

Robert shook his head. "Perhaps they haven't come. Anyway, there must be over three hundred people here. With luck, we won't see them, and they won't see us."

There was a momentary lull in both music and voices as the first dance, a Viennese waltz, was announced. The colonel and his wife led their most eminent guests out onto the floor; Prince Francis followed with a girl so embarrassingly plain that Louisa was overwhelmed with pity: for the girl with only her rank to recommend her and the prince who was obliged to honor it. But as they danced past, she saw that he was smiling and handsome, that his partner was enjoying her moment of glory. As more couples took the floor, she watched entranced, dazzled by jewels which sparkled and winked under those brilliant chandeliers, mesmerized by the swirl and sweep of soft chiffon and frothy lace.

Graceful ladies in rainbow colors, their hosts in scarlet and gold, narrow dark trousers slashed by a broad yellow stripe which somehow lent inches to them all; the other men, in evening dress of somber black and white, were quite outfaced, Louisa thought.

The music was hypnotic, drawing more and more dancers into its thrall, until Robert was touching her arm, reminding her that this first waltz, like the last, was his. Nervous, almost panic-stricken now the moment of truth had come, she hesitated, but he drew her on and into his arms.

The first few circuits were a blur of heady delight at realizing she could dance after all, of sheer pleasure in the music, and most of all joy at being held in Robert's arms in a public place with his smiling face so close to hers. She had a sensation of lightness, of floating round and round, borne up by the melody and those firmly guiding hands; as intoxication took the place of terror, she began to understand why he had been so eager to share it with her. She felt free, deliciously and delightfully so, and the Bainbridge family, complete with Rachel Tempest, were forgotten.

"I thought you said you couldn't dance?" Robert demanded as the music ended, and she laughed with delight, in love with the whole world. Looking down at her, Robert thought that he had never loved her more; she was beside him at last, just as he had longed for her to be, happy and unself-conscious and very, very lovely. On a wave of possessive pride he escorted her back to their table, smiling down into those brightly shining eyes; quite without thinking, he slid his arm around her waist.

As Tommy shook his head in an eloquent mime of reproof, across the room two pairs of eyes watched in almost horrified fascination. Arthur Bainbridge tapped his wife's hand, inquiring with a smirk whether she had seen a ghost. Irritably Rachel snatched her hand away and turned at once to her sister-in-law.

"It couldn't be anyone else, could it?"

"I hardly think so. The right height, the right hair—"

"It *can't* be her!" Rachel hissed. "Not with *him*. I don't believe it!"

Sophie glanced around again. "It is, you know. I told you I saw them together at Christmas, at the exhibition."

Peering between the palm fronds, Rachel said contemptuously, "I suppose that's another of her sister's gowns—poor Blanche must be working all hours for her. Wait a minute . . ."

Sophie craned her neck. "What? What is it?"

"She's wearing diamonds—no! Look, Sophie, that little brooch. Wait till she moves—there—did you see the flash? Diamonds, I'll lay my life on it!"

"Don't be silly, Rachel! They must be paste. Where would *she* get diamonds?"

Almost unconsciously, Rachel fingered her tiny drop earrings and the pendant at her throat. "Where do any of us get them?" she murmured under her breath, but her sister-in-law either was too innocent to understand or genuinely did not hear.

"They must be paste," she said again. "She looks very fine, though, doesn't she? You'd never think she was just a governess."

But Rachel was watching Robert Duncannon, that seemingly unattainable man; reading every gesture, his laughter and attentiveness, the ease with which he conversed with her former companion. She was suddenly seized with fury. The captain had attended her little soirees on occasion, but never had she seen him so animated; that he should be so besotted by that plain, dull old spinster was insufferable; and yet, watching her again, Rachel saw that she was far from plain in that elegant gown, far from dull in the way she spoke and smiled.

"What I'd like to know," Sophie said, "is how she managed to get an invitation. Papa had trouble enough getting tickets for all of us."

From the infinite superiority of her married state, Rachel clicked her tongue at Sophie's naïveté. "I'd have thought it was obvious," she said nastily. "She's his mistress, of course."

On an indrawn breath, her sister-in-law turned shocked eyes back to the dance floor. "Oh, goodness, Rachel, do you really think so?"

"He'll never marry her, of course—well, he couldn't possibly, could he? I mean, the Elliotts are *nothing*," she said disparagingly. "They don't even have *money*. Her mother only keeps an old boardinghouse on Gillygate. Or is it a bawdy house?" she whispered slyly. "One can never be quite sure."

Sophie's sudden giggles covered Hugh Darnley's departure from behind Rachel's chair. Faintly disturbed, he went in search of Robert Duncannon.

"To smile like that—with your heart in your eyes—is folly," said Tommy as the next dance paired him momentarily with Louisa. "It reveals too much."

She laughed. "I can't help it—I'm having such a wonderful time."

"Take care," he whispered, passing her back to Robert, but she smiled at him, refusing to see danger among that pleasure-loving crowd.

"I'm promised to Lady Haygarth next," Robert said. "She has a multitude of nieces, so don't worry if I don't get back to you immediately."

Before he left, however, a young lieutenant presented himself with a deferential air and begged the honor of any dance Louisa might have free. Privately she suspected Robert of connivance, but he resolutely refused to meet her eyes and with a twinkling grin took himself off.

As the young man escorted her through the crowd, Louisa caught sight of Hugh Darnley, soft spaniel eyes anxious as he first followed Robert's retreating figure and then turned back toward herself. Something in his demeanor made her hesitate, but the music was beginning and her partner was waiting; with what she hoped was a reassuring smile, Louisa gathered up the train of her gown and took the floor.

Although shy, he was a more than adequate partner. Trying to suppress a niggling anxiety, Louisa feigned ignorance, asking him to explain the standards and banners ranged beside the orchestra. She was audibly impressed by the two glittering stars of swords which faced the entrance to the ballroom, even more so by the names of famous battles and campaigns adorning the corner pillars: Dettingen, Peninsular, Waterloo, and Balaclava. They were names to conjure innumerable history lessons, but suddenly those lessons were real; she recalled that they had danced before Waterloo, that some young lady—Irish, Robert said, from Kilkenny—had begged leave to gird on Wellington's sword. It had always seemed a rather melodramatic gesture, yet suddenly the atmosphere of that fateful evening, almost eighty years before, was imaginable; her partner's smooth young face aroused her pity, and a fleeting glimpse of Robert, eyes shining as he waltzed with an elegant middle-aged lady, caused her heart to lurch painfully.

With a sharp mental admonition, Louisa forced herself to smile; grasping the young lieutenant's hand more firmly, she followed him into the turn, and there, without warning, for a brief, heart-stopping moment, was Rachel Tempest.

FIFTEEN

*T*hose few seconds blunted the rest of the evening, dulling the fine, shining edge of it, so that she danced and smiled mechanically, all the time imagining those eyes boring into her back. Robert introduced her to colleagues and acquaintances, and because his reputation was that of the rather solitary widower, there were indulgent, knowing smiles, whispered queries, and more than a few critical stares from disappointed mothers of marriageable daughters. Doing his best to make her laugh, Tommy tried to provide something of a smoke screen, claiming her for a polka and a lancers, flirting quite outrageously as they danced, and when she protested that the Misses Conyingham would be growing jealous, he simply laughed, saying that the sisters were all in all to each other, the despair of every bachelor for miles around. He took Louisa in to supper, letting Robert take charge of Flora and Amelia, but when, under the influence of some excellent champagne, she tried to press him further about the sisters, he maddeningly refused to be drawn.

Supper, laid out in the adjoining concert room, was a delight to the eye, designed to tempt even the most jaded palate; until she spied the Bainbridge party, Louisa had at least been trying to eat, but at sight of Rachel, in frothy lilac lace and playing to the crowd, what remained of her appetite fled. A distressed glance from Hugh Darnley broke through her bright facade, threatening to undo the act she thought she had perfected, and to drown that sudden burst of self-pity Louisa drained her glass. She wondered suddenly what Tommy had said to his ladies to explain her, the stranger in their midst, and knew, in spite of their self-absorbed indifference, that their curiosity would be aroused once Rachel started to talk. Abruptly she asked for another glass of wine and, despite Robert's look of concern, drained that too.

By the time they left the Assembly Rooms, shortly after two, she was more than a little tipsy and positively silly with relief. The sudden giggles which assailed her in the carriage just as suddenly deserted her once they were home; the two flights of stairs assumed Matterhorn proportions, but she climbed them unaided, then collapsed in a state of utter exhaustion. With infinite patience, Robert undressed her and put her to bed, propping pillows behind her for fear she would be sick. He wanted to stay, but he was in uniform and Harris was waiting up for him; after two journeys downstairs to reassure the waiting cabbie, he eventually left at half past three and, satisfied Louisa was sleeping naturally, took the cab back to Fulford.

When he arrived the following afternoon, Louisa was still in bed, complaining bitterly of a raging headache. Robert laughed, even louder as she held her head and whispered to him to stop, but within a few minutes he had the fire lit and before long was standing over her with toast and coffee.

"You'll never make a drinker, my love," he said with a regretful shake of his head. "This dreadful illness is merely the result of the wine you drank last night—on an empty stomach. I said you should have eaten."

"I couldn't."

"So, you're paying for it now. With a hangover. What you need is some fresh air, so get yourself dressed and we'll go out." He peered through the window. "I think we'll have a row on the river—that will blow the cobwebs off, and I could do with some practice."

"What on earth for?" she groaned, envisaging seasickness on top of everything else.

"A few of the chaps are organizing a water picnic for Saturday. And you, my love, are invited."

"Me?"

"Yes, you," he said with a laugh. "You were quite a success last night. *Quite* a success." He sat on the bed and kissed her naked shoulder. "I've been taken to task already for being so secretive. They all want to know where you've been hiding for the last two years. Don't panic!" he exclaimed at her alarm. "I maintained my discretion, didn't tell them a thing. You're being referred to now as *The Mysterious Lady in Blue,* which is rather romantic, don't you think?"

In spite of his amusement, however, Louisa was more worried than impressed.

For several days Robert rode the crest of a wave, refusing to heed Darnley's reproachful eyes or Tommy's reports that in certain circles Louisa was a topic of far greater interest than the ball itself. She had suspected as much. Hoping the ball and its accompanying stir of discussion would be no more than a nine days' wonder, she had planned to drop out of sight again; an intimate social occasion such as the picnic promised to be was the last thing she wanted. Feigned illness was unnecessary, however; on the Saturday it rained, and, thankfully, the event was called off.

Gradually Robert's euphoria waned to a more acceptable level, and outside interest faded, or seemed to. Less than a fortnight later, much to Louisa's relief, a far more exciting topic was on everyone's lips; the whole city was rejoicing over the duke of York's betrothal to Princess May of Teck.

The young couple were to be married within two months, a matter of days before the Royal Dragoons were due to leave York for Dublin, which meant the regiment would be able to take part in the city's celebrations. The city had taken Prince George to their hearts ever since the dukedom had been conferred upon him; it was obvious to all that the young prince was far more suited to future kingship than ever his elder brother had been; the fact that Princess May's brother had been resident in the city for almost two years was an added cause for celebration: even the humblest citizen felt honored by the connection.

Buoyant as a child at Christmas, Robert arrived that afternoon to share the news with Louisa. He hugged and kissed her with the taste of wine on his lips, so obviously thrilled that she looked at him in some amazement. At first she thought he was slightly drunk, and was on the point of refusing to walk out with him, but then she realized his pleasure at the betrothal was quite genuine and was even more surprised. With her, his attitude toward the regiment tended to be sardonic, as though the military games they played were his chief source of amusement; often he reported conversations and attitudes with a waspish cynicism, giving Louisa the impression that if he could think of anything better to do with his time, he would willingly do it.

"But he's a brother officer," Robert explained as they walked the path toward Clifton, and for the first time, under the influence of wine and subtle questioning, he talked seriously about his life with the Royals. She began to understand something of the deeply fraternal feelings which underlay his usual flippancy, that he could berate them, denounce with genuine anger their reactionary attitudes, and beneath it all still need them. They were his family; in effect he was wedded to them far more firmly than he had ever been to Charlotte. The men might change, but the idea of the regiment was almost tangible as he spoke of it, having a reality and dependability that the ordinary world lacked. For a fleeting moment, Louisa recalled his angry words on the night of their argument, and she knew that it was this life that he wanted her to know and understand, to be part of in the small way that women were permitted to be. But it was an intimate world, and she could see how difficult it must have been for him to maintain the secret of their relationship for so long. Anonymity would be impossible.

"There'll be quite a party tonight," Robert went on. "In fact," he added with a laugh, "it was already getting nicely underway this morning. It's fortunate I managed to escape."

"No doubt you'll all be disgustingly drunk by midnight," Louisa commented tartly.

Determined to maintain his joviality, Robert squeezed her hand. "Don't be a wet blanket, Louisa; it's not often the mess is in complete uproar."

"I suppose you'll play those silly games that schoolboys find so amusing, like taking each other's trousers off and having battles with bread-buns and champagne?"

He laughed uneasily. "What on earth makes you think that?"

"Oh, Robert, it's no secret! I worked in a big house for five years: young gentlemen are all the same. I've heard the noise and seen the mess they cause. They wouldn't think it so funny if they had to clear it up afterward. Nor would you," she added furiously and to cover her feelings began picking bluebells with unnecessary ferocity.

He frowned as he watched her under the trees, feeling belittled by that sharp, governessy reproof and annoyed by her failure to understand a piece of harmless fun. He stood quite still for several minutes, wondering what she was doing wandering about in the long, damp grass, keeping him waiting.

"Why are you doing that?" he asked eventually, suppressing a mounting irritation.

"What?"

"Dirtying your gloves and gown."

"I'm not. I'm picking bluebells."

With a theatrical sigh, Robert shook his head. "Now who's playing childish games?" he asked with heavy irony, striding through the long grass toward her. "Come on, darling, don't be silly. Let's get back to the apartment. I haven't that much time, you know."

"Time for what?" Louisa asked with obdurate calm, her attention still turned toward those long, slender stems.

"Time," he repeated suggestively, cupping the soft roundness of her bottom, "for something we're both in need of."

Ignoring his words and that familiar caress, she straightened and moved a pace or two away, then turned to regard him. In his immaculately tailored three-piece suit, with curly-brimmed hat fashionably tilted, Robert stood beneath the trees in a pose of unconscious elegance. It was impossible to mistake him for other than what he was, equally impossible to imagine him indulging in ridiculous horseplay. Yet he had played the fool with Louisa often enough, indulging in games which owed little to elegance and everything to sensuality.

The trees, the dappled sunlight, reminded her of the first time, in Blankney, and she frowned slightly, considering the differences that time and their relationship had wrought. She glanced down at her fine gown, remembering the old cotton dress she had worn that day, the burning fury which had so rapidly turned to urgent, ungovernable passion. Pique that their planned day should be marred by his anxiety to return to the mess turned to injured feminine pride. She would not be hurried home, not allow herself to be sandwiched like a meal taken on the run.

With a toss of her head, Louisa moved further into the wood.

She heard the swishing and tearing of grass beneath his feet as he strode after her; none too gently, he grabbed her arm and swung her around to face him.

"What are you playing at?" he demanded, an uneasy blend of desire and ill temper in his eyes. "If we don't go back now, there won't be time—and I want you. I'm on duty tomorrow, and the day after—"

"Don't you ever think of anything else?"

"No," he huskily confessed, his mouth closing hard upon hers. "Not when I'm with you. I want you all the time." Taking the bluebells, Robert dropped them in the grass, forcing her unwilling hand down between their bodies. "Can't you feel how much?" Touching her breast, he murmured suggestively: "Are we going home—or do you want me to take you here and now?"

"Stop it!" she cried, twisting away from him. "Do you think I'm your *whore,* to be ordered as and when you like? To be *used* in any spare half hour you might have between other pleasures?"

Stunned, he let his hands fall. "Don't be ridiculous!" he exclaimed with a forced laugh. "When have I ever—"

"Oh, but you have, Robert, you do it all the time! 'I've only got a couple of hours—let's go to bed.' "

"And you don't want to, I suppose?" he retorted angrily. "Your apparently insatiable desire is just an accommodating act, is it? The kind of act a whore puts on for her clients?"

Louisa's hand came up so fast he never saw it, only felt the weight behind that stinging slap and reeled with its force. Speechless for a moment, he simply stared at her; as he dropped his hand, she saw bright red weals across his cheek.

"That hurt!" he softly exclaimed.

"It was meant to!" Trembling, Louisa smoothed her dress, fingers checking every little button of its bodice. Robert moved not at all.

Eventually, as she bent to gather up that heedlessly scattered bouquet, he said: "I didn't mean that. I'm sorry. What was said just now—it wasn't meant."

"Wasn't it?" she muttered angrily. "Well, I certainly meant what *I* said. And as you are so obviously keen to get back to your other play-mates, Robert, might I suggest you take the quickest way back to the barracks and leave me to continue my walk. Alone. I don't want to see you," she added for good measure. "I intend to be very busy indeed. So don't bother to call."

"For Heaven's sake, Louisa! Don't you think you're—"

"I mean it, Robert."

Looking into her blazing eyes, he saw that she did. With a shrug he retrieved his hat and dusted it off. "Believe me, I'm sorry. But I'll not say it again. If you should need me, you know where I am."

With an elaborate and most unnecessary bow he turned, walking at an even pace through the trees and toward the river. Louisa was so angry she could have screamed. Instead she picked up a short dead branch and threw it at his retreating back. It fell short, but he heard it and, without turning his head, simply waved.

When she had calmed down, Louisa made her way back along the towpath toward Marygate Landing. It was hot in the sun, and she walked slowly, carrying the nodding bouquet of bluebells. There was no sign whatever of Robert, but she passed several small groups, nannies with perambulators, elderly couples out taking the afternoon air; and there were plenty of boats on the river, young men displaying their prowess before prettily dressed and parasoled ladies. Barges too; always plenty of those, she thought, gazing absently at one unwieldy and overloaded craft. Inadvertently she caught the eye of the helmsman. He was young and handsome, with a bright spotted neckerchief and bare brown fore-arms, and he whistled his appreciation as she passed. Scarlet with em-barrassment, Louisa tilted her parasol to cover her face, earning the derogatory glances of two middle-aged matrons on a bench nearby.

They probably think I'm a prostitute, she thought furiously, cursing her fine clothes. Ladies rarely walked anywhere alone. And ladies don't say what I've just said, she thought next, face flaming at the recollection, nor do the things I've done.

Passing under the railway bridge, she hurried along the path beside the embankment, almost sobbing with relief as she ran up the two flights of stairs to her apartment. Dumping the flowers anyhow into a vase, Louisa locked the door and stripped off her clothes, scrubbing furiously at her erring body with water cold from the tap. I hate him, she thought, blaming Robert totally for those heated words, for every single act of love, every erotic gesture she had ever made toward him. "The kind of act a whore puts on," he had said; and she winced again. Never before had she so much as questioned the rights and wrongs of her situation; because all was done in the name of love, it had seemed so good; but one phrase, one gesture, had soured it instantly, driving doubt and humiliation before it. Without him she would not have known the ways of whoredom, and without whores—how many? she wondered—he could not have taught her. Other than Charlotte, Robert had never mentioned previous sexual relationships, and in all innocence Louisa had imagined there were none. She cursed herself for a fool: there had to have been others, dozens, probably. How else could he know all that he taught so well? The act of procreation was simple and direct, a matter of instinct, she supposed, especially with a man; but there was nothing simple about Robert Duncannon, never had been, not after the first time.

With an angry determination not to cry, nor to brood, she donned a clean white cambric nightdress, made a cup of tea, and settled herself to read a new book, feet curled up in the chair. After three pages, however, she put it down, not having registered a single word. A headache nagged behind her eyes, and she closed them, aware of sudden overwhelming fatigue.

After the exceptional warmth of the day, heat still lingered beneath the eaves; the window which looked out over the river stood open, but there was no breeze, and the bluebells, standing with heavy heads in the hearth, pervaded the air with their cloying, almost narcotic scent. Within a very few minutes, Louisa was sound asleep.

Perhaps an hour later, a firm knock disturbed her dreams; in sleepy bewilderment she approached the door, wondering at the time and the identity of the caller. Suddenly convinced that it must be Robert, come to apologize, she snatched the door open, ready to order him away. But it was Edward, strangely unfamiliar on this weekday evening in his best black suit.

Louisa had not seen him for weeks, and then only to exchange the briefest of comments before she left her mother's house. While she wondered at his unexpected presence, his eyes took in her state of undress and slid uncomfortably away.

"I'm sorry," he said, already beginning to retreat. "I didn't mean to intrude. I'll come back later."

"You're not intruding," she informed him, the words clipped with anger. "I'm quite alone. Come in."

Having closed the door behind him, Louisa excused herself, returning from the bedroom with her robe. "I didn't feel well," she explained, "so I decided to lie down."

Edward studied her face, taut and rather pale, yet her brisk movements suggested that she was more upset than ill. "I can come back later, if you'd prefer?"

"Not at all," she insisted. "If you can excuse my somewhat informal attire, I'd rather you stayed. I don't often have the honor of visitors."

He found her brittle manner disconcerting and, in view of the reason for his visit, difficult. Unable to frame what he had come to say, Edward indulged in polite, inconsequential conversation, assuring her that all the family were in the best of health as far as he knew, that Emily and John had found a suitable house at last and intended moving to Leeds as soon as possible. John Chapman had been traveling there daily for some weeks.

Eventually, having run out of things to say, he simply sighed and looked at her helplessly. He saw her eyes soften, felt something of her distress mingling with his own, and then looked away, trying to close his mind against it.

Studying the bluebells in their green pottery vase, Edward thought of another spring, so long ago it hurt him to count the years between. A day like this had been, with sun-dappled woodland and shadowy paths flanked by a carpet of blue; a small girl clutching her first bouquet of short and mangled stems in a chubby fist, white apron grubby, golden curls awry, blue eyes full of laughter and delight. He saw himself, a boy of fourteen or fifteen, clasping that tiny hand, carrying her on his shoulders when the little legs were too tired to walk. It seemed a very short time ago, yet more than twenty years had somehow slipped away unseen.

"What made you pick them?" he asked, and suddenly she was no longer pale; color flooded her cheeks, and he wondered why.

Louisa laughed to cover her embarrassment. "I don't know. Because they were there, I suppose. I wish I hadn't," she confessed and then, as though that required an explanation, added: "They looked better where they were."

"Yes," he said softly. "They die so quickly, don't they?"

In obvious concern, Louisa leaned forward. "Oh, Edward, what is it? I do wish you'd tell me."

"Victoria Tempest," he said flatly, not looking at her. "She's very ill. I thought you'd want to know." As he caught her shock and incomprehension, his breath caught in his chest. He wanted to go to her, to comfort her with all the love of which he was capable; he wanted to turn back time so that, knowing what he knew now, he could change the pattern of events and wipe Robert Duncannon from their lives altogether. Even without his presence, Edward was so conscious of him here that every loving gesture, every word he longed to say, froze in his mind the moment it was conceived. Stiffly, hating himself, he apologized for the baldness of his statement, adding with formal and unnecessary parenthesis: "You came to care for her very much, I believe."

"Yes," It was a whisper, as though she knew there was little to hope for.

He sighed, conscious of an inexplicable sorrow for the child he had never met, knowing that if she lived she would be pitiable, a mindless creature for the rest of her days. But her chances of recovery were remote indeed. "Meningitis," he murmured and felt rather than heard the shock which brought Louisa's hand to her mouth. "Her father came in late this morning, called me into the office to tell me the doctor's judgment."

Recalling that painful interview, Edward paused, reliving his own pity and acute embarrassment. "He broke down completely. Wept like a child. It was dreadful—I've never seen a man so broken. He really worships that child."

"Worships her?" Louisa repeated in a high, unnatural voice. For a moment she stared at the ceiling as though considering the question. "I suppose you *could* put it like that," she said at last. "If you mean she's like a wax doll in a glass case, taken out from time to time, but never really played with—I suppose you could say he worships her. But he doesn't *love* her, I don't even think she's *real* to him. But then, nobody is," she added bitterly. "People are just objects to Albert Tempest, either attractive or useful. Dispensable, though, when they cease to please him. Like Rachel."

With an impatient gesture, Edward stopped her. "What's the matter with you? The man *wept,* for heaven's sake. He was genuinely distraught!"

"Oh, yes, he would be," she agreed, with a hard, mocking smile. "Albert Tempest is a creature of quite unbridled emotions, Edward, self-indulgent and blind to the sufferings of others. He sees nothing that isn't pointed out, and even then he accepts only what suits him!

"That child," she went on, "has had little warmth and even less companionship. Since Rachel left, the only person who seems to have given her as much as a second thought is Moira Hanrahan—and she had to come to *me* with her concern, because in her employer's eyes, Moira is less worthy of notice than the mat he wipes his feet on! And would *you* employ a cold, hard, middle-aged woman as your child's teacher and sole companion?"

Edward shook his head. "Probably not, but plenty do."

With a snort of disgust, Louisa said: "If Albert Tempest *really* cared for his daughter, he would have seen what Moira saw months ago and done something about it! He's a cruel man, Edward, if only by default. Thoughtless and cruel. I've no pity for him, none whatsoever."

Stunned by the vehemence of his cousin's words, Edward sat still and silent. Initially he suspected Louisa of exaggeration born of intense dislike, but then incidents from the past came back to him: summary dismissals of men with ailing wives or children, the almost constant ill feeling which prevailed in the print room. He escaped it simply because Albert Tempest was a printer and not a bookbinder, and Edward's standards were too high ever to give cause for complaint. Perhaps because they had never seriously crossed swords, Albert Tempest trusted him; had even, that very morning, put Edward in sole charge of the business for the few days he expected to be absent. And that had embarrassed Edward more than flattered him, for the print room foreman had taken it as a personal slight.

"I suppose," he eventually admitted, "that over the years my view of him has been restricted. He's hard, I know that. Which is probably why I was so shocked this morning. I couldn't quite believe it."

"He's more than hard," Louisa said quietly, her face a blank mask; but in the next moment, the mask crumpled. "That poor child," she whispered. "I tried so hard, really I did. Even in the beginning, when she was so difficult, I could see it wasn't her fault. And in the end—in the end, she was so lovable. If only—" She broke off and covered her eyes. "There was nothing I could do, Edward—nothing! That's what hurts so much."

He sat with eyes downcast, studying the small area of carpet which lay between them. It might well have been a mass of shifting quicksand: one foolish step and he risked being lost forever. Her feet, bare and vulnerable beneath the white hem of her nightdress, drew his gaze; he had the strangest desire to kiss them, to beg her forgiveness for the distance he had inadvertently created but deliberately maintained. A fleeting second later it dawned on him that, for the first time in his life, he was disturbed by Louisa's state of undress, although in the past he had been well used to seeing her so.

We were too close, he thought uncomfortably, recalling his own myopia; it hurt to realize that it had taken another man to open his eyes, to make him see her as she really was, yet it was still a shock to meet her face to face. The image of innocence he had held for so long was hard to dismiss, even harder to reconcile with the desirable woman she had become.

Edward knew his attitude in recent months had been interpreted as moralistic disapproval, knew also that this was partly true; but he remembered Christmas as the day she had presumed too much, presenting him with a book of verse whose philosophy ran contrary to everything he believed in and kissing his cheek as though nothing at all had changed. That brief and casual touch had stripped him naked, exposing wounds which were not even half-healed. Since then he had been overly aware of a need to protect himself against her; while she would not willingly hurt him, he was afraid she would do so out of blindness, for to her he was simply Edward, the edges of his manhood blurred by familiarity and, he had to admit, his own inability to define himself.

In that respect, however, he had begun to rectify matters. There had been too much grief and, for him, too much self-recrimination; the time had come for more positive things, and if the rest of his life was to be lonely, without benefit of the companionship he had always longed for, then he knew he must learn to accept it, and so must she.

A photograph of Robert Duncannon on the table beside him was sufficient reminder that Louisa was not alone, not without comfort in her moments of grief. And if her state of undress was anything to go by, he reflected, then the captain could well be arriving shortly. Smarting at the thought, he rose to his feet. "I'll let you know," he said, "what happens."

Louisa stared up at him, eyes wide in disbelief, pain and amazement plainly etched upon her face. Looking down at her, Edward felt all his fine resolutions begin to melt away. He wanted to stay, wanted to take her in his arms and hold her hard against his heart; even more, he wanted to take her home. Words hovered on his lips, all the doubts and sorrows of the last twelve months; he even took a step toward her, but then he closed his eyes tight, and common sense took over.

"I can't stay," he said at last, and his voice sounded taut and strained, even to himself.

"Why not?" she demanded, and he thought he detected a faint, high note of hysteria. "Do I embarrass you?"

"It isn't that," he murmured gruffly.

"Then what is it, Edward?" Again that high note in her voice. "Are you afraid to stay? Afraid you might be contaminated?"

Again he closed his eyes. No, he shouted silently, it's you I'm afraid of—you and the power you have to hurt me.

"It's me, isn't it? Isn't it?" she demanded fiercely and, when he did not immediately reply, added contemptuously: "You might as well admit it—I can see it in your face. You're ashamed of me!"

If she had repeated the accusation, taken just one more step toward him, Edward knew he would have slapped her; but as she turned away he took a deep breath, slowly uncurling his fingers from a crushed hat brim. With a great effort he kept a hold on his temper, forced himself to speak calmly and without rancor. It would have been easier to walk out, but he knew that if he did the tenuous link between them would be severed, perhaps forever.

"I have an appointment to keep. To view some premises in Piccadilly. I didn't want to tell you before, because it seemed—callous, I suppose." He struggled to explain himself, all the time aware that she was hardly listening. "I've been thinking for some time that I should leave Tempest's. I just wish this opportunity had come at some other time. Anyway," he added, "this place may not even be suitable. I shall have to see." With a glance at the clock, he sighed heavily. "I shall have to go, Louisa. I'll call again as soon as there's any news about the child."

In the safety of the lane he stopped for a moment, feeling ill; as he mopped his brow, he noticed his hands were trembling. Struggling to regain some sort of control, he swallowed hard and tried to breathe deeply, but the evening was warm, and the scented air, trapped between mellow brick walls, almost suffocated him. Eager to escape, he set off in almost feverish haste, disturbing a pair of lovers in the shadow of an overhanging lilac; apologizing, feeling like a leper, he hardly looked at them, continuing on uncertain feet toward the lower end of Marygate. On the landing he rested against a bollard, gulping at the sharp green smell of the river until his nausea passed.

Bargees and boatmen were idling, smoking pipes and calling to each other; from the prow of a keelboat a black and white dog barked at a group of ragged children playing on the opposite bank. There was a sane normality about it which placed the last half hour in the light of madness.

Now that it was over, he loathed himself, feeling not the smallest speck of pride in that convincing display of calm self-control. He almost wished that he had slapped her: it would at least have shown some degree of feeling. But her distress took him back to Tanner Row, to a small girl hurt and bewildered because some gang of urchins had called her filthy names, shouting obscenities as she ran for home. It had been a blessed relief to get away from there, but he had not forgotten the agony of those last weeks, nor ever would. It appalled him to think that Louisa might have a child whose inheritance would be no better than her own.

In many ways, Edward's childhood had been even more harrowing, although he rarely allowed himself to dwell on it. In retrospect, those early years were a haze of unanswered questions and bleak uncertainty; coupled with the bullying he had endured at school, he thought it hardly surprising that he had retreated into the world of books.

His mother's insistence that he take up a trade seemed to have been the beginning of a lifetime's acquiescence, a consistent deferring to other people's plans and desires. Although he enjoyed his work, he saw now that he had stayed at Tempest's out of sheer inertia; it was easier to ignore his employer's shortcomings than to take the risk of striking out elsewhere. The static world of books and poetry had kept his head down, in more ways than one, enabling him to blend quietly into his surroundings, gradually suffocating any latent embers of dissatisfaction.

The advent of Robert Duncannon into that safe and comfortable world had been unwelcome; the *fait accompli* of his affair with Louisa, shattering. And if all their lives had been shaken, he felt his own had suffered more than most; but out of the rubble of his dreams, Edward had managed to salvage something which would otherwise have been lost, and for that small blessing, he was grateful indeed.

During the long winter months he had not been idle. Armed with his father's family name, he had chased facts, worrying librarians like a terrier, until every possible scrap of information was unearthed. There were notebooks filled with hastily scribbled details covering several generations, people whose way of life was so far removed from his own that he was able at first to see no connection. Until that cold night when he had suddenly realized the unimportance of proving his father's identity. What mattered was that he was a product of that man's family, the inheritor of their failings as well as their virtues; in trying to fathom them, he began to understand himself, to see connections which had never been apparent on the Elliott side. And if the man with the thin, ascetic face was indeed his father, then it was suddenly clear why Elizabeth Elliott had treated her son with such apparent disdain. Not only did Edward favor looks other than hers; it seemed he had also inherited other characteristics. That scholarly air of absentmindedness, for instance, which, as Edward well knew, could be such an effective cover for cowardice. It was far easier to escape into a book, to pretend not to have heard, than to challenge the speaker; simpler by far to give in, to feign unselfishness for the sake of peace, and see the surrender as sacrifice.

Which was why he refused to give in now, either to Louisa or to Albert Tempest. He felt for each of them in their grief, but at this juncture it seemed imperative to ignore their separate calls upon his sympathy. Louisa had her lover, he reminded himself, and Albert Tempest would always survive, with his help or without it. In his world, no one was irreplaceable.

Edward looked at his pocket watch and stood up, straightening his shoulders. It was time to look to the future, his own future, and if he tarried much longer, those premises in Piccadilly would be taken by someone else.

SIXTEEN

*T*hose who understood the nature of Victoria Tempest's illness said her death would be a blessing, but it was impossible for Louisa to see it in that light. Haunted by visions of the child's suffering, both past and present, she found the argument with Robert paled into petty insignificance, leaving her wondering what on earth had given rise to those harsh exchanges. Anxious only to forget the whole incident, to bury her distress in the reassuring comfort of his arms, she wrote the very next day, no more than a brief note, but he came that night in answer to it.

On both sides, the last remnants of pride and determination crumbled within minutes, and knowing nothing of the crisis at the Tempests', he simply took her into his arms and into bed.

Although he made no further verbal apology, Robert's eagerness to make amends was obvious; but even while he listened to the outpouring of troubles afterward, he seemed incapable of understanding the guilt and grief which oppressed her.

At first he tried to chide her out of it. Then, as the days wore on, an unmistakable note of impatience crept in; resenting it, Louisa became edgy and bitter, half-regretting that too-easy forgiveness. A suspicion that perhaps she had been right about his motives made her draw physically away from him, which made his patience even shorter.

Edward called each evening, for a few minutes only and with news of the child. She would have welcomed his company and a chance to talk, but he was busy, he said, and seemed reluctant to spend more time in the apartment than was absolutely necessary. Despite his calm reassurance, nothing would sway Louisa's conviction that the little girl had pined for affection, in her weakened state becoming prey to the illness which had her so firmly in its grip. At night she tossed and turned, beset by the milestones of the past year, examining each event with the glare of hindsight, convinced she should have done more, written to Rachel, gone to see her, forced the girl to do something about her sister's situation. Yet Rachel had seen her sister on several occasions, she knew that from Moira; was she willfully blind, Louisa asked herself, or simply ignorant? Was she too proud, or too afraid to hammer on her father's door and demand admittance? And when, just ten days later, she had the news of Victoria's death, it was no comfort to be told by Robert that children died every day from the effects of poverty, no comfort at all to hear that Albert Tempest's child had not gone hungry from necessity, that there had been food and clothes and fuel to warm her and a very secure roof over her head. Louisa had lived under that roof herself and knew what it was like, and she knew Victoria Tempest had died from another kind of poverty entirely, one that Robert seemed quite unable to understand.

Moira came, missing the captain by minutes, but even that failed to register properly; in the midst of their shared grief, Louisa forgot her expensive silk tea gown and the aroma of cigars lingering in the room. The funeral was to be on the Friday, but Moira was not sure Albert Tempest would be fit to attend; at the news of his daughter's death he had been taken with some kind of seizure, she said, and since then was confined to bed, the doctor visiting every day. Rachel had called while her father was sleeping, and Mrs. Petty had been under the strictest orders not to disturb him. Moira felt sorry for them both; Albert Tempest was but a shadow of his former self, and Rachel so upset, her pretty face all blotched and swollen with weeping.

Recalling Rachel's propensity for tears, and her father's self-indulgent temper, Louisa could feel no sympathy for either of them; only outrage that Albert Tempest should go on living while an innocent child lay dead in her coffin.

Nevertheless, when she saw him at the funeral, it was a shock. Heavily veiled, she sat in a shadowed pew at the rear of the Priory Street chapel; among the many mourners Edward sat near the front as a representative of the Tempest work force, while on the other side of the aisle sat Moira and Mrs. Petty, both in new though ill-fitting mourning. Rachel, smart in couture black, sat with bowed head between her father and a middle-aged couple, Rachel's aunt and uncle, Louisa presumed, from Bradford.

As the little coffin was borne out, Albert Tempest staggered, ashen-faced and so obviously ill that his brother-in-law and another man took his arms, supporting him down the aisle. He seemed oddly shrunken, a gray and feeble replica of the man who had once had the power to terrify. She shuddered at the memory, looking down in her reluctance to meet those yellowed eyes, and when she raised her head again Rachel was with him in the lobby, taking her father's arm like a reconciled and most dutiful daughter. He made no demur, but turned to her in pathetic gratitude, while their various relatives stood by, nodding like a bunch of donkeys.

Bitterly Louisa looked on at a scene which seemed to be played for full sentimental effect. Waiting for the crowd to clear, she could think of nothing but the total bankruptcy of that supposedly touching reunion. Too late, too late! were the words drumming through her head; why couldn't you make things up before?

Oppressed by the weight of human folly, eager for clean, fresh air, she pushed her way through the gathering at the head of the steps. Rachel and her father were being assisted into the leading carriage, while to one side stood the entire Bainbridge family, all endeavoring to look suitably mournful and succeeding only in showing their collective embarrassment. With a little snort of disgust, Louisa turned away, looking for Edward.

She found him at the foot of the steps, exchanging polite conversation with a couple whose faces were unknown to her. Not wanting to be introduced, she hung back, but Edward noticed her immediately, excusing himself to speak to her.

With a sigh, he squeezed her hand. "Are you all right?"

"I think so," she whispered, her eyes on the leading carriage. "But I hope he suffers! I hope they both realize what part they had to play in that child's death, and never, ever, forget it!"

"Keep your voice down," Edward murmured, glancing around. "That's no way to talk here."

"You don't understand!"

"Perhaps I don't," he agreed, "but it's neither the time nor the place. The child's dead, Louisa. Bitterness won't bring her back."

For a moment she chewed her lip. "Of course it won't," she conceded at last. "But I just wish—oh, how I wish, Edward!—they could have swallowed their pride a little sooner than this. It's all so pointless— arguments in families, people not speaking, others suffering. And then, when it's all too late—" Voice breaking, Louisa shook her head. "Why," she pleaded, "does it have to take a tragedy to make people *see?*"

Very gently he ushered her away from the crowd at the pavement edge. Sighing, he shook his head. "I don't know. But there again," he admitted with weary reproach, "there are a lot of things I don't understand."

Amid the quiet buzz of subdued voices, the impatient shifting of horses' hooves, it seemed to Louisa he waited expectantly, waited for her to see how closely her criticism of the Tempests applied a little closer to home; at last, it did. As realization dawned, remorse flooded through her like a hot tidal wave.

"I'm sorry," she got out at last.

"So am I," Edward murmured with infinite regret. For a long moment, neither of them spoke; then, as though it cost him very deeply, he said: "We should talk."

Overwhelmed, wanting to tell him everything, knowing it should have been said a long time ago, Louisa simply squeezed the fingers which still held hers.

"Are you going to the cemetery?" he asked and, when she shook her head, looked back at the rapidly forming procession. "Well, I should go, but I very much doubt whether they'll miss me by the graveside. Look, if we walk together at the back of the crowd, I'm sure we can slip away unnoticed."

"Where are we going?" she asked as Edward slowed his steps on Castle Mills Bridge.

"My new workshop," he replied, watching the cortege wind its mournful way past empty cattle pens outside the Walmgate walls. "It's not far. When you've seen it, we'll go somewhere and have tea. I think we both deserve it."

Lifting the heavy veil from her face, he smiled reassuringly, tucked her arm in his, and guided her around the corner and into Piccadilly, a narrow cobbled street which bore no resemblance to its fashionable London counterpart. The vernacular architecture echoed the changing fashions of at least three centuries; crumbling, jettied buildings with age-skewed doors and windows glanced sidelong at less than classical Georgian facades, while stables and agricultural factors nudged elbows with houses both private and public. A strong smell of beer assailed their nostrils as they passed the entrance to a timber-framed alehouse, for a moment overlaying the odor of horses and the ever-present pungency of the Foss, running parallel only yards away. A group of soldiers were lounging in the doorway, supping ale from pewter tankards, their comments appreciative but ribald as Louisa edged her way past.

"Don't ever walk this way alone," Edward muttered grimly as he hurried her along, and with the close proximity of Walmgate in her mind, Louisa nodded a fervent assent.

Producing a large iron key from an inner pocket, he guided her steps toward an ancient house which might have been modern in the latter years of the fifteenth century, its quaint upper story tilting drunkenly toward the street. Cracked and peeling stucco made it more than a match for its neighbors, but with a smile and something of a flourish, Edward unlocked the heavy oak door and pushed it back for Louisa to enter.

He had been busy; she could see that. The room's worn, stone-flagged floor was empty and clean; part-brick, part-timber walls were freshly whitewashed, as was the beamed ceiling; a new flight of wooden steps led to an upper floor, while along the wall beneath the window was a smooth new workbench and a stack of what seemed to be pine shelving, waiting to be fitted. By contrast, the vast brick fireplace on the opposite wall contained an ancient range which looked to have lain unused for years. It was the only jarring note in what was otherwise a quaint but attractive workroom.

Edward was watching her closely, and as she turned to meet his gaze she saw the sparkle of pride and amusement. "Will it do, do you think?"

"It's amazing!" she confessed. "How ever did you keep all this to yourself? And you've worked so quickly—"

"Well, not me, exactly," he interrupted "I've had a carpenter in to do the essential jobs. And as you can see, he hasn't finished yet."

"But it's *lovely*," she sighed, taking everything in again. "I don't know, Edward, you're such a dark horse, sometimes."

"Perhaps it runs in the family," he commented.

Stabbed by that small dart, Louisa turned away. "What's upstairs?"

"Nothing much, junk that might come in handy. I got rid of the rubbish. But I haven't got round to cleaning it properly yet. Down here was the first priority."

"You know, I never thought you'd leave Tempest's," she said wonderingly. "Didn't imagine you could afford to. But you must have been planning this for a long time."

He shook his head. "Not at all. A couple of months, perhaps, no more than that. I suddenly realized I was in a rut—working hard for someone else, almost carrying the place for the last few years. The book-binding side, anyway. So I did a bit of arithmetic and decided it was just about feasible, then started looking for premises. As you can imagine," he laughed, "this place came pretty cheap!"

Fingering the new workbench, glancing around, he added softly, "But I wish I'd thought of this years ago. Probably couldn't have afforded it before my mother died, but I wish I'd thought of it and planned it then. My only regret now is the timing. I doubt I'll be ready to move in for a few weeks yet, but I feel bad about leaving the old man when he most needs me."

"Well, don't," Louisa said tersely. "He wouldn't think twice about getting rid of you if it suited him—no matter what your circumstances."

For a moment Edward pursed his lips, then, with a sudden click of disapproval, said: "There you go again—so bitter. It was never like you to hold a grudge." When she did not respond, he added more gently: "It's more than just the child's death, isn't it? Won't you tell me?"

Avoiding his gaze, on a deep breath she nodded. When she did look up, however, he saw pain and guilt and sadness; and he knew that, whatever the cause, it would inevitably hurt him too. For a moment, wondering at this meeting's wisdom, Edward closed his eyes. When he opened them she had moved closer, her hand half-extended toward him, and in the black garb of mourning he thought how pale she looked, like a grieving widow; there were even tears beneath her lashes. With a deep, sad sigh, conscious that all his fine resolutions were in danger of fleeing forever, Edward reached out, folding her hands tight within his own. In that quiet solitude he could hear the rapid pulsing of his blood, was suddenly aware of the weeks and months and years since they had been as close as this. Wanting desperately to hold her, he said breathlessly, "Why are you so afraid to tell me things? You never used to be."

The held-back tears escaped. "I'm sorry," she gulped, bending her head against his shoulder. "Oh, Edward—I'm sorry—so sorry!"

For once, instinct prevailed; the sudden, fierce joy that consumed him as he drew her into his arms was almost painful in its intensity; his fingers tingled as he touched her hair, her neck, the smoothness of her back. Longing to crush that delicious softness until her body merged with his, he held her delicately, savoring the infinite pleasure of the moment. Lips touched soft curls, the velvety curve of an ear, tasted the salty warmth of tears on her cheek. "There's no need to cry," he murmured, even while he savored the taste; she buried her face against his shoulder and sobbed.

"You don't understand," she got out at last. The words were muffled, but he heard them.

"What don't I understand?" he whispered.

"You don't know what happened—when I left Blossom Street."

"You're absolutely right, love," he murmured soothingly, no longer really caring. "But it doesn't matter now."

"Oh, but it does," she insisted, drawing back to look at him. While she brushed awkwardly at her eyes, Edward found a handkerchief and, seating himself more comfortably on the bench, tenderly dried her tears.

"You see, now they're together again, they'll talk—about the past, about what parted them in the first place. And in the making up they'll find other people to blame—they certainly won't blame themselves. I'll be the scapegoat, Edward—you can count on that!"

With a sigh he drew her comfortingly against him. "I think you'd better give me this story from the beginning."

Despite her agitation, he was aware of his own euphoria; felt that as long as he could go on holding her, touching her, nothing else could matter, and wondered why he had never felt like this before. The reasons behind her distress confused him, and whereas once he had been desperate for those answers, now he was strangely reluctant to hear them. With a smile and a sigh he touched her forehead with his lips. "Now," he said gently, "begin with Albert Tempest. What's his part in all this?"

Louisa shuddered, but he thought it merely the last vestiges of her sobbing fit. When she leaned against him, with a whispered plea that he should hold her tight, Edward did not object.

Sitting there on the bench, stroking her back, he listened as she began to talk about that afternoon at the Bainbridges', putting the entire story in chronological order, including the fact that she had not seen Robert Duncannon for months and the reasons why. Recalling the wrong conclusions drawn, Edward at first felt ashamed, then, as he heard her halting confession of that appalling sexual assault, he wanted to hit out, block his ears, anything but comprehend the terror and humiliation she had been forced to endure. He felt her pain like a physical thing, and despite her reticence in the telling, Edward was not so innocent that he lacked the imagination to understand all that had happened in the drawing room of Albert Tempest's house.

Anger, cold and stark, broke deep inside and chilled him to the bone. He began to shiver uncontrollably, held her hard and fast for warmth. "Oh, God," he swore with trembling passion, "he'll pay for that! He'll pay for *all* of it!"

SEVENTEEN

*A*nger and bitterly wounded pride left no room for regret.

Despite his original plan, which was to wait until the worst of the present crisis was over, the following day Edward penned a brief letter of resignation, stating with some satisfaction that he intended setting up in business on his own. Sealing the envelope, he went out immediately to post it on Fossgate. Albert Tempest would no doubt receive it by late afternoon, too late for any kind of action. There would be all evening and the long quiet hours of the Sabbath for him to ponder and fume and stew; Monday morning would see him back, no matter what his state of health.

The chain of events Louisa had described burned in the back of his mind, but he refused to consider them. Determined to clear as much work as possible, he summoned his senior assistant and, ignoring the man's pop-eyed surprise, informed him that he had given notice. He outlined his handover plans and began by showing him the orders and accounts, trying to suppress angry frustration at the younger man's slowness.

They worked on into the afternoon, until Edward sensed his assistant could absorb no more. With a sigh he sent the man home, surprised a moment later to see that the young apprentice was still working.

"Now then, Dick, what are you doing? I thought you'd gone long since."

The lad was tall and lanky; awkwardly, he towered over Edward. "Well, Mr. Elliott, sir, since you said you'd be leaving, I thought maybe you could deal with a bit of help. Strikes me there's a lot to do."

"Mmm," Edward gruffly acknowledged, secretly wishing the boy and his absent superior could swap places. Had Dick been out of his apprenticeship, there would have been fewer anxieties. He glanced at the clock; it was already past three. "I'll be here for a good while yet. You can stay if you want. I'd appreciate it."

The boy glowed with pleasure. "Right you are, sir." And with that he returned to his task, preparing the cut edges of unbound books with a sharp steel scraper.

At the end of each stage, Dick brought the books to Edward to be inspected. Edward ran sensitive fingers over each cut edge, cast an experienced eye at the clamps before the black lead polish was applied, and finally pronounced the edges ready for their coating of egg white. He went to the safe for the book of gold leaf, inspecting his hands as he did so. It pleased him to see they were steady; no sign of the tremors which had disturbed his work on more than one occasion in the last year.

Opening the book of gold leaf, he ran his fingers through his hair several times, allowing the engendered static to attract a single leaf of delicate tissue; swiftly and surely, he applied it to the unbound book, pressing it into place with a piece of polished agate. When it was dry it would be burnished; he always looked forward to the moment when he could riffle the pages, watching the light catch the glitter, close it, and see a solid block of gold.

With the unbound set complete, Edward gave a satisfied sigh. "Covers tomorrow, I think." The set was for a valued customer in the East Riding; it was suddenly a matter of personal importance that the gentleman not be disappointed.

"It's Sunday tomorrow, Mr. Elliott," the lad reminded him.

"I know."

"Will you be coming in, then?"

"I will." Automatically he began tidying things away, and the boy followed his lead.

"You expecting a spot of trouble on Monday, Mr. Elliott?" The apprentice's tone was sympathetic and deferential, but Edward looked up sharply. There was some alarm in the boy's face; Edward forced a smile.

"I think you know Mr. Tempest well enough," he said with a certain wryness, "to know he won't be pleased by my resignation."

"Aye, sir, I do."

"Well, he's going to want to know why I'm resigning. And when I tell him, he's going to be even less pleased. I rather think I shall be told to leave immediately."

Dick's face fell. "I'm sorry," he said at last. "Place won't be the same, sir."

"I was leaving anyway, Dick; a few days less are neither here nor there."

"Begging your pardon, sir—why are you bothered about getting this order away? I mean, if you're leaving, why should you worry?"

Edward smiled enigmatically. "Just call it professional pride. The gentleman's been a good customer. I don't want to let him down."

At the door, as Edward locked up, the boy said, "If you could do with a hand tomorrow, I'll come in, willingly."

Touched by the gesture, he glanced up. "There's no need. It's the Sabbath and your only day off. Your parents won't thank me for asking you to work."

"Oh, they won't mind. Besides, I'd like to see you get them books finished in decent time. I'll be here at eight as usual."

Edward smiled. "Make it nine."

They parted company by All Saints, and as the boy loped off up Coppergate, Edward smiled slightly, reminding himself that the world was not only comprised of Fossgate; but there were good things, even there.

The market, filling the length and breadth of Parliament Street, was still in full swing, a noisy, colorful melee of carts and stalls, hucksters, peddlers, and auctioneers all vying for attention. Farmers' wives on the butter stalls were crying their wares, customers walking the line with pennies at the ready, testing here and there as fancy took them. Having eaten nothing since breakfast, Edward was hungry, yet it was a pleasant evening and he was strangely averse to the idea of going home. After being shut inside all day he felt in need of air and a quiet place in which to think.

On impulse he bought a breadcake, returning to purchase a quarter each of butter and cheese. A buxom young woman with fair hair and rosy cheeks caught his attention, inviting him to try her wares. Flushing slightly, he fished in his pocket for a penny, scooped a little of the sample to his tongue, and pronounced it excellent. As she weighed and patted his order into shape, he chose a piece of white cheese, shaking his head at her attempts to sell him more.

Further on he bought an apple, threading his way through the crowds without haste, avoiding tired children and scolding mothers, frequently sidestepping his way past bulging baskets and gawking laborers, eager for entertainment now their working day was over.

Davygate was quieter, Lendal deserted. Descending the steps by the bridge, he walked along the Esplanade toward Marygate Landing, pausing to look across the park to where Louisa lived. For the moment, however, he did not even want to see her.

His anger of the day before had given way to numbness, a kind of suspended disbelief which had enabled him to fall into bed like a dead man, sleeping long and sound until daybreak. Dreaming of Louisa, he had woken to lonely reality, to bitterness and regret and a sorrow which swept through him like sudden bereavement. Allowing himself tears, he had felt cleansed because of them, and now, accepting those turbulent emotions as inevitable, he was able to consider Louisa's story with something approaching detachment.

Gradually he had had the whole of it, from the events of that fateful afternoon and evening to the captain's attempt to exact revenge; omission and embarrassment had revealed more than she intended about Blankney, but he had held her closer then, unwilling to exhibit his pain.

He loved her deeply, that much had never been in question. Yesterday, however, had brought him face to face with a different and far greater awareness, one he had fought against for longer than he cared to realize. To need her touch had seemed wrong, so wrong it had never been fully acknowledged, yet the soaring delight of those first few moments had cushioned him against the force of later pain; and how could that be wrong? While he held her, it had seemed as though his very bones would melt in flames which licked at lips and loins and fingertips. Remembering, it was suddenly easier to understand the force which bound her to another man, easier to understand the appeal of verses he had once thought blasphemous.

A scrap came back to him: "And if the wine you drink, the lip you press, End in the nothing all things end in. . . ."

He sighed. The old unbeliever had something there, Edward supposed; begin with nothing, end with nothing, and the rest is illusion . . .

Remorse crept in, however, as he realized how nearly the bonds of love might have been his, and legitimately so. She loved him, he knew that, however much he might have doubted it in the past year. His aloofness had hurt her, and he sent a swift prayer for absolution at his pleasure in that small admission. When he might have declared his love and married her, he had let her go for five long years, to live and grow and change in an alien world, so that when she returned she was no longer a girl but a self-contained woman, and he the stranger, shy in her presence.

He walked for a while, then ate his frugal meal, watching the river flow past on its inexorable journey to the sea. It had a long way to go, he thought, as he himself had, yet there was no hurry, only a sense of peace. Tomorrow would come, and it would go; the next day similarly, and all the days after that. Whatever Albert Tempest said or failed to say, did or failed to do, the river would still be here, and in the distance the Minster, soaring like the visible act of faith it was.

In unconscious prayer, he left all in the hands of God. There was nothing else he could do.

EIGHTEEN

S hortly before eleven o'clock, as the apprentice was applying sealing wax to that important parcel of books, a hired carriage drew up outside Tempest's shop on Fossgate. Leaving his task, the lad went quietly and unobtrusively into Edward's little office.

"He's here, Mr. Elliott. Mr. Tempest, sir," he added, as though clarification might be necessary.

"Very well," Edward said calmly enough, although his heart began a sudden pounding, and hands which had yesterday been so steady were already trembling. Firmly he grasped both pen and ruler, turning his attention to the ledger on his desk. "Please return to what you were doing, Dick. Mr. Tempest won't like to see you idle."

Beneath heavy brows, the boy's eyes widened in astonishment; dumbly he nodded and, leaving the door slightly ajar, went back to the work-room.

Edward heard a shuffling, the mingled voices of his employer and the lad who served behind the counter; Albert Tempest's office door opened and closed again; a moment later it reopened. With obvious and considerable anxiety, the shop boy put his head around Edward's door.

"He wants to see you, Mr. Elliott. In five minutes. I tell you what, sir, he don't look right good. Not right good at all."

"If you mean Mr. Tempest," Edward said briskly, "I thank you for letting me know. Meanwhile, attend to the counter, else some urchin will be away with the takings!"

"Yes, sir!" The door closed, loudly, it seemed, in that sudden silence. Edward looked at his pocket watch, sat back in his chair with hands clasped, and tried to breathe deeply. Now the time was upon him, he felt physically sick with loathing. He dreaded having to set eyes on the man, having to confront him; was tempted, for a second, simply to walk out. But Louisa had borne more than angry words; for her sake he had to see this through, to finish once and for all what Robert Duncannon had attempted a year ago.

The second hand on his watch came around for the third time; heavy with dread, he stood up, straightened his tie, and exchanged his overall for the jacket he always wore to work. Smoothing back the wayward lock of hair above his forehead, he automatically ran a hand over his beard, glad he had close-trimmed it the night before. It gave him a harder, less vulnerable aspect.

With yet a minute to go, he tapped on the inner office door and, without waiting to be bidden, walked in. The swivel chair was turned toward the clock; heavy eyebrows rose in surprise above sunken, feverish eyes. Slowly, as though it cost him effort, Albert Tempest turned to face the man who had been running his business for almost three weeks. A hand, which shook more palpably than Edward's ever had, indicated the letter before him.

"What's this, then?" The voice had less power, but the man's basic contempt was clearly audible. "What half-baked notion prompted this? Where's your sense of duty, man? I've employed you all these years, and in the midst of grief and sickness, you threaten to walk out! I suppose you're after more money?"

"I want *nothing* from you," Edward said quietly, but with such emphasis that Albert Tempest's head came up, eyes narrowing in weary speculation. "And the letter's no threat—it's my notice of resignation, to which I believe you are legally entitled."

The mind behind the eyes continued to calculate, then suddenly changed tack; attempting a hearty laugh, he said: "Nay, Edward, you're not serious! What's this 'legally entitled' nonsense? You worked alongside me twenty years back—when the old man was still alive. Surely we know each other better than this?"

"We don't know each other at all, *Mr.* Tempest." As his anger rose, Edward's hands threatened to betray him; he clasped them behind his back.

Astounded, confused, his adversary stared up at him open-mouthed. For a moment it seemed he would struggle to his feet, but the effort was too much. "But you can't leave now! I need you, for a few more weeks, anyway. Whatever it is you're planning, Elliott, surely it'll wait," he demanded pettishly, "until I'm back on my feet again. Anyway," he added, the eyes narrowing in fresh calculation, "what's brought all this on?"

The question had come, as he had known it would. Edward felt a surge of satisfaction so powerful he almost laughed. "Do you *honestly* want to know?" he demanded. A swift step forward and he saw fear leap in those yellowed, foxy eyes. "Be glad I'm leaving you to it," he whispered grimly. "Be glad of your sick and sorry state. Death's laid a hand on you already—he doesn't need me to help finish you off!"

Edward leaned closer, and the gray, sagging face recoiled. "Yes! I can see your fear, and smell it! Did you enjoy the fear in Louisa's eyes? Did you stop to pity *her,* a vulnerable, defenseless woman, under your roof and *your* protection?"

"Not so defenseless," Albert Tempest stuttered, and Edward reached for him, ready to drag him bodily from the chair. With an effort he stopped himself, dropped the hand that could have killed.

"No, thank God! But that absolves nothing. You would have satisfied your lust on her if you could!"

"She tempted me—"

"Tempted you? Tempted *you,* an old man? Oh, your vanity amazes me!" With a harsh laugh, Edward shook his head. "No, what tempted you was a titillating bit of scandal so old it should have crumbled years ago. But you hung on to it, didn't you? Until it might prove useful. With your taste for dirt and perversion, you never forgot. You couldn't resist raking it up, could you?"

"I never said a word!" he expostulated. "It was only to keep her quiet—I swear it!"

"You disgust me!" Edward spat out. "And I thought you an honest, upright man!" His contempt was blistering. "But I promise you this: I'll do all in my power to hurt you where you'll feel it most—in your pocket! I think you'll find you won't have your special customers long!"

He stood back, ready to leave, but the cowering figure behind the desk roused itself malevolently.

"What makes you think you'll have any customers at all?" he demanded. "By the time I've finished with you, you'll wish you'd kept your mouth shut! She's a whore—I said it, and she's proved it. Taken on with that fancy dragoon. Friend of the family, he called himself. Some friend," he sneered. "It's all over York already, or so my Rachel tells me."

Hatred grabbed Edward by the throat. For a moment he had difficulty breathing. Knowing only a desire to see Albert Tempest in Hell, he grabbed at the door, desperately resisting the urge to hit out, to go on smashing that gloating face until it could speak no more.

He was suddenly aware that the door was open, that a ring of interested faces were gathered outside. With a tremendous effort, he pulled himself together.

"You know," he said tautly, "I'm glad you raised that subject, Mr. Tempest. I'd almost forgotten what a connoisseur they say you are. Of whores, that is. The captain's an old friend. He tells me you have a regular Friday night appointment at Mrs. Dodsworth's. Just off Bootham, isn't it? I don't know the place personally—I never developed a taste for prostitutes, myself."

Albert Tempest gasped and choked, half-rose to his feet, and then subsided, dragging frantically at his collar. Veins at neck and temple pulsed and throbbed, empurpled lips gabbled for speech.

Appalled and disgusted, Edward turned on his heel. He almost knocked down his assistant and the print room foreman.

"For God's sake, one of you get in there and loosen his collar. And you'd better send someone for his doctor." He scribbled the name and an address on a scrap of paper. "It's on Micklegate."

With that he went through to the privy in the backyard and was violently sick.

It seemed an age before the doctor came.

Afterward, he entered Edward's tiny office, a small, spare man, elderly but with the brightness of youth in his brown button eyes. "You had an argument, I believe? Do you mind me asking what it was about?"

"I sent him a letter of resignation," Edward said shakily. "He came here to challenge it. I'm afraid the matter became very personal."

The doctor shrugged. "Not your fault, I daresay. Mr. Tempest had a most choleric disposition. But still," he added, "I suppose you'll know that better than I do. I warned him a couple of years back—when his wife died, you know. He had a turn then. Take things easy, I told him, sell the business." The old man shook his head in wonderment at other men's folly. "Wouldn't listen, though. They never do."

"Will he live?"

"After a fashion. Of course, he won't walk again, and I doubt he'll ever speak." With a thin, dry smile, the doctor doffed his hat. "Well, must be off."

Almost as an afterthought, he paused at the door. "Don't blame yourself, young man—this could have happened anytime. Those who live by the sword, you know . . ."

As the doctor let himself out, Edward began to laugh.

NINETEEN

*I*n soft, dusky pink, Louisa stood by the window arranging roses in a shallow bowl. From tight little buds to full-blown blooms, each subtle tint echoed the color she wore, and against the light her hair formed a burnished aureole.

She turned slightly, and her cheeks were flushed with pleasure.

"Where on earth did you find them? They're beautiful."

"Oh, they were growing almost wild in the garden," Robert said negligently. "I thought you'd like them." He leaned back in his chair, long legs stretched out before the empty hearth, silently appraising the lovely picture she made.

"Did you walk all the way from Fulford?"

"I didn't," he said with feeling. "It's far too hot."

"Nonsense!" she laughed. "You just didn't want to be seen with a bunch of flowers!"

His mouth twitched into a smile, but he was reluctant to admit it.

"You look quite radiant," he murmured. "Perhaps I should bring you roses more often?"

"Perhaps you should," she agreed. "There's some fresh lemonade. Would you like a glass?"

He nodded, following her with his eyes, unconsciously chewing the inside of his lip. She looked better, sounded brighter than she had for almost a month, but there was still that element of constraint. It was almost as though she blamed *him* for the Tempest child's unfortunate illness; he supposed, on reflection, that he had not been as sympathetic as she had expected, but it was hard to be less than honest, especially when the Tempests had been such a source of trouble and irritation.

"Edward called the other evening," Louisa remarked brightly. "But I imagine you've heard the news already."

And he's another, Robert thought, recalling Louisa's air of relief the other day; all because she'd persuaded him to leave Tempest's. That name again, he thought with annoyance. Devil take the lot of them!

"What news was that?"

"About Albert Tempest!" She looked eagerly at him, eyes sparkling, lips curved in a self-satisfied smile.

He shook his head. "I haven't seen Darnley today. Why? Has the old man been struck down by the wrath of God at long last?"

"You might say so," she acknowledged with a certain grim satisfaction. "A seizure. Massive, Edward said. He won't recover." She sat down and raised her glass to Robert's. "A pity this isn't champagne— we should be celebrating!"

Her laughter was high-pitched, excited; also faintly distasteful, Robert thought. He frowned. "When was this?"

"Monday morning. He did the same to Edward as he did to you. Couldn't resist it, Edward said—and you made the same comment. Remember the quick character assassination as you turned to leave? He used the same trick on Edward," she said contemptuously. "But Edward was prepared. I'd told him *everything*—Mrs. Dodsworth's, the whole story. And Edward flung it *all* in his face. Imagine it," she breathed with avid relish. "I wish I'd been there!"

"It's a damned shame you didn't tell him at the time," Robert commented. There was something indecent in her satisfaction, as though something had festered too long; repelled, he studied his glass and drank deeply, wishing it were something stronger. Albert Tempest deserved to suffer, and Robert had wished him dead on more than one occasion; nevertheless, this gloating of Louisa's was gross and unfeminine, and he was less than eager to hear her dwell on it. She persisted, however, in relating all the details of Edward's confrontation, together with the elderly doctor's prognosis.

"So," she concluded, "after all the ranting and raving, he'll be confined to his bed, silent and helpless as a baby. How ironic!" Draining her glass, she chuckled with vindictive amusement. "And I can't see Rachel nursing him, can you?"

"Oh, I don't know about that," he said with deceptive softness. "She might find a certain twisted pleasure in it, don't you think?" With one raised and quizzical eyebrow, he stared long and hard at her.

Louisa flushed angrily. "If you were a woman, you'd understand!"

"No doubt. But I'm not, and there are certain depths I'd prefer to leave unplumbed."

"How dare you!" White now, and shaking, Louisa leapt to her feet. "After what he did to *me*? You *saw* the marks—how can you wonder at the way I feel? And don't forget his child!"

Almost languidly, Robert rose from his chair and went to find the brandy. Pouring a generous measure, he said wearily: "So, revenge is sweet, is it? Well, I'm sorry my dear, but it doesn't become you."

"Oh. I see. So, for the sake of seeming gentle and kind—and eternally desirable—I must pretend to be sorry, must I? Sorry for that—that grotesque parody of a human being? Is that it? Is that what you want? Pretense?"

Her voice had risen alarmingly. Wincing, Robert drained his glass. "Oh, for God's sake, Louisa, stop it! Please!" He reached again for the bottle, but before he could pour another measure, her voice, vibrant with sudden anxiety, made him pause.

"Put that brandy down," she pleaded. "Put it down, and I promise I'll not say another word on the matter."

He held her gaze, and the bottle, for a long, tense moment. Reluctant to give way, he was forced to concede, even to himself, that it was important to do so. Yet again, he was drinking too much, but over the past weeks their relationship had been strained almost to the breaking point; he had stayed away unnecessarily on many occasions, making pressure of work and the new drill season his ready excuse. And when he had come, in hopes of reconciliation, she had either made her excuses in bed or accepted him dumbly. And in less than a month, Robert reminded himself, he would be in Dublin. He was suddenly afraid that perhaps she might refuse to join him.

Slowly he replaced the bottle in the cupboard, put his glass down, and went to join her.

"Not another word—promise?"

"I promise," she said with a sigh, leaning her head against his shoulder.

"Can we put all this behind us now? Truly?"

"I'll try."

Lifting her chin, Robert looked deep into her eyes, seeing lingering shadows which troubled him. Very tentatively, he kissed her. "I do love you," he whispered.

"And I love you, too!"

Her little cry, the sudden desperation with which she embraced him, were gratifying. For the first time in weeks she was as eager for love as Robert himself; and afterward, reassured, he simply lay on his side and watched her.

It was good to be close again, he thought; it would be better still when he had her safe in Dublin. Now he knew the date of his own departure, he could plan hers; would count the days until he could thankfully close the door on all Tempests and Bainbridges; and, he thought vehemently, on kissing cousins too. Especially those with haunted, lovesick eyes.

Carefully he reached for his watch, glancing anxiously at the time. Past five, and later than he thought; another hour and he must be on his way back to the barracks. Reluctant to move, not wanting to disturb her, for a few minutes he watched little motes of dust dancing slow gavottes in a golden beam of sun; then with a gentle squeeze he roused Louisa from sleep, kissing her shoulder as she murmured in protest.

"Sorry, darling, but I have to move. My arm's dead, I swear it!" He flexed the fingers of his left hand, wincing as the blood tingled back.

"Time to go?"

"Mmm, soon. It's nearly twenty past five."

"Oh, Lord!" she exclaimed, gathering the bedclothes around her. "I've just remembered—Moira's coming at six!"

"What for?"

"I don't know. She sent a note this morning." Pulling on her robe, Louisa began to search for scattered clothes. "I expect it's just a social call, but she'll be wondering what's to become of her, now Albert Tempest's in hospital. I should think the house will be closed up."

With a cynical little laugh, Robert rolled out of bed. "Don't you believe it: Rachel will be in there before the hearth goes cold. It's a far better house than that poky little villa in Fulford."

"Well, I'm afraid Moira will be out of a job whichever happens. Rachel never did like the poor girl."

"Why don't *you* offer her a job?" he suggested, adding, as he buttoned his shirt, "It's a long way to Dublin on your own, and I'm thinking you could use a maid when you get there."

"Do you mean that?"

"Of course I do!" Robert laughed. Drawing her into his arms, he kissed her lightly. "It really is time we changed your thinking, darling. Life in Dublin is going to be rather different from here."

For a moment Louisa drew back. "Are you sure you'd *want* Moira?"

"The question is—are you sure *you* want her? She'll be *your* maid."

"I really hadn't thought of it." Fastening her petticoats, slipping the pretty silk tea gown over her head, Louisa's voice was muffled. "She's a good little Catholic girl, remember?"

"They're all Catholics in Dublin—just about, anyway. Any Protestant in need of that kind of a job is bound to be too genteel for my taste, I can tell you. Anyway," he added to the mirror, adjusting his tie, "think about it. Ask her, why don't you? She might not want to leave York."

"But how ever will I explain about *you?*"

Robert turned to look at her, his head cocked quizzically to one side. "Oh, come now, Louisa, is she really so stupid? She *must* know there's a man about the place. How many times has she been here?"

With a deflated little sigh, Louisa sat down on the bed. "Of course, I really hadn't thought about that. What must she think?"

"Not a lot, I imagine," he replied cheerfully. "Or she'd keep well clear, now wouldn't she?"

Quite deliberately Robert stayed until Moira arrived. Sheer astonishment banished the weariness in her eyes, and as the introductions were performed, she bobbed a small curtsy which both amused and charmed him. Taking formal leave of Louisa, he winked mischievously behind the girl's back and nodded his confidence in the forthcoming interview.

When he had gone, Moira gave vent to uncontrollable giggles. Louisa tried, unsuccessfully, to keep a straight face, but before long the two of them were laughingly reliving the captain's visit to Blossom Street a year ago and Albert Tempest's broken teeth.

"Oh, miss!" Moira gasped, holding her sides, "I'm sorry, I really am! Sure, and I'd no idea! I thought—begging your pardon—there must be somebody. But I'd no idea it was *him!* Oh, but I'm pleased for you—honest I am. He's such a *lovely* gentleman."

Laughing again, Louisa shook her head. "Don't be deceived, Moira," she said at last. "He has quite a temper and doesn't care to be crossed."

"Sure, don't I know that?"

"Make sure you never forget," Louisa warned, going on to explain the forthcoming move to Dublin and Robert's suggestion that Moira might consider a position with them as lady's maid.

It was obvious that Moira would have been pathetically grateful for any offer; but such a superior position, subject to a month's approval with fare paid back to York, was beyond her wildest dreams. Moved almost to tears by Louisa's generosity, Moira promised faithfully to work hard and always do her best and never to mention the Tempests, especially in the captain's hearing.

"Because he doesn't want to be reminded of them ever again," Louisa stressed. "Not even by me."

"Never," Moira breathed earnestly, crossing her breast for good measure. "I'll never say a living word—may I hope to die."

"Not just yet, I hope," Louisa smiled, leaving her chair. "Why don't you start by making us both some tea—you know where everything is. There's something I must attend to in the other room. Then we can talk about what you're going to do and where you'll stay between now and then."

In the bedroom, Louisa smiled as she tidied sheets and pillows, glad, despite the compromise, to be back on good terms with Robert. She was also warmed by the thoughtfulness of his suggestion. Obvious though the idea now seemed, it would never have occurred to her. As Robert so often said, she really would have to alter her attitudes. It was good, too, to be able to do something for Moira, although the benefits were by no means one-sided. In spite of her slapdash and often careless ways, the girl was good-hearted and cheerful, never downcast for long. In the strange new world that loomed ahead, Louisa reflected, Moira would provide a much-needed point of familiarity, a link with York and home.

TWENTY

*T*wo days before the duke of York's wedding to Princess May of Teck, an advance squadron of Royal Dragoons set out on horseback for Dublin. From Robert, Louisa knew they were to make the journey by easy stages: Leeds, Huddersfield, Rochdale, and Wigan, arriving in Liverpool on the Saturday. Easy stages or not, it seemed a tremendous undertaking to her, and she made her way to Micklegate Bar for the novelty of seeing them pass.

In plain navy dress and matching, broad-brimmed straw hat, she mingled with the crowd by the Windmill Inn, feeling her heart begin to hammer as she set eyes on the Tempest house for the first time in almost a year. Unconsciously, it being the darkest and plainest, she had donned the very same dress she had been wearing the night she left; her fingers strayed to the collar as she suddenly recalled that other gown, soiled and torn, which she had insisted her mother throw away. It was painful being on Blossom Street again, although Albert Tempest was securely ensconced now in the Retreat. At least Rachel did that much for him, she thought, wondering if he knew how much the Friends were charging and if, sensing the intelligence which no doubt survived in that paralyzed body, Rachel had told her father he was in an asylum for the insane.

Her eyes dwelt on the upper windows from which she and Rachel and Victoria had looked on that winter's day, seeing perhaps this very same squadron out on exercise. A sudden vision of the child, plump and sweet-smelling, golden ringlets bouncing as she raised her arms to her father in greeting, brought a lump to her throat.

She looked away and was suddenly jostled as the crowd craned eagerly for sight of the dragoons. They were heard well before they were seen, but as they appeared, little murmurs of disappointment rippled through the assembled onlookers; the dragoons were not clad in their gay scarlet tunics; indeed, they made a grave and somber group in beribboned frock coats so dark they looked black. But as the squadron emerged from the shadow of the bar, sunlight danced on burnished gold helmets, touched the tips of lance and harness, and glossed the necks and quarters of their mounts with a most impressive sheen.

The crowd raised a little cheer; handkerchiefs were waved, individual names shouted; Louisa saw one girl sobbing desperately and was suddenly glad Robert did not ride with them. A few yards further and a dog dashed into the road, barking frenziedly. The leading officer, whose name she could not remember, reined in as his charger, black with a lot of thoroughbred in him, shied and reared. For a second or two the horse danced, crablike, across the sets, then his rider had him back under control, walking sedately on despite the yapping at his heels. There was a sudden burst of applause, followed by laughter as the dog appeared to notice the other horses for the first time and, with its tail between its legs, shot for cover. The officer's face, Louisa noticed, was red but undeniably relieved; beneath some flourishing moustaches, his men were smiling.

The day of the royal wedding was proclaimed a public holiday, and apart from some two thousand of the city's most deserving poor, who were to be fed and entertained by either the lord mayor or the York Central Mission, the majority of employed citizens took themselves off to the coast for the day. The North Eastern Railway ran twenty special trains in honor of the occasion.

Having only one bachelor guest who preferred to stay in York rather than return to Nottingham, Mary Elliott persuaded him to accept a midday rather than an evening meal and, once it was cleared away, retired to bed for the afternoon.

Edward returned to work through deserted streets. Banners fluttered from each and every flagstaff, the sun shone, and church bells pealed joyously all over the city; but there were so few people to be seen it was almost eerie. Every shop on Fossgate was closed, including Tempest's, and as he passed he wondered how long the business would survive without a driving force behind it. Rachel Tempest had installed a manager, but from gossip he had from his former apprentice, Edward understood that things were not going well. Indeed he had evidence of it, for already orders were coming in from some of Tempest's former customers, who were finding the old firm unable to deliver the kind of work they had come to rely on and expect. Fine art books were gratifying and lucrative, but they would always be too few; he needed more bread-and-butter work if he was to survive and hoped his recent advertisement in a local trade journal would produce the desired result. What remained of his savings would subsidize the business for a while, but he knew he had to be making a profit within six months; it was an anxiety, but not an undue one, for overall he found the challenge exciting and uplifting.

With a sigh of satisfaction he entered his workshop, leaving door and window open to the warm breeze; he wondered briefly what Louisa was doing, for the captain would be at Strensall today for the review. He had read in the paper that over five thousand troops were to be inspected by Major General Williamson, the commanding officer of the northeastern district; it would be quite a sight for those who were interested, and he wondered if she would be there. He knew she had promised to take her mother and Bessie to a torchlight tattoo on the Knavesmire that evening; she had asked Edward to join them, but he had refused, making tiredness and pressure of work his excuse. In reality, he thought he would prefer to walk around the town, for York was celebrating the marriage of its own duke and future king, and there were sure to be some excellent illuminations to mark the event. He had already picked out the words "George" and "May" and "God Bless our Royal Duke and Duchess" on the Mansion House, surmounted by a crown, the arms of the city and civic insignia; tonight they would be blazing in gaslit brilliance. The Victoria Ironworks in Walmgate, as befitted iron founders to the queen, were intending an even better display, and there were bound to be other, smaller exhibitions of pride and loyalty, all worth the viewing.

As he began to sort through a batch of leather which had arrived the previous day, the bells began to peal again, and he raised his head to listen, trying to distinguish one parish from another. He was suddenly aware of being alone, in a deserted street whose workers were most likely sharing the public holiday with their families, while two young people were being joined in marriage in a royal chapel two hundred miles away. As he wished them happiness and strength for the future, Edward was swamped by a sudden nostalgia for the past, for what might have been; and then he longed for the bells to stop, for they were but a clamorous counterpoint to his loneliness.

Slowly Robert picked his way toward them, walking his charger carefully through the crowd. Seeing him, Louisa felt a surge of possessive pride; in red and navy and gold, he made a magnificent figure on horseback, and she stood quite still, enjoying the way people looked up at him, the awe with which they drew aside to let him pass.

A smile lit her face; she knew and could not control it, and as he drew close, she saw that he was smiling too.

"How did it go?" he demanded, yet she could see from his smile that he knew the weeks of practice had been worthwhile, that the review had gone well and no one had disgraced the regiment.

"Wonderful! Marvelous, in fact, and you were the very best! I could see you and Gay Gordon quite clearly through the opera glasses."

He laughed. "Opera glasses! Well, I'm glad they came in useful."

"What have you done with Gay Gordon?" she asked, stroking his present mount's smooth, dappled gray neck.

"Oh, he's still at Strensall," Robert said. "Munching quietly, the last I saw of him, lucky beast. I've hardly eaten all day. As soon as the review was over, we had to get this little lot organized to come down here, and what a performance it's been. Still, I did manage a quick bite in the mess when I went to collect Dandy. He's best for this kind of work—doesn't mind the crowds so much."

Robert reached down to pat the gray's shoulder, and even in the fast-falling dusk, Louisa could see the lines of strain around his mouth and eyes. "You look tired," she said softly.

"I am," he admitted. "And we've this show to get through yet. There must be thousands here tonight—makes the crowd at Strensall seem pretty paltry. Still," he added with a thoughtful glance around, "I shouldn't imagine there'll be any trouble."

"Were you expecting any?" she asked in surprise.

He smiled and shook his head. "No. Overenthusiasm, perhaps. There's a lot of people, and they all want to see the marching bands. The problems arise when they start pressing forward for a better view. Where's your mother, by the way?"

"She and Bessie are quite near the front, I think—"

"Well, get them together and follow me. Harris is quite unprofessionally keeping a place for you by the enclosure. Much better view from there, and you'll be safer, too."

Louisa did as she was bidden, having no difficulty in keeping Robert in sight. They traversed the edge of the crowd, already dense around the huge arena where the massed bands of several regiments were beginning to assemble. On the still night air, the scent of crushed grass was heavy; away from the crowd it was cool, and she hugged her shawl closer, glad when they reached the top corner of the square, where, beside the railings, Harris had preserved a small space.

He was a plain man, with the most lugubrious expression Louisa had ever seen, yet she remembered his kindness and the devotion with which he attended Robert and greeted him with a warm smile; nodding a brief acknowledgment, he listened to what Robert had to say and then returned to the three women.

"I'm to stay with you, miss," he murmured deferentially. "Make sure you come to no harm."

"Then I'm sure we shan't," she said and was rewarded by the merest glimmer of a smile.

As the bands began to play a varied selection of popular tunes, Mary Elliott wanted to know which was the band of the Royal Dragoons.

Harris shook his head. "Our band's not here, ma'am. Our men are here to keep order. They're the ones in front of you—all round the square—the ones with lances."

"Of course," she laughed. "I should have realized—how silly of me! They're *very* smart."

Bessie nudged Louisa discreetly, pointing to the men interspersed between the dragoons. "What're they carrying?"

"Torches," Louisa whispered. "As soon as it's dark, they'll be lighting them."

As the band of the 4th Lincoln Regiment advanced, Harris identified them, much to Mary Elliott's delight. "I should have known them," she confided. "I was born and raised in Lincolnshire, you know."

The drums and fifes of the Dublin Fusiliers advanced next, to the music of an Irish march, followed by the Royal Scots, the Durham Light Infantry, and the Northumberland Fusiliers; together, they played two rousing tunes: "Marching on the Enemy" and "See the Conquering Hero Comes," both of which delighted their vast audience.

Mary Elliott squeezed her daughter's arm. "Oh, doesn't it make you *proud,*" she murmured fervently, and Louisa was bound to agree.

By half past nine it was dark; a trumpeter sounded the "First Post," and simultaneously torches were fired, the lines of dragoons with their scarlet tunics and long lances were thrown into sudden and startling relief; pennons fluttered in the rising heat, and as the last notes of the bugle died away, drums and fifes began a quick march across the grassy square, flanked either side by torchbearers. Silently the massed bands advanced to meet them, and in the center, bands and drums, with flaming torches intermingled, passed through each other's lines to accompanying gasps of awe and amazement from the gathered crowd.

Nothing quite like it had ever been seen before, and as the bands gathered again in the center to play "Rule Brittania," the crowd roared its approval.

With the "Last Post" and the national anthem, the tattoo was over, and as the dragoons followed the bands into the enclosure, Louisa began to look for Robert, but it was some while before he appeared. Harris held the gray while he dismounted.

"Nothing too serious," he replied in answer to Louisa's inquiry. "A few drunks, anxious to make a fight of it. But they'll soon cool, with a night in the cells to look forward to. And the magistrate in the morning," he added with a grim smile. "Are you going to watch the fireworks display? Everyone seems to be going over toward the grandstand. I'm sure Harris will accompany you."

While Mary Elliott and Bessie sauntered slowly away in that direction, Robert pulled Louisa into the greater cover afforded by his servant's back and the bulk of his horse. "Grief, but I've missed you this week," he whispered as he held her close. "I'd give anything to be with you tonight, but it's not possible. We've to be away back to Strensall by five in the morning, and I'm utterly exhausted as it is." He kissed her longingly, then released her with a sigh of regret. "I'm free on Sunday, so with luck I'll get away from Strensall before dusk on Saturday. Expect to see me then. I must go, my love."

In one easy motion, he remounted, returned Harris's salute, and guided the gray away and around the crowd, to where a torchlit group of mounted officers were assembling.

Robert spent Saturday night at the apartment off Marygate, and Sunday packing what few of his belongings remained there. He talked at great length about the journey Louisa and Moira were to make a month hence and wrote copious notes and lists of instructions. Ten days later, at the head of his own squadron, he was leaving York by Micklegate Bar for the five-day journey to Liverpool, although Louisa was not there to see him go. By the end of that week, the last of the regiment's goods and chattels were packed and ready to leave York by train; on the Monday, Louisa saw a squadron of 6th Dragoon Guards on Gillygate, and then she knew, with sickening realization, that Robert had really gone.

TWENTY-ONE

*I*n the end, it had all happened with such speed, she had barely been able to take it in. Of course, she had known he was to leave, and soon; but his visits were brief and rare latterly, and whether he had sought to spare her, or genuinely had not known until the last minute exactly how and when he was to go, she could not decide. Either way, the realization had been something of a shock, giving her no time for grief or protracted heart searching; a quick good-bye, and the promise to meet her in Dublin, and he was gone, almost before she was aware of it.

Moira helped Louisa to pack and clean the flat in readiness for her removal to Gillygate, in what she saw as the final week of her life in York. Although she knew she would be back for holidays, and in case of emergency could be home in a matter of hours, she felt as though she was leaving the city for good. It was heartbreaking, far worse than the first time, when, at the age of nineteen, she had left in a spirit of excitement and adventure.

Now, with each passing day, Robert slipped further and further away, and with him went reassurance, so that the future loomed large and black and immensely foreign.

Even his letters seemed strange, full of the iniquities of Island Bridge Barracks, which he swore should be razed to the ground, and his eagerness to get the men out to the healthier air of the Curragh; almost as an aside, he commented that at least the house was livable. Letty wrote at greater length, apologizing for Robert's brevity, explaining that he was working quite ridiculous hours since his arrival, that she and Georgina had seen little of him, but that he was anxious for things to be perfect for Louisa. The refurbishing project had almost taken her by surprise, she wrote, as the house was transformed, nothing like the gloomy place it once had been, and she was sure Louisa would love it.

Louisa was less than sure and found her sleep was frequently disturbed by nightmares in which a faceless Charlotte pursued her along endless, shadowy corridors. More than one dawn saw her sitting by an open window at the top of the Gillygate house, watching the early sunrise touch the sky with pink and gold.

The morning before her departure she again woke shivering and afraid. Striving to fight fear with reality, she began to count, as in childhood, all the secure and comforting things this room represented: this bed she had shared with Blanche and later with Emily; a few feet away, in the other featherbed, her mother lay sleeping, plaited hair buried deep in the pillow, fluttering breaths even and undisturbed. Across the landing, Edward slept, and in a tiny boxroom hardly bigger than a linen closet, Bessie was no doubt snoring. Another hour or more until she rose to light fires and begin the long round of cleaning and cooking, washing and ironing. But today was Sunday, she realized; Bessie's easy day, without guests, when she would sleep till seven.

With sudden and shocking awareness, Louisa knew that tomorrow they would all be gone.

Panic set in, quickening her heart; abruptly she sat up, hugging her knees to still the violent tremors which racked her like an ague. Her eyes registered each separate item in the room, all the things she had known since childhood: the great double chest which had once held their underclothes; wardrobe, mirror, washstand; the window with its gingham curtains . . .

No, she thought firmly; they will be here, and tomorrow I shall be gone. The difference was subtle, but enough. With an effort, she forced herself out of bed and to the window, peering out at walls and ramparts, the trees which at this time of year obscured the view of the Minster.

There was a movement across the landing, the sound of soft footsteps on the stairs. It came to her that Edward, this week, had probably slept even less; she had been aware of the odd, careful movement several times in the early hours.

As it had so often recently, her mind leapt back to that day in his workshop, and guilt began to nag again like an unsound tooth. Albeit for what had seemed the best of reasons at the time, she knew she had wronged Edward. Her conscience was not at all salved by the realization that her mother had been almost equally to blame for that withholding of the truth. Their instincts then had been to keep silent; now it was clear how wrong that had been. He should have been told in the beginning, allowed to make his own decisions regarding Albert Tempest and his job. And that was another mistaken assumption, Louisa reflected wearily. Financially, even then, Edward could have taken the risk. That he had voiced his forgiveness, reasonably and philosophically, did little to ease her sense of guilt.

In the final analysis, she knew why his unspoken appeal for honesty had touched so deeply: it was because she needed him to understand her bitterness and grief over Victoria's death. Because she needed *someone* to understand, needed a comfort that Robert simply could not give. Knowing all about Albert Tempest, still he was incapable of appreciating the long-reaching effects of that assault. She supposed it was because he was a man; but so was Edward, and some deep, long-buried instinct had told her that *he* would listen, *he* would have patience and sympathy and all the words she so desperately needed to hear. Just as he had never let her down in childhood, so he had responded on the day of the funeral, offering love and tenderness, taking her into his arms like a grieving child.

And like a child, comforted by the long-lost familiarity of scent and touch, Louisa had let all the barriers fall. Oh, the sense of relief at the time—and the guilt afterward, knowing that release of pain had been bought at his expense.

Sitting by the window in the early-morning chill, soul-searching, hating herself, she had a sudden unnerving sense of déjà vu; except the recall was real, not imagined. Sleepless then, she had been mourning Edward's leaving, hating him for not loving as she loved, blaming him for his abandonment, that weak, unfeeling surrender. Sleepless now, was he hating her for leaving him?

With a sharp mental admonition, she shook her head. It was years ago, when she was just a girl, and Edward's love then, as now, was fraternal and platonic. Concerned for her welfare, not heartbroken by a callous desertion. As she had been.

Nor had that leaving ever been satisfactorily explained. Almost overnight, it seemed, the decision was made and acted upon; when pleaded with he simply said his mother had retired; alone as she was, she needed him. But his mother had taken that house months before, and Edward had been grateful enough for Louisa's company during the period of his grief over Maud. And there lay another duplicity, Louisa realized: while sympathizing over his broken engagement she had secretly rejoiced, the intensity of her love fueled by fantasies in which Edward realized he loved Louisa more and asked *her* to marry him instead. He had turned to her for comfort, but other than holding her close occasionally and confiding rather more of his feelings than was sensible, he steadfastly refused to respond in any other way.

A sudden hot flush of embarrassment started in Louisa's breast and flooded her entire body. She glanced at her mother's sleeping form and wondered whether she had sensed that girlish passion, had taken the necessary steps to put Edward out of reach. At twenty-seven years old he had been a man, grieving and possibly, in her mother's eyes, vulnerable to such temptation. And there was another factor: they were first cousins.

Words and phrases from that time came back with disturbing clarity. Her mother's commands to "let Edward be, for goodness' sake," as she leaned over his shoulder or snuggled up to him in his chair, confiding secrets. And another time, lifting her face to be kissed before going up to bed: "Edward, she's too old and too big to be treated like a child. Don't encourage her."

So the goodnight kisses had stopped. And the bud was effectively nipped, for shortly after that he was gone from the house, with Aunt Elizabeth demanding enough to occupy most of his free time, discouraging her niece's visits as she did so. Although Blanche, like Emily, had always been welcome there.

Swamped by that remembered heartbreak, Louisa turned abruptly from the window. She stood for a moment by her mother's bed, staring down at that contentedly sleeping form. Whether Mary Elliott had sent her nephew away or the exile had been voluntary, Louisa knew she would never say. Her mother's memory was notoriously unreliable when it came to matters which might prove embarrassing; yet it was suddenly important to have the facts. One way or the other, Louisa *had* to know.

In the kitchen Edward was pouring a cup of tea. He looked up in surprise, then, with a smile, reached for another cup. "Did I disturb you?"

"No. I haven't slept much all week. Change, I suppose," she murmured, unwilling to admit to nightmares or doubts that she was doing the right thing. Sipping at the fresh tea, she said: "This place is hard to leave."

"I imagine it must be," he agreed, not looking at her. He sat down with his back to the window, his face in shadow.

"I thought of something just now," Louisa said abruptly. "About the time when *you* were leaving here, when you went to live with your mother. Why was it that you went?"

Bewildered for a moment, he studied her face, then shifted uncomfortably in his chair. "You know why," he said. "My mother was alone— she needed me."

"I know that was the explanation given at the time. But it suddenly occurred to me that there may have been another reason. Was there?" She sensed from his unease that there had been something; but despite his evasiveness and the blood which rushed to her cheeks, Louisa pressed him further. "Was it because of me?" she demanded through gritted teeth. "Did Mamma make you go because of me?"

She heard his indrawn breath. When he spoke, however, his voice was very controlled, very even. "Why should you think that?"

"I don't know," she admitted, suddenly feeling foolish. "I just did. But I wish you'd tell me—I need to know. Don't lie to me, please."

"When have I ever lied to you?"

She flushed again. "You might evade the issue. Please, don't."

"Is it so important?"

Louisa nodded, not knowing why it was so vital to have the truth confirmed, when every instinct told her she knew already. On a knife edge of impatience and dread, she waited for him to speak.

"It's a long time ago—I don't even remember exactly what it was all about. In fact, my clearest memory is one of surprise. Your mother seemed angry and upset, and I remember wondering what it was I'd done. At that time, I was overly concerned with my own sense of loss, and I'm afraid my mind did not function easily with regard to anyone else's problems."

"What did she say to you?"

"Goodness, Louisa—it's ten years ago! I can't recall what was *said*. I only know she wanted me to leave. She stressed my mother's position— if you remember, she'd just retired and taken that little house—and she said something about you girls growing up, needing more room, that sort of thing."

"Edward, I'm not a child, and neither were you at the time. That's not what she meant, is it?"

"I don't know what she meant," he said stubbornly, "and I didn't ask."

"Oh, you knew what she meant," Louisa whispered, "and I don't have to spell it out!"

"No," he said quietly, "you don't have to spell it out. In fact, I'd rather you didn't."

"Weren't you insulted?" she demanded. Recalling the romantic innocence of those days, when marriage had seemed little more than an extension of playing house, and the fulfillment of love a matter of sleeping cozily in the same bed, a blush of shame swept through her on his behalf.

"No," Edward said quietly. "I was astounded. Nothing could have been further from my mind. Nothing," he repeated softly. "But I suppose her fears were understandable. She was only doing what she thought was right—it's a mother's duty to protect her daughters in whatever way she thinks fit."

For a moment Louisa was too shocked to speak, too angry to do more than inwardly rage. "Protect them!" she exclaimed at last. "Against what? Against whom? Against someone who loved them—against someone who loved *me!* That's what it was all about, wasn't it? Me! Why?" she cried. "Was I so wicked, even then?"

"This conversation," he said painfully, "is pointless, Louisa. Let it cease now, for pity's sake. Why be so upset about something which happened so long ago? It doesn't matter anymore—it's dead and gone."

"Is it?" She went over to the window, staring out at the little pots of herbs ranged along the wall which divided their yard from the next. "When you left—I didn't understand. I felt betrayed, bereft of the only person who'd ever really cared about me. No one offered me the slightest scrap of comfort at that time, Edward—not even you. I remember," she said bitterly, "trying to see you, waiting for you on your way home from work. But all you would say was that it was for the best." Her vision of the trees and grassy ramparts blurred. "I thought you didn't love me anymore," she whispered, "and I couldn't bear it—it tore me apart. I loved you then, with all my heart and soul, and you didn't understand!"

"You were just a child," he murmured in protest.

"No, you saw me as a child, didn't credit me with a woman's feelings, a woman's understanding. You should have explained!"

"How could I?" he pleaded, his voice torn with pain and suppressed anger. "It would have been like—like corruption! Your love was so trusting, so innocent. How could I taint it with ideas like that? Ideas even I, as a man, found defiling. You would have turned from me in disgust."

There was an appalled silence between them, a minute or more in which both considered the enormity of what had been said.

At last, from his shadowed corner, Edward softly added: "I didn't think of you in that way; I couldn't put even the suggestion of it into your mind. So I said nothing. What was there to say? And in the meantime, I suffered too. Don't think it was easy to leave you, to keep silent. It wasn't. I loved you, too! And knowing how miserable you were made everything else that much harder to bear."

As a young girl, aware only of her own heartbreak and immature longings, Louisa supposed she had seen things from a selfish point of view; as a woman, looking back at the years Edward had given to an old and self-centered parent, she wanted to weep. In the face of that sense of honor and duty, her resentment of Elizabeth Elliott seemed so petty it shamed her. Not understanding, she had ceased to trust Edward;

and in ceasing to trust, she had clamped her emotions so severely that the old responses died.

"Oh, Edward," she whispered, going to him. "I'm sorry. I didn't know—why didn't I know? If only you could have told me." The parallels of pain caused by truth withheld hit her with such force she sank to her knees before him, laying her face against his shoulder. He made no move, either in comfort or rejection; and she knew with most painful awareness how much he had suffered on her behalf. Shakily, trying to thrust the knowledge away, she said: "We've hurt each other badly, one way and another, haven't we?"

He turned to her then, holding her to him and hiding his face against her hair; she felt the awful raggedness of his breathing, the struggle for self-control; and if there had ever been any doubt as to the depth of Edward's feelings, it was swept away in that embrace. All the love she had ever felt for him, suppressed under a tight cork of remembered disillusion, welled up like a swift spring tide; wanting to tell him, with the words on her lips, she bit them back. What was the point of telling him she loved him and always had, when she was beholden to another man?

With returning calm, that tight little kernel of newfound wisdom drove her away from his side. Leaning over the sink, she splashed her face with cold water and, with the towel still in her hands, stood looking out at the bright new morning. Suddenly she wanted to embrace it, ached to draw great breaths of that soft, rain-washed air deep into her lungs, to escape from the confines of this house with its tangled, suffocating emotions. Birds were singing in the trees, free and unfettered; a blackbird pecked at a few crumbs in the yard, then flew up toward the ramparts. Between the trees, Louisa saw it land on the wall, turning its head this way and that as though admiring the view.

As it disappeared toward the deanery garden, she mused aloud: "I must have sat by my window every morning this week, about this time, wishing I could see the Minster. Foolish, isn't it? When you want to see it in the summer, it's impossible for the trees, and in the winter you forget to look." With a weary sigh, she added: "There must be a moral in that somewhere . . ."

Edward stood up. By the door he paused and turned. "I've had enough of morals for one day, I think—quite enough." There was a suspicious huskiness in his voice, and he paused to clear his throat. "Understand this," he added with painful emphasis. "It's too late for games of truth and consequence, far too late. Tomorrow—" With a shrug, he broke off, wrenching the door open with unnecessary force. "I'm going out, for a walk."

"Edward, wait!" She hurried after him, stricken by that sudden anger. "I'm sorry, truly I am."

With his hand on the banister, he stood for a moment, frowning. "Look, I don't want to hear any more. Let's just forget the whole thing."

"All right." Very tentatively, she laid her hand over his. "Can I come with you? I promise I won't say a word."

"If you like."

When she came down, Edward was waiting by the front door, umbrella at the ready. Determined to ease the tension between them, she made a joke of his caution, and in the same spirit he smiled, swinging the offending article like a cane as they briskly walked the shadowed length of Gillygate. The streets were magically free of rumbling carts and bustling humankind, alive with birdsong. A stalking cat, distracted by their echoing footsteps, eyed Edward and Louisa with disgust, while a pair of sparrows fluttered to the safety of a projecting lintel.

He slowed his steps as they passed beneath the squat, thick-set mass of Bootham Bar; out of habit, Louisa would have walked on, up Petergate, but he touched her arm, leading the way through a covered alley on their left.

"If it's the Minster you want to see, this is the view to have," he smiled, and they emerged into a narrow lane of shuttered, brick-built cottages. At the foot of Precentor's Court, the great west front of the Minster rose before them like a giant ship in full sail, dwarfing the soot-stained flotilla of houses which stood off around it.

Louisa paused, smiling in admiration. From a distance, she thought, the Minster was often simply *there,* visible from each point of the compass for miles around; close to, its soaring perfection caught the breath, lifted the eyes, and slowed the hurrying step. Mutually caught, aware of their own insignificance yet by no means diminished, the two stood silent, dazzled afresh by that supreme illusion of light and grace, designed to raise souls, as well as eyes, to God.

Unwilling to disturb even the birds in a nearby garden, they walked the cobbles with care and quietness; united in thought and feeling, there was no need for words. Between gathering clouds, the rising sun shone out, casting the west front into sudden shadow, but along the length of Minster Yard it was briefly brilliant, and Louisa gratefully raised her face to its warmth. Lifted by the Minster, her spirits were alight, no longer oppressed by the past, nor even by thoughts of an uncertain future. To be happy *now* was the thing, to be aware of it; and she was, here, this minute, with Edward beside her. It mattered not at all that less than half an hour ago he had reproved her for grasping at straws of understanding, that tomorrow she would be gone. For the moment

York, in all its somnolent, early-morning beauty, was here to be enjoyed; the empty streets, that brilliant light and long, dramatic shadows, were theirs alone.

She thought how fragile happiness was, a fleeting thing; but the city was forever, solidly reassuring, a place where nothing ever really changed. It had stood, in one form or another, through invasions, plagues, massacres, and civil wars, for eighteen hundred years; it would survive her leaving, still be here, undaunted, when she returned.

A cloud crept over the sun, shadows disappeared, and the Minster's brilliance dimmed. In that diffused grayness, Louisa noticed movement. Beneath the low Tudor archway of St. William's College, figures were stirring, urchins no doubt too poor to claim a roof in that teeming, sagging tenement. At their approach, a child was pushed forward to beg, a girl, by the tattered remnants of skirt and shawl; she wore a pair of gaiters around her thin legs, but no shoes.

They stopped, each appalled by the child's pathetic form, her dirty, ugly little face. Louisa swallowed hard; no matter how often she saw such abject poverty, she could never get used to it, never forget that there were thousands living like this throughout the city. It was rare, however, to be approached so directly.

"Have you a mother?" she asked as the child stopped some yards short of them. The girl stared blankly, and Louisa repeated the question. Eventually, pointing back toward the doorway, she nodded. As Edward searched his pockets Louisa slipped off her shawl, ignoring his staying hand.

"They'll only take it from her," he said, as she handed it over.

"And will they let her keep the money?"

"I suppose not," he murmured.

The child ran back. Avid hands reached out, and she was gone from sight, into the shadows. Edward sighed.

"Are we fools, Edward?"

"Probably. If so, I'll always be one." He sighed again. "It's obscene."

With the first spots of rain, Louisa shivered. Despite her protests, Edward slipped off his jacket and draped it around her shoulders, raising the previously despised umbrella with the merest ghost of a smile.

"Kindness should not lead to pneumonia," he insisted, and she slid her hand gratefully into the crook of his arm.

They walked back through the park on the north side, but the lush green lawns and flowering shrubs went unnoticed. The rain began in earnest, pattering a steady tattoo on their makeshift roof and drawing them closer, while the even crunch of gravel underfoot seemed to stress their solitude.

"In a way, I'm glad," he said at last. "That—back there—has put things into perspective."

Understanding, Louisa nodded and pressed his arm. "Yes, it has."

"I shall miss you," he said with quiet sincerity. "I think you know how much. But I won't die of it."

She laughed, a little shakily. "Promise?"

"I promise," he added gravely.

They walked on in silence, then, with the incident still on his mind, Edward said, "They say Dublin's even worse—the poverty, I mean. The worst in Europe."

Inwardly she recoiled at the thought. "Don't—it's bad enough here." A moment later, with as much brightness as she could muster, she said: "You'll write to me, won't you? Every week? Tell me all you do, how many books you sell, every change you make to the workshop. Then I'll be able to see you in my mind and imagine you there."

Keenly she looked at him, noting the fine lines around his eyes, shadows beneath the cheekbones accentuated now by a close-trimmed beard. Was he really so much thinner, or had that previously luxuriant growth disguised it? He looked harder, less the romantic poet than the lean, tense man of business. Disturbed, she squeezed his arm, reassured by its muscular solidity beneath the linen of his shirt. "And you mustn't work too hard. Give yourself some time off. Go to Whitby again if you can—the sea air will do you good."

A warm smile deepened the lines around his eyes; in a curiously intimate gesture, he covered her hand with his own, as though he needed to sustain that pressure. "If I have time, I will. What I plan to do is go back to Lincolnshire."

"To see your father?"

"If he is my father."

"And if he's not?"

Edward shrugged. "If he isn't, then he isn't—there's nothing lost."

"Nothing?"

His smile faded. "Only a little more time."

Early next morning, Moira arrived with her trunk, and, damp-eyed, Bessie saw them all into the carriage which waited to take them to the station. Strangely devoid of any emotion, Louisa subjected herself to another embrace and, with a sigh, stepped into the carriage with her mother and Edward, forcing a smile and a wave as they drove away.

At the station she was all efficiency, ignoring her mother's anxious fussing and Moira's nervous excitement. Edward, with a grim frown, ordered the girl onto the train and his aunt to oversee Louisa's personal possessions; between them, he and Louisa saw the rest of her trunks and bags safely stowed. With ten minutes to go and nothing more to occupy them, for a helpless moment they simply stood and looked at one another.

Beset by sudden panic, Louisa bit her lip, wondering what she was doing, why she was leaving, when all she wanted to do was stay. She caught the same sense of bleak despair in Edward; then he reached for her hand and gripped it hard. The feeling passed, and she breathed again.

"That's it," he whispered, "fight it. Don't give way, please don't give way."

"I won't," she promised.

"Good. Otherwise your mother will go to pieces, and I've got to get her home!" He laughed shortly. "Remember that!"

Arm in arm, they walked back to where Mary Elliott stood by an open carriage door. Moira was busy arranging Louisa's things in what she hoped were the most convenient places. It was a first-class compartment, reserved exclusively for them.

Alternately weeping and smiling, Mary Elliott issued last-minute instructions as though her daughter had never traveled before. Desperate to be gone, her stomach tied in several different knots, Louisa glanced at the slow-moving clock a dozen times; then, too soon it seemed, doors were being slammed up and down the platform.

Suddenly it was all too quick. She kissed her mother and hugged Edward, feeling his arms tighten in a fierce embrace. She was conscious of the buttons of his jacket biting through the fine silk of her gown, the sharp, clipped hairs of his beard prickling her cheek; and then the unexpected softness of his mouth on hers. A sharp tingle of surprise ran through her, and she clung for a moment, kissing him back.

"Don't forget," he whispered as he released her. Briefly his fingers touched her cheek. "If anything should go wrong, if you should need me . . ."

She shivered suddenly, embracing him again. "I won't forget." As she stepped into the compartment, a porter hurriedly shut the door.

While the train shuddered and creaked, slowly picking up speed around the long western curve, Louisa hung out of the window, seeing her mother waving from the platform, a scrap of white lace in her hand. But Edward had already turned away and did not look back.

Book Three
1893–1896

Rain on the windows, creaking doors,
   With blasts that besom the green,
And I am here, and you are there,
   And a hundred miles between!

O were it but the weather, Dear,
   O were it but the miles
That summed up all our severance,
   There might be room for smiles.

From "The Division,"
by Thomas Hardy

ONE

*A*ugust was a miserable month of gray skies and pouring rain, a month of umbrellas and galoshes, forlorn and solitary walks along muddy lanes and sodden towpaths, a month in which the chill of autumn descended before the full glory of summer had bloomed.

Edward felt Louisa's absence even more keenly than he had envisaged, and although that last week she had spent in the Gillygate house had been the first for many months, there he missed her most, standing often by his window in the early morning, looking out at weeping trees and remembering the unexpected closeness of those last, precious hours. Knowing she would go had heightened every awareness, so that even while sitting some distance apart, he had felt his soul reach out and mesh with hers; and the same awareness had been with her, making her more open to him than she had been since girlhood. Recalling it, Edward's heart swelled with love, swelled until he thought it would burst.

The pain of loving her, missing her, was agonizing; every moment at home he was conscious of it, conscious too of his masculine jealousy, a black hatred of the man who had claimed her, who took her to his bed each night and forced his way into her secret heart. Despite his efforts to ignore, forget, wipe out that side of their relationship, Edward found it impossible; and while he knew very well that Louisa could not have gone to a man who abused her, it was easier to pretend that than picture her welcoming Robert Duncannon with open arms. Easier by far to imagine mute acceptance than cries and moans of pleasure.

He hated the wild visions which kept him awake; hated the sordid depths of his own imagination, the physical reactions he found so hard to ignore. If he had suffered badly on first discovering that illicit affair, Edward suffered more deeply now, simply because now he knew he loved Louisa and wanted her for himself. How *could* she leave?

That question was asked over and over; it became the punctuation to every conscious thought, in his mind at sleeping, still there at waking, so that he dragged himself out of bed unwillingly, spoke little to Bessie or his aunt, while haggard cheeks and hollow eyes gave evidence of suffering he thought so cleverly hidden.

As though by tacit agreement, nothing was said. Bessie was covertly sympathetic, saving all the best portions of whatever she cooked for him. Despite his lack of appetite, Edward allowed himself to be fussed over and cajoled, knowing she meant well and wanting to respond to that motherly affection. His aunt, however, was less disposed to such kindnesses. Had he not know better, Edward might have suspected she knew of his uncomfortable conversation with Louisa in the early hours of that Sunday morning, for behind the grim set of her mouth, in the swiftly dried tears and pained, averted eyes, he saw as much guilt as sorrow at Louisa's going. It was not an emotion his aunt normally allowed herself to feel, and he knew she hated it, blaming him in return. He felt almost honor-bound to recover from his grief as quickly as possible, in order that things might return to normal.

The idea crossed his mind one evening after a particularly wearing stretch of silence; it made him smile, and at the unaccustomed pull of muscles which had lain unused for weeks, Edward shook his head. I'm being ridiculous, he thought, nursing grief like a babe in arms; and with an effort he forced himself to list the things for which he knew he should be thankful. The next day he deliberately walked along Walmgate, opening his eyes to the poverty and squalor; although his journey thinned his pocket, by the end of the day Edward knew just how valuable were a sound roof, good food, and kindly companionship. That night, before he went upstairs to bed, he dropped a kiss on Mary Elliott's forehead, and for the first time in weeks, she smiled at him.

The work for which he had been unable to summon any enthusiasm began to catch his interest again. It was still no more than a steady trickle, but in his eagerness to concentrate on things other than Louisa and her absence, Edward completed every order well ahead of schedule. With time on his hands he turned to carpentry jobs, fixing extra shelves for his tools, repairing gaps in doors and windowframes in preparation for the winter, and undertaking the mammoth task of cleaning and sorting the storeroom above. In attempting to discover why the range would not burn properly, he investigated the chimney, finding birds' nests, loose brickwork, and at the level of the upper story a baby's shoe packed in with loose mortar. For a moment he was terribly shocked, fearing what else he might find: clothing, perhaps, or the blackened bones of a tiny child; he searched, scrabbling at the light, crumbling bricks inside the flue, but there was nothing more.

Holding that twisted shape of hardened leather like some fragile, injured thing, he showed it to an old stonemason who had premises a few doors down. Examining it with gnarled, arthritic fingers, the old man smiled as though at a most familiar object, advising Edward to put it back. A good-luck charm, he said, built into the house with the chimney; he had come across many in the course of his work and always replaced them. Superstition, of course, but you never knew.

Uneasily, not wanting to give in to such barbaric ideas, Edward took it back with him and placed it on one of his new shelves. There it stood for many weeks, like some kind of black reproach; every time it caught his eye he thought of the child whose shoe it had been, the child who had lived here perhaps, grown to adulthood and subsequently died, centuries past; whose bones were no doubt moldering in some nearby churchyard. Unsettled by these considerations of life and death at a time when his spirits were still low, eventually Edward gave in. With the chimney repairs almost complete, he returned the shoe to its former hiding place, curiously relieved as he smoothed new mortar around concealing bricks.

After that, the chimney drew excellently. Assured of a warming fire throughout the chill months ahead, and with incoming work no more than he could handle in three or four days of the working week, he began to think of taking a few days off.

One thing held him back, however; one thing which was still a source of considerable anxiety. As the debate on the Home Rule Bill continued its heated progress, Edward watched the newspapers anxiously. On the second day of September the bill was carried through the Commons with a meager majority of thirty-four votes. It was hardly a triumph, and its ultimate defeat by the Lords seemed a foregone conclusion. Torn between his sympathy with Gladstone's ideal of Home Rule for Ireland and fear of the trouble its implementation would cause, Edward waited on tenterhooks for the results of that second vote.

As he had both feared and hoped, the House of Lords turned the collected opinion of their elected brethren upside down; a mere forty-one peers and bishops were in favor of loosening the kindom's hold on that recalcitrant island, while the rest of those hereditary rulers, all 419 of them, were overwhelmingly against such radical ideas. It mattered not, however, how hard Gladstone ranted against the dead wood of the upper house, how loud his calls for the destruction of that power of veto; the Lords could smile, secure in the knowledge that any such decision by the Commons could be similarly thrown out. They were immovable and they knew it. Regretful though he was, Edward's sigh was one of relief. Since Parnell's disgrace and death a couple of years before, the Nationalist elements were tigers without teeth, whereas the Unionists' fangs seemed to have sharpened by the week. The Conservative member for Dublin University, Sir Edward Carson, would, no doubt, Edward thought, be celebrating not only a most successful lobby, but the downfall of the liberal government. For after this, Gladstone was most surely finished.

But the true irony of the news that week lay not in Ireland, where it seemed the native Nationalists had accepted their lot without a fight, but in England and very close to home. An important review of troops by the duke of Cambridge which was to have taken place in York had had to be canceled, those troops being absent, quelling riots in the pit districts of the West Riding. A coal strike had rapidly escalated into full-scale rioting, from Barnsley in the south of the region, through Pontefract, to as far north as Leeds; troops had been called in from all areas, a hundred dragoons coming from the south coast resort of Brighton. By the end of that violent week, Lord Masham's collieries were wrecked, his pit yards in flames, and five men had been shot dead. In Heckmondwike a mob was charged by police brandishing cutlasses.

Considering the true nature of Robert Duncannon's job—so different from those picturesque displays on the Knavesmire!—Edward shivered, but for the moment it made Ireland's problems seem very small beer indeed.

Nevertheless, he wrote assiduously to Louisa, begging for news. As with her other letters, he suspected her reply of being well tailored for his benefit, although she did include a macabre anecdote calculated to amuse rather than confirm any latent fears. A couple of days after the announcement of the Lords' decision, in one of the outlying areas of Dublin, she wrote that a horse had been murdered; but the act had been dismissed as one of political spite. She added that Robert was quite incensed by the news; even more so because she laughed. It had availed nothing to explain that her laughter was caused by the conclusions drawn, not the act itself; Robert's sense of humor was somewhat lacking where horses were concerned.

Setting the letter down without a smile, Edward concluded that, with regard to Robert Duncannon, his own sense of humor was similarly lacking.

He wondered whether she was happy. From her letters it was hard to tell. There was a stilted quality about the early ones which spoke of things hidden, difficulties she was perhaps trying to gloss over; but the problems, if there were indeed any at all, could have been either practical or personal. With no sense of guilt whatsoever, he prayed for the difficulties to multiply and become unbearable; prayed that she might miss him, suffer as much as he was suffering. Then, surely, she would return to York.

With too little work to occupy him, Edward was suddenly desperate for a change of scene. He thought about his friends in Whitby, and then he thought of Lincoln, wondering whether it was time to renew that very brief acquaintance made back in February. He considered whether to simply turn up, as he had done then, or to write first, reminding the elderly cleric of his months-old invitation. In the event he wrote a brief letter, stating his intention of taking a few days' holiday in the area and asking for a convenient date on which they might meet and explore the village church together.

Setting Edward's latest letter down on her dressing table, Louisa sighed. He wrote well, she thought; too well, since every line was eloquent of home and family, evoking images and scenes she would do well to forget. Even his elegant copperplate had made a pleasing picture on the page, flowing as easily as the words, each loop and curl perfectly balanced, his signature simply "Edward," without the emphasis of line or flourish. He did not even sign himself "Your loving cousin," as she did when replying; no stress, no pleading, no mention of love, not even that he was missing her in the smallest way. There were times when she thought he was being brave, sparing her what depths of misery he might be feeling, and others when she wondered if she had imagined the revelations of that late summer dawn or the poignancy of their last hours together. Louisa knew only that she was missing him far more than she had either expected or imagined, knew also, with a sense of disloyalty, that he left a gap in her life that Robert simply could not fill. A gap, ridiculously, that she had hardly been aware of before that last day in York.

It's your own fault, she silently admonished her reflection in the glass; you should have left well alone, instead of raking up the past.

"The past is dead," she said softly, looking into her own blue eyes and then beyond, at the reflected image of her bedroom, its dusky pinks and creams, rose velvet drapes at the deep Georgian window, the matching cover on the newly made double bed.

Not that it had taken much making this morning, she reflected sadly; with Robert away yet again she had slept alone, and alone, Louisa barely disturbed the sheets.

She missed him, too, but in a different and in some ways more profound manner. Not just his physical presence, which was reassuring in itself, but the Robert she knew and remembered in York. Here, albeit in subtle ways, he was different. Not less caring, not even less attentive; but busier, infinitely busier, his comings and goings abrupt and often unannounced, so that even Letty was sometimes thrown into a spin, her meticulous housekeeping disrupted by demands for meals late at night, or sudden absences when she had planned a dinner specially for him. He said it was because the regiment was so newly arrived that there were many unexpected demands on his time; then summer maneuvers at the Curragh were cut short by the Home Rule Bill. Anticipating trouble, troops were being moved, not only into Dublin but all over the country. It was the military's task to keep whatever outbreaks of trouble there were isolated, and Robert's job to see that those orders were followed to the letter.

Edward's graphic description of the riots at home, coupled with shorter reports in the Irish papers, brought a surge of thankfulness to Louisa's heart; had Robert been in York, he would have surely been involved, and in greater danger, it seemed, than he was here in Ireland. Ironic, she thought, that the expected quarter should give so little trouble and the unexpected so much. Or was it simply as Robert explained: that expected problems could be nipped before they grew, whereas the others caught everyone unawares and blossomed out of hand. Whichever, she was glad he was here and not in York; and if the job kept him busy at her expense, it was better that way. In that little apartment off Marygate they had eaten the lotus; here the sharp wind of reality was blowing, and if his attention was often elsewhere, his love all too brief, then she must learn to put up with it, stop moping for times and places which were never likely to be again.

Telling herself these things, however, did not make that reality any easier to bear. Despite the blossoming friendship with Letty, Louisa was both lonely and homesick, her days barely filled by the self-imposed task of teaching Georgina. The house was Letty's responsibility, that was agreed from the start, and Louisa was pleased to leave it that way; her position with regard to the servants was difficult enough without attempting to impose her will on theirs. At first, with staunch Catholic disapproval, their hostility toward the captain's mistress was scarcely veiled. Letty said it was best to ignore it; they would come around in their own ways and in their own time, but Louisa eventually realized what sheep the under-servants were, taking their lead from the elderly martinet of a butler, McMahon. He was a relic from Robert's mother's time, never losing an opportunity of referring to that honest, good-living Protestant lady, daughter of such a noble house.

While never denying her mother's virtue, Letty simply laughed at that, privately informing Louisa that her mother had had something of a reputation of her own, preferring to live separately in Dublin as a kind of literary hostess, surrounded by a wide circle of friends who shared her passions for painting and poetry. She had possessed a marvelous sense of humor, allowed both children and servants far too much license, and turned a consistently blind eye to her husband's peccadilloes. The estate at White Leigh, Letty stated bluntly, was well populated by families whose eldest sons and daughters bore a striking resemblance to each of the three legitimate Duncannons.

Faintly shocked, Louisa first smiled and then laughed, sharing Letty's slightly rueful amusement; she wondered why Robert had never revealed those facts about his family, about the "friends" he had consorted with as a boy. But, recalling the high regard and affection he had had for his mother, she wondered whether those facts were incompatible with his image of her and were conveniently forgotten.

Once again, however, she was struck by the gulfs which existed between people of Robert's class and those of her own. With money and position, it seemed virtually any behavior could be overlooked as singular or eccentric, while those who had their livings to earn must toe a very narrow social line in order to survive. Grossly unfair though it was, Louisa hardened herself to embrace life on Robert's side of the gulf; in his wake, perhaps she *could* flout the rules and get away with it.

Armed with Letty's knowledge, Louisa first of all began a concerted campaign to win over the elderly butler. She never crossed him, was unfailingly pleasant, and only once took him up on something he said. "Oh," she remarked with feigned innocence, "you mean the time when Lady Duncannon gave all those marvelous parties? The captain and his sister were talking about it only the other day," Louisa lied, "and I must say I wish I'd been here then. Such a fascinating lady, so Bohemian!"

Whether McMahon understood the reference to artistic gypsies or not Louisa could not tell; he certainly realized that his little game was over. Slowly he began to thaw, and with the relaxation of his thin-lipped disapproval, the other servants followed suit.

Having worked in a grand house herself, Louisa understood their motives; understood also that it was purely cultural differences which prevented them from seeing what English servants would have spotted immediately: that she was of a different class from the Duncannons. In Ireland, to be English and Protestant ensured immediate elevation; and drawing on past experience, Louisa knew that within the household, at least, the part she played was convincing enough. Even Moira, bolstered by pride in her new position and reluctant to lessen that by telling the truth of her own past, unwittingly added authenticity to her mistress's role. Exaggerating with the best, Moira gave the impression that her previous post had been with one of the most elevated families in York and that the Elliotts themselves owned one of the largest hotels in that city. Although it connected Louisa with "trade," which would have been unforgivable in the cream of English society, it made her out to be wealthy in her own right, which was almost acceptable. That she had received an academic education was another plus, making the time spent teaching Georgina a matter of simple eccentricity.

What Louisa dreaded, with an anxiety which often kept her awake at night, was her introduction into Irish society, an introduction which Robert often referred to, but as yet had had no time to implement. "This winter," he kept saying, "when the troubles have died down and we're back in Dublin on a permanent basis, we'll get out and about and have a great old time, I promise you. And White Leigh—you *must* see White Leigh."

White Leigh, she thought, her spirits plummeting to new depths: White Leigh in all its grandeur, with Sir William and Lady Anne viewing her disparagingly; and in the background somewhere, like a malignant, doom-laden ghost, Charlotte Duncannon, Robert's true and legal wife.

"Oh, Edward," she whispered to the letter spread so innocently across her dressing table, "what have I done?"

TWO

*D*espite the warmth of the invitation which came from Lincolnshire, Edward's journey in the third week of October was not without trepidation. Walking down to the village from the little halt, he hardly noticed that August's wreckage had disappeared under the golden veil of autumn. Orange rosehips and dark red haws, lush blackberries nestling in hedgerows of yellowing willow and purple elder were all subservient to the rehearsal of his opening words. Beneath that anxious framing, his poet's eye was dulled, missing brown earth and bleached fallow fields, the gleaming bronze and gold of distant woodlands. A young rabbit scuttled noisily into the hedge as he passed, but Edward's eyes were on those great iron gates at the bend in the road, his thoughts once again on the family which had given him life.

As before, he passed them by, going straight to the inn to register his arrival and leave his things. Remembering their visitor from the last occasion, the landlord greeted Edward like an old friend, pulling a pint of ale and setting down a plate of cheese and pickles before him. Even the wife was friendlier, informing Edward that there would be roast mutton with red currant sauce for supper and steamed apple pudding to follow. The landlord was so voluble, Edward began to fear he would never get away.

Eventually, feigning great reluctance to leave, he pulled out his pocket watch and sighed heavily at the time. "I shall have to go, I'm afraid— I have an appointment to keep."

"Ah," the older man murmured knowingly. "With the vicar, I expect. Come to see them monuments again, have you?"

Edward smiled with relief. "Indeed I have. Didn't get a chance to discuss them last time. I'm hoping the vicar will be able to give me the benefit of his knowledge today."

"Oh, he'll do that all right. Like nothing better, don't the old vicar. Does him good to have a body to talk to—he's a bachelor, you see.

Family don't bother with him much, and there's just him and his old housekeeper, Mrs. Pepperdine. Good woman, she is, but it's not the same as having a wife, is it sir?"

"No," Edward agreed. "It's not the same."

And as he left the little snug, he thought: Will that be me one day? In thirty years' time, when my hair is thinning like my conversation, and what remains of my family is scattered and gone, will that be me?

His footsteps crunched noisily on the gravel drive, while ahead of him the mellow Jacobean house seemed to sleep in the autumn sun. Red virginia creeper almost covered the south and east walls, fallen leaves making a shiny, jeweled carpet beneath. Awaiting an answer to his knock, Edward had an almost uncontrollable desire to walk through those gloriously shaded leaves. Giving in to another temptation, he picked one up and smoothed it between the pages of a small notebook, replacing it in his pocket as the door was opened.

A small, stout, elderly lady asked him inside as he gave his name. He was expected, she said, and led him across the enormous hall to an oak-paneled door. His heart was hammering as she announced him, and then she was standing back, and Edward's legs somehow took him forward into a book-lined study where a log fire was crackling and sunlight streamed through mullioned windows; from a battered old leather armchair a slight figure in clerical black stood up and came toward him with hand extended.

All Edward's finely wrought phrases deserted him; like a callow, tongue-tied schoolboy he shook hands and accepted the proffered chair, his mind a total blank. In response to the usual civilities regarding the weather and his journey down from York, Edward managed adequate replies; before he had truly recovered his composure, however, it dawned on him that he was being questioned, gently but quite directly, about himself.

"I know York well," George Gregory said. "Through the church's business mainly, although I have made personal visits. My interest, as you already know, is mainly in medieval architecture. It's a beautiful city, although, like Lincoln, many of its churches are in a sad state of repair these days. And too many are threatened with quite the wrong kind of restoration, I'm afraid."

Having watched the demolition of two supposedly crumbling medieval churches, one replaced by a soulless modern building, Edward was bound to agree; for a while the two men lamented modern trends, lauded one or two of York's finer restorations, and then the older man brought the subject back to Edward. Had he lived in York long? Was his father also in the bookbinding business?

It was a seemingly casual question, but as Edward glanced up into those pale gray eyes he thought he saw more than ordinary curiosity, more than a simple need to place him in the social scale. Indeed, it seemed to Edward that the older man hung quite anxiously on his reply, exuding the kind of sympathetic encouragement any father might extend to his son.

Swallowing hard, he said: "Sadly, sir, I never knew my father."

"Sad indeed" was the softly phrased comment. "He died, I presume . . . before you were born?"

"He may have done," Edward whispered. "But I'm not aware of it. In fact, I have to say that I know nothing whatsoever about my father. My mother never spoke of him—ever."

So afraid was he to break the silence which followed, Edward scarcely even breathed; he could feel the anxious throbbing of his pulse, and even the air between them, lit by a beam of sun, seemed tangible and taut.

At last the other man moved. As he dropped the hand which had shielded his face, Edward thought for a moment the thin face seemed thinner, the gray eyes infinitely sadder and darker. "I'm exceedingly sorry to hear that. Every man should know his father—for good or ill."

"I've always thought so. Unfortunately, I could never persuade my mother of that small fact."

"May I ask her name?"

"Elizabeth Elliott." Again the sudden flinch, the lengthy silence. "She was born," Edward went on, not from any particular need now to prove her identity, but simply to keep talking, "not too many miles from here, in Blankney. She had four older brothers and a younger sister—"

"Blankney, you say? I thought it was—" But whatever he thought was bitten off. "Are you sure it was Blankney?"

"Yes. They moved to Metheringham later, when my mother was about ten years old, I believe."

"I knew someone—by that name—who came from Metheringham."

"Perhaps it was my mother," Edward said gently, drawing a small *carte de viste* from his inside breast pocket. The photograph showed a young, unsmiling woman in a plain dark crinoline; she had light eyes and dark hair, center-parted and caught up in the ringlets fashionable at the time; her features were regular, possessing the well-shaped generous mouth common to most of the Elliotts. Had she been smiling, Edward felt, she would have been pretty; but the photograph showed that slight downturn of the lips, a feature which was well pronounced by the end of his mother's life.

"Ah, yes. Elizabeth." The name was no more than a breath, but such feeling was in its softness that Edward paused, arrested in speech and movement by that almost palpable emotion. "I loved her, you know—but then she went away." For a moment the older man gripped his hand. "My fault, not hers."

Covering his emotion, he briskly paced the room, returning to the fireside to tug sharply at the bellpull. "We'll have some tea, I think. Then you must tell me all about her—what she did, where she went, what happened to the pair of you. You've kept me waiting a long time, young man," he added with mock severity, "and now you are here, you must tell me *everything*."

Over tea Edward related the bare facts, as he knew them, of his mother's life and death; a knowledge so pathetically small, it shamed him in retrospect to realize how lacking his interest in her had been. Perhaps because of her refusal to divulge the only facts which were important to him, he had paid little attention to what else she might have offered. And what Edward had always wanted was his father's story.

Before he would tell it, however, he wanted Edward's life, and that was a tale more difficult to relate, punctuated by halts and hesitations and, because of that blanket of silent sympathy, moments when he had to move about the room in order to stop himself crying like a child. The elderly cleric was an excellent listener, his questions surprisingly shrewd, displaying a familiarity with city life that Edward had not expected.

Skimming his adult years, and determined above all things to reveal nothing of the circumstances which had led to Mary Elliott's lapse into truth, Edward simply said that his aunt had given him the family name, and from there he had pursued his own research. While he was talking, describing his determination to unearth as much of the truth as possible, it suddenly occurred to Edward that he had been accepted; that this man knew Edward was his son just as surely as Edward had known his identity that very first day.

Breaking off, he said: "Tell me, sir—did you know? That day in the church, did you know who I was?"

"I don't know," George Gregory said slowly. "I'm not sure. It was the name, you see—it gave me a shock. It's not common in these parts, and simply to hear it uttered brought Elizabeth immediately to mind. And then, of course, there was something about you, something very familiar. Enough, at least, to make me seek further conversation with you. It was really quite frustrating to be denied that opportunity.

"I hoped for a while that you'd return, but didn't really expect it. And then, a few weeks ago, I had your letter. Don't ask me why, but I had the strongest feeling that you were connected with her, and through Elizabeth, with me. I suddenly recalled something—something I'd seen for a fleeting second as we shook hands that morning—*your* recognition of me."

"And so you knew?"

"No, I *hoped*. But seeing you again, now I know. I also know why your face seemed so familiar the first time." With a wry smile, George Gregory said gently: "We're not unalike, you and me, are we? And once upon a time—during my rebellious period, when I first joined the church— I too wore a beard."

For several moments, without constraint or embarrassment, the two men simply looked at one another, weighing and assessing, finding balance on either side, sensing the easeful warmth of fellow feeling and knowing the liking went beyond that of mere blood ties.

Overcome by a sudden surge of gratitude and affection, Edward felt his throat constrict; bereft of words, he could only smile.

Rather gruffly, his father offered him more tea, noisily shifting cups and plates, complaining at the lack of hot water. He rang the bell again, and with the advent of the required hot water his recovery was complete. Almost casually, as though speaking to a very old and trusted friend, he began to talk about his early life.

Originally there had been never a thought of entering the church. Up at Cambridge, reading law, he was, he said, a typical undergraduate home for the Easter recess, determined, after a largely misspent three years, to cram for those all-important final exams. Along with most of his friends he had spent too much time drinking and running up to town, reading Shelley and Byron in preference to dull legal tomes and generally imagining himself a wild degenerate of the first water. "Whereas in reality I was—we all were—so terribly innocent."

It was his sister's infatuation with the son of family friends which led to his meeting with Elizabeth. Bored, leaving his sister to her own devices, George had wandered away after luncheon for a walk in the grounds; and it was there he met Elizabeth.

Sitting beneath a tree in the spring sunshine, book in hand and beautifully attired, he assumed she was either a guest of the house or a local inhabitant allowed to make free with the park. Nodding to her as he passed, he stopped to speak on the way back, asking from a polite distance what book it was that so held her attention. It was a book of poetry, and the poem she was reading was Thomas Gray's famous "Elegy in a Country Churchyard." Wanting to impress, the young man had begun a discourse, sadly somewhat woolly and sentimental, stopping only as he noticed her change from polite interest to supercilious disdain. At that point Elizabeth Elliott had told him quite brutally that he knew nothing of the subject, demolishing his gems of literary and stylistic appreciation in a few short, pithy sentences. Her true appreciation of the poem's reality left him speechless with admiration, hardly able to believe that beauty such as hers could be matched by the same degree of intellect. He never suspected that her articulate arguments were rooted in personal experience, that she was in fact both more and less than what she seemed.

With the wisdom of age and the confidence of having spent a lifetime correcting those early misconceptions, Edward's father admitted to an early and unforgivable blindness. Servants, he said, were less than real to him, having none of the refinements possessed by such as himself and largely illiterate; he could not imagine a maidservant recognizing much other than her name, and in his youthful, masculine superiority, it was incredible that one could be as intelligent as and more mature than himself.

Despite his attempts to prize information from her, Elizabeth kept her identity a secret. She made rather a game of it, which added piquancy to their subsequent meetings; and although the suspicion that she was simply playing with him became something of a torment, the whole situation was far too pleasurable to relinquish.

The years seemed to roll away as his father talked; Edward could see the lively, animated young man he must have been, imagine the attractive, witty, teasing girl by his side. But that image, preserved by the older man for almost forty years, did not match his own experience of his mother—not until he realized that Elizabeth Elliott was not a girl, not even then; she was a woman, years older than the immature and impressionable student she was leading on. It hurt to see how that deception still held, for he liked George Gregory, feeling a natural affinity with him which had never existed between his mother and himself. In a curious way, however, it helped the separate pictures come together; he knew then that they were talking about the same woman.

Back at Cambridge, George succeeded even less with his studies, living only for the end of term when he could see his beloved Elizabeth again. He even extracted an invitation to stay at the house for a week, and it was during that time, he murmured sadly, that he had discovered her identity. On the second day of his visit he came face to face with her in the drawing room.

The shock was shattering. To see her there, so unexpectedly, was one thing; to realize she was simply a servant, albeit a very superior one, was another. Worst of all, however, was to hear her addressed by surname only, like some faceless, characterless being who existed rather than lived.

"Her blankness frightened me," George admitted, "for she looked what she was supposed to be, and that was not the Elizabeth *I* knew. But to see my own dear love, with all her wit and sensitivity, laboring in virtual bondage to a dull, plodding woman who wouldn't have known a sonnet from a sow's ear—it was abominable! I wanted to shout and protest, tell them it was all some dreadful mistake. But I said nothing. I think I spilled a cup of tea."

In the hours that passed between that teatime and their next meeting, the young George Gregory set foot on the road to understanding. Elizabeth's fine clothes were expertly remade castoffs from her mistress's wardrobe, a perquisite, like the free afternoons, of her privileged position, a position she had achieved simply because of the education and natural refinement which had fooled George in the first place.

He told Edward that when Elizabeth eventually arrived at their usual meeting place the next day, she was contrite and pale-faced, full of apology and ready to flee; but after all that had happened, to him at least, he was not prepared to let her go. Bit by bit he elicited her story and was so moved by what he saw as the tragedy of wealth and position reduced in a single stroke to numbing poverty that he loved her even more. He proposed marriage, swore on his own life to redress the wrongs she had suffered, never dreaming how utterly impossible that would prove to be.

"It was a very emotional afternoon," he said succinctly, but the youthfulness had gone. Once more he was a man in his sixties, his age accentuated by the dress of his calling.

Edward understood, and in the silence which followed he thought of his mother and her lifelong bitterness at a promise broken; considered his own existence, which should never have been, except for the heightened emotions of a solitary afternoon. And he thought of Louisa, in Ireland with Robert Duncannon.

Distracted by his own private tragedy, for a moment Edward lost the thread of what the older man was saying. Something about the fury of his father, Sir Alfred, at the failure in those final exams, and drastic cuts in his allowance.

"Just in time," he said, "I managed to stop myself from blurting out my true intentions. With a vast reduction in finances, I knew I could not afford to marry Elizabeth just then—so with promises to my father that I would work like a slave for the next two terms, I knew I must ask Elizabeth to wait."

The thin, blue-veined hands splayed out in a sudden gesture of appeal and despair. "Unfortunately, when I did next see her—and remember we had been meeting frequently all summer—she said she couldn't afford to wait. At first," he admitted with sad irony, "I was too stupid to understand. She had to spell things out for me, I'm ashamed to say. Well, at least I didn't panic—not then. In fact, I seem to recall feeling rather idiotically proud of myself. I said we must elope, and she agreed. We made plans, which, as you know by now, never came to fruition."

Although he knew he should have been prepared by Mary Elliott's account of what had happened to her sister after that, Edward was profoundly distressed by his father's side of the story. With his attention fully concentrated on that thin, ascetic face, he felt every word, every phrase, as though that callous old man, his grandfather, had also mutilated him. Which in a way he had.

"That our liaison was discovered is obvious. How and by whom, I can still only guess at—but that's not important. What is important is that my father was informed. And you know, even after all these years, what was said during that interview with him still provokes feelings of—revulsion, I think. Yes," he repeated distastefully, "revulsion is the only word to describe it. He used the baldest, crudest terms. My own father, whom I had loved and respected without question, destroyed every scrap of innocence, all my youthful, romantic illusions, in one fell swoop. He made what had been the most perfect, beautiful experience of my life seem like an act of corruption—vile beyond anything I had previously known or suspected.

"His words were an act of corruption in themselves," the old man said slowly, "because, to my eternal regret, I believed him. He found the chink in my armor when he told me her age. I knew she was a little older than myself, but had no idea by how much. I was stunned when he told me she was thirty and offered to prove it. I was just twenty-one. His description of her as a scheming, calculating, experienced woman, playing upon the innocence of a boy, was suddenly all too plausible. And, as though he read my mind, before I could tell him of her condition, that she expected my child, therefore I *must* stand by her, he said she would claim that, true or not, in order to entrap me. It was wealth she was after, wealth and position; love had nothing to do with it. And anyway, how could a woman of her age and experience fall in love with a raw, gullible fool such as me?"

Edward winced at that. Not at his father's raw innocence, but at what seemed to him an accurate assessment of his mother's character. Thirty years old, her looks beginning to fade, and the sudden decision to play George Gregory for all he was worth. Perhaps she had been fond of him, but Edward saw the gift of her virginity to that young man as the kind of ace his mother would use. And having lost the game so painfully, she would never offer her body again.

Unaware of Edward's thoughts, his father went on: "It shames me, looking back. I *was* gullible and foolish—he knew me so well. But, in trying to cure what he saw as my youthful folly, my father went too far. He stunned my love for Elizabeth, but he also managed to kill other affections. I hated him and despised myself. Although I had promised to marry her, I didn't even want to see her again. My father suggested a polite note, canceling any further meetings. I couldn't even do that. I just wanted to get away—on my own—away from everyone."

His mother, desperately concerned for her son's health, had suggested a few days in the south, with relatives. Willingly George went and stayed for several weeks. Eventually, he said, he tried to write to Elizabeth, succeeding only in wasting vast amounts of paper. In the end he knew he had to see her, but by the time he was ready to face up to his responsibilities, she was gone. His inquiries, discreet though they were, had come to his father's ears. He was interviewed again. Little was said on that second occasion; he was simply shown the document Elizabeth Elliott had signed, acknowledging receipt of a large sum in return for quitting the county.

"Q.E.D.—the argument proved. I believed it for years," the old man confessed wearily. "After that, I went into the church. For all the wrong reasons, of course—partly because I knew my father would hate the idea and partly because it seemed a safe retreat. Law to me at that time seemed no more than an empty farce in an unjust world. And I was the matching empty vessel. I don't think I even believed in God at that time: it was just something to do.

"It wasn't until I arrived in Lincoln—years later—that I began to seriously question what had happened. It was a very poor parish indeed, and as a young curate I heard so many heartbreaking histories, baptized so many fatherless children who were destined to die within the year, it brought me to my senses. Life there made me think, it made me *feel* again. I finally understood *why* Elizabeth had made her promise and accepted that money. She hadn't lied to me—she *had* been expecting a child—my child. And for the first time I saw that appalling situation through her eyes. Saw the choice she faced when I broke my promise and deserted her. You see, women in that position can't afford fine principles and a man's sense of honor. Women will lie, cheat, and steal to survive and protect their children—use any means at their disposal. I can't say I blame them. And nor must you," he added gently.

"Oh, I don't blame her for that," Edward said. "Not now. I just wish she hadn't been so embittered by what happened."

Sighing, the older man nodded, and for a while there was the silence of much shared consideration. Eventually Edward asked whether he had ever tried to find her, and with another painful sigh his father described a journey made when Edward would have been six or seven years old. When the hotel on Tanner Row was flourishing, and a confused little boy had been brought back from those elderly relatives in Darlington and taught to call his mother "Auntie."

"I went to Metheringham and made some discreet inquiries. I heard a lot about the Elliotts, most of it confirming what your mother had told me all those years before—more proof, if I needed it, of her honesty. I heard the Elliotts were fine people, if a little proud for village society, and that in latter years they had enjoyed a small return of fortune. Certainly when your mother's parents were pointed out to me, I could see they were not poor—not as I had come to understand poverty. My informant was under the impression that of four children who had left the village, the two daughters were quite well placed. He understood they were in business somewhere in the north. York, however, was never mentioned. Ironic," he said, sighing again, "to think how much time I must have spent in that city, never knowing she was there."

"Didn't you inquire of my grandparents?"

"No. They didn't need my help, and I was too ashamed to make myself known to them."

Edward closed his eyes against a sudden surge of pain. "I'm sorry for that," he said softly. "I spent every summer with them when I was a child."

The irony of that hurt them both; but, even as the old man begged his forgiveness, Edward was surprised. Moved also; there were tears shining on those thin, pale cheeks.

"There's no need for forgiveness," Edward murmured; and in his heart the words were repeated: no need, because I understand.

Understanding him, liking him, feeling the healing power of warmth and truth, Edward knew his only regret would always be that they had come so late into each other's lives. Although he was saddened by the past, by a pain and loneliness which far outweighed his own experience, he felt that something had been completed, made whole. Because of this meeting and all those yet to come, neither of them would ever be quite as lonely again.

THREE

By the end of that beautiful month the Royals were ensconced once more in Dublin, the whole regiment looking forward to winter's easy period, to weeks of comparative rest, entertainment at the city's fleshpots, and, for the officers at least, relaxation on the hunting field.

Having settled his men as well as possible into the less than salubrious surroundings of Islandbridge Barracks, Robert was determined to put all such concerns behind him for a while. Louisa had been extremely patient, and he wanted to make up for the lengthy absences, for the visits which had scarcely been long enough for dinner and bed, much less sensible conversation. Eager to conclude his army business and go home at the end of a very tiring week, he had one more item to deal with, regarding a prisoner held at Mountjoy Gaol. There was a statement to make and papers to sign, and after that he was free.

With relief he rejoined Harris, and they returned to the waiting carriage. For a moment, feeling exhaustion take its grip, Robert closed his eyes; then, minutes later, at a sudden jolt over tramlines, he opened them again, seeing with irritation the amount of late-afternoon traffic. With dusk, it had begun to rain, a fine drenching mist which had shoppers rushing for cabs to whisk them home for tea; a self-defeating idea, Robert thought, since every cab was now caught up in a jam which extended the length of Sackville Street.

Just visible at the head of a side turning was St. George's, where once upon a time he had sworn eternal vows of love and fidelity to a woman who could scarcely have understood the meaning of such words; it seemed another life, another existence, he thought. Had Charlotte been sane, he might have persuaded her to divorce him; but in sickness she was blameless and he the guilty offender. Under the circumstances it was an academic point, but it embittered him, nevertheless; hating this part of town, he wished the traffic would clear, but it was a slow journey that evening, the coachman easing his way through every gap. Across a sea of bobbing umbrellas by Rutland Square, his eyes fastened on the lights of a mansion facing him, the house owned by Charlotte's uncle, where Robert had courted her in ignorance and had been trapped like a fly in that cleverly constructed web of secrecy and deceit. Not since his marriage had he seen them, nor did he wish to see them now; but they would know he was back in Dublin, as he was sure they knew everything about Charlotte; and with Louisa in his house and on his arm, they would know, too, that he was not destroyed.

With a sudden lurch of the carriage, the house was lost to view; they crossed the river, black and busy with traffic of its own, heading south down Grafton Street, thronged with cabs and carriages in the gathering November gloom, and then turned east, past endless iron balustrades on Stephen's Green, past dripping trees and ornamental lakes already lost to view. Here the traffic was clearer, and the streets, with faded Georgian grandeur, announced the presence of an equally fading gentility. Too many of the old aristocracy were feeling the pinch of high taxes and low land rents; they were retiring to impoverished country estates and selling their town houses to the up-and-coming middle classes. Doctors and lawyers were the newly rich in Dublin, and Robert did not entirely approve: regretting his marriage minutes ago, he had valid cause to thank Providence for it as they entered Fitzwilliam Square. Without Charlotte's money, he could never have afforded to restore and refurbish the Devereaux house. It was ironic, he thought, as the carriage drew up before that elegant facade, that a couple of years ago he had hated it fiercely and had wanted to sell; whereas now, with Louisa installed and awaiting him, it had become the home he never expected to have, especially after William's inheritance of White Leigh. For him, Louisa had laid the ghost of those early weeks with Charlotte, dispelled it more thoroughly than paint or paper ever could.

Georgina rushed to meet him, and he swung her around in the hall, earning a disapproving sniff from McMahon as he did the same to Louisa; breathless with laughter, she stood back, while Letty backed away, refusing to come near her brother until he promised to do no more than kiss her cheek. As though in defiance of the old butler, Harris managed a smile as he hoisted a couple of bags and prepared to take them upstairs.

"Something comfortable this evening, Harris," Robert called. "I'll be up shortly to change."

In the drawing room Robert hugged all his ladies again, delighted to be home. Sitting down in his favorite wing chair before the fire, once again he allowed his eyes to take in what was a very lovely room. Tall windows, overlooking the square, were framed in rich green velvet, the panels between exquisite plasterwork depictions of songbirds and wild roses; cream damask walls provided a perfect backing for his favorite Stubbs portrait, and the Adam fireplace was in itself a dream of classical perfection.

As was his daughter. Dainty as a piece of Dresden, she smiled up into his face, and unable to resist her, he drew her onto his lap, listening attentively to all her news.

He was fascinated and quite unaware of the delightful picture the pair of them made: himself still uniformed in red and gold; his daughter in blue, fair against his dark good looks.

Watching them, Louisa was filled with love and happiness, wondering in that moment how she could have doubted him or questioned the wisdom of coming to Dublin. Of course it was right; she loved him so much, and he loved her; it was simply that he had a job to do, and that job took him away from time to time. She must learn to be less selfish, more understanding of the demands which were made of him.

She sat quietly to one side of the sofa, listening with amusement to Georgina's piping excitement, delighted to see the sparkling adoration in the little girl's eyes and feeling a surge of possessive pride. The child was so quick and bright, she was a delight to teach; and so happy by nature that Louisa could not help but love her. Having been granted the position of honorary cousin, Louisa's only regret was that the relationship could never be closer; but Georgina regarded Letty as her mother, and her father was the only person who had her total and uncritical devotion. For him she would do anything.

When, after half an hour, Letty said it was time for bed, there was the instant threat of tears; but as Robert pointed to the clock and said he must go up and change for dinner, Georgina curbed her trembling lip, and in her best, most wheedling manner, asked whether he would put her to bed.

"No, you little minx, I've told you I must change. But," he added kindly, hoisting her into his arms, "I'll carry you up the wooden hill. Come on, away we go."

Reaching for Louisa's hand, he pulled her to her feet, and, laughing, the three went up the stairs.

At the foot of the second flight she kissed Georgina's cheek and let Robert take her up to the nursery; she stood for a moment, listening to their mingled voices, then took the corridor which led to her own little apartment at the back of the house. As usual, when he came down, Robert would go into the main bedroom at the front, although he used it mainly as a place to keep his clothes. Like the rest of the house, it had been redecorated, but in spite of its warm russets and golds, he complained of its coldness and never slept there; nor had Louisa any desire to cross the threshold. As though by mutual consent, the fact that he had shared that room with Charlotte was not mentioned; and that it was designated his room at all was purely a matter of form. When he had organized the refurbishment of the house, Robert had had bathrooms installed, one of which was in the old dressing room between the master bedroom and Louisa's, its communicating door cleverly disguised. She was sure it was no secret and wondered why he had bothered; but, with illogical reasoning, he insisted it kept up appearances, while the fact that he always slept with her seemed not to worry him at all. Although, when she thought about it, Louisa realized that when Robert was at home not even Moira entered her room in the early morning.

With a wry little smile for his secret orders, she admired her reflection in the glass; the gown she was wearing was the first Robert had bought for her, its rich autumn tones making it always one of his favorites and the soft velvet flattering her figure. She patted her hair, tucking a stray curl into place, then turned to survey the room. Everything was neat, dressing table tidy, a posy of dried flowers now in place of summer's roses, and on a side table within reach, a box of Robert's favorite cigars. The smell of them clung to curtains and draperies, and Moira consistently turned up her nose each morning as she came to open the windows, but Louisa never minded. Indeed, she rather liked that faint aroma; even days afterward it reminded her of Robert.

The hidden door clicked open, and he came slowly into the room, eyes smiling, nimble fingers already unhooking the tight collar of his uniform jacket.

Leaning against the paneling, he let Louisa come to him and with a throaty laugh crushed her in his arms. "Lord, have I missed you!" he exclaimed, kissing her hungrily. "It's been a hell of a week, you've no idea," he murmured between kisses. "I thought I'd never get home. I'm filthy, I need a bath, I have to change—I'm absolutely *starving*— and," he kissed her again, "all I want is you."

Louisa laughed, stripping him of coat and shirt. "Then get your bath— dinner's waiting. You can have me later."

"I can't wait!"

"Yes you can!" she insisted, slapping those teasing hands away. "For goodness' sake, go and get your bath!"

"Only if you come and talk to me," he pleaded.

She pushed him into the bathroom. "Don't be such a spoiled baby— we can talk later. Anyway," she added, touching the rich velvet of her gown, "one drop of water on this, and it'll be ruined."

"I'll buy you another."

"Oh, go on with you, you're wasting time!"

But when he called to her a few minutes later, she went to stand by the open door.

"I was thinking," Robert said, soaping arms and shoulders, "that we really should get down to White Leigh pretty soon. Oh, don't look so aghast—we'll have to go sooner or later, and in my book it's better to get the unpleasantness over first. That is, of course, if unpleasantness there's going to be. Personally I don't think there will be any. I had a letter from William the other week, asking when I'd be going down, and wasn't it about time Letty and Georgina paid a visit. So I took the bit between my teeth and told him about you."

Feeling the blood drain from her cheeks at the very idea of White Leigh, Louisa swallowed hard. "What did you say, for Heaven's sake?"

"The truth, more or less." Rinsing the soap from his body, Robert reached for the towel and stepped out of the bath. "I told him that you were living here as a member of my household and that if he wanted to see me at White Leigh, then he must also be prepared to accept you. And more to the point, that his *wife* must be prepared to accept you. She's the fly in the ointment, Louisa, not him. Will's like my father—couldn't give a damn who's doing what and with whom, as long as they're happy." With an air of total unconcern, Robert began to shave.

"Oh, Robert, how could you? You shouldn't have said that—your sister-in-law will hate me for it!"

"Anne hates *everybody,* particularly me. There's no point in trying to be tactful with women like that: they think it's a sign of weakness and kick you in the teeth at the first opportunity. She's like the worst kind of mare, that woman—you've got to keep the whip hand all the time. Will hasn't the first idea." As he waved the cutthroat razor in an eloquent gesture, Louisa winced again.

"Oh, don't," she pleaded and a moment later added plaintively: "Do we *have* to go?"

"Yes. I have some business to attend to, and I refuse to waste free and precious days by going alone. *Anyway,* I want you to see the place, Louisa. It's where I was born, for heaven's sake—where I spent the best years of my life—I *want* you to see it." He splashed his face with cold water and dabbed himself dry. "We've usually spent Christmas there, you know, but I've no intention of doing it this year. Christmas is going to be us—you and me and Georgie—and Letty, of course. And we're going to spend it here; not at White Leigh. My brother won't like that, and he'll be offended if we stay away completely—which is why I feel we should go *now,* rather than leaving it till spring."

"If I was your brother, I'd be offended by your letter," she said as Robert went through to collect the clothes Harris had left out for him.

"Nonsense!" he said with a laugh. "Will and I understand each other."

On the threshold of that other room, feeling the presence of Charlotte's ghost as surely as if she stood there, Louisa said: "And what about the *real* fly in the ointment, as you put it? What about—" About to say *your wife,* she changed her mind; he hated the reference, and she had no wish to destroy his good temper. "What about Charlotte?"

Without vehemence, Robert shook his head. "There's no need to worry about her," he said gently and, buttoning his trousers, returned to Louisa. "Don't look so stricken—you won't even see Charlotte."

But Louisa was frightened. Slipping her arms around his neck, she clung to him, feeling the dampness of his skin after the bath, his reassuring warmth and masculine strength. "I love you," she whispered, kissing the curve of his shoulder, and with fear in her heart swallowed the begging words which sprang to her lips.

"And I love you." With a tender kiss, he extricated himself from that clinging embrace. "Trust me," he said.

In the misty, fading light of a November afternoon they drove up the straight, single street of a village as plain and unremarkable as any in Ireland; it was the third day they had passed since leaving the railway station in Waterford, and Louisa was amazed only by its similarity to the others. Dublin, with its elegant Georgian streets, was a place with which she could identify, a city bearing, on the surface at least, a recognizably English stamp; but these villages were nothing like those of Lincolnshire or the Yorkshire Wolds. There was nothing pretty about them, no gardens to soften rough walls and sagging thatch, no endearing quaintness to relieve the harsh reality of poverty in its barest, bleakest form. In England, to be poor in the country was infinitely preferable to poverty in the city; here there seemed little to choose between the two. The most she could say for this particular village street was that it was tidy, and the cottages along the roadside seemed in better repair than most.

She expected to see open country at the end of those twin rows, to pass through this place as they had passed through others; but the carriage slowed, ahead was the darkness of forested land, and the village street became a broad driveway which led between open gates and an avenue of huge, foreign-looking trees.

The darkness was sudden and total. Alarmed, she gripped Robert's hand, feeling, rather than hearing, his little hiss of laughter against her cheek.

"Araucarias, my darling—also known as monkey-puzzle trees, which sounds far less frightening and reduces them, don't you think, to the ridiculousness they deserve."

"I've never seen so many or so tall."

"Yes, our great-grandfather had rather an obsession about his specimen trees: they had to be bigger and better than everyone else's. It shows an appalling lack of taste, I feel."

"They always frightened you as a child, Robert," Letty said wickedly.

"Did they? I really don't recall."

She laughed, while Georgina said firmly: "Horrid trees, Daddy; I hate them."

"I can't say I'm very fond of them," Louisa admitted, inordinately glad when they came out into the open.

Ahead, standing on a slight elevation, through the pale swirls of mist she saw the house, gray and somewhat spectral in the half-light, as insubstantial as a dream—or nightmare. With its pediments and pillars, balustrades and tall windows, there was an illusion of vastness about it, an illusion which was both impressive and chilling on that dank November afternoon.

"Not the best light in which to see the ancestral home," Letty observed with irony, "especially for the first time. Let's pray for a little sun tomorrow."

"And a good warm fire tonight," Robert muttered.

"Oh, yes, indeed, do let's hope that Anne's little economies haven't extended as far as the firewood!"

Letty laughed at the private joke, but Louisa's heart sank. She found herself thinking of the Gillygate house with a longing which brought a lump to her throat; a small town house it might be, with no pretensions to elegance, but at least it was warm and welcoming, even on the coldest night. This house looked cold and grand, like an ice palace without a heart. Wondering how Robert could love it, she returned the pressure of his hand and tried to summon a smile.

As the carriage drew up before a broad flight of steps, some of Louisa's awe diminished; close to, White Leigh House was smaller than it appeared at a distance, less the spectral palace and more the elegant and imposing country residence, quite solidly built of limestone. Nevertheless, Letty's exhortations to pack warm clothes rang in her ears, together with the truth that it was cold and drafty and that the east wing's roof leaked like a sieve.

As the steps were let down, Georgina leapt out and ran up the broad flight to where her cousin Harry was waiting with his parents. At least she's pleased, Louisa thought, following Letty and shaking out the skirts of her new traveling clothes. The skirt and jacket were plain and dark and very expensive, but she was glad of the confidence they gave; Lady Anne Duncannon could not accuse her of being cheap and flashy, whatever other criticisms she might make. Nor could she sigh over Letty's appearance today, for Robert's sister had given way to persuasion and indulged in two new winter outfits. Louisa thought she looked very distinguished in heathery tweeds.

On a deep breath she mounted the steps, hanging back with the right amount of tact as Robert and Letty were briefly embraced. Without waiting to be introduced, however, Sir William came forward and shook her hand, welcoming Louisa with such genuine warmth, she had no difficulty finding a responding smile. Grateful for that small kindness, she knew she would like this big bear of a man, whatever Robert said about his weaknesses. Broad, bearded, with a florid complexion and unruly red hair, he exhibited little in the way of family resemblance, except perhaps in warmth and charm, Louisa thought, that essence the Duncannons seemed to possess in such abundance.

Not so his wife. Her clipped, very English way of speaking contrasted sharply with her husband's soft, meandering phrases, while her eyes— so like Blanche's!—swept up and down Louisa's form, taking in every minute detail of her looks and appearance.

"So this is Miss Elliott," she murmured, barely touching the tips of Louisa's outstretched fingers, "of whom we have heard so much." The slight stress on the final word made her greeting sound like an insult, and Louisa felt the color mount to burning in her cheeks. Robert's sudden indrawn breath was distinctly audible, and, afraid to meet his eyes, she looked down, thankful for Letty's intervention, her overbright tones and inconsequential chatter as she ushered her sister-in-law into the house.

Glaring at Anne's retreating back and then at his brother, Robert gripped Louisa's elbow with a firmness that hurt and steered her inside.

There was more trouble later. When he saw Louisa's room in the ill-famed east wing, Robert was furious. Whipping back the bedclothes, he ran his hand between the sheets.

"This bed is damp," he said. "You can't possibly sleep here."

He was almost out of the door before she could call him back. "Robert, please don't make a fuss. At least there's a fire, and with a couple of hot water bottles I'll be all right."

"You'll have pneumonia," he muttered.

Determined to rectify matters, he went in search of his sister-in-law. Louisa shivered. The room felt cold in spite of the fire, and as she took stock of her surroundings, she realized that it was indeed a gloomy place.

The carpet was sadly worn, the window hangings dusty and frayed, and in the far corner among the shadows black mildew spotted the silk-covered wall. She touched it with her fingers, finding it loose and damp, and, as she raised the lamp above her head, noticed a whole section peeling away below the cornice. It was a sad sight. The eighteenth-century Chinese silk had been very beautiful once, she could see that, but those exotic birds in spiky foliage were faded now, the whole room ruined beyond repair by the damp seeping in from above.

She sneezed, and the sound seemed unnaturally loud. Apart from the crackle of logs in the grate, the silence was total, almost uncanny. She might have been all alone in the house. It certainly seemed she was alone in this part of it. Or was she? With another shiver, this time of nerves, Louisa thought of Charlotte and wondered where her quarters were. If Anne Duncannon would place a guest in this wing, perhaps she would also house a mad relative here?

Louisa moved back to the fire and set her eyes upon the door. So tense was she that Robert's return startled her, and, trembling with sudden relief, she sat down suddenly in a fireside chair.

"Don't be making yourself comfortable here," he said abruptly. "You're moving to the west wing—a little closer, thank God, to me."

Swallowing hard, standing up, Louisa began to gather her things.

"No, no, no—leave that—a maid will see to it. Come on, let's get down for a drink, for Heaven's sake."

"But what about—" She broke off, glancing down at her traveling clothes. "I haven't changed."

"Nor can you until your room's prepared. We'll have some tea—or you can—and change later."

With a backward glance, Louisa followed him out of the room. Dreading the thought of another confrontation with Anne Duncannon, she inquired tentatively: "What did you say, or shouldn't I ask?"

"Don't ask," Robert growled. Suddenly protective, he stopped before the doors which led into the main body of the house and squeezed her shoulders. "Lady Anne is no lady, believe me. *Don't* let her upset you, Louisa. And if she does," he advised, "don't show it. Raise that pretty little chin of yours, my darling, and look down your nose at her—it's no more than she deserves. And remember, you're *my* guest."

"But this is her house, Robert."

"My brother's house," he corrected. "And also my childhood home." Dropping a light kiss on the end of her nose, he smiled suddenly. "Come on, let's go down and give her a run for her money!"

Not for the first time, Louisa thought how well he thrived on conflict, on a challenge, on the chance to thumb his nose at an adversary and get away with it. As a soldier, she supposed he needed that, but she found the trait disquieting; and as some kind of camp follower, which was perhaps how Anne Duncannon chose to see her, there was danger in being dragged along in Robert's wake.

With a wry twist of her lips, Louisa nodded. "I'll do my best," she whispered. Before he could open the doors, however, she tugged at his arm. "Tell me something first—where are Charlotte's rooms? I only want to know," she added quickly, "so I can avoid the area. I don't particularly want to run into her or her nurse."

"But you won't," he said. "Don't you remember? She hasn't lived in the house for a long time—not since that last little debacle a couple of years ago. William had a cottage built for her in the grounds. She has her nurse and a couple of servants, and the change has done her good. Or so they tell me," he added dryly. A moment later, searching her face, he said: "You haven't been worrying about her, have you?"

"Well, yes, actually, I have," she admitted tautly, allowing anger and disappointment to show. "Silly of me, no doubt, but I *didn't* know, and nobody thought to tell me."

With a heavy sigh, Robert shook his head. "She's not a subject we discuss every day, is she? There's been a lot of water under the bridge since then, and anyway, I thought you knew."

"I didn't know," Louisa repeated, and despite his apology, the matter rankled.

Her new room was at the far end of the west wing, next to the servants' staircase, much smaller than the first but also warmer, with the furnishings in better repair. It was the fifth bedroom, with an empty one between herself and Mr. Crabtree, young Harry's tutor, and another between him and Robert.

"A matter of discretion," Robert explained as he escorted her upstairs to change. "Anne did not wish to embarrass you—she said—by making you the only woman in this part of the house. So she very kindly gave you a grand room in the other wing."

"And who lived there before, I wonder?"

Ignoring her waspish tone, he said evenly, "That part of the house was quite livable a couple of years ago. It's deteriorated badly in the last twelve months."

"Why isn't it repaired? It seems a shame to let everything be ruined."

"Oh, for God's sake!" he exclaimed. "Don't you start trying to tell me what should and should not be done! We did this roof four years ago, then the main house, and then there was the cottage to build. And after that, damn me if the Devereaux house didn't need a new bloody roof along with everything else. I couldn't refurbish *that* place on my army pay—and contrary to popular misconception, Charlotte's fortune is *not* a bottomless pit!"

"No," she said quietly. "I'm sure it isn't." His reproval hurt her, but that information, so angrily revealed, left a sour taste in Louisa's mouth. He never discussed money with her, nor did she expect him to; but she had assumed, rather foolishly it now seemed, that Charlotte's subsidies were restricted to White Leigh. Assumed that a sharp sense of integrity prevented Robert from diverting her income to his own use.

The maid had laid out Louisa's russet velvet, always one of her favorite gowns; now, however, she eyed it with prickling suspicion, wondering whose money had paid for that. A long time ago, the day Robert first told her about Charlotte, he had said he was not a wealthy man; but wealth was a matter of degree, and to Louisa, a hundred a year was untold riches; horrified at the cost of even one such gown, she had long ago stopped asking the price. That the clothes she wore, the bed she slept in, even the pictures she had chosen to adorn the walls of her rooms in Dublin might have been paid for with Charlotte's money filled Louisa with such shameful distaste that she shuddered.

For a moment she simply sat, regarding the gown, wondering what she should do. It was impossible, here and now, to have the matter out with Robert; equally impossible to refuse to dress for dinner; and anyway, she thought, looking down at her expensive traveling clothes, it was more likely Charlotte had paid for those. Furious, humiliated, hating both herself and Robert, Louisa stripped off the jacket and skirt, the ruffled silk blouse, and shrugged herself into the soft velvet with hardly a care for its seams and folds.

Tight-lipped, clutching a fine paisley shawl against the chill of those dark corridors, Louisa went down to dinner with Robert.

At his sister-in-law's direction, Robert took a seat next to her, with Letty and Louisa opposite; Sir William, as always, at the head; and a single, three-branched candelabra between them at one end of that vast table. A couple of oil lamps glowed on the sideboard, but the silent footman was simply a darker shape in that shadow-vaulted room. Logs crackled cheerfully in the distant grate, making little impression on the group at the table.

Remarking on the distance, Robert shivered in the chill. "Lord, but it's cold in here. Do we have to sit so far from the fire? I'm sure we used to be much nearer."

"That was years ago, Robert, to accommodate your ailing father," Anne murmured reprovingly. "This is the correct position for the table— a room must have balance."

"Balance, you call it? I call it *cold*. And who can tell the difference in the dark? If the chandeliers were lit, I could understand your argument."

His sister-in-law sighed dramatically, touching her napkin delicately to her lips as the soup plates were removed. "The cost of candles, Robert, is quite extortionate these days. You've no idea how we try to economize."

Beside her, Louisa felt Letty twitch with suppressed laughter; less amused, Robert gritted his teeth. In very clipped tones, he said: "Obviously not."

Lady Anne seemed not to notice the dangerous ground she trod; or was she, Louisa wondered, simply acting a part, being deliberately provocative? With the arrival of the fish, which was surprisingly hot, she said languidly, "The Blamires have had electricity installed at the castle; so much more convenient—light at the flick of a switch."

At that, Letty's foot nudged Louisa's, threatening to release hours of tension in a burst of unseemly laughter. Her napkin firmly covering her mouth, she stared hard at the innocent salmon on her plate.

With just the hint of a quiver to her voice, Letty said: "How are the horses coming on this season, William? Any cub-hunting yet? Robert was saying only the other day—weren't you, Robert?—that he hoped to ride out with you one day."

Thankfully rescued, the conversation continued quite sensibly along Sir William's favorite lines for some time. Only after dinner, when they were briefly alone, did Letty and Louisa relive that moment, chuckling and giggling like naughty schoolgirls. The laughter acted like a tonic, however, boosting Louisa's flagging spirits and placing Anne Duncannon's daunting presence in its proper perspective.

"May anyone share the joke?" Robert inquired as he and William rejoined them.

"It's an old one, Robert dear," Letty said lightly as William helped himself to coffee. "I've told it many times, and you never laugh, so I'll not repeat it now."

He looked hard at his sister and then at Louisa, thawing under her twinkling smile; for a few minutes they were all relaxed, chatting pleasantly of nothing in particular; then Anne Duncannon rejoined them. Louisa's amusement quickly faded, for those barbed remarks, ostensibly so innocent, were this time directed at herself.

Almost as though interviewing a servant, she questioned Louisa directly about her work as a governess, wanting to know the names of her previous employers and whether it was through those North Riding gentry that she had been introduced to Robert.

Annoyed, he answered for her. "No. In fact we met in York. We were both guests at a small birthday celebration in the home of Major and Mrs. Bainbridge, whose names I'm sure you've never heard before, Anne, so why the intense interest, for goodness' sake?"

"I was educated in England, Robert, as you are well aware. It merely occurred to me that I might be personally acquainted with some of Miss Elliott's former employers." Quite smoothly, almost without pause, she went on: "I suppose your father was a minister of religion, Miss Elliott? Just about every governess I ever heard of claimed to be a vicar's daughter, I can't imagine why . . ." Both tone and glance managed to imply that most governesses were inveterate liars.

For a moment Louisa simply held that poisonous look with her own cold stare; it seemed they all hung on her reply. Then, with a tight little smile, she said evenly: "That's probably because most of them *are* clergymen's daughters. And as you're probably well aware, Lady Duncannon, so many of the Anglican clergy these days are younger sons of impoverished gentry." She let that small observation sink in, then said, "However, I've met quite a few governesses who claimed to be the daughters of country doctors. I myself claim to be the daughter of a Bradford wool merchant—which is original, I suppose, if nothing else. And now," she added, rising to her feet, "if you'll excuse me, I simply must retire: it's been an exhausting day."

Glad of the chance to escape, Letty offered to show Louisa to her room; on the stairs, however, Robert caught up with them. Having bidden his sister goodnight by the doors to the west wing, he whispered to Louisa, "Shall I come to you or you to me?"

"Neither," she responded tartly. "I'm not going to be caught out, wandering round the corridors at dead of night, like somebody in a music hall farce! And neither are you."

"I see. And who, may I ask, is likely to catch either of us?"

"I wouldn't know, Robert, but in case you'd forgotten, a certain Mr. Crabtree rooms between us."

"I doubt he'd notice if the roof fell in."

"No, and that's an end of it."

"Very well. I'll see you for breakfast in the morning. Eight-thirty."

FOUR

As always, dragged as though by a magnet, Robert rode out early to the cottage. It stood, well sheltered by trees, not very far from the east gate. A simple place, like those in the village but larger, it had two chimneys and a tiled roof and also a small garden. With no intention of entering, he sat astride his horse for a few minutes, peering through the trees and the gray, clinging mist.

Thin spirals of smoke rose from the chimneys, and through the kitchen window he could see signs of movement, probably the general servant who lived in, making breakfast for the household. Later a woman from the village would come, as she did each day, to do the heavy work. It was a good arrangement and one he wished had been thought of earlier; it might have saved much in both argument and tragedy. Isolated with her nurse and the two servants, Charlotte seemed better than she had been for years; and, more to the point, White Leigh itself was quieter, the occupants no longer disturbed by those occasional outbursts of violence.

Harness jangled as the horse shook its head and stamped, and in that freezing air the sudden snort of impatience became a cloud of denser fog. With a sudden shiver, Robert touched the reins and guided his mount carefully through the trees. Back on the path, with space before them, he urged the horse forward, keeping its eagerness to a steady trot across the hard earth.

He was out for the best part of an hour, making a circuit of the grounds and returning at a canter up the long avenue of araucarias. The sun had risen, dispersing much of the mist, but it clung stubbornly to groups of trees in the shallow bowl which surrounded White Leigh, leaving a silvered rime everywhere. Vast lawns glittered in the ellipse of gravel drive, and the simple, classical lines of the great south front shone like a stage set against a backdrop of cedars and conifers beyond.

Its beauty touched him as it always did, and he reined the horse into a walk, determined to bring Louisa out immediately after breakfast, to see White Leigh as it should be seen. A view such as this, he thought, was worth all it cost to preserve; and despite William's name on the title deeds, it would always belong to him in his heart.

With Anne Duncannon's sly innuendos in her mind, and thoughts of Charlotte lurking in the small hours, Louisa slept very poorly. Aware of the bed's strangeness and every creak and groan of an old and unfamiliar house, she regretted most bitterly her refusal of Robert's companionship. Pride might have buckled, but integrity would not: here, Robert's wife had been granted refuge, however unwillingly; and as a tolerated though hardly welcome guest, Louisa could not defile that. Perhaps more to the point was her realization that the shadowy figure which stood between herself and Robert was no longer mythical.

Fully awake before first light, she felt weary and disinclined to rise, but with the arrival of tea and biscuits and the making up of the fire, her spirits lifted. Shivering in the chill, standing as close to the fire as she dare, Louisa dressed in her warmest clothes and prepared to face the day.

There was no reply to her tap at Robert's door and, when she looked inside, no sign of him. Feeling put out by that desertion, and more than a little sorry for herself, she wandered disconsolately in search of breakfast. Despite the maid's directions, or perhaps because of them, she missed the breakfast room entirely, opening elaborate double doors on a large blue salon. At the far end, a small figure in white cap and apron was opening the last of the window shutters, letting a soft, diffused light reveal the portrait which dominated the room. About to apologize and retreat, Louisa found her attention arrested; the painting was so very different from the formal and rather dull collection of forebears above the staircase that she moved slowly toward it, intrigued by the identity of the sitter.

The raven-haired woman was a beauty, her flamboyant crinoline of deep, vibrant blue underlining all the room's lighter tones. Or it had done once, Louisa thought; for the salon, by comparison with the painting, was now somewhat faded and shabby. Seated, half-reclining against the curved end of a chaise longue, the subject's informal pose and décolleté gown suggested warmth and femininity, echoed in the soft curves of shoulders and bosom, the round white arms of the artist's sitter. There was amusement in her eyes and a pretty blush to her cheeks, as though the painter had paid a too-extravagant compliment; she had the bloom of youth and the freshness of yesterday, although, by the style of her gown, Louisa knew she had been painted many years before. At least thirty, she judged, and probably before Robert was born.

There was scarcely any need to wonder who she was; there was sufficient likeness in that fine Irish coloring and bone structure to tell which side of the family Letty and Robert favored; but even as she considered, Louisa heard footsteps behind her.

She turned, and Robert in boots and breeches was at her shoulder. His cheeks were ruddy with fresh air and exercise, his hair and jacket damp; glancing between Louisa and the portrait, he smiled slightly. "My mother, Elizabeth Devereaux. Or had you already deduced it?"

"Yes, I think so. A very beautiful woman."

"She was, wasn't she? Before I was born, of course. I suppose she'd have been in her mid-twenties then. Still," he added wistfully, "she was very lovely, even as an older woman."

For a long moment neither of them said anything; then Louisa asked, "What age was she—when she died?"

"Not very old; forty-five or six, I think. I remember William was just twenty-one, and Letty a couple of years older." He paused and sighed. "I was fifteen and away at school." In that succinct utterance was a wealth of grief and regret. A moment later he said, "She loved this room. I always think of it as it was when she was here—full of light and laughter and people." Slowly he shook his head. "It doesn't seem that long ago, yet how things change."

His sadness touched Louisa, banishing, for a while at least, all her silent recriminations. Touching his arm, she said gently: "Things do change, dearest: nothing ever stays the same."

"No, more's the pity." He smiled suddenly, but it was forced, his eyes suspiciously bright. "Come on, let's find breakfast. I've been up and out for the last hour; I'm starving!"

That night, after a day spent touring both house and grounds, Louisa slept more soundly though, again at her insistence, alone. As planned, Robert and William were out soon after breakfast, riding to join their neighbors, the Blamires, for a day's hunting.

Left to their own devices, the women were having a quiet morning, Georgina having elected to join Harry for his morning's lessons with Mr. Crabtree.

"Elected to disrupt them," Letty said, laughing, as she poured their mid-morning coffee.

"No," Louisa said thoughtfully, "she has a natural love of learning, I'm sure of it. Not just superficial, either—she really wants to *know* about things. For a child of her age, I find her questions quite profound."

"Oh, Miss Elliott, you don't need to tell *us* that!" Anne Duncannon exclaimed. "The child is quite infamous for her questions—far too precocious for her age. Answer one of her inquiries, Miss Elliott, and I guarantee you'll be there all day. It's a most unfortunate trait and should be squashed. I'm always telling Letty that."

"But questions are the sign of an inquiring mind, Lady Duncannon, and as a teacher I feel they should be encouraged."

"In the classroom, perhaps," came the frosty reply, "but it's hardly fitting for society, is it? But as you're not *of* society, perhaps that doesn't matter to you. Still," she added sarcastically, "I suppose you have heard the epithet that well-bred children should be seen and not heard?"

"I have indeed. An ideal which is convenient only from an adult point of view. An ideal—and I'm sure you will agree—designed to separate a child's world totally from the real world in which *we* live." As her adversary nodded, and Letty suppressed a smile over the coffeepot, Louisa went on: "It seems to me to preserve innocence at the high expense of so much else."

"I'm not sure I follow your argument, Miss Elliott . . ."

"How many young women—ladies—of your acquaintance are at all prepared for the pitfalls of the real world? Even in the rather rarefied atmosphere of society, Lady Duncannon, all is not sweetness and light. Surely you agree? Men inhabit that world—yet how many young girls understand that good looks and good manners often cover a multitude of darker sins? They walk into marriage knowing nothing, bear children in ignorance, express horror when they encounter real illness or real poverty for the first time. They are not equipped to understand or to cope. And yet they go on rearing their own daughters in much the same way."

With a cold and dangerous smile, Anne Duncannon nodded. "Ah, yes, I think I recognize the argument now. My sister-in-law holds similar beliefs, don't you, Letty? No wonder the two of you are such close, bosom friends! Though I dread to think," she added as she rose to her feet, "what you'll do to that child between you, with your freethinking views!

"Despite this pathetic pretense of being Georgina's governess, I know what your relationship with Robert is, so don't try to deny it!"

"I wouldn't insult you by doing so," Louisa said bravely, "and I didn't think Robert had tried to pass me off as anything other than his mistress."

"I'm afraid I was the one who said you were a governess, Louisa; I'm sorry," Letty said, wincing as Anne's strident voice cut across them both.

"Precisely! And what an insult—to insist that *I* should receive *you*—when the last five years of my life have been *ruined* by having to look after his *wife!*" Ignoring Letty's remonstrations, she went on: "He simply dumped her here—did you know that?—when she was pregnant. 'Until she has the child,' I said, 'no longer.' But he left her here, twisted William round his little finger until he agreed, and simply walked away from the lot.

"So we had two babies to care for—Harry was barely two—and a madwoman hell-bent on suicide. Murder, too, for all we knew—we hardly dared sleep for what might happen. Harry still has nightmares, poor lamb, still asks whether that mad creature has gone away for good. So don't preach to me about inquiring minds and preparation for the great, wide world—I'd rather have my child brought up in happy ignorance!"

"I'm sorry—I—"

"Sorry? You haven't an inkling, Miss Elliott, not an *inkling* of what we've endured! And let me ask you this, if you're so concerned about Georgina—what sort of a girl is she going to be? Even supposing she's inherited nothing of her mother's blood—and if you ask me, that would be a miracle!—how is all this going to affect her future? Her mother mad—and she knows it, thanks to Letty—and her father living quite openly with his mistress? What will she think? What will she say, in unguarded moments? And, more to the point, *who* will want to marry her?"

Into the ensuing silence, Anne Duncannon dropped more vitriol. "My brother-in-law, Miss Elliott, will ruin his daughter's life—and yours—as thoughtlessly as he's ruined everyone else's. If I were you, I'd go back to England while you still can, while you still have a scrap of reputation to cling to."

"Desert him, you mean? Let you think you've won?"

"Won?" Anne Duncannon repeated with a low, bitter laugh. "This isn't a *game,* Miss Elliott. And if you think it is, then I suggest you take a walk to the east gate before you leave White Leigh. Talk to Mrs. Hanrahan—take a look at what *he* married—and then try preaching to Robert.

"And I sincerely hope," she added softly from the doorway, "that he doesn't tell you what he so frequently tells me—that you have that demented creature to thank for the roof over your head and the clothes on your back."

The silence which followed her departure was thick and suffocating. Nausea threatened. In need of air, Louisa walked unsteadily to the window and raised the sash, drawing great drafts of cold, damp air deep into her lungs.

"I'm sorry," Letty said. "I expected a lot of things from Anne, but not that. You mustn't take any notice: she's very bitter."

"I'd say she has a lot to be bitter about—wouldn't you?"

"Yes and no." With a long sigh, the older woman said quietly: "The trouble with people like Anne—and Robert—is that they only ever see their own side of things. Much of what she says is true, but—"

"Is it true that Charlotte supports us, too?"

"No, no, of course not."

But Louisa did not believe her.

That afternoon, greatly subdued, they took the children for a long walk through the woods, while Anne went off to her dressmaker in Waterford. Letty maintained that her sister-in-law's attack was purely strategic, a means of sowing dissension in Robert's camp by ensuring Louisa's refusal to visit White Leigh again. Louisa was not convinced, however, and despite a long discussion which lasted half the afternoon, Charlotte remained obsessively at the forefront of her mind.

On the way back, as Letty opened the gate into the enclosed kitchen garden and the children dashed ahead, Louisa said: "Will you take me to see her?"

It was cold and drawing dusk, and in her heathery tweeds the older woman shivered. "My dear, Robert would have my hide!"

"Does he have to know?"

"He might easily find out."

"Then tell him I threatened to go alone. I will, you know, if you don't take me."

"But it's teatime," Letty protested weakly, seeing two small figures disappear inside a lighted kitchen doorway.

Moments later, however, Letty was stepping inside the same door and shouting to the children to behave themselves—she would see them in half an hour. Taking Louisa's arm, she guided her across the cobbled courtyard and past the stables, peeping in to verify her brother's absence.

"I call most days when I'm here," she admitted as they took the deeply rutted road toward the east gates. "Not that it makes any difference: she doesn't appear to know me. Still," she said with a sigh, "Mrs. Hanrahan appreciates the gesture—they don't have many visitors, as you can imagine."

"It must be a terrible strain, looking after someone like that, week in and week out. Does she ever have a break?"

"Well, she's never taken a holiday, but she goes into Waterford one day a week, to see a relative, I believe." After a small pause, Letty said: "Of course, nobody likes to admit it, but Mrs. Hanrahan is just a tiny bit strange herself. And it's become more pronounced since they've lived in the cottage. I mean, everybody says how wonderful she is, looking after that poor girl like a mother, but I honestly do think Mrs. Hanrahan regards Charlotte as her daughter. She's very possessive and totally protective. Robert couldn't get near Charlotte these days, even if he tried."

"And does he? Try to see her, I mean."

"Well," Letty said evasively, "he likes to know what's going on."

A small path curved away from the road and into the woods. A mixture of conifers and evergreens, designed originally to screen the estate's high brick wall in winter, also provided excellent cover for the cottage.

With hot cheeks and clammy hands, Louisa stood back while Letty tapped at the door; she felt sick and terrified, half of her wanting to turn and run, while the other, dominant half seemed incapable of movement.

A well-built young woman answered, bobbing a curtsy to Letty and standing back while they entered the small living room. "I'll be fetching Mrs. Hanrahan," she murmured.

"Only if it's convenient, Mary."

Squeezing Louisa's arm, Letty gave her a twinkling grin and whispered, "Too late now—you wanted to come."

Before she could reply, an inner door opened and a middle-aged woman emerged, gray hair so severely scraped back from her face that for a moment Louisa thought she was bald. She was massive; as tall as Letty and powerfully built, with a wide, pale face made paler by the severe black dress she wore. Shortsighted brown eyes peered suspiciously for a moment in the half-light, but then she smiled at Letty, and the smile was warmly welcoming.

Introduced as Georgina's new governess, Louisa was inordinately glad of the plain brown cloak she had donned before setting off that afternoon, and the close-fitting bonnet which was more sensible than fashionable.

Offered tea, Letty refused, but they stood in conversation for several minutes; eventually Mrs. Hanrahan asked whether they would like to say hello to her charge.

"She's a good girl today; we've been doing a nice jigsaw this afternoon—nearly finished it between us. Come through," she instructed, going ahead of the two women into a cozy sitting room which reminded Louisa of a nursery with its large, secure fireguard and its absence of ornaments. A slender girl was sitting cross-legged on the rug, bending forward over a board and a simple wooden puzzle; she was wearing a child's white pinafore, and her waist-length, silvery hair was caught back in a large pink bow.

Lovely hair, Louisa thought, wondering whose child she was, even as her eyes flicked rapidly in search of that demented creature, Robert's wife.

As the nurse stepped forward, lowering her massive bulk to kneel beside the child, realization began to dawn; it seemed that time slowed, that the woman took forever to kneel, to raise her hand so gently and kindly to that pale, silvery hair.

Words were uttered, words which seemed to have no meaning, and then Letty was going forward, bending over, whispering Charlotte's name. Louisa thought she might faint; took hold of a chair back and blinked and swallowed hard. The girl did not look up; Letty and Mrs. Hanrahan might not have been there at all. Louisa studied her, amazed at her slightness, trying to assess how tall she was, trying to see past those thin wrists and childish clothes and envisage her in a ballgown, with her hair piled high in curls and ringlets. Could this be Georgina's *mother?* were the words which rang in her brain. Robert's *wife?* Had this frail, bloodless creature really wreaked such damage?

Louisa moved, trying to get a better view, and at that Charlotte did look up. At once the hair and the bow and the childish pinafore were incongruous; the face was small, but not a child's, the eyes old, calculating, all-knowing. It seemed to Louisa those pale eyes stripped her bare; like a rabbit before a stoat, she could not have moved had her life depended on it.

Sensing the tension, Letty and Mrs. Hanrahan turned at the same time, and in that moment Charlotte leapt up, scattering the wooden pieces. Seizing the board, she threw it at Louisa. It missed her face but struck her painfully in the breast. Whether Charlotte would have leapt after it, attacking her, was impossible to say: Mrs. Hanrahan seized that writhing figure in her massive arms and yelled for Mary. Within seconds the servant was there with bottle and spoon, pouring liquid down Charlotte's throat while Mrs. Hanrahan forced her tight-clenched jaws apart.

In the kitchen, Letty handed Louisa a glass of water and urged her to sit down; but, trembling in every limb, Louisa wanted nothing but to leave.

"I must make sure she's all right, first."

"Who? Charlotte?"

"No, Mrs. Hanrahan."

Breezing into the kitchen, her rosy cheeks all smiles, the serving woman seemed not at all perturbed. "Half an hour, they'll both be fine," she informed Letty and, with a kind smile for Louisa, added: "Don't be feeling guilty, ma'am; you don't need to be doing anything to set Miss Charlotte off. She has her little turns every now and then, no matter what."

But Louisa felt more than guilty: sane or insane, she felt Robert's wife knew her through and through. Knew who she was and what she was.

As they prepared to leave, the young servant said confidentially: "I expect it was Mr. Robert being here this morning, and yesterday. I saw him myself—on horseback he was, just outside. I daresay she saw him, too."

FIVE

*E*ach shock, every impression of that day and those preceding it, seemed indelibly printed at the forefront of her mind. Feverish, unable to control the involuntary tremors which seized her, Louisa would have taken to her bed had she not been afraid Robert might want to sit with her. His company, his solicitous, probing questions, were the very last things she felt able to face. Dressing for dinner, she thought of packing to go home; not to Dublin, but to York. York and Gillygate and Edward: the three were synonymous with home and comfort and sanity. She longed for them with a passion which made her cry.

Letty came, suggesting something on a tray. Louisa refused. Sighing, the older woman asked what, if anything, Robert was to be told, for he was bound to notice the change in her.

"If he asks, tell him I'm ill and want to go home. I *hate* this place!"

"And Anne?"

With a cold cloth over her eyes, Louisa shook her head. "She can go to blazes, for all I care!"

Thankful of the candlelight, of the flickering shadows, thankful too for the added presence of Mr. Crabtree and one of the Blamires that night, Louisa struggled through dinner, eating little, saying less, feigning polite interest in the men's lively conversation. They had had a good day's riding with convivial company, if little success at the hunt itself, and with the rising of the ladies after the meal, it seemed they would sit long over the port.

Louisa drank her coffee in the small drawing room, then begged leave to be excused. As she left the room she caught the sound of Letty's voice, though not what was said; Anne Duncannon's words, however, rang clear as bells.

"She didn't have to go, did she? And *you* didn't have to take her, Letty."

Nauseated, she climbed the marble staircase to her room, feeling the weight of the day in every step. Convinced that sleep would elude her, she in fact fell asleep almost immediately, to be woken again sometime after midnight by the sound of a door being opened and closed.

Startled, the disturbing mists of the dreamworld in her mind, she saw a man's dark shape pass between herself and the glowing ashes of the fire; on the point of crying out, she was silenced by Robert's whisper.

"It's all right—it's only me." Leaning over the bed, he kissed her cheek; she caught the rich, sweet aroma of wine and cigars and knew he was a little drunk. "Sorry I'm so late, darling—it went on longer than I'd thought. Letty tells me you're not well, a bit of a chill. I must say I thought you were quiet over dinner, then thought it must be young Blamire, talking his head off like a fool."

He was so reassuringly normal that for a moment she forgot his early-morning vigils at the cottage; wanting to hold him, to feel his safety and strength beside her, Louisa buried her face against his neck. "I want to go home," she whispered, desperately fighting the tears.

"What, now?" he chuckled. "In the middle of the night?"

"Yes, if we could. But we can't, can we?"

"No, my darling, we can't. Besides," he murmured, nuzzling her cheek, "I want to make love to you."

She drew back. "Didn't you hear what I said? I said I want to go home—leave—get away. I can't stand this place; I'm sorry, but it's hateful to me. Can we go tomorrow, please?"

His evening coat off, Robert began loosening his tie; the starched collar and front of his shirt crackled in the silence. Suddenly it stopped. "We can't leave tomorrow—I've promised to look at a horse with young Blamire. And anyway, I said we'd stay until Saturday."

"But that's three more days!" Appalled, Louisa gripped his hand. "Robert, I can't tolerate any more of this, really I can't. We *must* leave."

He shook his head. "Not tomorrow—Blamire wants my advice about that hunter, and I promised to look it over."

"Surely," she began, but Robert laid a finger across her lips.

"No, Louisa, I gave my word. Also, I have some business to attend to in Waterford. I *may* be able to clear it up tomorrow, after we've looked at the horse, in which case we'll go home on Friday morning. I'm sorry," he said gently, "but it can't be done before."

Without an argument, without confessing the sordid details of the day, Louisa knew she could not shift that stance of his. She simply nodded and turned away.

"Stay in bed tomorrow," he advised, stroking her hot cheek, "and get over that chill; otherwise you'll be in no fit state to travel anywhere."

. . .

Their train journey down had been via the coastal route, through Wicklow and Wexford, but the change in arrangements meant an inland return, with less spectacular scenery. Louisa stared out of the window, but her eyes registered nothing: in her mind were the cottage in the woods and the child-woman Robert had married. She could hardly bear to look at Georgina: her pale, ash-blond hair was so like her mother's.

The child was unusually quiet, her deep blue eyes solemn and strangely watchful. After a while, Robert drew her onto his knee, holding her close within the crook of his arm.

"I think my little one's tired," he murmured, pushing back a stray lock of silvery hair. His fingers lingered in the loose, soft tresses, and an unexpected dart of pain stabbed at Louisa's vulnerable heart. Wincing, she turned away.

The little girl slid off her father's knee and leaned against her, touching her hand with tender solicitude. Still unable to frame the beginning of Louisa's name, she said: "Have you got a headache, 'Ouisa? Auntie's got a headache, too."

Catching Letty's eye, Louisa let a shamefaced laugh escape. "Yes, dearest, I do have a headache. But don't worry, I expect it will soon be better."

"Well, thank the Lord for that," Robert muttered. "I was beginning to think long faces were the fashion."

Beyond the little town of Kildare they passed the Curragh, its open expanse of racecourse and military training ground barely visible through a drenching blanket of mist and rain. Robert said that was the place he would be spending the summer and pulled a face; his expression was even more wry as they approached the outskirts of Dublin. Peering through the darkness, he pointed out the lights of Islandbridge Barracks.

"And that place needs more than just a new roof: it should be pulled down and completely rebuilt. I've never seen such an old ark—Noah would think twice about billeting his animals there, believe me." Indicating the darkness beyond, he said: "And over there—across the Liffey—is Phoenix Park. Famous for displays and field days throughout the entire British Army!"

"Is it really?" Louisa asked. "Why?"

"My dear," Letty answered dryly, "with more than twenty thousand troops weighing this little island down, the powers that be have to find something for them all to do and somewhere in which to do it. Phoenix Park is traditional, like cricket, garden parties, and afternoon tea."

"And the odd assassination," Robert muttered darkly, not to be outdone. "Although that seems out of fashion at present."

With the merest ghost of a smile at his sardonic humor, Louisa nodded. Minutes later the train was pulling into the station by the Liffey, and Robert steered them through the bustling crush of humanity to where their carriage waited in the forecourt. As they made themselves comfortable, Letty pressed her hand.

"For all Dublin's iniquities," she whispered, "it's good to be back, don't you think?"

Unable to speak, Louisa simply returned the pressure; but as the carriage wound its way through traffic along Victoria Quay, she looked out across a black expanse of water and thought longingly of York.

The carriage turned down Patrick Street, its gray, greasy poverty illumined by the hanging lanterns of dozens of market stalls. Bacon, sheep's heads, and barrels of pickled herring were for sale among racks and rows of secondhand clothes, items which looked as verminous as their vendors. The reek of rotting meat and vegetation mingled with other unsavory odors, permeating the air of the carriage and bringing nausea to Louisa's throat. Fumbling in her reticule, she found a powder puff and held it to her nose, while Letty, hardened by innumerable visits to streets such as these, simply smiled. Georgina coughed and pulled a face; Robert lit a cigar and cursed everything roundly, including their coachman, while above them, somewhere in the darkness, rang the bells of St. Patrick's Cathedral.

Even Walmgate, Louisa thought, with its dirt and grime and miserable little courts, was never like this; never such filth and degradation on the open street; never poverty on such a massive scale. The whole area surrounding both cathedral and castle was the same, Robert said; it made journeys to and from the most prestigious social occasion something of a trial, but it was one of the city's curses which had to be lived with. Had they come by the eastern route to the other station, he added pointedly to Louisa, their carriage drive home would have been both shorter and pleasanter.

In Fitzwilliam Square the little park was shrouded, street lamps lighting drenching veils of mist beneath the trees. With the restored beauty of the Devereaux house facing them, Louisa thought she had never been so thankful for a journey's end. It was not the home she truly longed for, but it was a refuge and a most attractive one. Above the broad central doorway a magnificent fanlight shone a warm welcome across the square, an oil lamp glowed on its ornamental bracket by the steps, and railings curved protectively to either side. Below was a big, modernized kitchen and comfortable servants' quarters, and to the rear of the house a large, secluded garden with mews at the back. It was a dignified town house in an equally dignified Georgian square, which might have been a thousand miles from the obscenities of Patrick Street.

Louisa was grateful for its warmth and comfort and the modern amenities Robert had installed; its elegance and simplicity appealed to her strong aesthetic sense. She wished, however, that she could truly love the house, wished it could feel like home.

Chronically and desperately homesick, shocked to the core of her emotions by the visit to White Leigh, Louisa felt honor-bound to keep the misery to herself. White Leigh she could not, dare not, discuss with Robert, and the other she did not care to: to be homesick seemed so ungrateful.

He saw it, of course. When the feverish chill had subsided and still Louisa's eyes were dull, her smile forced, he tried hard to cheer her, to tell her the ache for home was natural and would pass. Unconcerned at first by her lack of response, Robert retained his good humor, instructed Letty to keep her as busy as possible during the day, and meanwhile accepted a number of invitations to social gatherings due to take place over the Christmas period.

Initially, however, he arranged with his sister to give a small dinner party, largely for Louisa's benefit and as a way of introducing her to people who might prove useful in the future. On the military side, he thought the Kellys would make a good start. Captain Kelly was recently attached to the regiment and also recently married. His wife, the widow of a brother officer, was a very pleasant woman and refreshingly down-to-earth; Robert felt instinctively that she was the one most likely to understand his sister's eccentricities and to offer both Letty and Louisa the benefit of her patronage. She was also the mother of three grown daughters: the youngest might possibly make a dinner partner for Darnley, who, in spite of his good looks, remained obstinately unattached wherever he went.

Darnley Louisa knew and liked, and also Tommy. They would provide the cushion of familiarity. Tommy would no doubt bring his latest inamorata, a pretty young widow from Blackrock; and to please his sister, Robert thought he would invite their neighbor, a young Irish doctor by the name of Molloy. He was well connected, with a string of wealthy patients; but he also worked among the poor, and that was what interested Letty. Robert was not at all sure he approved of her increasing involvement in these charitable works, but with his wit and good humor, Molloy was hard to dislike.

To make up the round dozen, Robert hoped the Loys would accept. Gerald was a distant cousin on the Devereaux side, of an age with himself, and at school they had been quite good friends. Over the years they had dropped out of touch completely, but with Louisa in mind, and needing more than one social string to his bow, Robert had called on his cousin quite soon after his arrival in the summer, and while mentioning Louisa only obliquely, he managed to make the circumstances clear.

For long enough, Robert had been dropping hints in the mess, and with Tommy released from his vow of silence, it seemed most people were now aware of his true situation. Only Darnley had mentioned it directly; and all he had said was "Now I understand." Once, Robert would have scorned even tacit sympathy, but loving Louisa as he did, he wanted it understood that she was his mistress only because she could not be his wife.

Perhaps out of curiosity, the Loys accepted his dinner invitation, and Robert was delighted to find Gerald's wife a devotee of the hunting field. She was surprisingly young, no more than twenty; and built, as Robert laughingly remarked later, like a little whippet; but what she lacked in womanly contours she made up for in personality and daunting self-confidence. If she was aware of the Duncannon household's peculiarities, she gave no sign of it, greeting Letty warmly as her husband's cousin and accepting Louisa as the family friend she purported to be.

Mrs. Kelly's fine hazel eyes were perhaps somewhat guarded, watching all and revealing little. She exchanged a few words with Louisa, as she did with everyone, and while Robert took care to keep Louisa in the conversation, for discretion's sake he let his sister play the protective role. It would not do to reveal all at this early juncture.

He was pleased to notice later that Mrs. Kelly seemed to be taking Louisa under her wing and that she was responding with at least a small degree of warmth. It was very difficult, as Robert himself realized, because so many of the other regimental wives had known the Bainbridges and might, therefore, know more of Louisa's background than would ever be openly admitted here; but he was confident she could carry it off. Her spirit was rebellious enough, he was sure, to tell them all to go to blazes, if she so chose.

As a beginning, the evening was a great success. The meal was excellent, Letty's Chopin faultless, and afterward their guests had been relaxed enough to join in what became an informal musical evening. It was with genuine praise and thanks that the last ones left, and with a warm and very satisfied smile, Robert turned and hugged his ladies.

"Well, a small start, but a good one."

"I'll say so," Letty agreed, squeezing Louisa's arm. "You're on your way, my dear, unless I'm very much mistaken. Didn't you hear Mrs. Kelly? 'I'm at home on Thursdays, Miss Duncannon. I do hope yourself and Miss Elliott will call.' And Amelia Loy asked when we were at home, so that means—'' Letty broke off suddenly, smiting her forehead with a mock groan of despair. ''Oh, what am I saying? I hate *at homes*— I loathe all that effort of making conversation about nothing! I must be mad, Louisa!'' But she hugged her again and kissed her brother's cheek.

''I think Louisa struck exactly the right note, don't you? Quiet, modest, pleasant—they liked her, Robert, didn't they?'' She smiled fondly, as at a well-behaved child.

''They did indeed,'' he agreed, kissing Louisa's cheek.

He did wish, however, that she could have looked a little more pleased.

SIX

*T*he weeks wore on toward Christmas, and those stark impressions of White Leigh began to fade. Although her image of Charlotte was still as clear as ever, refreshed by Georgina's bright hair and quick, lithe movements, Louisa found she could banish that picture for lengthy periods as long as she kept busy. At first, morning lessons with Robert's daughter had been a trial, made more difficult by the child's acute sensitivity to every mood; it had taken a supreme mental effort to overcome those negative emotions, but overcome them she had, and she and Georgina at least were on a happier footing.

Letty thought it wise not to talk about White Leigh and, practical as ever, tried to involve Louisa in her own work. Two afternoons a week she went with a group of women into the slum area surrounding Patrick Street; they ran a soup kitchen for the poor and needy, and Letty supervised, under Dr. Molloy's direction, a small dispensary. With gallows humor, she said it was good for the soul: one afternoon in those surroundings was guaranteed to cure self-pity, even the most deep-seated variety. Louisa was bound to agree, but, while she counted her blessings in abundance, she found those horrendous images of poverty and disease another source of fear and depression.

It was endless, hopeless, like bailing sewage from the Liffey, as she once remarked bitterly to Letty, who laughed; and the native Irish mostly terrified her. She had never seen such wretchedness: beggars, maimed and ugly, lay in wait on every corner, ready with a gap-toothed grin or vicious, well-aimed spittle; and gangs armed and dangerous, roamed the poorest quarters. Even Moira, giving up free time to accompany her mistress like a bodyguard, recalled Walmgate in terms of rosy endearment. But Letty accepted it all with a shrug and a smile. This was Ireland, she said, where poverty was endemic and blood feuds a way of life; one simply did what one could. Louisa thought her a saint and said so; regrettably, she did not think herself the stuff of which saints were made, hating the smell of the clothes she kept for such visits and hating even more the carbolic baths they were forced to take afterward. She never felt clean, was always afraid, as she climbed into bed each night, of something lingering. Letty said she would grow used to it; Louisa knew she never would. Robert, meanwhile, complained of what he called the "eau de carbolic" and bought her bottles of expensive French perfume to disguise the smell.

Beset by the unchanging routines of the regiment, Robert had problems of his own, largely concerned with his men's welfare. Conditions at the barracks were hardly any better, he said, than the stews of Patrick Street, and in the midst of a running battle with the military authorities, he had little inclination to listen to similar complaints during his time off. Quite simply, he was happy to have Louisa under his own roof, and while they were together he wanted all unpleasantness shut out. She did her best to comply, but suppressed as it was, her homesickness increased. She missed York and its comfortable familiarity like an amputated limb; and Dublin, full of strangers only Robert knew, was no substitute.

The painful contrast between the Patrick Street afternoons and the false, forced, cozily insulated at homes, made everything worse. The regimental wives were rank-conscious to a point Letty found laughable; their unwritten codes hard to follow, their snobbery unbearable. It soon became clear that Mrs. Kelly was by far the kindest of her peers, and not even her attempts to smooth a way for Louisa would ensure acceptance in that very tight clique. Letty's reciprocal afternoons were attended only by that august lady and her daughter, by Tommy's empty-headed little widow and a very junior wife who seemed to find herself there by mistake. Amelia Loy called from politeness and invited them back as a matter of form; but while Letty managed to listen intelligently to the society gossip, Louisa was quite beyond her depth. She understood little of hunting's finer points and less about the Irish gentry. They were foreigners to her, every one of them, full of prurient, un-English curiosity about each other and open contempt for their cousins who ruled from across the water. Louisa found it shocking. What they thought about her, she had no idea. Probably not very much, she told herself sternly: most of the time, by the women at least, her presence was ignored.

Gradually her cheerfulness and natural resilience wore thin; what she had summoned quite easily in August became by December an increasingly threadbare mantle she donned every evening as she changed for dinner. And, with masculine myopia, Robert seemed not to notice.

He was very busy up to Christmas, and although when he was at home he always slept with her, they did not often make love. This was something of a relief to Louisa, whose fatigue seemed unconquerable, despite the number of hours she slept. She imagined, on the occasions when he kissed her tenderly and then turned away, that he was as tired as she was herself. It was a surprise, therefore, that he pressed his attention one night and then lost his temper at her halfhearted acquiescence. After some harsh words, in which oaths and York and homesickness were liberally mingled, he left to sleep in his own room.

She was too miserable to weep and too aware of his absence to relax. Most of the night she dozed and dreamed, and the dreams were nightmare distortions of her everyday life: crippled beggars leering and touching; red, laughing military faces; a sneering Irish voice saying over and over, "The goods are bought and paid for—bought and paid for—bought and paid for . . . ," and a hand dragging her backward, back to some nameless terror . . .

She woke in tears, with Robert leaning across the bed and shaking her. "Come on, now, wake up, it's only a dream." It was dark, but he was fully dressed; she could feel the prickly serge of his working dress against her face as he held her close. "I didn't mean to disturb you. I crept in looking for my watch chain. Then you were crying and shouting," he said, sounding amused. "I thought you'd wake the whole house."

"I'm sorry," she whispered against his shoulder.

"There's no need—you couldn't help it."

"I mean about last night."

There was a momentary tension in the hands that held her. "Ah, yes. Well, so am I. I was more tired than I realized," he admitted with a sigh, "which is probably why I lost my temper. However, I didn't sleep very well."

"Nor did I," Louisa murmured. Reaching up, she touched his face, feeling its freshly shaved smoothness beneath her fingers. "I do love you, Robert, really I do."

A muscle in his jaw tightened. With a short little laugh, he said: "Can I have that in writing, do you think?"

"Oh, Robert, *don't*. I wish I could explain—I don't understand it myself—I—" she broke off, unable to continue.

For a second his fingers bit deep into her shoulder; she heard his rather tremulous indrawn breath and its sudden release. "Darling, I have to go. I wish I could stay, but Harris is waiting. We'll have to talk later."

With a brief kiss he released her, and Louisa leaned back against the pillows, watching him search for the missing watch chain among the items on her bedside table. There won't be time, she thought with sick frustration; there never is. And in a house full of people, no privacy either.

At lunchtime, while she was rinsing hands and face of chalk dust from the schoolroom, Moira came into her room with the noon post. "A nice fat letter from Mr. Edward, ma'am."

With a cold murmur of thanks, Louisa took the envelope. "You know, Moira, it's very irritating to be told who my correspondent is before I've had a chance to open the envelope myself. I wish you wouldn't do it."

"Oh, sorry, ma'am. It was only that I thought it would cheer you . . ."

Awaiting a reply while Louisa slit the envelope with a slim ivory paper knife, she earned herself a chillier dismissal. In high dudgeon she took herself off, closing the door behind her with rather too much force.

Ignoring the girl, Louisa withdrew the pages of the letter and sat down, instantly warmed by the sight of that familiar writing and comforted by the amount.

"My Dear Louisa," she read, "it was good to have your long letter after weeks without news. The regular notes addressed to your mother assured me you were in reasonable health, but I was beginning to fear Christmas would come and go without a personal word for me.

"Having read your dozen pages several times, I do understand why you felt unable to write before and am most sincerely sorry for all the drama and anxiety you have suffered of late. It is a difficult situation and will no doubt continue to be so; but, my dear one, at the risk of sounding hard and unfeeling, may I say that you should have expected it. Well, something like it, anyway.

"As to that poor young woman, his wife—well, dearest, what can I say? That others fare worse? In his way, I'm sure the captain does his best, and after all, she is not locked away in some lunatic asylum and conveniently forgotten.

"Regarding the financial side, I don't know his income, and nor do you. Perhaps you might ask? An indelicate subject for you, I know, but rather that embarrassment than all this worry, which might well be needless.

"Other than that, I cannot advise you. If you are indeed as unhappy as your letter suggests—and only you know the truth of that—then perhaps the time has come to consider your choices. You don't *have to stay,* you know. Home is still here, and we all miss you very much——"

Below that long line, the letter continued in darker ink, a résumé of work and home in Edward's usual flowing, graphic style. She could see the fussiness of his customers as he described them, hear her mother's voice and Bessie's as he related comments and occurrences; with a sigh she turned back to the beginning and read the first two pages again.

Warmth leapt again in her breast at the words "my dear one" and "dearest," coupled with anger at his ruthless fairness to all concerned, particularly Robert. And the phrase "we all miss you very much" reduced her to such fury that she crumpled the letter and let it fall. A hot storm of self-pity swept through her, and for several minutes, not knowing the number of pages discarded, the torment her letter and its reply had caused him, she raged against Edward, demanding of herself why he could not say "*I* miss you—*I* need you—*I* want you to come home."

She did not know, for Edward could not say, that his replies to her letters were tailored for the benefit of eyes other than hers, that he had no way of knowing whether her letters were read by Robert; and his inclusion of two small endearments was simply to soften the apparent harshness of his comments.

The sound of the gong jerked Louisa to her feet, and she hurried down to luncheon; immediately afterward, it being a Patrick Street afternoon, she returned to change into one of the old, plain skirts she kept for such visits. Like everything else, it was sponged and aired regularly, but the smell lingered, taking her mind off everything but the dread of what was to come.

Robert had had a particularly frustrating morning. It was pouring with rain, the drill ground was awash, and none of the people he intended to see were available. After an hour spent kicking his heels in the adjutant's office, a miserable lunch in the mess broke what remained of his patience; consigning all to perdition, he shouted for Harris and told him they were going home.

Thoughts of dry clothes and a warm fire consoled him throughout that wet, two-mile ride from Islandbridge to Fitzwilliam Square. He would have a good hot bath, followed by tea in the study with Louisa; just the two of them. They would talk things out, which was essential, and afterward he would take her out to dinner, again just the two of them, and after that . . .

As Harris took his cloak in the hall, Robert told him to get to the kitchen for a hot drink. "You can collect my things later," he said as he mounted the stairs. "Find some dry clothes yourself, first."

Shaking his head at that abrupt change of mood, Harris almost smiled. Filthy temper first thing, he thought, getting worse by the hour; then suddenly all sweetness and light. It was beyond his understanding, and he did not dwell on the matter; in the kitchen, however, Moira gave him cause to ponder afresh. Elbows on table, nursing a pot of tea, she was deep in conversation with the cook. At sight of Harris she set the tea down and adjusted herself to a more ladylike pose, while cook automatically reached another pot from the dresser.

He stood by the fire, warming himself, stealing surreptitious glances at the girl. Unused to the company of women, he felt awkward in this household of largely female servants, and although he liked Moira Hanrahan, he was never quite sure how to show it. She had the kind of face he wanted to look at all the time, because the expression was always changing, never the same for two minutes together. She could be mad, sad, glad, according to what she was saying, and it fascinated him, who had spent a lifetime keeping all feelings strictly to himself. Even in a city of pretty girls, she was pretty; and he liked her smile, too, which was never cruel, even when she teased him, which was often. At the moment, however, she was too put out even to tease.

"So after that, didn't I change my mind, and I thought—why should I go on an afternoon like this, with it raining cats and dogs? If they want to go out and catch their deaths and worse down Patrick Street, well, fine. But I don't have to—it *is* my afternoon off, after all."

Sympathizing, cook said she would not give up her time off for anything at all, and certainly not to serve pigs' trotters and cabbage soup to those dregs from the Liberties.

"Something upset you?" Harris asked gruffly as cook disappeared into the pantry.

"Not upset me," Moira said with a toss of her head; "made me mad. Tore me off a strip, she did, just because I gave her a letter and told her who it was from. She's such an old misery these days, and no mistake. Sure, if I'd known that, I'd have stayed at home. And there's me," she added crossly, "thinking the letter'd cheer her up."

Feeling sorry for the girl, Harris pondered; as a rule, he never commented on his master's moods, but after all, this was not the regiment, and tomorrow was Christmas Eve. A moment later, he said sympathetically: "He's been the same—like a bear with a sore head this morning. Probably had a bit of a row last night. They'll be right as rain tomorrow, just you wait and see."

Arriving home at five, the two women deposited umbrellas and galoshes in the hall, while McMahon removed their cloaks as though with tongs and took them away to some secret storage place. As always, his expression of severe distaste brought a rueful smile to Letty's face.

"And now the bath," she said as they mounted the stairs. "I can't wait—my head itches. I envy you your short crop, Louisa, believe me, I do!"

"Short hair wouldn't suit you, Letty," Louisa said with a tired grin.

"No, but it must be so much easier to wash!" Scratching comically, she disappeared into her room.

In the bathroom she shared with Robert, Louisa stripped off every item of clothing into a wicker basket and, pouring carbolic solution into the bath, stepped in for a quick but thorough wash. Draining the water, she ran more, this time to soak with scented bath salts and a bar of expensive soap.

With her hair washed twice, Louisa wrapped herself in her robe and her hair in a towel and with a contented sigh went through into the bedroom, where she knew a tray of tea and biscuits would be waiting.

Robert was also waiting. Fully dressed, with a half-smoked cigar, he lay at ease on Louisa's bed, viewing her unsmilingly beneath half-closed lids. On the table beside him, the table where he had searched for his watch chain early that morning, were the smoothed-out pages of Edward's letter.

"So," he remarked tersely, "have you considered your choices, *my dear one?* Have you decided whether to stay or go?"

Half an hour later they were still locked in heated argument, accusing each other of secrecy, defending themselves, still circling the points at issue. Louisa's hair was dry, but she was not dressed, and the tea stood untouched on the tray.

"I'll tell you again," Robert said angrily, "that I do not read your personal mail. I know where your letters are—in that drawer in the dressing table—and I haven't the slightest desire to read their contents. I would not have read this, except that I wondered what it was, lying crumpled beneath the chair. I'd scanned the first page before I realized."

"And so you read the rest," she said with virtuous contempt.

"Yes, I damn well did, hoping to discover what he was talking about. You still haven't explained why *my* personal affairs should be of interest to *him,* and I think I've every right to demand an explanation."

Wearily Louisa acknowledged the truth of that; she sat down, watching his angry pacing, and finally begged him to be still. "I had a lot on my mind," she said as he leaned against the mantelpiece, "and I wish you could appreciate that. Things happened at White Leigh—things I didn't want to tell you about—didn't want to worry you with. I couldn't discuss them with anyone here, nor did I want to worry them at home. But it got worse, Robert, so bad, I couldn't think clearly anymore. You thought I was just homesick, but it was more than that, and I needed *advice.* So, eventually, I wrote to Edward. Perhaps it was the wrong thing to do," she acknowledged bitterly, "but as you can see from his letter, he *is* fair—scrupulously so—and doesn't leap to stupid conclusions."

"Tell me what happened at White Leigh," he demanded, ignoring the gauntlet of her last comment; and as he listened to the carefully restrained account of Anne Duncannon's self-righteous attack, his mind leapt ahead, deducing, before Louisa said so, that she had been goaded into visiting Charlotte. With a single, half-smothered oath, he swung away to the window, looking out into darkness.

With many halts and hesitations, Louisa finished the tale; she could see Robert's face reflected in the glass, and it mirrored her own wretchedness. "I'm sorry," she said, meaning it. "I shouldn't have gone. I gave your sister-in-law her victory, didn't I?"

"You did indeed," he murmured. "But at least you know I spoke the truth." Making for the door, he said: "I think I'd better leave you to dress—it's almost time for dinner. Oh, and by the way," he added, without looking at her, "I'd like you to know that this house was not renovated purely for your benefit, nor is it run solely for you. I needed somewhere to live, other than White Leigh, and it was time I provided a home for my daughter."

Robert said, after dinner, that he had work to do in his study. Pleading a headache, Louisa bade Letty an early goodnight and went to her room, mortified by self-accusation and the hair shirt of failure. With the specter of that afternoon's experiences before her, she refused to lapse into self-pity and instead picked up Edward's letter, reading the first two pages through again.

If you are indeed as unhappy as your letter suggests—was she?—*then perhaps the time has come to consider your choices. You don't have to stay.* Perhaps not. But had she come too far?

In the cooler light of detachment, it seemed to Louisa that she had expected too much; or, rather, not knowing the waters into which she plunged, had foreseen different dangers. Dreading untold depths, she had found the pain of sharp rocks in the shallows and was now caught, wondering which way to turn. Was it easier to plunge on into deeper water and trust that she could swim or to suffer the greater pain of returning to a safe and familiar shore?

Only you know the truth of that, Edward said.

But I'm still not sure, she silently answered. Smoothing the letter, folding it, she returned it to the envelope. With her anger gone, she stood by the dressing table, looking into the drawer where her other letters lay, and was suddenly thankful for their lack of endearment. Edward was Edward: calm, detached, and fastidiously fair; not understanding that, Robert would always be jealous.

Sighing, she closed the drawer, and loneliness descended like a leaden weight. Christmas, she thought, and sighed again; it was too late to make decisions, and she was far too tired. On a resolution to be bright and cheerful over the festive season, she rang the bell for Moira; afterward, she thought, she would talk to Robert calmly, tell him how she felt, and between them they would decide whether she should return to York.

Moira came and helped her to undress. Glad of her company, Louisa chatted lightly about household arrangements and Georgina's presents; tomorrow they would be erecting the tree in the hall; the girl's face, as she left, was smiling again.

It was a little after ten, still early according to the hours Robert kept. Glancing at the clock, wondering unhappily whether he would keep to his own room, she settled herself before the fire to read. Half an hour later, resigned to loneliness and convinced the New Year would see her in York once more, Louisa retired to bed.

It was past midnight when he came to her, his body chilled and shivering, and with an outdoor dampness about his face and hair.

"Where have you been?" she whispered, while icy hands sought the warmth of her skin.

"Out—walking. I needed some air, and Harris was still up, so we went out. God, but I'm cold!" he said shakily, clasping her close along the length of him. Thighs and buttocks were frozen, and instinctively she wrapped herself around him, chafing tension from his back, warming face and ears with kisses. As heat blossomed between them, the shivering ceased, became the frisson of fettered passion; and lips which had been like ice were suddenly hot and questing.

Aroused, tense, she responded avidly, heart and mind racing, blood tingling like needles in her veins; she loved him, wanted him, could never live without him; this glory, this delight, this song in head and heart and womb was his, only his, this fusion the only thing worth living for, dying for, suffering for . . .

Too late did she recall what should never have been forgotten, too late whisper caution to one whose curbs were long disused . . .

SEVEN

fterward, lighting candle and cigar from a single match, Robert looked down at her and smiled. "It should always be like that," he whispered, "with nothing between us—nothing at all."

"Did you know?" she asked, thinking of the little device resting unused in her bedside drawer.

The picture of innocence, he shook his head. "Know what?" he asked, his hand caressing the slight roundness of her stomach. "I meant there should be no more secrets, that's all." But with what seemed to Louisa a most remarkable tenderness, he bent and kissed the area of her womb.

"Whatever either of us meant," he whispered reverently, "that was the best—the very, very best."

For a while, whenever Louisa thought about it, she was anxious; but with their relationship restored to its former ardent nature, it passed, and for the first time since her arrival she felt happy. Christmas was delightful, with toys for Georgina and silly games; they sang carols at the piano, ate too much, drank too much, and retired to bed early, all quite exhausted. Boxing Day was the servant's party. Cook had prepared a hot lunch and cold buffet supper for the family, and the party began unofficially sometime in the afternoon. By teatime the abstemious Harris had been persuaded to take a drink; by evening his inhibitions had fled. When Robert and Louisa went down in answer to McMahon's suspiciously serious invitation, Harris had the floor with one of the kitchen girls, while the coachman was seated in a corner, fiddling a foot-tapping Irish reel. Despite his height and military stiffness, Robert's servant was not making such a fool of himself, and the laughter and hand-clapping were that of encouragement, not mockery. Cheering him on, Moira grabbed his hand and joined in, steering him adroitly, as the music stopped, beneath a judiciously placed sprig of mistletoe. To cheers and applause, he bent his head and very graciously kissed the girl, then, catching his master's eye, blushed furiously and came to attention. Amidst gales of laughter, Robert simply instructed him to carry on.

It was honest, enjoyable fun, something Louisa understood and, having become well acquainted with all the servants, something she could enter into without fear of embarrassment. She began to hope that perhaps she might also feel at home with Robert's friends once she knew them better; but apart from Tommy and Darnley, the old faithfuls, that feeling resolutely eluded her.

They dined out a good deal during the twelve days of Christmas and attended a couple of informal subscription dances, but despite Letty's continuing support as ostensible friend and chaperon, there were undercurrents of hostility wherever they went. As though threatened by Louisa, the regimental wives were the worst, affecting not to notice her presence and, in Letty's company particularly, treating her like a paid companion. Although it was mildly offensive, that attitude was something she had grown used to over the years; in fact, she would have been happy to keep up the pretense as a blind to her real position, but Robert would not have it. He unfailingly took her arm, kept her beside him, drew her into conversations where she would rather have kept silent, and in dozens of small ways advertised his interest.

He seemed not to notice the snubs of his colleagues' wives, nor the lingering, sometimes insolent stares of the men. Louisa did, and it was a subtle form of torture to her; wanting to please him, however, she swallowed the instinct to flee and, summoning all her pride, glared challengingly back. That fighting instinct aroused Robert's admiration, and he encouraged it, coaching her in the art of small talk, the double-edged reply. "It's time you learned the art of self-defense," he told her, "because you're bright enough to slaughter the lot of them in a verbal fencing match." Louisa was not so sure, but she practiced sharpening her wits, wore the shoulder-revealing gowns he liked, even used a little cosmetic help to enhance her best features, and learned to smile, smile, smile, whatever the odds.

It was at the beginning of February, as Dublin's social season was flowering with receptions and levees at the castle, that Louisa's anxious and only half-acknowledged suspicions began to give way to chilling certainty. A visit to Patrick Street made her unexpectedly ill, the reek of brandy and port after dinner nauseated her, and breakfast was a meal she could no longer face. Missing her second monthly period, she sought a discreet appointment with the apparently unshockable Dr. Molloy.

With a professional air of detachment he asked the relevant questions, and on the point of ringing for his nurse he paused; normally, he said, he asked the nurse to be present while he examined his lady patients;

but in the interests of complete discretion, Miss Elliott might prefer
otherwise? It was something she had not envisaged, having to undress
for a man she knew better socially than medically, and she blushed
furiously as she asked whether an examination was absolutely necessary.

"If it's a thorough diagnosis you are wanting," he said gently, "then
yes, I'm afraid it is. This is not a social call—in this room we are no
more and no less than a doctor and his patient," he reminded her gravely;
then, with a merry chuckle at her expression, added: "You know, we've
seen so much together in the stews of Patrick Street, I never expected
you to be this squeamish."

That made her laugh; nevertheless, she was severely embarrassed lying
on the couch in her shift, even more so as he touched her breasts with
cold fingers and even colder detachment. With face and throat on fire,
Louisa studied rococo plaster cherubs on the ceiling, only afterward
thinking how appropriate they were, while those experienced fingers
probed further.

Dressed again, she faced him with something approaching composure,
convinced that he was about to dismiss her worst fears and say it was
a straightforward malfunction of the normal cycle. Instead, he looked
at her, hemmed and hawed for a moment, chewed his pencil, and
displayed all the symptoms of a man with awkward and possibly unwelcome news to impart.

"You're a young woman," he said at last, "in the very best of health,
I'm delighted to say—so there's nothing to be worrying about in that
way. It's a good, strong frame you have, too, so bearing children should
not be difficult at all . . ."

"It's definite, then?" Louisa whispered. "I am carrying a child?"

"Well, now, it's a little early to be absolutely sure—ideally, I should
see you again in another month to six weeks—but yes, I'd say so. You
have all the signs and symptoms."

To Louisa, those words were like the slamming of a door, a door
which had been propped carefully open to admit light and air and a
means of escape. Now there was no way out, no retreat; she was committed, irrevocably and forever. Only in that moment did she realize
how uncommitted she had been before, how much she had clung to
the idea that she could always go home if she wanted to. Now there
could be no return, not even for a visit.

Numbed by the enormity of just that one idea, Louisa barely took
in the doctor's brisk advice to go home and rest for a while. She struggled
to speak, found herself mumbling inane, automatic words of thanks—
for what?—as he came around the desk.

"It's a shock to you, I can see that; but sure, it's not the end of the world, and you'll not be abandoned, that I do know." A moment later, assisting her to her feet, he said, "You have a good friend in Letty Duncannon—don't forget that, now. And try not to worry yourself. In a few months' time you'll be the mother of a fine, healthy baby—not like those poor souls in the Liberties."

The statement was true enough, but small consolation, and Louisa resented that call to count her blessings. Affecting a composure she was far from feeling, she straightened her bonnet, pulled on her gloves, and bade the young doctor a dry good morning.

She came down into a large hall which was almost the twin of the Devereaux house's and stepped out into a sly breeze and pale, tremulous sunshine. It was an indecisive day, with a sky of washed-out blue and clouds which might or might not hold rain; the trees in the square seemed poised between winter and spring, and the patches of white beneath might easily have been snow. Standing there, not wanting to return to the house across the way, yet having nowhere else to go, Louisa felt everything echoed in herself. Peculiarly aware of her body inside its impeccably tailored clothes, it was as though her spirit had stepped slightly sideways and was looking down with scarcely veiled disgust at changes which were going on without permission.

Taking the far side of the square, she walked toward Stephen's Green, passing seven uniformed nannies, all with perambulators, on the way. There were more in the park, some with sturdy little children playing ball. Well-fed, well-dressed, their excited little voices reminded her of Georgina in the Museum Gardens just over a year ago. Meeting Robert's child for the first time, she had had her moments of envy, moments of longing for children of her own, but those longings went with marriage and security and a home of her own, not this state of limbo where she wore a different mask for every occasion. After months of playacting, months of not really being herself, not even with Robert, Louisa knew she was in danger of losing sight of the person she had been. Even as a governess, at the beck and call of other people's children, she had been used to having time to herself, time to read, time to be quiet, time to be at peace with the solitary soul within. In a strange land, among strange people with even stranger customs, she felt constantly bombarded, her very soul thrown out of kilter in its efforts to absorb and understand.

With a fervor which spread like pain, she longed once more for home and peace and time to think and knew she should have gone before Christmas, not waited to give it one more chance. Too late now! logic said with callous satisfaction; and a moment later she was wondering what her mother would say, wincing painfully at thoughts of Edward.

"You told me," she whispered aloud, her eyes tight shut against the children playing on the green; "but I didn't believe you."

Opening her eyes, she saw the vast expanse of parkland, groups of people in twos and threes, soldiers with swagger sticks, riders in the distance, and was sure they were friendly and happy and unconcerned. In the void which she inhabited, only she was alone and vulnerable, an unmarried woman with the seed of life within her, a marked woman, an outcast.

EIGHT

Needing time to adjust, Louisa said nothing. She told herself it was because her pregnancy could not be confirmed for another month, whereas in reality she was concerned as to Robert's reaction. The possibility of children had never been seriously discussed, and the only time she had tentatively mentioned it, he had airily dismissed her fears with an assurance that of course he would look after her.

While not doubting that, she was equally sure children were not in his scheme of things; even Georgina's requirements were incidental, despite his virtuous claim to have thought of her when renovating the house. Toward Louisa, Robert was loving, generous, and very possessive; he wanted her to be there for him, ready to fall in with his plans, his friends, his needs; how he would react to a child's demands upon her time and affection, Louisa dreaded to think.

Despite that constant anxiety, after the early nausea attacks, physically she began to feel remarkably well; a shade delicate first thing, but that was easily hidden. At Robert's insistence, after Christmas she had dropped one afternoon's work with Letty, which made life much easier on many fronts; it would have been impossible to keep up the social whirl of the season otherwise. Sometimes catching inquiring looks from Letty, she often wondered whether that very shrewd lady suspected her condition; obviously, Robert did not. He remarked one day that she was putting on weight; another that she was growing more and more beautiful. Glancing in the mirror, Louisa was bound to agree that she had never looked better: her eyes were clear, her skin glowed, and her hair was thicker and glossier than ever.

Lies, all lies, she thought, turning away; just like the bland little notes written every week to her mother and Edward.

In the second week of March she again visited Dr. Molloy. The original diagnosis was confirmed, as she had known it would be, the birth projected for the end of September. Feeling more than ever the exile, she walked out into the square, and through the railings were the nodding heads of early daffodils, reminding her unbearably of York. On the ramparts facing the station, just coming into bloom, would be mass upon mass of them, waving in the wind, ready to welcome the weary traveler, to greet the returning native home.

She stood for a moment, staring, letting the two pictures merge and blend; and then she shook her head and turned away, going back to the house for tea.

Considering ways and means of breaking the news to Robert, she felt it would be better to wait until after the seventeenth, when the season was officially over. Her condition was borne forcibly upon her during the final fitting of her gown for the St. Patrick's Day Ball; in only two weeks her waist measurement had spread more than an inch, and no amount of heaving at stays and laces would reduce it. The seamstress gave her some very hard looks, muttered ominously about the seams, and proceeded to let them out. She was there all afternoon, but no one was completely satisfied with the result. Trying the gown again in the privacy of her own room, Louisa realized that her bosom had deepened considerably, and tight lacing, coupled with the gown's restrictions, thrust her breasts upward into quite immodest display.

Chuckling appreciatively, Robert made several lascivious comments when he saw her.

"I can't go looking like this!" she cried, trying shawls, stoles, scraps of lace to hide what resolutely refused to be hidden.

"Nonsense," he said firmly. "You look wonderful—stunning, in fact. I've seen dowagers displaying more than that, and an acre of wrinkles besides." Turning her around to face him, he smiled and kissed her gently. "You're the most desirable woman I ever saw," he whispered, his blue eyes twinkling in the lamplight, "and to tell the truth, I'd as soon stay at home and make love to you as fight my way through that thrash at the castle tonight." He kissed her again, passionately, his hand cupping and caressing the firm white rise of her breasts.

With an effort, she pulled away from him and on a nervous laugh sent him out while she prepared herself for the evening ahead. As he closed the door, she sank down onto the bed. It was disconcerting to realize that, in spite of everything, she wanted him more than ever, as though her recalcitrant body was determined to have its own way, no matter what her mind was thinking.

Later, as she came down into the hall, Letty's eyebrows arched in surprise.

"Yes, I know," Louisa said uncomfortably. "That dratted woman made it far too tight, but," she sighed, "it was too late to do much about it."

"It's a lovely gown," Letty said, fingering the pale apricot silk, "and will stand out beautifully amongst all the green that's bound to be there tonight."

From a silver tray held by an impressive McMahon, Robert took little sprigs of shamrock. He pinned Letty's to the left shoulder of her ame-thyst-colored gown, his own to his lapel, and with a rueful grin surveyed Louisa's cleavage. "There's not a lot to pin this to, now is there? Here," he said, handing over the little bunch of tiny green leaves. "Stick it down the front of your gown—it'll give a bit of cover."

Louisa was still blushing in the carriage. She was reminded of the ball at the Assembly Rooms in York, but her chronic self-consciousness this evening was caused by so much more than a simple fear of strangers. Across the square, Dr. Molloy was waiting, having arranged to share their carriage as a matter of practical convenience. He bade everyone a happy good evening, but Louisa could not meet his eyes. Glad of the shadows within, she looked out of the window and let the others talk.

They passed the smart, well-lit thoroughfare of Grafton Street, with its exclusive little shops and tearooms, but beyond that they were soon in the dark, ill-swept area of the slums. Robert lit a cigar as the carriage slowed in a line of others, all making for the castle; the aromatic scent of tobacco went some way toward dispelling other unsavory odors. Hav-ing spent time amid that poverty, Louisa was almost immune to the sight and sound and smell of it, but she was surprised, nevertheless, to see the excited, jostling crowd outside the castle gates.

It was a cold night with a chill wind blowing, and many of those who waited to see the quality in all their finery were barefoot and dressed in tatters. There were seditious comments and ribald catcalling from both men and women, but there were unexpected cheers, too; far more cheers, Louisa felt, than anyone deserved.

"Jaysus," Molloy muttered as he helped Letty to alight in the cobbled castle yard, "what have they got to cheer about?"

It seemed they were all, except Robert, somewhat deflated by that delighted, laughing crowd.

Despite being described as a Grand Ball, despite the long lines of liveried footmen in silver and light blue, despite the introduction to Lord and Lady Cadogan, viceroy and vicereine of Ireland, the evening was a thrash, as Robert described it, of over seven hundred guests. Priceless diamonds winked and glittered like Christmas decorations; waltz music played endlessly to a heedless throng; voices brayed, every accent Ireland and England could produce shouted to be heard; cerise and pink and orange clashed with forty shades of emerald green, while champagne was quaffed like porter, and drunken fathers let daughters get away with murder in the last-minute race for a husband.

Her plunging neckline forgotten in that welter of very mixed tastes, Louisa danced and supped and talked with the best. The Loys joined them, and it was while they were all grouped together around their small and much-envied table that she noticed an amused smile suddenly freeze on Robert's face. He rose to his feet and, with stiff, unsmiling formality, bowed to an elderly couple who seemed anxious not to acknowledge him.

Interrupting glances of severe embarrassment and theatrical dismay from Letty and Gerald, Louisa asked who they were, but neither seemed disposed to answer.

"No one of any consequence," Robert said, taking her arm. "Come on, darling; this is our dance, I believe."

As he guided her through the crush to the floor, his eyes still followed that pair of neatly coiffed gray heads. The woman, Louisa noticed, was wearing a set of diamonds which put Lady Cadogan in the shade, and a fashionable gown of cerise and fuchsia satin which killed her complexion. Those hard, proud eyes, meeting Robert's as they brushed past, looked abruptly away.

"Who *was* that?" she asked as he led her into the waltz.

"Relatives of mine," he answered tersely, "by marriage."

"Anne's?"

"No, Charlotte's."

Swallowing an exclamation, Louisa danced on automatically, but her heart was pounding in consternation. "Did you *want* them to see us together?"

"Yes."

"Why?"

"Because I wanted them to know I've survived."

"But do they know about Charlotte?" she asked above the surge of the music.

"Of course they do," he replied, swinging into the turn. "Whatever they want to know, they're rich enough to find out."

Still a little shocked by that encounter, on the way back to their table after the waltz they bumped into Prince Francis fighting his way onto the floor with a pretty, flirtatious young thing in sugar-pink lace. He laughed as he saw Robert and made some comment about the impossible crowd; as his eyes flickered over Louisa's generous form, Robert begged leave to introduce her. It was graciously granted, but as she dropped a low curtsy, Louisa recalled her plunging neckline, blushing furiously as she regained her full height and saw the merry, appreciative twinkle in his eye.

"Oh, this *damned* dress," she muttered querulously under her breath; but, with the departure of the young couple, Robert was quietly laughing.

"Well, darling, that's one up to you—not everybody gets an introduction to the chief guest of honor!"

Letty was impressed, and Amelia Loy openly envious. Reminding Robert of the dance he had promised, she also begged him to engineer an introduction. Although Robert winked as he went off with her, Louisa was quite irrationally jealous. For Robert's sake she wished one could like his cousin's wife, but it was impossible. She was such a disconcerting mix of tomboy, flirt, and daunting duchess that Louisa was never quite sure of her intentions, nor how to react; but as Letty quietly pointed out, with her estates and huge inheritance expected shortly, Amelia Loy could be as haughty and capricious as she chose.

With his fine features and limited assets, Louisa wondered whether Gerald had married from love or a strong sense of self-preservation. In some kind of export business, Robert's cousin had the family's taste for country pursuits and very good living, without, apparently, the necessary means to indulge it. But despite the rather limited common ground of immediate family, Gerald had always been pleasantly attentive toward her, and Louisa quite liked him. He reminded her of Edward with his fair coloring and gray eyes, and without any real ground for support, she attributed to him the same gentle manners. This evening, however, Gerald having imbibed rather more than was conducive to either good manners or polite conversation, she thought those perpetually amused gray eyes had a tendency to leer, and with the departure of Letty with Tommy Fitzsimmons, his anecdotes became uncomfortably risqué.

Dismayed by an increasingly lurid commentary on several eminent guests, Louisa searched anxiously for signs of rescue. It seemed Robert was gone an inordinate length of time; at least three dances had passed since his departure with Gerald's wife. Suddenly she spotted Letty and Tommy, both towering over the crowd and coming their way.

"Oh, good," Gerald exclaimed, pulling Louisa to her feet. "They're coming to mind the table for a while. Come on, my beauty—let's take our turn while we have the chance."

Swallowed by the mass of dancers, Louisa could hardly protest before he whisked her away in a grip more enthusiastic than polite. Holding her firm, and far too close, Gerald pressed his cheek to hers and steered her expertly through the crush. Given a clear floor he must have been an excellent dancer, but breast to breast and thigh to thigh, Louisa was too disturbed to follow well. She stepped twice on his toes, then half-stumbled; without faltering he lifted her bodily into the turn, surprising her by his strength, for he was hardly taller than herself and not heavily built.

At the end of the piece, before the orchestra could strike up again, Louisa pleaded heat and fatigue and suggested a return to their table. Gerald smiled, grabbed two glasses from the tray of a passing footman, and proceeded through the nearest double doors into a carpeted but ill-lit corridor. Thankfully Louisa noticed many people had taken a similar opportunity for a cooler, quieter respite from the noise.

Somewhat guardedly, she accepted the glass of Champagne and tried not to shiver. For a few minutes they walked up and down, Louisa keeping a decent distance between them; but as she turned, with the tactful suggestion of another dance on her lips, Gerald grabbed her and, pulling her into a darkened alcove, pressed his mouth avidly to hers. Even as she pushed and protested, his fingers were at her breast.

"I'd like to strip you naked," he whispered hotly against her ear, while one arm held her like a vice and a growing hardness pressed into her groin. "I'd like to take you to bed and—"

"Damn you!" she hissed, digging nails into his neck and stamping hard with her heel on the arch of his foot. "You're disgusting!" Free as the strains of music ceased, she hurried along the corridor, through a sudden surge of laughing, breathless escapees from the dance floor, past serried lines of bored and yawning footmen, and to the ladies' rooms.

Sick and faint for a moment, she had to sit down and borrow a fan; her own was lost back there with Gerald Loy. An attendant brought a glass of water and smelling salts; one whiff of the concentrated ammonia and she was herself again, blazing with rage that a so-called *gentleman* could treat her like a common whore and expect to get away with it.

Robert's *cousin,* she thought, amazed at the depths of male depravity and knowing in the next moment that she could never tell what had happened, no matter how much she wanted to repay that insult. Pushed and jostled by the constant stream of ladies in and out, Louisa went into the corridor, where the air was fresher. After a few minutes she felt better, capable of going back to face the throng.

Poised on the threshold of the ballroom, looking for familiar faces and ready to pin on a smile, Louisa was suddenly aware of someone at her elbow. It was Dr. Molloy, dapper and unfamiliar in his crisp evening clothes and smoking a cigar.

"Are you all right? You looked rather white as you hurried past a moment ago." Through curls of blue smoke he looked keenly sideways, not quite believing her assurance that she was fine. "Try not to overtire yourself," he advised. A moment later, he murmured: "Have you told the captain yet?"

"No," she whispered, feeling foolish. "There really hasn't been a good opportunity."

"Well, I'm sure you're the best judge of that," he acknowledged with a frown. "But I don't think you should leave it too much longer."

There was an element of reproof in his tone which, coming after the incident with Gerald Loy, was ridiculously hurtful. Her eyes filled with sudden tears, and as she turned away, the young doctor took her arm.

"Come on, now, sit down here behind this lovely potted palm, and we can pretend to be hatching conspiracies to overthrow all this nonsense. Would you like a mineral water—no? Well then, perhaps you should tell me what's wrong. Secrets of the confessional and all that," he joked, while, under pretense of holding her hand, he actually counted her pulse. Frowning, he said: "You're overdoing things. It's time you were home and in bed."

"No, I'm all right. I *was* all right," she amended, "until a few minutes ago. Someone insulted me, and it upset me, that's all."

"Who?"

"Don't ask. A man. Anyway," she sniffed, "it was my own fault really, wearing this ridiculous gown. I've put weight on, you see."

"One does," he said dryly. "It's one of the features of the case."

"Yes," she said seriously. "I know, but I didn't think about it when I ordered the dress."

"You'll have a lot of adjustments to make—and not just to your clothes."

For a moment neither of them spoke. Without looking at her companion, in fact as though speaking to herself, Louisa said bleakly: "You know, I'm really quite glad about it. At least all this will be over. I won't have to smile and put on a face and pretend I'm enjoying myself."

"Do you hate it so much?" he asked, and then, answering his own question, said: "Yes, I imagine you do. You weren't brought up to it, I understand?"

"No. We lived very quietly at home. I miss that."

"I should think Miss Duncannon will be glad of a break, too," he commented dryly. Seeing Robert striding toward them, looking this way and that, the young doctor touched her arm. "He's looking for you, but don't smile too brightly. I'll tell him you're faint with the heat, and maybe he'll take you home."

"That's a shame," Robert said regretfully a moment later. "I thought you were having such a good time. Look—" he hesitated—"will you be

all right for just a few more minutes? I have a dance promised, you
see—"

"Speaking as a doctor," Molloy said firmly, "I really do think, Captain, that you should take Miss Elliott home now. I shall see Miss
Duncannon gets back safely."

For a moment, faintly nettled, Robert was disposed to argue; then
he glanced at Louisa and saw that she did indeed look very tired,
although it was scarcely past one o'clock and the ball would go on for
hours yet.

"Will you wait," he asked Molloy, "while I organize the carriage?"
The doctor nodded, and Louisa looked so relieved he began to think
there might be something seriously wrong. "I'll fetch your cloak," he
said gently, pressing her hand. "I have the ticket."

An attendant went to look for their driver, while Robert hoped he
was not too well refreshed, and returned anxiously to Louisa. Wrapping
the cloak around her, he thanked Molloy for his attention and bade him
goodnight; he thought, however, that there was a most odd expression
in the stocky Irishman's eyes as he returned the civility.

So intent was he on that particular puzzle, he said nothing while they
were waiting for the carriage; when Louisa asked whether he was angry,
Robert was in fact feeling cross, thinking that if there was anything at
all the matter with her, he would have Molloy's hide for not telling him
so.

"Angry?" he repeated. "No, of course not." He forced a smile. "Why
should you think so?"

In the carriage, he drew her close within the crook of his arm. "We'll
soon have you home safe and to bed," he whispered, "and you can
sleep till noon if you wish." She said nothing, but rested her head against
his chest; a moment later, as casually as he was able, he said: "I thought
Molloy seemed overly concerned about you, darling—there's nothing
wrong, is there? I know you haven't been quite yourself for some time,
but you're not ill, are you?"

"No, I'm not ill," she said in a small, queer voice. "I'm having a
baby."

"What?" he asked stupidly, not believing, understanding only the
half. "What did you say? Did you say—did you say you were having
a *baby?*"

It was not something Robert had ever seriously considered. Finding
himself ridiculously pleased and also vaguely alarmed at the prospect,
during the next few days he still had moments of total disbelief which
sent him hurrying to Louisa's side for further confirmation.

"Anyone would think you'd never been a father before," she said one time, laughing, and he rumpled his hair like one bemused, which he was.

"This may sound idiotic," he admitted, with unaccustomed bashfulness, "but that is exactly how I do feel.

"You see," he went on after some thought, "I never had this experience before. Charlotte was so strange, I don't think she even realized she was pregnant. *I* was the one who noticed, eventually, and by that time, she must have been about five months gone. I couldn't believe it—didn't *want* to believe it—but it was true. Then I called a doctor in, and he confirmed it, of course." Sighing, he said: "I felt—trapped— there's no other word for it. *I* didn't want a child, and by that time, having realized something of Charlotte's illness, I didn't want her either. Nor was I in any position at that time to care for either of them. The regiment was on the move; I never knew where I was going to be from one day to another. It was hellish."

Understanding from personal experience something of those emotions, Louisa nodded. Despite Robert's enthusiasm, she still felt trapped. But all she said was "Poor Georgina," and sighed.

"Yes, quite. But she wasn't Georgina then—she was no more than an idea, an idea I dreaded like nothing I've ever dreaded before. I didn't even think of her as *my child,* if you can understand that. *It* was something growing inside Charlotte—a monster, for all I knew—nothing to do with *me.* Which is probably why I wanted nothing to do with her as a baby. In fact, she must have been about two years old," he added quietly, "before I realized she was a lovely, pretty, charming little girl."

"Do you still worry about her? Being like Charlotte, I mean?"

Robert nodded, knowing it was a fear he would probably never lose. "But Letty decided—and I agreed—that she should not be wrapped in cotton wool, as her mother appears to have been. We wanted her to have something of the rough-and-tumble we enjoyed as children at White Leigh, which was one of the reasons for staying on there. She did have Harry as a companion, and the estate children to play with. But then—oh, I don't know—perhaps the pressures of White Leigh outweighed even those advantages.

"Anyway," he added, smiling and squeezing her hand, "Georgie will soon have a little brother of her own to play with."

"Or sister," Louisa reminded him, laughing.

"No, I'm sorry," he insisted with mock seriousness. "This time I want a son."

NINE

*H*e had his way. On a fine morning in early October, just as dawn was breaking, Robert's son fought his way into the world.

Hearing that protracted wail of protest, Robert ceased his caged, desperate pacing; he listened hard, but there was no sound from Louisa, whose smothered moans had tormented him half the night and whose final, agonized yell of pain had stricken him like a physical wound. Swallowing hard, he made for the door, paused to gird himself against the news that she was dead, and finally went along the landing to her room.

Before he could knock, the door was opened, Molloy was standing there, a broad grin on his unshaven Irish face, and behind him, pale and disheveled but very much alive, Louisa was smiling from the bed.

The doctor put up his hand, halting that automatic step forward. "It's a boy—and they're both just fine—but hold on, will you, while we have a little tidy up. Five minutes or so—yes?"

Unable to contain himself, he went along to his sister's door and rapped urgently; within seconds Letty opened it, robe flapping, hair awry, and a cigarette burning between her fingers.

"She's all right!" he whispered, hugging her, and in answer to her thrice-repeated question: "It's a boy!"

"Oh, thank God!" Letty exclaimed, relaxing like jelly in his arms. "What a night! Have you seen her yet?"

"Just a glimpse—five minutes, Molloy said."

It was a long five minutes. "Bloody Irishman," Robert complained, lighting one of Letty's cigarettes and pulling a face. "God, these are awful, Letty—how do you smoke them?"

"Quite easily, dear boy, especially at times like this."

There were footsteps on the landing; Robert stubbed out the cigarette and went to the door; a uniformed nurse beckoned him with a smile.

"Five minutes," Molloy said, drying his hands. "She's very tired."

Robert grinned. "Does that mean half an hour?"

"It most certainly does not," came the serious reply, but Robert was lost in the delight of Louisa's smile. He saw the pride of achievement and in her eyes the soft glow of love; she looked tired and happy and quite, quite different, Robert thought. Transfixed by the change, he kissed her tenderly, hesitantly, and with her hand in his, perched on the very edge of the bed. Almost hidden by blankets, beside her nestled a tiny cocooned bundle with smooth pink cheeks and a puckered little mouth which moved.

Amazed, fascinated, awestruck, for a moment Robert was quite at a loss. Louisa pushed the shawl back and released one miniature hand; it moved jerkily, then opened like a starfish; she touched the palm and it closed round her finger, displaying perfect pink nails with white tips.

She chuckled. "Isn't he clever? He knows me already!"

"I should think he does after all this time. I thought he was never going to make an appearance."

"Worth waiting for, though," Louisa murmured. "He's quite perfect, isn't he? And so beautiful. Not a bit red and wrinkled."

Greatly daring, he touched the waving, starfish hand; tiny fingers gripped his with incredible strength, and surprised, Robert laughed; the baby's face crumpled immediately, and from that little pink mouth issued a piercing wail.

"Well!" Robert exclaimed in some alarm. "There's nothing much wrong with his lungs, is there?"

The nurse bustled in, full of professional concern for her charges, and with an ease which amazed Robert, she lifted the tiny bundle in one smooth movement, cradling it in her arms. The noise diminished to a whimper and then ceased. "It's a fine boy he is, sir," she said proudly, "and a fine big boy he'll be—just look at the size of those hands." Robert peered obligingly, but they still looked very small to him. "Near ten pounds, too," she informed him accusingly. "No wonder Mother had such a hard time."

Feeling unutterably guilty, Robert stole a glance at Louisa, who stifled a laugh; and then, unbelievably, the nurse was offering him the baby to hold.

"There we are—in the crook of the arm, that's right—don't be stiff now, and mind his head."

The little face registered alarm, frowning at the indignity of being passed about like a parcel; Robert thought he was going to cry again and almost panicked, but as the nurse opened thick velvet curtains on a bright new world, the baby blinked several times, revealing cloudy, gray-blue eyes which for a moment seemed to hold a very adult wisdom.

But the effort was too much; he slept again, while the rising sun caught fine lashes and downy tufts of eyebrows, making an aureole of soft blond hair on his crown.

Overwhelmed suddenly, Robert felt his throat constrict with emotion; after months of waiting and talking and trying to plan, worrying from the distance of the Curragh, dashing back to town whenever he could, *this* was the reality, this little scrap of humanity whose tiny muscles twitched and moved of their own volition. The burden of responsibility was suddenly out of all proportion; as the nurse held out her arms, Robert was glad to be relieved of his burden and firmly ushered from the room.

Alone, he stood for a moment, gripping the banister. Fatigue and relief set his muscles trembling; it was on very uncertain feet that he went down to find Molloy and a nerve-restoring drink.

After weeks of indecision before the birth, they eventually agreed to name the baby William. It began as something of a joke, when Louisa said the baby was the image of her uncle; but as she had such fond memories of her mother's brother, it pleased her to think of his name being perpetuated. Robert laughingly agreed, saying his own brother was sure to think the child was named for him, so both families would be pleased.

"Pleased," however, was not a word she associated with the Elliotts. Her family in York regarded her pregnancy as a tragedy, and not one of them had hesitated to say so. Her mother, of course, was relieved at her safe delivery, acknowledging Robert's telegram with words to that effect, but Louisa had the feeling that, for Emily and Blanche, death would have been the only honorable solution. From Edward there came no comment at all, and there had been none for many months. Understanding, not blaming him, she was still grieved by his silence, for she missed his letters, which were a window on life at home, missed knowing what he was doing, missed the reassurance that he was still thinking about her, as she so often thought of him. Occasionally she would begin a letter, only to destroy it: why hurt him further? she would think, seeking some activity to divert the longing for home.

With winter upon them once more, there was little to do in the garden, which had been a most sustaining interest throughout the spring and summer. Gardening was Letty's passion, a delightful counterbalance, she said, to all the dirt and misery of the slums. In a garden you could see results—plan, execute, succeed—and all that was required was patience. Louisa thought patience on the scale of years quite a large requirement, but from knowing absolutely nothing about any kind of garden, she soon found an affinity with growing things which gave her immense pleasure and satisfaction. "It's the blood of your farming fore-bears coming out," Letty said, teasing her, while the only thing she bemoaned about Louisa's pregnancy was the fact that they could not visit the country houses she had talked about all winter. They had to make do with public gardens within easy striking distance, but even those, as time advanced, became forbidden territory. They had rented a villa south of Dalkey in August, and Louisa thoroughly enjoyed that month by the sea, strolling like any legitimate matron along the seafront.

"Next summer," Letty said, "we'll do all the things we couldn't do this year," and meanwhile Louisa hugged her baby close, finding comfort in that warm, plump little body.

He was filling out and growing fast, a fact which surprised few people in the household, since little Liam, as the servants persisted in calling him, was a hungry baby with an internal clock set to three-hourly meals. He loathed being fed from a bottle, screaming so loud for his mother that Louisa had long ago stopped relying on his nurse to give him the last feed. It was a restrictive and tiring routine which began at six each morning and ended just before midnight; and despite being able to rest in between, Louisa had little time or energy for anything else. But she continued to regard her time with Georgina as of paramount importance and, with Letty's help, kept up the lessons begun eighteen months before. At six years old, the little girl's bright intelligence shone; she could read fluently, write a good hand, and, under Letty's tuition, showed a talent for drawing and the piano. The visit to White Leigh in November the previous year had prompted requests for a pony of her own, and for her birthday Robert had bought a Shetland pony which she immediately named Dinky. Like all his breed, he could be naughty and stubborn, but with all his idiosyncrasies, Georgina loved him, showing a steadfast refusal to be daunted which terrified Louisa but quite delighted her father.

Along with the carriage horses and Robert's hunters, Dinky was sta-bled in the nearby mews; on fine days when he was free, Robert took Georgina out with him to Stephen's Green. Seeing them set forth always amused Louisa: Robert sitting tall and straight on his seventeen-hand gray, the horse moving at a slow, elegant walk; and beside him, little legs straddling the barrel-sided Shetland, Georgina bounced along at a trot.

Sometimes Amelia Loy went with them, and Louisa would watch through narrowed eyes as they passed the house, hating the girl for no particular reason and praying to see her take a tumble from that proud, strutting thoroughbred. But she never would; like everything else Amelia did, she rode with a ready crop and a very firm hand. Louisa could imagine her beating her animals, just as she verbally lashed her husband on occasion, and wondered how Robert could like her at all; he said she was amusing, entertaining company on a long day's hunt, and Tommy agreed wholeheartedly. Louisa wished, however, that the hunting was less attractive in Meath, that it was not so necessary for Robert and his friends to stay overnight as guests of the Loys.

The six weeks of the season that year were something of an embarrassment. Word of Louisa's confinement had been passed, mostly with scandalized titillation, from one drawing room to another. The more straitlaced were genuinely shocked, horrified by the Duncannons' lack of discretion in keeping mother and child beneath their roof; in their books, all three names were deleted from invitation lists. There were others who clicked their tongues and quietly advised Robert to conduct his affairs at a distance from the public gaze, and yet more who frankly envied his bravado. In every case, however, it was made distressingly plain that Louisa could not be publicly received, and because of her tacit approval of the situation, nor could Letty.

It was no great surprise to Robert; indeed, he had expected it, and at a family conference almost a year before, they had all discussed the relative merits and disadvantages of total discretion. To have retired from Dublin during the whole period of her confinement and farmed her child out to foster parents was the only way to preserve the appearance of respectability; but that idea was repugnant to each of them; and to attempt anything less ran so many risks of discovery that it hardly seemed worth the effort involved. Without being blatant, it was decided that Louisa should stay in Dublin and that, as a whole, they would face the social consequences.

Faced with the embarrassment, however, of invitations which were addressed to him, and him alone, Robert found certain ironies in their situation. As a man, he was not castigated; he could be accepted in the grandest society, and was; and, judging by the increased attention he received, his reputation appeared to be enhanced by that irregular relationship. Louisa, his equal partner in love or sin, was the fallen woman who should have known better, the woman nobody cared to acknowledge; and his sister, the innocent bystander, was treated as an accomplice after the fact. The true irony, however, was that neither of these women appeared to feel in the least punished by that judgment. Letty, particularly, heaved a huge sigh of relief, made a coarse comment to the effect that she could now take off her mental corsets, and threw herself eagerly into her own interests; while Louisa simply smiled that secret smile of hers and went to tend the baby.

Ultimately it was Robert who suffered the most. He was the one morally obliged to attend regimental entertainments, musical evenings, and soirees, and now he must attend alone; he was the one who had gone to great lengths to renew that circle of social acquaintances in Dublin, acquaintances who now called upon him to make up numbers at dinner or parties attending receptions at the castle. He could have refused, but at heart he did not want to. After several years of life in England, the pleasure of being back among his own people was still a tonic to be savored, despite his feelings of guilt at leaving Louisa behind. But it was more than guilt; even though it had been a trial to her at first, he genuinely missed her company, most especially the thrill of having a lovely woman on his arm and knowing he was envied. That had been a luxury long denied, and he hated to give it up.

TEN

There was some consolation, however, in knowing their social life was not completely curtailed. Private dinner parties with very close friends were permissible, and visits to theaters and public concerts which they attended as a couple, rather than part of a group. On those occasions Robert had to be content with a brief nod of recognition; no one would stop and speak. Louisa said it spoiled her enjoyment of the music, so, unless it was a program they particularly wanted to hear, they did not go. The friends who were prepared to entertain them were few: namely Tommy and Darnley, a couple of bachelor friends from Robert's school days whom he had met again through Gerald Loy, and of course the Loys themselves. What he could not understand was Louisa's great reluctance to accept those occasional invitations to the house in Mountjoy Square. Having refused two such because of some indisposition of hers, he insisted they accept the third, which came at the end of February.

"Frank O'Mara will be there—you like him—and Tom McNeill. I know he's not exactly your cup of tea, but he's not so bad underneath that brusque manner."

"Like your cousin," Louisa said, "he drinks too much and treats women like dirt. I'm not surprised he's still a bachelor—for all his money, I wouldn't have him if he came tied up in blue ribbon."

At first Robert laughed. Then, realizing what she had said, he asked: "*Does* Gerald treat women badly? I've never noticed. I always thought he had impeccable manners, especially where women were concerned."

"On the surface," she murmured enigmatically and refused to be drawn.

Like Fitzwilliam Square, Mountjoy still retained its air of prestige, lingering like some ancient oasis of butlers and brass plates and visiting cards on the edge of the city's slums. There was also the attendant presence of incipient decay, as though most of the inhabitants had yet to make up their minds whether to renovate and stay or sell up and move out. The triumph of hope over experience, Louisa thought, viewing with the clarity of a newcomer the encroaching poverty around. It seemed the newly rich had more sense than the old aristocracy, having moved out to fresher air and newer property in Ballsbridge and Rathmines.

The prestige of new paint and well-fitting sashes seemed not to bother Amelia Loy, however; noticing marked and dusty wallpaper in a drawing room which had seen better days, Louisa tried hard not to shiver. A draft from the window at her back had her discreetly drawing up the folds of her lacy stole and thinking longingly of the cozy rooms left behind. They were early arrivals, and without Letty, Louisa could think of nothing to say. Gerald avoided looking at her, as he always did these days, and his wife monopolized Robert without a care. It was a relief when the butler announced the arrival of the other guests; also something of a surprise to Louisa, who had not realized there would be other ladies present.

Within a few minutes, however, it dawned on her that "ladies" was a loose term; one of them might be an elderly peer's widow, but Louisa was certain she had begun life in far more humble surroundings and had used the stage as a springboard; the other was more difficult to place. Confident and hard-eyed, she could have been any age between thirty and forty and, by her voice and mannerisms, was obviously well born; but she wore no rings and her gown was hardly that of a *femme fatale*. It transpired that she was a neighbor of Amelia's from Meath; for a while Louisa wondered what her connection could be with Frank O'Mara, and then it dawned on her that Frank was very rich, and Amelia's friend was not.

Frank was about Robert's age, a softly spoken, unhandsome man, immensely kind but not very bright, and for that very reason both well liked and much put upon by all who knew him. Robert said he never had much luck with women, and it saddened Louisa to realize that two at least were in collusion against his better interests. It surprised her too that after the meal their hostess did not signal the ladies to rise; instead of coffee in the drawing room, the ladies supped port with the men and, as much wine had been consumed already, the conversation quickly became much freer than Louisa thought right or proper.

Tom McNeill, short, dark, and wiry, had a sharpness of wit which leaned toward the suggestive at the best of times; with drink inside him and Amelia's rather raucous laughter as encouragement, every comment contained a double meaning. Even the most innocent response was turned, and at every feminine blush he laughed louder. His companion, the full-blown, rather gaudy widow, took it in her stride, feeding him opportunities like a straight comic in a music hall; like everyone else, she was enjoying herself immensely. Having dropped more than one innocent but ill-phrased remark and found herself the butt of that drunken hilarity, Louisa sat quiet for some time. At one point she inadvertently caught Gerald's eye, and his smug little smile was very revealing. He's paying me back, she thought angrily and in the next moment was furious with Robert also, for making her accompany him, for being too drunk to realize how offensive she found the entire group. It was one thing to share that kind of joke in private, quite another with people she disliked intensely. Even Frank O'Mara, the silly innocent, was too far gone to keep his hands to himself; and that calculating bitch, Louisa thought, will have a proposal out of him before the night's out.

"I'm afraid we don't amuse you," Tom McNeill said from across the table. "Tell us, Bob, what can we do to amuse your pretty lady? She sits quiet as a mouse beside you—doesn't laugh, doesn't drink, doesn't talk—"

"I'm afraid you're right," Louisa said clearly, rising to her feet. "You *don't* amuse me. Not at all. I find your humor quite tasteless. In fact," she added, meeting each upturned glance, "you bore me. Goodnight."

With that she swept from the room, leaving Robert to suffer whatever followed. There was a babble of voices and laughter as an impassive manservant fetched her cloak, and moments later Robert joined her, his face flushed and angry.

He said nothing until they were seated in the carriage and on their way home; and then, in a voice which shook with barely suppressed fury, he accused her of prudery and a most lamentable lack of manners; she had not only embarrassed him, he said, but insulted his friends quite unforgivably.

They were traveling south down Gardiner Street, through the heart of the notorious brothel area; soldiers in every style and color of uniform strolled in groups along the pavements, while girls in crude finery gathered under street lamps, beckoning and calling the business of the night.

"Look," she said, pointing from the window. "See the soldiers, Robert? And those women? What difference is there between them and us? Answer me that."

Aghast for a moment, he stared at her through the gloom. "Have you taken total leave of your senses this evening? How can you liken such people to us? There's no comparison at all!"

"Isn't there?" she demanded stonily. "There's no difference in the eyes of the law, and none in the eyes of your precious society, as far as I can see." Pointing again, she said bitterly: "*That* is how I felt this

evening—no better than a common prostitute, in the company of prostitutes!"

"If I were you," he said between gritted teeth, "I'd take that back—"

"I will not!" Shaking off the hand that gripped her arm, she declared
passionately: "Blame your fine friends and those gently bred cousins of
yours! And blame *yourself,* Robert, for taking me there in the first place."

"I didn't know those women were going to be there—"

"But you didn't object to them, did you? And you were as vulgar as
the rest."

"Now wait a minute—"

But, in full flow of self-righteous fury, Louisa gave him no quarter.
"And as for that common little trollop, Amelia Loy," she went on, "I
don't care how far back her family goes, she's no more a lady than that
jumped-up chorus girl. And the same goes for that fine friend of hers—
I'd like to bet she's been through every eligible man in County Meath,
and a few more besides! I feel so sorry for poor Frank: he deserves better
than that, and you know it."

"Will you stop this? I don't give a damn about Frank O'Mara right
at this minute; I want you to listen to me—"

"No," she declared emphatically, *"you* listen to *me,* Robert Duncannon. I never want to see your cousins again—*ever.* Or that McNeill
creature. Invite them to the house if you wish—it's your privilege—but
don't expect me to be there to entertain them. I might not be welcome
in polite circles, Robert, but I swear to you, I'd rather live like a hermit
than mix with people like that."

"My God!" he exclaimed with a bitter little laugh. "You're so bloody
middle-class!"

"Perhaps I am," she acknowledged, "but at least I have manners and
a set of principles. Being your mistress hasn't made me lose sight of
them—not entirely, anyway."

With that furious exchange hammering one more nail in the coffin
of their social life, Robert made no more attempts to involve Louisa.
Almost as a matter of principle, he continued to see Gerald and Amelia,
often finding himself in the not-entirely-unwelcome position of escorting
some otherwise unaccompanied female friend or acquaintance. It both
amused and annoyed him to realize that Amelia was actively trying to
pair him with another woman.

One evening when she was extolling the virtues of a particularly
attractive girl, he said: "Don't be an idiot, Amelia. I'm *married,* in case
you'd forgotten. Quite apart from any other consideration."

Her thin features registered a little *moue* of disappointment. "But of
course, one tends to forget, you're so often alone." She sighed. "And

how is *la petite bourgeoise?* Although she's not exactly *petite,* is she? More the Amazon, I think."

"Now stop that," he said sternly, as though to a child. "Showing your claws just doesn't become you."

"I wish I knew what did become me," she said archly, "in your eyes, that is. In fact, if I thought anything I did would dent that iron heart of yours, Robbie darling, I'd be more than gratified."

"I'm sure you would," he said sardonically and turned away.

"I mean it, Robert."

Surprised, he looked back; she was smiling that pert, teasing little smile, but her eyes were quite uncertain.

"I don't *need* anyone else," he said quietly.

"No?" she laughed, twirling the stem of a glass between her fingers. "Well, when you do, just let me know."

ELEVEN

After a mild, wet winter, March was bitter, with frosts and gales and heavy blizzards; spring took a shock and, with everything delayed, burst forth quite suddenly into summer at the end of May. Within a week it seemed the sheltered garden of the Devereaux house was alive with perfume and color: yellow tulips, blue hyacinths, lilacs and laburnum, the tall spikes of irises and fat purple cushions of aubrietia edging lawns bright green in the sun.

Having felt at odds with everything for weeks, Louisa's listless spirit bloomed again, and in a surge of renewed energy she began to make plans for the summer ahead. While baby Liam gurgled happily at Georgina from his cradle beneath the lilacs, she and Letty pored over seed catalogues and guidebooks; Robert would shortly be away to the Curragh for the drill season, and with him gone they could more or less please themselves. And at eight months old, Liam could quite well be weaned, Louisa thought, which could leave her freer to take trips with Letty.

They planned visits to Glasnevin's Botanic Gardens and Wicklow's beautiful Glendalough and, if Robert would sanction it, a week in Killarney before the summer visitors overran it. "It's a pity we couldn't stay over at White Leigh," Letty said, understanding Louisa's refusal, "because the gardens are superb in the summer." Hearing the name, Georgina set up a clamor to see her cousin Harry; it was eventually decided that she and Letty would go for a few days alone, a plan which would suit everyone, including Robert.

By the middle of July, with the two of them away and Robert back in Dublin for a couple of days, it suddenly occurred to Louisa that, in spite of weaning the baby, her monthly cycle had not readjusted itself, and, more worrying still, that she was putting weight on rather than losing it. She felt well, looked well, had no early-morning nausea; but still the creeping suspicion grew. While Robert was preparing for an early return to the Curragh next morning, she stood in front of the pier glass and examined her silhouette. It was suspiciously rounded in the area of her abdomen. With a sinking heart, she pulled on her robe and went into the bathroom, where Robert was shaving. She stood for a moment, holding on to the doorjamb, knowing instinctively that for him it would not be welcome news and yet needing his loving reassurance, needing above all things to tell him, and tell him immediately. After the harrowing effort of keeping her last pregnancy to herself, she could not do it again, not even for a week.

"I think I'm having another baby," she said hollowly.

The smooth sweep of the razor stopped abruptly, drawing blood beneath his chin in a long, thin line. There was silence for several seconds, and then as he wheeled, grabbed a towel to stanch the cut, he swore long and volubly.

"Do you want me to cut my bloody throat?" he demanded after that string of curses; Louisa burst into tears and fled.

Moments later, half-dressed, he was by her side, apologizing even as he dabbed at his face, drawing her to him with his free arm. His eyes, however, were singularly lacking in delight.

"Are you sure?"

"No, not absolutely. It's hard to tell, what with the baby and—and everything. But I think so."

Staring hard into her face, he said, "You *can't* be. I thought, while you were feeding the baby, that—" He broke off, not entirely sure of himself. "And since then—well, you always said everything was all right—"

"I thought it was! It seems I was wrong, though, doesn't it? I'm sorry—I didn't plan it—it's as big a shock to me as it is to you, for Heaven's sake!"

"All right, all right, calm down, I didn't mean—" Sighing, he squeezed her shoulder and, looking down, swore softly at the amount of blood on the towel. "God, Louisa, you really choose your moments, don't you? Just look at that. Anytime you want to polish me off for good, just do that again. I'll probably get the jugular next time!"

"I'm sorry, I didn't realize, didn't think what you were doing."

He laughed softly. "That goes for both of us, I think." Ruffling her hair, he kissed her cheek. "No use crying over it, darling, especially as it's not certain. You'd better get yourself over to see Molloy and let me know *immediately*."

As ever, the clock was against him; with a train to catch, he dressed hurriedly, sharing toast and coffee with Louisa in her room. The small meal put color back into her cheeks, and he smiled ruefully as he kissed her good-bye. "I think I know what Molloy's going to say—you've got that luscious glow about you again. I should have noticed." Kissing her again, lingeringly, he said, "Or maybe I did. Thanks for last night—it was the best we've had in a long time."

To her, the comment seemed indelicate under the circumstances; flushing uncomfortably, she shook her head and pulled her robe closer. Robert sighed and pecked her cheek. "Write to me. I'll try and get back next week—if not, it may be two. Take care, and give my love to Georgie." At the door he paused and looked back. "What will it be this time, I wonder? Brother or sister?"

Georgina was disappointed. Having one little brother, she had told her father that it would be very nice to have a baby sister to play with; but the week-old baby boy in his crib seemed so appropriate at Christmas, she forgave Louisa everything, adoring the child with the same wide-eyed wonder she had displayed at Liam's birth. A practiced father this time, Robert held his new son with a pleasure far greater than expected, looking down into a face Letty swore was the image of his own. Scoffing at such nonsense, swearing babies looked like babies and no one else, deep down he was pleased; and certainly this little scrap had dark and curly hair, fine black lashes, and eyes which might clear to the color of his own.

A general consensus said he must be called Robert for his father, and Bobby he became, a child for whom the sun seemed always to shine; he rarely cried, even from the first, and was content to rest in anyone's arms. That supreme contentment under which he thrived was fortunate, for in spite of a much easier birth, Louisa was slow to recover. Two children in less than fifteen months had sapped her strength, leaving her tired and very depressed. Dr. Molloy prescribed plenty of rest and a fortifying diet, but still she lost weight and, more worrying still, her interest in life.

Letty often came across her in the nursery weeping over her two babies, sometimes sobbing as though her heart would break, although when questioned she would not, or could not, say why. Abandoning her charity work, the older woman took over supervision of the nursery and her niece's lessons, which along with her usual housekeeping duties made her feel, as she remarked to Robert, less the maiden aunt than a bowed-down mother of three. Robert himself felt totally helpless, his initial irritation at such groundless misery soon changing to the most abject concern. An interview with Dr. Molloy did nothing to relieve his anxiety. It was a distressingly common complaint, he was told, often following childbirth; but its frequency did not lessen its serious nature. To prevent any possibility of tragedy, Molloy said, she must be watched all the time, and under no circumstances whatsoever must she be allowed to conceive another child.

"At least," he added weightily, "not until I see a complete recovery, and even then not for a year or so. You do understand what that means?"

"I think so," Robert murmured, resisting the inference nevertheless. "At least, I understand what *you* mean." For a moment, trying to assess Molloy's position, his likely reaction, Robert paused. Then he said, in worldly, man-to-man tones: "But in this day and age, there are ways and means—surely, as a doctor . . ."

"Would you have me struck from the medical register? As a doctor, I must tell you that I do not—cannot—approve." Meeting his gaze, the younger man allowed himself to show a brief if eloquent sympathy; then, turning away, he added: "I can tell you, they're unsafe and unreliable. There is only one way to ensure conception does not take place— a priest would call it celibacy. I call it common sense, Captain, because there's certainty in nothing else."

"Certainty, no," Robert ventured, "but a percentage of success."

With stern disapproval, the young Irish doctor shook his head. "In other circumstances, I might say 'Fine, take your own chances,' but not in this situation. And certainly not now. It's a peculiarity of Mother Nature, Captain, that women who have recently given birth are immensely fertile: *one* mistake is all that's needed. Embrace abstinence for a year," he advised with grim humor. "Like fasting, they say it does wonders for the soul."

"Mine's already damned," Robert said acidly, "by your church's reckoning, at least."

"By yours too, I should think," came the quick reply, but he was smiling again, enjoying the sparks they inevitably raised between them. On a more serious note, before he left, Molloy asked leave to refer Louisa to a colleague. "He's a specialist," he said, "and very well thought of."

"What kind of specialist?" Robert demanded suspiciously.

Recognizing delicate ground, the younger man tried to backtrack, unsuccessfully. "In this kind of disorder," he said. "For my own peace of mind as her doctor, I'd like confirmation of my diagnosis. And Stevens might well suggest some treatment I'm not yet familiar with."

"Why don't you just say it, Molloy? His specialty is mental illness. You think she's mad, like—" Hurting, furious, he broke off, turned away. "She's not, you know, not a bit of it. She needs taking out of herself, that's all, cheering up. If only," he added miserably, "there were some way of doing it."

"I didn't say she was mad, nor do I think it. But she won't talk to you or Miss Duncannon. She won't even talk to me. Stevens is a stranger— and quite brilliant—she may well talk to him."

"No, I won't have it," Robert said vehemently. "There wasn't a specialist yet could help my wife, and believe me, we've tried them all!"

"You haven't tried him" was the reasonable reply. "And your wife, if I might venture to point out, is a totally different case."

But Robert was not assured. He felt as though the most terrifying nightmare of his life was being reenacted, and, fluctuating between belief and disbelief, his nights and days became a blur of unreality. Molloy called each afternoon that week and went away still shaking his head and insisting on a second opinion. His patience at an end, Robert cornered him, demanding an explanation.

"But I'm *not* an expert," Molloy told him yet again. "I can diagnose physical illness and be right most of the time; I can tell you the effects of poverty and malnutrition, even describe the various afflictions of wealthy women of a certain age. But I cannot assess Louisa's state of mind, because I can get nothing out of her, or too little to suggest a remedy. I confess she seems a *little* better: I'm not as anxious as I was, and I doubt she'll injure the children in any way, but—"

"Oh, good God!" Robert exclaimed, feeling the walls close in on him. "Don't even think it." Pouring himself a drink, all resistance shattered, he simply said: "Whatever his name is—get him."

Crisis at Islandbridge interrupted all private considerations, however; there was an outbreak of dysentery at the barracks, which surprised no one who had seen the sanitary arrangements there, and Robert least of all. But it was no time for gloating at being proved right; the sick men had to be removed to the fever hospital and the rest to huts at the Curragh. Afraid of endangering the children, Robert stayed away from the house for three weeks, and while colleagues dashed back and forth enjoying the latter end of the season, he conducted lengthy correspondence with Letty and Dr. Molloy.

"You will be relieved to know," wrote Molloy at the end of March, "that Stevens does not consider the problem to be serious. Indeed, I have seen a great improvement myself recently and would bear out his diagnosis. He would like, however, to see you personally, so I will say no more at present. . . ."

Robert rang the bell for Harris and asked him to bring fresh coffee and a large brandy. Standing over the potbellied iron stove, he shivered and shook as though with an ague, wanting to rush home immediately, wanting to see Louisa, talk to her, make love; wanting solid, physical reassurance that she was indeed better. Never again did he want to see such misery in her eyes, never again feel that terrible chill around his own heart as he looked at her.

Reading the letter through again, however, he realized that no one had actually said she was recovered. Improved, yes; and the problem, whatever it was, was not considered serious, which seemed to promise an eventual return to normal, without being specific. Depression descended again like a leaden weight.

When Harris came, Robert drank the brandy quickly, following that blood-tingling warmth with a mug of hot coffee, and while the other man fed logs into the stove, paced the small area which comprised his quarters. Outside, the sun was setting in a clear, cold sky; frost, which had lingered all day in the shadows, would be reinforced during the night. Shivering again, drawing his cloak around him like a blanket, he thought longingly of home. Once, the bare wooden walls of his quarters, with the attendant lack of ease and warmth, would have been beneath his notice; but the last three years had conditioned Robert to a more sybaritic way of life, and he missed most sorely the comforts of his own hearth.

In the chilly solitude of a narrow bed, thoughts of Louisa were never far away; cold and sleepless, he would have gladly exchanged anything for the simple pleasure of sharing her warmth. Wanting her, he tried to recall the last time they had made love and knew it must have been at least six months before; and while acknowledging the necessity for abstinence, it irked him like a hair shirt. Rationalizing, he told himself that physical desire was no more than a part of their relationship, by no means its sole reason for being; but it seemed immensely ironic that the mistress he had taken four years ago should have become so much his wife that even sex was now forbidden.

Wife, mistress, sister, children; the responsibility of caring, of keeping them clothed and housed and fed; of listening to their myriad tiny problems and solving the dozens of major ones: it was becoming too much. Stuck at the Curragh, the most miserable place on earth in winter, miles from anywhere, without a scrap of anything worthwhile to look forward to, Robert felt very sorry for himself indeed. He should take a few days off to go home, he knew that; but, much as he wanted to be with Louisa, the thought of all that misery held him back.

Next morning, in the midst of tedious paperwork to do with the men who were sick, Harris brought in the mail and requested permission to speak.

"Yes, Harris, what is it?"

"Well, begging your pardon, sir, but I wondered whether we would be going back to Dublin at all."

Slightly irritated, Robert laid down his pen. *"By we,* do you mean the regiment? If you do, the answer's no, not for a long time."

Clearing his throat, Harris said: "No, sir, I meant—begging your pardon—would you yourself be going back to Dublin anytime soon?"

"I shall be, but I can't say exactly when. Not at this moment, anyway. Why do you want to know?"

Coloring with sudden embarrassment, Harris said: "Well, sir, it's to do with me leaving the colors—sort of."

"Oh, good grief, yes—I keep forgetting about that." Opening a drawer in his desk, Robert sifted through some papers. "Seven years—and six of them with me—it'll be hell breaking a new man in," he joked. "Can't you do another seven?"

"Wish I could, sir; wish they'd let me."

"Ah well, regulations." Robert sighed. "When exactly is it? End of May?"

"The twentieth, sir."

"You know, there's been so much going on," Robert muttered, finding at last the details he was looking for, "it's been pushed to the back of my mind. But I haven't forgotten what we discussed at Christmas," he added, glancing up. "Was it that you wanted to see me about?"

"Well, no, not exactly." Scarlet with embarrassment, Harris came to attention. "I'd like your permission, sir, to ask for Miss Moira's hand in marriage. I know she's a Papist, sir, but she can't help that, and she is clean and hardworking. What's more, I know the ladies have taught her to write a good hand and figure accounts—I think she'll do me very nicely. You did say, sir," he added into the stunned silence, "that I'd find it hard going on my own, and thinking it over, it makes sense. So if it's all right with you, sir, I'd like permission to ask."

"Oh, my God," Robert murmured into his hand. Covering a smile, he said: "Does the girl know of your intentions, Harris? I mean, is she likely to agree?"

Relaxing somewhat, the younger man nodded. "Oh, I think so, sir. Miss Moira likes me well enough. I think she knows I'd have offered before, if I'd had anything to offer—if you see what I mean, sir. Army life's no life for a woman, in the ranks, that is," he added hurriedly, "and I know she misses her hometown—so if I was to look for a public house in York, she'd say yes like a shot."

"She'd be a fool to turn you down," Robert said quietly. "Yes, Harris, you have my permission to ask for her hand." Smiling again, he added: "And kindly take two days' leave. You deserve it!"

"When, sir?"

"Ah, yes." Flicking through the mail on his desk, looking for handwriting which might be pertinent, Robert shook his head. "See me about that this evening, will you?"

"Yes, sir, and thank you, sir!" With a very crisp salute, Harris marched from the office, looking at least six inches taller than when he had entered. Watching his retreating back, Robert's smile faded.

I know she misses her hometown—the words echoed hollowly in his head. Was that Louisa's problem? he wondered; after almost three years away, was she simply heartsick for home and family? In the beginning, he had promised to take her back, but since then, what with pregnancies and children, there had been no opportunity. We must make that opportunity, he thought, his mind jumping back to Harris and his proposals for the future.

Sober, thrifty, hardworking, Harris would make a success of his venture, of that Robert had no doubt at all. With no collateral except his faith in the man, Robert had offered to invest in that long-standing ambition to own a small public house in a garrison town. Without that material help, Harris would have found it exceedingly difficult, for army pay, even that of a privileged servant, did not allow for vast savings. Even so, Harris had gathered a surprising little nest egg, and Robert's investment would not be large. It remained only to find a suitable property, and that could not be done until Harris finished his time in May.

Perhaps then, he thought, we might go across to view the place and spend a few days in York.

Picking up the mail on his desk, he sorted through it again. There was a lengthy epistle from Letty, a few bills, and a slim envelope addressed in the spiky hand he had come to recognize as Amelia Loy's.

Curious, he opened that one first, and his face relaxed into a smile as he read her note. She and Gerald were invited down to Kilkenny by some boring but hospitable cousins; if he could inveigle a few days off, would he like to join them for the hunting? It was so long since they'd seen or heard from him, Amelia said, she was beginning to think the Curragh no more than an excuse.

"Admit it," that spiky hand ordered, "you've joined some Trappist order in the bogs of Connaught! Even so, I trust this will be passed on and that vows of poverty, chastity, and silence will not prevent a handwritten reply."

He laughed at that, amused more by the accurate analogy than anything else; on an impulse, he wrote straight back, promising to join them for a day and a night at least the following week.

TWELVE

With the worst of the regimental problems ironed out, and the prospect of cheerful company and a day's hunting to fortify himself, Robert thought it was time he went back to Dublin. Dreading the meeting with Molloy's colleague, Dr. Stevens, he made that appointment first, needing to know the worst and best of Louisa's situation before seeing her.

Like Molloy, he was no more than thirty years old, a tall, thin, intense-eyed man with a high, domed forehead and narrow jaw. His handshake was firm and protracted, and Robert felt, rather guiltily, that the long fingers absorbed as much as those piercing eyes. In the manner of a man whose time is valuable, after a very short silence, he launched at once into a frank assessment of his patient.

In his opinion, he said, the depression was a common one brought about by childbirth; not particularly severe in itself, but complicated by other factors. He did not consider the patient to be of a melancholic disposition, nor was it likely that she would be permanently affected; nevertheless, he added, he was still very much concerned.

Robert cleared his throat. "Why is that?" he asked, having an uneasy feeling that the cause was about to be placed squarely on his own shoulders.

With eloquently raised brows and a sigh which spoke volumes, the doctor said severely: "Your situation is hardly the usual one, Captain. Miss Elliott is not your wife, and yet she lives with you as such—there are two children of the union, are there not?"

"Now, look here!" Robert protested, rising to his feet; but the tall doctor waved him down.

"Calm yourself," he ordered. "I'm not here to make petty moral judgments, but to give you my considered medical opinion. My fees, incidentally, are not small, so please don't waste my time."

"I'm sorry," Robert murmured, feeling as though he had just been carpeted by the colonel.

"You are prepared to listen? Good. Then let me tell you this: it took some considerable time to discover what lay at the heart of Miss Elliott's problem, several interviews before I was able to gain her confidence. At first, loyalty stood in the way, loyalty to you, Captain." He paused for a moment, and when he looked up, again there was that disapproval in his eyes, as though the man before him had performed some deed unmentionable between gentlemen. "She's an admirable woman—in spite of the irregularity of your union—a fine woman with a strong moral sense. And it's that very moral sense which is destroying her. Why? Because she feels *guilt*. Her children are evidence of her wrongdoing, yet she loves them dearly, as she most surely cares for you."

For a while there was silence, while Robert was so swamped by shock and his own brand of guilt he could think of nothing at all to say. Eventually Dr. Stevens said: "Perhaps if you could have lived quietly somewhere . . . away from the pressures of society, away from public condemnation, she might have come to terms with it. As things stand, I find it hard to find a solution. To abandon her—even if you could find it in your heart to do so—would be worse, yet to continue the physical side of your relationship is, I think, as bad. She is afraid, you see, very much afraid, of bearing more children. Not because of the physical pain," he added quickly, "but the moral, emotional pain—the *guilt*."

When he could find his voice, Robert whispered, "Is she—are the children—in any kind of danger?"

"No, I don't think so. No," he repeated more firmly, "she's unhappy, but I don't sense that destructive urge in her; rather the opposite, in fact. And now the postnatal melancholia has lifted, she is getting better. Now she understands *why* she is unhappy, she is coming to terms with it. But no more pressure must be put upon her. You do understand that?"

"Yes, I understand," Robert said bleakly.

"There is one other thing—her family. I understand she is in communication with her mother, but feels condemned by the rest. I don't know how you stand with regard to them, Captain, but if someone could be persuaded to write and explain the situation—if *they* could be persuaded to forgive her and say so—then I feel that would set her squarely on the road to recovery. Society's opinion would perhaps matter less."

Her family! Robert thought, with Edward clear as day before him; hot, jealous anger burned the ice away, and suddenly he felt betrayed by all Louisa had confessed to this man. Doctor or not, he had no right to know the inmost secrets of her mind, no right to probe where he, Robert, had never been.

Through tight lips, he said: "I couldn't possibly begin to explain. Perhaps my sister might."

"Persuade her," Dr. Stevens said. "It is important."

It was the middle of the afternoon when he came out of the consulting rooms in Merrion Square. Although it was but a short walk from there to the Devereaux house, Robert turned in the opposite direction, toward a pub he knew near Trinity College. It was a wild, blustery day, with raindrops scattering in sudden gusts, but the fight against it seemed the most positive, enjoyable thing he had done in weeks. Blood was tingling in hands and face within seconds of entering that tiny, smoke-filled room; not wishing to draw attention to himself, he ordered a large whiskey and downed it quickly, relishing the gasp of heat in his chest; ordered another and sipped it, holding the glass like mulled wine between his hands. Several students were arguing noisily in one corner; they turned to him for a good-humored judgment, but he was in no mood for their idiotic and fanciful philosophies; with a taut smile he shook his head and left.

He entered the house almost stealthily, going straight to his study and sending McMahon to fetch Letty. While he waited, he poured himself another drink and sat down, at last feeling the tight knot in his stomach begin to unravel. Not too far, though, he told himself sternly, pushing the bottle across the desk; too much and he would fall apart completely, and that would never do.

Letty came in quietly; startled, he turned, and she was leaning against the door, shaking her head. "Oh, Robert, don't start that habit again, please."

Angry, he slammed the glass down. "One drink! Am I not allowed that after what I've just been through?"

She sighed. "You've been to see Dr. Stevens, then? What did he say?"

"Enough. None of it very good. Oh, she'll get over it—not *very* serious, he said. Except," Robert added bitterly, "she'd be a bloody sight happier, apparently, if I walked out and joined a blasted monastery!"

Used to his obscenities, Letty merely set her lips and said tersely, "We'll have less of the barrack-room adjectives, Robert—in this house, anyway!"

Leaning back in his chair, he propped his booted feet on the desktop, another habit she disliked intensely. With challenge in his eyes he watched her pace the square of carpet before him, waiting for the inevitable comment. When none came, he said flippantly: "It would appear she's suffering from an attack of the vapors, sister dear, brought on by the nasty things people say and do. Or rather, the nasty things she *thinks* they're thinking, since to my knowledge no one has actually said a damn thing to her face!"

"You have been drinking, Robert, I can tell. Don't bother denying it," she said furiously, "because if I thought you were stone cold sober, I'd kill you right now!" Brandishing the heavy brass poker, Letty stabbed at the fire, holding it, between thrusts, like a weapon. "How you can speak so, I've no idea. If I thought you meant it, if I thought you didn't care—"

"Oh, for Christ's sake, Letty. Of course I care!"

"You have a most delightful way of showing it."

"I know, it's part of my natural charm—or so you tell me."

She came at him with fire in her eyes; for a second the poker threatened; and then on a long breath she lowered it slowly to the desk. Leaning forward, his sister hung her head like someone exhausted. "Please," she said quietly, "don't fight with me. I'm trying to help you. I need to know what was said. What was *really* said, not some sarcastic interpretation. I've been as worried as you, Robert, thought the same things, spent sleepless nights remembering Charlotte and all the things she said and did after Georgie was born. So *please,* if there's anything I can do, tell me."

Dragging his mental faculties together, trying to quell the bitterness, Robert eventually managed to relate most of what had been said that afternoon. Acrimony crept back, however, as he recalled that final plea to write to her family; confessing that to his sister cost him much in injured pride, and her eagerness to fulfill that duty was no pleasure at all.

Glancing at the time, he rose slowly to his feet. "Where is she?" he asked. "I suppose I ought to see her."

"Indeed you should!" Letty remarked sharply. "What's the matter, don't you want to?"

For a moment Robert could not reply; then, covering nothing, he said, with simple honesty: "I dread it."

It was impossible to say more; impossible to discuss with his sister the remorseful secrets of his private life. Understanding though she was, he could not describe to her the effects of those early days with Charlotte, the sexual fear and guilt thus induced, which Louisa had salved so miraculously. In her eager response he had found the balm he needed, and in her laughing delight a happiness which bound him more securely than any marriage vow. It was hard to believe that she wanted him no longer, that the passion they had shared with such abandon could be so pitifully reduced; and yet he did believe it. The change in her had begun in slow and subtle ways, with the confirmation of her second pregnancy; and since Bobby's birth had come the abject misery, expressed in constant flooding tears and an abnormal anxiety over those two babies. He had watched her clasp them to her bosom as though the Grim Reaper himself stood on the threshold, as though the weight of all human frailty bowed her down; had tried to comfort, and been rejected; talked, and felt the walls had better ears. Even Letty, sharing friendship and a common gender, had achieved little more than himself.

Remembering her old fear of gossip, the attitudes he had so often dismissed as *bourgeois,* Robert believed the doctor's diagnosis, equating what he understood as guilt-ridden misery with sexual revulsion.

In his mind, it was Charlotte all over again: fear and loathing, the total rejection of all that made him, in his own eyes, a man.

He found her in the nursery with all three children. Georgina was playing with Liam, leading him on staggering, chubby legs around the room. Beneath a shock of thick blond hair, his bright eyes shone with delight; seeing Robert, he gurgled happily, proudly walking a few steps unaided and, clutching his father's knees, looked up with a broad, toothy grin.

"Isn't he clever, Daddy?" Georgina cried, hugging Robert's arm. He kissed her upturned face and picked up Liam with suitable words of praise and surprise at his progress; over the child's head, however, he caught Louisa's uncertain, tremulous smile, and his heart lurched with sudden pain.

Laying Robert's little namesake in his crib, she came toward him, lifting her face to be kissed. With dry lips he touched her cheek, commented lightly on how well she was looking, praised each child in turn, listened to Georgina's excited news, and was immensely relieved when the nursemaid arrived to prepare the little ones for bed.

In the drawing room, his daughter insisted on playing her latest pieces at the piano, but once she had gone upstairs, an awkwardness descended upon them all. During dinner, Letty did her best to keep up the conversation, drawing her brother out regarding the problems at the Curragh; work, however, was the last thing on his mind, and Louisa seemed tongue-tied almost to the point of idiocy. He wondered whether she knew of his appointment with Dr. Stevens; he knew it was not a subject he would raise himself.

For a while Letty played Schumann for them, but the romance of his music held undertones of sadness which echoed unbearably in that quiet room. Stretched out in his chair before the fire, Robert smoked a cigar and stared into the flames; Louisa held a piece of embroidery.

Eventually, without saying goodnight, Letty simply closed the piano and went to bed.

Having managed perhaps half a dozen stitches, Louisa folded her work and returned it to the basket. Hearing her sigh, Robert looked up, noting the heightened color along her cheekbones. She was wearing a blue velvet gown, one he had never seen before, which suited her very well; and this evening her hair was particularly pretty. Apart from her silence, she seemed so much recovered, so much her old self that he was tempted to think the rest a nightmare from which they would all very shortly wake. He remembered there had been moments like this with Charlotte, however, and hardened his heart to temptation. No doubt her silence was that of embarrassment, he told himself; nervous apprehension at thoughts of having to share the same bed and wondering how to phrase rejection without giving offense.

He smiled at the irony, and, seeing it, Louisa colored even more. Her fingers trembled over the work basket, arranging and rearranging its contents.

"Well," she said brightly, "it's perhaps time we went up, too. It's been a long day for me, and you look quite exhausted."

"I am," he admitted, sighing, "but I don't think I'll come up just now. I'll have a nightcap first."

"You won't be long, will you?"

There was a plaintive quality in her voice which touched several raw nerves. Rising abruptly, he went over to the table where a decanter and glasses stood; pouring a generous measure, he said shortly: "I may be— I'm not sure."

In the silence which followed, the ticking of the clock sounded like a death knell. It seemed an eternity before she moved, and when she did, he could not believe she was coming toward him. He almost flinched at her touch, turning his eyes from that tearful, appealing gaze, wishing she would simply go to bed and leave him to suffer alone.

But she slipped inside his guard. Embracing him, she whispered: "I've missed you so much."

For a moment, gripping her shoulders, he wanted to shake her. What was she trying to *do?* he thought on a surge of anger; didn't she *know?* Was the responsibility for her well-being to be entirely *his?*

With a great effort, Robert tried to compose himself and, searching for gentleness, found only a voice which shook with frustration. "I've missed you, too."

"Then won't you come to bed?"

"No, I don't think so," he said hoarsely, wanting to caress her and determined not to. "You've not been well—you need your rest."

The arms which had held them together dropped slowly away. Her underlip quivered for a moment, and then she blinked and smiled. "Yes," she said lightly. "Yes, I'm sure you're right. I'll go on up, and see you tomorrow."

"Yes," he repeated, not sure whether it was gratitude or regret which brought that sudden shiver to his spine. "Go on up now. We'll talk tomorrow."

Next day, however, the household was full of different news. Harris and Moira were engaged to be married and, while the happy couple were inclined to be prosaic about that as-yet distant union, in the servants' hall it was cause for celebration.

Upstairs, in spite of genuine and hearty congratulations, that betrothal cast long shadows ahead. To Robert it was a very real reminder that, after six years, he was losing the best servant he had ever had; and more than that, for within the strictures of their official relationship, Harris had become a trusted friend. There was never any need to explain things to Harris: he knew and understood. The very idea of having a stranger in his quarters and in his home set Robert's teeth on edge; it was symptomatic of change, change on every front, and he hated it.

At first Louisa received the news with genuine pleasure; Moira was so happy, and after months in which the smallest ray of light had failed to penetrate, it was good to have something to be happy about. Good to have something to lift her spirits even slightly after the bitter disappointment of Robert's homecoming.

The tunnel of black and terrifying despair was behind her, she knew that; but in the shadows which remained were other anxieties, fears she was too insecure to tackle alone. She needed Robert's help to determine a path for the future, needed a hand to hold when the going was hard; needed, above all, a chance to speak honestly, in much the same way as she had spoken to Dr. Stevens. Professional sympathy and detachment, coupled with the sure and certain knowledge that he was bound by confidentiality, had enabled Louisa to give voice to what was troubling her. After weeks in which the simplest problems had been agony to contemplate, the most banal questions impossible to answer, it had been blessed relief to talk again. The expression of truth, which was often critical and sometimes shameful, had been hard to one so accustomed to swallowing the unpalatable and saying nothing; but having done so once, she could see its importance.

Robert was not the easiest of men to pin down, particularly when he had other things on his mind; and for that reason alone, she regretted the sudden and early removal to the Curragh. Had he been living at home, with no more pressing concern than the next day's hunting, it would have been easier to broach, a simple matter of awaiting the right moment. But, over periods of no more than two or three days, with everyone wanting a piece of his time, and problems of which she knew nothing occupying his mind, the difficulty seemed insurmountable.

Being told that further children were to be avoided at all costs was to Louisa a most mixed blessing. Having had two in quick succession, and having suffered because of it, she had no desire for more. Indeed, the very thought of being pregnant again could reduce her to panic; not simply for her own suffering, but because she knew, deep down, that Robert had wanted neither child. Once he knew about Liam, of course he had been delighted; but the reality had become a burden to him more than a pleasure.

Wondering whether he had been told she must bear no more, Louisa's answer had come last night. In retrospect, she knew she should have pressed him, overridden that hurt and angry pride of his; knew she had let one vital opportunity slip through her fingers. But in truth, she herself had been so very hurt, so cut to the heart by his crass insensitivity, that to struggle against it was quite beyond her. She had passed a bitter, sleepless night, and so, without doubt, had he.

Resting in her bedroom after luncheon, it seemed to Louisa that there was far more than mere brick walls between them, more than the distance from Dublin to the Curragh. Loving him, wanting him, she found the means of communicating that without bald words eluded her. And the time when bald words could have been uttered without loss of grace or femininity was long gone. She could say "I love you," but unless they were in bed together, touching, how could she imply that she wanted him physically? To say "I want you," in the middle of the afternoon, over tea, was far too gross. A man could say that, and from Robert those words had always provoked a pleasurable thrill; but ladies never did. On the other hand, Louisa reflected, ladies were supposed to endure, not enjoy, so where did that leave her? Guilty of being less than the lady she imagined herself to be, and far less than the one Robert wanted her to seem in public. It left her, as always, in the company of women she invariably despised, those who were coarse, grasping, and vulgar, women with whom men could be free, because they deserved no particular respect.

Once, such thoughts had never clouded her horizons. To love and be loved, to share the physical expression of that love, in whichever and whatever ways there were, had been all that really mattered. But in those days their love had been private, a secret between the two of them, inviting no comment, no judgments, because hardly anyone knew. Was guilt, then, a matter of public contempt—and innocence one of public approbation? The consensus of the majority? If society said *This is the way we behave, therefore this is right,* was all other behavior wrong?

In searching for answers, she searched the innermost depths of her being and knew it was not so. While one half of society gorged itself, the other half starved. In Ireland, the Catholic majority believed in the intercession of the saints, while the Protestant minority accused them of worshiping graven images. Always there were two sides to every argument; even Christ said to render unto Caesar what was Caesar's and to God what belonged to God. He did not condemn the woman taken in adultery; but He said *Go and sin no more.*

That cold, dark, terrible despair seemed eloquent of judgment; under its weight she had wept the penitent's tears, made promises which, in the clear light of day, she had no desire to keep. She loved Robert; her body cried out for his touch, for his warmth and vitality, the reassurance that he loved her still . . .

No more children, the doctor said. *Go and sin no more,* intoned the Gospel. Where, for Heaven's sake, was the compromise?

THIRTEEN

*A*fter a hellish couple of days, Robert made his escape on the Sunday evening. Having booked one of his hunters on the train in advance—"Just in case I get the opportunity," he told Letty—he had one of the grooms take it over to the station to be boxed and had Harris pack stocks, breeches, cutaway coats and mahogany-top boots for his trip to Kilkenny later in the week.

Saying good-bye to Louisa, he felt guilty; she clung for a moment as he kissed her cheek, and though none were shed, tears were shining in her eyes. Georgina was cross and sulky at his going, demanding to know when he would be back and wanting it to be soon. Waving him off from the steps, his sister quite simply looked grim.

"Think you should have stayed a bit longer, sir," Harris observed as soon as the luggage was stowed and they were away.

"Oh, for God's sake, Harris," Robert said shortly, "don't you start that as well! If I don't get away for a few days' exercise, there'll be crimes committed, I promise you."

With a little half-smile lifting those lugubrious features, the younger man said: "There's always the Sudan, sir—crying out for officers, they are."

"Don't imagine I haven't thought of it," responded Robert with dour humor. "Right at this moment, the idea of marching through the desert, knocking hell out of whoever gets in the way, has a certain perverse appeal." He joked, but there was more than a grain of truth in what he said. From reports which were still coming in, it seemed the advance toward the Nile valley would be a determined, careful, and lengthy campaign, and, as Harris so rightly said, the Egyptian Cavalry, under Kitchener's general command, were crying out for British officers. It was tempting, very tempting indeed, but for the moment domestic and financial responsibility was running high; to keep his finger on the pulse, Robert needed to be in Ireland, so in Ireland he must stay.

For the time being at least, he reflected, he would have to make do with other escape-routes, however short, and close his mind to the rest.

On the Monday he made his presence felt in stables and mess hall, and Tuesday on the parade ground; in between he cleared an accumulation of paperwork, sent a telegram to the Loys in Kilkenny, and set forth to join them early on Wednesday morning.

It was a glorious spring day, the sort when even the meanest of God's creatures feels good to be alive. Rabbits scuttled across green fields, wild primroses were in bloom along the trackside, and in the distance Kilkenny's hills were purple against a cerulean sky. With a groom, Amelia was there to meet him, looking like a daffodil in a green velvet habit with yellow facings. As always, she made him smile.

"So the monastery did let you out, after all," she declared, pecking his cheek in cousinly fashion. Giving orders to the groom, she assured Robert the man was capable and invited him to sit beside her on the driving seat of the trap.

"Will I be safe, with you driving?" he inquired, laughing.

"I doubt it, but it'll be exhilarating, at least!"

He climbed aboard and, as though noticing for the first time, said: "Where's Gerald, the lazy hound? Still lounging over breakfast?"

"Gerald isn't with us," she announced airily. "His business, you know, takes up far too much of his time."

Out of sight of the station and any curious passersby, Robert laid his hand on her knee. "You know," he said, with a slow, laconic smile, "I was rather hoping you might say that."

The affair went exceedingly well, for a while at least. It answered pressing physical needs, provided a certain spice which had been missing from Robert's life for some time, and seemed to put a feather in Amelia's cap.

They saw each other frequently to begin with, usually as houseguests in the country homes of mutual friends; but as the hunting season drew to its close and the intensity of training at the Curragh increased, such opportunities were rare. They risked a hotel on a few occasions, and Amelia's Meath estate twice, but the latter was inconvenient for the Curragh and also rather too dangerous even for one addicted to such dangers. She loved the aura of sin and secrecy, that much was obvious, throwing herself into every encounter like a hungry animal, almost devouring Robert in her eagerness. It was typical of everything she did, yet he often found himself wondering, especially afterward when she lay unrelaxed beside him, whether Amelia really enjoyed sex. She seemed insatiable, and for a while that was very flattering; for a while, also, it gave him reasons why she wanted a man other than her husband.

Quite early in their relationship he asked her; she said Gerald was boring, uninventive as a lover; accused him too of having married her for the estate, which Robert found hard to believe. In the early days of their acquaintance, he had thought his cousin very fond of her. How things stood between them now, however, was anyone's guess. Robert was sure he was by no means the first of Amelia's lovers; indeed, he had been convinced for a long time that Tom McNeill claimed that dubious honor, while two more had danced notable attendance since. Certainly he saw very little of Gerald that summer, but whether his cousin was genuinely besieged by business matters or he knew and simply did not care, Robert had no idea.

Occasionally, seeing him to exchange a few words in passing, Robert was aware of guilt at the betrayal of their youthful friendship; after a while, however, he became adept at feeling nothing at all. Between himself and Gerald's wife, love was not the currency of exchange—sex was. He imagined Amelia would tire of the game before long, as he was already beginning to; and ultimately they would part as amicably as they had come together, with no real emotion involved. If an example was needed to reinforce that theory, he had Tom McNeill to look to, still *persona grata* at all Amelia's gatherings.

As far as his home life was concerned, in Robert's eyes the affair was equally successful. The summer drill season was a period when he was away a good deal, anyway, so the odd day or night spent elsewhere was never remarked upon. In the past he had usually taken Harris home with him, but with his leaving the regiment in May, it was a habit Robert did not begin with the new man.

When he did go home to Fitzwilliam Square, he was in far better humor; and although there had been initial pangs of guilt, since then he had told himself it was for Louisa's benefit in the long run and persuaded himself into virtue. With excitement both behind him and ahead, it was easier by far to tolerate his sister's earnestness and Louisa's obsession with the children. Much as he adored his family, the atmosphere of the Devereaux house was too often that of quiet, middle-class sobriety; less of the Good Book than gardening catalogues, admittedly, but the women's interests bored him to distraction.

Louisa, however, was beginning to mystify him. She gardened with Letty, looked after the children, sat in the evening in her modest cotton gowns with her embroidery, for all the world the archetypal, respectable matron. Her conversation was sparse, on occasion sharply ironic, but never personal. Obviously she was recovered from the deep melancholy of the winter and showing no signs whatever of a return to that state; in fact she seemed, to all intents and purposes little changed from the Louisa of a year ago; except that she was not pregnant. Yet subtle differences impinged upon him, changes which, while not exactly worrying him, gave rise to a certain amount of serious reflection.

In the spring, when reproachful tones and tears were the last things his conscience could stand, she had been very emotional on a couple of occasions. With determined brightness he had successfully talked her out of it and, as before, left her to sleep alone. Then, looking back, he recalled a period of excessive quietness, one visit at least when she had hardly spoken to him at all. That had given him cause for anxiety, thinking word of his affair was out; but with Letty more or less her usual self, he realized he was safe.

Since then, except to discuss Georgina or the boys, she rarely asked him anything, and as though obeying a set of rules, he never mentioned his social life; what was left was very limited.

At the end of August, with his squadron's maneuvers finished, Robert took a planned two weeks' leave, joining his family at their rented villa by the sea. With the forthcoming upheaval of the regiment's move to winter quarters in Dundalk to look forward to at the end of September, it was a good time for rest and much-needed recuperation. Since February, work had been intense at the Curragh, and summer had been particularly unsettling, with Harris's departure for York in May and Darnley away to the Sudan in June. In different ways, he missed both men, particularly envying Darnley his freedom to pursue whatever course ambition dictated. Tommy said he was mad: he envied no one the harsh inconveniences of a desert campaign. Training on the lush green expanse of the Curragh was bad enough, even with the fleshpots of Dublin to look forward to; home situations were far too cushy to exchange for the hard reality of death and disease in a foreign land.

"You're getting soft, Tommy," Robert had said; but Tommy, heavier and less agile than in the days when he had earned that terrible facial scar, had laughed and delivered a dart of his own.

"I can't see why you're so damned keen," he retorted, "with a mistress at home and another panting after your every move—you're in clover, man! My little filly's just thrown me over for a pansy hussar and a gold ring. With my broken heart, I'm the one who should be volunteering for the desert, not you!"

The strange thing was that, in spite of the jest, Robert believed his friend was upset at losing his latest love. But avoiding commitment had become such a way of life with Tommy that Robert thought him incapable of any other.

That conversation, and the reason behind it, was very much on his mind when he arrived at the villa in Dalkey. As Moira opened the door to him, he was even envying Harris the simplicity of his life. Working as a cellarman in York for the experience, and looking for the right little property, Harris was single-minded enough to achieve all he set out to do. And as Louisa had so rightly remarked on the day of the betrothal, he could not see Harris letting passion get in the way of it. His old servant's letters bore that out: there had been plenty of pubs on the market, but none of them quite what Harris wanted. They were either too expensive or not in the right quarter, and despite his eagerness to find a place, marry, and begin work, Harris would not let that come between him and his better judgment.

Miss Letty and Miss Louisa were out walking along the seawall, Moira told him, and the children were having their afternoon nap; but there was a letter for him, she added with twinkling brightness, sent on from Dublin that very morning.

"Is it good news, then?" he asked, recognizing Harris's careful hand.

"It is indeed, sir. He's found a place, a bit run-down but otherwise fine—and wants me to go ahead right away!"

"That *is* good news!" Robert smiled. "Not long to the wedding, then?"

Moira blushed. "Well, that depends on getting the pub, sir."

"Oh, we'll soon have that sorted out, Moira, don't you worry. A September wedding, eh?" With a little laugh, he winked at her and went upstairs.

Reading his mail, Robert was bound to agree with everything Harris said. The pub was on Fishergate, small, run-down, and absolutely filthy—although he had never been in, Robert remembered the place—but structurally sound and going very cheap. Dirt was no problem, hard work would cure that; but as Robert was investing his money too, Harris wanted him to see the place before agreeing to buy.

Thinking it over, Robert's initial reaction was to write back and tell him to go ahead anyway; but on reflection, he realized he had two weeks' leave, and a visit to York might do Louisa the world of good. She had been critical and cutting with him recently, and a trip home might sweeten her temper. Always providing, he thought gloomily, that she could be persuaded to leave the children for a few days.

Over dinner that evening he told them Harris's news, and for his sake and Moira's both Louisa and his sister were delighted. Almost as one, however, they remarked on losing the girl so soon.

Robert laughed. "You've known about it since last March. How can you call that 'soon'?"

"Well, a betrothal isn't a marriage, is it?" Louisa said. "The date was dependent on Harris finding what he wanted, and that could have been anytime. Now we know, and it's a surprise, that's all. We've been carrying on regardless of Moira going—and time's slipped away without realizing." For a moment, as she studied her empty plate, an ironic smile passed her lips. "Time does slip away like that, doesn't it? I was only saying today—wasn't I, Letty?—that it's just three years since I came to Ireland." She looked up, and Robert caught a fleeting glimpse of something—pain, mockery, accusation?—which disconcerted him.

"So long?" he laughed. "Is it really three years?"

"Liam will be two in just over a month," she said defensively and, switching to the attack, added: "Or had you forgotten?"

"No," he lied, "I hadn't forgotten."

"Then how could you think it was less than three years?"

He laughed again, uneasily. "It just doesn't *seem* that long. This year's flown."

"Time does, when you're enjoying yourself."

Pursing his lips, Robert looked down at the table. Embarrassed, Letty scraped her chair as she stood up.

"Shall we take our coffee outside, onto the terrace? The evening's lovely, and the garden's full of scented stocks."

Determined to break the tension, Robert agreed. Taking Louisa's arm as they crossed the threshold, he said: "Harris wants me to go and look at the property before he agrees to take it. I don't really think that's necessary, but it occurred to me you might like to go over for a few days. We could make a little holiday of it."

Stiffening perceptibly, Louisa withdrew her arm from his grasp. "No, I don't think so," she murmured.

Amazed by that refusal, Robert paused, unsure whether he had heard aright. "Why ever not?"

"Because," she said, seating herself in one of the wicker chairs, "if I went home to York now, Robert, I very much doubt whether I should want to come back.

"I'm sorry, Letty," she went on into the stunned silence. "I don't mean to hurt *you* by that. You've been a good friend to me, and I hope you always will be. But it's true—if I were to go home, I couldn't bear to return to Dublin."

"My dear," the older woman said, looking up at her brother and pressing Louisa's hand, "I quite understand. However, I won't interfere, and that's all I'm going to say on the subject." Patting the cushions of her chair into shape, she added firmly: "Nor do I intend to give up this lovely evening in favor of a discreet retirement to bed. If you need to discuss the matter further, Robert, might I suggest a little stroll along the promenade?"

For several seconds Robert was too stunned to move or answer. Starting to speak, he thought better of it, eventually forcing his wooden limbs to carry him across the terrace and away from the women. Stiffly he descended the steps to the garden, walking the twilight-shadowed area of lawns and shrubberies alone. He felt no pain or anger, only a kind of stinging shock, like the aftermath of a most unexpected slap in the face. From behind him, beyond the house, the hushed murmur of the sea blended with those soft voices from the terrace, making it impossible to decipher words or intent; he could imagine, however, a damning discussion of his shortcomings, both real and fallacious.

Did they know about Amelia? The thought hit him from nowhere, making his heart pound, bringing guilty heat to face and throat; with trembling fingers he lit a cigar, drawing the smoke deep into his lungs. A pity if it came out now, he thought, just as he was planning a strategic withdrawal from that particular field.

He shivered suddenly and moved on, returning at an apparently aimless, meandering pace to the steps. Letty had her eyes conveniently closed, but Louisa returned his gaze unsmilingly, with just a hint of challenge in that lifted chin. He stood for a while without speaking, unhurriedly smoking the last of his cigar.

Finally, with an air of having come to a great decision, he said: "I think we'd better take that walk."

To westward over the land, the sun had set, leaving a sky streaked like an artist's palette with pinks and golds on an indigo ground. Over the sea it was already dark, the black and incoming tide visible in foaming white rivulets on the curve of beach below. The sound of it shushing and sighing over sand and shingle was much louder here, drowning the silence between them, filling the space that time had created. It was late for the usual evening promenaders, and they were virtually alone, surrounded by a greater privacy than any four walls could provide.

"Tell me, then," he said at last, "why you want to go home."

"I didn't say that."

"No, but what you did say left no doubt that that was what you meant."

There was a strengthening breeze blowing off the sea, cool and refreshing after the sultriness of a warm afternoon. As they rounded one of the bluffs of that rocky, indented coastline, it buffeted the stiff brim of Robert's straw hat and he removed it, turning to look at Louisa with searching eyes. "Well?" he prompted, but she was busy with her own bonnet, trying to anchor it, unsuccessfully, to her short curls.

Eventually, with an impatient gesture, she took it off and went to lean against the seawall. Looking down at the rocks far below, and with the wind ruffling her hair, she said: "Do you want me to go? Home, I mean—permanently?"

He had to stand close to hear what she said; as understanding dawned, he felt something very akin to fear grip him with surprising force. "No," he slowly replied, "*I* don't want you to go . . ."

"You amaze me," she remarked with bitter humor. "I've had the feeling for a long time that I was no more than an encumbrance in your life. A bit of a joke, really—the mistress you no longer sleep with!" She laughed, shaking her head at the irony, but Robert could not summon so much as a smile.

"For *your* sake," he said.

"Really? Are you sure?" Even through the gloom, that piercing look of hers made him shiver. "Are you sure it's not because there's someone else? Knowing you as I do, Robert, I find it hard to credit such lengthy celibacy to *my* account!"

"Thank you," he replied shortly, his bitterness managing to equal hers.

"Not at all."

"Would you believe me if I denied it?"

"No."

"Then there's no point in telling you I love you?" he demanded. "Or that I've done my best to abide by what both Molloy and Stevens told me?"

When Robert thought about that time, the fear he had experienced in comparing that situation with Charlotte's, there was no need to simulate any emotion. The pain and bitterness were real, as was his anger at blind fate. For the first time he gave vent to those feelings, holding nothing back in a lengthy affirmation of all that had gone through his mind while Louisa was ill. Even at some months' distance, it was a relief to talk about it; a relief to have it out, quite literally, in the open, against the sound of wind and waves and with that clean salt taste on his tongue.

"All I could see was Charlotte," he said again, stressing an image she knew and understood, "and to be told you must never bear another child—" He broke off, thinking not of children but of the passion they had shared, and wishing, now, that he could have spoken of it then.

"But you didn't want more children," she said bleakly.

"I wanted *you*," he declared hotly, grasping her shoulder and turning her to face him. "But I was told it would do you harm, that you were afraid, guilty—damaged mentally by what I'd done!"

"Oh, God!" Louisa whispered, leaning heavily against him. "That's not true. Whoever told you that—it's not true. I was afraid—yes—and I did feel terribly guilty about the children, about us, but I still wanted you in spite of all that—I still needed you!"

Clasping her tight against him, rocking her in his arms, he fought down guilt and remorse, silently cursing the hurt and angry pride which had driven him to Amelia Loy, with her voracious, shrew-like appetites. There was no comparison, he thought, between those spoiled and greedy demands and the love Louisa gave so freely. "We should have talked," he said miserably, knowing it was no fault but his own, yet clinging to the idea that absence had contributed.

"I tried to," she sobbed against his chest. "I *needed* to talk to you, Robert, but you wouldn't listen."

"I know, I know—I'm sorry. If I'd been more at home, we'd have got together, helped each other." Kissing her hair, her face, he whispered: "Can you ever forgive me?"

Tentatively at first, he touched her lips, and then, as longing seized him, kissed her with mounting hunger. Not wanting to let go, yet needing more than kisses, he murmured endearments and promises, plans for the future; but he sensed a holding back, her body's eagerness restrained by thoughts he did not want to put into words. "Let's go home," he urged, "back to the villa. I want to be in bed with you, not out here in the cold. You're shivering, too."

Slipping off his jacket, Robert draped it round her shoulders. "Come on, now," he smiled. "Let's go home."

She gripped his hands, staring up into his face. The night wind was getting stronger, whipping at her dress, tossing the curls back from her forehead; it was cold and fresh, tangy with salt and the smell of seaweed, and up from the rocks came the hiss and boom of the tide.

"Tell me honestly," she begged, "that there's no one else, hasn't been anyone else."

He closed his eyes, and for a moment the desire to confess was overwhelming; but then sense prevailed. Louisa loved him, and love could forgive much—but not Amelia Loy. Drawing her close, with his mouth against her lips, he whispered: "No, there's never been anyone else."

FOURTEEN

*F*or the first time in many months, since well before Bobby's birth, Robert realized, they shared the same bed. At first there was a deep reticence in her, which he guiltily ascribed to suspicion; at pains to overcome it, he was particularly tender, but that awareness, coupled with the need to be careful, resulted in a less than satisfying reunion. She said she was happy just to sleep with him, and for a few days Robert did his best to think the purest of thoughts before he went to sleep. But abstinence and close proximity were uneasy partners for both of them. After almost four years, that little cone-shaped device obtained in Leeds was obviously past its useful life; and whether it could be replaced in Dublin was a matter for discreet inquiry. If not, Robert said, then a trip across the water must be made; and while they were discussing that subject, he resurrected the idea of a holiday in York.

But again Louisa was peculiarly reluctant. She seemed unable to give a concise reason, and with both Harris and Moira in need of a speedy response to his letter, Robert let the subject drop. He wrote that his new partner in the licensed trade should go ahead with the purchase, that he should fix up whatever was essential and return to Dublin as soon as convenient for the wedding. Vastly amused, especially by the idea of being "in trade," Robert did not seriously expect the partnership to last very long. His investment was more in the nature of a loan, made with the proviso that Harris might buy him out as and when he was able to do so; although, if anything should happen to Robert, the return on that investment would be payable to Louisa. The very remote possibility of war, with Harris recalled to the colors, was also covered, in which case Moira would either continue the business or sell up, again paying Louisa the agreed proportion.

The wedding itself was finally arranged for the end of September, which involved a great deal of to-ing and fro-ing between Dalkey and Dublin during the second week of their stay. Excitement was in the air, and romance, the women planning Moira's trousseau as though she were a member of the family, buying Irish linens for the bottom drawer, and generally indulging themselves. Even Robert was not immune. Although Moira would have liked him to give her away, it was finally decided that, as a Catholic, McMahon should have that honor, while Robert preferred to stand as Harris's best man; and Georgina, more excited than all of them put together, was to be bridesmaid. It would be a small wedding in the church where Moira attended Mass each Sunday, with a reception below stairs at the Devereaux house.

In the midst of all the preparations for the wedding, and Robert's move with the regiment to Dundalk two days afterward, Louisa's birthday was quite overlooked. She was aware that the date fell some ten days before the big event but, in the light of present happiness, had an almost superstitious dread of mentioning it. Awareness of her thirtieth year, marking the end of youth, heralding the approach of middle age, had been with her all summer, like a deep-stressed line beneath Robert's neglect. The passage of time, while she seemed to be standing still, was frightening, as was the conviction that he had found someone younger, prettier, more lighthearted with whom to enjoy his precious hours of freedom. With two babies, she felt defenseless, trapped; she could have slipped so easily into despair, except that the memory of true and total darkness, so recent, kept her upright and alert.

York was on her mind constantly that summer. Seductive and repelling, like a siren song of certain danger, it seemed the longer she fought it, the stronger it became; only love of Robert was stronger, and with lack of nurture, that love was in danger of dying. Her words to him that evening in Dalkey were not exaggerated, and his response had come like a blessed draft of water, restoring life, restoring faith, bringing love to stem that call for home. Because she could never go back. Not to live. Not with two children.

But she was happier now, more confident of the future, despite the fact that Robert would be away for the winter. At least, she reflected, with proper quarters and the drill season over, he should be able to take plenty of leave. In the past year he had taken far less than the statutory six weeks, when usually, along with most of his colleagues, he managed to elicit something like two and a half months. With any luck he would have a couple of weeks either before or after Christmas, and probably the same at the end of February; and Dundalk was not much more than an hour by train, more convenient than Belfast, where Tommy's squadron was to be sent.

Happier, but nevertheless reluctant to acknowledge the milestone of her birthday, Louisa dropped no hints to anyone and, until the arrival of the morning mail, had almost managed to forget it herself. There were letters from her mother and Edward and what felt like cards from her sisters. Despite her regret for the day, each envelope gave her a mixture of surprise and pleasure; after that long gap in which she had heard from no one but her mother, each little missive from home brought a sentimental lump to her throat, even the ones from Emily and Blanche. Tempted to open them, she pushed them unread into her drawer, to savor later, and went down to breakfast.

As had become usual when he was at home in Dublin, Robert had been out earlier; he was already at the table, still in his riding clothes, opening his own mail over a second cup of coffee.

He seemed preoccupied, barely acknowledging the kiss Louisa dropped on his forehead. As she helped herself to bacon and mushrooms from the sideboard, he pushed the letter aside and gave vent to a soft but eloquent curse.

"What's wrong? Army business?"

"No, I wish it were." Disregarding the fact that she was just about to eat, Robert lit a cigar, staring through the curls of smoke at an obscure point, with a deep frown of concentration.

"What is it?" she asked again; and with a little flutter of alarm: "Not bad news, I hope?"

He sighed. "Yes, it is, rather. The trouble is, I'm not sure what to do about it." After a short pause, he said: "Mrs. Hanrahan, Charlotte's nurse, has just died. A sudden heart attack, William says."

From her own divination, Louisa understood enough of that intimate relationship to realize that such a bereavement could only spell trouble at White Leigh. And inconvenience in Dublin, too, with the wedding and Robert's departure so soon upon them.

"I should go down—William would like me to—but I really don't see how I can. And if I do go, what use will I be? I'm sure they're as capable of interviewing replacement staff as anyone . . ."

Remembering the vicious blow she had received from Charlotte, Louisa shivered. "That won't be easy. Where will they find another Mrs. Hanrahan?"

"Heaven only knows, but they'll have to find somebody, and soon— the girl, Mary, won't be able to manage on her own." The frown deepened as he considered the problem; then, with a sudden shrug, Robert stood up. "I'd better find Letty, see what she thinks about it."

Letty thought he should go down to the funeral, if only as a mark of respect for many years of devoted service; Louisa agreed, but she wished Robert could have asked her opinion first. Where Charlotte and White Leigh were concerned, however, Robert never invited her comments; it was as though all the fractured stress of that first visit stood between them. Either that, Louisa thought, or a continuing sense of guilt on his part. Whatever it was, the problem ensured that her birthday was truly forgotten.

By the end of the day, having read Edward's letter twice, and been touched both times by its simple sincerity, Louisa was aware of a quite profound disappointment. Other than her family in York, no one had remembered.

Robert made an overnight trip to Waterford for the funeral, returning gloomier than ever. Charlotte was distressed and inconsolable, which did not presage well. Owing to his commitments elsewhere, he could not interview possible nurses, so he had simply left instructions with his brother. Letty, meanwhile, offered to go to White Leigh should William need a second opinion.

Immediately on his return, Robert was away to the Curragh to prepare for the regiment's removal to Dundalk; he came back for the wedding, stayed the night, and left again next morning. After a couple of days' honeymoon in Blackrock, the bridal couple set sail for home.

Waving from the quayside at Kingstown, Moira and Harris barely identifiable among the throng aboard the steam packet, Louisa felt quite unreal, like someone made dizzy by a speeding ride at a funfair. Indeed, that afternoon had all the atmosphere of a funfair; it was sunny and warm, and the quay was crowded with all manner of people, sightseers as well as those waving fond farewells. There were poor women in shawls, wealthy ones with fashionable hats and parasols, burly dockers in steel-rimmed clogs, uniformed ship's officers, gentlemen in frock coats and tall top hats. The atmosphere was excited and emotional, handkerchiefs waving, dabbing tears away; and with the casting off of the final ropes, there rose a spontaneous cheer from the crowd. Very slowly the ship eased away from its berth. Moira waved frantically, Harris smiled, and gradually, slowly, oh, so very slowly, their faces became less and less distinct, while the ship itself became more and more visible as a whole.

As it gathered way and headed for the harbor mouth, the crowd began to disperse. Faces were sad, expressions flat; the quay an ordinary, cobbled, workday place, its carnival atmosphere gone.

With a great sense of anticlimax, the little party from Fitzwilliam Square went home.

Upon arrival, with the babies grizzling, Georgina tired and tearful, Letty anxious about Charlotte, it suddenly hit Louisa that Moira was gone. No smiling face to greet them, no welcome cheerfulness to banish children's tears and whisk them up to the nursery for tea; no cheeky anecdotes from the kitchen to disapprove; no one to share treasured moments of sweet nostalgia.

Moira was a married woman, with a home of her own and a business to go to: Moira was going back to York.

Back to autumn in the Museum Gardens, falling leaves along the riverside, white walls sharp against a clear blue sky; home to Minster bells, crooked doorways, and narrow, winding streets, to the scent of chrysanthemums at Christmas and daffodils in the spring . . .

FIFTEEN

*B*arely had Robert arrived in Dundalk than he was receiving pressing letters from Amelia. She had not seen him in more than a month, she wrote, and unless he made an effort *very* soon, desperation might send her fleeing back to Gerald's arms.

It was all couched in the lightest of terms, and for a while Robert stalled in much the same fashion, pleading pressure of work, making vague allusions to the hunting season proper, once he could get away. By the third such missive, however, he had detected an underlying seriousness which alarmed him. It was not going to die an easy, natural death after all; he was going to have to kill that relationship stone dead, and the prospect was not a pleasing one.

By the middle of November, he could stall no more: Amelia arrived in Dundalk one Friday afternoon, unannounced, just as he was about to set off for Dublin. For the benefit of the adjutant and other interested ears, she spun an excellent story about Gerald and business and traveling down together. Robert was furious.

"Are you *mad?*" he hissed once they were outside. "You'll be the talk of the regiment!"

"That doesn't bother me in the slightest, darling," she said brazenly. "If the mountain won't come to Mohammed . . ."

"This particular mountain is on his way home, Amelia, where he is expected for dinner."

"Send a telegram, tell them you've been detained. I've taken a suite at the Adelphi," she said, tapping his arm provocatively. "We could have dinner there."

He stood for a moment, looking down at her, wondering how so small a frame could contain such a determined, foolhardy spirit. Although he would much rather have gone straight home, it occurred to him that he should take the opportunity to call a halt to the game, to make her see, once and for all, that the stakes were too high.

Over dinner in her suite, Amelia was lively and witty as ever, apparently oblivious to his lack of conversation; she drank a great deal, almost matching Robert glass for glass, but, like himself, showed no signs of being drunk. For a girl in her early twenties, he thought with a faint shudder of distaste, she could certainly put the stuff away. Once that brazen impudence had been exciting; she could ride, swear, gamble, and drink as well as any man he knew, while her young girl's face and body lent a paradoxical air of innocence to everything she did. Playing the *enfant terrible* was all very well; but one day, he reflected, it would backfire, or she would grow old, and perhaps even Gerald would tire of the little harridan then.

Waiting for the remains of their meal to be cleared away, Robert searched for words and phrases to ease the forthcoming unpleasantness. There were none which were not trite or hollow or singularly inappropriate to the tone of their relationship so far. Which had been, he considered, basically honest.

Having decided that, and settled on a tone of firm frankness, he said over coffee: "This won't happen again."

"No, Robbie darling, you're quite right, it won't. I shouldn't have bearded the lion in his den and promise not to repeat the scenario. But it was desperation, you see, as I tried to tell you in my letters." Smiling sweetly, she put up her hands, removed a pin from her hair, and shook the dark mass free. Seconds later, she was seated across his lap and running her fingers through his hair, kissing his neck and ears and cheeks, and making her expectations very clear indeed.

He tried being stern, but she laughed and, ignoring his protestations, divested him of sufficient clothes to make donning them again seem foolish. For a little while it was amusing, and then, with his shirt open to the waist, Robert took hold of her wrists and held them fast.

Very seriously, as she tried to shake free, he said: "Stop it, and listen. This affair is over: it has to be. We've had a lot of fun, you and I, and so far nobody's been hurt—we've been very lucky. But one more incident like today, Amelia, and we'll both be in the divorce court, with Gerald citing me as corespondent!"

"What nonsense," she said petulantly. "Gerald doesn't care a fig."

"Doesn't he?" Robert asked. "I'm not so sure about that."

"I am. And, what's more, I don't care if he does. If I was free, it wouldn't matter who I saw, or how often—would it?"

"Don't be childish. You wouldn't enjoy being dragged through the humiliation of a divorce, with every intimate detail reported in the press. Imagine," he added sardonically, "what would the servants think?"

With a mutinous toss of her head, she refused to answer, and Robert pressed the argument home. "Don't you think it would be wiser to let the whole thing drop while we're still ahead? To part the friends we've always been?"

Again there was silence. She hung her head like a reproved child, hiding her face behind that mane of dark hair. "You don't want me anymore," she said in an unexpectedly small voice and, with a quick glance, added plaintively: "Why not?"

Dumbfounded by that quick change from hardened sophisticate to little girl lost, Robert could only shake his head. If ever there was a time for honesty, this was it, yet he was suddenly most reluctant to hurt her. Very gently, as he would with Georgina, he pushed the hair back from her face. "It's not that, believe me—rather that I can't afford to take the risks anymore. You might not care about Gerald finding out, but I do care about Louisa. The silly woman loves me, you see, and I cannot bear to have her hurt. It's as simple as that."

"And you love her?"

"Of course. When did I ever pretend otherwise?"

"Then why did you come to me?"

Suppressing a dry little smile, he said: "You know the answer to that as well as I do." After a momentary pause, he added: "You were bored, and so was I. It was a pleasant diversion for both of us."

For a long time, as though digesting the words left unsaid, she looked down at the slim brown wrists held within his hand. Then, with a catch in her voice, she murmured: "It was more than that for me. I think I've fallen in love with you."

Robert's heart sank. For a moment he allowed himself to believe her, and then, thrusting credulity aside, shook his head. "No, you don't. You've had a good time, little girl, and you don't want to go home, that's all."

Vehemently she denied it and then began to cry, heart-rendingly, against his chest. He suddenly saw her for what she was: a spoiled child without discipline, who had exchanged a father's indulgences for a husband's. A husband, moreover, who was Robert's own age, old enough to know better than let his wife run around like a first-class whore. She should have had her bottom smacked a long time ago, Robert thought harshly, and wondered whether this incident might teach her a much-needed lesson.

But he was not sufficiently hard-hearted to leave her in such distress. He cuddled her and petted her and ultimately took her to bed. For the last time, he swore to himself, making love with unaccustomed gentleness. She was passive and soft, and it seemed strange, with her, not to have a fight on his hands, not to feel she was bent on devouring him whole. It was also very enjoyable, and as he collapsed afterward, he had few regrets.

When his thoughts cleared, another strangeness became apparent: for the first time she was relaxed, too; genuinely satisfied, instead of clamoring for more.

A little after one, Louisa heard him come in, but he went straight to his own room. For a moment she wondered whether to call out or go to him, but she was sleepy and warm, and the effort was too much. Minutes later, she was dreaming of other things.

Next morning he was oddly vague about the business which had kept him in Dundalk, and for a fleeting moment she thought he might be lying; but then Letty started talking about the situation at White Leigh, and the matter went from her mind. It was a miserable end to the week, dull and gloomy outside, not fit for the ride Georgina longed to have; Robert seemed preoccupied by Charlotte, who was not, according to recent letters, responding well to the new nurse; and the baby was teething. They were all, it seemed, edgy and irritable, and for the first time in months Louisa was quite pleased to see him away again on Monday morning.

Going up to the schoolroom shortly afterward, she found Georgina by the window, in tears.

"What's the matter, dearest?" Putting an arm around those slender shoulders, Louisa drew her nearer the warm fire. "Why the tears?"

For eight years old, Georgina was tall and leggy, but she sidled gratefully onto the proffered knee, snuggling against Louisa's comforting bosom. "Daddy's horrid," she sniffed, "and I don't love him anymore."

"Oh, deary me, why ever not?"

"He doesn't love me!" she declared, bursting into a fresh bout of sobs.

"Oh, my love, of course he does! He does love you—you're the apple of his eye, sweetheart, truly you are."

"No, I'm not. He *promised* to take me riding, 'Ouisa, he truly, truly did. And I promised Dinky, and then he *wouldn't*—" she sobbed again— "and told me I was cheeky for saying it!"

"But it was awfully wet, wasn't it—not fit for going out. You might have caught a nasty cold."

"Not *so* wet," Georgina insisted, "and Daddy rides when it's raining. He goes out whenever he wants to—it's *not fair*."

"Oh, my sweetheart," Louisa said, sighing, "there's an awful lot of things in life which aren't fair, an awful lot. We just have to learn to put up with them."

"But he *promised*," she said indignantly, staring up into Louisa's face. "He shouldn't have, should he? That makes it a horrid lie, doesn't it? And that's *wrong*."

The child's black and white view brought another sigh to Louisa's lips and struck a chord deep down, which for no obvious reason made her feel faintly uneasy. Perhaps it was the extent of her own compromise, she thought; which was a difficult balancing act at the best of times.

"Yes, it is wrong," she conceded at last, "and he shouldn't have promised. But sometimes," she added wearily, "we promise things in all good faith, then outside things come along and make it impossible for us to keep to it. Like the weather—which we can't do much about."

"Well, it's still not fair," the little girl said, but the assertion was less vehement. Taking her hand, Louisa led her through into the nursery, and in the midst of Liam's prattling baby talk, Georgina at last recovered her good spirits.

Writing to Edward that afternoon, Louisa confessed to a certain gloominess, "brought on by the weather, no doubt," and mentioned the current anxiety over Robert's wife.

"Both Letty and William—and most certainly Anne!—think she should be committed, but, as ever, Robert won't hear of it. He hasn't been down to see her, however—Letty has and is most concerned. The new nurse—the second since Mrs. Hanrahan died—is more capable than the first, but far less pleasant apparently, and the servant Mary is now threatening to give notice. Charlotte is violent again, which must make things difficult all round. It seems an endless problem, which as far as I can see will only be solved by putting her in permanent, professional care. But Robert has this fixed idea about asylums and cruelty, and a strong sentimental streak which I'm sure obscures his better judgment sometimes.

"Anyway," she went on, "I really shouldn't bother you with all these problems, Edward . . ."

Sometime later, reading the complete missive through, she paused at that point; of late it seemed she bothered him more and more with day-to-day problems in the Duncannon household. Originally she had tried to avoid that, describing places she had visited, giving observations on life in the Irish capital; but with the advent of children, their correspondence had ceased, and since then, probably because she had little to write about other than her everyday life, it had become much more intimate.

She still had his first letter after Bobby's birth, written in the spring; could still feel stupidly emotional, reading the first few lines. "Forgive me," Edward said, "for being angry and hurt. From the very first, it seemed I was watching my dearest, most beloved friend place her head in a noose, and with news of your condition, I saw the rope tighten invincibly. I didn't want to acknowledge it, so I turned my head away and pretended the deed was done. Now I see how badly that hurt you—that in spite of all you have, you still need your family, even at a distance, even through the pitiful contact of words upon a page. So I beg your understanding, and pray our correspondence might resume."

It had resumed, and with those letters was created a new paradox in her life. Knowing she was forgiven had made life bearable, but as time went on, his letters fed and fueled that latent homesickness, which surfaced so painfully at Robert's suggestion of a holiday there.

Her mother's often-expressed desire to see those little grandsons had an equally profound effect. She longed for her to know them, yet feared the consequence of taking them back to York; and even though she had invited her mother to Dublin, Mary Elliott steadfastly refused to make the journey.

"I've never crossed the sea before," she wrote, "and I'm too old to start now." Those sentiments projected Louisa into the future, imagining her mother a helpless invalid, growing old and sick and lonely, her family scattered.

Which was ridiculous, as Letty often pointed out; Mary Elliott had companionship in Bessie, and neither Emily nor Blanche lived a thousand miles away. Nevertheless, having no great faith in either of her sisters, Louisa was aware of a gnawing sense of guilt, a feeling that she might never see her mother again and would suffer more because of it.

Standing by the nursery window, with the last blast of wind and rain upon the glass, she looked out over the square at bare trees and wet, scurrying leaves, and the days of the Marygate apartment seemed halcyon indeed, with her family within reach and Robert never further away, even in the summer, than the five miles' distance of Strensall. Although he must have worked hours which were as long and inconvenient as now, it did not seem so. Everything was closer, of course, unlike the Curragh, which was thirty miles away; and in those days he had been with her every hour that he could spare, whereas now he seemed to spare so little. Although the social life in Dundalk must be poorly provincial compared to Dublin, Louisa thought, there would always be the excuse of having to attend this or that social function for the regiment's sake. And now December was almost upon them, cubbing would be over and the hounds ready to quarter the countryside of Meath like soldiers after a red-haired rebel.

"Perhaps I should have learned to ride," she observed to Liam, "and taken up hunting." But he was busy banging alphabet bricks together and could not have answered even if he would. With a throaty, confiding chuckle, he presented his mother with a brick, then two more; dutifully she built them up, and with delighted glee he knocked them down.

The roster for December had Robert marked down for duty over Christmas. It was unfortunate, but, as he explained to Louisa, he had escaped the last three years and could not in conscience complain. She was sad for the children's sake, knowing the festival would not be the same without him, but a peculiar sense of detachment prevented her from being too upset on her own behalf. She was coming to expect these things; indeed, absence had become so much the norm, she sometimes wondered how they would react if thrown together for a long period of time. The numbing routine of her days continued, hardly broken even by her weekly visits to the Liberties. Familiarity with those back-street hovels had made them ineffective as a blessing-counter; and she was well aware that it was only Dr. Molloy's friendship which saved her from the worst snubs of the other helpers. He was held in such high regard by his little army, and Letty was so well respected, that no one dared do more than express a little coolness. But the odor of contempt was there, and Louisa hated it; only a dogged refusal to be bested kept her going.

Saturdays and Sundays, which had been red-letter days once upon a time, created yet another area of conflict in Louisa's battle-strewn soul. That Robert's discreet inquiries had proved fruitful, that she was now in possession of a newer, though by no means more attractive, device, did little to alleviate the situation. The seedy-looking medical man off Sackville Street had made her flesh crawl. She had the feeling he supplied the nearby brothels as well as ladies eager to broaden their horizons, and this suspicion imbued the tough little cone of wire and rubber with every degree of sinfulness. She could not escape from the feeling that what she was doing was wrong, that everything in her life was wrong, and that it was all concentrated in that one basic act.

Aware that something was amiss, Robert did try, unsuccessfully, to elicit the reason. But, with nothing solved, after a few days' leave in mid-December, he returned to Dundalk on the seventeenth. He would be back, he said, at the end of the following week; but not again until New Year's Eve.

"We'll celebrate then," he promised, in an attempt to cheer her, and with that he kissed her cheek and was gone.

Two days later, while Letty was out with Georgina, Louisa thought to take the opportunity to wrap the children's Christmas presents. She laid out paper, presents, sealing wax, and ribbon on the dining table and was just about to begin her task when the doorbell rang. It was the hour for afternoon callers, but other than Dr. Molloy or one of the kinder charity ladies, Letty had few visitors; with a little exclamation of annoyance, Louisa listened for voices as McMahon answered the door. Masculine tones reached her ear, not identifiable; thinking it must be the doctor, she was halfway across the room when McMahon entered. With exceptionally stiff formality, breathing disapproval from every pore, the elderly butler announced Mr. Gerald Loy.

A fleeting moment of sheer revulsion prompted Louisa to say she was not at home; then curiosity overcame it, together with a sickly apprehension that something was wrong. Gerald had not been to the house in more than a year, and never during the day. Perhaps, knowing he was Robert's cousin, the army had sent him to break some terrible news: a riding accident; insurrection in the streets; Robert the victim of a Fenian's bullet . . .

"Perhaps I'd better see him," she said in a voice which shook perceptibly. "Show him into the drawing room."

She waited a moment, clasping trembling hands together, wishing Letty were there; feeling hot and cold by turns, she went down the hall, past the as yet untrimmed Christmas tree, and into the drawing room. Gerald was standing by one of the tall windows, looking out at the bleak and rain-swept garden. His expression, equally wintry, underscored all Louisa's fears.

Discarding the niceties of social convention, she simply said: "You'd better tell me why you've come. If it's about Robert, just tell me what's happened."

For what seemed an eternity, those pale gray eyes searched and studied; and then, against all expectation, he laughed. Not pleasantly, but he saw some amusement in the situation which Louisa failed to catch. "It *is* about Robert, but—forgive me—not *quite* the tragedy you seem to expect." Again the bitter grimace of amusement. "A tragedy, but not of life and limb. Unfortunately."

"What do you mean?" Formed as a demand, the phrase came out as a whisper; and limbs which had trembled with tension now gave way to weakness. Sinking into a chair, her eyes never left him, searching every fleeting change of face and gesture, until he sat too, and strutting arrogance gave way to self-pity.

"He's taken my wife," Gerald announced in hollow tones.

"Taken your wife? Taken her where?" she asked stupidly. "What do you mean?"

"*Taken* her," he repeated with sudden fury, "away from me. Slept with her—had carnal knowledge, sexual intercourse—whatever you like to call it. The fornicating bastard, my own cousin, too!"

She wanted to scream and yell at him, say it wasn't true, but everything inside her—instinct, suspicion, foreknowledge—said it was.

"I've suspected it for a long time," Gerald went on, more quietly now, "but I didn't know for sure, didn't want to know, if truth be known. I love her, you see, the bad little bitch—God knows why, but I do. She thinks I married her for the estate, but that's not true. The trouble is, she doesn't believe me, and I can't convince her. I keep trying with the business—really just to prove I don't need her money—and she thinks that's boring, thinks because I don't spend every minute of the day with her, I don't love her, don't want her. But I do, and the more I try, the less I succeed . . ."

His voice tailed away on a pathetic, pleading note, and Louisa wanted to kill him, to squash that submissive, almost criminal weakness out of existence. He was begging for sympathy, but she had none; had he been stronger, wiser, less addicted to sexual titillation, she might have found it in her heart to pity him, but his weakness left Amelia Loy open to other temptations, and, tempted by Robert, she had not so much as paused before reaching out.

"I've given her everything," he said, "denied her nothing, and now . . ."

"And now she doesn't want you anymore," Louisa cut in, her voice like steel knives, "and I can't say it surprises me. So kindly spare me your bleeding heart and tell me what makes you think Robert's in-volved."

"Oh, I don't just suspect, Louisa, I know. Amelia told me."

"Told you what?"

"Why, that she wants a divorce."

"A *divorce?*" On a sudden gasp of incredulous laughter, Louisa shook her head. "What for? To marry Robert?" She laughed again, almost hysterically. "Are you mad? Is she completely *insane?* He's the most irrevocably married man I know, Gerald—you too, I should think. What does she hope to gain by a divorce, for Heaven's sake? She cannot marry *him!*"

"She wants her freedom; she says she's in love with him, that he's the only man who's ever—" after a momentary pause, he finished lamely, "made her happy."

Louisa felt physically sick. "And what does Robert say?" she asked. "Has anyone tried asking him what he thinks of this wonderful idea?"

"I haven't had a chance to see him yet . . ."

"Then why did you come to me?" she demanded bitterly. "What do you hope to gain by telling *me* the sordid details?"

"I thought perhaps you might—" he hesitated, uncertain of his ground, slightly afraid of her, "might persuade him to give her up."

"What? Me?" For some time she stared at him and through him, making Gerald Loy drop his gaze uncomfortably. "I very much doubt my ability to make your cousin do anything," she said at last, "and quite frankly, I don't see why I should even try. As far as I can see, they're very well matched. I wish him well of her, Gerald, and her of him."

"You don't mean that!"

"Oh, but I do," Louisa declared, giving a sharp tug at the bellpull. "And furthermore, I have no intention of doing your dirty work for you. See Robert yourself, challenge him to a duel, or something, make headlines in the newspapers, I really don't care."

With the arrival of the butler, Louisa bade a curt good afternoon and swept past them both on an angry rustle of petticoats.

SIXTEEN

*A*s though the past half hour had been no more than an ordinary interruption, Louisa went back to the dining room and continued wrapping presents. The task occupied a very tiny portion of her conscious mind, as did Gerald, and Robert, and Amelia Loy. The main part of her mind was not thinking at all; it was quite blank with shock.

She was aware, as she worked, of feeling quite calm and was dispassionately surprised by it. Surprised, also, by the feeling that something was missing. At first, she did not know what it was. Then, tying the last bow, stacking the last box, it dawned on her that she was no longer confused, because everything was crystal clear; no longer under tension, because the mainstay had finally snapped. And in that strong prevailing wind there was only one direction in which to go. The rocky shore was quite forgotten.

While she was upstairs, Letty and Georgina returned. The little girl immediately bounded up to the nursery, and when Louisa was not there, came knocking at her bedroom door, full of secrets and excitement over the shopping expedition. Seeing her, Louisa's resolve faltered for a second; the preserve of shock sustained a small but painful blow at the realization that in leaving Robert she would also have to part from his daughter. And his sister, her dearest friend.

She was trembling as she went down to join Letty for tea in the drawing room. With heavy curtains drawn against the early dusk, lamps lit, and the fire burning brightly, it was hardly the same room in which she had received Gerald Loy a mere couple of hours before. On a silver tray the tea things gleamed, and a plate of muffins stood by the fire, keeping warm. With a bright smile, Letty launched immediately into an account of her afternoon, the crush in Grafton Street, the ridiculous price of things, the difficulty of persuading Georgina toward gifts within her pocket's limitations.

Handing Louisa a cup of tea, however, she noticed the trembling hands, the ashen face, and was quickly contrite. "My dear, you look dreadful. What on earth's happened?"

"Letty, would you mind terribly if I was to go home?"

"Yes, of course I should mind. I'd miss you dreadfully, you know that. But if you thought it was for the best—well, you know I'd never try to stop you." After a pause for thought, she said, "We've talked about this before, but something has happened, hasn't it? Won't you tell me?"

"Gerald Loy called this afternoon." It was a bald statement, unrevealing as it stood, but for a while Louisa could say no more. She sipped her tea, holding the cup between both hands, needing the warmth in fingers which were still icy with shock.

Showing a patience she did not feel, the older woman waited for the rest of it, and as it came, piecemeal, she moved to the sofa where Louisa sat, enfolding her close, like a child. Less shocked, but far more surprised, Letty gave vent to exclamations and curses, frustrated by her brother's folly.

But as her first rage subsided, Letty's good sense began to reassert itself. "The thing is," she said angrily, "we only have Gerald's word for all this, and he only has Amelia's. She's such a nasty piece, Louisa, I'd not put it past her to be making the whole thing up."

"Gerald said he'd suspected it for a long time," Louisa whispered, "and to tell the truth, in the summer, so did I. But Robert *denied* it, and I believed him!"

"He *might* have been telling the truth, you know. Amelia could just, conceivably, be making trouble for Gerald. We should give Robert the benefit of the doubt, for the time being, and ask him, direct."

"There's no doubt at all in my mind." On a heavy, weary sigh, she said: "I've had enough, Letty. I can't take this kind of life anymore. It's not for me."

"It's not like you to give up so easily, to give in without a fight."

The smallest vestige of a smile lifted Louisa's lips. "No? As I see it, Letty, there's nothing left worth fighting for."

"You won't give Robert a chance to defend himself?"

"He lied to me, Letty. If he can do that once, he can do it again. I don't even want to see him."

Before dinner, while Louisa went upstairs with the intention of packing, Letty sent a telegram to her brother, telling him to return at once, by the very next train, if possible; Gerald Loy had called, and Louisa was leaving for York.

In the mess, two hours later, Robert frowned as he took the envelope. Reading the message, he felt the blood drain from his extremities; for a second, light-headed, he gripped the arm of his chair. Someone asked whether it was bad news, and he nodded, said he would have to return to Dublin immediately. With two large brandies under his belt he felt better, arranged to swap duties for the succeeding two days, saw the adjutant briefly, and set off for the station.

From Amiens Street he took a cab, arriving home just before midnight. Letty was waiting up, watching from his study window; she let him in quietly and poured him a drink. Within seconds his front of innocent dismay was seen through, and seconds later, demolished. With a plummeting heart Robert saw how thoroughly he was caught and by what devious means.

"A woman scorned," he said at last, pouring another drink. "Strange how the old adages are always the most true. Should have taken more note of that one, Letty, shouldn't I?"

"You're a fool, Robert; you should never have become involved with her in the first place."

"You're quite right," he said humbly. "I should have had more sense. Still, it happened—there's no point denying it now—and Madame Loy is hell-bent on revenge, methinks. I don't for one minute believe that Gerald will divorce her, nor will he give her grounds to divorce him. He'd be an idiot if he did."

"It would seem he came here to plead with Louisa, to persuade *her* to persuade *you* to give Amelia up."

"Well, good for him," Robert said sarcastically. "He's got what he wanted, had what he wanted—months ago. Well, weeks," he amended with a shamefaced grin, "if we're being technical about it. If only the stupid idiot had come to me first. We could have avoided all this."

With a little *humph* of derision, Letty lit another cigarette. "But that was never Gerald's way, was it? A bit of a sneak, our Gerald, if I recall correctly: no guts, at least not where it mattered."

Buoyed up by the brandy, Robert laughed. "Letty dear, you really are so devastatingly shrewd!"

"Aren't I though? And let me tell you now, Robert, you'd better get yourself up those stairs with a damn good explanation, otherwise Louisa will be gone tomorrow, and the children too."

Draining his glass, he went to the door; there, momentarily, he paused. "Tell me, would you forgive me? If you were Louisa, that is?"

"Well now, there you have me," she said sadly. "I really don't know."

He expected her to be in bed; if not asleep, then surely awake and tearful, stricken by the afternoon's events. He envisaged himself comforting her, telling her all that had happened and why, begging her forgiveness, promising a new, clean start; anything, in order to put things straight between them.

The first thing that met his eye, however, was an open trunk, almost full with children's clothes and toys. It stood inside the doorway of her room. In nightdress and robe, Louisa was searching through a cupboard; several drawers stood open, the chosen contents neatly folded across a chair.

Although she must have heard him enter, she did not turn around; nor, when he stated hesitantly that Letty had sent for him, did she so much as reply.

He closed the door behind him. For a minute or two, unsure of himself, Robert simply stood quietly and watched her. He spoke again; there was no response; accused her of being childish, to no avail. Afraid that his temper was mounting, he sat down, determined to say his piece, explain what must be explained, whether she wanted to listen or not.

With honesty the only policy left open to him, Robert began with the evening at Dalkey, telling her the reason for his lie. He said he had seen Amelia perhaps a dozen times in all, a fact he regretted, even before Louisa asked that fateful question. He went through it all, including that unexpected visit of Amelia's to Dundalk.

"I told her it was over, and I told her why. And to reinforce the argument, to my eternal regret I said we must not meet again in case Gerald heard of it—he might divorce her. That point was discussed at some length. I'm sure," he added, "that it was that conversation which planted the idea in her mind. She tried to engineer another meeting after that, but I was quite firm and refused point-blank to see her. I had another letter last week. Again I wrote, quite strongly, and said she must not contact me again.

"I can only assume that she's organized this little plot as a means of revenge, to spoil things between you and me. On the principle that if *she* cannot have me, then nor will you.

"If you leave, Louisa," he said to her resolute back, "you'll be ensuring her victory. It's what she wants. But it's all bluff: she won't divorce Gerald, or, should I say, he won't divorce her."

"I really don't care, Robert. Whatever she does is quite immaterial to me. I have my passage booked, and I've said my good-byes," she added falteringly, "and tomorrow all this will be behind me. I'm going home to a sane and sensible way of life. And I'm never coming back."

"You can't mean that! You mean you'll let Amelia Loy win her little victory, just like that?"

"It has very little to do with Amelia Loy!" Louisa declared. "You talked about honesty, Robert—and you lied in the same breath."

"I didn't want to hurt you!"

"But you managed it, nevertheless. Anyway, I don't want to talk about it. Will you go now, and let me get on."

"No, I damn well won't!" Breathing heavily, he fought to regain control of himself; he wanted to tell her he loved her and no one else, wanted to say how important she was to him, far too important to let go without a struggle.

"You can't do this, you can't just *go* without listening to me, without talking it over. I *need* you, Louisa."

"Yes, I've noticed," she said flatly, folding a plain gray dress and taking it to the open trunk.

"Does what we've shared mean nothing to you?" he demanded, grasping her arm as she brushed past. "The children? Our life here? Letty and Georgina?"

"I might well ask you," she said hotly, meeting his eyes for the first time, "the same question!" Shaking off his restraining hand, she returned to the wardrobe; but she was trembling, and he could see he had shaken that cold implacability.

With some idea that physical contact could transmit what words were failing to, Robert pursued that small advantage. Taking a step toward her, he caught her by the shoulders as she turned. "I love you," he whispered hoarsely, "and I won't let you go like this." But as his lips grazed hers, Louisa pushed out with all the force of angry repugnance, and catching him off balance, sent him staggering back. Coming up against the edge of the bed, he fell awkwardly across it, jarring his shoulder against its carved wooden foot.

Furious, inflamed by the sight of her wiping her mouth, he leapt to his feet and struck her hard with the flat of his hand.

That resounding crack shocked him: it seemed to go on forever, as she slid senseless to the floor. White marks across her face turned livid even as he watched, while his fingers stung with the force of the blow.

In bitter remorse he bent and gathered her into his arms, cursing himself, his temper, his strength, even the brandy consumed so thoughtlessly. She moaned and it was a blessed relief, struggled feebly as he removed her robe and lifted her into bed. A moment later, as he shed his clothes and lay down beside her, she was crying and shivering with shock, but he warmed her with his body and kissed the tears away, silencing her protests with broken, begging pleas. He was aware only of how much, how very much, he wanted her; and in the belief that passion could rekindle love and need and all the things they had shared and somehow lost along the way, he forced himself into her, roused beyond thought or care by that tight, closed, struggling rejection. He was harshly demanding, forcing her mouth even as he opened that more secret place, arousing a response at last simply because he knew every inch, every sexual trigger of that lovely, passionate body beneath him.

Thrusting blindly to a huge, shattering, mind-consuming climax, he was aware of nothing but success; and even afterward, before sleep took reason away, with their bodies relaxed and slippery with sweat, he was sure she was his completely.

Book Four
1898–1899

So thoroughly and long
  Have you now known me,
So real in faith and strong
  Have I now shown me,
That nothing needs disguise
Further in any wise,
Or asks or justifies
  A guarded tongue.

Face unto face, then, say,
  Eyes my own meeting,
Is your heart far away,
  Or with mine beating?

From "Between Us Now,"
by Thomas Hardy

ONE

*H*igh gray walls and taller trees; massive gates of cast iron which seemed set to remain closed against the world. From the carriage window Robert stared at them, the fingers of his free hand drumming absently against his thigh.

Anxious to have the visit over, to be away from this place with its disturbed and disturbing inhabitants, Robert thought of White Leigh, whose gates were rarely shut and never locked, and knew he would have to go there soon, if only to pay dutiful respects to William and Anne. Almost two years since he had made his last hasty visit, and that at William's insistence, not even to say good-bye. On a bitter January day, in the throes of uniform fittings, interviews, and travel arrangements for the Sudan, Robert had dropped everything to answer that peremptory summons. Whether tactical or simply coincidental, the moment had certainly been well chosen; he had neither the time nor the inclination then for protracted arguments, and face to face with Charlotte for the first time in years, Robert had simply given in.

An arthritic old man, draped in oilskins far too large, struggled to open the gates; as his carriage went through, Robert tossed a coin, which was caught with amazing agility. Amused, he leaned carefully back, wincing as his injured shoulder made contact with hard upholstery.

It was perhaps half a mile to the house through open parkland, a drive which on a dry day might have been pleasant, but the lingering glow of autumn was barely a glimmer through the mist, its last embers almost extinguished by mud and rain. The carriage ground to a halt before a surprisingly well-kept mansion whose stuccoed facade showed few signs of neglect. Impressed, Robert gathered his cloak around him and, declining his coachman's offer of help, managed to alight with painful independence. The knives which seemed to stab at his shoulder with each and every movement were an irritating reminder that he was supposed to be convalescent, but with gritted teeth he mounted the steps unaided.

The door was opened eventually by a girl whose bright eyes and flushed cheeks suggested a hurried journey from distant quarters. Meeting Robert's gaze, she quickly looked down and, once the door was closed behind him, carefully folded her hands out of sight. Apologizing for keeping him waiting, she said Sister Cuthbert was expecting him, and would he please to come this way?

He followed her to the foot of a broad, cantilevered staircase, then stopped with an apologetic shake of the head. "I find stairs very fatiguing. Do you think I could wait here?"

The girl's quick glance seemed to take in, for the first time, the useless left arm in its sling; with an embarrassed nod she ascended the stairs alone, and as he watched that slight figure in ill-fitting black, he wondered what other duties she performed, whether she was servant or novice in this strange household. With sudden and incongruous discomfort, he was reminded of his visit to Mrs. Dodsworth's several years before, and the little servant girl whose presence in that house had filled him with such revulsion. The two houses could not be more dissimilar, nor their reasons for being, yet the feeling persisted that this was no more a place for innocent youth than that other had been.

Deliberately he looked round, studying the hall's single painting of Christ healing the sick and, in a niche which was surely designed to hold a classical marble statue, a painted plaster saint. A slight disturbance of the air, a faint rustling like dry leaves, made him turn. A fully fledged nun this time, her ageless face a painting by Rembrandt, descended the last few stairs and came to stand before him. The starched white coif and wimple reflected light into her face and eyes, and, feeling the impact of her serenity, he stared in frank appraisal. Unlike the girl, she met his gaze quite openly, although she did not offer him her hand. The voice was unmistakably that of a well-bred Englishwoman. In his surprise, he heard only half of what was obviously a standard speech about the work of this obscure little order of nursing nuns; and as she repeated her offer to escort him on a tour of the house, he declined rather abruptly. With a smile of apology, Robert explained that his sister had described its facilities in excellent detail, and, much to his regret, his state of convalescence did not allow for a protracted visit. If it was convenient, he simply wished to see Mrs. Charlotte Duncannon.

Wasting no words, and like the mistress of the house she undoubtedly was, Sister Cuthbert simply turned and bade him follow her. She led him through glass doors into a beautiful conservatory, flourishing like a small jungle with exotic plants and shrubs. Beneath tree-sized palms, several ladies sat at small tables; except for the two nuns reading identical black-bound books, the scene could have been the palm court of an expensive seaside hotel. Momentarily nonplussed, Robert ventured a comment on the number of visitors.

"Patients, Captain. The less disturbed ones, of course."

With raised eyebrows, Robert followed the quietly rustling figure down a long corridor. Molloy, he reflected, had always claimed his colleague Stevens to be brilliant, and one of a new school of thought where the treatment of insanity was concerned; and Letty had extolled the nuns' every virtue; but still Robert could not quite believe it.

"And the others?" he asked.

"Each case is treated individually," she replied. "Your wife, as I am sure you are aware, was exceedingly disturbed when she came to us. But with care and patience, and under the guidance of Dr. Stevens, we have managed to gain Charlotte's confidence. She has periods of quite rational calm, you know, and as time goes by, we hope to extend those periods."

"You hope for a cure?"

The nun shook her head. "I'm sure you realize the unlikelihood of that, Captain. But by kindness and God's Good Grace, we can help her to be less unhappy."

The faith she wore like a cloak was touching Robert, and he resented it, even suspected a hint of accusation behind her words. On a reflex he bridled and said defensively: "My profession takes me away a good deal. Of necessity I had to leave Charlotte in the care of others."

"Life is hard enough," she said, appearing not to notice the guilty color which flooded his cheeks, "without any of us making judgments. Only God may do that."

She halted before a closed door, and Robert's apprehension rose like bile. He had not seen Charlotte in almost two years, and his last sight of her, cowering like a terrified, hunted animal, had shocked him to the core. One look had been enough to convince him that she was totally beyond the help of any half-trained nurse. But there had been no time to do more than leave joint power of attorney with William and Letty; he had had to abandon all arrangements to them.

"Charlotte enjoys painting," Sister Cuthbert said. "Did you know that?"

He was astounded. Even more so when she opened the door on a studio ranged around with easels, the walls covered with the strangest works of art he had ever seen. Some were no more than childish daubs; others, well executed, were disturbing in both content and perspective; a few bore the marks of vibrant, clashing color; one was simply black.

"Sister Matthew is our inspiration here—I must introduce you to her. She's a most talented artist and a wonderful teacher. There she is with Charlotte."

For a second it seemed his heart skipped a beat; his eyes searched the far row of easels and spotted an incongruously smocked nun, her charge painting furiously in grim and silent concentration. His eyes flicked over that small, intent figure, then returned. Charlotte was so radically changed, so unmatched to any of his memories that he hardly recognized her. Although he knew she could not be much past thirty, she looked much older, with the spinster spareness of middle age. Her hair, once so long and lustrous, was pulled severely back from her forehead in a single short braid, steely rather than silvery in that cold northern light. Like her mouth, her face seemed pinched and thin, totally devoid of what little color she had once possessed; yet there was a lively intensity of movement in hands and eyes, a truly miraculous transformation when he recalled his last sight of her at White Leigh.

That terrified and terrifying creature had gone, but with illness and the passing years her beauty had also faded. He found it hard to believe that this ordinary-looking woman had once captivated and appalled him, even driven him to the brink of desperation. It did not seem possible. A few short paces separated them, yet he might have been invisible, so absorbed was she. Relief washed over him and then subsided, leaving him drained of any emotion; it was strange to think this woman was, in the eyes of church and state, his wife. He supposed there had been too much water under the bridge of his life, a veritable flood of events which had shifted the wreck of his marriage to a point of minimal importance. Only in very low moments did he acknowledge its existence; and when Sister Cuthbert referred to his wife, Robert immediately pictured Louisa, who had been, and always would be, the wife he had truly wanted. Sadness washed over him then, tinged with a darker trace of resentment; without Charlotte, he could have married Louisa and made her happy.

Sister Cuthbert attracted the nun's attention, and she nodded, signifying with a motion of her hand that she would speak to them shortly. For a moment Robert was tempted to look at what Charlotte was painting, then changed his mind; if the work expressed her thoughts and feelings, it was better not to look too closely. He shivered, wincing as his shoulder made itself known again, and made a slow retreat to the door.

Satisfied by his visit, and utterly exhausted, Robert declined the offer of tea and returned to his carriage. The journey, the gamut of emotions, had been too much: Letty, as usual, was right; he should have waited a little longer. But when death stood near to claiming him, he had made certain promises, promises which must be fulfilled as soon as possible, before life became mundane again, before he forgot the simple euphoria of survival. The journey to Charlotte was shortest and first; but later there were other journeys to make, longer and infinitely more difficult to face.

"I trust you had a pleasant drive, sir?" McMahon murmured as he arrived home. "Miss Letty is hearing Miss Georgina in the drawing room."

Thanking him, Robert followed the rousing notes of a faultlessly played mazurka, feeling his spirits lift as he crept quietly into the room where his sister and daughter were seated together at the piano. Letty's iron-gray hair was as carelessly pinned as ever, wayward strands falling forward as she turned each page of music; and Georgina had grown so much in two years that it amazed him still to see her blond head on a level with her aunt's shoulder. She was thin like Letty, all arms and legs like a young foal; but her face had character already. She would never possess her mother's vapid beauty, and for that Robert was profoundly grateful.

Unexpectedly, and in spite of everything, their presence was a comfort to him. He had been afraid, once he had taken time to think, that with Charlotte gone from White Leigh, they would return there; but they had stayed and he was grateful. Without them, without Louisa, this house would have become again what it had been once before: empty, forlorn, and soulless. He still had a home, if not Louisa, and she had left part of herself here in memories which were startlingly fresh.

After two years he could hardly believe it, could not understand the sense of bereavement which had come with his return; it was as though Louisa had left only the week before, and those long months abroad were no more than the stuff of fantasy and nightmare. He could not escape the feeling that she *should* have been there; that if he closed his eyes and opened them quickly, she would be there, her eyes alight with laughter at the practical joke.

After an early dinner, physically and mentally exhausted by the day, Robert made his excuses and went upstairs. Before ringing for McMahon to help him undress, he went through into Louisa's old room, lit the bedside lamp, and slowly scanned the room. Little had changed. The decor of deep rose and cream still gave an illusion of warmth and femininity, and the pictures she had chosen still echoed her love of birds and flowers and wide open spaces.

The window reflected his fragmented image; but for a moment he stood looking beyond it, remembering the garden below in the height of summer, as she had first seen it, with rose arbors in full bloom, close-clipped lawns, and heliotrope in flower along that south-facing wall. With a sigh he pulled the curtains together and, turning to her dressing table, ran gentle fingers over china and cut crystal, pretty scent bottles he must have bought for her once upon a time. In one of the drawers were a few lace-edged handkerchiefs embroidered with her initials, and a lavender sachet whose redolence did not disappoint him. Even on another woman that old, traditional scent could always conjure her, rosy-cheeked as a country girl, with her bare arms and flapping sunbonnet, striding across those broad Lincolnshire meadows.

He sank down on the bed and lit a cigar, wondering why it was he should picture her like that, when that was no more than one day in five long years. Perhaps it was the sexual memory, he thought, so deep it seemed physically implanted, so rich it could rouse him even now. He considered it and found the idea both more and less than what he sought; connected, but not the answer itself. Instinctively he felt it had something to do with the person she was, with his very first impression in the depths of a city winter, of sun and open skies, and a warm generosity of spirit oddly at variance with time and place.

But that was not the woman who had lived here, not the woman who had refused to listen, refused to forgive, who had taken herself and his children away from here, and never a word since.

Why had she changed so? he asked himself; and in the next instant, with sudden insight, he wondered whether she had really changed at all, whether in fact he had tried too hard to mold her into something she could never be. He had wanted her to be his wife, and in his mind he had had an image of the two of them gracing various social functions; Louisa elegant, witty, and beautiful and himself outrageously envied for the lovely woman on his arm. But she was not his wife and never could be, and as his mistress there had been too many barriers to cross.

She had tried, and he could not fault her there; but the children had been their downfall. They had altered every single aspect of his relationship with Louisa, in ways and to extents he still found incredible. Fettered by them, her bright, lively, independent spirit had changed almost beyond recognition, and with the wisdom of hindsight Robert saw what folly it had been to imagine he could hold her in such a way. On occasion, that excess of domesticity had been claustrophobic to him; but he had been able to walk away from it. Louisa never could.

And in walking away from him, she had had to take the children with her, shouldering that responsibility alone.

He had never seriously believed she would go. That farce with Amelia Loy had never been much more than that in his mind; it was so lacking in any real substance, he could not believe Louisa would take it so much to heart. But she had, and in this very room he had found her, packing with methodical calm, for all practical purposes deaf, dumb, and blind to his plans and entreaties.

Thrusting aside what happened after that, Robert stood up and paced the room, stubbing out the remains of his cigar in the empty fireplace. He looked in the wardrobe, knowing all her fine gowns would still be there. She had taken so few personal things with her. Only two days ago he had discovered that of all her jewelry Louisa had taken but one item with her: the little diamond and sapphire brooch he had bought for her in York.

The scent of lavender caught him afresh; he stood with head bowed and eyes closed, regretting the blind folly which had spurred him on, the angry pride which so hated to be crossed. And if the drink that night had lent a little Dutch courage, it had certainly dulled the edge of his perceptions, so that he reached for her in the only way he knew, firm in his belief that he could stop her leaving, and in the aftermath of love convince her of his good intent. But it had not turned out that way, and when he woke, many hours later, she was already gone.

He had known then, with absolute certainty, that she would not be back. Known also, in the darker recesses of his mind, that what he had done the night before was unpardonable. He could forgive himself for Amelia Loy, but he could not forgive the rest.

Letty had taken her and the children to Kingstown, seen them safely aboard the steam packet, and then returned to berate him. Blistered pride made him cover rage and pain with cold, detached calm, while he went through the motions of sending telegrams to York, requesting confirmation of the children's safe arrival. Except as a matter of life and death, however, Robert could not have followed, nor even set pen to paper as a means of reparation. He was crippled by his own folly; even told himself it was for the best.

His sister raged; Georgina verged on hysteria, begging him to go and bring Louisa and the children back. When he refused, they both accused him in their own ways of a cruelty and callousness he almost wished were fact. Clinging to the last vestiges of self-control, he returned to Dundalk to set other plans in motion.

Within three weeks of Louisa's departure for York, Robert was on his way to Cairo. It was ironic, he thought, how tempted he had been during the whole of that spring and summer of '96. With Kitchener's campaign going so well, he had longed to be out there amid the action;

and yet for Louisa and the children he had stayed. Had he ignored those responsibilities, there would have been no Amelia Loy, and Louisa would probably have accepted the situation and stayed in Dublin with Letty and Georgina.

There was, in fact, such a thread of irony running through the whole of his experience out there that the memory of it brought the ghost of a smile to Robert's lips. The model they worked from might have been the Indian Army, but the reality was somewhat different. It was hard, unremitting work; rewarding, but not without its moments of frustration and despair. In less than two years, however, Robert knew he had learned more about soldiering than in an entire career spent at home; and in the Sudanese campaign especially, those months in the desert with Haig and Broadwood and Kitchener taught him more about human nature than even he had previously suspected.

Uncomfortably close to the idea of dying, it seemed life was stripped to essentials, that all obscuring trivia fell away, revealing people and situations for what they really were. He saw that guilt and resentment were unnecessary burdens, akin to the chairs and bedsteads some officers insisted on lugging everywhere; and selfishness a petty luxury, windy and tasteless as inferior Champagne. Certainly he had learned much about himself and, with regard to his most personal and intimate relationships, was not overly impressed by the record. Whether he could change very much was another matter, but he desperately wanted Louisa to know what he had discovered.

Drastic changes might not come about on that front—he was prepared to accept that—but with regard to his career they could well be forcibly imposed. As things stood, he was a man with a most uncertain future. If his arm and shoulder healed well enough to leave no permanent disability, all well and good . . . If not, then he would be permanently retired at the age of thirty-seven.

Depressed by the thought, and in considerable physical pain, he closed the door on Louisa's gowns and wished it were possible to lock away the past with the same finality. With a heavy sigh he rang the bell for McMahon.

TWO

*H*e woke, sweating, having dreamed again of that carnage at Omdurman. Wave upon wave of horsemen, charging straight into the teeth of the British guns; then the dervishes on foot, being possessed, masses rushing heedlessly on, regardless of that hail of bullets. Twenty minutes which seemed as many hours, twenty agonizing minutes when it seemed McDonald's infantry must break under the onslaught . . . and then, mercifully, the order for cavalry squadrons to attack; the fierce joy of the charge, pride in his own men's response, absolute conviction of success . . .

But the dervishes did not turn and flee. They fought where they stood, viciously, like tigers. All except one; one who knelt and begged for mercy . . .

Shivering, Robert pulled on his robe and reached for his cigars. Opening the window, he stood and looked down into the square, trying to banish the memory of that cringing face and knowing it would be with him till his dying day.

Despite the heat of battle, despite the dozens upon dozens he had cut down with savage pleasure, that pathetic, crouching figure had momentarily halted his sword; and as he swept on past, the hidden scimitar swirled and caught him. He remembered the scream as the betrayer was cut down by one of his own men, but recalled little else, had no idea how he kept his saddle, how he had avoided being killed in the rain of cross fire. Mercifully, however, that battle had been the last. By three in the afternoon, after almost nine hours of constant conflict, the worst was over. The victorious army, half the strength of its adversary, made camp on the banks of the Nile. There, Robert's exhausted, beaten horse had dipped its head to drink, and as it did so, the strength which had kept him in the saddle deserted him; he slipped down into the warm, muddy water, where he would no doubt have happily drowned had it not been for the determined efforts of two of his fellahin, the same two who had escorted him from the battlefield. He was a big man and they were small, but they dragged him, wet and bleeding from that ugly, open wound, into the hastily erected casualty tent.

A few days later he had embarked with the other wounded on the long journey by barge and rail and truck to the military hospital in Cairo. En route he heard many tales of men wounded and killed by tricks similar to the one which could have been the end of him. Robert knew that only sheer, headlong speed had saved him from the full force of that potentially lethal blow. Even now he could hardly imagine how he had been wounded at such a height from the ground: the man must have leapt and struck, all in the same movement; and a blow which might have severed vital organs at waist height, or bared his thigh to the bone, instead had glanced across his right shoulder, cutting deep into the muscle of his upper arm. He knew he had been almost un-believably lucky to escape with his life, and yet that momentary mistake angered him still. A split-second in which he had forgotten almost eighteen months' experience in the East and obeyed a reflex learned in childhood: *Pax—I surrender.* He should have remembered that none of them surrendered, not in Holy War, which was how the Khalifa's Mus-lim troops regarded that incursion of Christians into their land.

"Still," he said cynically to Molloy an hour later, "I suppose General Gordon stands avenged at long last—even though it's taken us ten years to do it—and we've ruined Omdurman and the Mahdi's last resting place, just as those devils ruined Khartoum."

"But more to the point," Molloy said slyly, "the British have triumphed in the Nile valley and stopped the French in *their* colonial aspirations!"

Robert laughed. "Right! So we're all due for a big pat on the back, in spite of losing the Khalifa!"

"Will he give any more trouble, do you think?"

Robert shook his head. "Shouldn't think so—he's a spent force. They'll catch up with him eventually."

Molloy sipped his coffee. "Will you go back?"

Consciously easing his shoulder, Robert paused to consider. "I don't know. It depends on this damned thing. If it heals well, I'd prefer to return to the regiment. I think I've had enough of sun and sand to last me a lifetime!"

Laughing, Molloy set down his cup. "Well, now, let's have a look at it." Warming his hands at the study fire, he unfastened the sling and helped Robert with his jacket and shirt. Running expert fingers over those damaged muscles, he persuaded his patient into movement, watch-ing the response with keen concern.

Some minutes later, there was a knock at the study door. Letty came in, apologizing for the intrusion. "I'm sorry, I thought you were finished. I'll come back later."

"It's quite all right, we nearly are," the doctor murmured, gently touching Robert's outstretched arm. "Bend the elbow, now, and if you can, try to touch the back of your head."

"You jest, of course!" Robert exclaimed to the mirror, but he bent the elbow as required, gritting his teeth as fingertips grazed the tip of his right ear. "That's as much as you're getting, damn you!" he swore and, gasping, leaned against the mantelpiece.

Seeing the rivulets of perspiration on his skin, Letty swallowed hard and turned away, forcing down an urge to fuss.

"That's excellent," Molloy said. "We'll be having you to hounds in a week, and whirling that saber like an expert the week after, make no mistake."

"Sword," Robert muttered darkly. "And save the blarney for your other patients, Molloy. I want the truth."

"I'll do my best," the other man said agreeably. "But you've done that shoulder a lot of damage, as I'm sure you're well aware. It's healed very well, despite those army butchers, though I wish," he murmured thoughtfully, touching those angry, puckered scars, "they could have foregone some of the fancy embroidery."

"They were stitching people up," Robert countered grimly, "left, right, and center, in a tent full of flies on the banks of the Nile. The battle had been going on since sunup, and by the time they got to me, it was dark. I'd lost a lot of blood, and I was singularly fortunate not to lose my arm as well! So don't talk to me about aesthetics, Molloy. As far as I'm concerned, those army butchers did a bloody good job."

"Oh, they did, they did indeed. I'm just concerned about the range of movement—"

"So am I. I expect you to tell me how to regain it."

"Robert, please," Letty murmured, handing him his shirt. "It's not Dr. Molloy's fault. Don't be so aggressive."

"I'm sorry." Exhausted, he sank down into a chair, fumbling with buttons and collar studs.

"It's all right," the younger man smiled. "Pain shortens the best of tempers." Accepting more coffee from Letty, he said: "Exercise is what you're needing, every day and plenty of it. Nothing too sudden or strenuous, you understand—just gentle and consistent movement. Get rid of that sling—which could be doing more harm than good, now— and use your arm as much as possible. It will tire you, so be sure and get plenty of rest. You must send him early to bed, Miss Duncannon," he instructed with a twinkle, "and no wild hooleys yet awhile!"

"I'll do my best," she promised and, seeing her brother in difficulties with his cravat, bent to help him. His skin was still tanned, but beneath that superficial veneer Robert was waxen with pain and fatigue, and she was hurting for him.

"I'll be going," Molloy said. "I'll call again in a couple of days, and in the meantime, keep up with those exercises."

Letty saw him out and, returning, poured Robert a glass of sherry.

"A little early in the day, isn't it?" he asked sardonically. "To what do I owe the honor?"

"Drink it. It'll do you good."

In mock amazement, he raised his glass to her. "Well, cheers, I never thought I'd hear *you* say that!"

"It's sherry, Robert, not brandy." Drawing an envelope from her pocket, Letty paused momentarily. "The post just arrived—with a letter from Louisa."

He stiffened immediately, then winced; setting his glass down, he said: "For me?"

"No. It's a reply to one I wrote some weeks ago, after we'd heard you were safe in Cairo. The lists of wounded were in every paper, and I wanted her to know you were alive and recovering."

"Good of her to reply so quickly," he remarked with heavy sarcasm.

"Yes, I wondered why she didn't write straight back." Drawing out two small sheets of paper, Letty handed them across to him.

Robert scanned the lines quickly. She was relieved to know he was safe and in hospital—had great faith in his powers of recovery—Letty must not worry too much about him. He smiled dryly at that and read on. Her mother was ill—very ill—had been for some time—nursing her at home—no time to write more—children well . . .

Looking up, Robert sighed. "Oh, I see."

"Doesn't sound very good, does it?"

He read the letter through again, absorbing every hasty line. "No," he said at last, "it doesn't sound good at all. In fact," he added bitterly, "it couldn't be worse."

"Why?"

For a long time Robert did not answer. He sat back in his chair and closed his eyes, suddenly realizing how very much he had been depending on Mary Elliott to help him do what must be done. With Louisa he had no direct contact; she had ignored every letter, and he had no faith in a sudden change of attitude now. Through Mary Elliott he had hoped to gain some kind of access to his children, and through them to Louisa herself. If she would not accept a written apology for what had happened two years ago, he must see her face to face. But if Mary Elliott was ill to the point of no recovery, he would soon be without a go-between in York.

Another problem presented itself: before leaving for the Sudan, Robert had made arrangements for an allotment of money to be paid each month into Mary Elliott's bank account, for the children. If she was ill, that money would be frozen; and with her death would end his only means of supporting them. Louisa could be starving, and her children in tatters, but she would not accept money from him.

"I have to see her—and soon."

"Who?"

"Mary Elliott, of course."

As soon as Letty left him, he went to his desk and with great difficulty penned a few lines to Louisa's mother. With the excuse of business to transact with Harris, he said he would be visiting York in the near future and would like to take the opportunity of visiting her. He had heard via Letty that she was unwell, but trusted it was no more than a temporary indisposition and that their meeting would see her restored to her usual self. Unless he heard to the contrary, he would see her shortly, certainly within the next ten days.

Despite his sister's remonstrations, Robert booked his passage and embarked upon a regime of alternate rest and exercise which was like a military training plan. He sent a telegram to Harris, requesting bed and board for a few days, and prayed Mary Elliott would be well enough to receive him.

THREE

*A*fter seven hours' sleep, dead to the world, Louisa woke reluctantly to a cup of tea from Bessie.

"She's still asleep, and she's all right just now. I'm off to my bed."

"All right, Bessie, I'll be up in a minute." Forcing her eyes open, Louisa struggled to stay awake and tried not to think of the hours which must be faced before she could decently get back to bed again. Like an automaton she washed and dressed, went down to the kitchen to make Edward's breakfast, trailed back upstairs for the children, washed them, dressed them, fed them, and waved Edward good-bye at the door.

"I'll see you about eight, probably," he said as he left. "I hope you have a better day."

"So do I," she murmured fervently; but every day seemed worse than the one before.

Ignoring first the protestations, then the stony silence, Louisa bathed her mother as a nurse would, helping her out of bed, changing the sheets, and making her patient comfortable for the day. Then it was back downstairs, to put the sheets in cold water to soak, wash her hands, change her apron, prepare a soft-boiled egg and thin slices of bread and butter in the somewhat vain hope of tempting that jaded appetite. She arranged the tray with a starched linen cloth, gilt-edged china, and silver spoons; mashed the tea, lightly tapped the top of the egg, and with a weary, heartfelt sigh, edged her way carefully into the hall.

Although she almost ignored the two letters lying on the mat, the thought that one *might* be for her mother made her set the tray down and pick them up. A cream envelope was uppermost, for Edward; and the thick white one, clearly postmarked Dublin . . . was addressed to Mrs. Mary Elliott.

For all its labored style, the handwriting was familiar enough to set her trembling. Unable to tear her eyes away, Louisa sat down for a moment on the stairs; the heavy paper seemed to have ROBERT written across it in huge letters. It was as though his presence had grown suddenly, frighteningly close. From the brutal brevity of that announcement in the *Gazette,* through Letty's joyful missive that he was alive and in Cairo, to this note from Dublin, it was like watching through a telescope and seeing the approach of an executioner.

She did not wish him dead. No, not that. And she was glad he had survived with all his limbs intact: the idea of Robert maimed, permanently disabled, was not repugnant but heartbreaking. She would have pitied him, and blamed herself. Alive, at least she could still detest him, call him despicable, wish on him another Amelia Loy . . .

But why had he written to her mother? And *what* had he written?

Gingerly, as though the envelope contained some secret, explosive device, Louisa placed it face down on the breakfast tray, tucking the edge securely beneath a plate.

Mary Elliott was in a fretful, peevish mood. She complained that her bones hurt, particularly her back and beneath her arms, where she said Louisa had *hauled* her out of bed. Irritated, biting her tongue, Louisa set the tray down, gently assisted her mother into a sitting position, and propped her up with pillows. Hiding Robert's letter under a book, she recited the usual litany about eating up and getting well and received the usual negative responses.

"Well, Mamma, don't eat if you don't want to, but you've got a letter this morning, and unless you eat *all* the yolk and at least half a slice of bread, I shall leave it where it is."

"A letter?" Mary Elliott demanded. "Who from?" For a moment all her old vivacity was back, and the milky blue eyes almost sparkled.

"How should I know? I haven't looked beyond the address. Come on, eat up and I'll get it." She broke into the egg and spooned soft white and deep orange yolk into her mother's mouth. Like feeding a baby, she thought, angry at the indignity of illness and age, only too aware that those tiny, claw-like hands trembled too much to hold a spoon. Louisa knew, as they all did, that it was just a matter of time. The word was never uttered, of course, not even by the blunt Dr. Mackenzie, but it was obvious even to those with no medical knowledge that Mary Elliott was suffering some sort of cancer. Painlessly as yet, but with silent, inexorable, horrifying speed, it was devouring her almost before their eyes.

That ever-present knowledge was like a form of cancer itself, eating away in Louisa's mind. With pity, sorrow, anger, and exhaustion, it was central to everything, subjecting all other concerns, all other emotions to very minor places in her consideration. Faced with her mother, even Robert's letter was important only as a means of bribery.

"Is it from John Elliott? You know his writing well enough."

"You can see for yourself who it's from," Louisa said, "when we've finished this egg." It was more than half gone, and no real difficulty so far; that simple satisfaction momentarily outweighed everything else. She waited while her mother chewed a piece of bread with agonizing slowness, felt the effort it cost to swallow, and instinctively offered a sip of tea. The rest of the bread was waved away, but energy and determination lasted long enough for the egg to be finished, and, with a sigh of real pleasure, Louisa patted her mother's forearm, feeling the awful absence of flesh beneath that crisp white sleeve. "You've done marvelously this morning," she smiled. "I wish you had a letter every day."

Determined not to be flattered, Mary Elliott gave a half-smile and a little grunt of disparagement. "Wouldn't be the same. Anyway, I wish you'd stop talking about it and just go and get it." Despite the feeble voice, her eyes held all their old command, and Louisa marveled at the way her mother could slip from vague, almost meaningless rambling to this sharp lucidity. And back again.

"I told a fib," she said apologetically, with the envelope in her hand. "I do know who it's from, I'm sorry to say. It's from Robert."

Mary Elliott's eyes darkened perceptibly, the sparse flesh covering her small, bird-like features suddenly creasing into a thousand wrinkles. "Well, give it to me!"

"Don't you want me to open it for you?"

"No, I don't. I'm quite capable of opening my own letters, thank you. Pass me a knife."

Biting her lip, Louisa did as she was bidden and stayed to watch the ensuing struggle. Crossly, and with great difficulty, Mary Elliott achieved her objective, then turned on her daughter.

"Well? What are you waiting for? It's me he's written to—not you."

With another leather-bound ledger complete, Edward rubbed his eyes and glanced at the clock: it was a little after seven, and the kettle was hissing gently over the glowing coals of his small fire. He brewed another pot of tea, warming his hands around it before arranging another batch of materials on his bench. It was bread-and-butter work which occupied him, work he preferred to do in the evenings when his concentration was less acute. He measured and scored, trimmed and glued almost mechanically, keeping a notebook and pencil by his side ready to jot down any odd lines of verse which came to him. While his fingers were busy, his mind was also, refining and polishing words with a craftsman's thoroughness. Although he had written a vast amount since Louisa's return, over the years he had become increasingly fastidious; much was destroyed, the best kept in the strongbox with the gold leaf, and very little submitted for publication.

But his mind that evening was occupied less by words than by figures; by a tortured form of mental arithmetic which steadfastly refused to give the answers he desperately needed. Financially, as in every other respect, their joint resources had been stretched to the limit over the past few months, and while Louisa did her best to economize, that huge house ran up bills which were becoming increasingly difficult to pay.

The hotel had struggled on as a business for well over a year after Louisa's return; but with children in the house and whiffs of scandal spreading like sulfur fumes, even their regular guests had begun to thin alarmingly, making closure just a matter of time. Deciding to wind it up before bankruptcy set in, they had talked about moving, even looked at a few properties six months ago; then his aunt had lost interest, and with the onset of her illness she simply wanted to stay where she was. Edward understood that and sympathized, and for a while had accepted the contributions she made to the housekeeping bills; but with no real idea of her savings, and knowing they could not be vast, he wanted to reserve what little was left for the offices of a decent burial.

In front of Mary Elliott he maintained that money was not a problem, and indeed his own business had expanded to the point where he could barely cope with it single-handedly; he was working ridiculous hours just to keep up with orders. The problem lay in the fact that he was owed considerable amounts of money, largely by new customers of whose reliability he was unsure; his credit at the bank was none too healthy, and he was repeatedly warned not to take on more than the business would stand. Only his need to provide drove him into that kind of gamble, and he was increasingly anxious about it. With accounts falling behind and paperwork mounting up, Edward knew he needed another pair of hands to take the bulk of the sort of work upon which he was presently engaged. He needed someone like his old apprentice, by some miracle still working at Tempest's, and needed him desperately; but Edward could not afford to pay his wages.

There was no answer to it. While his aunt lived, they could not move house; and until they moved to less expensive accommodation, the crisis would only deepen. Edward finished the ledger and cleared his bench; he should have worked another hour at least, but was quite beyond it. Gathering his coat and scarf, he banked down the fire and set off for home.

Even as Louisa set his dinner on the table, he could tell that something more than the usual daily frustrations had upset her. Her silence was that of rigid self-control, and with inner determination, he resisted the urge to ask. Instead, he waded through a dumpling stew which boasted rather more vegetables than meat; but it was tasty and he was hungry, and he had no intention of letting it go to waste. While he slowly ate a steaming baked apple with cinnamon and custard sauce, Edward stared at the letter in front of him. It was postmarked Lincoln and was from his father; although he looked forward to reading it, he knew it would have to wait a little while at least.

"What is it?" he asked at last, pushing his empty plate away. "What's happened?"

From her chair by the fire, Louisa finally spoke: "Well, apart from the fact that Mamma's been quite cantankerous today—absolutely *hateful,* in fact—she had a letter this morning." For a moment she hesitated, then, indicating his own missive on the table, she said: "It came with yours—from Dublin—from Robert. But don't ask me what it said," she added defiantly, "because she wouldn't let me see it."

The name stabbed at him. He looked away, not wanting her to see his face, while he told himself that this was only the beginning of something he had expected for a long time. Fighting for mastery of his own painful emotions, Edward took in very little else of what Louisa said.

"Postmarked Dublin, you say?"

"Yes."

"Then you must expect to see him," he said, unable to keep the bitterness from his voice. "He'll be here, sooner or later; you can depend on it."

FOUR

Although he had slept tolerably well on the overnight packet, and ate a good breakfast before disembarking, the train journey was more tiring than he had imagined, and by the time he arrived in York, Robert was white with exhaustion. Concentrating on finding a porter, and with his shoulder throbbing abominably, he did not notice Harris's lanky form striding toward him; unexpectedly, and most thankfully, the familiar voice hailed greetings, large hands grasped his with painful enthusiasm and then took charge of the baggage.

The steps were a trial, both down and up, but in the entrance arcade were several cabs awaiting fares; with a sigh of relief Robert leaned back against sagging upholstery and let Harris stow the small trunk and leather bag. Amidst thuds and creaks the job was done, Harris climbed inside and the cab pulled out, its wheels protesting against sanded granite sets.

Almost against his will, Robert looked out at the city which had haunted him, off and on, for years. Here, for a short while at least, he and Louisa had been truly happy. But that afternoon, against a dirty yellow sky and wet, dark, depressing streets, the stark smell of the city walls seemed fraught with menace, a bold and strangely potent reminder of old defiance not yet dead. Beside the road, at the foot of those massive ramparts, like loose and blackened teeth, the tombstones in the cholera ground made him shiver.

"*Without a city wall,*" he quoted, remembering the Easter hymn. "But wouldn't you think, Harris, they'd move the poor bastards? It looks like some gruesome medieval warning just as you leave the bloody station—heads on gateposts, that sort of thing. Hard to credit they were put there within living memory and not in the blasted Dark Ages." Getting no reply, he leaned back and closed his eyes.

After a moment, he prompted: "So what do you make of these people, Harris? Don't you find them obstinate and backward? Does living in a walled city give them archaic ideas?"

Harris shifted uncomfortably. "Don't know, sir. Can't say I've ever really thought about it."

"You should, Harris, you should. I think you'll find I'm right."

He winced in sudden pain as the cab jolted over tramlines at Nessgate Corner; full of concern, Harris said with forced brightness, "We'll soon be home, sir. The missus has got you a room all ready, and a nice hot meal. Then you can get your head down for a couple of hours—do you the world of good."

There were more jolts, several of them, over Castle Mills Bridge; grim with anxiety, Harris uttered a few terse comments as he paid the fare, and such was the state of his other passenger that the cabbie forebore to reply. Leaving the man to unload the luggage, Harris ushered Robert through into the snug, where a cheerful fire was blazing; a moment later he was back from the bar with a glass and a bottle.

"Here we are, sir, a drop of your favorite." Pouring a glassful, he pushed it across the table. "Get that down you and we'll think about getting you up those stairs and to bed. You'll feel more like eating later."

"Grief, Harris, are you intending to carry me?" Robert muttered. "I don't knock it back like that anymore."

"All the better then—it should kill that pain all the quicker. Honest fair, sir, you shouldn't be traveling in your state of health."

"That's what my sister said."

"And she was right. Come on, sir, get that down."

"All right, Harris, all right! Good God, man, do you want to choke me?"

"No, sir, I want to get you up them stairs."

Robert downed what was left in the glass and struggled to his feet. He caught a brief glimpse of Moira behind the bar and answered her anxious, fleeting smile before negotiating a steep and narrow staircase and a landing which sloped like the deck of a ship. He muttered something about being drunk again, and Harris laughed, saying it was the house which was drunk; a fitting condition, he supposed, for a pub.

There was no need to fetch his luggage; Harris knew of old that the captain slept in nothing more restricting than his skin. With the ease of long practice, he gently removed overcoat, jacket, waistcoat, and boots, standing back while Robert unbuttoned his shirt and trousers and the long underwear Letty had insisted on for the sea voyage.

"Feels like a blasted hair shirt," he muttered as Harris peeled the fine wool from his shoulders, and smiled grimly at the sudden indrawn breath and low whistle which followed. "I know it's not a pretty sight, but believe me, it looks worse than it is." With an attempt at levity, he pointed to the long, jagged scars which stood out white against the tanned skin of his wrist and forearm. "Remember these? That old *riding accident?* You never believed that for a minute, did you, Harris?" As his old servant smiled and shook his head, Robert pointed to a deep, crescent-shaped indentation above his right knee. "This one was before your time, though—a mess if ever I saw one. Got that at the same time as Tommy Fitzsimmons had his face cut open." With a long sigh, as he slid between cool clean sheets, he murmured: "I wonder how old Tommy's going on? Haven't heard from him in ages."

"He'll be managing just fine, sir," Harris observed, straightening clothes and producing hangers from a curtained alcove beside the chimney breast. With a sudden grimace, he explained that fancy furniture had been low on their list of priorities; while building up the business, he and Moira had felt it fitting to concentrate their money on the public rooms. "But as you can see, sir, we gave the place a thorough going-over. And we had a man in to paint the woodwork and hang new wallpaper. Still, we'll get to proper furniture eventually."

"You've done wonders," Robert commented, glancing around at the pale yellow walls and dark green skirtings. The bedside table might be an old trunk with a cloth over, but it served a purpose, and the bed was comfortable. He had no complaints at all.

"Well, sir, I'll leave you to sleep. Dinner's a hot-pot, and it'll keep."

Drowsy already, Robert murmured: "Don't let me sleep too long. I've a lot of things to do . . ."

It was almost five o'clock when he sat down to eat his meal at a place set for him in the tiny snug. Refreshed by his sleep and reasonably free of pain, once he caught the aroma of that hearty mutton stew, Robert realized he was famished. Harris set a full plate before him and, to wash it down, a pint of dark and creamy porter, the best he had tasted in years. In the course of her work, Moira kept appearing briefly behind the serving hatch, her cheery smile the only recognition of his rapidly clearing plate.

"Help yourself to that when you're ready, sir," Harris said as he returned with coffee and the same bottle of brandy he had produced earlier. "I'll just pull myself a mug of ale."

A moment later the two men were seated comfortably by a well-stacked fire, exchanging the preliminary courtesies which had of necessity been cut short earlier. Glancing around, it was obvious to Robert that the years of rigorous military training had been allowed to slip not one iota; brassware and copper shone as though for a field day, the mahogany bar counter gleamed, and the stained glass to either side of the serving hatch sparkled its reflections of the fire. Complimenting his host on the quality of his beer, Robert ventured a comment that business must be good; with a deprecating smile Harris said it was improving all the time. The roughest faction, mainly itinerants rife in the area on cattle market days, had been quickly discouraged, making way for a better clientele of farmers in from the country and a hard core of noncommissioned officers from the Cavalry Barracks.

"We did have a few of the foot soldiers," he added, "but the usual trouble started. I tried to be fair about it—taking no sides—but once it got round that I was ex-cavalry myself, the other johnnies stopped coming in."

The talk hovered for a while on the relative merits of army and civilian life; there were certain aspects of his former occupation that Harris missed, but not many, and not enough to have bred regrets. The one thing he was sorry about was the fact that his old master had taken himself off to the Sudan alone.

"Not that I could have gone anyway, sir, even if I'd still been with the colors—but I always thought, if there was anything, we'd sort of be in it together, if you know what I mean."

More deeply touched than he cared to admit, Robert looked down into his glass and smiled. "Yes, Harris," he murmured. "I do know what you mean. But you know," he added in a brighter tone, "you did come with me in a way. When I was stuck out there in the desert, scouting for Kitchener and wondering what ghastly mess my blackfellas were going to produce for supper, I thought of you and the rabbit stews we used to plan! *Where's your rabbits now, Harris?* I used to say to myself. *Where's those plump little chickens and game birds we used to buy at the poulterers on the Fulford Road?*" The blue eyes twinkled with sudden humor, and Harris pulled a rueful face.

"I still wish I'd been there, sir." His quiet sincerity left an uneasy silence in its wake, while the inevitable questions about what had happened at Omdurman hung awkwardly between them. Harris was strangely embarrassed; Robert less so, having already given versions of the truth to Letty and Molloy.

Eventually, on neutral ground, Harris said: "The papers made quite a thing of that stupid charge—when they finally got hold of it. Made the 21st Lancers sound like conquering bloody heroes," he added with more than a touch of derision. "But it sounded a bit of a cock-up to me, sir."

With raised eyebrows and a faint, quirky smile, Robert nodded. "I'm glad somebody could read between the lines," he said admiringly. "It's all everybody else wants to talk about—the honor and glory bit." Shaking his head, he added, "Kitchener was so bloody furious he didn't even report it in the press dispatches." In fact, Robert had heard from one of Kitchener's own staff that it was only the press correspondents' eagerness for a story which had made that abortive charge generally known: in their enthusiasm for the "victory" at Omdurman, they had blown a fiasco into a colorful and glorious act of bravery. The bravery of those raw and untried troops was not in question, of course; wisdom and discipline, however, were different matters. It was not at all what the great man had intended; and in the aftermath of that fiasco, although the town of Omdurman was taken, their chief objective, which had been the capture of the Khalifa, was a failure. As far as Robert was aware, they were chasing him still.

Thinking of the charge, he sadly shook his head. "What a waste," he murmured. "What a desperate waste it was. Of men and good horses, and—well, bravery. All for nothing."

"Why, sir?"

With a short, mocking laugh, Robert said, "Well, I know it's easy to be wise after the event, Harris, but they were all green as grass, virtually a scratch force, fresh out from England. They were told to head the Khalifa's main force away from Omdurman—and I suppose a headlong charge seemed the most obvious way of doing it. But apparently the order to charge was never given—the whole lot just set off, spontaneously. I suppose they just couldn't wait; it was what they'd all left home for, the silly buggers."

Harris winced. "Carnage," he whispered.

"Absolutely bloody right!" Robert exclaimed. "And in the end, they had to dismount and use their carbines, which isn't nearly so much fun as rushing headlong into the gallop! But by then," he added, sighing, "it was far too late to have any effect. The blasted dervishes retreated, joined up again with their main force, and attacked the rest of us coming down behind the lancers. Kitchener," he murmured dryly, "was not best pleased. And nor were we. We'd had a tough morning, without facing that little lot for a second time."

"Was that when you got the—er—"

"Scimitar across my shoulder? Yes, Harris, it was." With a wry smile, Robert drained his glass. "But that's another story—for later. I really should be getting on my way."

"How's Mr. Darnley going on, sir? And his Serene Highness? He went out as well, didn't he?"

Robert laughed. "Oh, the prince is doing very well—recommended for the D.S.O. no less!"

Aware that he himself had been similarly recommended, Robert tried to shrug the subject aside, winced, and ended up laughing. "And Hugh

Darnley," he added with amused envy, "came through the whole blasted show without so much as a scratch! Don't know how he did it. He's still out there, of course—and loving every minute."

Just at that moment, Moira looked through the serving hatch and announced that it was past six, the public bar was empty, and she was going to make a pot of tea.

As Harris opened a door in the screen which divided the two bars, Robert, with an abrupt change of subject, asked whether Moira had seen much of the Elliotts in recent weeks. The other man shifted uncomfortably, pursing his lips in the fashion Robert recognized as the precursor of an evasive answer. Biting back irritation, he reminded himself that their relationship had undergone considerable changes since the days when he could order a straight reply.

"Not in recent weeks, no," Harris eventually admitted. "We get very busy, you see, sir, and can't afford much help. Except for shopping, the missus doesn't get out much at all."

"But she has seen Louisa?"

"Oh, yes, she had a letter not long after Miss Louisa came back to York. And she went to see her a couple of times, that I do know. But Miss Louisa's never been here, and I don't know if she's heard from her lately. I'll ask if you like."

"No, it doesn't matter. It's recent news I'm in need of, Harris, not history!"

"I'm sorry, sir," the other man murmured, but his tone was somewhat aggrieved.

"Oh, I didn't mean to bite your head off—it's just that I have to see Mrs. Elliott. From the sound of things, she's not long for this world."

Harris was shocked. Moira also. Having had nothing from him other than the telegram requesting board and lodging, they had no idea of the real reason for his visit.

"I haven't heard from Miss Louisa for a long time," Moira confessed. "Perhaps that's why."

Unreasonably irritated by that lack of persistence, Robert found himself thinking she should have kept in touch, if only as a link between himself and his children. After all Louisa had done for Moira, and all he, Robert, had done for Harris, she might have tried a little harder, he felt. And now there was nothing for it but to go in like a stranger, knowing lamentably little of the situation.

Using as his excuse the fiction that the Elliotts were expecting him, he said he had to leave. While Moira went up to fetch his outdoor clothes, Harris stepped out to find a cab.

Some minutes later he returned, out of breath and coughing. "No wonder it's like a grave in here," he commented when he could find his voice. "It's brewing up like pea soup outside. Had to go across to the rank by the cattle pens—there were only two, sir, and both drivers were in the City Arms. Anyway," he finished anxiously, "I got the least drunk of the two, so I hope you don't end up in the river."

"I've not come all this way to end up in the river!" Robert said. "I'll get to Gillygate somehow, Harris, even if I have to walk."

"I'd not recommend that," Moira laughed. "The fog will poison you for sure."

They saw him into the cab, Harris giving the dark and almost formless bundle in the driving seat his instructions. The only answer he received was a ghastly, racking cough, but the old horse set off in what seemed the right direction, and Harris crossed his fingers as he waved them away.

FIVE

*f*og, isolating, thick, and sulfurous, took the city in its grip, slowing movement, muffling sound, furtively distorting each awareness, every sense. The short distance between Fishergate and Clifford Street seemed to take an age, punctuated only by the cabbie's cough and the slow, hesitant clopping of the horse's hooves. Unsure how far they had covered, Robert leaned out and identified the castle's looming wall in the feeble glow of a street lamp; a few yards further and those hesitant hooves stopped altogether; he leaned forward again and saw the rising steps of the Police Station, although its entrance was obscured from sight. With an inward groan he consulted his watch, and five minutes later, having made no more than twenty yards' progress, he decided to walk.

The cabbie's grumbles were quieted by a sudden shout and running feet; heedless of the fog, figures dashed blindly past Robert and up the steps, shouting something about an accident on Nessgate. With a movement of blankets and shawls that could have been a shrug, the cabbie rasped something obscene and let his fare go; with some relief, Robert walked on, guided by the long line of traffic backed up from the notorious few yards known as Nessgate Corner. There seven thoroughfares converged, and there the treachery of the fog had claimed its first victims of the night.

People were hurrying as he neared the scene of the accident, and horses stamping and whinnying, tossing about in the confines of shafts and traces; several uniformed policemen ran past him, and a man in heavy tweeds and gaiters; then he caught the high-pitched screams of a horse in agony. Pure instinct made Robert push his way through the crowd, but a few seconds later a shot rang out and the screaming stopped; a muffled murmur of human voices dispelled the silence which followed. With his view of the roadway obscured by the chaos of carts and carriages, he was unable to see what had happened or where; but when he tried to cross at the far junction, the dreadful scene was laid out before him, only partially veiled by the fog.

Two burly policemen were trying to calm a massive dray horse with an open wound in its side, while the shaken driver fumbled with snarled traces and a broken, blood-stained shaft. The vet in tweeds and gaiters was still crouched beside the other horse, lying at an ugly angle amidst the shattered remains of a light victoria; a young man knelt in the gutter, head in hands, a middle-aged woman comforting him.

But the young fool's horse was out of its misery, Robert thought, and liable to cause no more problems, other than the removal of its carcass; the dray was terrified and dangerous, its massive hooves lifting as it tossed and reared, the load of heavy grain sacks about to fall at any moment. Angrily Robert pushed his way past a restraining blue uniform and with a few choice words prevented the carter from releasing his horse.

"Can't you see he'll run amok? Just give me the feed bag and don't release those traces till I tell you!"

Instructing the nearest bobby to hold the horse's head down, Robert gently ran his hands over its muzzle and sweating neck and, murmuring softly, slipped the feed bag over its nose to mask the smell of blood. Still using the meaningless phrases he employed with his own animals, he coaxed the huge head down until it was against his chest and the blinkered eyes were unable to see the distressing scene behind him. Comforted by the smell of food and persuaded by those confident hands, the big dray calmed sufficiently to be led out of its own mangled shafts and into a narrow alley behind the church. There, in the comparative peace of that ill-lit walkway, the horse shook and shivered while sweat dripped off its belly like water from a leaking faucet, but it stood still while Robert examined its wound and the trembling carter stammered his thanks.

With the arrival of the vet and confirmation that the injury was not unduly serious, Robert continued on his way. The accident had shaken him, however, and he was reluctant to pass the other animal with the gaping holes in its head and chest. He felt his way along the smooth stone of the church wall and through a covered passage which brought him out at the Spurriergate end of fashionable Coney Street, where brightly lit shops made it easier to see and the warm press of bustling humanity had to some extent dissipated the fog. But, he reflected with bitter irony, those fashionable capes and high silk hats had not prevented them from gawking, as Louisa would have said, at the tragedy on the corner.

His assistance with the dray had cost both time and energy; renewed pain in his shoulder made it impossible to hurry, yet he was all too conscious of the passing time. Edward could well be on his way home, and it suddenly occurred to Robert that he would look a fool if entry to the house was denied him. Passing a florist's, he went inside to purchase a large bouquet of red and gold chrysanthemums; armed with an excuse for calling, he proceeded toward Gillygate.

Shrouded by linen blinds, the windows of Elliott's Commercial Hotel offered no chink of light to guide those who made their way like blind men along the length of that wintry northern street. With his hand halfway to the doorbell, Robert paused and looked up, searching for the cheerful sign which had caught his attention once, a lifetime ago it seemed, on his way to Strensall. But the fog was thickening all the time, and he could barely distinguish the first-floor windows; the sign, he was sure, had been above them. The door's brave green paint was dulled and peeling, the window boxes still inhabited by sad little skeletons of summer flowers; the whole house seemed so unnaturally quiet and dark he was suddenly afraid he was too late, that even while he hurried in response to the letter, Mary Elliott had passed sadly out of reach.

Daunted, he turned away, glad of the cover the weather afforded. In the shelter of a haberdasher's doorway he stopped to gather his courage, to collect thoughts which were already running wild. He shivered, longing for the harsh dry heat of Egypt and the Sudan, longing in a way which brought a wry twist to his mouth. Latterly, with dust and grief and exhaustion stinging his eyes, he had dreamed of York, of misty days and falling leaves and the peaceful sound of church bells; and now the taste of those dreams, like the fog, was bitter on his tongue.

Easing her aching back, Louisa paced the stretch of carpet between bed and window, trying to block the moans and cries of pain which issued from her mother's lips. She parted the heavy curtains and raised the blind, trying to peer through the fog, willing Dr. Mackenzie to hurry. For perhaps the twentieth time in less than half an hour she glanced at the clock and returned to the bed, bending once more to hold those frail, wasted hands between her own. Exhausted, feeling her own life force ebbing in seemingly direct ratio to her mother's survival, she prayed with the fervency of desperation for that indomitable spirit to falter, to release its hold on her and the husk of a body to which it clung.

Ashamed, she shook her head, summoned the dregs of courage, and focused it upon her mother. Gradually, the fevered movements subsided, the cries became mere whimpers, and Mary Elliott seemed to sleep.

Afraid to let go, afraid, almost, to look away, Louisa prayed for the doctor to come; and as though in answer to that prayer, the faint tinkle of the doorbell reached her ears.

Silence followed, then the low murmur of voices. Anxious at first, then furious that Bessie should keep Dr. Mackenzie talking, Louisa released her mother's hands and headed for the stairs.

"If that's the doctor, Bessie," she softly hissed, leaning over the banister, "don't keep him talking. Bring him up."

The older woman met her at the turn of the stairs. "It's the captain, ma'am. Do you want me to get shut of him?"

"Who?" Louisa demanded as her legs buckled suddenly. Sitting down, she asked faintly: "Who did you say?"

In the shadows at the foot of the staircase, a tall figure appeared. "It's me, Louisa—Robert."

For a moment she saw only the flowers, and those enormous hothouse blooms, red and gold, gold and red, surged and seemed to fill the hall. Gripping the banister, she took a deep breath, willing herself not to pass out. Edward, she reminded herself, had said Robert would come, and here he was; but under no circumstances would she break down and make a fool of herself, under no circumstances give Robert Duncannon an excuse to be sympathetic.

"It's all right, Bessie," she said, detaching herself from the other woman's concern. "Show the captain into the parlor—I'll be down shortly."

"Yes, ma'am," Bessie muttered, her footsteps heavy with disapproval as she descended to the hall.

Retreating into her mother's room, Louisa stood with her back to the door, shaking like an aspen. With military eloquence she cursed him under her breath, cursed him for coming back, cursed him for going away, cursed him for all his sins, both real and imaginary. And when her trembling abated, she went to the mirror and swore again. Her hair, trimmed by Bessie these days and kept short from convenience rather than fashion, was lusterless and flat from too many days cooped up in an overwarm room; and she had lost so much weight it seemed an elf's face looked back at her from the glass. Angrily she splashed her face with cold water from the ewer, pinched her pale cheeks, and quickly bent to the fire. With a smear of soot on her fingertips, Louisa touched her eyelashes, washed her hands, and donned a clean starched apron kept close by for emergencies; brushing her hair into a semblance of fluffiness, she surveyed her appearance afresh. With the feeling of going into battle, she rang the bell for Bessie to come up.

"I'll be back," she said, "just as soon as Dr. Mackenzie arrives. Mamma should be all right—he can't be long."

With no more than a grunt of disapproval, Bessie settled herself in the chair at the side of the bed. Louisa went downstairs.

The parlor fire was unlit and the room was cold. With a little dart of satisfaction, Louisa saw that the muscles along his jaw were twitching, with either nerves or a determination not to shiver. He still wore his heavy overcoat and scarf; the long-stemmed chrysanthemums, wreathed in tissue, lay on the table beside his hat and gloves. Apart from lighting the gas mantles above the fireplace, Bessie had obviously left him to his own devices.

But if he was trembling with nerves, so was she. Her breath caught in her throat as she apologized for the chill; her voice wavered as she explained that since her mother's illness they had all been too busy to give the room much use. Her eyes never left his face, and his raked hers more hungrily than ever. If she had lost weight, then he was thin to the point of gauntness, and, without the softening cover of flesh, those strong bones stood out harshly; but in spite of that, she thought nervously, his presence could still fill that little room, still make her heart beat faster with a single glance.

She moved, and so did he, but with a stiffness of his right side which was painfully revealing. For a moment, under the influence of that pleading gaze, Louisa longed to comfort him; seized with the desire to touch him, hold him, forgive him everything, she looked away, took a deep breath, and hardened her determination. If he had suffered, then so had she; in payment for their sins they were even. Almost.

"Letty told me your mother was very ill. I had some business to conduct with Harris, so I decided to call. How is she?"

His voice had not changed: still rich and deep and melodious. Feeling the familiar lurch and flutter of panic, Louisa took another deep breath before replying. "Not exactly up to receiving visitors," she said with as much detachment as she could muster. "She's been in pain, on and off, for a few days, but it's much worse today. Much worse," she repeated, feeling tears in her voice and hating them. Swallowing hard, she went to the window and raised the blind. "We're expecting the doctor, but I expect he's held up with the fog."

"It's very bad near the river," he said quietly. "There's been an accident on Nessgate, and a terrible jam of traffic at the bottom of the street here. He could be caught up in either." Touching her shoulder in tentative sympathy, Robert added: "I'd like to see your mother, if I may?"

She jerked away from him as though stung. "I'd rather you waited until the doctor's been. She's in so much pain, I doubt she'd know you just now." Shivering suddenly, Louisa rubbed the backs of her arms and moved toward the empty fireplace. "It's cold in here. I'd better light the fire."

Going through into the kitchen, taking the shovel with which she usually cleaned out the ashes, Louisa thrust it into the fire and scooped up the top layer of burning coals. "Move the fire screen, Robert, and don't get in my way!" she called as she came down the hall.

Staring aghast at the flaming mass, he stepped back and swore. "What a bloody stupid thing to do! You might set yourself on fire!"

Setting fresh coal to the blaze, Louisa gritted her teeth. "But I didn't, did I? And it's the one sure way of getting this fire going."

The doorbell rang, silencing further comment. As Louisa scrambled to her feet, the stocky little doctor marched in and through the hall without any preamble.

With his coat still on, warming his hands at the crackling, fitful fire, Robert wondered why he had come and whether he should leave. It was a difficult time, obviously; although, he reflected, under present circumstances no time could have been right. Imagining, over the years, a dozen different reunions, he had never pictured waiting alone in this cold, gloomy, unlived-in room. Its old air of smiling welcome was gone; indeed, the atmosphere of the whole house had changed. He felt an intruder, awkward and unwelcome, a stranger for whom Louisa must don a polite, company face, when grief and worry had obviously stripped her resources bare.

Pain and death; he had seen enough of both to realize that pain, real pain, was always ugly. To experience it personally was bad enough; to watch another's agony even worse. For Louisa's sake as much as her mother's, he hoped the little doctor carried morphia with him.

The darkness of his thoughts depressed him. On the point of gathering his things and going, Robert heard footsteps on the stairs.

"Now think on what I've told you," the Scots voice said emphatically. "Get some rest! Let Bessie sit up with her tonight—or Edward. And when he comes in, tell him I want to see him. I'm away home now for my tea."

The door closed. In the narrow hallway he found Louisa leaning against the wall, one hand pressed to her mouth.

"I'm sorry I've come at such a bad time," Robert said gently. "Should I go?"

She shook her head, but he was unsure whether she wanted him to stay or was simply unable to speak. Her distress was so apparent, his heart broke for her; he wanted to take her in his arms and let her weep, but after that flinching away only minutes ago, was afraid to touch her.

"I'm sorry," he whispered again, and there was all the regret of two long years in those words. "So terribly sorry."

"And so you should be," she said with low, angry force. "Why have you come back? After two years, Robert, why couldn't you just stay away and let us all forget you ever existed?"

It was a vicious blow, and he flinched from it; but, other than telling her what she was not prepared to believe, there was no short answer to that question. "I need to talk to you—sometime, whenever you have time to listen—about the children, if nothing else."

"There's nothing to discuss. They're *my* children, and they bear *my* name. You have no legal claim to them—none whatsoever."

"I don't want," he said slowly, "a *legal* claim to them. I'm their father, for Heaven's sake. I simply want to make sure that they, and you, are all right and adequately provided for."

"They're all right. I'm all right. We are adequately provided for. Does that satisfy you?"

"Not entirely, I'd like to see them." Taking his courage in both hands, Robert added unsteadily: "Especially my baby daughter—the one you never saw fit to tell me about."

In a choked voice, with her back turned rigidly to him, she said, *"My* daughter, not yours."

In the silence which followed, above the sound of his own breathing, he thought he heard a voice which could have been Liam's. "Might I see them?"

"No, not just now." Taking a handkerchief from her pocket, Louisa wiped her eyes and nose; tears were pouring down her face like silent rivers. "They're in bed. I must see to Edward's dinner," she added irrelevantly, walking away from him. "Have you eaten?"

Bemused, he nodded. "Yes, not long before I came out."

"Well, then, if you want to see my mother, you'd better come up now. She'll no doubt be asleep soon."

"Did the doctor give her something?" he asked as they mounted the stairs.

"Yes. And he's left a prescription. I don't know why he wants to see Edward," she remarked wearily. "He must think I can't read. It's morphia."

On the threshold of the room where they had first set eyes on one another, both paused. He wondered whether the same memories caught at her and, listening for the sound of children's voices, thought how strange it was, coming back to the beginning after all these years. But the children, wherever they were, were quiet now; Louisa whispered to Bessie and let Robert go in alone.

He heard the sudden swish of her skirts and realized she had gone. With a sigh he blinked hard, then took a deep breath, allowing his eyes to register reality. Nervously he tried to prepare himself for the inevitable shock of seeing Mary Elliott on the verge of death; but death as he had witnessed it already, in cleft skulls and severed limbs and hoards of devouring flies, bore no relation to what was happening here. In that quiet, familiar, firelit room, he was reminded of a more distant time when, tossing and turning with fever, a motherly, rosy-faced woman had insisted on keeping him alive.

So the shock was greater than he had expected. The tiny, withered figure in that enormous bed seemed scarcely more substantial than a brittle autumn leaf. Asleep, she could have been a stranger. Only when she opened her eyes at his gently whispered bidding did he recognize a remnant of the woman he had known.

As he reached the foot of the stairs, intending to collect his coat and take his leave as unobtrusively as possible, Edward came in, fog clinging to his clothes like a shroud.

For a moment Robert tensed, but even in the poor light of the hallway, he could see the other man's demeanor was troubled rather than hostile. Edward did not offer his hand, but after regarding him steadily, managed a sad, rather quizzical smile.

"So," he murmured as he unwound a long woolen scarf and removed his soft-brimmed hat, "you finally arrived."

"You don't seem surprised."

"I'm not. I've been expecting you." He led the way through into the parlor, and, totally bemused, Robert followed him. "Won't you sit down, Captain? And let me get you something to drink. This household doesn't run to spirits, but the elderberry wine is very warming." From a cupboard in the corner he produced a dark bottle with a handwritten label and held it up to the light.

"How did you know I was coming? I didn't know myself until a few days ago."

Edward smiled as he poured two glasses of the rich, ruby-red wine. "Well, it stands to reason you were going to turn up sooner or later. Your letter was another clue, of course. And Louisa confirmed your arrival half an hour ago when I came in for my dinner. I've just been to see Dr. Mackenzie."

"I see."

Silently Edward raised his glass, and for a few moments the two men regarded each other without speaking. One was amazed, not only by the other's serene control of a difficult situation, but also by his apparent agelessness. Clean-shaven, he seemed at least ten years younger; and for the first time, seeing those regular features fully revealed, Robert realized what a handsome man his adversary was. The other weighed and examined, seeing a face much older than he remembered, and considerably altered by life and experience. Where once those eyes had challenged, now they questioned; movements which had been lithe and graceful were uncharacteristically stiff, and there were deep-etched lines of pain round eyes and mouth, touches of frost in the crisp black hair. Recalling that recent injury, Edward could identify its place from the way his companion held himself; but his compassion was tempered by Louisa's suffering, and he did not refer to it. He waited, quite deliberately, for Robert to break the silence.

"I gather the good doctor wanted to see you about Mrs. Elliott."

Gravely Edward nodded. "It's the beginning of the end, he thinks. A matter of hours, if she's lucky, days if not." He stared into the leaping flames which were finally beginning to warm the room and slowly added, "But he's concerned about Louisa, too. She's at the end of her tether—absolutely exhausted. The trouble is, when Aunt Mary's awake, and in pain, it's Louisa she asks for."

"I can understand that," Robert said, recalling the insignificant aches and pains Louisa had soothed in the past. It was a gift she had, intangible and inexplicable, but no less real for all that. Aware of the nagging ache in his shoulder, he shifted position and sighed. "I wish," he added hesitantly, "I wish there was something I could do. Something—anything. Your aunt was kind to me—beyond anything I deserved."

"She understood people," Edward said. "And human nature."

"And never judged."

"Oh, I don't know. She did sometimes, and she wasn't *always* right."

Unaware of the source of that heartfelt comment, Robert glanced quickly up, but his companion's eyes were downcast, his manner reflective, as though he recalled personal judgments just as important but far more arbitrary than her peculiar fondness for Robert Duncannon.

"I just wish I could do something," he repeated.

"We all feel that. That's the worst part of it," Edward sighed, "knowing there's nothing to be done. Except watching and waiting—and praying for the end."

"You'll let me know? I'm staying with Harris for a few days." He drained his glass and stood up. "There's a lot I want to discuss—with Louisa particularly—but it's waited a long time, and I daresay it will wait a little longer. Now, I really must go and let you get to bed."

"I'll not be seeing my bed for a few hours yet," the other man admitted with a weary smile. "I must let Bessie get some sleep: she was up all last night and half the night before."

For a moment Robert stood deep in thought. He looked at his watch and peered through the window at the fog. Tentatively, afraid of being snubbed, he said: "I can spare a few hours, all night if necessary. If it's simply a question of someone being there and watching over her, then I can stay awake and watch with the best."

With a small, ironic smile, Edward looked out of the window, then brushed past him into the hall. A moment later, closing the front door, he said, "You might as well, I suppose. I doubt you'll get back to your lodgings tonight, anyway."

By half past ten Robert had stood like a schoolboy under Bessie's stern gaze and listened to her instructions, repeated them three times, and settled himself, not too comfortably, with a selection of books and journals Edward had provided. Under the influence of that heavy dose of morphia, Mary Elliott slept peacefully on.

Edward came into the room and stood gazing down at his aunt. "I don't know how much he's given her, but it could start to wear off in the early hours. Wake me anyway, by two at the latest. You know where my room is; at the top of the next flight."

Robert nodded, and Edward glanced at the clock. "I'm going down to make Louisa some cocoa. Can I get you anything?"

"No, thanks. Bessie made me some coffee to keep me awake. How is Louisa?"

"Too tired to sleep, I think. Still—" He shook his head and left.

Robert heard him return a little while later, heard Louisa's door open and close, but though he listened intently, he did not hear Edward come out again.

Despite the small fire, Louisa was huddled in a shawl, her face pale and drawn against the stacked pillows. Her eyes were huge and dark-shadowed, and she looked so frail in the flickering candlelight that Edward felt his heart lurch with concern. Not half an hour previously, as he mentioned Robert's offer, she had been aggressively scathing, telling him, yes, Robert could stay; of course he could do as he wished, he always did! But the boldness had evaporated; he could see she regretted that angry impulse, that, with time to think, the shock of his arrival had finally penetrated.

He handed her the mug of cocoa, watched her clasp reddened, work-worn hands around it for warmth, and felt the impersonal barriers created by words and work and sheer fatigue begin to crumble. For a moment he wondered whether it had been the wrong thing to do, letting Robert Duncannon back into their lives, however temporarily; then he reflected on past awareness, knowing it had to be. He had always believed Louisa must face him again, must come to terms with what he suspected she still felt for him and, more important still, with the consequences of her actions. For two years, like a child hiding its face against adult reproach, she had hidden from the world and ignored the existence of Robert Duncannon; but she could not cover her face forever, and now he had come to seek her out. Much as he longed to help her, Edward knew he could not, for Robert Duncannon was a subject they did not discuss.

"I looked in on the children," he told her, sitting on the edge of the bed. "They're sleeping soundly."

For once, however, the children were not Louisa's prime concern. "And what's *he* doing?"

"Nothing particularly—just sitting there, drinking coffee and reading a book. I'm quite sure he won't fall asleep, if that's what you're worried about."

She closed her eyes and grasped his hand. "Why did he have to come?" she whispered. *"Now,* of all times!"

He smoothed her hair. "I don't know. The first opportunity, I suppose."

"He wants to see the children."

"I imagine he does," Edward sighed. "You know, there's a lot we have to discuss. Not immediately—not even in the next few days—but soon. It would be better to agree to that: it will save a lot of argument and heartbreak in the long run."

"I don't want to."

"No, I know that. But you're very tired, and now isn't even the time to be thinking of it. I'll go now," he said gently, "and we'll talk some more tomorrow." He made to stand, but Louisa clung to him, begging him not to leave, and like a frightened child refused to give a reason. With a sigh, Edward agreed to stay until she went to sleep.

Making himself comfortable with his back against the pillows, he let her nestle in the crook of his arm. Unutterably tired, longing for his own bed, the seductive comfort of her warmth and closeness made him loath to hurry away. After a little while he extinguished the candle and slipped off his shoes; within a very short time he was curled beside her and fast asleep.

SIX

*f*eeling the heaviness of imminent sleep, Robert yawned deeply and stood up, pacing the half-dozen steps to the window, where, more from habit than any real curiosity, he lifted the blind and glanced out at the fog. It was just as dense as before and totally silent; there had been no traffic for several hours, and a long time had elapsed since the last faltering drunks had set off home, cursing and laughing, from the public house a few doors away.

Mary Elliott was still sleeping, breathing stertorously, oblivious to Robert's presence and the small light beside his chair. Having grown used to the immense change in her, he was able to look at her now without shock or revulsion, and having seen the smile and the recognition in her eyes, was able to reconcile both past and present. In the time that he had spent alone with her initially, he had simply knelt by her bed and talked to her, all the while holding those frail fingers between his own. She had looked at him and smiled, managed to murmur his name once or twice, but he had no way of knowing whether she understood what he was saying. Not that it mattered; he was sure she knew he would do his best for Louisa and the children, insofar as he was allowed to do anything at all, and equally sure that his journey had not been in vain.

But she had slipped into the welcoming arms of oblivion and since then had barely moved. The end, he was sure, could not be far away.

He took out his watch and saw that it was twenty minutes past two, sighed, and returned the gold hunter to his pocket, wondering whether to call Edward or not. He had said to call him at two, but Robert knew full well he was not in his room, and sheer embarrassment held him from entering Louisa's. Although he had long since conquered his anger, and even half-convinced himself that it was inevitable they should be living in the closest and most intimate of terms, still he burned with shame that she should make it so obvious. Edward had intended to sleep elsewhere, Robert reasoned, but she had kept him by her side on purpose, simply to underscore a point made clear two years before.

And then, as he bent to mend the fire, he heard movement, turned quickly, and saw Edward with crumpled suit and tousled hair, leaning against the doorjamb.

"I fell asleep," he said simply.

For a moment Robert did not answer, his eyes taking in the evidence of that unmistakably creased jacket. "No matter," he replied evenly. "I told you I could stay all night if need be." But his tension was dispelled, and as Edward went downstairs to make some tea, Robert could have laughed with relief.

By the time Edward returned, he had regained control of himself; the two men sat at either side of the hearth, drinking their tea in quite companionable silence. Edward had combed his hair and straightened his tie, but his eyes were heavy, Robert noticed, and a faint stubble on his chin gleamed gold in the firelight. He ran exploratory fingers over his own jaw; it felt unpleasantly rough, and his eyes were prickling with tiredness; he was wondering idly whether he could borrow a razor before morning, when the other man glanced across at him and smiled.

"There's hot water downstairs, and I have a spare razor if you'd like to shave."

"Do you read minds?"

"Not usually," Edward smiled, "but I understood the gesture. We both look a little worse for wear. By the way, how is your shoulder now?"

"It's fine, much easier for sitting still and doing nothing." After a moment he asked, "But how did you know it was bothering me earlier? I never mentioned it."

Edward shrugged. "Oh, from the look on your face and the way you were sitting. And there was a letter from your sister, so I knew something of it."

"You're very observant," Robert remarked.

After a while they fell to talking quietly, about the battle and Robert's experiences in Egypt, carefully skirting his reasons for going there. The possibility of his return was discussed, as were his chances of rejoining the Royals.

"So you don't want to retire?"

"Lord, no. The army's my life. I've never known anything else, and I've no desire to give it up yet. I got a taste of promotion while I was out there, you know," Robert chuckled. *"Major* Duncannon for the duration of my service with the Egyptian Cavalry, and I must admit it whetted my appetite. I'd very much like to be gazetted as such—with my old regiment, of course!"

"Of course," Edward echoed with a smile. "So you've no plans to retire to a little place in the country and take up farming for a living?"

With a soft laugh, Robert shook his head. "I don't think so, in spite of the fact that I was virtually born and bred to it: It's all very well, but after a few weeks I'd be bored to distraction. I'd not care for it on a permanent basis—not yet awhile."

"Nor me," his companion agreed. "I love the city—*this* city—too much. I'd feel like an exile, I think, if I had to leave."

Their glances met, and in that moment both men were equally aware that Louisa would have loved nothing better than an isolated cottage in the depths of the country; almost guiltily their glances fell away, and like two conspirators surprised by a third party, they changed the subject.

By four in the morning, Robert was nodding gently; Edward touched him lightly on the shoulder. "The bed in the dressing room is made up with fresh sheets. I think you should lie down."

For a moment he protested, but the thought of sleep was suddenly too attractive to ignore. Standing in the doorway of the little dressing room, he looked back, seeing the fireplace and the light and the bed as though for the first time.

"How strange," he slowly remarked. "It was exactly like this that I first met Louisa." He paused, and Edward looked up, alert suddenly and questioning. "A winter's night—someone ill. And I was still feverish, I suppose, because I cried out in my sleep—Louisa came to wake me. She was sitting with her mother that night, in the dressing room. It was when everyone had the flu, do you remember? And then she came back for some reason—I forget why—and we sat, she and I, just as we have tonight, either side of that very fireplace, in the same two chairs, talking."

After a moment Edward said: "So that's how you met? I didn't know, and I often wondered."

"Yes. Right here in this room. That's where she was sitting—in the chair facing you. And I remember thinking how lovely she looked in the firelight, but how desperately uneasy she was," he added with a smile, "talking, in the middle of the night, to a total stranger!" But even as the memory amused him, regret and sorrow mocked. Abruptly he turned away. "Well, goodnight."

"Yes, sleep well."

He woke to the sound of voices in the next room, but light was filtering through chinks in the curtains, so he knew it must be past eight o'clock. He lay still, trying to distinguish what was being said, whether anyone was weeping, but he could make out only the heavy Scots rumble of the doctor and a lighter voice that was probably Louisa's. There were footsteps on the stairs, and the same voices receding; a few minutes later more footsteps returned, and seconds later there was a sharp tap on his door.

Almost certain it was Louisa, he hitched the blankets around his injured shoulder before calling her in. Without meeting his eyes, she set hot water and a razor on a washstand and informed him that breakfast would be served downstairs in approximately half an hour. She was almost gone again before he could collect his thoughts.

"Louisa!"

She paused, her hand on the door. "Yes?"

"Your mother—how is she?"

"As well as can be expected—isn't that the phrase?" With an edge of sarcasm, she said, "Was there anything else, sir?"

Hating her, he shook his head. About to say that dressing himself took forever, just in time he bit the words back; he was too conscious of its ugliness to want her to see that healing wound and afraid he might seem to play for sympathy should he draw attention to it.

As every morning, his shoulder and arm were unbearably stiff; with difficulty he eased himself out of bed and pulled on his trousers and, with even greater difficulty, managed to shave. Shirt and waistcoat were no real problem, but the stiff collar and tiny studs almost defeated him. As Robert knotted his tie, he was white-faced and trembling.

They breakfasted well, if silently, in what had once been the guests' dining room. Stealing glances at Louisa, he was glad to see that, in spite of the dark smudges beneath her eyes, there were two high spots of color on her cheekbones, which, even if summoned by resentment at his presence, were certainly an improvement on yesterday's pallor. Her hair was soft and fluffy as though newly washed, and she was wearing a plain navy dress which accentuated her slenderness. Yesterday he had been shocked by her appearance; this morning he was relieved to see a spark of life and spirit in her glance.

Hearing sudden squeals and high, piping voices, Robert knew the children were close by, probably in the kitchen; he heard the distinct patter of small feet in the hallway, and for a second his heart raced so desperately he could hardly breathe. Edward caught his eyes and gave a most uncertain smile.

"I was wondering," he said, "how long they would take to escape."

Before Louisa could reach the door a small, towheaded boy thrust his way through, halted in consternation at sight of the stranger, then rushed at his mother, hiding a suddenly rosy face against her skirts.

The color in Louisa's face spread and deepened; avoiding Robert's gaze, she addressed herself to his son. "Mind your manners, William, and say hello. You know who this is, don't you?"

Gentle hands stroked that round, fair head; watching them, Robert saw she still wore the same two rings, his signet and the plain gold band he had bought for her in Dublin. For some reason it cheered him, and he smiled at the little boy who reluctantly showed his face. In two years he had grown a great deal, but he was more like Louisa than ever, with the same determined chin and bright blue, questioning gaze. Was there also a spark of recognition? Robert wondered, aware of the pulse throbbing in his throat and an unbearable tension as they all awaited the boy's reply. It seemed an eternity before he shook his head, defiantly, Robert thought, and turned again to his mother.

Two years for the child was half a lifetime, Robert reminded himself; but shame and regret assailed him, and he had to look down, clearing his throat of a sudden, choking obstruction. Disturbed, totally lost for words, he took refuge in silent anger, blaming Louisa for everything. Two years was a long time, and she might have told the children anything—or nothing at all, he thought bitterly. Either way, whatever he said would be wrong.

She whispered something and tried to push Liam forward, but he stood resolutely against her. "How d'you do," he said at last with solemn formality.

From somewhere, Robert summoned a smile and an adequate response. That defiant blue gaze continued to assess him, and he swallowed hard. "I'm sorry you don't remember me, Liam—we used to have a lot of fun together in the old days. Do you remember being in Dublin—the big house in the square?" There was a sudden frown at that, as though the child tugged hard at something on the edge of his memory. "We often played there with a ball," Robert went on in desperation, "with Georgina. Do you remember Georgina?"

Slowly Liam nodded, and Edward said: "Letty and Georgina came to stay with us last summer."

Ignoring him, Robert said: "Georgie sends her love to you, and your Mamma," he added, looking up at Louisa. "She wanted to come with me, but I said I'd bring her another time. Georgie's my little girl, but, like you, she's grown a lot. When I went away, you were very small—only two—that's a long time ago, isn't it?"

"I'm big now," Liam confided in a rush. "I'm going to school soon. Bobby isn't—he's not three yet—and Tisha's only a baby."

Startled, Robert glanced up. "Tisha?"

"Letitia—I'm sure Letty must have told you we named the baby after her."

He dropped his gaze. "Yes—yes, she did. I'm sorry, I wasn't connecting the two names." Letty *had* told him, in the letter which relayed news of the birth itself. Previous to that, he had known absolutely nothing at all about it; and even now he found it hard to forgive his sister for that withholding of the truth. She said she had not known herself until latterly, that Louisa had not wanted him to know at all; but Robert was not entirely sure of that.

He had written to Louisa, begging forgiveness for his behavior, offering to move Heaven and earth for leave, if only she would consider a reconciliation; and waited in vain for a reply. Not a single word from her in all that time: it was hard to understand, let alone forgive.

"May I see her?" he asked.

"If you wish," she replied, displaying no more emotion than if he had asked to see a book or a picture or a bundle of old clothes.

She bent toward the child, telling him to go and ask Bessie to bring the baby downstairs; but Robert cut across those softly voiced instructions, his anger more telling because it was so restrained. "If I wish?" he demanded. "Do you think I shouldn't want to see her? She is my daughter, isn't she?"

He was aware of a hand pressing into the crook of his right shoulder.

"Please," Edward whispered warningly, "not in front of the child!" With that he ushered Liam from the room.

Rage boiled inside him while he stared at Louisa's white, closed face. He wanted to hit her, hard, knowing if he did he would probably half kill her. He could hardly believe that this cold, emotionless woman was the one he had loved so passionately, refused to believe he had done anything to warrant such calculated cruelty.

Edward came back, and Robert looked up, ready to vent his fury. "Well?" he snapped. "Is she my daughter—or is she yours?"

Edward's head jerked up, his mouth compressed into a thin, hard line; for a second, caught offguard, his eyes glittered with icy contempt. For the first time Robert saw all his own pain and anger reflected in the other man's eyes, all the resentment and hostility he had expected the night before.

There was a muffled exclamation from Louisa. "My God, Robert! Do you have to judge everyone by your own disgustingly low standards?"

With an apology to Edward on the tip of his tongue, he bit it back. "Low standards?" he repeated with mocking amazement. "Do you include yourself?"

Edward's voice rapped across them. "Stop it! Immediately! You're worse than children," he snapped, "indulging in petty insults," and as Louisa rose to clear the table, he motioned her back to her seat. "Just a moment, Louisa, there's something I have to say." He paused, tugging at his chin, his eyes flicking from one to the other. "At the moment, we're all three of us very tired. One way and another, for all of us, the past few months have been . . . difficult. We've all suffered, I have no doubt, and at the moment, emotions are running high.

"There'll never be," he continued heavily, "an ideal time to discuss what must be discussed, but I think just now is probably the worst time we could have chosen. And it's quite unseemly that we should be letting tempers get the better of us when Louisa's mother is lying upstairs . . ."

Sobbing suddenly, Louisa shot out of her chair, but before she could reach the door, Edward grabbed her arm.

"Sit down and listen to me; I'm not going to say this again." While she fought to bring her tears under control, he said to her, "Between you, you and Robert brought three children into this world—and I'm not going to stand by and see them suffer because you two want to indulge in some kind of protracted war. It's time you started thinking about *them*," he said emphatically, his glance resting on Robert, "instead of yourselves and your past mistakes."

"I agree," Robert murmured, amazed and not a little daunted by his obvious control over Louisa; indeed, of the whole situation. Lighting one of his small cigars, he blew a fine blue haze of smoke into the room. "So what do you suggest?"

"Leave it a few weeks. At least until we here have had the chance to get over—well, whatever it is we have to get over in the next few weeks. I'm sure you understand."

Trying to ignore Louisa's quiet sobs, Robert nodded. "And in the meantime—a truce?"

"Of course," Edward replied with patient restraint. "A truce." He turned to Louisa then and, with a gentle but very firm gesture, pulled her hands from her face. "I hope you agree to that?" As she nodded, he told her to dry her eyes; it amazed Robert that she did.

With a swish of her skirts, she left the room. There was an awkward silence in her wake; Edward gave a heavy sigh while Robert studied the curling smoke of his cigar. About to speak, he broke off at the sound of scuffling outside the door, and as Edward opened it, he saw Liam standing there with his reluctant little brother. Shyly, he simply stood and stared, three fingers jammed into his tiny mouth.

Robert half-rose, then resumed his seat, aware of his own rather daunting height. Anxious to avoid another embarrassing round of introduction, he leaned toward them and smiled. "Well, now, this must be Bobby. I swear I hardly know him, he's grown so much. And he's so hungry, he has to chew his fingers. Come over here, and let's see what we've got." Wishing he had remembered to buy a quarter of sweets as well as those chrysanthemums, Robert quickly cut and buttered a piece of bread, spreading it thickly with strawberry jam.

Despite his superior age, Liam still hung back, unsure of the big man with the sun-browned skin and flourishing black moustache. Not so his little brother. Bobby climbed confidently onto the proffered knee, beamed like a rococo cherub and thrust out an already sticky hand for the finger of bread. Robert looked at them: one dark, one fair, and both strikingly attractive children, likely to grow into handsome young men. But as soon as Louisa carried Tisha into the room, Robert knew she was going to be beautiful. At fifteen months, with clear, translucent skin, rosy cheeks and a perfect little rosebud mouth, she had all the delicate perfection of a china doll. She stared at him from beneath glossy dark-gold curls, a wide, unblinking, inscrutable gaze, and Robert knew he was lost.

Suddenly, her gaze shifted; and immediately she struggled to be free. "Dadda," the tiny heartbreaker demanded, reaching out her arms to Edward. "Want Dadda."

SEVEN

*E*dward did not go to work that day, nor the next, and on the night Mary Elliott slipped peacefully away, Louisa had slept some twelve hours, unaware of her mother's passing.

In retrospect, that was what grieved her, beyond thankfulness, beyond relief, beyond the dreadful aching hole she felt somewhere in her breast, beyond any of the emotions she thought she should have felt. It seemed unnatural and unfair that, after all they had suffered together, her mother should leave the mortal world without Louisa even being aware of it. Initially she could not forgive Dr. Mackenzie for the sleeping draft he had insisted she take that night, and even railed against Edward for agreeing with him. Angrier than she had seen him for a long time, he told her to stop behaving like a spoiled child: rest was what she had needed, still needed. Standing over her like a martinet, he watched while she swallowed more of the foul-tasting medicine.

Louisa knew she had behaved badly, reacting in bizarre and eccentric fashion to quite ordinary situations; the children were puzzled and upset, and as though they could not give up the habit, Bessie and Edward took turns to sit with her each night until she fell asleep. And sleep she did, all night and half the day, the sleep of total and utter exhaustion.

Robert had planned to return to Dublin, but with Mary Elliott's death he said he would stay on for the funeral, and since that first evening, had called several times. While confined to her bed, Louisa was spared the necessity of seeing him, although he was never out of her awareness, his presence like an upraised sword on the edge of her vision.

For the moment, however, she had peace and solitude. Blanche had been and gone, Edward was out, Emily had thankfully whisked the children back to Leeds with her the night before, and Bessie was in her beloved kitchen, preparing food for the funeral tea. But when we move, Louisa thought bitterly, she will go too, because we can't afford to keep her. And because Emily is moving up in the world, and really *must* have a housekeeper, she will go to them, to a nice, decent, respectable family with a marriage license framed on the wall.

For the past two years, although she had kept silence on the subject, in myriad small ways Bessie had managed to register strong disapproval, making it more than clear that had it not been for loyalty to her old and dearly loved mistress, she would be searching for another place. And that, more than anything, had hurt Louisa, for Bessie was more family than servant, a human fixture who had always been kinder and more reliable than either sister; more affectionate, even, in the difficult years between child and adult, than her mother.

With Mary Elliott gone, however, and a move from the Gillygate house imperative, Bessie had no reason to stay. Despite the antipathy, Louisa knew she would miss her, and Bessie's going was symptomatic of upheavals which, however necessary, she did not want to face.

Self-pity attacked, and she gave in to it, for a moment wishing she smoked like Letty or drank like Robert, so there could be some outward and visible sign of the grief and tension within. She dreaded the funeral, not least because it meant facing people she had avoided for a long time. People like Mrs. Chapman, who had fueled more gossip than Louisa cared to contemplate, and one prune-faced neighbor who never lost an opportunity to lift her nose and swish her skirt aside if she saw Louisa in the street. Another had actually hissed the word *whore* at her in the butcher's; and while that kindly soul had glared at the old witch and given Louisa an extra half pound of shin, that had been the end. After all, she reasoned, to a certain extent they were right; and not only had she broken all the rules in the book as far as they were concerned, she had also had the brass-faced cheek to come back and advertise the fact. With her pregnancy becoming more obvious then, she had given up, leaving Bessie to do the shopping and her mother to take the boys for walks. Except for Edward's insistence, she might have given up going out altogether; but from the very beginning he had refused to let her become a hermit and done all in his power to deflect the prurience of local curiosity.

Even within the family he had consoled and supported her, pricking Blanche's self-righteousness and curbing Emily's tendency to condescension; and although there had been harsh words on occasion, delivered mainly as jolts to her bouts of self-pity, from Edward there had been none of the recriminations with which she lacerated herself. Up to her mother's illness, Louisa felt she had been recovering, but the agony of that raked up all the old guilt and more: had she stayed in Dublin, the hotel would still be viable; Mamma's health might not have broken down; Edward need not have worked so desperately hard to support them . . . The list went on and on.

The irony of it, when she had imagined from the distance of Dublin that a return to York would provide all the answers, bit into her even now. In their own ways, people here could be just as cruel as anywhere else: human nature was no different, whatever the class, whatever the language used to express it. The only consolation, throughout everything, was in Edward's undemanding, unconditional affection and in her love for the city itself. In the very early hours of a summer's morning, or at dusk, Louisa would walk her favorite paths, watch the changing of the seasons, and for a brief while, at least, leave all her troubles behind.

Half-dozing in her mother's favorite chair, she was startled into wakefulness by the jangling of the front bell. She heard Bessie's footsteps and an irritated sigh as she approached the door, silence for a second, and then her voice, heavy with disapproval, as she invited Robert to wait inside.

"It's the captain, ma'am," she said to Louisa, eyebrows drawn together over a gimlet gaze. "Are you at home?"

"No, Bessie, I don't think I am."

"At home or not," Robert said, coming into the parlor, "you're up and dressed, and I need to speak to you."

Bessie bestowed on him a look which would have crushed a less determined man, glanced at Louisa for further instructions, and, receiving none, gave a sniff as she swept out which said they must both go to hell without her assistance.

"I don't—particularly—want to speak to you."

"Well, it's time you did. There are things we have to discuss before I return to Ireland." Removing hat and coat and gloves, he took the chair which faced her. "Edward tells me you're thinking of moving house."

"Yes, that's right. We can't afford to keep this house on."

"So I understand. But do you have to move in with him?"

Amazed at his temerity, for a second Louisa simply stared at him. "I don't think that's any of your business!" she said, furious that he should even think to interfere.

"The children are my business."

"Oh, no. They're *mine,* as I said before. I'll provide for them somehow, Robert, don't you fear!"

"How?" he demanded. "You're an unmarried woman; without employment, how will you provide?"

"I was an unmarried woman, without employment," she said with low, controlled fury, "when I first came back here, *two years ago.* I had every intention at that time of taking a job—any job—to feed and clothe my children. I had no intention of being a *burden* on my mother, or Edward, or anyone else!" Breathing hard, pausing to let that sink in, she glared at him with such venom that for a moment Robert recoiled. "But before I was able to do that—I was looking, you understand—I discovered I was *pregnant!*

"*You* made me a burden on this household," she said quietly into the silence, "and it's thanks to you that Edward has had to support me all this time. If you could have just let me go that night—just accepted that I had had enough and could take not one thing more, Robert—if you could have done that, I might have been able to forgive you."

"I know," he murmured with abject contrition. "I'm so sorry for that, Louisa, you've no idea—"

"I don't want to know! *Your* sorrow at this juncture does not concern me!" Rising abruptly to her feet, Louisa went to the door. "I think you should go."

He stood, but did not gather his things. "Please, listen to me. I've had two long years to think about that night—and all that went before it—and I know what a blasted fool I was. But you wouldn't listen to me then, Louisa—just as you don't want to listen to me now. What I did was unforgivable, but believe me, it happened only because I loved you so much, *because I didn't want you to leave.*

"You have to understand that," he whispered, taking a step toward her. "You have to believe that it was love and—and dread—which drove me then, not anger."

Not wanting to accept it, still she saw the sorrow in his eyes and the memory of their last night together, when he had taken her without consent. Reliving all the rage and humiliation of that night, she stiffened under the hand which touched her shoulder and knew there had been hatred, too. Not in him, perhaps, but in herself, for the weakness of the body which had committed the ultimate betrayal and responded to him.

But it would not happen again, however hard he tried to remind her of other, better days. Moving out of reach, in a voice which was not quite steady, she said: "All right—I believe you. I hope that makes you happy."

"Do you mean that?"

"I've said so, haven't I? But remember this, Robert—it's over. I've changed. I'm no longer the woman I was two years ago—"

"I've changed, too," he said quickly, taking hold of her hand. "That's what I've been trying to tell you. I've learned a lot from those mistakes, from my time out there in the desert. I've changed, Louisa, but I still love you, and I—"

"No! There can be no going back, not now, not ever! I don't want your kind of life, Robert, and, if truth be told, I never did!"

"On your terms," he said desperately. "You could stay here, in York— I'd buy a house for you—"

"No!" Backing away from him, shaking her head, Louisa took refuge in her mother's chair and blocked her ears. That fragile self-control, so carefully held together, was crumbling through her fingers like sand. She had an overwhelming desire to scream at him and was afraid that if she did, the scream would go on and on and on . . .

"Louisa . . ." He was bending over her, much too close; she pushed at the air, fending him away.

"Don't—don't touch me. I don't want you near me—just stay away—"

He sat down. "I'm sorry," he whispered. "I shouldn't have said anything. It's the wrong time, the wrong place." He leaned forward, head in hands. "As always, there's never enough time—I'm never with you long enough to find the right moment." Looking up, he lit a cigar, and the scent of it was poignant, unbearable, reminding her of happy, faraway evenings and the aftermath of love. "What I'm trying to say is—if you can bear to hear it—that I still care about you and the children. I'd like the chance to spend time with them occasionally. I hope you won't deny me that. And, whatever happens, the offer is still open, will always be open, should you change your mind."

Unable to speak, she simply nodded, with the feeling that she would agree to anything if only he would go away, leave her in peace.

For some minutes he said nothing at all, and then, leaning back against the sofa cushions, looked as exhausted as she felt, Robert started to talk about Letty, about a plan he had discussed with Edward, for inviting his sister over to accompany Louisa on a short holiday. The thought that she had been discussed behind her back, by Edward and Robert of all people, roused her anger afresh, but she had no energy with which to express it and moments later was aware that the idea was absurdly tempting. She had not seen Letty for almost six months, and to see her again, talk to her, get away from everything for a while, might help restore a better perspective.

She wished she could have seen Georgina, too. Loving her, she had missed the child for a long time after leaving Dublin and, since the heartbreak of that parting, had thought often of Anne Duncannon's words uttered all those years ago at White Leigh. What did we do to her? she wondered, thinking of that quiet and thoughtful girl, the child-ish exuberance tamed by tragedies not of her making. Loving her little brothers, depending on Louisa, the shock of losing them, with her adored father's abrupt departure so very close behind, must have left indelible scars. Only Letty remained a true, fixed point, and for that Louisa was thankful. But she often wondered, guiltily, what went through Georgina's mind when she visited them in York and how Robert stood these days in her affections.

"How is Georgina?" she asked. "Was she pleased to have you back?"

"Yes, I think so," he said; a little guardedly, Louisa thought, glancing quickly up into his face. Holding that glance, he added softly: "She hoped, when I told her I was coming here, that I would bring you back."

EIGHT

Scarcely a handful of mourners had paid their respects at Elizabeth Elliott's funeral, but at her sister Mary's were dozens of people, neighbors and shopkeepers from Gillygate, old regulars from the hotel, and friends she had made over the years whom her daughters barely knew.

Shaking beneath dense black veiling, Louisa clung to Edward's arm as they followed the coffin with Blanche and Emily and into the huge chapel. To her, the gathered mourners were not individuals but an amorphous mass with eyes, eyes that touched and probed, stripping away the crepe and veils and leaving her naked in terror and grief. She shivered and trembled and tried to concentrate on the service, but that was worse, impersonal and anonymous, conducted by a curate who had no acquaintance with Mary Elliott and behaved as though performing a tedious and distasteful task. To hear her mother referred to as "Our sister here departed" was no better than an insult; she looked at Blanche, her face and hands so neatly composed, and Emily weeping quietly into her handkerchief, and each time she heard that phrase repeated, wanted to scream in protest.

She began to be afraid she would give voice to it, pushed a scrap of lace and linen between her teeth and bit hard, covering her mouth with her fingers. Edward gripped her other hand fiercely, and she knew he was suffering too. At the hymn they stood, both unable to sing; Blanche's voice, steady at first, quavering like Emily's toward the end, rang in her ears. Louisa wanted to yell at them both.

Out. Out past that sea of faces and into swirling mist. Fresh agony struck: how would they ever find the grave? Angels with outspread wings loomed at her, obelisks appeared for a moment and then were swallowed whole; great slabs of marble and granite, nightmare trees dripping crocodile tears reached out; the coffin with its bearers moved off, disappearing into the fog. Blanche and Emily were indistinct, then gone . . .

Edward was tugging gently at her elbow. "Not much more, then we can go home. Come on."

"I can't!" She was shaking, too terrified to move.

Out of the rapidly swelling crowd, Bessie appeared, grief suspended as she reached for Louisa's hand; but Louisa flinched from the expected touch. "No, leave me alone!"

"It's all right," Edward said calmly, and his voice was soft and warm; gently, he pulled her arm through his and squeezed her hand. "Don't panic. Just tell me what's wrong."

"They've gone; we'll never find them, never find the grave!"

"Yes, we will." His voice was so sure, so confident. "All we have to do is follow the path. I know the way."

As she took her first hesitant step forward, she caught sight of Robert a few yards ahead, on the edge of the crowd but towering above them, face anxious, eyes willing her on. Her knees threatened to give way at every step, but leaning on Edward, heartened by his murmured encouragements, she made her way past white, anonymous faces down the path Emily and Blanche had walked. Bessie was in front, with a man whose jaunty figure and black billycoat hat raised a weak smile beneath her veil. He turned, his face anxious at first, then cheeky as it burst into a broad grin. His saucy wink brought an unexpected gurgle of laughter to her throat.

"Oh, John Elliott," she whispered to Edward. "I might have known the angle of that hat would be John."

"Typical," he replied, referring to the wink, but there was gladness in his voice as he pressed her hand. "Good of him to come. It must have been the very devil of a journey."

"He was very fond of Mamma. I knew he'd come if he could."

To one side of the open grave, flares were lit, dispelling wraiths of fog beneath the trees. Supported by her husband, Emily was weeping copiously; even Blanche was dabbing her eyes with a scrap of silk, but, strangely, Louisa had no desire to weep.

The curate mumbled his way through the last of the service, and she simply ceased to listen. Lifting her head, she noticed a few withered leaves clinging to the branch above them and thought of her mother in the past endless weeks, clinging so tenaciously to life. But the suffering was over, the spirit set free, having no more to do with this mere disposal of mortal remains. Its importance fell away, and spring was in her soul, and the scent of roses; she was suddenly warm and glad, relieved of fear, relieved of grief and sadness and the terrible memory of lingering death. She wanted to embrace them all, fill them with her sure and eager certainty: they were wrong to be weeping when Mary Elliott had been set free; wrong to weep for a soul at peace.

The joy she had experienced buoyed her through the ordeal of condolences. Edward kept her close beside him, forcing people who would commiserate with him to acknowledge Louisa at least. Sometimes strained through tight lips, sometimes surprisingly genuine, the wash of words flowed over her, leaving little mark. She had a sense of familiarity, as though she had done this before; the sight of Robert, head bowed in conversation with John Elliott, suddenly provided the answer: those early days in Dublin, when he had taken her practically everywhere with him. He had forced her through dozens of similar ordeals, but she had never acquired the necessary immunity to sly looks and whispered gossip. Unlike Robert, she would never be gregarious; her life and nature precluded it, but she would strive, for the children's sake, to regain something of her former confidence. And for her mother's sake, she thought, still warmed by the glow of that fleeting presence. It was a small beginning on the road back to life, but with help, she knew she would get there.

Only one incident pierced that new resolve. She overheard Emily ask her mother-in-law if she would come back to the house for some refreshment; Mrs. Chapman's audible sniff and contemptuous refusal went home like a shaft from a bow, wounding Louisa inordinately. She felt herself shrink and wither, but Edward grimly ushered her into the waiting carriage.

Turning back to Emily, he said quietly, but within earshot of the pruriently curious Mrs. Chapman: "Don't ask all and sundry back to the house, Emily—we are a little short of space. Your mother's *friends,*" he added with heavy emphasis, "and immediate family only.

"The old battle-ax," he muttered as he climbed in beside Louisa. "I don't know how she lives with herself." Summoning a smile, he patted her arm. "You've done marvelously—I'm so proud of you. What happened to you by the graveside? I felt your spirits lift and—"

There was a tap at the opposite window. Sheltered from prying eyes by the body of the carriage, Robert waited to speak to them, with John Elliott by his side.

"Look, I won't come back to the house—you've enough to handle without my presence causing more raised eyebrows. I'll head off back to Harris's place, and—" he smiled ruefully—"John here feels in need of something warming, so he's coming with me."

Through the open window, John gripped her hand and held it for a moment against his cheek. "I'll come on later, love, if that's all right. When the crowd's shifted. Can I beg a bed for the night, do you think?"

He grinned. "I don't need no clean sheets—nothing like that—a couple of blankets'll do me just fine."

"Of course you can. It's good to see you."

"Aye, well," he murmured, his eyes suddenly misty, "we'll have a little talk later, eh? Take care, now."

Robert touched her arm. "Moira sends her love, by the way—most sincerely. And her condolences. She would have liked to be here with you, but couldn't. You understand?"

For a moment Louisa furrowed her brow. "Too busy?" she ventured.

"No, a small matter of religion."

"Oh, of course." Louisa sighed. "I'd forgotten that. Yes, well—send her my thanks, Robert. And my regards."

"I'll do that." Hesitating a second, he suddenly took her hand and brushed it with his lips. "You deserve a medal," he said.

"It's kind of you to say so," she answered bleakly, "but the day's not over yet."

"The worst part is." He turned to Edward. "Letty's arriving the day after tomorrow. She'll want to see Louisa straight away, I know. May I bring her?"

Edward nodded. "Of course."

With a smile and that so-familiar half-salute, he was gone. Louisa turned to find Edward's eyes upon her, his gaze uneasy, questioning.

The children were upstairs in the nursery with Emily's four, looked after by a huge-eyed slip of a girl who reminded Louisa of her sister before marriage and children had thickened her figure. She was unsure whether the girl was employed as nanny or skivvy in Emily's household, but did not ask; she was good with the children and polite enough, although her heavy West Riding accent with its strange dialect words and absence of *t*'s was hard for Louisa to comprehend. Young as they were, even Emily's children were adopting it, and that seemed stranger still.

Sighing, trying to recall when they were all last gathered as a family, she took a tray of tea through into the parlor. Once again the absence of her mother's face hit her hard; she would have liked to be here, Louisa thought, just to see us all together. Although Emily had visited regularly, and Blanche came when she could spare an afternoon from the business in Harrogate, they never came as a pair. From the tone of their conversation, however, Louisa deduced they saw each other from time to time in Harrogate. It was, after all, only a short train ride from Leeds. And York, Louisa thought with irony.

But Blanche's excuse, as always, was lack of time. Now a *modiste* in her own right, she had opened a small establishment in Harrogate three years before, working virtually single-handed to begin with. For a long time, York had seen nothing of her at all. Recently, however, she had taken much grander premises in Montpellier Parade, employing a full staff of seamstresses and assistants, all of whom, according to Blanche, were absolutely devoted to her. Nor were they the only ones. The maid who looked after her in the pleasant apartment overlooking the stray was a similar treasure.

Louisa wondered how much of that was true and how much a desire to impress the gathered company. For all her admirable talents, Blanche had never been very lovable, except perhaps in her mother's eyes. Now that her success seemed assured and she had a little time to take stock of her life, perhaps she noticed her lack of friends. For a moment Louisa pondered the question, and also wondered whether men in general or one man in particular had any place in her sister's life; with her dark, symmetrical features and severely elegant clothes, she cut a striking if not very feminine figure, and her business acumen was no detraction. But men had never figured much in Blanche's life, and if they had, Louisa reasoned, then surely she would be less obviously disgusted by her sister's position.

Feeling like the servants they discussed, she served the tea and returned to the kitchen. She felt better, keeping busy, in spite of Edward's constant pleas that she sit down and rest. She cut sandwiches and cake for the children, calling the girl down from the nursery; minutes later, intending to call her again, she went silently into the hall. John Chapman, the up-and-coming cabinetmaker, with his well-tailored black suit and gleaming new watch chain, was standing at the foot of the stairs, his hand upon the young girl's waist. And she, the silly, goggle-eyed creature, was gazing ardently back at him. So that's the way the land lies, Louisa thought with more regret than satisfaction. As she ostentatiously cleared her throat, the two sprang apart, guilty confirmation in John's dark flush and the girl's haste to perform her errand.

"I was just—er—inquiring after the bairns. You know, if they were behaving."

"Don't be a fool, John," she whispered harshly. "Don't you think one scandal in the family is enough? Besides," she added contemptuously, "what *would* your mother say? Hmm?"

Sheepishly, and without further defense, he returned to the parlor. Louisa went upstairs intending to apprise the girl, quietly but in graphic detail, of her future.

"Yes," Emily was saying wistfully as her husband rejoined them. "I've always liked that little writing desk. I seem to remember Mamma saying she brought it back from Lincoln after her mother died. It's terribly old-fashioned, I know, but . . ."

"I could do with a couple of occasional tables," Blanche said frankly. "There must be a dozen dotted about this house. I shall have to have a word with Louisa about it. You know, Edward, when you move, there simply won't be room for all this stuff. You'll have to get rid of it."

"And so many ornaments," Emily added. "Do you think I could take those glass vases? They're such a pretty shade of turquoise, and they'd look so nice against the new wallpaper in the parlor, wouldn't they, John?"

"We haven't even begun to *look* for another house," Edward said sharply. "And until we find one, it's impossible to say what we shall need, what will have to go. And the decision as to what will be kept and what *sold,*" he added heavily, "will have to be Louisa's."

"Oh?" Blanche challenged. "Why's that? There are *three* daughters, Edward, and if you'll pardon my pointing it out, you are only a nephew."

"I'm also the executor of your mother's will."

There was a stunned silence. Suddenly they were all asking questions at once, and in the midst of it, as though on cue, Louisa came in.

Edward motioned her to a chair, but she looked like someone on trial, guilt and remorse written all over her. He was exceedingly glad he had managed to field the money question. While she supposed her mother's estate was negligible, she would survive this interrogation; but if her sisters knew there was close on a thousand pounds in Mary Elliott's bank deposit, their wrathful indignation would know no bounds. Personally, he was surprised: under the circumstances he thought his aunt might have named something for each of them, a small token, if only for the sake of sentiment; but there was nothing.

"Why didn't you tell us there was a will?" Blanche demanded. "I asked you only the other day!"

"We weren't sure there was one," Edward replied, diverting attention from his cousin. "If you recall, I was out the afternoon you called, at the solicitor's and the bank."

"You weren't out when *I* came!" Emily said indignantly. "And you never said anything to me!"

"You never asked."

"Well, I'm asking now. What did she leave, and who to?"

With deliberate slowness, Edward took a copy of the will from his inside pocket. "It's here," he said, scanning the short and familiar contents. "You can have a look at it, if you like, but to summarize—

apart from a bequest of fifty pounds to Bessie, everything is left to your sister Louisa. And I do mean *everything*—furniture, linen, pots and pans—everything.''

Emily sank back like a deflated balloon. ''Oh,'' she whispered. ''And I always thought she was going to leave the silver to me. I must have spent years cleaning it.''

With her usual hard edge of practicality, Blanche asked: ''So how much did she leave in terms of hard cash, Edward? Just as a matter of interest, you understand?''

''Enough to bury her with,'' Louisa cried and left the room.

Furious, Edward chewed his lip, resisting the urge to follow and tell her the truth. But he would never, he realized, be able to reveal suspicions which were almost certainty: that for the past two years, Robert Duncannon had been paying an allotment of £12 a month into Mary Elliott's account. While she was able, his aunt had made withdrawals against that amount, providing the children with clothes and shoes and contributing to household expenses. It had been done secretly, but with the noblest of motives, while Louisa refused to accept Robert's offer of an annuity and swore she would never take a penny from him again.

Even without the residue of that considerable sum, Mary Elliott had saved a surprising amount. Edward almost smiled at the irony of these last months, when he had driven himself to the limits in an attempt to keep them solvent, refusing every offer his aunt had made. He had wondered at her frustration, and now he knew; understood also Robert Duncannon's need to see her before she died. But the irony amused rather than annoyed him; even in the bank, that tidy sum would bring in interest for Louisa of almost fifteen shillings a week, which was more than some men were paid for hard physical labor. He knew it would give her financial independence and the freedom to decide what her next move must be; and if she should *choose* to make her home with him, Edward thought, with a small thrill of pleasure, he would know the past was over indeed.

NINE

*H*eavy rain, which had made the usual Sunday afternoon walk an impossibility, rattled a sharp tattoo against the parlor windows. Bessie hitched her shawl closer and peered at her knitting; with a yawn she put it to one side and reached for a taper to light the lamps.

"Don't know how you can see to read, Mr. Edward," she muttered. "And that child is falling asleep. If she nods off now, she'll never settle tonight."

Edward shifted slightly, adjusting the baby in the crook of his arm and pulling her thumb away from her mouth. "Just one more page, and then it's teatime."

On either side of him on the sofa, the boys snuggled closer, peering eagerly at the next colored picture, of gray skies and a heaving sea, a small fishing boat with a brown sail and frightened men in long, colored robes.

Liam knew the book by heart. "Jesus isn't scared," he said, pointing to the man in white standing in the bows. "He's telling the storm to go away!"

"Can you read it?" Edward asked, pointing to the words. " 'Now it came to pass on a certain day . . .' "

" 'That he went into a ship with His disciples,' " Liam continued, but even though Edward knew he was reciting, rather than reading, he let him continue, picking up toward the end of the piece as Liam's memory failed him.

" '. . . Then He arose, and rebuked the wind and the raging of the water, and they ceased, and there was calm.' "

"Saint Luke, chapter eight, verses twenty-two to twenty-four," Liam finished proudly.

"Very good! What comes next?" He turned the page to the poem which followed, the poem with its sepia illustrations of a storm-tossed sailing ship on one side and the same ship in calm waters on the other.

" 'Twas a wild, wild night at sea:
And the captain and crew of the Bonnie Marie
Were all as grave as grave could be:
For the waves rolled by,
So great and high;
While the wind whistled loud,
And dark hung every cloud,
And the good ship labored heavily . . ."

Edward smiled, prompting: " 'But the little cabin boy . . .' "

"But the little cabin boy, with a happy smile,
Went about his work, and sang the while
Of Him who spake and the worlds were made:
Of Him who spake and the winds were stayed,
And the storm was stilled on Galilee."

"And do you know the rest, or shall I read it?" Edward asked. Liam shook his head, hugging his knees as he listened to the last verse.

Into the ensuing silence, Bobby's piping voice said anxiously: "That man's gone on a ship."

Edward's heart lurched. Then Liam said: "He'll be all right. Jesus will look after him."

Edward thought he heard Bessie say the devil looked after his own, but when he glanced again, her lips were pursed and she was studying her knitting.

"Besides," added Liam importantly, "he's the captain. I know 'cause he told me."

"He's not that kind of captain," Edward felt constrained to say. "Captain Duncannon is—" Is what? he thought, while the words echoed around his head and he hated himself for being unable to utter them, for being unable to tell two young boys that *that man* was their father. "Captain Duncannon is in the army," he finished lamely.

"Well, I'm going to go on a ship when I'm big," Liam announced. "I'll sail away for ever and a day." He slid off the sofa and followed Bessie into the kitchen.

"Where's Mammy?" Bobby asked wistfully. "When's she coming back?"

"She only went yesterday," Edward said, stroking the boy's dark curls, "so it'll be a few more days before she's back. She's gone to Scarborough with Auntie Letty."

"Why can't we go, Daddy?"

He sighed, pulling the child closer. Sometimes it was *Uncle;* more often, like Tisha, it was *Daddy;* even Liam was picking it up, wanting to copy the other two. At first Louisa had been very keen, like himself, to correct them, but of late such niceties had fallen by the wayside, along with so many other things. Had it not been for Robert Duncannon's return, he supposed it would not have mattered too much; but Edward had to remind himself that he was not the children's natural father, however pleasant it might be to imagine so.

He was desperately torn between past and present, between a deep-seated belief that it was vital for every child to know its own father and a growing conviction that security and affection were at least as important; torn to the extent that it was hard for him to decide a course of action and stick to it. The children loved him, and despite his constant striving for detachment, he loved them too. But he had no right to them and no claim upon Louisa. If she asked for advice, he could attempt to give it; but he could not tell her what she should and should not do.

Faced with Robert and his sister two nights ago, Edward had felt a mixture of heart-soaring joy and excruciating embarrassment when Louisa had declared her intentions to them. He wanted her to stay with him, of course he did; and that she wanted to share his life too was as much as he had ever dared to hope. But he was sensitive enough to appreciate the blow to Robert Duncannon, a blow, moreover, which was delivered before witnesses. And Louisa was not indifferent to its effect: he had the feeling that she was using the occasion to maximum advantage, and he doubted the purity of her motives.

No matter how vehemently she stated her desire to have nothing more to do with Robert, the fact that he still disturbed her was obvious. Deep down, perhaps below the level of her conscious mind, Edward believed, Louisa was still in love with the Irishman. He suspected that what truly rankled with her, beyond that affair with the other woman, was his abrupt abandonment of *everything* in favor of some piffling little foreign war. She had used that phrase so often; had even, at news of his wound, said defiantly: "It serves him right."

True or not, Edward had little sympathy to spare for the other man. He would never forget the night of her return, when she and the children had arrived like waifs of the storm, seeking shelter and safety. For long enough he had suspected that things were far from well in Dublin. The tone of her letters had revealed so much more than even Louisa imagined, and Edward was attuned to every subtle shift and change of fortune in that distant city. The bruises on her face had ensured instant sympathy from his aunt and Bessie, and in the first flush of her need to confess and be comforted, Louisa had revealed much of the cause of that stinging blow. But horrified though he was by that act of violence, Edward had cause enough to be glad of the other man's hasty temper; and only afterward, weeks later, when he had time to consider and assess, did he begin to realize that the affair was by no means closed.

In some respects he welcomed Robert Duncannon's return. For Edward the past two years had been uneasy in the extreme, like living on a knife edge, always wondering what would happen when the day came, always reluctant to reveal too much or love too well for fear of losing all in the end. He wanted Louisa to make up her own mind, without pressure from himself or anyone else; and most important of all, whatever love she had to give, he wanted it untainted by either gratitude or guilt.

But the children were caught between the three of them, and no matter the difficulty of making hard and fast decisions now, they could not be set aside to await a more propitious day. Their future hung in the balance, and unfair though it was, he could understand why Robert Duncannon wanted his own position made clear. He wanted access to his children and the chance to support them financially, points which Louisa was inclined to dismiss out of hand on the grounds that they were *her* children, and she did not want them to be confused by a complicated web of embarrassing relationships.

On the sidelines, both he and Letty had weighed in with occasional comments, but apart from an agreement that Robert could see them, the rest was still very much unresolved.

Wide blue eyes full of trusting innocence gazed up at him. "Why can't we go with Mammy?"

"It's not a very good day for playing on the sands, now is it? I tell you what, we'll go in the summer, when the weather is better. But right now," he added, "it's time for tea. Off you go and wash your hands."

Tisha whimpered as he lifted her up, soft little arms clinging round his neck. Edward smiled as he cuddled and kissed her, delighting in the sweet baby smell, the feel of her satiny skin against his cheek. No matter how detached he tried to be, it was hard not to play the part of loving parent. No father could have been more anxious than he during the hours of Tisha's entry into the world, no father more proud and relieved when he was allowed in to see mother and child for the first time. Although he adored all three of them, he supposed it was because he had lived with Louisa throughout the whole of that last pregnancy that Tisha was so special to him. Illogically, but very deeply, he felt she was his child, which was why the brutal callousness of Robert's question had hurt and angered him so much.

Setting the little girl into her high chair by the kitchen table, Edward watched while Bessie tied a toweling bib around her and waited for the boys to cease their chatter.

"Hands together," he said quietly and was rewarded by a beaming smile as Tisha squashed pudgy fingers against each other. "For what we are about to receive, may the Lord make us truly thankful." There was a chorus of "Amen" and, on Bobby's part at least, an unseemly rush for the scones and cake.

"Bread and butter *first,*" Bessie reminded him, tapping his hand away. Instead of crying, he simply set his mouth and grabbed two slices of bread as recompense, while Edward looked away, trying to hide his amusement.

Bobby had character, and with his sunny disposition it was easy to be charmed by him; despite that, Edward was more deeply drawn to the elder boy. He had arrived in York on a bitter December evening when he was even younger than Bobby was now, and Edward knew he would never forget his first sight of Liam, never forget those huge, frightened eyes set in a face as pinched and white as his mother's. And he was so like her that Edward's heart had gone out to the child at once. Still a baby, Bobby had settled at once, sleeping contentedly through his brother's quiet sobs, sobs which Edward had heard in the middle of the night, while Louisa slept the sleep of the utterly exhausted. He had gone in to him at once and, short of suitable reading matter, proceeded to make up a long and very silly story about a cat which had three homes. At first Liam had wept even harder, telling the strange man to go away, he wanted his Mammy, his Daddy, he wanted Georgie and Bridget, and a whole host of other names, all foreign to Edward. But, gradually, he had begun to listen, and gradually a little smile appeared through the tears as the story took his imagination. From such small beginnings their friendship had grown, but he had hated to have Louisa out of his sight in those early days and continued to ask for his father for quite some time.

It was hard to tell what went on in a child's mind, especially one as young as Liam, but Edward suspected the boy of recalling far more than he was prepared to admit.

With tea cleared away, he left Bessie with the children and went to church for the Sunday evening service. There was a visiting preacher whose sermon was somewhat shorter than usual, and, mindful of the still torrential rain, Edward hurried home. He took a shortcut through the farmyard at the end of Lord Mayor's walk and, avoiding several unsavory puddles, made his way up the dark lane at the foot of the ramparts, through the backyard, and into the house by way of the kitchen door.

Clearly startled, Bessie paused guiltily in the act of wrapping a china teapot, then pushed it defiantly into the half-filled tea chest by her feet.

"What on earth are you doing?" he asked as he shook his dripping umbrella and stood it in the sink.

"Packing."

"I can see that."

"I know I shouldn't be working on a Sunday, Mr. Edward, but I don't know how I'm ever going to get this packing sorted with them children under my feet all day. And if it's left till the last minute, Miss Louisa will be out of her mind, she will."

"But we haven't even found a house yet."

"I'm only packing stuff that's never used, and I'm jotting it down, so she knows what's what."

Edward sighed. "I suppose you're right, Bessie," he conceded. "There haven't been enough hours in the day lately." He sighed and pulled at his chin. "I don't know, I've done more on Sundays these last few months than I've ever done in my life, but I'd thought that with the funeral over—" He stopped and sat down. "I thought perhaps we could return to normal, Bessie."

"Normal!" Bessie exclaimed. "Huh! In the last two years, Mr. Edward, I've forgotten what normal is."

He glanced sharply at her, but she continued wrapping delicate china in tissue and newspaper and packing it into the chest. "That's most unfair."

"Aye, well, maybe it is, maybe it isn't. But she should never have come back here, in my opinion, bringing trouble and scandal on your good name and driving her poor mother—God rest her soul—into an early grave."

Angrily Edward stood up. "Well, Bessie, if that really is your considered opinion, then perhaps it's as well you're leaving us. No doubt the Chapmans will endorse everything you say, and you can gossip over Louisa's misfortune to your heart's delight. But," he added heavily, "might I also tell you how much you disappoint me. I never, ever, thought I would live to hear you bring her down this way!"

Without warning, Bessie burst into noisy sobs. "And I never thought," she began as she sank into the nearest chair, "I never thought she would ruin her life like this." She wept into her apron, her back turned to Edward, but he was too angry to feel any sympathy; while saying very little of a direct nature to Louisa, he knew the older woman had managed to make her life more difficult than it needed to be since her return.

"I don't know why it shocks you so," he said coldly. "You've spent the best part of forty years with this family, and despite their constant striving for respectability, neither my mother nor my aunt was married. It can't have bothered you then, so why does it bother you now?"

"I was only a lass then, and I was real proud just to have a good place. I'd have fought tooth and nail for your mam," she vowed, straightening her back. "She was such a *lady*. When you saw her walking down a street in her best black—straight as a ramrod she was—nobody would ever have believed she wasn't what she said she was. She aimed high, and she made sure everybody else knew their place."

What she said was undeniably true, but the admiration in her voice chilled Edward. "You didn't live with her latterly," he said quietly.

"No, I came here with Miss Mary, because she needed me. And we worked hard, both of us. We worked hard," she repeated vehemently, "to build this place up and bury the past. We worked hard to give them lasses a good start, not to have it all pulled down round our ears twenty years later, just because Miss Louisa decides she doesn't like it with her fancy man after all!"

She was weeping again, but in spite of his anger Edward said nothing; Bessie's resentment had been corked tight for a long time, and now it was pouring out along with her grief for his aunt. It was better coming out now than later, in front of Emily and the Chapmans.

"It was bad enough her going off with him like that, but at least nobody knew and we could say she'd got a good place as a governess in Ireland. And then she had to come back with two bairns and another on the way—and didn't she make liars and fools of us all then! Oh, she thinks she's hard done by, that one—people talking, pointing the finger—but I've heard them, and I'm telling you now, it weren't just Miss Louisa they were blacking. No, it was her mother an' all. Not that they knew aught—but they were making plenty up!"

"That must have hurt badly."

"Aye, it did. I thought all that were past, Mr. Edward. I thought all that were past." She shook her head sadly, wiping her eyes with her apron. "I can't take it no more—I just can't, and that's a fact. I'm sorry for her—deep down I am, no matter how mad she makes me—but you're going to have to sort yourselves out. I'm an old woman, Mr. Edward— I want a bit of peace. I want to do me work and nip to the shops without feeling like I'm off to fight a war."

Her words sent a sharp mixture of guilt and surprise running through him. What age was she? Late fifties, he supposed, but she hardly seemed to have changed in all the years he had known her, and it shocked him to hear her refer to herself as old.

"I'm so sorry," he said sincerely. "It hasn't been easy for any of us, but I hadn't realized how hard it's been for you, Bessie. You've always been such a tower of strength," he added with a little smile "I suppose we all thought you were indestructible."

"Aye, well I'm not. I'm only human, Mr. Edward—and I'll tell you this for nothing," she added, wagging an admonitory finger at him. "So are you."

"Meaning?" he asked softly.

Bessie looked down, and for a moment her fingers played with a scrap of tissue paper. "Well," she said at last, "I suppose you'll think I shouldn't say this, me being no more than a servant and an old spinster woman at that. But I did help bring you up, Mr. Edward—you and Miss Louisa, come to that. *And* I've seen a bit of life, here and there."

He chewed his lip, wishing she would get on and give voice to whatever home truth was hovering on her tongue. "Yes?" he prompted.

She took a deep breath. "Well, it's just this, Mr. Edward—can you tell me what you're doing? I mean, what do you hope to gain from all this? That little madam will have you at her beck and call till your dying day, if you'll let her—just like she always did. And for what? What will she ever give you in return? Peace of mind? Never! Not while that jumped-up good-for-nothing comes calling. And don't tell me he comes to see his *children*—what thought did he ever have for them bairns? What thought did he ever have for his other little lass—or his sister, come to that? Duty? He don't know the meaning of the word! For all you know, he could have bairns to different women up and down the country."

"Have you quite finished?"

"No, I have not. It's time you told him to clear off, once and for all. And if you're going to be living under the same roof, then it's time you made an honest woman of her—stop people talking, once and for all!"

"I see," he said tautly, thrusting hands in pockets as he crossed the room. "If you don't mind, Bessie, I'll continue to conduct my life in the way *I* see fit! Meanwhile, I think I'll take your earlier advice and do some packing. I'm sure there must be whole shelves of books upstairs that I can live without for the next few weeks!"

By the following morning the storm had passed, but there was still a stiff breeze blowing off the sea, and where the tide met each curving bastion, huge waves curled and smashed along the promenade. White spray leapt high into the air, falling back in great turquoise troughs, only to rise again seconds later. Excited, mesmerized, Louisa could not tear her eyes away. The sky was blue, and in spite of wanting but three weeks to Christmas, the sun was shining with spring-like fervor.

"The children would have loved this," she said to Letty, wishing with all her heart they could have been with her. Although it was good to be away from York, she missed them terribly, seemed to spend half her time wondering what they were doing and whether they were missing her, too.

"I'm sure they would," came the brisk reply. "Can't you just see them running through the spray, soaked to the skin, and being carried off by the next big wave? No, my dear, that sea is for looking at from a safe distance—and we're too close by half!" she declared as the wind tugged at skirts and scarves. "Let's go before that tide comes any closer. I'm sure we can watch from the safety of the spa, behind glass, with a warming drink to comfort us!"

"You've no adventure in your soul."

"Perhaps not. I prefer to view and run away—and return to view another day."

"It reminds me of our visits to Dalkey," Louisa admitted with a hint of wistfulness as they climbed the cliff path to their hotel. "Georgina always loved it so." A moment later, slightly out of breath, she said: "Robert said she wanted to come with him. I imagine she was cross at being left behind a second time."

"She was indeed. But I promised to bring her next time. That is," she added quietly, "if there is a next time."

Turning sharply, Louisa stopped to look at her friend. "Oh, Letty, don't take it like that, please. We must *always* be friends. It would break my heart if I thought I wouldn't see you or Georgina again."

"And Edward?"

"What about Edward?"

"Well, perhaps he'd rather not see us at all."

Unable to answer immediately, Louisa turned and went inside. In the dining room, awaiting luncheon, she said: "Edward likes you, and Georgina. I can't see why he wouldn't want you to visit us. And anyway," she added firmly, "you're *my* dear friend, so what does it matter?"

Sipping at a very dry sherry, Letty raised her eyebrows quizzically, but did not reply. Looking out at the broad expanse of the bay beyond the windows, she appeared to be enjoying the view; presently, however, glancing back at her friend, she said, "You're obviously feeling much better. Beginning to look a little more like the Louisa I remember. And perhaps after a few days' rest and good food like this, you'll even put on a little more weight. I thought it was a ghost I was seeing when I arrived in York the other day."

"You're exaggerating."

"Indeed I'm not, and you know it. You were in such good health in the summer—seeing you again was quite a shock to me." With gentle concern she added: "The last few months must have been hell for you."

Louisa shrugged and looked away. "I suppose they have. It didn't seem so at the time, but . . ." she paused. It was too difficult to explain, even to Letty. But after a moment she said: "Now the worst of it is over, I can see how dreadful it was. Like being ill and not realizing how ill you've been, until the day you know you're better. Do you know what I mean? The comparison is frightening."

"Is it over?" Letty asked, her slate-gray eyes managing to give the question more than one meaning.

Her friend looked out of the window and over the boiling sea. "I think so. They say time's a great healer—and I'm sure it is. It's bound to be a while yet before we get over Mamma's death, but once we find another house and can get away from Gillygate, I'm sure that will help."

"I'm sure you're right. But what about Robert? Is it really over between the two of you?"

"Oh, Letty, you know it is! It was over two years ago."

"Are you absolutely sure about that?"

"For goodness' sake, Letty, what are you trying to do? Persuade me to go back to him? To return to Dublin and all I left behind? No, thank you!"

"No, I don't think I am. I suppose I'm asking whether you still love him, whether you don't regret saying good-bye."

"I don't regret it," was the quick reply. "I don't regret anything, except the length of time it took to reach that decision."

"Will you never forgive him?"

With a weary sigh, Louisa shook her head. "It's not a question of forgiveness, Letty—not anymore. We were wrong—both of us—to imagine the rules didn't apply. *If* we had been able to marry, it might have worked; I might have been accepted as his wife. If I hadn't had children, maybe *that* would have worked. But it's all hypothesis," she said bitterly, "and the only certainty is that in the end, nothing was right. It all just fell apart."

For a while there was silence between them, then Letty remarked: "Amelia Loy went back to Gerald, you know—it was all hot air."

"I remember, you told me."

"He was a bloody fool: he should never have got involved."

"There are a lot of things Robert should never have done, Letty, and I can't say being a fool makes him any less culpable."

"So, you haven't forgiven him?"

Louisa pursed her lips, remembering things no one but herself and Robert would ever know. "For Amelia Loy—yes," she said enigmatically and refused to be drawn further.

With the arrival of their meal, Letty ate appreciatively, but after the soup Louisa did no more than pick at the fish, and her plate of roast pork and applesauce went almost untouched. Staring out at the fading afternoon light, she thought about Gerald Loy and the night of the Grand Ball at Dublin Castle. Despite the momentary revulsion and a more lingering sense of insult, at the time the incident had been buried among a welter of other events; since then, illogically, like the visit to White Leigh and her memories of the whores on Sackville and Gardiner streets, it had become symbolic of all she hated about Robert's way of life. There were some pleasant vistas in her mind's eye, but, like the views along the Liffey, too superficial; one was always aware, Louisa thought, of a certain olfactory unpleasantness. And he was too easily bored. Life must always present a challenge to him, an element of danger; which was why, she supposed, he had gone to the Sudan.

"It's not for me," she said quietly, "that kind of life. I'm too ordinary for it, too dull. And now I have my children to think of—and Edward. Where I'd be without him, Letty, I do not know. Dead, probably—or in Bootham."

Remembering the shock of realizing she was pregnant with Tisha, Louisa was still for a moment. It had come in the same week as the news of Robert's departure. She had thought she would go mad. Without Edward, without the reassuring strength which had pulled her through some of the bleakest months of her life, Louisa knew she would have given in to overwhelming despair. He had listened and comforted, reasoned with her, even bullied her on occasion; anything to make her think of the future and stop dwelling on the past. Caring for the children, he had forced her to do the same, when in her apathy Louisa would gladly have left them to Bessie or her mother. If nothing else, he had insisted, they were her reason for living. Without that realization, and particularly without him, she knew she would never have survived the second blow of her mother's protracted and fatal illness.

"I owe him my life, and because of that," she said firmly, "I'm quite determined *not* to make the same mistakes again."

The coffee arrived, and while Louisa poured for them both, Letty studied her friend carefully. "But is gratitude enough?" she asked at last.

"Enough for what?"

Letty hesitated, and for a moment her shrewd eyes were particularly keen. "Well . . . for the rest of your lives."

Slowly Louisa shook her head, disappointed and hurt that Letty, who had given up so much for her brother's child, could not understand the depth of love behind her decision. "If it was only gratitude, I'd have repaid what I could out of Mamma's legacy and be looking for a cheap little terrace house to rent. For myself and the children. That's what Robert would *like* me to do—so he can call and visit me from time to time. So *very* convenient," she said bitterly.

"Sure you're not using Edward to hide behind?" Letty asked softly, sipping her coffee.

There was a stunned silence. Banging down her cup, with coffee slopping into the saucer, Louisa said: "No, of course not!"

"Please don't be angry. Can't you see I'm only trying to be sure you know what you're doing? You're my friend, Robert's my brother, and I love you both. I don't want to see you making more mistakes, hurting Edward as well as yourselves. He's a fine man—did I know him better, I'm sure I'd be fond of him, too. He doesn't deserve to be caught up like this—"

"I love Edward!"

It was Letty's turn to be stunned. "You do? Then why don't you marry him, for Heaven's sake?"

With eyes downcast, Louisa shook her head. "He hasn't asked me. And anyway, it's not as simple as that, Letty." She struggled for words to explain the tangled emotions the suggestion aroused and failed abysmally. "I doubt I'll ever marry," she said at last and with a negative gesture called a halt to further questions. "I can't explain, I'm sorry. But do please understand that I'm going to live with Edward because I want to share my life with him—because I need him, and he needs me. And because I know he loves my children as though they were his own; and, unlike Robert, he'll never let them down."

Sadly, Letty nodded. "Yes," she said slowly, "you have a very good point there."

They sat without speaking for some time. Against the gathering twilight their faces were reflected in the glass, with an almost empty room behind them. A solitary waiter hovered, ready to clear their table as soon as they left. Noticing him, Louisa reluctantly rose to her feet. "I think we'd better go. Shall we have a walk in the grounds before it gets dark? I could do with a breath of air."

A graveled walk ran between shrubs and trees before winding steeply toward the promenade below. In their winter sleep, the gardens were drab and gray, but the smell of earth and leaves was invigorating after the warm, stale air of the hotel.

"You know," Louisa confessed, "I'd like a garden. That's one of the things I really loved about the Devereaux house. Not that we could afford anything like that," she said with a laugh, "but it would be nice to find somewhere—a little cottage, perhaps—with a proper garden. Flow-

ers and vegetables,'' she mused wistfully, ''and a place for the children
to play.''

''Your farming forebears again,'' Letty teased. ''I'm sure you're just
a simple country girl at heart.''

''You could be right,'' Louisa admitted. ''But there are worse things
to be.''

TEN

inding a house with a garden, even a plot of land which could be transformed into one, was not easy. Within the city such houses tended to be old, run-down, and ridiculously expensive; on the outskirts the new purpose-built terraces had no gardens at all, and the outlying villages such as Acomb and Clifton were too far distant from Edward's business in Piccadilly. Fulford might have been ideal, but because of the barracks, property there was rarely advertised on the open market, being snapped up immediately by the military.

Although Bessie had agreed to stay for the move, she was anxious to take up her new post with the Chapmans before Christmas; and for reasons of their own, both Edward and Louisa wanted to be away from Gillygate by the same date. Having chased a number of possibilities throughout the city only to be disappointed, Edward was beginning to despair of finding anything remotely suitable within their allotted time-span; he had almost made up his mind to let Bessie go and postpone the search until spring, when one of his customers mentioned a cottage for rent at Clementhorpe.

"The old couple who had it have just moved into one of my new houses on Ebor Street," the man said. "Shouldn't think you'd want it—it's an old place, needs a lot doing to it, don't even know if it's got running water—but it does have a stretch of land with it. Near the old ropewalk on the riverbank, know where I mean? 'Course, it's liable to flood when the river gets up," he sniffed. "Shouldn't want to take it on myself."

Edward had been to look at those new houses off Bishopthorpe Road. "I should think the bottom end of Ebor Street might be subject to the same," he commented mildly.

"No, no, much higher ground," his customer protested. "River'd have to be damned high to flood *my* houses. Anyway, please yourself." He fished inside an inner pocket and produced a scrap of paper. "Here's the landlord's name—can't say I know the chap. Anyway, it might be worth a look if it's land you're wanting."

"I'm sure it will be worth a look," Edward said with a smile. "Thanks very much indeed for your trouble." He wrapped two new ledgers securely in brown paper and handed the parcel over. "Thank you again, Mr. Clayton."

"Aye, well, let me know when you decide you want one of my new houses. You'll not find better-built property this side of Leeds Town Hall, you know!"

Edward laughed. "Give me a patch of land with one, and it's a bargain!"

"Nay, I can't do that. I want land for building on, not making fancy gardens. I expect it's your wife's idea, eh? These women and their notions—I don't know!"

Noncommittal, Edward showed him to the door, thanked him again, and returned to his bench. It was very strange, he mused, how in the course of their search for a house people had simply assumed Louisa to be his wife; but Louisa had not corrected them, and he was certainly not about to. Illusion it might be, but it had its uses.

He looked at the address on the piece of paper, studied the time, and decided that, if he left early, he could ask for the keys of the cottage this evening; then, first thing tomorrow, he and Louisa could view the place in daylight.

On Fossgate he saw his old apprentice ahead of him, carrying what appeared to be a parcel of books; by the corn dealer's on Pavement he caught up with the young man.

"Special delivery, Dick?" he asked with a smile.

"Oh, hello, Mr. Elliott, sir—you're early this evening!"

"Special errand—I'm looking for another house to rent. One with a garden. You don't know of any, do you?"

"Nay," Dick laughed. "The only garden I know is George's field!"

"Aye, well, it was worth a try." Edward laughed as they crossed the road in front of the church. "Are you walking with me? I thought your way home was up Coppergate?"

"Oh, I aren't off home yet, sir. I've these to take to Blossom Street, to Mrs. Bainbridge. Miss Tempest, as was, sir."

"Yes, I know Mrs. Bainbridge. Taken up reading, has she? I didn't know she was a bookworm."

"She never used to be," Dick agreed with a grin, "but she wants to look at these. Not just any old books, Mr. Elliott—they're *the* books, and I have to take them over."

"Not the manager?"

"No, sir."

"Doesn't she trust him?"

"I don't know sir," Dick said uncomfortably, as though suddenly aware of an indiscretion.

"I'm sorry," Edward murmured. "I shouldn't have asked that. I didn't mean to take advantage of an old friendship."

The young man beamed proudly. "That's all right, Mr. Elliott, I know I can trust you."

They crested the hill of High Ousegate in companionable silence, negotiated the traffic on Nessgate Corner, and headed down toward the bridge. At the foot of Micklegate, Edward began studying doorplates until he found the office he wanted. As he turned to bid his companion good-bye, the young man stopped abruptly, with the air of one who has come to a momentous decision.

"I know this might sound funny, Mr. Elliott, but . . . I wish you well in the business."

"Why, thank you, Dick. That's most kind of you."

"No—I mean—well, what I mean is this. If you ever think of taking anybody else on, like—I mean, I wish you'd think of me first."

"I most certainly will," Edward said sincerely. "If I'm ever in a position to take someone on, I assure you your name would be the first that came to mind."

"Really?" The broad grin of pleasure threatened to split his face in two. "Well, I mustn't keep you. Thanks a lot, Mr. Elliott!"

He strode away, Edward noticed, far more lightly than he had walked up Fossgate. For a moment he stood and chewed his lip, considering the information his old apprentice had so unwittingly revealed. Whether Dick realized it or not, something was wrong at Tempest's. Since the old man's death, Rachel had run through a succession of managers, not all of them bad, but most, like the business itself, victims of her whims and caprices. And her husband, Edward thought, the so-called *sleeping partner,* slept so soundly he was never seen on Fossgate except to stand the men drinks at Christmas. He wondered what made her keep the business on when it would have been far more sensible to sell it as a going concern at her father's death.

Answers eluded him, but he was certain of one thing: Dick had seen the writing on the wall and wanted something better. Edward wished he were in a position to offer the lad employment now, but the time was not quite right. Perhaps in a few months, when he and Louisa were settled, when capital and income could be assessed with some degree of accuracy.

With a slight shrug he dismissed the matter from his mind and entered the doorway on his left.

The landlord was a chartered accountant, obviously a busy man. Edward was kept waiting, but the interview was brief enough.

The questions of name and occupation disposed of, the accountant asked whether Edward was married; with the slightest hesitation, he nodded.

"Yes," he said quietly, "with three children."

"Can't say I was very keen on him," Edward confessed as Louisa cleared away the remains of their meal. "Youngish chap—probably inherited the property, and now he's got rid of the old couple he's banging the rent up. Old Clayton said it was run-down—so don't get excited, Louisa, it doesn't sound very promising at all."

"It's on the right side of town," she commented. "Probably nearer work than you are already. And the rent's only half what we're paying here."

"But this house is sound, *and* we have gas and running water. The cottage might have neither. And don't forget the river," he added. "It probably floods down there every winter."

"Oh, don't be such a pessimist," she said affectionately. "We haven't even seen it yet. Maybe it's delightful!"

"And maybe it isn't," Edward insisted, but he smiled nevertheless.

A bitter wind was blowing, and the sky was heavy with unshed rain as they set forth the following morning. To save the toll they crossed the river by the old bridge and turned down Skeldergate, a narrow thoroughfare of ancient warehouses fronting the river, and a hotchpotch of dilapidated shops, pubs, and tenements rising steeply toward Bishophill. It was busy at that hour, with drays and carts of every description loading coal and grain and bonded goods, men shouting instructions to one another, and horses straining in their shafts, plodding greasy cobbles with heavy hooves. Despite the cold, barefoot children on their way to school hovered in the hope of a few minutes' employment, vying with those who waited at gates and doorways in the hope of something more permanent.

Disturbed by idly curious eyes, still too aware of the anxiety which was coiled like a snake throughout every public venture, Louisa kept her veiled eyes down, carefully gathering her skirts over puddles and broken pavements. Something about Skeldergate reminded her of Dublin, of the wharves and warehouses beside the Liffey. The musty smells of grain stores and flour mills were the same, the dankness of the river and the unmistakable odor of poverty itself: cabbage and offal, inadequate privies, and unwashed, overcrowded humanity. But at the end of the street, where the iron span of Skeldergate Bridge joined St. George's Field with the Clementhorpe shore, Dublin receded and York became entirely itself again. Musty, throat-catching odors gave way to the much sweeter, more cloying smell of chocolate.

Terry's confectionery works lay across the road, and along the wharf barges containing cocoa beans and sugar were steadily being relieved of their cargoes. Gantries spanned the cobbled road, and like the sections of a giant, endless caterpillar, heavy sacks swung up and across on moving chains, disappearing into the open maw of the factory warehouse on their right. Taking a firm grasp of Louisa's arm, Edward marched her smartly beneath that hazardous mechanical creature. Having once seen a man killed at that very point, he had less faith than those who strolled so casually beneath. Beyond the factory was a boatyard with a metal bridge over the slipway; beyond that a glassworks and the new houses mentioned by Edward's customer, Mr. Clayton. Then the riverside began to open out, and on the far side of the ropewalk with its conglomeration of sheds and machinery was a stretch of cultivated land and what looked like a small farmhouse. At first Louisa thought all the land was attached to it, then she saw it was divided into small allotment gardens; by far the largest plot, however, lay beside and behind the cottage's rusty brick walls.

As though stayed by a common hand, the two halted at the iron-barred gate, taking in the slightly off-center front door, two empty ground-floor windows with dormers more or less in line above, and a low, pantiled roof.

"Roses around the door," Louisa said.

"And at least two tiles off the roof," Edward said with a laugh. With an effort he pushed open the gate; it squeaked on rusty hinges and left red dust on his black leather glove. With an air of martyred resignation he followed Louisa up the uneven brick path.

"Winter jasmine," Louisa breathed, "and honeysuckle. Oh, and look— fruit trees. What a wonderful garden this will make, Edward. We could grow our own vegetables, maybe even sell them!"

The key was large and the lock in need of attention. "Can we just look inside first?" he begged as he struggled to open the door. "This place," he muttered darkly, "looks about as good as my workshop before I moved in, and that's not intended as a compliment!"

The floors were stone and the walls roughly plastered and whitewashed. It was clean, but there was a suspicion of damp in the air, as though it had been empty for months; the evidence of past flooding lay in a gray tidemark several inches above the floor.

"What did I tell you," he said triumphantly, but Louisa had already found the kitchen, a large low room with windows front and back and an old-fashioned range filling most of the chimney breast. Filling each alcove completely were long painted cupboards in crazed dark brown. Mentally she saw them stripped of old paint and finished in fresh bright green, with yellow gingham curtains fluttering at the windows and the scrubbed deal table from Gillygate providing a familiar centerpiece.

There was a scullery and pantry built on at the back, and what looked like an earth closet at the foot of the garden; she wrinkled her nose at the thought of cleaning it out, then brightened again as her eyes caught the new sink with its lead piping and only slightly dulled brass tap.

"Look!" she exclaimed to Edward, but he was right behind her. With a laugh he reached across and lifted her veil. "Running water!"

"No gas!" he countered.

"I don't care—we've plenty of oil lamps. Let's look upstairs," she said eagerly, but Edward insisted on seeing the other room first.

Whereas the kitchen was almost square in shape, the parlor was oblong, with a larger window overlooking the garden at the back. The fireplace was tiled with blue and white delft, stained and crazed around the old grate, but the hardwood mantelpiece was in good condition, Edward noted, in spite of the water which must have swilled around it in the past. White patches on the walls revealed the size and placings of several pictures, and a bigger patch, almost the area of one alcove, told of a cupboard or dresser which had recently stood there. In spite of the emptiness and its unfortunate proximity to the river, the house had a certain appeal to which he was not immune; he thought of the elderly couple who had possibly spent their entire married lives there. Could smooth square walls and the brightness of gaslight replace the memories of a lifetime?

Aware that he was drifting into probably misplaced sentiment, Edward shook himself and looked up at the beamed ceiling. "A nasty thought occurs to me," he said suddenly, interrupting Louisa's declamation on the joys of gardening. "There are probably only two bedrooms. You see, there are no supporting walls down here."

With an exclamation, she gathered her skirts and dashed back into the narrow hall. He followed her more carefully up the steeply winding stairs, but at the top, off an equally narrow landing, were four small bedrooms, their dividing walls, as he eventually established, constructed of lath and plaster. Less than solid, and certainly not soundproof, they were at least adequate to their needs. He could hardly believe it. Determined to show no enthusiasm as yet, Edward cast a jaundiced eye into several damp corners and commented on the cost of heating such a house with ill-fitting doors and rotting windowframes, but Louisa was overjoyed, hugging him with excitement.

"If the landlord won't put things right," she pleaded, "we can afford to do it, surely?" She squeezed his arm. "Oh, please say yes, Edward— it's lovely, really lovely!"

"Even though you're shivering with cold and it's started to rain, and the river will probably flood us out?"

"Yes, oh, yes!"

"We'll have to get rid of a lot of furniture—"

"Send it to the salerooms!"

"And that so-called garden," he added, glancing back at the overgrown wilderness beyond the window, "will take a month of Sundays to clear. And I won't have time to do it." He shook his head and tried to control the smile which threatened to give him away. "I really don't—"

"Oh, I'll find a boy—a couple of boys—to help me. It's what I've dreamed about, that garden, and in a few months' time, Edward, you won't even recognize it! Is it yes?" she demanded, almost bouncing with childlike glee.

As he looked into her bright, excited eyes, his smile escaped him; the look on her face was what he had longed to see for two weary years, and he could keep up the pretense no longer. "How could I say no?" he said, laughing.

With a little moan of delight she kissed him, hard and full on the mouth, her gloved hands cupping his face between them. "Oh, I *do* love you," she said with gay spontaneity, but both the words and the kiss were what she might have bestowed on any of the children, and while his heart thudded out a crazy tattoo, he was glad she had given him no chance to respond.

In the next second she was standing by the window, identifying shrubs and trees, eagerly planning what she would do first. "You must find out where those people are living now, and I'll call to see them, ask what's worth keeping and what's past its best."

Unable to trust his voice, he went up behind her and put his hands on her shoulders; she leaned back against him and touched her cheek to his. "Will you do that?" she asked.

"Whatever you want," he said softly. He wanted to tell her that he loved her too, and again the memory of what he had said in the accountant's office came back to him. But the time was not right, he felt, to apprise her of that.

They were both trembling, more with cold than anything else; his fingers tightened. "Come on, love," he sighed. "It's too cold to linger. And I must try to get some work done."

"What about the keys?"

"I'll call at the office this evening and tell them what we've decided. Then," he said with mock enthusiasm, "it's just a question of work, work, work! There's an awful lot to do, and we won't be ready to move in before Christmas. Yes, I know," he added as she turned to face him. "I know we wanted to be out of Gillygate before then, but I don't think it's going to be possible." At her crestfallen expression, he made what he felt was probably a rash promise: "We'll be in for New Year—how's that?"

First of all Edward had a load of coal delivered; after that, with the children bundled like miniature coachmen, Bessie and Louisa went down every day before Christmas to supervise workmen and clean the cottage. Tiles were replaced and the locks overhauled, outer doors repaired as far as possible and rehung in their age-skewed frames; and all at Edward's expense. The landlord, as he had suspected, was reluctant to undertake the work immediately, and Edward had no desire to see Louisa and the children freeze until spring. On the morning of Christmas Eve, two workmen arrived with a load of whitewash to repaint all the interior walls.

Edward let them in and gave them their instructions, then returned to Gillygate where Bessie was packing her own few things in preparation for the noon train to Leeds. A separate crate, containing china and pictures for Emily, stood in the hall.

"Tell her I'm sorry about the blue vases and those little figurines," Louisa said, "but I don't want to part with those. And if there's anything in the way of furniture she wants—well, she'll have to let me know before Thursday, because that's the day we move. And what we don't take is going straight to the salerooms. Blanche has already told me what she wants."

Tearfully Bessie nodded. "I'm glad I'm going before you move," she confessed. "I'll be able to remember the old place how it always was. Empty houses always put me in mind of death somehow."

Edward hired a cab to take Bessie and her luggage to the station; the parting with Louisa and the children in Gillygate was painful, yet, curiously, among the tears was a feeling of reconciliation. Their embraces were poignant, full with the knowledge of bonds being torn, of love and loyalty which were suddenly stronger by far than the irksome frustrations of recent times. Aware that a link with her mother was going, and another, the house, would be gone within the week, for a moment

Louisa let emotion outweigh reason and was tempted to call a halt to everything, to beg Bessie to stay, to cancel the move and give backword on the cottage; but as they stood in the open doorway, the curious eyes of a passerby looked in, curtains twitched across the street, and indecision fled. With a brave smile for Bessie's wave, Louisa gathered the children close and watched the cab down the street. Only then did she take them inside.

By mid-afternoon on the 28th of December the house on Gillygate was finally cleared. With Tisha balanced against her hip, Louisa mounted the stairs for the final time, her footsteps echoing hollowly on the naked wooden treads. She went up to the second floor and into Bessie's room, small and bare, with only a mark on the wall where the bedstead had rubbed as witness to her long occupation; Edward's room, which for a while had been Uncle Will's, with its empty rows of shelves; and the larger room she had shared as a child with Emily and Blanche, its window revealing the Minster's towers, clear behind a tossing web of twigs and branches. All clean, all empty, not a scrap of paper or a mirror to reflect them, not a candle end or a duster, not even a forgotten broom to speak of the women who had lived and worked there for twenty years. She stepped back, and the sound multiplied; she sighed and heard it repeated as though by ghosts. Pursued by memories, she tiptoed down to the next floor, examining each empty room in turn with no more than a cursory glance. Until she came to the best room, the one that fronted Gillygate; and there the ghosts of her mother and Robert were waiting. She stood for what seemed a long time without moving, clutching Tisha to her breast while silent tears poured down her cheeks. It was as though all that had happened here was continuing; she could feel it in the air, hear it, smell it like dying roses, a presence which had strangely been released with the emptying of the house. She had to leave; wanted to; although now the moment had come, like watching a loved one waving from a train, she found it hard to turn away.

Tisha twisted suddenly and patted Louisa's face. "Mamma," she said plaintively, her baby lips quivering at the sight of her mother's tears.

"Yes, darling," Louisa sniffed, wiping her eyes with the back of her hand. "Mamma's coming now."

With one last look she turned and closed the door.

For more than a week while they were working there, Bessie and Louisa had lit fires in every room in an attempt to dispel the damp; after two days of occupation and what seemed to Louisa a most profligate use of coal, the cottage was beginning to feel dry and warm, and with at least the larger pieces of furniture in place, it looked attractive. Packing cases still stood in what would eventually be Tisha's bedroom, but the kitchen was stocked with essential crockery and utensils, and in the parlor Louisa had reerected the children's Christmas tree with its red streamers and silver star. Few of the chocolate animals and fancy biscuits remained, but most of the tiny glass ornaments her mother had kept for years had survived the move, glinting in the firelight as she came into the room.

For a moment she stood quite still, enchanted by the blazing coals in the grate and their dancing reflections on pure white walls and ceiling. Despite its cheapness, the whitewash was clean and effective, throwing furniture and hangings into stark relief; Louisa was so taken with it she was almost convinced it was preferable to the heavily patterned wall-papers currently in vogue. Her mother's best winter curtains, of heavy maroon velvet, glowed with plummy richness, and although the Turkey carpet was past its best, along with the furniture it seemed to have taken on a new lease on life in this low-beamed room. Each item looked different, yet formed part of a cohesive whole which seemed to truly belong here.

Her first impression, that the cottage would prove a haven, was suddenly intensified; it would respond to love and care and in return give back all the peace and contentment she craved. After years in which an atmosphere of crisis had prevailed, unhappy years which had seen the mangling of so many hopes and dreams, Louisa felt endowed with unexpected bounty. Running her fingers over the worn sofa back, she thought of her mother and wished she could have been there to see the cottage, to share the happiness which seemed to beckon like an old and valued friend; and it hurt that she could not.

The date was poignant, too. Like the two-faced mask of Janus, the last day of the Old Year seemed to necessitate a looking back as much as a looking forward, an accounting of old sins and sorrows before the baptism of the future. She supposed that in a year's time Mary Elliott's death would be less painful, just as the second anniversary of leaving Robert had been easier to bear than the first; both partings had been necessary, and, in many ways, not before time; what hurt was coming to terms with life afterward.

But that was part of the penance where he was concerned, she reminded herself, part of the two years' hard labor for presuming to flout laws unwritten as well as those carved in stone. And now, please God, it was over; this place the safe harbor after the storm. Here she and Edward could be happy, the children unfettered by noise and traffic and the cruel gibes of neighborhood urchins. They had a garden to play in, woods and meadows downriver as they grew older, and sufficient income to keep them all from fear of the workhouse. It hardly seemed possible, yet it was all there, just waiting to be enjoyed.

She heard the front door open and was momentarily startled; then Edward came in, laughing and stamping his feet.

"Have you seen it?" he demanded, pulling her with him to the window. "Look," he said with a smile, thrusting back the heavy curtains. "It's snowing."

Great fat flakes were floating gently down and, like feathers lying softly one upon another, were gradually blanketing soil and paths and shrubs and walls; the black railings were tipped with it already, and across the river on New Walk, a solitary street lamp was enveloped in a mist of white.

Louisa hugged his arm. "It's like fairyland," she said, touched as much by his delight as by the beauty outside. "What were you doing out there?"

"Finding some laurel," he laughed, "and a lump of coal. We're a bit new and a bit remote to expect first-footers, so I thought I'd better be ready to let the New Year in myself."

"Goodness, I hadn't thought of that. Who came last year? Oh, yes, it was the butcher's boy," she chuckled, "busy bringing luck to the whole street! He was as drunk as a lord by the time he got to us. Do you remember—Mamma was afraid he'd never get home and gave him money instead . . ." With a long-drawn sigh, she murmured: "New Year's Eve—how things change in a year."

"It's been hard going," Edward agreed, resting his arm across her shoulders. "Let's hope and pray things are going to be better from now on." For a long time they stood looking out at the thickening snow; then he said, "In a couple of hours, it will be 1899—the last year of this century. It sounds rather momentous, doesn't it? Significant, some-how—as though we should finish it well, balance the books, put our metaphorical house in order . . ."

There was a question in his voice, and she glanced up, seeing his eyes, shining with the snow's reflection, upon her. With a smile she smoothed back a lock of hair from his forehead. "We've made a start, haven't we?"

He answered her smile, but his eyes seemed troubled. "I want you to be happy," he sighed, "and I want the children to be safe and secure. I don't want anything else to hurt or distress you."

Louisa pressed her cheek against his jacket and breathed deeply, trying to control wayward, seesawing emotions. She could smell fresh air on his clothes and the scent of Pears' soap on his skin. Hugging him tight, loving him so much she thought her heart would break, she whispered, "Nothing can; while ever I have you, nothing can."

"Oh, my angel, I wish that were true, how I wish it were true!" There was a catch in his voice. Almost roughly, he grasped her arms and held her away from him; and for one startled moment she saw bitter conflict in his eyes.

"Sit down," he said brusquely, taking the chair to one side of the hearth. He sat forward, hands clasped tensely between his knees, the firelight illuming only one side of his face, sharpening nose and cheekbone and jaw, deepening each small furrow of anxiety into stern lines of arraignment.

"You know, our solitude here is quite illusory," he began. "We're not in the depths of the country, Louisa, far from it. There's a city out there, and thousands of people. A lot of those people know us both. Among my business acquaintances, I suppose it's fairly common knowledge that I'm a bachelor, although," he added softly, "there have been one or two since I've been house-hunting who've assumed I'm lately married. And I haven't denied it."

"Well?" she asked, but her voice sounded squeaky with nerves. Afraid of what he was about to say, she clasped her trembling fingers together and hardly listened as he told her about his interview with the landlord, about the direct lie he had felt bound to utter.

"But it made me think, Louisa, about things that, through force of circumstances, we haven't yet considered. For instance, what happens when Liam goes to school? What will you say when you register his name and address and have to give his next of kin?"

"I don't know, I haven't thought about it."

"Well, love, we *must* think about it. What do we do? What do we say? Do we let people assume we're married, or do we clarify the situation, laying ourselves open to further gossip? Because our situation is hardly conventional at the moment—there's no longer a third adult in the house to play chaperon—and people, being what they are, will simply put the blackest interpretation on it." He tugged at his chin, the eyes which held hers more anxious than ever. "I'm sorry, but they will."

Louisa jumped up from the sofa and began to pace the room as though pursued, as though sheer physical movement could prevent those unwelcome ideas from taking root. But take root they did, and, coming hard on the heels of that fleeting happiness, they made her want to rage and shout in protest.

"Why," she spat out, "should we have to say *anything?* It's no one else's business! We're doing nothing wrong—in fact our lives couldn't be more scrupulous. You're not even *keeping* me. We're living independently, but in the same house, that's all!"

"I know that. You know that. The rest of the world doesn't. And while it doesn't bother me what people say, I do worry about the children. They're the ones our situation will affect, that is, if we do nothing about it. Just as you and I were affected when we were young. Do you want that for them?"

Pain, like a knife, ran through her then. "No," she cried, "of course I don't!" She continued her anguished pacing, feeling as though the black sins of all the world sat on her shoulder. Hating herself, and furious with Edward for destroying those happy illusions, she had no eyes for his sorrow.

With a sigh that seemed wrung from the depths of his soul, he said at last: "There is a way to put an end to speculation."

"Oh, and what's that?"

"We could get married," he said flatly. "Make things legal and incontrovertible. Nothing need change between us—I simply want to put an end to gossip before it starts."

For a second Louisa's heart leapt and plummeted all at once, leaving her breathless with amazement. "What a thing to say," she said at last, faintly, wondering why she felt so desperately hurt by the suggestion. "Marriage—for nothing more than respectability's sake? I never heard such a thing! It's—it's immoral," she stammered. "I'm astounded you could even think of it!"

"It wasn't considered lightly, I assure you," he replied with sudden asperity. "I've thought of little else for days. I thought, for the children's sake . . ."

With a sharp gesture, Louisa mumbled an apology and turned her back, reluctant to face that kind of logic. Chewing her lip, fighting for mastery of her voice, she said: "It isn't right, Edward. I'm sorry, but it isn't. If we were to marry—" Courage failed her and she broke off, unable to say that it would have to be wholeheartedly, a real marriage, or not at all.

"Yes?" he prompted.

"I was about to say," she hesitated, "that anything less than a real marriage would be like cheating."

"I don't see it like that!" he exclaimed, rising to face her.

"But I do."

"I know you still love *him,* but I'm thinking of the children!"

"Forget Robert," she said angrily. "I'm thinking of us!" At the sudden flicker of hope in his eyes, Louisa winced and shook her head, feeling the denial wrenched out of her like a premature birth. "I can't, Edward—not now, don't you see? I can't!"

He meant so many different things to her, and she loved him in as many ways; he had the protectiveness of a brother and the understanding of a friend; in times of stress his arms were a sure retreat, warm and comforting without the guilt and tension of sexual demands. And yet, Louisa realized, there had been times when she wanted him, moments which would have taken no more than one serious move on his part to break those fragile barriers. But she knew such responses were simply the result of another man's tuition, the crying out of her body for the fulfillment it had been coached to expect and enjoy. To use Edward to such base ends was worse, far worse than the sin of her relationship with Robert, and to marry him for respectability's sake would demean everything.

Had she loved him less, it would not have mattered; because she loved him more than she trusted him to understand, she could not explain.

While he finally retreated upstairs in hurt and weary exasperation, Louisa shivered, chilled by his departure. To have argued so soon in their new house, and at the turn of the year, seemed depressingly ominous. The little parlor's magic was destroyed. Sadly she banked down the fire and, setting a spark-guard around it, she went into the kitchen to make some tea. While the kettle hissed, she pulled her chair close to the range and slipped off her shoes, resting her feet against the warm oven door.

She felt exhausted, drained. Although Edward's motives were pure, his logic almost unassailable, she could not agree to those terms, nor could she make clear her own. On the one hand, his coldness crushed her; and on the other, the weight of his generosity was similarly unbearable, leaving her bowed between. She was hurt that in his detached, male way he could not see that.

He imagined, of course, that she nursed secret hopes of a reconciliation with Robert, whereas nothing could be further from the truth. The difficulty lay in the fact that she could not explain to Edward, who loved her, exactly what it was she still felt for the father of her children.

The punishment for what they had shared felt like a public flaying from which she was still unhealed; and if its severity truly equaled the crime, then what they had done was horribly and grievously wrong. If penance was necessary to forgiveness, then Louisa felt she had already paid the price; but should the requirement be true remorse, she suspected her errant soul was still unshriven. For the beginning, for those months of happiness in Marygate, she could not be sorry; nor could she regret the friendship with Letty and Georgina which had flowered amidst the wreckage of her love for Robert. And as for the children, innocent and beautiful, while they would always be living reminders of that unblessed union, she could not regret them either.

It was Robert she regretted; Robert with his charm and powerful sexual appeal which it seemed could still stir desires she had thought comfortably dead. The knowledge shamed her, denting her small and fragile store of self-respect. And if she could scarcely face that unwelcome aspect of her own character, Louisa could not admit it to Edward, whose love and esteem were as essential to her now as food and drink to a starving child. Even if she were to admit it, he could never understand, for the crippling torments of sexual desire had surely never been his.

But he loved her all the same. She knew it even though he had never said as such; and her silence hurt him. Recalling the flicker of hope in his eyes, and then that crushed look of weary resignation, Louisa wanted to weep. She loved Edward; loved him, trusted him, understanding his aloofness and that strangely romantic idealism. Like Chaucer's *verray parfit gentil knight,* he had a pure and beautiful soul; he would give her his heart and his life. But what had she of value to give him in return?

In the silence, something stirred. Listening, she thought she heard the sound of bells and went to the window to open it. On the still, crisp air, across that frozen blanket of snow, came the sound of the Minster bells chiming the last of the Old Year and, on a sudden, joyful peal, heralding the New.

Louisa was far from certain why she wept. It might have been for her mother, or for Robert and what should have been buried two years past; it was most probably for sheer loneliness.

ELEVEN

Most of that winter, Edward was anxious about her. The strength and determination she had possessed since childhood were at such a low ebb, she reminded him of something stranded and defenseless, prey to any attack, both real and imaginary. She suffered a string of petty illnesses, and as he nursed her through the worst of them he watched her covertly, wondering whether the cottage would prove to be the permanent haven she needed or only a temporary resting place. There was unfathomable pain behind those large, expressive eyes, and a downward turn at the corners of her mouth which might have been the result of natural grief for her mother or a longing for things which could never be. Despite her attempts to salve his feelings that night, he was still convinced Louisa had turned down his proposal because at heart she loved and wanted Robert Duncannon, and her agreement to pretend they were married for the children's sake left him just as uneasy as ever.

But the warmth of her welcome when he returned each night was genuine, and her delight in their new home was equally unfeigned; each small improvement was proudly shown, and her enthusiasm for every carpentry job he completed was unbounded. The string of coughs and colds she suffered seemed to pass the children by; they thrived physically and emotionally, playing outside in all weathers, as noisy and boisterous as only happy, healthy children can be. That cheered him, but although he liked the cottage, after the noise and bustle of Gillygate it took him some time to grow used to its quietness and sense of isolation. He could not ignore the fact that, apart from the children, he and Louisa were quite alone, and for a long time it disturbed him.

At night, with that fragile partition between them, that thin plaster wall through which he could hear her moving about, hanging up her clothes, or climbing into the big double bed with its myriad, torturing little squeaks, Edward was often awake till long after midnight. Tense, wanting her, he prayed for sleep. Several times he thought he heard her crying, a low, muffled sound which might have been the sobs of wind and rain beneath the eaves, and immediately visualized her face pressed to the pillow, heart breaking with secret anguish. On each occasion he left his bed, stopping once halfway to the door, another time with fingers on the latch, knowing that the new rules of this household, unwritten and unspoken though they were, forbade him to go and comfort her.

But as the short winter days began to lengthen, as February's frosts gave way to a blustery March, he began to notice changes as subtle and welcome as the burgeoning spring.

Inspired by the first daffodils, Louisa started work in the garden, and Edward soon found a strong-looking boy to help with the heavy digging. The fastidious appetite which had given him such cause for concern began to improve, and the healthy outdoor exercise put color into cheeks which had for too long been drawn and pale; there was a new spring to her step, and at the end of each day her smiles had the happy glow of achievement. Watching her in the garden or with the children, he could not recall a time when she had been more relaxed or more beautiful; and when she looked up and smiled at him, Edward's heart swelled with love. It was impossible to speak of, so he wrote it in his poetry and meanwhile savored each precious, fragile moment, the silly things which amused them both, the minor problems they solved together. As tension and anxiety receded, so the little noises beyond the wall took on the nature of a nightly ritual to be listened for in the surrounding quietness. Gradually, more comforted than disturbed, he grew to love the isolation, and slept.

As weeds and thick, tussocky grass were dug out and burned, and shrubs and trees pruned into shape, Louisa's correspondence with Letty increased; before long, plots for different vegetables were cleared and marked, and the beds of hardy perennials near the house severely disciplined. Letty suggested coming over to York for a few days with Georgina, and the visit was fixed for the beginning of May. Just after Easter there was a letter from Robert to say he had been passed fit for service again and that he would be rejoining his old regiment at Hounslow; he said he would like to visit them once he was settled; but, whether from tact or a reluctance to have him at the cottage alone, Louisa referred him to his sister, and Edward was inordinately glad the three would be coming together. They would be staying in town, as lack of space absolved Louisa from offering accommodation, and Edward hoped that would set the pattern for any future visits. He quite liked Letty and felt sorry for the little girl, but while he had had no objection to their staying at the Gillygate house, he was aware of an irrational need to keep the cottage and his relationship with Louisa inviolate; and if he could, in conscience, have prevented Robert from visiting them at all, he knew he would have done so.

Letty and Georgina arrived on the Thursday, and Robert joined them the following evening. Torn between a desire to watch Louisa's reactions to him and a deep-seated reluctance to be drawn into the Duncannons' joint and very powerful Irish charm, Edward was moody and morose, unable to summon his usual shield of calm detachment. Aware that he was putting up a very poor front, he made the excuse of pressing work on the Saturday, telling Louisa he would not be back until evening; and when he did return at five, found himself quite unreasonably furious that they were all out.

It had been a clear, beautiful day, and it was natural that the adults should have taken the children out to enjoy themselves; nevertheless, the image of a happy, carefree family group which excluded him wormed its way under Edward's skin and bit deep, releasing a jealous and bitter resentment which shocked him even as it grew in strength.

He went upstairs to wash and change, came down again to await their return; tried reading, but the words danced before his eyes; was hungry and made himself a sandwich; thirsty, and poured a glass of water. He paced the house, then, with anxiety dogging him like a crouching beast, went out into the chill and gathering dusk to look for them along the riverbank.

The children's piping voices were instantly recognizable above the steady thud of horses' hooves. They were singing and laughing in the back of a little wagonette, urging their driver on.

On the still evening air, he heard Robert's voice; and a moment later he was reining in as he recognized the figure on the narrow dirt road.

"So, you're here at last," Edward called, his voice taut with anger. "I've been wondering where on earth you'd got to." Ignoring Robert's reply, he went to where Louisa was sitting in the back of the wagonette, looking directly up at her as she leaned out to speak. "Where have you been? Don't you know what time it is?"

With laughter still in her voice, she said: "About seven, I suppose. Why?"

"Why?" he echoed angrily. "Why? Because I didn't know where you were, and, rather foolishly, I suppose, I was anxious about you!"

"I'm sorry, Edward, I didn't think—"

"Then perhaps it's time you started thinking!" His glance took in the children's faces, pale in the twilight, their shoulders wrapped in shawls against the chill evening air. "It's time those children were home and in bed."

"We traveled further than we intended," Robert said with quiet emphasis. "And we were returning as fast as decently possible in this light. I'm sorry, we should have left a note, I suppose. It's my fault—didn't think." There was a momentary pause. "Won't you hop in? Then we can get the children home."

Edward shook his head. "No thanks. I'll see you back at the cottage."

When he got back, lamps were lit in kitchen and parlor, and the horse, hitched to the iron railings, was cropping patiently at the grass beside the road. As he walked up the path, Robert came out to meet him, leaving his sister and daughter saying their farewells.

"Sorry about that—sheer carelessness on my part," he insisted. "It was very spur of the moment, and I did think we'd be back before you."

Still irritated, Edward simply nodded his acknowledgment of the apology. "Will you be here tomorrow?"

"No, I have to get back to London. Although I imagine Letty is making some arrangements. Look," he added tersely, "can we talk a moment?"

Outside the gate, Robert turned to the horse, making a pretense of adjusting its bridle. "You're angry, and I think I know why. It's because I'm here. Don't bother to deny it," he added with a sharp sideways glance, "because I'd feel the same in your shoes. But remember—you did agree."

"I haven't forgotten," Edward said stiffly.

"Good, because I shall want to see the children as often as possible while I'm able to do so."

Something in his voice made Edward glance keenly through the gloom. "You're going away again?"

"Perhaps, I don't know. It's a feeling I have, a suspicion. No," he added, "it's more than that—it's a calculated guess." He ran his fingers down the horse's neck, and it turned and nudged him, whickering gently as though reminding him that it was well past supper and time to be off. "This trouble with Kruger in the Transvaal—it may be nothing, but I have a feeling it could develop. I haven't said anything to Letty or Louisa, so I'd rather you kept it to yourself. But the point remains that I could be gone before the summer's out."

As a follower of world events in several newspapers, Edward knew the suspicion was not unfounded, and he felt the other man could well be privy to other, more direct information. The glow of satisfaction which spread warmly through his veins, however, was quickly quenched by the biting quality of Robert Duncannon's next words.

"So—about the children. Louisa informs me that she does not want them confused by the intricacies of our relationship. They don't remember me, and they seem to be under the impression that *you* are their father." He paused, and Edward heard the sharpness of his breathing. "I want you to know," he went on, with the same menacing restraint, "that the only reason I'm prepared to give in to her blackmail—and it *is* blackmail, no matter what you prefer to call it—is because I cannot see them as often as I would wish. And, of course, I may not be in the country very much longer."

"Blackmail? I don't know what you're talking about!"

"Don't you?" Robert demanded. "Then I suggest you ask Louisa."

Tension crackled between them for a moment. Between frozen lips, Edward said, "I will, but I'd prefer an explanation from you."

"Well, you're not getting one. I don't want to discuss it any further."

Abruptly Edward turned and went inside.

Passing the women in the doorway, he was forced to make some conventional remark, but as Georgina hugged Louisa with passionate affection, he shot a furious glance above the child's head before bidding them all goodnight.

When she had put the children to bed, Louisa came into the parlor to ask whether he would like something to eat, but he was reading determinedly and gave no more than a noncommittal reply. A short while later she returned and touched his shoulder, reminding him that it was warmer in the kitchen and supper was ready. Although he followed her with a great show of reluctance, Edward was too hungry to ignore the spread she set before him; with one basic need satisfied, and residual warmth from the range taking the chill from his bones, he was better fitted to tackle the subject at hand.

"It's not like you to sulk," she observed.

He regarded her gravely. "I was angry. I still am."

"I'm sorry," she murmured, lowering her eyes. "It's my fault. I should have known better than to keep them out so long."

"Never mind, forget that. What happened this afternoon? I understand there was a difference of opinion."

Glancing guiltily up at him, she colored to the roots of her hair. "Yes, there was. It was before we set off." She was silent for so long that he waited with bated breath, knuckles showing white where he gripped the arms of the chair. "It didn't arise before, you see—but today I thought it might, so I asked him whether . . . I asked him," she repeated, "if he would mind the children calling him *Uncle*."

"And?"

"He did mind. Very much. But I told him the truth would only confuse them—and it would, Edward," she said with direct and forceful appeal. "You know it would. Now Liam's at school—can you imagine what he might *say?*"

"Only too well, but go on. There's more, I believe?"

"No, that's it. I said it must be so, whether he liked it or not."

"And he accepted your argument, just like that?"

Again her color deepened. "Well, no. Not exactly. In fact he argued the point—so much so I eventually said that if he wanted to go on seeing the children at all, then he must accept my terms."

"You shouldn't have done that," he said quietly. "You had no right—"

"I have *every* right—"

"We *agreed.* At Christmas you said he could see them. You imposed no conditions then—"

"I wasn't fit to *think* straight at Christmas!" she said angrily. "What with Mamma's death—him turning up—moving house—my God! What do you think I am? They're *my* children, Edward. I'm not going to have their lives disrupted and made hell just because their father's taken a sudden interest in them! They don't even know him—they hardly saw him in Dublin, never 'mind *here.*"

Thinking of his own father, and the relationship which had become precious to them both, Edward shook his head. If he embarked on that, he knew he would plead like a prisoner at the bar for the rights of another man. With a bitter sigh, he said: "They'll have to know one day, Louisa. You can't in all honesty keep it from them."

"Then one day I'll tell them—but not now."

"The longer you leave it," he said softly, "the harder it will be."

Without answering she stood up and began to clear the table; he noticed her hands were shaking and, when he looked up, that she was crying.

His anger evaporated. Distressed for her, for the situation, for himself who must stand in perpetuity as an observer, Edward took the tray from her hands and put his arms around her. "Oh, God," he whispered as he held her close, "what are we doing to ourselves?"

"I don't know," she sobbed. "I feel wicked—evil—but what else could I *do?*"

"Hush, don't say that. Don't even think it. You're not wicked—it's just a mad, ridiculous, terrible situation." With his cheek against hers, he inhaled the scents of lavender and warm skin; her arms tightened across his shoulders. For a second, guilt fled; there was nothing else, only the two of them. We should put things straight, he thought; marry and make things right; give love and share it.

"Louisa—" he whispered, but she stiffened at once, listening for something else, something his bemused senses had failed to catch. It came again, a small cry from above; then Liam's voice, clearer, shouting for his mother.

Louisa leaned her forehead against Edward's cheek and sighed. "I'm sorry," she murmured shakily. "I shouldn't—" Breaking off, she left whatever it was unsaid and patted his arm. "I'd better go and see what's wrong."

Alone, Edward leaned heavily against the table, breathing deeply and pondering the irony of that little voice. Again he had been about to mention marriage; perhaps he had been saved from making a fool of himself a second time. Despite that racing of the blood, the fleeting illusion of youth and excitement, he reminded himself with bitter stoicism that he was neither more nor less than a middle-aged bachelor of entrenched habits; far too old a dog to start jumping through hoops, whatever the provocation.

Inwardly cursing Robert Duncannon and all he stood for, Edward shook his head and went to the pantry. Pouring himself a glass of bottled beer, he drank deep to clear the terrible dryness in his throat; it slaked his thirst, but not the need which lingered like burning sand in his blood.

Hearing Louisa's foot on the stair, he turned abruptly and went outside.

TWELVE

*J*ust five weeks later, on a balmy summer evening, Robert stepped off the London train, gathered his single piece of luggage, and checked into the Royal Station Hotel. It had been a tedious, sticky journey from Hounslow that afternoon, and he was eager to bathe and change before walking down to Clementhorpe to see Louisa and the children.

With a thick white towel wrapped around his waist he stood before the mirror, splashing the remains of shaving soap from his chin and jaw; his eyes caught the tail end of that long, puckered scar, and he turned to look at it, flexing the muscle with an ease that brought a small, satisfied smile to his lips. It was still pink, and would never be less than ugly, but his determination with those painful exercises had ensured he was not disabled by it. In fact he felt very fit, and since his return to the regiment was aware of a pleasurable sense of fulfillment. The training season was well under way, and he was enjoying every minute of it, his sense of discipline and eye for detail sharpened by the thought of impending war. As in the Sudan, training now had purpose to it, potentially a matter of life and death for each man in the field, no longer precision for the sake of display or discipline to curb unruly crowds at pitheads and race meetings. Despite the wound and his extended absence from the regiment, there had been whispers that his field experience and the medal awarded for action with Broadwood's cavalry had put him in line for promotion; soon the rank of major would no longer be honorary, but permanent, and that thought provided the necessary balance for all that was missing in his private life.

When he looked back to those depressing November days, Robert realized that his motives in trying to put things right had been less than altruistic. Physical pain and a crushing sense of failure had driven him to make whatever peace he could, more as a salve for his own conscience than out of true regard for the consequences. At a six-month distance from that time, he was not at all sure he had done the right thing, although room for maneuver had been so desperately limited. With all the talk of Louisa and Edward moving from Gillygate to set up home together, Letty had assumed marriage was afoot; but Robert was not so sure. Originally he would not have been surprised to find them wed before his return; that it was not so made him wonder why, and in wondering he had begun to think that perhaps it was because Louisa loved him still. Just a little bit, beneath the anger and the bitterness and that blistering resentment; but she was not indifferent to him, and that was what mattered.

He had asked what her intentions were, the day of the picnic; and with one sharp negative she had dismissed the idea that she and Edward might one day marry. In the midst of the row about the children, however, it was less than surprising that she had given no explanation. Perhaps, Robert thought, when the time was right he would ask her again. He did wonder whether she was playing games with him, deliberately humiliating him in ways guaranteed to hurt, in revenge for past sins. If so, he reasoned, then she was using Edward to further those ends, and he would have said, once, she was incapable of such callousness. Now he was no longer sure; he asked himself whether any man could plumb the depths of a woman's mind or thread a way through the maze of twisted logic toward what they liked to call poetic justice. He was certain of only one thing: a man's sense of honor meant nothing to the average woman.

With a sigh he donned his clothes and sent down for a light supper to be served in his room; there was no point in dressing for dinner downstairs, only to change again for his visit to Clementhorpe. Although he had written telling them to expect him the following day, Robert could imagine they would be out.

Replete and refreshed, he strolled up Queen Street in the gathering dusk, sniffing the scents of new-mown grass along the ramparts. He passed the small and rather forbidding school beneath the Micklegate walls, where Liam had recently begun his first term, and wondered how the child was coping. He would have preferred to educate his sons privately, but as Louisa was never slow to point out, technically the children were hers, not his, and they would receive the kind of education suitable to their status in life. At least until they were older. Should one or all of them prove worthy of a higher education, Edward had assured him he was quite as keen as Robert that they should receive it, no matter what the cost.

At the corner with Blossom Street he paused, staring with sudden and avid curiosity at the Tempest house across the road. It was the first time he had set eyes on the place since leaving York with the regiment, and he wondered how poor Arthur was coping with marriage to a woman like Rachel. Not much of a welcome in her bed, he decided with more amusement than pity; he had never cared much for young Bainbridge; he was the worst kind of amateur soldier, vain, cocksure, and empty-headed. Briefly Robert wondered whether he was still with the hussars or whether Rachel had made him give up that smart blue uniform for real work in her father's business.

And then he wondered how Louisa felt, passing this corner every day as she brought Liam to and from school; that house had always given her the cold shivers, ever since . . . He made a mental note to ask her whether she had ever bumped into Rachel or, since the move to Clementhorpe, had seen anything of Moira and Harris. They were just across the river, after all.

Along Nunnery Lane, the shadows in the moat were indigo, the bright new leaves of chestnut trees like vivid green fingers holding candles in the dusk; high above the trees, the crenellated city wall was touched with pink. The familiar scent of horses in a stable on his left, freshly cut grass, and all the heady newness of early summer attacked Robert's senses like wine. Two young girls in white Whitsunday dresses and cheaply trimmed straw hats passed him, their voices high with excitement. No doubt they were out to meet two similarly eager young men, and Robert was filled with envy for their innocence, for the as yet unmarked page of their future lives. A sentimental desire to wish them well possessed him; with lingering, frankly admiring eyes he tipped his hat and was rewarded by two dimpling smiles; the burst of delighted, half-fearful laughter behind his back was saddening, however. For all that he had, for all the sensual beauty this summer evening had to offer, he was alone, not for the want of opportunity, but for need of a woman who had turned her back on him.

And when all was said and done, he knew he could forget her intransigence, the blistering words, the utter boredom of domestic life; but he had only to watch her cross a room or catch a hint of her perfume as she passed by to recall in minutest detail how she looked and smelled and felt after making love. It was the subtlest form of torture, yet for that he had taken an extra half-day's leave and the early train in order to indulge it.

Unsure which of the new streets led down to the cottage, Robert took the longer way that he knew, past the confectionery works and along the riverside. It was lighter there, the past pale glow of the western sky reflected on the glassy water; a solitary rowing boat was drifting slowly downstream toward the confluence with the Foss, no doubt some boatman or bargee returning to his craft moored in the basin at Castle Mills. A touch of red caught his eye beneath trees on the far bank, and he saw with a pang of unexpected nostalgia a pair of young soldiers walking their girls across St. George's Field.

After the metallic echo of his footsteps on pavements and cobbles, his footfall was suddenly absorbed by a sandy bridleway overhung with beeches and tall elms. Further on he saw the pantiled roof over a wall thick with flowering shrubs, and then the iron railings beside the path; there was the squeak of the gate and Edward appeared, his face quite clear in that open space. He was laughing as he turned back, the first genuine, carefree laugh Robert had ever heard him utter. He was so surprised, he stopped; and then he was curious, reluctant to leave the shadow of the trees under which he stood.

"Leave that weeding," he heard Edward say, "or you'll be bent double tomorrow. And you needn't come to me for sympathy!"

"I'm coming," the disembodied voice called back. It was Louisa, of course.

Edward appeared again, bareheaded and with turned-back shirt-sleeves, as though he had been helping her. He leaned on the gate, smiling as he held out his hand to the invisible figure in the garden. He has good teeth, Robert thought, with surprised irrelevance, knowing he had never noticed before.

Relaxed and unaware, Edward chaffed Louisa to hurry, and she came at last, laughing, pulling off stained gloves, and untucking her dress as she stepped out onto the path. That merry, dimpling glance at her cousin burned jealousy into Robert's heart; for a second he simply stood trans-fixed, hating them both, then, afraid they might start toward him, stepped back into deeper shadow.

But they went no further than the grassy riverbank.

"I'd nearly finished," she said with lighthearted protest as Edward helped her down a steep and hidden path.

"I know, but it'll be dark in no time, and I want to see the river and this marvelous light before it goes completely. A few minutes, that's all."

"You're quite mad," she said with a laugh, dropping down beside him in the grass.

He could see only their heads and the line of their shoulders, close together; then Edward's arm came up around her, his broad hand resting against the curve of her neck. Like a pair of lovers, Robert thought as he turned away, not caring if he was seen.

It was already hot when he returned the next morning. All the doors and windows stood open, and Louisa was in the kitchen preparing dinner.

Her cheeks were flushed, but as always she looked prettier like that, he thought, never distressed and unattractive. She was wearing a broad starched apron over a white-spotted navy-blue dress, and looked neat and cool and capable, rather like one of the nurses on the steamship home from Cairo. The image appealed to him.

As before they greeted each other casually, from a distance of several feet. Robert stood in the shady doorway, where a slight breeze played, watching her rinse crisp green lettuce leaves in a bowl of icy water; her hands dripped as she shook them, and he longed to feel their coolness against his brow. Catching the glance, she smiled and reached for a large jug of fresh lemonade.

"Here," she said, pouring Robert a glass, "have a drink. You look as though you could do with it."

Thanking her, he followed her with his eyes; embarrassed, Louisa turned away. With the memory of the riverbank in his mind, he stood quite still for a moment, pondering afresh the question which had tormented him half the night: *had* the situation drastically changed, or was it simply that he had watched them unobserved? But she was hardly likely to answer him, Robert reflected with a sigh; attracted by the sound of children's voices, he went outside.

Beneath trees in the little orchard, on grass white-spotted with daisies and fallen blossoms, the boys had erected a makeshift tent of clotheshorse and blankets; while they crawled in and out, disturbing and rearranging, the baby sat calmly by in frilled pinafore and sunbonnet, like an amused little queen surveying her unruly subjects. From time to time she plucked a daisy from the grass and ate it. He crouched down, intending to dissuade her, but Liam called him to see the tent, eager and so remarkably transformed from the hesitant, suspicious child he had come to expect that Robert had to go.

Surveying that round, fair head, and listening to his elder son's assessment of the problem of the blankets, Robert was amazed at the change in him. He could date it, he realized, to a precise point in his last visit, the afternoon of the picnic. Before it, the boy had been reluctant to speak to him and even less eager to make any kind of physical contact. Asked whether he would like to ride alongside Robert on the driving seat, he had backed away as though from a plague. Until the moment Robert had noticed him on his own, watching the placid old horse cropping contentedly at the grass. With the excuse of checking its tether, Robert strolled casually toward them. He began by talking about the horse, its size and breed and what it was suited for, running his hands over various points and showing Liam its hooves and shoes; went on to talk about his own horses in Ireland and the chargers which must be specially trained for cavalry use. The child had listened carefully, but at a distance, torn between fascination and obvious mistrust. Despairing of the game, Robert sat back on the grass and returned his son's stare, trying to fathom the cause of that desperate inner struggle. The fact that he did not immediately run back to his mother was heartening. Eventually Robert had said quite baldly: "You don't know what to call me, do you, Liam? You remember me, and you remember the horses—but you can't *quite* remember who I am. Isn't that it?" Very slowly the child had nodded.

The recollection of that moment brought another lump to Robert's throat; he stroked the soft fair hair, and the boy smiled up at him. "Come on, Uncle Bob," he said brightly, "you come in as well."

"No—no, I'm far too big for that little tent. I should knock it down, and then you'd have to start again. I'll sit here outside for a while."

He watched them playing, Liam the leader and Bobby his faithful follower, and wondered whether it would always be so. With age, boys tended to quarrel; he had with his own brother.

"And you, little miss," he murmured as the baby crawled toward him, "will you be like your namesake, with an independent streak a mile wide?"

Attracted by another daisy, Tisha paused, her perfect features the very picture of concentration. Chubby fingers hovered, descended, and picked the tiny yellow and white flower; it went straight into her mouth.

"Should she be doing that?" he asked Liam. "Eating daisies?"

"Oh, she's all right," Liam stated with airy unconcern. "She likes them."

"I think I'd better ask your mother," Robert replied doubtfully, glad of an excuse to go inside, out of the sun.

As he reached for that little stranger, his daughter, she turned an imperious blue gaze upon him; a second later those rosebud lips enunciated the clearest, firmest negative Robert thought he had ever heard. With a laugh he picked her up and was rewarded by a piercing scream; wincing, he took her in to Louisa.

"Here's one who'll never be taken advantage of," he muttered thoughtlessly as he handed her over.

Tight-lipped, Louisa soothed the child and sponged her face and hands. "I think it's time for a little lie down."

"Yes, please," Robert agreed, holding his head. "Just show me the way."

"What's the matter? Aren't you well?"

"I'm most decidedly unwell," he admitted, sinking into a chair.

Giving him a searching look, Louisa took the baby upstairs; when she came down, she said: "Demon drink, Robert? I thought you'd given that up."

"Not entirely. And last night I bumped into an old acquaintance."

"Oh? Who was that? Anyone I know?" Taking the lettuce she had washed and drained earlier, she began arranging it in a large glass bowl. On the table were spring onions and watercress and a crock of large brown eggs.

"Arthur Bainbridge."

"Rachel's husband? What on earth was he doing in London?"

It took some time for Robert to explain the circumstances of that meeting on Blossom Street, as the tale was threaded by some necessary half-truths; exhausted by that mental effort, he had quite forgotten the reason for beginning it when she said: "And one drink led to another, I suppose?"

"Yes," he admitted. "I suppose it did."

"Well, I hope you can manage some dinner. It's all cold—I couldn't face cooking a hot meal today, and by the look of you, you couldn't have eaten it, so it's just as well." Cracking and peeling two large hard-boiled eggs, Louisa removed the yolks and mashed them into a bowl, adding salt and sugar and vinegar and several tablespoons of olive oil.

While she was stirring the salad sauce he watched her, amazed at her ability to cope with meals, domestic chores, and the demands of three young children. The kitchen was bright and spotless, as he was sure the rest of the house would be. Remembering her work in the garden, late the night before, he realized she must rise early and work solidly throughout the day; what amazed him most of all was the fact that she appeared to be happy doing it.

"How on earth do you manage on your own, without help?"

"Quite well," she said with more than a touch of pride and challenge in her voice. Chopping sprigs of parsley, she sprinkled it over the mixed salad in the bowl, set the sauce to one side, and fetched a large stand pie from the pantry. "Not that I have time these days to sew fine seams and play the piano—but I enjoy what I do. It's very *satisfying*, Robert, to be appreciated."

"Meaning I didn't appreciate you?"

"You took me for granted, Robert. And really, to be honest," she added dryly, "I didn't actually do very much in Dublin, did I? Apart from bear children, that is."

He sighed. "You never let up, do you?"

With a little laugh, Louisa shook her head. "What do you expect? That I should fall into your arms, say it was all a big mistake, and won't you take me away from all this?" She stood for a moment, arms akimbo, watching him. "This is where I belong, Robert. What else could you possibly offer me that I might want? I've tasted it all—and it went very sour."

"I could think of something," he said with brutal frankness. "Or is that provided, too?"

She went white. In her eyes there was more pain than fury, and instantly he regretted those goaded, hasty words. Even as he apologized, bracing himself for a torrent of abuse or the short order to leave, Louisa turned away.

"I'm sorry," he said again, hating himself. "That was unforgivable— I don't know what made me say that—" As she leaned against the table, Robert caught her arm, and before she could jerk away, made her face him. "I didn't mean it," he said softly.

"It doesn't matter," she said in a queer, controlled voice. "You can think what you like."

"I don't want to think that!" His eyes raked her face, hating that blank, shuttered expression. "Look at me," he ordered, shaking her, "and tell me I mean nothing to you! Tell me you could see me dead and not weep one single tear—tell me that, and I'll go away and never bother you again!"

"Let go, you're hurting me."

For a second his fingers bit deeper into the soft flesh at the top of her arms; then, with a coarse oath, he dropped his hands and stepped abruptly back.

When he could find his voice, which was far from steady, Robert said: "Why do you make me so bloody angry? You know, it was precisely this sort of situation which led to that . . ." He shook his head, not wanting to complete the sentence, not wanting to admit that for one terrible moment he could have forced himself on her again.

But while he glared at her in angry frustration, Louisa's eyes were on the window. "Edward's here," she whispered on a sharp release of breath, "so please don't say any more."

As Edward came in at the front, Robert made a swift exit through the kitchen door, and when he returned with the boys some ten minutes later, Edward was washing his hands in the tiny scullery. None of last night's easy humor remained; he was polite and wary as ever, and at the table, taking their cue from him, the children were on their best behavior, subdued by the atmosphere and the unaccustomed grandeur of eating in the parlor.

They discussed the weather and the garden, and Robert praised the simple but excellent meal. Afterward, while the boys were sent to lie on their beds for an hour, and Louisa gave Tisha her dinner in the kitchen, the two men took their coffee outside.

Searching for something to say, something neutral which would break the ice between them, he mentioned having run into Arthur Bainbridge the night before. As a means of deflecting interest in himself and the nature of that spurious army business, he had bombarded Arthur with questions about himself, his family, and all the mutual acquaintances he could bring to mind. Over several drinks in Arthur's club, he had heard the story of Mrs. Bainbridge senior's demise and Sophie's subsequent role of martyred companion to the old major.

Repeating that conversation, Robert managed a little laugh. "Happy families! And Arthur's talking about applying for a regular commission, he's so sick of them all. I get the impression Rachel drives him mad."

"Fancy Sophie being still on the shelf," Louisa remarked as she came out to join them. "I'd have thought she'd be like Rachel—marrying the first to come along. Whatever happened to Lily? Is she still at home?"

"Far from it," Robert chuckled. "She married some eccentric old boy with estates in the East Riding. Big interests in bloodstock and racing, apparently, but they live in absolute squalor, according to Arthur. He said he'd rather have slept in the stables when he visited last—they were a damn sight cleaner than the house!"

"I can imagine that," Louisa said dryly, "from what I recall of Lily!"

She poured fresh coffee, and after a while the conversation lapsed quite comfortably. Robert's headache had gone, and with it the hard edge of his anger; as always, he regretted losing his temper and wondered how to apologize. Beginning to feel the soporific effects of a late night and a pleasant meal, he leaned back, finding the uncushioned Windsor chair lacking in sufficient comfort. What they really needed here, he thought, was a long garden seat; propped up by cushions, he could have stretched out his legs and gone to sleep . . .

Later Robert suggested taking the children on the river for the afternoon. There were several steamboats which ran up and down the river to the outlying villages; it might be pleasant to take them down to Bishopthorpe to see the palace. Louisa, however, was less than keen. Although she did not say so, he knew she was alarmed at the prospect of them all being seen together by some mutual acquaintance; on a day like this, such trips were bound to be popular. Robert did not press the matter and was most surprised when Edward suggested he might take the boys on his own, if he wished.

Dressed alike in sailor suits and straw boaters, with sturdy knees peeping from beneath short cotton trousers, Liam and Bobby waved a cheerful farewell to the others at the garden gate. They linked hands with Robert, Bobby skipping delightedly as far as the bridge, when he complained his legs ached and he had to be carried. Liam walked stoically on, like Livingstone seeking the source of the Nile.

There was quite a queue of people waiting on King's Staith for the pleasure steamer; with one look Robert deferred the idea and, almost before it had registered with the boys, hailed a cab and piled them into it. For a moment he considered swearing them to secrecy, sealing the pact with an ice cream; then it dawned on him that they could hardly be expected to keep secrets at their age but, with the promise of an ice to divert them, might possibly forget a visit to a boring shop, especially when no immediate purchase was made. They would not forget the cab ride, however. Bouncing with excitement, the two boys laughed all the way to the Mansion House and were most disappointed at having to alight.

At the top of Stonegate, the thirteenth-century facade of the Minster's south transept stood white and gleaming in the sun, framed by a deep blue sky and the shadowed narrowness of the street before it.

"Is that where we're going?" asked Liam. "To the Minster?"

"Not today, but we will another time, if you wish." Fragments of a conversation about this place, years before, came back to him, and he said whimsically: "Imagine, hundreds and hundreds of years ago, Roman soldiers marched up here, where we're walking now."

The bright little face turned and looked up at him. "Like the ones in the Bible?"

Startled, for he had hardly expected Liam to know who the Romans were, Robert agreed, but when his son asked if they had marched to the Minster, like the ones from the barracks on Military Sunday, Robert smiled and shook his head. "The soldiers we're talking about were here an awful long time before the Minster was built. No, when they marched up here, they were going into their fortress."

"I wish it was still here!" Liam exclaimed. "Me and Bobby could go and explore it."

Robert laughed. "Well, perhaps it still is there—some of it, at least. But we'll never see it, little man. It's buried forever beneath that great pile of stones!"

"Someone might dig it up?"

"I doubt it—they'd have to move the Minster first!"

While they walked, Robert was peering into deep, dark windows, for the names emblazoned on boards and painted on stucco meant nothing to him. The shop he wanted was on a corner a little way up, a deeply jettied medieval building abutting a neighbor with a straight

Georgian face. The boys drew his attention to it, seeing before he did the ship's figurehead bent beneath the upper story, thrusting the whole building forward, like the prow of a ship, into the street. The female figure, with its strangely narrow face and breasts, tapered like a mermaid into the massive supporting beam.

Fascinated, full of questions, both Liam and Bobby demanded to be picked up so they could touch the smooth wooden figure.

A female voice, old and high and quavery, startled them all. Sharply the boys withdrew exploring fingers, and for a split second even Robert thought the figure had spoken. Then came a peal of merry laughter, and a wizened face peered around the jamb of a deeply shadowed doorway.

"You want to know about my little mermaid?" With a twinkle in her eye, the old lady set down her knitting, and, sure of her young audience's awed attention, she said: "She came off a sailing ship, she did, more than a hundred years ago. She's crossed the oceans, faced storms and tempests, and been becalmed in the Coral Seas. She's seen whales and sea serpents, and defied all the monsters of the deep—she knows more than I'll ever know, nor you too, young sirs, I shouldn't wonder!"

Round-eyed, Liam whispered: "Is she really a mermaid?"

"She is that."

"But how did she get here?"

For a second the old lady's eyes widened, and she lowered her voice; she seemed suddenly very young. "Nobody knows."

"Was it magic?" whispered Liam, while his little brother stared in open-mouthed wonder.

"I think so," she nodded.

Then she smiled at Robert and winked, and her face creased into a thousand tiny wrinkles. He coughed to hide his amusement; ordering a garden seat after that was something of an anticlimax.

There were samples of the wire-workers' trade everywhere, but the old lady showed him the chair on which she had been sitting in the doorway, insisting he try it for comfort and strength. It looked too light and fragile to last, but it bore his weight easily. Impressed, Robert decided the size he wanted, placed his order, and gave the address to which it was to be delivered.

He was almost sure his sons were still too impressed to notice; once outside, his suspicions were confirmed. "Was she a witch?" Liam asked in hollow tones.

"Of course not—she's just an old lady."

"I think she's a witch."

"Yes," Bobby confirmed. "A witch."

Afraid they might have nightmares, Robert relented. "Well, all right then, but a nice witch. A good witch, not a bad one."

Satisfied with that, the two boys were ready for the boat trip and their promised ices.

THIRTEEN

*R*obert had dinner with them the next day, leaving to catch the late afternoon train for London. He would spend the rest of the week at headquarters in Hounslow, he said, before rejoining the main body of the regiment for field exercises on Salisbury Plain. Despite political uncertainty, summer's maneuvers promised to be too intense to allow for much leave of absence; but he would see them again as soon as he could.

Louisa's eyes were troubled as she watched his tall figure receding beneath the trees. "Do you think it will come to anything?" she asked Edward.

"Who knows? According to the papers, the government seems to be trying to play the situation down. But this Kruger fellow sounds like such a hothead, I don't think he wants to listen." Edward squeezed her hand reassuringly. "If he does provoke a war, I can't see it lasting long. A handful of farmers against a well-trained army? He doesn't stand a chance!"

With a short, nervous laugh, Louisa agreed. "And our people out there have to be protected, I suppose. But still," she reflected with a sudden shiver, "they were only farmers last time, weren't they? Where was that place they beat us before?"

"Majuba Hill," he said quietly, "in 'eighty-one." Trying to lighten the atmosphere, he forced a smile. "How on earth do you remember that? You were no more than a child."

"I was fourteen. And I do remember it." Hoisting the baby onto her hip, she turned and went into the house.

Torn between a need to reassure her and the desire to have Robert firmly occupied elsewhere and for a considerable time, Edward followed more slowly. But this visit had gone much better than the last, he thought; and among the Bainbridge anecdotes had emerged a nugget of firsthand information which explained much regarding the failure of

Tempest's as a business. Edward had heard the gossip, of course but, true to his principles, had refused to believe it; in this case however, sad though it was, "common knowledge" was right: Arthur Bainbridge *was* a gambler, a heavy and compulsive one by Robert's reckoning, and he must have seen enough of them to judge. So, thought Edward, either Arthur was spending the profits, or Rachel was honoring his debts; whichever way it was, no fortune was vast enough and no business strong enough to withstand that particular vice for long. They were heading for bankruptcy, that much was certain, and judging by his own increase in orders over the last few years, the word was out already.

"I'll make a point of seeing Dick tomorrow," he said to Louisa. "If things are as bad as they seem at Tempest's, I don't think he'll hesitate over my offer."

"I should think he'll be very relieved," she replied. "Jobs are not so plentiful these days."

"Nor are good workers," Edward grinned. "I'll be getting a bargain if he agrees. And what's more, I like him; we work well together. You can never be sure with a stranger."

Louisa strolled out into the garden and sank thankfully into one of the recently vacated chairs. Although the sun was well past the meridian, it was very close and hot, even in the shade. She let Tisha struggle down from her knee and smiled as the child immediately held up her arms to Edward.

"She's tired."

"I'm not surprised," he said, "in this heat." Slipping off his linen jacket, Edward loosened his tie and sat down next to Louisa. He lifted the little girl onto his knee, quite unperturbed by the tiny fingers which explored his face as thoroughly as they did his waistcoat pockets. He let her listen to the ticking of his watch, secure in its silver casing; but, afraid the child might stab herself, removed his tiepin and handed it to Louisa.

"Poor Rachel," she said musingly, her eyes on Tisha.

"You can sympathize?"

"Oh, yes. She was always so demanding, so much the child, you see. It was the moon she wanted, Edward—and sixpence to go with it. Money, clothes, romance—that's what she thought she was getting when she ran off with poor Arthur. I don't know who got the worst of the bargain, though."

The depth of compassion in her voice touched him. Rachel had been no friend to either of them, and he was sure her propensity for malice had blackened Louisa's name in quarters which might otherwise have remained ignorant and friendly. In the present situation she could have been forgiven for gloating; since Albert Tempest's demise, however, that root of fear and loathing had withered and died, and her own suffering seemed to have killed any latent desire for revenge.

The exploration of his pockets had ceased. He glanced down at the golden head nodding against his chest; with thumb in mouth, Tisha was falling asleep. Easing her more comfortably against his arm, Edward leaned back, regarding Louisa through half-closed lids. After the inevitable tension of the last two days she looked tired but relaxed, lazily wafting the heavy air with a painted paper fan. With a faint sigh she unbuttoned the high neck of her broderie anglaise blouse and slowly pushed back the sleeves, revealing skin pale gold and freckled from hours spent gardening under an afternoon sun. Beautiful like a rose, Edward thought, seeing soft pink lips and cheeks and the damp little tendrils which framed her face like curling bronze leaves. He was suddenly flooded with love and contentment, felt he could have extended that moment forever: the warmth of the sun and the child in his arms, scents of earth and grass and growing things, the boys' light voices in the orchard, and Louisa, beautiful, embodying all of it.

As though she read his mind, she looked at him, reached out her hand, and touched his own. With a soft, sad smile she said, "I'm so glad I've got you."

The next morning Edward sent a note around to his old apprentice and met him by arrangement in the saloon bar of a public house just off Walmgate. It was a rambling place full of tiny, low-ceilinged rooms, darkened like the varnish on paintings centuries old by decades of tobacco smoke and jostling shoulders. The place was popular, for the food, like the beer, was good and reasonably priced; Edward often took his midday meal in the dining room behind the main bar. After a glass of light ale, he stood Dick a hearty portion of the landlady's specialty, smiling with benign satisfaction as he watched his young companion tucking into the steaming steak and kidney pudding.

Dick's gratitude at the offer of a job was effusive, his sense of relief quite patent; he had, he said, been looking out for another place for quite some time.

"I've been thinking for weeks that it couldn't last much longer—my job, at any rate. I mean, we're running out of everything, and no fresh supplies coming in—we used the last of the gold leaf a fortnight since. I've just been waiting for Mrs. B. to tell me that's it. Every time she comes down, I think she's going to say something, and she's down nearly every day lately. Still," he said with a shrug, "the printing side seems all right—ticking over, at least."

"Yes, I think she's clinging on to that," Edward agreed. "Although she'd have done better to let it all go—sell it—a year back." He sighed and shook his head. "I'm sorry—it's sad to see an old, established firm go to the wall like that. And I'm sorry I couldn't offer you anything sooner, Dick. But I had my own affairs to straighten out, and I needed to be sure my business would stand another man's wages."

"I'm glad you decided it could, Mr. Elliott—I really am."

Edward smiled. "Oh, yes, I'm quite certain now. The thing is—when can you start?"

"I wish I could say tomorrow." The lad grinned, mopping up the last of his gravy with a thick slice of bread. "But it'll have to be next week. I'll have to give notice."

"Yes, of course. Do it right."

As their plates were cleared, Edward glanced at his watch, asking whether Dick had time to see his workshop; after a moment's hesitation he nodded, and the two men left by the pub's back door, threading their way through the maze of alleys which led into Piccadilly.

"I'd like to move," Edward confessed. "Get a place more central to town. This place is cheap to rent, and handy for me living at Clementhorpe, but it's out of the way for people who like to call in person. Not many will venture through this little lot," he said with a laugh, indicating the squalid tenements and warehouses which backed onto the Foss, "which means they have to come the long way round by the castle—and it's too far for some. But who knows, perhaps the two of us can build things up, and maybe next year we'll talk about a workshop in town."

"I'll do my best," Dick promised as the alley widened out into a cobbled street. "You can count on me, Mr. Elliott."

"I'm sure I can, Dick," Edward murmured, his voice trailing off as he spotted Louisa waiting for him outside the workshop. Bobby was sitting on the step, drumming his heels in the dust, and Tisha, placid as ever, sat like a little doll in her perambulator.

Instantly he knew something was wrong; in his alarm he hastened his steps, forgetting the young man by his side, not thinking how much or how little his former apprentice knew about Louisa and their private life.

"Have you been waiting long?" he asked, unlocking the door. "Yes, darling, hello," he said to Tisha, waving her arms and demanding his attention.

Louisa smiled at Dick, hanging back as they went inside; Edward hurriedly introduced her as "Mrs. Elliott" and asked the young man to wait. While they went into the cool workroom, Dick squatted on his haunches, talking to the children outside.

"I'm afraid your father's ill," Louisa said gently, handing him a telegram message. "I thought I'd better open it—just in case . . ."

"Yes," he murmured. "Yes, you did quite right." He sat down, reading and rereading the few words sent from the vicarage by his father's elderly housekeeper. A strange woman, he thought, and found himself ridiculously moved by her unexpected kindness in sending for him. "So she does know," he said, voicing the thought out loud. "I often wondered whether she did."

"What does she know?" Louisa asked.

"Who I am." He smiled.

Faced with the problem of having to leave his work and go to Lincolnshire, Edward was momentarily at a loss; it was Louisa who solved the problem for him. Calling Dick inside, she put the situation to him and asked whether he could possibly take over there and then.

"No, of course he can't," Edward said, and, chewing his lip, the young man shook his head.

"But there's so little work for me to do at the moment," he put in, "I'm sure I could ask to do half time. I can't see Mrs. B. objecting to that—she won't have to pay me so much. And I could start work here as soon as I finish there."

"And I could be here for a few hours each day," Louisa added. "To see to any inquiries and do the paperwork. If you could show us the ropes, Edward—me this afternoon and Dick this evening—you could get off to Lincoln in the morning."

"I've got a better idea," Dick said. "Show us both now. It's not going to make much difference whether I go back to work this afternoon or not."

Within a couple of hours, Louisa had grasped most of what she would be able to do, and, with a list of notes and instructions pinned above Edward's desk for reference, she prepared to leave. Bobby relinquished his paper and glue with a great show of reluctance, and Tisha cried piteously as Edward handed her back to her mother.

"I'll have your things all ready for you," Louisa said as they parted, "and a meal on the table at eight. Try not to be late. You'll need a good night's sleep."

"I'll be home at eight," he promised with a smile. "Thanks, love."

He watched them down the street and then went back inside. Dick was working steadily, as though he had been there for years; as he glanced around at Edward, however, there was a quirky little smile playing at the corner of his mouth.

"Do you know something, Mr. Elliott? I'd no idea you were a family man—no idea at all!"

"Oh, yes," Edward said after a slight hesitation. "I have been for a long time."

Since his first visit six years before, Edward had returned several times as a guest at the vicarage. Each time he dreaded calls by wealthy parishioners or members of his father's family; and try as he might, although they were also his own kin, Edward could never quite see it that way.

Without doubt, the rest of the family were unaware of his existence, and every instinct warned Edward that should they meet, he would not be welcomed, either as relative or friend. So far his visits had been unmarred by any such embarrassment, but with his father as ill as he evidently was, the situation was ripe for change. He dreaded it, dreaded having to introduce himself, having to explain his presence in the house or—God forbid!—at the bedside of a dying man.

The train rattled its way across the flat Lincolnshire countryside, and with every click of the wheels Edward urged it on. If death was waiting, let it wait a little longer.

With a heavy heart he alighted at the halt and began the long walk into the village. Fields which were bleached and fallow on his first visit now whispered with verdant life. A tiny breeze rippled across meadows and leafy, waving wheat, relieving in some small measure the unremitting heat of the sun. As he approached the imposing main gateway to the hall, Edward saw a pony trap emerge, two ladies in floating pastel finery seated in the back. With a feeling of dismay he watched their parasols bobbing all the way down the road into the village; as he passed the church his suspicions were confirmed: the same trap and its driver stood beneath trees on the vicarage drive. For a moment he almost walked on; then, with a deep breath, turned in at the gate, after the hot June sun glad of the drive's cool green shade.

To his relief, as the door opened there was no sign of the ladies; with a warning glance the housekeeper greeted him quietly, took his small suitcase, and showed him into the study.

"We have visitors," Mrs. Pepperdine said with an apologetic smile. "The squire's wife and daughter. If you'd rather not meet them, Mr. Elliott, just stay here. They won't disturb you, and I doubt they'll stay very long."

Edward thanked her and asked about his father. As he had suspected, it was his heart; for some time the old man had been subject to small attacks, but this latest one, she told him gravely, had been very serious.

The vicar's doctor, she said, had confined him to bed, and for once he was pleased to stay there.

Left alone, Edward browsed among his father's books, picked one at random, a treatise on Romanesque styles, and sat down to read; but the words jazzed before his eyes and he laid it down again, leaning his head against the chair's smooth leather wing. Sunlight streamed through mullioned windows, and in those beams a million dust motes moved in slow, hypnotic pavanes. A clock ticked in the silence, and above his head somewhere a floorboard creaked. In this room he was always reminded of that first visit, in the autumn of the year Louisa went to Ireland. The trees outside in full summer leaf had been yellowing then, especially the beeches; he remembered watching the leaves fall, one by one, remembered his heart's sadness, and found it echoed now.

He and his father had talked for what seemed like minutes but must have been hours; and afterward, sitting in silence, divided only by a beam of Indian summer sun, Edward had been struck by the separate facets of one character as reflected in different eyes. Who ever knew one person entirely? he wondered, thinking of all the people in his life, the praise and blame, sins and virtues. His mother, Mary Elliott, Louisa and her sisters, Robert Duncannon, his own father . . .

He heard the ladies leaving; the polite murmur of voices as they were shown to the door reached his ears, but not their words. Edward imagined them composing their faces, gesturing with feigned regret, and his inner tension mounted. The housekeeper came in and offered him tea, but little comfort: the nurse had said her patient was exhausted by his visitors and must rest for a while.

At seven, just before dinner, Edward was finally allowed upstairs. He stood for a moment on the broad landing, bracing himself. The housekeeper knocked and went in first, stood back with a smile, and let him pass. In that pleasant, comfortable room, shining with late evening sun, his father lay in bed, well propped by pillows, alert and smiling despite his obvious frailty. Relief washed through Edward's veins, taking fear and tension with it; his whole body felt ridiculously soft and pliable as he crossed the room.

"Good to see you, my boy," the old man whispered; and as Edward bent to take his hand, he saw the brightness of unshed tears. "Silly woman shouldn't have sent for you—long journey for nothing—but I'm glad you're here."

"I'm glad to be here," Edward replied. "It's been too long. I should have come before. I wish you'd told me you weren't well."

Very slowly the old man shook his head. "I was all right, then suddenly—" his hand dropped to the bed. "They say I mustn't talk, so make yourself comfortable and tell me all your news."

Although they exchanged letters regularly, Edward had not been to Lincolnshire for almost a year; Mary Elliott's illness and subsequent unheavals had led him to cancel one visit and postpone a later invitation. It had been impossible for him to come, yet he regretted not doing so. With the business very much at the forefront of his mind, he talked enthusiastically for several minutes, extolling Dick's virtues and outlining plans for the future. While he was explaining Louisa's part in helping during the coming few days, the nurse came in on a sharply efficient rustle of starched apron and headdress and announced firmly that visiting time was over for the day.

Vulnerable in his nightshirt, the vicar raised his eyes to Heaven and submitted to her ministrations. As she began plumping the pillows and tucking in a stray inch of sheet, Edward smilingly left the room.

Next morning, however, with a fire brightly blazing to combat the room's early chill, and sherry to fortify them, they had a much longer conversation. It was still rather one-sided, as the vicar was not supposed to tire himself, but he wanted to know about Louisa and the children, and Edward was eager to describe their progress over the preceding months. Quite naturally he concentrated on the positive aspects of their life: the cottage, its garden, his contentment; but in a momentary lapse he mentioned Robert, suddenly realizing that the matter of his return was not one he had cared to mention in his letters.

"I'm not at all sure we made the right decisions—and the matter of the children worries me very much."

Edward stood up and moved about the room; paused by the window, staring out over lawns and flowerbeds toward the beechwoods beyond. "You said in one of your letters that the move from Gillygate would be good for Louisa, yet at the time I could only see the financial sense of it. And I must confess I thought her insistence on a garden was something of a whim. I was wrong, though: it's been the saving of her. She's quite her old self again."

But Edward was silent for such a length of time after that, so locked in contemplation, that his father said: "What is it that's bothering you? You mentioned the children just now . . ."

"Yes." Edward sighed, knowing they were a subject he had long needed to discuss. The matter of the deception, which had been so easily slipped into, and the problems Edward foresaw as a result, still nagged at a corner of his mind, yet to discuss it with Louisa was difficult, and with anyone other than his father, downright impossible.

"Whenever I try to talk it over with Louisa, all she will say is that their situation is not the same as mine was—and I accept that. I was fostered out, and my mother never found it convenient to acknowledge

me as her son until I was an adult. And even then," he added bitterly,
"her will managed to make it very ambiguous indeed!" He broke off.
"Oh, I'm sorry, I shouldn't be saying this to you—"

"Who else would you say it to? Go on."

"What I mean is this—I feel very strongly that Louisa's children should
know who their father is. Louisa's parents were not married, either, but
she knew her father, and what's more, *knew that he was her father*. She
doesn't seem to understand the importance of that. Of course our situation is complicated by the fact of my presence in the house—the fact
that I love them dearly and wish to God that Robert Duncannon would
just—"

"What? Die?"

"No—no, I don't wish him dead. I just wish he could relinquish his
hold on Louisa. I wish," he added miserably, "that she didn't still love
him."

George Gregory smiled and shook his head. "I don't see the logic
there. What makes you think she still loves him?"

"Oh, lots of little things—things she says and does, seeing them
together." With a certain dry amusement, Edward embarked upon the
story of his proposal. It embarrassed him, but only in the telling did
he feel his father would understand.

For a long time the old man said nothing; then, musing aloud on
the problem, he remarked on the strangeness of women. "They can be
very oblique, you know. It's their vulnerability, I suppose—makes them
tell you only what they think you want to hear. Yet they imagine you
should understand the rest," he said with a chuckle, "and are offended
when you don't.

"But I've heard some rum stories in my time," he went on. "Confes-
sions from women of all ranks which would turn your hair. They will
reveal to a clergyman not only their souls, but sometimes the most
intimate details of their lives—desires and aspirations they wouldn't
dream of admitting to their husbands. And in effect, Edward," he added
weightily, "that's what you are. Without the benefit of a conjugal relationship, you stand—far more so than Robert—in the place of a husband, and as father to her children."

"But if that's so, why wouldn't she—?" He frowned in perplexity.
"You see, we've always been close, and . . ."

"But circumstances have changed—drastically. Her reasons may be
far less obvious than they appear. Perhaps she feels that she's accepted
too much from you; perhaps she needed time to give you something in
return. Something free and without obligation on either side—her time
and caring." Pausing while that point went home, the old man sipped

carefully at a fresh glass of sherry. "A question of too much, too soon. And she was still grieving then. You must understand," he added gently, "that the healing of the mind, unlike the body, can take a long, long time."

Responding to the wisdom of personal experience, Edward nodded, for a moment lost in contemplation of his father's words. "Yes, I can see that. She's much better—much calmer—than she was at the beginning of the year."

"A word of warning, however," the old man said, more gently still. "While I think I appreciate the reasons behind that rather peculiar proposal of yours, might I suggest you don't repeat it?"

Surprised, Edward scrutinized his father's face, finding concern tempered by a small spark of amusement. He frowned. "Why do you say that?"

"Well, my boy, think about it. If a proposal of marriage, with all it entails, is the highest compliment a woman can receive, your suggestion could be regarded as something of an insult. *I'll give you my name, but not myself.* Hmm?

"Oh, I'm sure it wasn't," he added kindly, overriding Edward's protests, "but it *might* have been, for all your altruistic motives. And another thing," he added seriously, "if the marriage was to have been performed in church, it would certainly be an insult to the sacrament."

"I doubt it would have been," Edward murmured, feeling reproved.

"I know you love Louisa," the old man said softly, "and I can't help wondering—don't you *want* to marry her?"

The unexpected question caught him on the raw. It was something Edward had often asked himself, and never yet had he come up with a satisfactory answer. It was bound so much in what he imagined Louisa felt for him and in her relationship with Robert Duncannon. Thrusting his hands deep in his trouser pockets, he strode about the room; twice he opened his mouth to speak and twice thought better of it.

"I *don't* want to change things," he said at last, knowing it was near enough the truth. "I don't want to upset the balance of what we have already. I'm happier now than I've ever been, with my own home and family and my own business. Louisa and I make good, affectionate companions—were it not for the children, I'd be content to leave it that way."

"Are you sure?"

"Of course I'm sure!" he retorted; but a second later he was shaking his head, resuming his seat in an attitude of despair. "No," he admitted, covering his face, "I'm not sure."

Not sure of Louisa, not sure of himself; and the path they trod was so precarious, their steps so uncertain, any resting place seemed preferable to the dizzy pinnacle he occasionally glimpsed ahead, to the agonizing depths he knew lay below. Nor was he sure whether his desire to consolidate their present position was merely symptomatic of age or a basic facet of his own cautious nature. Every time he thought about those hard-won gains, however, he was less and less inclined to risk them.

Expressing those thoughts, he heard his father sigh. "You speak as though life were a static thing," George Gregory said. "As though an idyllic moment could be preserved like a specimen in a bell jar. It can't. Specimens are dead; the very essence of life is that it moves and changes. Children grow up, situations alter, people die."

"But I'm afraid of losing what happiness we have! When I look back, when I see how barren my life was before, I know I can't go back to that."

With all the patience of age, the older man shook his head. "So you would clutch what you have and smother it?"

"No!"

"Then move forward—have faith. Let the Holy Spirit guide you, as you were guided once before, when you first came here. The devil doesn't have things all his own way, you know," he added gently. A moment later, with a whimsical smile, he said: "And sometimes, Edward, through the heat of all we desire for ourselves, the still small voice does speak . . . if only we have the ear to listen."

Recognizing the words of a familiar hymn, Edward smiled and felt his tension dissipate. "It doesn't always say what we want to hear, though, does it?" he asked ruefully.

"Have faith," George Gregory said again. "Have patience. You gave me a new lease on life—but I have a feeling it's running out at last. Oh, don't worry, I'm not afraid. And I do believe that lease was only intended to cover the period when you needed me most."

A cold chill touched Edward's heart. "Please, Father, don't say that."

"*Change,* Edward; *nothing stays the same.*" Leaning across to his son, the old man touched his arm. "Your life," he said intently, "has many years to run. Don't waste those years."

Despite his father's fatalistic acceptance of approaching death, during the days of Edward's visit his improvement was marked enough to earn even the nurse's grudging approval. As his own anxiety began to subside, Edward convinced himself that the old man had had no more than a bad scare, that he was destined to survive a few more years: he could not abide the thought of losing such friendship.

With hours of unaccustomed leisure at his disposal, he took to strolling each afternoon across the fields and through the beechwoods, in a green dappled silence where nothing much stirred bar the leaves and an occasional muted flutter of wings. He used the time for thought and reflection, realizing for the first time in months how busy he had been, how taken up with immediate practical problems in York. Beneath all that activity, the fears and apprehensions revealed to his father had been buried, surfacing in dreams and nightmares, making his heart race uncomfortably for the most trivial of reasons. He had even been unaware of how tired he was; yet, strangely, with the cessation of effort fatigue descended like a lead weight, leaving him depressed and joyless, incapable of summoning more than flat relief at his father's evident recovery.

He walked and read and slept, astonishingly well and without disturbing dreams. By the end of the week he was sufficiently recovered in spirit to be slightly amused at the reversal in roles: he had come to cheer and comfort his ailing parent and ended by being comforted himself.

On the Saturday afternoon as he prepared to leave, however, Edward was conscious only of grave unease. With the aid of a stick, the frail old man managed the few yards to Edward's bedroom, sitting in a wicker chair while his son completed his packing. He was fully dressed for the first time, looking almost his old self in dog collar and clerical black, but Edward could not rid himself of the feeling that he might be seeing his father for the last time. It made his promises to return soon sound hollow and insincere, at least to himself; he found himself repeating them several times.

"Now I've got Dick, it won't be as difficult," he said yet again. "I should be able to get down one Saturday for an overnight stay at least. Just as soon as we've got the business sorted out. It shouldn't take long."

"Don't worry, I shall be all right. I'm glad we had these few days—it's done us both a power of good. I'll be up and about in no time."

The words were said, Edward felt, to ease the parting; the hands around his were papery and cold, the smile forced, the light gray eyes suspiciously bright. For a moment the chill and empty years of childhood engulfed Edward like a tidal wave; he embraced his father awkwardly, hurt by the frailty of age.

"Take good care of him," he murmured gruffly to Mrs. Pepperdine as she saw him to the door. "And please—if . . ." He could not complete the sentence; but she nodded sadly. He sensed that even her optimism was slipping, that she too had seen the shadows gathering around his father.

As he walked down the drive, Edward was already plotting ways and means of returning, and soon; but on his way to the train he found himself noting each bend in the road, every twisted tree, all the small features of that undramatic landscape, as though he might not see them again. He thought of death and burial, wondering whether it would be politic to attend his father's when the time came; the family would all be there, and his identity would fall into question, causing ripples of unrest if not a downright furor. He shivered away from it.

When he arrived home, it was almost dark, night clouds gathering early with a suggestion of rain. Along the river the air was moist already, and the unaccustomed chill struck through to his bones. Through the undrawn parlor curtains he saw a lamp was lit, and pushing the gate open with its familiar, uncured squeak, he saw Louisa jump up with a wave and a welcoming smile; she was at the door before he reached it.

Over a pot of tea in the parlor, she chatted eagerly about the week's achievements and minor hitches, then, sensing his tiredness, suddenly broke off; she would explain in detail the next day, she said, when he was rested.

He appreciated her sensitivity. Although he was relieved to be home, there was no joy in it; the fatigue which had dogged him all week seemed denser than ever, blunting everything except the desire to get to bed and sleep. It was an effort to smile, an even greater one to speak. He managed to say his father was much better, then relapsed into silence, his gaze blankly surveying an abandoned pile of sewing on the opposite chair.

He stirred as Louisa rose to her feet to close the curtains. "I'm sorry," he murmured, drinking the last of his cooling tea. "I'm not much company, am I? We'll talk tomorrow."

"It's Sunday," she averred. "We've got all day." Her hand reached out to touch his hair; quite unexpectedly she leaned over the chair back and hugged him, laying her cheek next to his. "I've missed you," Louisa whispered. "The house felt so strange at night, I hardly slept a wink."

"And I've done nothing but sleep," Edward said dryly. Her skin felt soft and warm against his own; he was conscious one moment that his jaw was rough and needed a shave and in the next that he wanted to be in bed with her, wrapped around and inside all that warmth and silkiness. Her hand lay over his heart; afraid she would feel its frantic pounding, he lifted it, very slowly, to his lips and held it there. For what seemed an inordinate length of time Edward fumbled in his mind for every mental switch used over the years; none worked. He wanted her, needed her so badly he ached with it.

"Dearest," Louisa whispered, "you're hurting my hand."

Abruptly he released her fingers. "I'm sorry."

"What's wrong?" she asked, kneeling in front of him, looking up with such tender appeal into his face that he had to close his eyes. "What is it? Your father?"

"No," he replied, more sharply than intended, "I'm just tired." The celibacy he had embraced rose in his mind to mock him. In that moment he envied Robert Duncannon and every philanderer he had ever despised; envied their physical knowledge, that easy familiarity which began, he was sure, with some basic instinct he did not possess. He wanted her, but did not know how to say so, even less how to show what he felt. He knew neither how to begin nor where to end; he was afraid of rejection, but most of all he was frightened of his own inadequacy.

Leaning forward, Edward took the hands which rested so trustingly across his knees; for a moment he held them tight within his own.

"Go to bed," he said tersely. "We'll talk about it some other time."

FOURTEEN

*D*uring the following few weeks, Edward was busier than ever. With Dick's departure, Tempest's ceased to operate the bookbinding side of its business, while old customers, recalling Edward Elliott's expertise and good service, flocked in with fresh orders. It meant late hours and full Saturdays for both men, while Louisa, with little to do in the garden at that time of year except sit and watch it grow, pulled her weight by keeping the accounts up to date.

The early heat wave which had descended in June gave way the following month to electric storms and days of continuous, torrential rain. It was chilly and damp even in the house, and Louisa was glad to sit at the kitchen table with her pile of ledgers in the quiet hour after lunch. She often thought about Edward's strangeness that evening of his return, and his tense, uncommunicative silence since, attributing it in generous moments to natural anxiety and sheer pressure of work. Most of the time, however, she felt hurt and rejected. During the week he was generally too tired to talk, and his Sundays were taken up with the usual trips to Sunday school with the boys, evening service at the new church on Scarcroft Road, and afternoon walks when the weather was fine. Sometimes they went downriver, through meadows and fields toward Bishopthorpe, and sometimes to the cemetery with flowers for the family grave. Louisa always saved a single bloom for little Victoria Tempest, placing it on that neglected plot in the Nonconformist section with a short prayer for her innocent soul. She tried to be Christian about the other occupant mentioned on that granite obelisk, but other than a bare acknowledgment of his need for a lifetime's prayer, Louisa could barely bring herself to look at his name.

Whichever way they walked to the cemetery, either through St. George's Fields and over Blue Bridge, guarded by its massive Crimean guns, or along the main road, Louisa's past caught up with her in other ways.

Blue Bridge and New Walk were always littered with splendidly attired young soldiers out on Sunday leave, soldiers whose popularity with local factory girls increased noticeably as talk of war touched everyone's lips. Louisa would look at the laughing groups, hear the flirtatious, sometimes ribald comments, see the tender looks which passed between isolated couples on the riverbank, and think of herself and Robert and all the others who had frequented the Bainbridge house just a few short years before. Although these were a new generation and a different class, the situation was not so far removed from her own experience; she often wondered why that year seemed a whole lifetime past. Remembering Tommy Fitzsimmons and Hugh, and the party where Robert had kissed her that very first time; recalling Rachel and Arthur and gauche, tactless Sophie, still unmarried, but perhaps the only one with illusions still intact. It made her feel tender and bitter at the same time, while Edward knew none of it, simply steering her and the children around boisterous groups, taking her arm with proprietary care.

Walking by Castle Mills and along Fishergate, Louisa was dogged by memories of Dublin, her eyes drawn to the little public house owned by Moira and Harris. In some ways she would have liked to see them, but a deep sense of embarrassment prevented her from going in.

She was thinking of Moira one damp and windy afternoon while Tisha and Bobby were resting, thoughts prompted by a midday letter from Robert in which she and Harris were mentioned. The letter lay open on the kitchen table beside a stack of Edward's invoices; even while she worked Louisa was distracted by its contents, her mind straying toward Moira and those ever-present threatenings of war, like thunder in the distance.

Disturbed by the squeak of the garden gate, Louisa automatically glanced out of the window; surprise at an unexpected caller intensified to sheer amazement when she saw who it was. Armed with a large furled umbrella, dressed in smart maroon and black with a matching, beribboned hat, Moira was approaching the front door in the manner of a wary recalcitrant bearing a flag of truce.

It was a strange interview, Louisa thought afterward as she washed the china cups and plates of their token afternoon tea, although less awkward than their previous meeting in Gillygate. The gap of almost two and a half years had given both a chance to consolidate their altered roles, to approach each other with some semblance of ease, and Moira's arrival this time as a kind of supplicant went some way toward redressing a most uneven balance.

The first time they had both been aware of Moira's great change in status, of the leap from servant to wife of established property owner; most of all were they aware of her new and unassailable respectability. In the face of Louisa's fall it had created a barrier that neither was able to surmount. It was not that Moira was unsympathetic; it was simply that she was used to looking out for her own interests and had had no practice at defending others. Louisa understood that, even while it saddened her. She had not expected to see Moira again.

At that time, Louisa recalled, she had been pregnant but not obviously so; quite naturally her condition had not been mentioned to the younger woman. Now it amused her, as she replaced cups and saucers to the dresser, to recall her expression at seeing Tisha for the first time. Bobby had shouted, as he tended to do when he thought he had been up there long enough, and she had gone unthinkingly to bring both children down. Moira's first reaction to the little boy was to remark upon his likeness to his father; then, noticing the baby in Louisa's arms, her eyes and mouth had formed three round Os of astonishment. Tisha was so round and fair and perfect, she could have been anyone's child, and Louisa quite deliberately left the unspoken questions hanging in the air. She fielded all references to Edward and their relationship with consummate ease, actually enjoying the younger woman's consternation, the recently acquired manners which prevented her from asking outright. She was happily sure that Moira had gone away with the impression that Louisa was now respectably married. Honor had been in some small measure avenged; Louisa thought she might even return the call after a decent interval.

In fact, she would definitely return it. If war was declared, which seemed increasingly likely, Harris would be recalled to the colors, leaving Moira to fend alone. That she would do so quite capably Louisa had no doubt; nevertheless, she felt sorry for her, understanding the motive which had driven Moira to call and ask such a small and unnecessary favor.

If Harris was going to war, Moira said, then she wanted to be sure he was in the best and safest place; and in her opinion that place was by Major Duncannon's side. She knew him and trusted him; nobody else would do. The trouble was, Harris himself was too proud to write and ask for his old position; he said it wasn't right to trade on old comradeship; if the major wanted him, he would ask for him, and that was that.

Knowing Robert as she did, Louisa felt there was hardly any need to ask; he had always trusted Harris implicitly and would pull every string imaginable to get him back. Louisa promised to pass on the request and did not elaborate upon their present relationship.

Later, idly watching the boys at play while she prepared vegetables for their evening meal, Louisa wondered whether Moira regretted her own lack of children. It could have been imagination, but while they talked, Louisa thought she had detected a certain sad envy in the younger woman's glance; the irony of it made her sigh.

For Edward the weeks continued to come and go with frightening speed. His intentions to return to Lincolnshire were put off, first from necessity and then, as work began to even out, from a half-acknowledged reluctance to relive what he had gone through before. Almost as an antidote to reflection, he concentrated on the business and talked of little else. Appeasing his conscience in regular, weekly letters which were full and bright and overly cheerful, it did not occur to him that he rarely mentioned Louisa until in one reply his father remarked on it.

Folding the letter back into its envelope, Edward sighed. Since that last visit, with its disturbing aftermath, he realized he had been neglecting her, deliberately putting pressure of work between them. Although she had not complained, he suddenly felt guilty. After all, he reasoned, that inner conflict was not of her making.

He went outside to where she was half-sitting, half-lying along the seat Robert had ordered for her on his last visit. Edward was so used to seeing her there on fine evenings that it surprised him to recall what a length of time had elapsed since then. Although, as a somewhat costly present, the seat still annoyed him, he had to admit that it was comfortable and a fitting match for the bronze wire rosary he had himself installed across the path. The mass of blooms it carried were fading now, their scent slightly musty after a late-afternoon shower of rain.

"I'm sorry," he said, looking down at her; and as she laid aside her book, her gentle, inquiring smile caught most painfully at his heart. Wanting to kiss those soft lips, Edward tore his eyes away, knowing full well why he had been devoting so much time elsewhere.

"Sorry? What on earth for?"

"I seem to have been neglecting you," he said gruffly, seating himself as far away from her as possible.

"Oh, don't be silly—I know you've been busy."

"I'll take the day off on Saturday," he promised. "We'll go somewhere, take the children to the coast for the day. It will do us all good."

"That would be lovely," Louisa said with a sudden, dimpling smile; then, as another thought struck, she frowned. "But what about your father? I thought you were keen to get back to Lincolnshire?"

"He's much better—taking services again, so he must be feeling stronger. I'll go down later."

"Well, if you're sure. I don't mind waiting . . ."

"No, we'll have our day this week. See if you can get to the station and find out what day-trips are on. The children will enjoy it."

Louisa patted his hand as she rose to her feet. "And so will I," she said softly.

It surprised her to realize how much she was looking forward to that day out. Spirits which had been somewhat jaded suddenly bloomed into song; she found herself humming as she washed and ironed, scrubbed and cleaned; even the task of Edward's accounts, which had become less of a challenge as time went by, suddenly became interesting again. Children came and went, friends Liam had made at school, all home for the holidays and delighted to find a garden in which to play. They made a lot of noise, but Louisa tried to be benevolent, reminding herself that the orchard must be paradise compared to the streets in which they usually acted out their games. Only one thing really rankled: Liam had begun to object to his name, which had apparently caused unfavorable comment at school. It was different and "foreign." In front of his friends he wanted them to use his proper name, he said, which was not too hard for Louisa to remember to do, but impossible for Bobby. They had several fights over the matter.

Saturday dawned in debatable English-summer fashion; jerseys were packed as well as towels, and, armed with a couple of large umbrellas, they set out for Scarborough. It was the first Saturday in August, and the train was crowded with trippers, families and courting couples, all determined to brave the weather and enjoy themselves. At the coast an east wind was blowing off the sea; it made for a clear sky and plenty of sun, but it was sneakily chill, like unexpected blobs of ice in fizzy lemonade. They were glad of shawls and jerseys, and Louisa employed one of the umbrellas to shade her already freckled face from the sun. But it was a lovely day in every sense; Edward was more relaxed than she had seen him for a long time, stripping off his jacket and making sandcastles for the boys, rolling his trouser legs and paddling barefoot with Tisha in the shallow, retreating waves.

With tired eyes and tingling skin they sank gratefully into their second-class compartment, the rhythmic clickety-clack of the wheels soon soothing any latent fractiousness; within a very short time, all three children were fast asleep. An hour later, as the train slowed down in preparation for the long curving entrance into York, Edward began to wake them; but crossing Scarborough Bridge, Louisa's eyes looked back to the little apartment she had once shared with Robert. In the excitement of setting off she had forgotten it, and suddenly she wished she had not looked at all; the sight of that small bedroom window kindled violent memories.

As Louisa opened her eyes she caught Edward's still and steady gaze; it was as though he read her mind. Blushing furiously, she bent to gather the children's things, fussing unnecessarily with all the paraphernalia of their day out.

On the way home, Edward was very quiet.

The following Saturday he set off early for Lincoln, leaving Louisa feeling lonely and unsettled, unreasonably as though she had been deserted.

Determined not to be mawkish, she cooked breakfast for the children, getting them washed and changed, deliberately choosing a favorite dress for herself, one which was smart in an austere way, its slightly puffed sleeves a concession to current fashion.

During the week, Louisa did her shopping locally on Bishopthorpe Road, but on Saturdays she looked forward to the bustle of the market, keeping an eye open for bargains in linen or crockery. Thanks to the garden, she no longer needed to carry heavy bags of vegetables, but she bought fresh fruit, butter and eggs, and soft, crumbly farmhouse cheese. The children enjoyed the antics of peddlers and hucksters, and the promise of oranges and apples, and a bag of sweets if they were good.

It was a warm, hazy morning, lovely along the towpath with its trees in shady summer leaf, uplifting to all but the most jaded spirit; within minutes of setting forth Louisa began to feel better. The river was still and low, keelboats and sailing barges moored well out, gangplanks stretching precariously over the mud-flats like so many skeletal fingers; ahead, the iron span of Skeldergate Bridge was beginning to open for a tall-masted boat coming slowly downstream. The two halves of the bridge parted and rose, and the boys ran on to see it, clapping their hands delightedly as the boat sailed majestically through; the helmsman waved to them as he passed, which sent their spirits even higher. It was quite a disappointment to them to be ushered on up Skeldergate, to cross by the free bridge higher up.

The market was dusty and noisy, busy with carriers' carts coming in from the country, farm wagons full of produce, and townsfolk elbowing their way up and down the long rows of stalls which filled the city's broadest street. There were secondhand stalls overflowing with clothes and boots and shoes; old books, cheap jewelry, glassware, and tattered furniture; further on a full dinner service was being auctioned before a laughing, gaping crowd. The huckster tossed plates and cups into the air like a juggler, catching each piece deftly and throwing it on to his lugubrious assistant with the instructions to "Wrap it up, George!" The boys loved it. Louisa always had difficulty tearing them away; all the way around the market they shouted to each other in imitation, dissolving into fits of giggles at the grins of passersby. She quieted them eventually with a bag of luscious red cherries and the promise that they should share them the minute they got home, as long as they were good. From the butter market she bought two pounds each of butter and cheese and a dozen brown eggs and, with purchases almost complete, made her way through narrow Newgate and into the Shambles.

After the broad, sunny expanse of Parliament Street it was dark and shady, the jettied medieval buildings on either side almost meeting overhead and blocking out the sky. Nevertheless, it was warm and very crowded, with a press of customers queuing outside every butcher's shop. The unglazed windows were open to the street as they had been since medieval times, sectioned carcasses hanging from blackened oak lintels and displayed across every broad windowledge. The smell of raw meat was pervasive and unpleasant; Louisa breathed carefully through her mouth rather than her nose, while the boys pulled faces and fidgeted to go home.

With the Sunday joint purchased at last, well wrapped in newspaper at the bottom of her bag, Louisa gave the boys small parcels to carry and steered Tisha's perambulator toward High Ousegate and home. She paused at the crest of the hill to peer into a shop window at the price of children's boots and shoes and, setting off again, almost ran into a couple coming sharply out of the high-class tailor's next door.

"Well, that's that one settled," the plump, elegant woman said. "I promise Father and Rachel won't hear a word of it, but don't let's have any more silly talk of leaving."

Astonished, Louisa stopped, studying the man's profile, the sheepish, sideways glance at his companion before he took her arm to cross the road. Louisa turned sharply back to the shop window, not daring to look again until they were safely ahead. It was definitely Arthur Bainbridge; hangdog and dissipated, but undoubtedly him. And the woman was Sophie, less recognizable with her deep bosom and comfortable seat, although her voice was still that of a slightly breathless little girl. By the look of her as she steered her brother into Coney Street, Sophie was delivering some well-intentioned advice; but, recalling Robert's comments some two months previously, Louisa judged Arthur less than capable of taking it.

The feeling of defenselessness which had touched her at Edward's leaving returned in force that night. Everything she did seemed to underline his absence, from setting the table at teatime to preparing the children's bath. It was a job he generally undertook, afterward taking the children up for a lengthy bedtime story while she poured water for her own bath, usually a rather hurried affair.

Without him, however, the children were washed, dried, in their nightclothes, and in bed almost before they realized it; sulky faces accepted her goodnight kisses. Feeling almost as miserable and resentful as her children, Louisa went downstairs, determined to enjoy the peace of a leisurely bath.

Usually, conscious that Edward was waiting, she performed the essentials and was into her nightdress within half an hour; it was a pleasure indeed to lie and soak, to take time over hair and nails and pad about without clothes in front of the warm range. The last time she had looked at her body, really examined it, was with dismay at its gauntness; but months of contentment had wrought their changes. Breasts and hips had filled out again, and if her waist was also a little thicker, at least her skin showed few of the marks of childbearing. It was still silky and fine to the touch; unlike her hands, she noticed with a grimace. They were roughened by housework and gardening, no longer smooth and white like a teacher's; nor a mistress's, she thought with savage satisfaction.

The telltale squeak of the garden gate put her on instant alert; poised like a statue with her nightdress half on, Louisa stared at the closed gingham curtains as though sheer will would enable her to see through them.

The light tap at the door came like a releasing signal. Galvanized into action, she pulled on the white cambric nightdress and searched feverishly for her robe. It was missing. So was her shawl. Feeling immensely foolish, she opened the front door no more than an inch, hiding behind its reassuring solidity. There in the soft lilac dusk, looking as though he had materialized straight from Savile Row in an immaculate pale gray suit, stood Robert. His smile at least had the grace to seem a little uncertain.

Caught between a reluctance to keep him standing there, where the curiosity of any strolling passerby might be aroused, and a profound aversion to his seeing her in such a state of undress, Louisa hesitated and then invited him in.

"I'm not dressed. Go through into the parlor while I go upstairs and change."

He smiled quirkily, opened his mouth to say something, then evidently thought better of it. With a slow, sardonic nod, he indicated his agreement. Louisa fled.

Laying hat and gloves on the parlor table, Robert glanced around at white walls and gleaming furniture, the old sofa he remembered so well from the Gillygate days. Peering at a framed photograph of Mary Elliott, he smiled sadly and sat down, wondering what she would have thought of the present situation. Would she approve of Louisa hiding in Edward's shadow, or was her intention in leaving everything to her eldest daughter a hope that she might strike out on her own, as she herself had done? There was little likelihood of that now. He had the feeling that Louisa would defend her right to this place till death if necessary, facing flood or fire or acts of God, no matter who came or went from her life in the meantime.

The ambience of the cottage, its whole environment in fact, was so exactly right for her, Robert thought; he sensed it more each time he came. But was Edward the man she needed? The area of that relationship was like quicksand, so smooth on the surface, but subtly moving and shifting underneath; it was impossible to gauge the depth of it, difficult even to discern a safe approach.

Edward wanted her, he was convinced of that; what Louisa felt for him, however, was more difficult to judge. He wondered sometimes whether she had set Edward on a pedestal so high that in her mind the man was no longer reachable, or whether her rejection of himself as a lover had led to some ridiculous vow of nun-like celibacy. It might even have been a genuine fear of further childbearing, but, from what Letty had to say on the subject, Robert did not think so. It seemed to him that marriage, in Louisa's case, should be the cure for a plethora of ills, and he could not understand what it was that held her back.

At one time he had wondered whether, deep down, she still wanted him; but with the absolute rejection of every single approach, that theory was unhappily discounted. With concern for the future suddenly thrust upon him, however, Robert wished the situation were cut and dried, Louisa married and happy, the children legally protected, and himself on the far side of the world with a genuinely clear conscience. For too long he had been obsessed with what had happened in Dublin, and that theoretical freedom of Louisa's had tantalized him unbearably. He still wanted her, and no matter how many women came in between, he probably always would; at this juncture, however, ties and responsibilities were things he could do without.

He heard her feet on the stairs, then odd sounds from the kitchen, water being poured at intervals down the sink, then an odd scraping noise, like metal across stone. About to investigate, it suddenly occurred to him that he had interrupted Louisa in the course of a bath; reluctant to embarrass her further, he resumed his seat and waited, wondering where Edward could be.

Eventually, somewhat heated by her efforts, Louisa arrived with a neatly set tray of tea and cakes.

"So," she commented, in exactly the manner he had of beginning a conversation, "what brings you here tonight, and unannounced?"

"I'm on my way to Ireland," he said, watching her face, her hands, the strong tea describing an elegant arc between china spout and gold-rimmed cups. "I haven't been home for some time—thought I should organize a few days' leave before it became impossible."

"Impossible?"

"Well, more difficult," he amended, pursing his lips. "Things are getting busier all the time. It looks as though leave may be rather difficult to come by for a few weeks, so I thought I'd better come and see you. I'm not at all sure when there'll be another chance."

Although he was reluctant to explain in detail, his tone alerted her. Looking up at him, regarding him gravely with eyes which were wide and apprehensive, Louisa said: "War? Is it to be declared, then?"

"No, not necessarily. Not yet, at least. It simply means—" Breaking off suddenly, Robert ran his fingers through his hair. "As I was leaving," he said slowly, "I was given some rather confidential information. Not to be repeated," he sternly warned. "As from next week, the regiment will be on a war footing. We've been preparing, unofficially, for some time, but now it's official. We *have* to be ready in case Kruger goes too far—which he will eventually. At the moment it's just words: the consensus of opinion is that he's simply waiting for the spring—*their* spring, that is. It's winter now in South Africa. He's waiting for the new grass to grow—to feed his horses—and playing for time in the interval."

"And when will that be?" Louisa asked bleakly.

"A month—two, perhaps. Certainly by the end of October. I'm afraid it seems inevitable. I had to see you while I had the chance. But," he warned again, "you must not repeat what I've told you. If you should see Moira or Harris, you know *nothing*. He'll be getting his papers soon enough, I'm afraid."

She was very quiet and still, her eyes downcast, like someone who has received news of a bereavement, Robert thought. Then she left her chair and moved slowly away from him, absently touching ornaments and flowers in her progress round the room. In the soft twilight she moved with unconscious grace, like a ghost of her former self in a faded pastel dress paler than hair or skin. He was reminded of that afternoon in Blankney; the thin cotton dress worn for coolness; the absence of stiff, restricting underclothes; and suddenly his mouth and throat were terribly dry, his fine theories vanishing on a dangerous surge of desire.

"Where's Edward, by the way?" he asked, making quite a play of searching for cigars and matches.

She was standing by the window looking out at the river, its silvery surface reflecting the last of the evening light. Absently she answered: "Lincoln. Visiting his father—he hasn't been well."

"Who? Edward?"

"No, his father."

Drawing the curtains, Louisa came back to the hearth and, reaching up for the oil lamp on the mantelpiece, set it down on the small table between them. She bent to remove the glass globe and pipe, and Robert touched a match to the wick; as it flared into life they stared at each other across the array of gilded china. Her expression changed from soft, inward-looking sadness to sharp anxiety; blinking, she set the globe and pipe back with trembling fingers and stood upright. Very definitely Robert wanted her; determined as she was not to show it, he suspected she wanted him too. The idea set every sense on edge.

Blue spirals of smoke from his cigar were sucked into the heat from the lamp; above it her face and pastel blue dress shimmered like a mirage, just as tempting, and probably just as unreachable . . .

She cleared her throat and looked away. "Would you like some more tea?"

Locked in that joint awareness of Edward's absence, it seemed neither could think of a thing to say. The chink of china and teaspoons accentuated the silence; while in the distance, across the river probably, came the sound of raised voices and wild hilarity. Louisa commented on it, wondering aloud whether they had been to Harris's place. A moment later, still searching for conversation, she asked whether Robert would be able to ask for him back.

He nodded. "There are a few strings I can pull. I'd like him back for my own sake. If we're going to the Cape, I want someone with me I can rely on. But don't," he said with a smile, "tell him I said so."

There was another lengthy silence, broken by several of Louisa's sighs; eventually she voiced polite regrets that the children were in bed, that he was unable to see them. It seemed like a cue for him to leave.

Rather abruptly he said: "I need to talk to you, Louisa, which is why I'm here. I didn't expect to find you alone, but I intended to ask Edward if I might have some time with you. To talk."

"What about?" she asked suspiciously.

"Well, the fact that I'm going away, for one thing. I may be gone for some time—who knows? And before I go, I would really like to have things clear in my mind, so that I know," he added with deliberate emphasis, "exactly what it is I'm leaving behind."

"I see. And what—exactly—does that mean?"

"I want to know why you haven't married him," Robert stated baldly. "And I'd rather not be told—yet again—that it's none of my damn business, because I happen to think it is. That's all I want to know, but I do want an answer."

Fury and indignation leapt to her eyes. "Oh, you do, do you? That's all you want to know? Fine, but I can't see why it should concern you. The fact that I *don't want* to get married is *my* business. I don't have to explain my reasons to you, nor anyone else, come to that."

"Not even to Edward?" he asked, goading her.

"Leave him out of it!"

"But I can't," Robert said reasonably. "He lives with you. Some people might put a very unkind interpretation on that."

"You've got a filthy mind!"

"No, I haven't. I said *some* people—I didn't say me."

"If that's what you think—"

"I *don't,* Louisa. My thoughts on the matter are quite the opposite, I do assure you, although I can't help wondering why, in the circumstances. I mean, where does Edward fit into all this? If you're genuinely enamored of the single state, Louisa, why does he live here? As I understand it, you're not financially dependent on him, yet you must have to make certain concessions to his needs—cook his meals, iron his shirts—all the things a housekeeper could do quite well. Why should it be you, unless you feel so strongly that you can't live without him? And if you feel like that, why not marry him and put him out of his bloody misery? Are you so tied up with yourself, you can't see how much he wants you?" He paused to let that sink in, then said: "But you've never been able to see it, have you?"

Abruptly she turned away, leaning tensely against the mantelpiece. He could see her face in the mirror, mouth tight, eyes downcast, livid color along her cheekbones.

"It's not like that," she got out at last. "Not like that *at all*. He needs me."

"I'm well aware of that," he said with heavy irony, but the comment was lost. "I needed you once—very much. I still do," he murmured, though more to himself than her. Better than anyone, Robert knew he was in no position to offer Louisa an alternative. Living in quarters, moving around as he had been for months, and with the threat of war on the horizon, there was no place for a woman, let alone her children. Wanting her, he had had to learn to make do with pale imitations; but even sexual gratification, he realized with a sigh, seemed to be grabbed on the run these days, somewhere between Hounslow and Salisbury Plain. He wished, again, that they could make love once more, if only to erase forever that last night in Dublin, to know and be assured that she had forgiven him, that they could part friends.

"You needed me in the beginning," she admitted with great reluctance, "but not latterly. And certainly not now."

"Oh, you're wrong there," he whispered, taking a step toward her. "I need you now, Louisa, far more than I've ever needed you before. Not forever—perhaps never again. But once—just once—to prove you've forgiven me, darling, for all the stupid things I did . . ."

"No—no!" she exclaimed, hunching her shoulders against that tentative touch; but with all the instincts of a former lover, Robert knew the source of that bitter tension; he felt it in himself and burned for its release.

He could feel her body's heat, yet she was shivering as though frozen; wanting to hold her, caress her, soothe that hurting spirit into some kind of peace, he made her turn to face him and, seeing her distress, pulled her roughly into his arms. "I don't want to hurt you," he murmured against her hair, "and I don't want to come between you and Edward. If you want him, marry him, for God's sake, and with my blessing. Let him bring the children up as his—that doesn't matter anymore. Just come to bed with me now—one last time—and let us part friends. We owe each other that," he whispered, bending his mouth to her lips, "if nothing else . . ."

She could not have reacted more violently if he had struck her. With a gasp of outrage she twisted away, swept up his things, and flung them at the door. "Get out—now!"

"Louisa! For God's sake, I—"

"Get out—get back to your whores and loose women friends! Let *them* pander to your needs and leave me my self-respect!"

"You call it self-respect?" he demanded incredulously. "This farce? You can respect yourself, while that poor bastard pants like a dog for the want of you? Just who are you trying to convince!" While Louisa breathed hate and fury from the doorway, he gathered up his scattered things and straightened his tie. "It's no good playing the outraged virgin with me—I know you too well."

Her hand came up to strike him, but Robert blocked it, gripped her shoulders, and shook her hard. "If all I wanted," he got out between gritted teeth, "was a quick ride on a willing mount, believe me, I'd know where to go for it. But I didn't come here for that. I came because I *loved* you. And, God knows, because I wanted something straight and settled between us. What a fool I was!''

After he had slammed out of the house, Louisa stood where she was in the center of the room. Although he had done no more than shake her, she felt battered and boneless, like a loosely stuffed doll, her head a hollow, aching void. The clock chimed ten as she sank into her chair; then eleven, and there seemed no time between.

Eventually she dragged herself up, automatically straightening cushions and antimacassars before going to bed. With her hands on the sofa back, she noticed the stub of Robert's cigar in the empty hearth.

''I hate you,'' she said without passion and went upstairs.

She fell asleep that night in Edward's bed, curled up like a ball between sheets which still retained a faint, comforting smell of him.

FIFTEEN

T he sister of the boy who helped Louisa in the garden called after dinner the following day, to take the boys to Sunday school. It was a prearrangement, and they were ready and waiting in their best sailor suits, Tisha grizzling because she wanted to go wherever they were going, her ill temper increased by their teasing and Louisa's sharpness of manner. When Mary Ann asked if she might take the baby as well, it was with only cursory hesitation that Louisa agreed. The girl loved taking Tisha out in her pram, and Louisa trusted her; with flat relief she watched them go.

In the kitchen she eyed the dinnerpots with distaste. She had no inclination to wash them and, suddenly, no desire to stay within the confines of the cottage. Pushing the crockery to one side, she washed her hands and face and went upstairs to change her dress. Within minutes she was ready. In the orchard there were cornflowers and oxeye daisies growing wild; gathering a bunch, Louisa wrapped them in a piece of newspaper and set off for the cemetery.

Mary Elliott's name had been added to the memorial stone in the spring, below that of William and Elizabeth, together with the words "Her End Was Peace." The words always brought a lump to Louisa's throat, but for the first time she knelt by the grave and wept like one newly bereaved.

"Oh, Mamma, Mamma, what am I to do? What *am* I to do?"

No answer presented itself; there was not even a suggestion of the rose scent which had come so comfortingly to her in the depth of winter. The dead, if they were able to see and hear from beyond the grave, seemed set to ignore her pleas. Either that, Louisa thought, or they were too appalled by the mess she had made of her life, the pain she unwittingly inflicted on others. She had hurt Robert badly, she knew that; hurt him out of her own fear of being kind to him. His physical presence was so powerful, his sexual appeal a magnet which drew her in spite of herself. He could rouse, excite, and satisfy with a consummate ease which was no more than second nature; he would have taken her to bed, made love for hours, and kissed her good-bye in the morning with affectionate regret. That was his idea of making up and making friends, Louisa thought bitterly, while her body mocked and ached with the thought. Unlike her, he had no conscience; the next time they met he would greet Edward and herself in his usual bland, friendly manner; and then he would go away to his war imagining everything was all right. His complacency infuriated her. He had no conception of the emotional battles already fought, the constant struggle to keep resurgent desire at bay, nor the terror she experienced at having to fight the same ground again.

But still, part of her wished she had given in, relaxed in his arms, invited him to stay.

In her weakness, Louisa wondered whether marriage was indeed the answer, whether Edward could love her in the way Robert so brazenly suggested. But Robert judged all men by himself, and something inside her recoiled from calculated seduction. If Edward wanted her, it must come from him, not to be inspired by a base appeal to baser nature. Her religious faith might be a puny thing compared to Edward's staunch adherence, but she was idealistic enough to believe the church's ordinances when it came to baptism, marriage, and death. And when the church proclaimed that marriage was for the procreation of children, a remedy against sin, and for mutual society, help, and comfort, Louisa could not gainsay it. That Edward had no apparent need for such remedy was no comfort at all.

"Why did you keep us apart?" she whispered to her mother's name. "Would it have been so wrong for us to fall in love and marry then? There'd have been no Robert—none of all this anguish."

Drying the last of her tears, Louisa laid the little bouquet of meadow flowers by the headstone and rose to her feet. With a silent request for some kind of benediction, she read their names like a prayer and turned away.

Counting the hours to Edward's return, she decided to say nothing of Robert's visit. The face in the mirror, however, seemed to tell its own tale, pale and hollow-eyed from anguish and restless, dream-filled sleep. Attempts to redress those effects with powder and rouge proved an abysmal failure; in the end Louisa settled for a pretty lace blouse that Edward particularly liked and a determinedly bright manner which might cover the hours between his return and bed.

Although it was late when he arrived, Edward was obviously cheered by his father's good recovery, more relaxed than she had seen him for weeks. While he related the highlights of his weekend, her brightness became less forced, the smile she wore a natural expression of her pleasure at his return. It was rather disconcerting, therefore, when Edward remarked with some concern that she looked peaky.

"Oh, I'm all right," she said with a quick smile. "Just a bit late going to bed, that's all." Remembering where she had slept, she colored in sudden embarrassment and looked away. "I was lonely without you."

"I missed you too," he said softly, drawing her into the crook of his arm. In surprise at that unexpected gesture, Louisa turned her head, and the kiss which was intended for her cheek caught the corner of her mouth.

For an instant they both froze, shocked by the current which flashed between them. With the blood pounding in her throat, Louisa looked away first, afraid that he would see her soul laid bare and be repulsed by its naked hunger. It seemed to her they stood there a long time, she with her eyes downcast, not daring to look up, and Edward rigid beside her. She heard him begin to breathe again, felt the stomach-churning uncertainty as his hand slowly fell away. It seemed an eternity before he moved or spoke, and when he did, mentioning a present he had bought for Tisha's birthday, his voice was tight.

Paying less than half attention, Louisa said goodnight and climbed the stairs on heavy limbs. In the privacy of her own room she sank down onto the bed, bending instinctively against overwhelming misery. Her lips burned, but her body was leaden with disappointment. Right or wrong, she wanted to be loved, wanted its physical expression; and having rejected what would have come so easily from Robert, it seemed unbearably cruel that Edward should withhold from her all but the smallest gesture of affection. Apparently Robert's capacity for hurting them both was undiminished; like a crackling flame, every time they turned to each other the searing heat of his memory turned them back. Louisa rocked like someone holding a grievous hurt, aching with loneliness and longing, and the knowledge that this was her punishment for loving too well and too unwisely; and Edward's, too, for loving her.

Although the atmosphere was taut between them for several days, the celebration of Tisha's birthday eased it considerably. That evening, when the children had gone to bed, he told her that Tempest's had closed. As he passed, the place was being boarded up, and he had heard of no other buyer. But there was more: rumor had it that Rachel's husband had disappeared.

The words she had overheard and forgotten between Arthur and his sister returned with force; suddenly Louisa knew the rumors were true and said so. Although the knowledge saddened her, she had cause to be grateful for the topic of neutral conversation it created.

Within a couple of weeks there was an advertisement in the weekly paper to say that the Blossom Street house was for sale, together with its contents; as Edward read the details aloud, he grinned mischievously.

"Dick tells me she's moved in with the Bainbridges. What do you think of that?"

A sudden vision of Rachel as captive audience to the boring old major, reliving the Crimean campaigns of his youth, brought a rueful gurgle of laughter from Louisa. "Oh, she'll *hate* it! She might have been enamored of their way of life at one time—but I daresay the gilt's worn off that particular gingerbread by now. Oh, dear." She laughed again. "Poor Rachel!"

"And not a word of her husband," Edward remarked, shaking his head. "I bet you anything Robert was right—I think poor Arthur's gone off to do the only thing he ever succeeded at."

"You think he's joined up?"

"I do indeed—haven't you seen the news?" Folding the paper back for her, Edward handed it across, and Louisa's eyes were immediately caught by a large illustration of a mounted British soldier, with Majuba Hill in the background. The headlines announced the Boers' refusal of the latest British demands for voting rights among their nationals working the goldfields; the article began: "In the event of war between England and the Transvaal . . ."

Louisa's heart sank like a stone as she immediately pictured Robert, knowing his predictions had been accurate. Her eyes scanned the page; further information that the War Office planned to dispatch 49,000 men from England and India to the Cape, including large forces of cavalry and field batteries, only served to underline all that he had said.

Since his brief visit almost a month before, there had been no word from him, not even a card on her birthday. As he generally wrote quite often, even Edward had remarked on it. The silence worried her, and again she felt guilty at parting on such bad terms. Several times she had thought of penning some sort of explanation, yet constantly recoiled from the idea. Her inner turmoil was bad enough, but easier to bear when left alone; taken up for examination, it writhed like the snakes of Medusa, abhorrent and frightening. But she would have to write *something,* if only a single word of apology. He could not be allowed to go away without a word. After all, for all his faults, Robert still loved her; had it been otherwise, he would not have made that journey in the first place.

That planned letter was never written, however. The following day Edward's father died. The sheer unexpectedness of it after his gradual and apparently good recovery was a great shock. As always when deeply hurt, Edward retreated into himself, calm and quite unreachable during the few days before the funeral.

It was planned for mid-morning, which meant traveling down the day before. Edward had exchanged telegraph messages with Mrs. Pepperdine, arranging to stay at the vicarage for the night. Apart from confessing his anxiety at coming face to face with his father's family at long last, he gave the impression of being very self-contained. With a brief embrace he told Louisa Dick was in possession of the workshop keys and bade her good-bye.

"I'll be thinking about you—all the time," she called as he walked away. It was foggy along the river, with a struggling, opalescent sun still rising on the right. Louisa stood shivering by the gate until he disappeared into the enveloping mist, wondering whether her sense of foreboding was simply an extension of grief and the morning's damp chill or something more sinister. She had a most irrational desire to run after him, to enfold that strange defenselessness of his and arm him with her love.

Edward arrived home again the following evening as she was putting the children to bed, his whole demeanor so bruised and battered she ached at the sight of him. The dinner she had cooked was no more than picked at; when he abandoned it with a sigh, she pushed her plate away also.

"Go and sit down in the parlor," she said gently. "I've made a fire in there. I'll bring you a drink through in a minute."

There were still a few bottles of her mother's elderberry wine in the cupboard. Not as good as the bottle Edward had shared with Robert all those months before, but good enough. With a silent message of thanks to Mary Elliott, Louisa opened one and filled two glasses to the rim.

He was sitting, not in his usual chair, but bent forward on the sofa, elbows on knees, and staring into the fire. Sitting down beside him, Louisa handed him the wine and told him to drink it.

"It'll do you good," she said, pushing back the lock of hair from his forehead. "Now, tell me. What happened?"

"Just about everything," he said dejectedly. "They'd read the will, of course, and put Mrs. Pepperdine through hell before I got there. But at least she had the good sense to tell them no more than they were entitled to know. Grief! but that nephew of his—the one who inherited the title—he's an arrogant swine. I'm just glad my father referred to me only as his friend. If he'd acknowledged me as his son—as apparently he wanted to—I'd never have heard the end of it. As it was," Edward added bitterly, "he was talking about contesting the will's validity almost before we'd got the funeral over with. Thank God the solicitor who drew it up was there—he soon squashed that idea."

"I don't quite understand . . . ?"

Apologizing, Edward shook his head. "I'm sorry, I'm getting ahead of myself—not thinking straight at all." Taking a large draft of the wine, he said slowly, "My father's estate has been divided up three ways. Apart from small bequests—mainly to servants—a third goes to Mrs. Pepperdine, who's been his housekeeper for nearly thirty years, a third goes to charity, and the rest to me. It's hard to say how much just yet, but the solicitor thinks in the region of £2,000."

"All of it?" Louisa asked in amazement. "Or do you mean just to you?"

"Each. Two thousand each."

"But that's a fortune! I thought he was a poor man."

Edward shrugged. "By their standards, I suppose he was. Nevertheless," he added, his voice suddenly as tight as the fists clenched before him, "the nephew was fairly hopping with rage. He wanted to know who the hell I thought I was, battening on to an old man in his senility. God knows," he exclaimed, startling Louisa by his vehemence, "there was nobody with more wit and good sense than my father—and to suggest that—"

Louisa took his glass and set it down. Squeezing his shoulder, she said: "They're not worth it, Edward. Don't distress yourself."

"That solicitor knew more than he was letting on, though. There was a note for me: he gave me it just as he was leaving. He just said, *'Your father asked me to give you this—'* "

Suddenly, to her great dismay, Edward's self-control deserted him. He hid his face in his arms, like a child who had been bitterly hurt and does not know why. Her heart twisted within her, feeling all his sorrow and humiliation. Money meant so little to him: however much it was, it would never compensate for the loss of a loved and trusted friend, the father he had longed for all his life and discovered such a few short years ago. Edward had loved him, and to be accused of avarice for the sake of gain hurt him like nothing else could.

"Don't," she said again. "Don't distress yourself. They don't count— none of them do. Whatever they think doesn't matter. You needn't ever see them again."

He turned then, hiding his contorted face against her breast. "It isn't just that," he whispered brokenly.

"I know." Hurting for him, Louisa held him close, cradling his head in her arms. "It was what you meant to each other—I know. If it's any comfort, dearest, you've still got me—and the children. I know I'm not much, but I do love you."

"You're *everything* to me," Edward said fiercely. "If I should lose you, too—if you should go away . . ."

"How could I leave you?" she demanded, suddenly angered by that lack of trust. "I *love* you. Why won't you believe that?"

On that passionate declaration his arms tightened, and through the pintucked layers of blouse and chemise, she felt the pressure of his lips against her breast. It was like being burned by a deep, secret fire, one she did not want to relinquish. A little moan escaped her as he raised his head; and another as he kissed her throat.

With a long, deep sigh, like a man at the close of an arduous, exhausting journey, he eased her back against the cushions and for a moment looked wonderingly down at her.

"Do you?" he murmured huskily.

Her fingers touched his face. "You know I do."

He smiled then, and nodded; and without another word simply nestled his head between shoulder and breast, his hand possessively at her waist. Tension coiled her every nerve, but he seemed quite relaxed, breathing with deep and steady regularity, neither moving nor speaking for so long she began to think sleep had claimed him. She told herself it was natural, that after two exhausting days of harassment and grief he was simply relieved to know he was home and safe.

No lamps were lit, and in the fire's dull glow all should have been peace and contentment; but a little cinder of need, lit by the pressure of his lips, burned resolutely within. If she had only known ten years ago, Louisa thought, what seemed so obvious now, but with no Robert in between . . .

"Why the sigh?" he murmured.

With a wry smile, Louisa shook her head. "I thought you'd fallen asleep."

"No, just extending a very precious moment. And listening to your heart, so steady and strong."

In the light of her thoughts, those words were imbued with unbearable poignancy. For a moment it was difficult to speak. Then, with feigned lightness, she said: "It's a very foolish heart. It wishes, sometimes, for things which just can't be."

"What things? Tell me."

"Oh, I don't know," she said, a little breathlessly. "That I could turn back the clock, I suppose, be what I used to be, instead of what I am."

"Don't wish that. I wouldn't change you."

"Wouldn't you? Wouldn't you go back ten years and start again?"

Edward raised himself to look at her; with a tender smile he shook his head. "I might have done once, but not now. You see," he said simply, "I love you just as you are."

For a moment his fingers tightened around hers, crushing the rings she wore. They felt tight and painful, and for the first time she wanted to take them off, discard them, lock them away in some secret place along with the woman she once had been. As though he read those thoughts, Edward looked down at her hand, worrying the two rings between finger and thumb.

"Do you really need these things?" he asked quietly; and when she shook her head, told her to take them off.

With difficulty, she did so, thrusting them deep into her pocket. Her third finger looked white and thin and very naked without them, but she was aware of a most ridiculous lightness, as though fetters had been broken and she was free. He kissed the palm, and then each fingertip, one by one; and then, very deliberately, bent his head and touched her lips. It was a gentle kiss, but, like that accidental contact weeks before, it sent a sudden flame through both of them. Their eyes met, and this time Louisa did not look away. For a long, long moment he continued to regard her, as though needing to know, positively and absolutely, that he was the one she really wanted. Gentle fingers touched her eyes, her hair, her face; he traced the outline of her mouth and smiled as she smiled, with tender satisfaction.

"I love you," he said again, and clasped her to his heart. For some time nothing more was said between them; even kisses were unnecessary, so close was their embrace, so deep was their awareness of each other. In that moment, all barriers fell. Physically stirred, she felt the same need in him; yet that leap of the blood was nothing compared to the sense of hearts and minds and souls being reunited; of coming home, and finding peace and rest and absolute contentment. With no more need for pretense, apprehension fled; and in its fleeing Louisa wondered how she could ever have questioned the breadth and depth of Edward's love.

Sharing those thoughts, he said: "I've always loved you, but it was a long time before it dawned on me just how much. As you said that day before you left for Ireland—do you remember?—about not noticing the Minster when it was there all the time. Sometimes things need to be taken away, don't they, before we realize just how important they are."

Pressing herself closer, Louisa murmured: "Why did you never say, before?"

He laughed, softly. "Oh, my angel, what a question! Give me a week, and I might answer that! No," he amended gently, "let's just say that while you were wishing for a return to innocence, I've been regretting my celibate years."

"Does that worry you?" she asked, looking up at him.

"It has done—yes."

Moved by that honest admission, by what she saw as his deliberate refusal to mention Robert, Louisa suddenly saw how difficult life had been for him, especially these last months in the cottage. Her eyes examined him for any lingering trace of bitterness or anguish, but there was none. Nor, she thought with tenderness, did he show the years which had divided them when she was young. With his fine features and pale skin, Edward could have been touching her own age; and even his eyes, which betrayed the strain of the past few days, held all the uncertainty of an untried, beseeching lover.

"Oh, Edward," she whispered, loving him so much she thought her heart would break with it, "how could I be so blind?"

Looking deep into her eyes, he said softly: "Probably because I didn't want you to see—I didn't want to spoil what we already had."

"But I *should* have seen! I thought I knew you so well, I thought—"

"Don't," he whispered, laying a gentle finger against her lips. "Don't tell me what you thought. We were both wrong, and it doesn't matter now. I haven't been unhappy—far from it. The worst thing was the fear of losing you."

For a long moment, words would not come. She kissed his hands passionately, pressing each palm against her mouth. "You shame me, Edward . . ."

"No," he said fervently. "I *love* you."

Holding her very close, he repeated those words over and over, as though, having broken the seal on his tongue, it was necessary to compensate for the years of silence. And between the words, like pauses in a poem, his lips touched her skin; soft, sensitive, searching, each little touch raising thrill upon thrill of pleasure. Opening the neck of her blouse, she felt, given the chance, that he would probably kiss every inch of her body, and shivered with delightful anticipation. Turning her mouth to his, wanting him, needing to show it, she urged the same quickening in him. She had a sense of carefully banked-down fires bursting into flame; his skin was hot, his lips burned against hers, and by the eager press of his body as they lay together, Louisa knew at last how very much he wanted her. Giving herself up to that passionate embrace, for the first time since Robert's visit she was genuinely, wholeheartedly glad that she had sent him away.

But Edward was not Robert, and from long experience his passion was a governable thing. Trembling, with his fingers lightly tracing the line of her breast, he slowly shook his head. "I love you," he said again, and she recognized too the change in emphasis.

"And I love you—always and forever."

He kissed her very gently. "Then marry me."

Louisa's heart and soul leapt in unison; she thought of all the false starts and wrong directions, roads which had led to pain and grave misunderstanding, and it seemed she was being offered a most undeserved and overwhelming second chance.

"Yes," she whispered at last, against his mouth, knowing life had never been more beautiful, Edward never more the lover she had always wanted.

Drawing back, with the suggestion of a smile lighting the glance which traversed her face, he murmured unsteadily: "If you are going to marry me, I think you'd better make it very soon. I'm beginning to doubt my ability to wait!"

"There's no need—" she began, but he silenced her with a light, chaste kiss.

"Oh, but there is," Edward insisted. "After all these years, my angel, you and I are going to do things *right*."

SIXTEEN

They were married eight days later by special license, in the church of St. Mary, Bishophill Senior, at three in the afternoon.

A quaint little gritstone church, its brick tower, pointed gables, and dipping, layered roofline spoke of changes and additions which stretched back over a thousand-year life to Saxon times. It stood within the city walls at the head of a steep slope, overlooking the chimneys, roofs, and warehouses of Skeldergate, its tiny graveyard a haven of autumnal peace amid that dusty, workaday bustle.

Escorted by John Chapman, Louisa walked past ancient, weathered tombstones to the south door, her eyes catching names and dates spanning three centuries, while her feet scuffed the fallen yellow leaves of another year's dying. The golden, hazy day reminded her for a moment of other such days in other years, the years of another life to which it was suddenly important to say good-bye. By the door she paused and, leaving John in some consternation, went around the church to the shadowed north side. From there, beyond the gleaming sliver of water visible between those rusty roofs and blackened chimneys, she could see the Minster, its glorious towers rising clear and white; beyond them lay Gillygate and childhood, and somewhere to the left, upriver, was the little apartment she had shared with Robert. She said good-bye to that and, in her heart, to him. When he knew of her decision, she was sure he would understand; she felt that perhaps he had been trying to tell her something of the kind on his last visit, although at the time she had misunderstood, sensing only the physical longing he found so difficult to hide. From now on it would no longer matter; secure in Edward's love, in the fact that at long last he knew and understood the very mixed feelings Robert inspired, Louisa prayed that one day they could meet again as friends.

John Chapman cleared his throat as he approached and glanced at his watch. "Come on, Louisa. It's time we went in."

She looked at him, well fed and very middle-class in a good suit which did not quite disguise that added weight, and wondered where the bashful young carpenter had gone. For all his age was little more than hers he seemed much older, and was certainly ill at ease. Was it the occasion, she asked herself, or a continuation of the basic antipathy he had always felt toward her? But it hardly mattered, she thought; determined nothing should mar the day, Louisa smiled at him and took his arm, grateful for the part he had offered to play and trying to like him for a few minutes at least.

Walking into the old church with its smell of candles and beeswax and age, she felt fresh and sweet and new, like the scented carnations she carried, a last-minute gift from Edward. They were a delicate shade of pink, matching the blouse she wore and the trim of her new velvet hat. There had not been time to order a new costume for the wedding, but the pearl-gray jacket and skirt bought in the spring had rarely been worn, and even Blanche pronounced the outfit acceptable. To Louisa it was more than that, and when she saw Edward's eyes as he turned to watch her approach, she knew she looked beautiful indeed. Still in the black of mourning, he seemed paler than ever, his hair a dark, burnished gold in light diffused through medieval glass. Her "verray parfit gentil knight," Louisa thought, and having eyes only for him, she was but dimly aware of her two sisters and the elderly cleric welcoming that small congregation.

Without benefit of choir or hymns, the ceremony was short. She gave her responses clearly, promising as she had practiced, over and over, to love, cherish, and obey; Edward's words, however, moved her almost to tears. As he slipped a new ring on her wedding finger, she felt that fullness overflow. She glanced at him while they knelt together, and for a fleeting second he pressed her hand in reassurance. Afterward, raising her hat's tiny veil, he embraced Louisa with brief intensity, and then Emily was kissing her too, fussing like a mother hen; even Blanche allowed the semblance of a tear as she patted Edward's cheek and exhorted him to look after Louisa properly now.

The signing of the register was almost an anticlimax after that. The little party walked back along the riverside in the hazy autumn sunshine, all of them strangely quiet, locked in private thoughts and speculations which broke into the sharp laughter of relief only as they reached the cottage. Bessie was there to welcome them, her kind old face flushed and tragicomic as she laughed and wept by turns. Bemused but excited, Bobby and Tisha milled among the adults, demanding to know what was happening. Receiving no definite replies, they demanded cake and sandwiches instead, but access to the tea table was denied until Liam arrived. *He* was visibly astonished by the sight of his two aunts in their best gowns, his mother looking like a princess and almost giddy with laughter, and everyone suddenly patting his head, kissing him, and wishing him a very happy birthday.

Louisa drew him onto her knee. Cuddling him, smoothing his soft blond hair, she longed to let him into the secret, even while she knew he was too young to understand. Her eldest son, and Robert's, although he did not realize it; and at last she had married the man Liam thought was his father. Even while she wished him a happy birthday, Louisa felt she was cheating her son, although the fortunate coincidence of his birthday that week had seemed the best way of explaining everyone's presence and the air of celebration.

Very gently she explained that he was going to Leeds with Aunt Emily and Uncle John; along with Tisha and Bobby, of course, but it was to be a special treat for his birthday. She sensed from his expression that it was a treat he would rather have done without, and was tempted, suddenly, to call the whole thing off. Torn, glancing at Edward, happy in smiling conversation with John Chapman, she knew she owed this night, at least, totally to him; with no distractions, no lengthy bedtime stories, no children crying in the night. Hardening her heart, she kissed her best-loved child with sudden intensity and, taking his hand, took him to her sister.

Within the hour they were all gone, leaving Edward and Louisa with the dregs of the Champagne and a considerable amount of clearing up. Bessie had washed most of the china, but there was still much to side away and a fire to light. After the warmth of the afternoon, the cloudless sky and blazing early autumn sunset promised a cold night with perhaps a touch of frost.

Distracted from her task, Louisa called Edward to her side, and from the window which overlooked the garden they watched the haze of red, like fire in the west, spread and deepen over distant roofs and chimney stacks; stood and watched until the apple trees in the orchard were no more than black silhouettes.

With his arms around her, Edward nuzzled her neck. "Come on, Mrs. Elliott," he murmured with gentle, teasing pride. "This and better might do. Let's clear these things away and get that fire lit—then we can settle down. There's a new book I brought home yesterday," he added slyly, "which I rather hoped you might read to me."

For a moment she thought he was serious. "A new *book?* What is it?"

He smiled, kissing her. "A first edition, very valuable. It's by some chap called Milton—*Paradise Regained,* I think it's called . . ."

She laughed then and kissed him back, holding his face between her hands. "In that case, Mr. Elliott, I'd better hurry. I understand it's an awfully long poem!"

While Louisa washed the last of the dishes he went outside, strolling to the top of the garden in the cold, still air. The smell of autumn, more pronounced with every passing day, reminded him of his aunt and those revelations so many years ago; and of his father, so recently buried. Stricken for a moment, he looked back to that early summer visit, recalling the old man's serene philosophy and trying to hold it in his mind like an amulet against these sudden bouts of pain. Life was changing, as his father had predicted; although it seemed uncanny those changes should be brought about by the fact of the old man's death. But in a way, Edward thought, it was peculiarly fitting.

Fitting also that he and Louisa had given themselves this week of readjustment and discovery. Curled up on the sofa before a warmly blazing fire, they had explored both past and present with unaccustomed honesty, healing the occasionally painful disclosures with love. Each night, however, it had been harder to part; so tempting, with no more than a thin wall between them, to set that earlier vow aside and give way to burgeoning desire. Although he had slept fitfully, Edward did not regret it; out of that new closeness he had found courage to ask the kind of questions he had never asked anyone before, and, reassured now, was less afraid of sudden impotence or simply making a hash of things. New to each other, they would learn, as she so wisely said, from one another's mistakes.

Aware that Louisa and his father had shared certain wisdoms he lacked, Edward offered a silent prayer of thanks for them both as he retraced his steps, past serried lines of winter vegetables and through the orchard, heavy with ripening fruit. A few apples had fallen already, and as he picked one up he sniffed it pleasurably, inhaling its cidery sharpness. Suddenly taken by the allegory of lost innocence, he smiled and bit into its rosy skin, savoring an unexpected sweetness on his tongue. He could see Louisa in the kitchen, moving unhurriedly about her tasks; the scrubbed white table with its lamp in the center and, where the door was open, a golden triangle of light spilling forth across the flags. It was a view he often saw and paused over and, like a stranger, envied; but for the first time he felt he truly belonged there, and knew she was waiting for him.

Smiling back at the moon, rising large and pale in the eastern sky, Edward tossed the core of his apple across the garden wall and went inside.

Making a play of searching for that mythical new book, he produced instead a second bottle of Champagne, saying that, with luck, they should each have more than the half-glass they had been left with earlier. "Although I must admit," he added with a slight grimace, "I think it's overrated. I'd have preferred us to drink to each other with your mother's elderflower wine."

"There's plenty of elderberry left, if you'd rather have that."

"No," he said gently, privately recalling an evening spent in Robert's company. "That's for consolation, not celebration."

"Is it?"

"I think so."

Handing Louisa a glass, he raised his own, watching her over its rim, feasting his eyes on her peach-like loveliness, hardly daring to believe she was his wife at last. Conscious of that lingering study, her hands made little fluttering movements, from the glass to a small table, from its cover to her hair and then to the lace-trimmed collar of her pink silk blouse. That she should also be stricken with last-minute nerves was a most flattering revelation; one which stirred his blood even as he smiled. Going to her, for a moment he simply enfolded her within his arms, kissing her cheek with affectionate and tender restraint.

After all the heightened tensions of the past week he wanted her desperately, but remembering the subtle pleasure of each slow discovery already made, Edward was reluctant to rush those final steps. Easing her down beside him, he was aware, at every point of contact, of an exquisite tingling running through him; touching her hair, her mouth, her breasts, he wondered whether she could feel it too.

There was answer in the little moan of happiness and relief as he kissed her, in the parting of soft lips under his. Conscious, in some distant corner of his mind, that he was losing control, Edward tried hard to concentrate, to think of the bed waiting upstairs, far more comfortable than this elderly sofa, and surely more appropriate. But the unexpected touch of her tongue triggered a leaping response; with a gasp he pressed himself against her, eagerly exploring the warmth of her mouth.

It was heady wine, headier by far than the neglected Champagne which stood, rapidly losing its bubbles, on the table beside them. He felt her hands run under his shirt and over his back, and the restrictions of clothes were suddenly too much; wanting to be rid of them, he fumbled inexpertly with the tiny buttons of her blouse, slipping off his jacket and waistcoat as she unfastened them herself. With his shirt open, he drew her back, and as she knelt between his knees, shivered at her touch. Untying each little satin bow of her chemise, slipping the narrow straps from her shoulders, he sighed as the soft lawn fell away. Caught by her fire-warmed beauty, by that strange vulnerability as she knelt there, he could only watch as she released the fastening at her waist, until, surrounded by that mass of virgin white, she took his hand, stretching out like an odalisque before him. With great reverence he bent and touched his lips to the tip of each full breast, unable to speak, scarcely able to breathe for wanting her.

Naked, he lay beside her, feeling skin that was cool against the throbbing heat of his loins; and where she led, he followed, until, like a slow-burning fuse, that heightened hour of flickering firelight, of soft words and butterfly touches, exploded at last in a short, violent consummation. Louisa arched and cried out as he flooded her, thrusting hard against him in a shared, sobbing climax which seemed to go on forever.

Slowly the violence subsided. He would think it was over, and then another tremor, deep within her womb, would find its echo in himself. Joined to her, kissing her, he was aware of a profound sense of completion, of wanting nothing more than this. As languor overtook them both he smoothed damp curls from Louisa's forehead and, raising himself on one elbow, looked down into her happy, beautiful face. Reluctant to speak lest he should break that fragile sense of being one and whole with her, Edward simply smiled. Her eyes, soft with love, told him all he wanted to know.

SEVENTEEN

*R*eturning from Leeds with the children the following afternoon, the headlines on every hoarding they passed were full of the most disturbing news. "WAR COMMENCED!" it was announced. "LAING'S NEK SEIZED BY BOERS!"

At the station they queued for the latest edition, like everyone else scanning the inside pages immediately.

"Majuba Hill to be occupied," Louisa read aloud. "Hurried flight from Newcastle—Natal to be abandoned down to Dundee and Glencoe—nearest British troops in Ladysmith."

"That's bad," Edward murmured. "They've managed to take advantage of us, after all."

"And before we were ready," she added with sickly apprehension. Soon—all too soon—Robert would be on his way.

As though he read her thoughts, Edward pressed her hand. "You *must* write to him—tonight, I think."

Having risen at five to oversee the arrival of a new batch of horses and check the attendant paperwork, Robert returned to the mess for breakfast. Tommy was already halfway through an enormous plate of bacon and eggs, his chin fairly dripping with grease. Wiping his lips on a napkin, he greeted Robert with his usual friendly grin.

"What do you think of them? Will they do, d'you think?"

Robert grunted a monosyllabic reply. His breakfast ordered, he sat back and yawned, suddenly aware of the fatigue the last few weeks had wrought. "We could have done with them a month ago. Like everything else the War Office condescends to allow. The way they're carrying on, you'd think this damned war was a great surprise to them!"

Tommy agreed. "They should've had *us* ready a month ago. By the time *we* get there, the damned war'll be over!"

"D'you really think so?"

With a laugh and a shrug, Tommy pushed his empty plate away. "Perhaps not. With any luck, they'll let us do the mopping up."

Easing the neck of his new khaki uniform, Robert forbore to comment. Of the reports he had read so far, not even the best were enough to rejoice over; Kruger was clever, and those Boer farmers were hard nuts, used to the climate, familiar with the territory, and most important of all, fighting for what they considered to be their land, hard won over several generations. They had a lot of advantages, and they were not about to give up easily, even if it meant fighting dirty, without any rules. As they were doing already, he reflected; while British troops waited for an official declaration of war, the Boers had taken matters into their own hands.

The vague, illogical uneasiness of months had grown into a positive but inexplicable certainty; without specific reason, Robert just *knew* that all the strong and unquestioning discipline of the British troops, all their bravery and patriotism, was not going to be enough to win this war with speed or ease. It would *not* be over by Christmas, no matter how often that phrase was repeated; nor would those Boers be squashed like recalcitrant natives. War was a job he was trained for, and part of him could not fail to be excited by the fulfillment of that task; but he was also very much afraid, and that very fear prevented him from furthering his argument with anyone else. At times he wondered whether it was the memory of being wounded at Omdurman a year ago, that brush with death which still gave him nightmares at unexpected intervals; and he accused himself of cowardice. Whatever the reason, the presentiment was strong; strong enough to sharpen his eye for detail and discipline, to make him determined that every man under his command should be as well trained and well prepared as it was humanly possible to be.

And was it the thought of dying, he asked himself, which made him so very sad about Louisa?

Her letter arrived by the afternoon post. It was waiting for him in his quarters when he returned to change for dinner in the mess.

As usual, Harris had laid out his uniform. Quiet and unobtrusive as ever, he eased off Robert's boots and poured him a large brandy, setting the tray with its glass and decanter on the small table by his chair. Almost as an afterthought, he placed the letter on the tray, giving the major a surreptitious glance as he did so.

Robert picked up the envelope, staring at the handwriting as though at a ghost.

"Will there be anything further just now, sir?"

"No—no, not for the moment. Give me a few minutes, will you Harris, before you draw my bath?"

"Of course, sir."

When he returned, almost half an hour later, the major was still sitting exactly as before, the opened pages of the letter resting against his knee. Pausing by the door, Harris glanced from those open pages to the photograph on the desk and slowly shook his head. What have you done now? he silently asked Louisa; and for a moment all the old affection and loyalty he felt for Robert Duncannon quite overcame any latent sympathy he had for her.

"Bit of bad news, is it, sir?" he asked, setting towels to warm by the fire.

Slowly Robert shook his head. "No, Harris, not really." He stood up, replacing the letter in its envelope. "Quite the reverse, in fact. An occasion, if not for unmitigated joy, then certainly for a measure of . . ." His voice tailed away, and with slow deliberation, he placed the envelope and its contents on the fire. As it blackened and curled, he said: "Relief, I suppose."

The days which followed were even more hectic, if that were possible, than the weeks preceding the outbreak of war. There was much to be done: stores to arrange for a three-week voyage, horses to train and examine for fitness, reservists to integrate among the regulars, inoculations against enteric fever to administer, and transport to arrange from Hounslow to Southampton. The news that the regiment was to be transported to South Africa by Liverpool cattle boat was greeted with very mixed feelings indeed; fine for the horses, everyone agreed, but less than ideal for the men. The officers in particular were most disgruntled.

"I don't know what you're complaining about," Robert said to Tommy one day in the adjutant's office. "No matter how bad it is, it'll be nothing compared to what we'll face when we get there." He was needled by all the pettiness and made the mistake of letting it show.

"Oh, there's no need to remind us of your extensive field experience," Tommy retorted. "We're all *very* much aware of it already. And if you don't mind me saying so, *Major,* a little weary."

"Tommy, just bugger off, will you? I've got work to do."

The adjutant raised his eyebrows but made no comment. As Tommy left, banging the door behind him, he leaned over Robert's shoulder to look at the rota of embarkation leave the two men were working on. "Nerves," he said at last. "This whole thing is getting to everybody."

"We'll all be better when we've been home and said the good-byes," Robert murmured, and with that put it out of his mind.

He went to Dublin first, spending two days with Letty and Georgina before making a long detour back to Hounslow, via York.

It was late when he arrived, and he was tired, despite using most of the journey in sleep. The drag on his emotions had been far greater than he had anticipated, and despite the forced brightness, he knew Letty sensed some of the fatalistic dread which clutched at his heart. Every time he looked at his daughter, with her sharp, intelligent face and too-knowing eyes, Robert wondered whether he would ever see her again. She had sensed it too, clinging to him and crying as he left.

His mind kept returning to Georgina, even while his eyes scanned the tossing, windswept trees in the moat. Leaves were blowing everywhere, spinning like moths past dim and isolated gas lamps, catching at railings which stood like guards beneath those massive ramparts, fleeing in huddles across the road. The sturdy cab horse shied a couple of times, jerking Robert from his reverie. It was well past nine, and no doubt the boys and Tisha would be in bed, sound asleep. In a way he was relieved; he did not think he could bear another such scene as the one with Georgina. Not that they would understand, as she did, but still . . .

Louisa was another matter.

Although the tone of her letter had been conciliatory, in the light of its contents he assumed it could not have been otherwise; and, remembering their last parting, he dreaded the coming one. Would she never truly forgive him? Would she stand, stiff as those cast-iron railings, and utter unfelt words, phrases she only thought he wanted to hear, simply because he was going away? And Edward: what would his reaction be? In possession of the prize, would he gloat?

Dreading it, Robert shivered, pulling his heavy greatcoat around him, glad the coming interview must of necessity be short: the London train left at eleven, and to be back at Headquarters by morning he must be on it.

The cab pulled up outside the cottage gate, and Robert stepped down; having made his arrangements at the station, he did no more than clarify them before going in.

"I may be only a few minutes; it might be an hour. Whichever—wait. You'll get your fare and a handsome tip. All right?"

"Right, guv'nor. Train at eleven, you say? If you're more than an hour," the cabbie added, with the suggestion of a leer at Robert's uniform, "I'll give a knock."

"There'll be no need for that, I assure you."

Edward answered the door, inviting him into the tiny hall without even the pretense of a smile. Both tense, for a moment the two men simply stood and regarded one another; then Robert saw compassion in his rival's eyes and for a fleeting second wanted to hit out. It was injured pride as much as jealousy, but knowing it made that look no easier to bear.

"I'm glad you were able to come. Louisa wanted very much to see you."

"I couldn't go," Robert said tersely, "without saying good-bye."

"She wants to apologize, I think, for treating you badly the last time you were here."

Sudden embarrassment dispersed Robert's anger. "Oh. She told you?"

"Well, she told me why you came."

"Look, I simply wanted to clear a few things up—no more than that. I wanted us to be *friends*."

"I know. I understand. It's what we all want."

"Thank God for that." Robert sighed and with a weary smile set down his hat and stick on the little table. "I suppose I should congratulate you . . ."

"Not if you don't want to," Edward said dryly.

Robert laughed. "No, you're quite right, I don't want to. With envy clutching at my throat," he added with disarming frankness, "the words would choke me. The stupid thing is—I knew all along she *should* marry you. It was the only logical thing to do."

The other man pursed his lips; then, with an ironic smile, said: "I only hope logic didn't have too much to do with it."

The sudden softening of his expression was most revealing. Regarding him for a moment, Robert smiled sadly. "Knowing Louisa, I shouldn't imagine it did."

"Well," Edward said, clearing his throat, "perhaps we'd better go through. She'll be wondering what plots are being hatched out here." Opening the parlor door, he stood back for Robert to enter.

Standing by the hearth, she looked anxious; then she smiled, that lovely curving smile which lit her eyes and a host of poignant memories. For the first time in this house she opened her arms and embraced him.

"I'm so glad to see you, Robert," she murmured, and he knew she was. Forgetting the years between, he wanted to kiss her, say foolish things; but most of all he wanted to go on holding her.

With an effort he dropped his arms. "I can't stay long," he said brusquely "I have a cab waiting outside. But I wanted to see you. To see you both," he added, including Edward in his glance.

Glad of the offered chair, for his knees were suddenly weak, Robert sat down, accepting a glass of wine, which he drank far too quickly, and a hefty slice of fruitcake which he did not want at all. For a few minutes they were all tongue-tied; then Louisa asked after Letty and Georgina, and he asked about the children; but those polite exchanges were no more than bandages, Robert thought, covering the rawness beneath. That they had done the right thing he had no doubt; he simply wondered why it hurt so much. In a strange way, the fact of their sexual intimacy disturbed him far less than that ongoing spiritual intercourse which he had been aware of from the very beginning. Now, however, it was far more tangible. They *knew* one another, he realized, in the fullest sense of the word.

In her new contentment, Louisa seemed to have come to terms with so many other emotions; she could look at him and smile, and all the bitterness and resentment were gone. Robert even felt she loved him in a dispassionate kind of way. That hurt, too.

At ease and confident, even Edward seemed to have grown in stature, exuding tolerance and sympathy as though that separate suffering in the same cause had somehow made them brothers. It had certainly made them equal; and after all, Robert reasoned, they both loved her, both wanted the best for her; and the best was here, with the children, in peace and security. He had known that for a long time.

With an eye on the clock, Edward said he would fetch Mary Ann's mother; on the strength of Robert's letter, arrangements had already been made for the children to be cared for while they saw him to the station.

"That's not necessary," Robert protested, but Louisa waved it aside.

"Nonsense—we want to come with you. I couldn't bear the thought of you getting on that train all on your own. There'll be all those others—" she broke off suddenly and shook her head.

"You silly bloody woman," he whispered as the door closed behind Edward. "After all that's been said and done, and you can't let me get on a damn train without—" Words failed him. Taking a step toward her, he held out his arms; she came straight to him, burying her face against his shoulder.

"I'm sorry—"

"What for, for Heaven's sake?"

"For being so horrid to you. I shouldn't have—didn't mean—"

"It's all right. It's not important, not anymore." She struggled to explain herself, but words were no longer necessary. "I *know*," he said gently, kissing the little curls on the crown of her head, "why you said what you said and did what you did. If you'd gone to bed with me that night, you couldn't have looked him in the face again. Am I right?"

She nodded, and Robert sighed, pressing her closer. "I just wish you could have said so at the time—it might have saved a lot of bitterness."

"I didn't know it then—didn't realize. It dawned on me afterward, and then I hated myself for hurting you. I wanted to explain, but I couldn't. I'm sorry."

He shook his head, still hurt by the memory. Full of love and pain and regret, he raised her face to his and gazed longingly into those deep, forget-me-not eyes. With quiet sincerity, he said: "I'm sorry too." Gently he pressed his mouth to hers; for a moment she responded, then drew away.

"I love Edward."

"I know. You always have."

Releasing her, he said, in an attempt at lightness, "It was about time you pushed him off that bloody pedestal. I must say he's a damn sight better for it. You never know, I might even get to like him—and that would be a novelty, wouldn't it?" She tried, unsuccessfully, to suppress a grin; pinching her cheek, he murmured: "That's better. Don't let's have any more sad faces; I can't bear it."

Louisa glanced at the clock. "He should be back any minute. Why don't you go up and see the children? I'll call you when he comes."

Lighting a candle at the foot of the stairs, she handed it to Robert; a gusting draft made it flicker suddenly as he ascended those narrow, winding steps. The wind was more noticeable at the top of the house, whistling eerily round the eaves and down the chimneys, and shadows danced ahead of him. Through an open door he thought he saw someone move, then realized it was his own shadow across a large brass bedstead. Unable to resist temptation, Robert looked into a room as white and neat and shining as the rest of the cottage. Apart from the lace counterpane and a faint scent of lavender, there was nothing soft or sensual or even particularly feminine about it; no perfumes or powder bowls or pieces of cut glass; even the washstand contained no more than the usual functional items and a single vase of honesty, fragile and silvery in the flickering light. It was so painfully virginal he could hardly believe it was Louisa's room; then he saw a woman's shawl across the seat of a chair and a man's jacket supported on the back. For a moment his heart twisted. But the woman who slept here, he told himself, was different indeed from the one who had shared his life before. In a way he was relieved: her memory would remain intact.

With a sigh of deep resignation, Robert crossed the landing to the children's room. Tisha was asleep flat on her back, golden curls framing her head like a halo, long eyelashes casting shadows over cherubic cheeks; one fist was poised with thumb extended, where it had slipped from her mouth in sleep. Leaning on the wooden side of her cot, Robert smiled down at her, briefly touching one warm, rosy cheek with the back of his hand; but as he turned to his sons, one dark, one fair, curled round each other in the center of their wide bed, he felt his throat constrict with sudden pain. Bobby turned away from the light, but Liam stirred, for a moment blinking and smiling.

"Night-night, Daddy," he murmured indistinctly, burying his face in the pillow. "See you in the morning."

"Not me, little man," Robert whispered. "Not me."

Tears pricked suddenly; hearing a light foot on the stair, he brushed them quickly away.

It was Louisa. Setting the candle down, he pulled the door gently to and embraced her. "Whatever else we did," he murmured huskily, "we made three beautiful children. Don't ever regret them, will you?"

"Oh, Robert, love! I never have, nor ever will."

"Take good care of them."

"Always." Holding him tight, she kissed his cheek. "Come on, chin up, it's time to go."

Her sudden briskness was intentional. Heartened by it, he straightened and took a deep breath; himself again, he followed her down the stairs.

In the hall, Edward was waiting with his coat on; through the open kitchen door, Robert caught sight of a pair of curious eyes, eyes which took in every detail of his immaculate officer's uniform, from the crown at his shoulder down to his knee-length and highly polished boots.

Louisa thanked the woman for coming over and said they would not be very long; anxious about the time, Edward hurried them out to the waiting cab.

The station, even at that late hour, was full of bustle and noise. Under that great curving arch, the wind howled in gusts, steam hissed, voices were hollow, and whistles echoed into infinity. As Louisa had suspected, there were many more khaki uniforms on the main platform that night, most of them standing by open carriage doors, surrounded by groups of relatives and friends. Railway guards and porters tried ineffectually to usher those who were traveling onto the train, while latecomers like themselves fussed with bags and trunks, nerves fraying by the guard's van.

With little more than ten minutes to spare, Robert strolled to the left-luggage office and, with a porter already at his elbow, directed the stowage of his single bag to an already reserved compartment. As though he was seeing them away, he guided Edward and Louisa in the porter's wake toward the head of the train. Heads turned as they passed; the men with varying degrees of envy or grudging respect, most of the women frankly admiring. Even in that new, dull khaki, Louisa thought, Robert cut a very handsome figure indeed; she was suddenly very proud to have borne his sons, and for once in York, cared not at all who saw them together.

Edward, seeing the light of pride and affection in her eyes, immediately smothered a sneaking twinge of jealousy. She needs this, he told himself; needs to feel proud and pleased that he's going away. That little air of glory surrounding Robert and every other soldier on the station that night was essential; the idea that they were going, like crusader knights, to defend an idea in a foreign land, was equally so; without it, leaving would be impossible. If we saw them on the field of battle, he thought, those uniforms tattered, smooth flesh hacked to ribbons, could we cheer and encourage and wish them well? If we saw them kill and maim, making widows of other men's wives, orphans of innocent children, could we send them away like this? Shivering suddenly, pitying the man who stood so straight before him, Edward thanked God he was required to have no part of it; knowing himself as a creator, he wondered how he would feel if asked to destroy. The poet in him seized on that, using the idea as a defense against these minutes of tension and pain.

Wishing he had changed his mind, wishing Louisa could have come alone, Edward stood back, reluctant to intrude; but Robert seized his hand and clasped his shoulder like a friend.

Behind that sudden and genuine warmth, for a moment other emotions darkened that steady, expressive gaze, as though he wanted Edward to understand something which must be shielded from Louisa. Opening his mouth to speak, Edward saw the slight negative gesture and swallowed the words, which would have been pitifully inadequate anyway. Exhorted to take care of Louisa and the children, he could only nod and press that firm hand harder, hoping the other man registered his understanding. In his dismay, he prayed that Louisa would not sense that terrible sadness.

He watched as they embraced; saw tears hover on those heavy lashes, the sudden twist of her mouth in response to something Robert said; and as the train suddenly clanged and jerked, his hard, lingering, defiant kiss.

The train was already beginning to move as he boarded it; a guard slammed the door, shaking his head in wry reproach; moving down the platform, hands linked in farewell, people jostled the two of them where they stood. Robert leaned against the window, not waving, simply watching, his eyes for Louisa alone.

Buffeted by wind which swept down the tunnel of that great arcade, Louisa clung to Edward, weeping against his shoulder. Although she did not voice her fear that Robert might not come back, he sensed it; and, fighting his own sorrows, held her close. Jealousy, old and only partly disinterred, nevertheless had struggled from its grave as Robert

Duncannon took his leave; he wondered whether they would ever be free of him.

He caressed her cheek, drying the tears. Touching his mouth to hers, he kissed her with such passionate intensity, wanting to erase the memory of that other kiss, to affirm that she was his, and his alone. There was love and desolation in her response, a sudden, desperate cleaving to all that was known and familiar in that lonely, echoing place. Her eyes took in the thinning crowds and returned to him; and, in answer to that unspoken plea, Edward tucked her arm in his, guiding her through the barriers and out toward home.

Because of the wind, they took the sheltered way through town and, with the white mass of the city walls behind them, traversed the narrow streets which led past the old station to Micklegate. Pausing at the dogleg junction of Tanner Row, only then did Edward realize where they were, suddenly remembering another such night, taking Louisa home in the snow. With startling clarity he recalled wanting to kiss her then and being afraid to do so. It was the night she had met Robert Duncannon for the very first time. Sorrow and regret assailed him; wishing he *had* kissed her, thinking it might have changed the course of their lives, he turned his head quickly and met Louisa's steady, compassionate gaze.

"We were different people then," she softly said, echoing words he had used himself. "I loved Robert—really loved him, in spite of all I've thought or said since. I realize that now. But it's over. He's gone," she whispered, with sad finality. "Without him, Edward, I might never have learned to love you." Touching his cheek, she added: "And without you, my darling, I might never have learned to forgive myself."

Drawing her into the shelter of a disused doorway, he kissed her with infinite tenderness, aware, as he had been that other night, that this was the place of their beginning, where he had loved and cherished and tried to protect that precious innocence. Like illicit lovers they embraced, and stood for a moment longer, gazing into each other's eyes. Knowing the ghosts of this place were finally laid to rest, Edward smiled and kissed her again.

"I love you, Mrs. Elliott," he murmured huskily. "Let's go home."